Crafter's
MARKET

The DIY Resource for Creating a Successful and Profitable Craft Business

[3RD EDITION]

Fons&Porter

CINCINNATI, OHIO

2017 Crafter's Market. Copyright © 2016 by F+W, a
Content + eCommerce Company. Manufactured in
USA. All rights reserved. No part of this book may be
reproduced in any form or by any electronic or mechanical means including information storage and retrieval
systems without permission in writing from the publisher, except by a reviewer who may quote brief pas-
sages in a review. Published by Fons & Porter Books,
an imprint of F+W, Inc., 10151 Carver Road, Blue Ash,
Ohio 45242. (800) 289-0963. First Edition.

fw

www.fwcommunity.com

Distributed in Canada by Fraser Direct
100 Armstrong Avenue
Georgetown, ON, Canada L7G 5S4
Tel: (905) 877-4411

Distributed in the U.K. and Europe by
F&W MEDIA INTERNATIONAL
Pynes Hill Court, Pynes Hill, Rydon Lane
Exeter, EX2 5AZ, United Kingdom
Tel: (+44) 1392 797680
E-mail: enquiries@fwmedia.com

ISBN-13: 978-1-4402-4683-8
SRN: R0832

Edited by: Abby Glassenberg and Maya Elson
Cover Designed by: Frank Rivera
Interior Designed by: Alanna DiLiddo

CONTENTS

Photo by Lisa Neighbors

FROM THE EDITOR

When I left my job as a middle school teacher in 2005 to become a mother I could never have imagined that I'd start a craft business. Although I've always been artistic and have enjoyed making things with my hands since I was a child, I thought my art and craft could only ever be a fun hobby. Today, I have a thriving sewing pattern business that helps to support my family. I work from home with flexible hours, and my business out-earns my former full-time salary. Plus I craft every day! I get tremendous satisfaction from helping other people to turn their talents into a fulfilling creative career, and I'm proof that it's possible.

One of my mantras is to show up every day and make things as though it's your job. This means approaching your crafty endeavors with the same discipline you would a "real job." Don't be afraid to share what you're making online and in person. If you follow this path consistently over time, crafting will in some way become your real job. Whether it's getting a licensing deal, writing a craft book, teaching workshops, selling wholesale, or having gangbuster holiday craft fair booths, treating your work seriously and with discipline pays off.

Crafter's Market is an immensely useful tool for business success. This book is for crafters of all types including knitters, crocheters, paper crafters, woodworkers, quilters, and more. The front section contains a variety of articles from craft business owners, each with a wealth of experience that they drew from to share valuable lessons. Read their best tips on getting press, working with retailers, choosing an ecommerce option, and more.

Following the articles are more than a thousand listings to help you connect with places to market and sell your work. You'll find dozens of book publishers, craft magazines, industry shows, craft communities, craft fairs, and marketplaces. I encourage you to put these listings to use. Reach out and see if you can get your work in front of new eyes this year. Success is the best motivator, so don't be afraid to take that first step.

Happy crafting!
Abby Glassenberg

[HOW TO USE THIS BOOK]

If you're picking up this book for the first time, you might not know quite how to start using it. Your first impulse might be to flip through and quickly make a mailing list, submitting your work to everyone with hopes that *someone* might like it. Resist that urge. First, you have to narrow down the names in this book to those who need your particular style. That's what this book is all about. We provide the names and addresses of places to sell your hand-made creations and publish how-to instructions, along with plenty of business advice. You provide the hard work, creativity, and dedication to making and selling handmade goods.

LISTINGS

The book is divided into market sections, from craft fairs to publishers. (See the Table of Contents for a complete list.) Each section begins with an introduction containing informa-tion and advice to help you break into that specific market. Listings are the meat of this book. In a nutshell, listings are names, addresses, and contact information for avenues through which you can sell your craft and hone your business.

ARTICLES

In this book, you will find helpful articles by and about working crafters, editors, and experts from the craft world. These articles give you a richer understanding of the marketplace by sharing the featured artists' personal experiences and insights. Their stories, and the lessons you can learn from other crafters' feats and follies, give you an important edge over competition.

HOW CRAFTER'S MARKET WORKS

We suggest you follow the instructions in the listings and explore the different methods and avenues you can use to successfully sell your handmade goods. Whether your interest lies in publishing, craft fairs, or growing your online presence, you will find instructions in the listing on how to reach out to the correct people.

WORKING WITH LISTINGS

1. **Read the entire listing to decide whether that publisher, craft fair, or website is a good fit.** Do not use this book simply as a mailing list of names and addresses. Reading listings carefully helps you narrow your list to select the most appropriate places to sell your work.

2. **Read the description of the company in the first paragraph of the listing.** Then jump to the Needs or Media heading to find out what type of artwork is preferred. Is

---

KEY TO SYMBOLS & ABBREVIATIONS

✹	Canadian market
◐	market located outside of the U.S. and Canada
⌂	market prefers to work with local artists/designers
b&w	black & white (photo or illustration)
SASE	self-addressed, stamped envelope
SAE	self-addressed envelope
IIRC	International Reply Coupon, for use when mailing to countries other than your own

it the type of craft you create? This is the first step to narrowing your target market. Only consider working with those places that need the kind of work you create.

3. Send appropriate submissions. It seems like common sense to research what kind of samples a listing wants before sending off just any artwork you have on hand. But believe it or not, some artists skip this step. Look under the First Contact & Terms heading to find out how to contact the market and what to send. Some companies and publishers are very picky about what kinds of samples they like to see; others are more flexible. Failure to follow directions in submissions may result in automatic rejection from a publisher or show.

4. Be sure to read the Tips. This is where editors and directors describe their pet peeves and give clues for how to impress them. The information within the Tips will help you get a feel for what a publisher might be like to work with or a show might be like to attend.

These steps are just the beginning. As you become accustomed to reading listings, you will think of more ways to mine this book for potential craft outlets.

PAY ATTENTION TO COPYRIGHT INFORMATION

If you are using this book to locate a publisher or find a magazine to work with, it's important to consider what rights publishing companies buy. It is preferable to work with companies that buy first or one-time rights. If you see a listing that buys "all rights," be aware you may be giving up the right to sell that particular craft in the future. See the "Copyright Basics" article in this section for more information.

LOOK FOR SPECIALTIES AND NICHE MARKETS

Read listings closely. Most describe their specialties, clients, and products within the first paragraph. If you are primarily a knitter, it probably won't be beneficial for you to apply as a vendor to International Quilt Market. If you design plushie patterns, look for a magazine that caters to sewing or general craft, not scrapbooking. Make sure your submissions and applications are targeted to maximize the potential success of your craft endeavor.

Browse the listings for new information. A publisher you thought was only interested in quilting patterns may in fact have an imprint dedicated to cross-stitch.

HANG IN THERE!

Building a professional business doesn't happen overnight. It's a gradual process. It may take two or three years to gain enough information and experience to be a true professional in your field. So if you really want to be a professional crafter, hang in there. Before long, you'll experience the exhilaration of seeing your name in print, your social media stats rise, your work pop up on Pinterest, and your sales steadily increase. If you really want it and you're willing to work for it, it will happen.

FREQUENTLY ASKED QUESTIONS

1. **How do companies get listed in the book?** No company pays to be included—all listings are free. Every company has to fill out a detailed questionnaire about their art needs. All questionnaires are screened to make sure the companies meet our requirements. Each year we contact every company in the book and ask them to update their information.

2. **Why aren't other companies I know about listed in this book?** We may have sent these companies a questionnaire, but they never returned it. Or if they did return a questionnaire, we may have decided not to include them based on our requirements.

3. **I applied to a show or sent a proposal to a company that stated they were open to reviewing the type of work I do, but I have not heard from them yet. What should I do?** At the time we contacted the company, they were open to receiving such submissions. However, things can change. It's a good idea to contact any company listed in this book to check on their policy before sending them anything. Perhaps they have not had time to review your submission yet. If the listing states that they respond to queries in one month, and more than a month has passed, you can send a brief e-mail to the company to inquire about the status of your submission. Some companies receive a large volume of submissions, so you must be patient.

4. **A company says they want to publish my artwork, but first they will need a fee from me. Is this a standard business practice?** No, it is not a standard business practice. You should never have to pay to have your work reviewed or accepted for publication. If you suspect that a company may not be reputable, do some research before you submit anything or pay their fees. The exception to this rule is craft fairs and shows. Most fairs and shows have an application fee, and usually there is a fee for renting booth space. Some galleries may also require a fee for renting space to exhibit your work.

[HOW TO STAY ON TRACK & GET PAID]

As you launch your craft career, be aware that you are actually starting a small business. It is crucial that you keep track of the details, or your business will not last very long. The most important rule of all is to find a system to keep your business organized and stick with it.

YOUR DAILY RECORD-KEEPING SYSTEM

Every artist needs to keep a daily record of art-making and marketing activities. Before you do anything else, visit an office supply store and pick out the items listed below (or your own variations of these items). Keep it simple so you can remember your system and use it on automatic pilot whenever you make a business transaction.

WHAT YOU'LL NEED:

- a packet of colorful file folders or a basic Personal Information Manager on your smartphone, computer, or personal digital assistant (PDA).
- a notebook or legal pads to serve as a log or journal to keep track of your daily craft-making and craft-marketing activities.
- a small pocket notebook to keep in your car to track mileage and gas expenses.

HOW TO START YOUR SYSTEM

Designate a permanent location in your studio or home office for two file folders and your notebook. Label one red file folder "Expenses." Label one green file folder "Income." Write in your daily log book each and every day.

Every time you purchase anything for your business, such as envelopes or art supplies, place the receipt in your red Expenses folder. When you receive payment for a sale or other crafty job (such as writing an article for a magazine), photocopy the check or place the receipt in your green Income folder.

GETTING PAID

Be sure to factor in the value of your time and supplies and then add 50 percent to arrive at your retail price. This 50 percent increase will allow you to sell wholesale without taking a loss.

For standard items offered in your inventory, be sure to receive payment upfront before sending the item to its new home. Once you have sent off the merchandise, you may have a problem collecting unpaid bills. If you are taking custom orders, consider how you'd like to handle payment. Will you require full payment before starting the work, or just a deposit? Decide how and when you need to be paid for custom work and be sure to collect the final amount due before sending the final product.

When writing for magazines or working with a publisher, you will most likely be asked to submit an invoice with the finished work. Some book deals may include a small advance prior to beginning work, and others may not. Be sure to understand the terms of a publishing contract or agreement before starting work. Pay close attention to how and when you will receive payment and ask if you need to submit an invoice or if you will be paid automatically upon completion of the work.

TAKE ADVANTAGE OF TAX DEDUCTIONS

You have the right to deduct legitimate business expenses from your taxable income. Art supplies, studio rent, printing costs, and other business expenses are deductible against your gross craft-related income. It is imperative to seek the help of an accountant or tax-preparation service in filing your return. In the event your deductions exceed profits, the loss will lower your taxable income from other sources.

To guard against taxpayers fraudulently claiming hobby expenses as business losses, the IRS requires taxpayers to demonstrate a "profit motive." As a general rule, you must show a profit for three out of five years to retain a business status. If you are audited, the burden of proof will be on you to validate your work as a business and not a hobby. The nine criteria the IRS use to distinguish a business from a hobby are:

- **the manner in which you conduct your business**
- **expertise**
- **amount of time and effort put into your work**
- **expectation of future profits**
- **success in similar ventures**
- **history of profit and losses**
- **amount of occasional profits**
- **financial status**
- **element of personal pleasure or recreation**

If the IRS rules that you sew for pure enjoyment rather than profit, they will consider you a hobbyist. Complete and accurate records will demonstrate to the IRS that you take your business seriously.

Even if you are a "hobbyist," you can deduct expenses such as supplies on a Schedule A, but you can only take craft-related deductions equal to craft-related income. If you sold two $500 quilts, you can deduct expenses such as fabric, patterns, books, and seminars only up to $1,000. Itemize deductions only if your total itemized deductions exceed your standard deduction. You will not be allowed to deduct a loss from other sources of income.

FIGURING DEDUCTIONS

To deduct business expenses, you or your accountant will fill out a 1040 tax form (not 1040EZ) and prepare a Schedule C, which is a separate form used to calculate profit or loss from your business. The income (or loss) from Schedule C is then reported on the 1040 form. In regard to business expenses, the standard deduction does not come into play as it would for a hobbyist. The total of your business expenses need not exceed the standard deduction.

There is a shorter form called Schedule C-EZ for self-employed people in service industries. It can be applicable to those who have receipts of $25,000 or less and deductible expenses of $2,000 or less. Check with your accountant to see if you qualify.

Deductible expenses include advertising costs, brochures, business cards, professional group dues, subscriptions to trade journals and magazines, legal and professional services, leased office equipment, office supplies, business travel expenses, etc. Your accountant can give you a list of all 100 percent and 50 percent deductible expenses. Don't forget to deduct the cost of this book!

As a self-employed "sole proprietor," there is no employer regularly taking tax out of your paycheck. Your accountant will help you put money away to meet your tax obligations and may advise you to estimate your tax and file quarterly returns.

Your accountant also will be knowledgeable about another annual tax called the Social Security Self-Employment Tax. You must pay this tax if your net craft business income is $400 or more.

The fees of tax professionals are relatively low, and they are deductible. To find a good accountant, ask colleagues for recommendations, look for advertisements in trade publications, or ask your local Small Business Administration.

REPORT ALL INCOME TO UNCLE SAM

Don't be tempted to sell your work without reporting it on your income tax. You may think this saves money, but it can do real damage to your career and credibility—even if you are never audited by the IRS. Unless you report your income, the IRS will not categorize you as a professional, and you won't be able to deduct expenses. And don't think you won't get caught if you neglect to report income. If you bill any client in excess of $600 (for example, if you are consistently writing for a magazine), the IRS requires the client to provide you with a Form 1099 at the end of the year. Your client must send one copy to the IRS and a copy to you to attach to your income tax return. Likewise, if you pay a freelancer over $600 to assist with any portion of your work, you must issue a 1099 form. This procedure is one way the IRS cuts down on unreported income.

REGISTER WITH THE STATE SALES TAX DEPARTMENT

Most states require a 2–7 percent sales tax on artwork you sell directly from your studio or at art/craft fairs or on work created for a client. You must register with the state sales tax department, which will issue you a sales permit or a resale number and send you appropriate forms and instructions for collecting the tax. Getting a sales permit usually involves filling out a form and paying a small fee. Reporting sales tax is a relatively simple procedure. Record all sales taxes on invoices and in your sales journal. Every three months, total the taxes collected and send it to the state sales tax department.

In most states, if you sell to a customer outside of your sales tax area, you do not have to collect sales tax. However, this may not hold true for your state. You may also need a business license or permit. Call your state tax office to find out what is required.

SAVE MONEY ON CRAFT SUPPLIES

As long as you have the above sales permit number, you can buy craft supplies without paying sales tax. You will probably have to fill out a tax-exempt form with your permit number at the sales desk where you buy materials. The reason you do not have to pay sales tax on craft supplies is that sales tax is only charged on the final product. However, you must then add the cost of materials into the cost of your finished product or the final work for your client. Keep all receipts in case of a tax audit. If the state discovers that you have not collected sales tax, you will be liable for tax and penalties.

Some states claim "creativity" is a non-taxable service, while others view it as a product and therefore taxable. Be certain you understand the sales tax laws to avoid being held liable for uncollected money at tax time. Contact your state auditor for sales tax information.

SAVE MONEY ON POSTAGE

When you send out postcard samples or invitations to openings, you can save big bucks by mailing in bulk. Artists should send orders via first-class mail for quicker service and better handling. Package flat work between heavy cardboard or foam core or roll it in a cardboard tube. Include your business card or a label with your name and address on the outside of the packaging material in case the outer wrapper becomes separated from the inner packing in transit.

Protect larger works—particularly those that are matted or framed—with a strong outer surface, such as laminated cardboard, Masonite, or light plywood. Wrap the work in polyfoam, heavy cloth, or bubble wrap, and cushion it against the outer container with spacers to keep it from moving. Whenever possible, ship work before it is glassed. If the glass breaks en route, it may destroy your original image. If shipping large framed work, contact a museum in your area for more suggestions on packaging.

The U.S. Postal Service will not automatically insure your work, but you can purchase up to $5,000 worth of coverage. Artworks exceeding this value should be sent by registered mail, which can be insured for up to $25,000. Certified packages travel a little slower but are easier to track.

Consider special services offered by the post office, such as Priority Mail, Express Mail Next Day Service, and Special Delivery. For overnight delivery, check to see which air-freight services are available in your area. Federal Express automatically insures packages for $100 and will ship art valued up to $500. Their 24-hour computer tracking system enables you to locate your package at any time.

The United Parcel Service automatically insures work for $100, but you can purchase additional insurance for work valued as high as $25,000 for items shipped by air (there is no limit for items sent on the ground). UPS cannot guarantee arrival dates but will track lost packages. It also offers Two-Day Blue Label Air Service within the U.S. and Next Day Service in specific ZIP code zones.

Always make a quick address check by phone before putting your package in the mail.

CAN I DEDUCT MY HOME STUDIO?

If you freelance full time from your home and devote a separate area to your business, you may qualify for a home office deduction. If eligible, you can deduct a percentage of your rent or mortgage as well as utilities and expenses such as office supplies and business-related telephone calls.

The IRS does not allow deductions if the space is used for purposes other than business. A studio or office in your home must meet three criteria:

• The space must be used exclusively for your business.

• The space must be used regularly as a place of business.

• The space must be your principal place of business.

The IRS might question a home office deduction if you are employed full time elsewhere and freelance from home. If you do claim a home office, the area must be clearly divided from your living area. A desk in your bedroom will not qualify. To figure out the percentage of your home used for business, divide the total square footage of your home by the total square footage of your office. This will give you a percentage to work with when figuring deductions. If the home office is 10 percent of the square footage of your home, deduct 10 percent of expenses such as rent, heat, and air-conditioning.

The total home office deduction cannot exceed the gross income you derive from its business use. You cannot take a net business loss resulting from a home office deduction. Your business must be profitable three out of five years; otherwise, you will be classified as a hobbyist and will not be entitled to this deduction.

Consult a tax advisor before attempting to take this deduction, as its interpretations frequently change.

For additional information, refer to IRS Publication 587, Business Use of Your Home, which can be downloaded at www.irs.gov or ordered by calling (800)829-3676.

[COPYRIGHT BASICS]

As creator of your artwork, you have certain inherent rights over your work and can control how each one of your works is used, until you sell your rights to someone else. The legal term for these rights is called *copyright*. Technically, any original artwork you produce is automatically copyrighted as soon as you put it in tangible form.

To be automatically copyrighted, your artwork must fall within these guidelines:

- It must be your original creation. It cannot be a copy of somebody else's work.
- It must be "pictorial, graphic, or sculptural." Utilitarian objects, such as lamps or toasters, are not covered, although you can copyright an illustration featured on a lamp or toaster.
- It must be fixed in "any tangible medium, now known or later developed." Your work, or at least a representation of a planned work, must be created in or on a medium you can see or touch, such as paper, canvas, clay, a sketch pad, or even a website. It can't just be an idea in your head. An idea cannot be copyrighted.

COPYRIGHT LASTS FOR YOUR LIFETIME PLUS SEVENTY YEARS

Copyright is exclusive. When you create a work, the rights automatically belong to you and nobody else but you until those rights are sold to someone else.

Works of art created on or after January 1978 are protected for your lifetime plus seventy years.

THE ARTIST'S BUNDLE OF RIGHTS

One of the most important things you need to know about copyright is that it is not just a singular right. It is a bundle of rights you enjoy as creator of your artwork:

- Reproduction right. You have the right to make copies of the original work.
- Modification right. You have the right to create derivative works based on the original work.

- Distribution rights. You have the right to sell, rent, or lease copies of your work.
- Public performance right. You have the right to play, recite, or otherwise perform a work. (This right is more applicable to written or musical art forms than to visual art.)
- Public display right. You have the right to display your work in a public place. This bundle of rights can be divided up in a number of ways so that you can sell all or part of any of those exclusive rights to one or more parties. The system of selling parts of your copyright bundle is sometimes referred to as divisible copyright. Just as a land owner can divide up his property and sell it to many different people, the artist can divide up his rights to an artwork and sell portions of those rights to different buyers.

DIVISIBLE COPYRIGHT: DIVIDE AND CONQUER

Why is divisible copyright so important? Because dividing up your bundle and selling parts of it to different buyers will help you get the most payment for each of your artworks. For any one of your artworks, you can sell your entire bundle of rights at one time (not advisable!) or divide each bundle pertaining to that work into smaller portions and make more money as a result. You can grant one party the right to use your work on a greeting card and sell another party the right to print that same work on T-shirts.

DIVISIBLE COPYRIGHT TERMS

Clients tend to use legal jargon to specify the rights they want to buy. The terms below are commonly used in contracts to indicate portions of your bundle of rights. Some terms are vague or general, such as "all rights." Other terms are more specific, such as "first North American rights." Make sure you know what each term means before signing a contract.

- **One-time rights.** Your client buys the right to use or publish your artwork on a one-time basis. One fee is paid for one use. Most magazine assignments fall under this category.
- **First rights.** This is almost the same as one-time rights, except that the buyer is also paying for the privilege of being the first to use your image. He may use it only once unless the other rights are negotiated. Sometimes first rights can be further broken down geographically. The buyer might ask to buy first North American rights, meaning he would have the right to be the first to publish the work in North America.
- **Exclusive rights.** This guarantees the buyer's exclusive right to use the artwork in his particular market or for a particular product. Exclusive rights are frequently negotiated by greeting card and gift companies. One company might purchase the exclusive right to use your work as a greeting card, leaving you free to sell the exclusive rights to produce the image on a mug to another company.
- **Promotional rights.** These rights allow a publisher to use an artwork for promotion of a publication in which the artwork appears. For example, if *The New Yorker* bought promotional rights to your cartoon, they could also use it in a direct-mail promotion.

- **Electronic rights.** These rights allow a buyer to place your work on electronic media such as websites. Often these rights are requested with print rights.

Work for hire. Under the Copyright Act of 1976, section 101, a "work for hire" is defined as "(1) a work prepared by an employee within the scope of his or her employment; or (2) a work specially ordered or commissioned for use as a contribution to a collective work, as part of a motion picture or other audiovisual work ... if the parties expressly agree in a written instrument signed by them that the work shall be considered a work made for hire." When the agreement is "work for hire," you surrender all rights to the image and can never resell that particular image again. If you agree to the terms, make sure the money you receive makes it well worth the arrangement.

- **All rights.** Again, be aware that this phrase means you will relinquish your entire copyright to a specific artwork. Before agreeing to the terms, make sure this is an arrangement you can live with. At the very least, arrange for the contract to expire after a specified date. Terms for all rights—including time period for usage and compensation—should be confirmed in a written agreement with the company.

Since legally your artwork is your property, when you create a project for a magazine you are, in effect, temporarily "leasing" your work to the client for publication.

Chances are you'll never hear an editor ask to lease or license your work, and he may not even realize he is leasing, not buying, your work, but most editors know that once the magazine is published, the editor has no further claims to your work, and the rights revert back to you. If the editor wants to use your work a second or third time, he must ask permission and negotiate with you to determine any additional fees you want to charge. You are free to take that same work and sell it to another buyer.

However, if the editor buys "all rights," you cannot legally offer that same image to another magazine or company. If you agree to create the artwork as "work for hire," you relinquish your rights entirely.

WHAT LICENSING AGENTS KNOW

The practice of leasing parts or groups of an artist's bundle of rights is often referred to as licensing, because (legally) the artist is granting someone a "license" to use his work for a limited time for a specific reason. As licensing agents have come to realize, it is the exclusivity of the rights and the ability to divide and sell them that make them valuable. Knowing exactly what rights you own, which you can sell, and in what combinations, will help you negotiate.

DON'T SELL CONFLICTING RIGHTS TO DIFFERENT CLIENTS

You also have to make sure the rights you sell to one client don't conflict with any of the rights sold to other clients. For example, you can't sell the exclusive right to use your image on greeting cards to two separate greeting card companies. You can sell the exclusive greeting card rights to one card company and the exclusive rights to use your artwork on mugs to a separate gift company. You should always get such agreements in writing and let both companies know your work will appear on other products.

WHEN TO USE THE COPYRIGHT © AND CREDIT LINES

A copyright notice consists of the word "Copyright" or its symbol ©, the year the work was created or first published, and the full name of the copyright owner. It should be placed where it can easily be seen, on the front or back of a piece of work.

Under today's laws, placing the copyright symbol on your work isn't absolutely necessary to claim copyright infringement and take a plagiarist to court if he steals your work. If you browse through magazines, you will often see the illustrator's name in small print near the illustration, without the Copyright ©. This is common practice in the magazine industry. Even though the © is not printed, the illustrator still owns the copyright unless the magazine purchased all rights to the work. Just make sure the editor gives you a credit line.

Usually you will not see the artist's name or credit line next to advertisements for products. Advertising agencies often purchase all rights to the work for a specified time. They usually pay the artist generously for this privilege and spell out the terms clearly in the artist's contract.

HOW TO REGISTER A COPYRIGHT

The process of registering your work is simple. Visit the United States Copyright Office website at www.copyright.gov to file electronically. You can still register with paper forms, but this method requires a higher filing fee. To request paper forms, call (202)707-9100 or write to the Library of Congress, Copyright Office-COPUBS, 101 Independence Ave. SE, Washington, DC 20559-6304, Attn: Information Publications, Section LM0455 and ask for package 115 and circulars 40 and 40A. Crafters should ask for package 111 and circular 44. They will send you a package containing Form VA (for visual artists).

You can register an entire collection of your work rather than one work at a time. That way you will only have to pay one fee for an unlimited number of works. For example, if you have created a hundred works between 2012 and 2014, you can complete a copyright form to register "the collected works of Jane Smith, 2012–2014." But you will have to upload digital files or send either slides or photocopies of each of those works.

WHY REGISTER?

It seems like a lot of time and trouble to complete the forms to register copyrights for all your artworks. It may not be necessary or worth it to you to register every artwork you create. After all, a work is copyrighted the moment it's created anyway, right? The benefits of registering are basically to give you additional clout in case an infringement occurs, and you decide to take the offender to court. Without a copyright registration, it probably wouldn't be economically feasible to file suit, because you'd be entitled to only your damages and the infringer's profits, which might not equal the cost of litigating the case. If the works are registered with the U.S. Copyright Office, it will be easier to prove your case and get reimbursed for your court costs.

Likewise, the big advantage of using the Copyright © also comes when and if you ever have to take an infringer to court. Since the Copyright © is the most clear warning to potential plagiarizers, it is easier to collect damages if the © is in plain sight.

Register with the U.S. Copyright Office those works you fear are likely to be plagiarized before or shortly after they have been exhibited or published. That way, if anyone uses your work without permission, you can take action.

DEAL SWIFTLY WITH PLAGIARISTS

If you suspect your work has been plagiarized and you have not already registered it with the Copyright Office, register it immediately. You have to wait until it is registered before you can take legal action against the infringer.

Before taking the matter to court, however, your first course of action might be a well-phrased letter from your lawyer telling the offender to "cease and desist" using your work, because you have a registered copyright. Such a warning (especially if printed on your lawyer's letterhead) is often enough to get the offender to stop using your work.

COPYRIGHT RESOURCES

The U.S. Copyright website (www.copyright.gov), the official site of the U.S. Copyright Office, is very helpful and will answer just about any question you can think of. Information is also available by phone at (202) 707-3000. Another great site, called the Copyright Website, is located at www.benedict.com.

[DEFEAT SELF-DOUBT, GROW YOUR BUSINESS]

....

by Tara Swiger

What's really holding you back from starting or growing your business? Crafters and makers often tell me that they don't know enough. They need to learn Instagram, or bookkeeping, or how to register their domain name.

And that may be true. You probably have a lot to learn about business (we all do!). But is that really what's holding you back, right now? Is that what's keeping you from taking the next step?

I doubt it. You probably know at least one action you could take, right now, to start or build your business.

So why aren't you doing it? Why don't we take action? Why don't we do the thing we KNOW we want to do? Why don't we act on all the knowledge we have?

Self-doubt.

Can you build a business? Are you capable enough? Smart enough? Hard-working enough?

It's easy to get sucked into a swirl of doubts and then freeze. Which direction should you go? Which step should you take next? How do you know if it's the right one?

Here's the secret of all successful businesses: **you have to act even when you don't know, even when you're not sure.** You have to act. There is never going to be the "right" answer. There's never going to be the "right" action. You have to just do it.

But telling yourself to "just do it" doesn't always work. Not when you're swirling in self-doubt. The sneakiest (and most dangerous) aspect of self-doubt is that we don't always recognize it for what it is. It often presents as the voice of reason. "Oh, you're not ready for that yet, wait a little bit." "You shouldn't try that yet, you don't want to fail."

But businesses are built on trying. They are only built on failing and trying again.

You're not alone in this doubt. Most of us, to one degree or another, experience it especially as we do something new, exciting, and risky, like start a business. The good news is, studies show us that it's possible to rewire this self-doubt into confidence. The doubt doesn't need to entirely disappear, you simply need to be able to take action in spite of it.

So how do we take action, build our business, while still feeling the doubt?

Here are five things to try:

1. DO THINGS!

You don't feel ready, and you're not entirely sure you can do something big and scary, I know! But guess what? The best way to build confidence in your ability to do things in your business is to do things in your business. You develop the habit of taking action, living through the consequences (more on that in a minute), and coming out the other side braver and more competent. In other words, do things before you feel you're ready: take on projects, say yes, commit. Then figure it out (don't back out, don't slack on finding the answer) and do the thing you agreed to do.

This is different than just telling yourself to do it. Instead, tell yourself, "I'm going to start doing this, even though I'm not entirely sure I can." And when self-doubt slows you down, remember—failure isn't final, it's data. You're not trying to do anything perfectly; you're simply experimenting to see what works and what doesn't.

2. LEARN THE RIGHT LESSON FROM FAILURE.

Studies show that **confidence is built on trying things and then failing at them** (check out *The Confidence Code* (Harper Business, 2014), if you'd like to read more about the research into how confidence is built). Yes! Failure is going to help you get past the self-doubt, but only if you learn the right lesson from it.

Often when we fail, we decide that we've learned (or proved) that we're failures. That we aren't capable. That we shouldn't try bigger and better things. Taking that lesson isn't going to help your confidence. It kills it, and you'll be less likely to take on the next challenge.

Instead, you can choose to see each failure, mistake, or flop as proof that you can do things and survive. You can try and fail and still be OK. Because that directly confronts the lie that self-doubt tells you: "You'd better not do that, or you won't be OK." When you challenge that directly, when you do the thing and yet still survive? That builds confidence.

3. COMPETENCE BUILDS CONFIDENCE BUILDS COMPETENCE.

When you feel capable and competent, you're more likely to take action. When you take action, you get good at taking action and you build your skills, which then builds your confidence. For example, once you survive your first few craft shows, you build competence in doing craft shows, and that makes it easier and easier to apply to more shows!

Often when we're in a new situation or confronted with a new challenge, we just forget that we're already competent. For example, if you're nervous to apply to your first craft show, but you've already made some sales online, you can use your competence at making, pricing, and writing about your work to succeed at the craft show.

4. LIST THREE THINGS YOU'VE DONE SUCCESSFULLY.

If you have a hard time kicking off the competence/confidence cycle, you need to first gather the confidence to do the thing the first time. How? Look at everything else you've done successfully. Did you successfully navigate a career? Do you feed your children? Did you graduate high school? No matter who you are or how old or young you are, you have a long list of things you've tried, survived, and succeeded at. List at least three things (list ten to get really fired up) you've accomplished and then write about the skills and smarts you needed to do those three things.

What from that list can you apply to your current business challenge? What skills or smarts can you use in this situation?

5. TAKE CONFIDENCE INTO YOUR OWN HANDS.

Are you waiting for someone to "pick" you? Someone to tell you you're good enough, that you should grow your business, that you should sell your work? Maybe you're waiting for approval from Oprah, or the big craft show organizer, or a fancy blogger. But that's not the path to confidence and action. In fact, studies show that confidence built on other people's praise is more fragile than confidence built from our own achievement.

You're going to become more confident and be able to take more action when you start taking action, grow your competence (actually get good at it!), and survive failures. Don't wait for someone else to approve of you. Don't wait for someone else to give you permission to take the next step. It's OK (and perfectly normal!) to feel self-doubt about your business, just decide to take action and build your business despite it.

TARA SWIGER

Tara Swiger is the author of *Market Yourself*, a workbook for crafters and artists who want to share their work with the world. Her podcast, blog, and workshops can be found at

www.TaraSwiger.com.

[BUILDING A COHESIVE BRAND]

....

by Arianne Foulks

I'm sure you know of some "overnight success" businesses. Their products are recognizable from a mile away, people clamor to buy, and they get regular publicity. These businesses seem like a snowball rolling downhill, gathering speed and getting huge.

What makes success come more easily for these business owners? They have created a strong brand that people relate to. With effective branding in place, building their business is now a journey of achievable challenges.

Branding is an area of business where makers often "make-do" with graphic design that is ill-fitting or unprofessional. Amateur-looking design or messaging that doesn't speak to the right people gives business owners a rough start, by making their work harder to promote. It's important to have a brand that is not only appealing, but that appeals to the exact type of person you're hoping to attract. A confusing, scattered, or slapdash brand ends up being a hurdle they have to overcome as their business grows. If you're new to branding, though, it's hard to know what you need.

If you think of branding as telling a consistent story about your business, the work should come more easily. Consider the story of these two talented artisans and how their understanding of their story brought them different outcomes:

ONCE UPON A TIME, THERE WERE TWO MAKERS ...

Toby sells handcrafted soap and artistic bottle openers at the farmer's market. His friends love his soap and encouraged him to sell it on Etsy. He is giving it a try, but finding it frustrating.

Lucy makes ceramics with geometric shapes and bright colors in her unique style. She recently turned her hobby into a business. Her launch went well, and she is now overwhelmed with orders.

BOTH OF THESE ENTREPRENEURS HAVE PROBLEMS

Toby feels like he is doing the right things to market his work, but he isn't getting any traction. When he gets publicity, the customers don't "stick," and he doesn't see a steady increase in sales.

Illustration by Arianne Foulks

Toby applies to craft fairs, but isn't accepted to any of them. People say he's charging too much for his soap, but he doesn't see a way to lower prices while he's struggling to make a profit.

Lucy is having problems, too. Her website crashes when too many shoppers visit the site at once. Blogs and news outlets pick up on her new product launches and spread the news further than she expects.

She is working feverishly to keep items in stock, as she has more demand than supply. It's hard for her to keep up with publicity, production, and new business prospects.

As you can see, Lucy's problems are quite a bit more fun to solve.

WHAT IS DIFFERENT ABOUT THESE TWO BUSINESSES?

They are both skilled artisans, producing a quality product with love and care. They are both hard workers, taking extra time to learn about running and marketing a business. It is working for Lucy, but not for Toby.

WHAT'S GOING WRONG FOR TOBY?

Toby is not sure where his customers are, since he doesn't know who they are. If you ask him why you should buy from him instead of Soapy Joe's booth, he can't give you an answer.

He hasn't focused his product line. He has a hard time selling bottle openers to his soap customers, and creating a logo that makes sense for both. His Etsy shop graphics don't match his market booth, and the packaging is different from item to item. His signs and displays look homemade. Toby doesn't have a cohesive brand.

WHAT'S GOING RIGHT FOR LUCY?

Lucy sure seems lucky! I'm sure you can tell by now that it's not luck that's working for her. She has a knack for telling her story. Her products make sense together, and her logo and packaging communicate her story visually.

Lucy knows who relates to her values and style, and she speaks directly to them on relevant blogs and social media platforms. She understands what makes her work unique and valuable and makes sure the press know as well.

Because of her storytelling and memorable brand, people want what she sells, and it's easy for them to share it with their friends.

CREATE A UNIQUE BUSINESS FOR YOUR TARGET CUSTOMER

Three things will serve as the building blocks for your brand:

1. Having a Unique Selling Proposition (USP)
2. Knowing your target customer
3. Building a strong brand identity using this knowledge

Your Unique Selling Proposition: What makes you different from even your closest competitors? Conveying this is key to making your product stand out. For example, there are hundreds of options when someone wants coffee. The reason so many people go to Starbucks is because of how well they've built their brand.

Your target customer: People will buy from you because of how your product makes them feel about themselves. To create this sort of emotional connection and tell your story effectively, you need to know your audience.

Standard practice is to narrow down your possible customers to one ideal imaginary person. Then relate directly to that person, making you THE only choice for them.

USING GRAPHIC DESIGN TO BUILD A STRONG IDENTITY

Once you've determined your USP, you can design a strong brand identity that will speak to your target customer.

Your brand identity includes the logo, fonts, colors, and graphics for your brand. It's also the voice and tone of your copywriting, the style and theme of your photography, the look and feel of your website.

All these things need to relate back to your unique selling proposition. When marketing your business, you should always consider your target customer's needs and preferences.

Once you know who you're talking to and what about, you can create and design the information that communicates your brand to the world. As you do, keep these things in mind:

- **Your logo must be simple.** You can't fit everything about your business into your logo. It should be a single clear idea that is easy to recognize and describe.
- **Your brand should be memorable and distinctive.** You want your customers to immediately recognize it. It needs to stand apart from others in your industry. Trends are fine when designing seasonal product lines, but you want your logo to stand the test of time.
- **Your graphic design needs to be versatile** because there are so many ways you'll be using your brand. Your logo should be effective in all sizes and in both print and Web applications.
- **Your brand identity should be appropriate.** Your logo must make sense for your type of business. A playful look and feel works for a children's toy maker, but doesn't for a sophisticated jewelry designer.
- **Keep everything cohesive and consistent.** Choose a set of fonts, colors, and graphics for all marketing and other materials. Make sure your design choices reflect your brand.
- **Make it polished.** To interest retail and wholesale buyers, as well as press, you need to look trustworthy and stable. If your packaging and other materials look too "homemade," it will be a turn-off.
- **Feel confident about your brand!** When all the pieces of your brand fit together, it's much easier to approach customers, stores, and press, expecting to receive a positive response.

A creative business like yours has a huge branding advantage because you're likely to have an interesting story to tell about yourself and your products. If you create a brand identity that tells your story with personality, customers will want to find out more about your business. And the work to build your business will be that much easier.

Photo by Jennifer Lacey Photography for Aeolidia

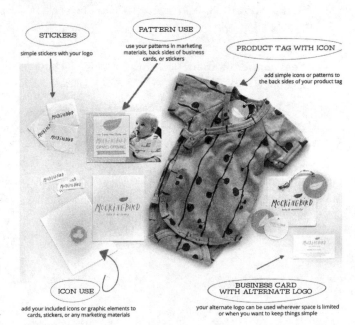

STICKERS
simple stickers with your logo

PATTERN USE
use your patterns in marketing materials, back sides of business cards, or stickers

PRODUCT TAG WITH ICON
add simple icons or patterns to the back sides of your product tag

ICON USE
add your included icons or graphic elements to cards, stickers, or any marketing materials

BUSINESS CARD WITH ALTERNATE LOGO
your alternate logo can be used wherever space is limited or when you want to keep things simple

Photo by TK

ARIANNE FOULKS

Arianne Foulks is a storyteller, idea hatcher, and yaysayer. She is captain and founder at Aeolidia, a Web and graphic design studio that has been working with creative handmakers and designers since 2004, helping them put their best foot forward online.

www.aeolidia.com

[10 TIPS AND TRICKS FOR PHOTOGRAPHING YOUR CRAFT]

....

by Gale Zucker

More often than not, the first glimpse the world sees of your craft is in a photograph. The imagery must catch eyes surfing the Internet, persuade juries, create followers on social media, and get subscribers to read your newsletter instead of clicking away.

If hiring a professional photographer is not in your budget, it's best to embrace photography as a crucial step in your process and create amazing photos yourself.

As a professional photographer with much experience in the world of handmade, I'm here with surefire tips to make your photos fabulous. These are easy techniques to try, regardless of what kind of camera you own. I guarantee that your images will take leaps forward if you use a few of these techniques.

First, a few basics: I am talking about digital photography. A film camera is great for art or fun, but not for business. A DSLR (digital single lens reflex) camera with a prime 50mm lens is ideal for photographing craft, but not required. A point and shoot, or even a good smartphone camera (shhh, don't tell anyone) with some photo edits can do the job.

1. PIXELS ARE FREE.

It takes time, expense, thought, and effort to arrive at your finger on the shutter release photographing your craft—so don't skimp on the exposures! It doesn't cost anything more to make ten, twenty, or a hundred alternative versions showing your work. Photograph and shoot and shoot some more—you can delete later. Try different angles, compositions, and move the subject around to change the light. I promise you, the more you shoot, the more success you'll have with your photos.

2. TURN OFF THAT FLASH.

Never use direct flash on your craft. There is always a better way. If nothing else, in a low light situation, steady your camera on a tripod or on a table, and hold your breath while you release that shutter. Make many exposures. You'll get some that are sharp. I promise.

3. SOFT INDIRECT SIDE LIGHTING IS BEST TO SHOW TEXTURE AND DIMENSION.

Find some nice open shade: a covered patio, an overcast day outdoors, the north side of a building, or a room with lots of windows but no direct sunlight streaming onto your shooting surface. If you are in a sunny location, you can diffuse light to create shade using white cloth, a white or translucent umbrella. Even a large white sheet of paper can block direct light. Avoid photographing near intensely colored walls or using colored material to create shade or your images will be tinted accordingly.

Photo by Gale Zucker

4. REFLECTORS TO SOFTEN AND FILL SHADOWS.

Even on a cloudy day, the light will be directional. Fill light into shadows by placing a white board or silver reflector at a low angle on the opposite side from the light source. The light will bounce back into dark areas, softening shadows and flattering the subject. Whether you purchase a folding reflector designed for use with photography or use a white foamcore board, the light bouncing back will greatly improve your photos.

5. GET CLOSE!

I know you are proud of your artwork and want to show every square inch of it, but getting close will make us want to touch it and own it. It is also a smarter way to use the tiny image real estate on a mobile device or screen. Try shooting your work from a few feet away and then keep shooting, getting closer and closer. Detail shots are the closers for getting buyers to make the purchase.

6. EVERY PICTURE TELLS A STORY—MAKE SURE IT'S ONE STORY AND IT'S YOUR STORY.

A good story has one main point and supporting material. Create imagery that narrates. Is your work soft and cuddly? Is it colorful? Is it detailed and etched? An image that tries to tell too many stories at once gets lost. Your styling and props should be the supporting material.

7. COMPOSITIONAL TIP 1: GEOMETRY.

Create graphic elements within your photos. Try putting your artwork in a basket or box or on a shallow plate or tray. Circles, especially, are pleasing to our brains.

8. COMPOSITIONAL TIP 2: ASYMMETRY

Avoid plunking your artwork dead-center. There's the popular Rule of Thirds you'll find mentioned in most lists of photo tips—and it works. I like to use diagonals to lead the eye around the image. We all get into photographic ruts—so be mindful while holding up your camera. Shoot your craft how you might normally and then keep moving around the subject, tilting your camera (those pixels are free, after all).

9. BACKGROUNDS ARE IMPORTANT.

Create a signature look by choosing a background or style that you'll use consistently. For your background, consider a limited palette of colors that go with your work. Or go high contrast with complementary colors to pop that photo. Flat, low textured surfaces such

Photo by Gale Zucker

as fabric work great as backgrounds, prints add ambiance for your work. Once you've found something that works, you'll have a photographic identity that will get you attention. (Sidenote: innovate, don't imitate. You don't want to get lost in a crowd of, for example, products shown on weathered barn wood.)

10. PHOTO EDITING.

None of the imagery you see published is straight out of a camera. It all gets a little touch up, a boost, or a significant amount of editing before it grabs your eyeballs. True, this adds a little more time to the process, but it is time well spent. The grand-daddy of all photo-editing programs is PhotoShop, which is expensive and dense to learn. Fortunately, there are user- and budget-friendly alternatives for photo editing, such as PicMonkey and Ribbet. These Web-based tools will allow you to easily color-correct, optimize, crop, clean up, add type, and make simple collages of your photos.

Good luck—and remember, pixels are free. Keep shooting!

Photo by Gale Zucker

GALE ZUCKER

Gale Zucker is a commercial and editorial photographer with the niche specialty of the handmade market and knitwear fashion. She's the co-author/photographer of the books *CraftActivism* and *Shear Spirit*, both from Random House. Her next book, *Drop Dead Easy Knits*, will be published September 2016 from Clarkson Potter. Gale has downloadable photography webinars for crafters and knitters available through Interweave, and she teaches Photography for Makers workshops. You can find her on the social media under her name galezucker.

www.gzucker.com

[A BUSINESS PLAN YOU'LL ACTUALLY USE]

....

by Kelly Rand

In 2016, Idaho-based sewist Angela Bowman launched *We Seam*, an online sewing community. The sewing website was a dream a long time in the making. And just like any other entrepreneur's dream, *We Seam* started with a business plan. But it was no ordinary business plan.

Business plans are an essential tool that helps guide business endeavors. Putting thoughts to paper regarding how to finance and market a business as well as understand a product's customer base helps keep a business nimble and growing. However, creating a traditional business plan can be cumbersome. It's an arduous process, and the thought of writing a business plan can make both business students and craft-minded entrepreneurs want to do anything except write one.

The U.S. Small Business Administration (SBA) describes a business plan as a "living document" that ". . . is an essential roadmap for business success." The SBA outlines nine sections to incorporate into a business plan. These sections are an executive summary, a company description, marketing analysis with customer research, how the company will be organized and managed, the service or product, a marketing and sales strategy, funding request, financial projections, and an appendix for resumes, licenses, and various other documentation.

Writing this type of traditional business plan can easily take a very long time and quickly rack up more than 100 pages of information. Because it can take so long to complete, it runs the risk of becoming worthless by the time it's finished. Caroline Cummings, Venture Catalyst with the Regional Accelerator and Innovation Network (RAIN) in Oregon, agrees. "[A business plan] has a connotation associated with it that you write once then you never look at it again, and then it's outdated the second you print it," she explained on the phone. All that time and energy wasted, frozen in time.

So how can a business plan be helpful if writing one is a waste of time? By slimming it down and shifting the focus.

Bowman had always assumed a business plan was a communication tool for gaining investment. In her mind, the document would be presented to people outside of the business, a bank or group of investors, for the sole purpose of raising funds. "It was all unapproachable and boring to me," she said on the phone.

Then one day, while researching business-process modeling for her then employer, she came across the Business Model Canvas by Alex Osterwalder, a business theorist and author of *Business Model Generation* (John Wiley and Sons; July 2010).

The Business Model Canvas is an efficient planning tool that helps map a new or existing business. The Canvas has nine sections similar to a traditional business plan including key partners, activities and resources, a value proposition, customer relationships and segments, sales channels, cost structure, and revenue streams. The main difference is it encourages the user to capture this information on just one piece of paper.

Bowman found herself drawn to the Canvas as a business plan because it was simple and a highly visual tool. "It's called a canvas for a reason," she explained. "The whole thing can be one big drawing if you want it to be."

Bowman completed the Business Model Canvas for *We Seam* in "just a few minutes." But, she explained, she had been thinking of the idea of *We Seam* for a very long time before creating a Canvas. "I had the idea nailed down," she said.

Photo by Kelly Rand

Whatever stage your business idea is in, the simple act of filling out a Business Model Canvas or doing some form of a business plan can be a beneficial exercise. "There's a lot of research that shows if you just go through the exercise of writing a business plan, whether it's three pages or thirty pages, you'll think more strategically about your business," Cummings explained.

Cummings is a proponent of another form of slim business plan. In an Etsy *Seller's Handbook* blog post from 2013 titled "How to Write a Creative Business Plan In Under an Hour," Cummings suggests treating each section of a business plan as if you were writing tweets to share on Twitter, the microblogging platform, where you only have 140 characters per post. "What [this] does is force you as a business owner to focus on what is really important about your market, about your product, about the problem that you are solving in the marketplace for someone," she elaborated.

Another way to view the business plan is to appreciate that it can have multiple audiences. While a traditional plan is mostly presented to an external audience and used to gain investors, a business plan can also be written for the business owner as an internal tool. "Really that's the whole point of creating a business plan," Bowman said, ". . . knowing your plan in your own brain. That's the true value right there."

Viewing the plan as a living document is also important no matter the format. This enables quick rewrites or periodic tweaks for internal or external use. Cummings likens it to being asked to speak for an audience, where the speaker needs to provide a bio. "I first find out who it is I am going to be speaking to and then I tailor those two or three sentences for that audience," Cummings said.

Cummings suggests revisiting a business plan quarterly or in the case of a significant event, such as being acquired by another company. Bowman revisits her Canvas every few months and often revises it every six months. Speaking to the Canvas's flexibility Bowman said, "You can tweak it to your heart's content."

Even with a slimmed-down plan, it is vital to include a value proposition. "You can't underestimate the importance of [the value proposition] because that is what you're going to lead with when someone stops you on the street and says 'what do you do?' And if you can't say it in one sentence, then you're in trouble," Cummings explained.

Bowman agrees that the value proposition is necessary and adds that the customer segments section is also vital to include. "Those two sections of the Canvas are the most critical in my mind because you need to define your value proposition and who your customers are," she said. "How can you relieve your customer's pains with your value proposition?"

A business plan doesn't need to be a soulless tome. Create a Business Model Canvas, a plan made up of a series of tweets or another form entirely, and the exercise itself can help your business become strategic and get on the right track to success.

KELLY RAND

Kelly Rand writes about the intersection of craft, entrepreneurship, and the handmade movement. Rand is a frequent contributor to *Handmade Business* magazine and her work has also appeared in *Bust* magazine, *Studios* magazine, *The Crafts Report*, and Etsy. Rand is the lead author of *Handmade to Sell: Hello Craft's Guide to Owning, Running and Growing Your Crafty Business* (Potter Craft, 2012). She consults on elements of craft and sustainable business. Rand has a BFA in illustration from the Savannah College of Art and Design. She resides in Washington, D.C., with her husband and daughter.

www.kellyrand.com

[CHOOSING AN ONLINE MARKETPLACE]

....

by Isaac Watson

The Internet is your oyster! Most business consultants and successful craft business owners suggest that the best customer experience is something you manage end to end—from the minute the customer loads your website to the minute they open the package on their doorstep. But for someone who's just starting out, setting up a dedicated website and online shop from scratch is a daunting task. In most cases, the easiest place to start is with an existing online marketplace that offers the tools and platform to sell your work without investing an unwieldy amount of time, effort, and money.

Online marketplaces have a lot to offer, even if they don't give you complete control. They are typically easy to set up, they offer access to an existing customer base that trusts and shops with them regularly, and they understand the needs of the craft business owner. Most online platforms fall under one of three categories:

INTERNET CRAFT FAIR

Like the in-person variety, these third-party marketplaces allow you to set up a "booth" or online shop. They handle payment for you, but you have little room for customization—you're selling under their umbrella brand using a rather rigid shop template. Aftcra, Art-Fire, Etsy, and Handmade at Amazon are all great examples.

ONLINE PRODUCTION HOUSE

Many illustrators, designers, and digital craftspeople use these services to sell their art without needing to worry about the actual production. Upload your artwork and choose your product offering, then they'll produce the item purchased (a T-shirt, mug, or art print, for example) and send it to your customer for you. Take a look at ImageKind, Society6, and Spreadshirt to get a sense for how these work.

E-COMMERCE PLATFORM

Use these services to create your own custom-branded shop, then integrate it into your own website. You are responsible for fulfilling orders yourself, but they still handle payment processing. Popular examples include Big Cartel, Shopify, StoreEnvy, and WooCommerce.

Before you begin evaluating online marketplaces, you'll want to make sure you're ready to sell online. Ask yourself these five questions to start:

1. **What are your selling priorities?** If you are focused on selling your crafts to local customers, an online shop may not be necessary. If you want to expand your audience to a broader market, selling online is a natural next step.
2. **Are your prices adequate?** Your retail price needs to accommodate materials, payment processing and marketplace fees (usually around 10%), and shipping costs, and still pay yourself appropriately. If you expect to sell wholesale in the future, your prices should also be able to handle a 50 percent wholesale discount and still be profitable.
3. **Are your marketing materials at the ready?** Taking the time to write stellar item descriptions and investing in the best product photos you can afford will have the biggest impact on convincing potential customers to click that "buy" button.
4. **How much time are you willing to put into marketing?** It's easy to think that all you have to do is list something and let the people come to you. But online marketplaces are not your sales rep—as the maker, you are the only person qualified to find your customer and bring them to your shop, so that puts you in charge of marketing efforts.
5. **Do you have time and capacity to manage and fulfill orders consistently?** Knowing how long it takes you to fulfill orders, relist items, order supplies, and produce more inventory can help you gauge what kind of commitment you'll need to make to this selling channel.

Once you're ready to research your online options, a simple pros and cons list may not cut it. Grab a sheet of paper and create a large grid with a row for each of the five questions below and a column for each marketplace you're considering, then see how each measures up.

1. **Does your target customer shop here already?** An online marketplace should provide access to the people that are most likely to purchase your work. If they serve a different audience, that's the first sign they're not a good fit.

2. **Why do you want to sell here?** Following the masses to an online marketplace isn't always the best idea. A platform where you can stand out will make it easier to find your customer instead of swimming through a sea of similar sellers.

3. **What does it take to sell here?** Know the true costs involved, including listing and processing fees. Read and understand the legal agreements and talk with other makers who use that platform to see what advice they have.

4. **What tools do they provide?** Some marketplaces have active editorial and social media channels that feature sellers and provide access to low-cost advertising, fulfillment services, wholesale networks, and more. These fringe benefits can set one marketplace apart from the rest or may be more trouble than they're worth.

5. **How will this integrate with your existing business?** If you sell out of something in person at a craft fair, managing that listing online should be as effortless as possible. Some platforms integrate with popular online accounting and inventory management software, or offer offline payment processing using their app and a smartphone.

Selling online is one of the easiest experiments you can run for your business, so if one marketplace stands out above the rest, it's time to give it a shot. By keeping an eye on your sales data, traffic analytics, and listing information, you'll have a good handle on what's working and what needs to change. Tweak your listings, experiment with advertising and adjust your product photos to see what delivers the best results. And if it comes right down to it, leaving one platform for another or maintaining multiple platforms at once isn't rocket science. Just remember—finding your customers and directing them to your online shop is the single most important thing you can do to have a successful online craft business.

ISAAC WATSON

Isaac Watson founded and runs Maker's Nation, a nonprofit offering business education and community support for creative small business owners. In addition, Isaac is a professional conference producer and event organizer who loves spending his spare time making with his hands, including cooking, puttering in his yard, renovating houses, and building a tiny cabin on a mountain. He lives in Vancouver, Washington.

www.makersnation.org

CUSTOMER COMMUNICATION 101

....

by John and Elizabeth Rappa

An earlier version of this piece appeared on the Academy of Handmade *blog*

You have a (largely) online business, and your main form of communication is writing via e-mail or messaging. No big deal, right? A customer messages you and you message them back. It seems simple enough. However, the content of those messages can be a little more complicated. We have a few tips and tricks that can streamline the process to ensure you are always at your best.

Customers are individuals, and as such each customer has different service requirements. Most customers require little or no communication or customer service before or after the transaction—and this should be your ultimate goal. Customers should have all the information available to them, from your product listings to your policies, to make an informed and smooth purchase from your shop.

However, sometimes customers require a little more service. Whether it is a customer with questions prior to a purchase or with problems during shipping or after receiving the item, you must present yourself and your business in a completely professional manner. Remember: when it comes to business correspondence, you are not you, you are your business. Each customer or potential customer can become a loyal patron of your business for years to come and as such deserves your complete attention and highest degree of professionalism.

Customers make purchases from your business for an item or service. Always keep that in mind: your purpose is to sell your items. The communications you receive can be anything from a blogger asking to review your items to a customer who needs help navigate a customization process. Everyone is a potential customer. Each person with whom you communicate could potentially tell their friends and family about you. You want to be sure you are putting your best foot forward in all communications.

You should treat the format of each correspondence like a letter. Your customers may not follow this same format when asking you questions. Often, online communications are treated like texting or messaging. This does not mean that you should disregard the basic format of business communication. If you have ever worked in an office, you are probably familiar with the proper letter-writing format, which follow a few simple rules.

Your communication format should be as follows:

Greeting
Thanking your customer for their time
Answering the question
Encouraging your customer to respond
Salutation
Name
Business Name

It is that simple. By following this format you ensure your correspondences are professional, concise, and courteous.

Here are two examples of business communications. The first is a reply to the customer in the same format as their question. The second showcases the proper letter-writing format.

CUSTOMER:

DO YOU HAVE THIS IN RED

REPLY #1:

Yeah

Notice that the customer did not provide a salutation or correct punctuation, nor did they sign their message. The one word colloquial response may seem to match the question, however, this kind of response is not professional and should be avoided at all costs.

REPLY #2

Hi (name of customer/customer screen name),

Thank you for contacting us. We do have this item in red, which you can see here (product link).

If you have any other questions or if there is any other way in which we can be of assistance, please let us know.

Thank you,

(Name/ Business)

In the second response you present a professional demeanor and encourage the customer to respond or reply. Regardless of the question, this format will serve you and become second nature when replying to any e-mail or message.

Another tricky thing to consider is tone. Do you know what tone your message takes? For that matter, what is tone? Tone is the general attitude that is perceived when reading a message. When writing a reply, if your wording or phrasing is off, it can be read as offensive or off-putting. You never want to seem sarcastic, unhelpful, or rude.

Reading and editing for tone is a skill that takes time to develop. If you are unsure about the tone of your message, have a friend whose opinion you trust read it or step away for a while before rereading it. Consider the following examples of two messages with different tones.

CUSTOMER:

I DON'T LIKE THIS. THE COLOR IS DIFFERENT THAN WHAT I EXPECTED.

REPLY #1

Hi (Name of customer),

Thank you for contacting us. The color is exactly what we show on our website. It isn't any different than what you see. You must know that computer screens can vary. Do you want another color?

Thank you,

(Name/ Name of Business)

REPLY #2

Hi (Name of Customer),

Thank you for contacting us. We appreciate you reaching out to us. As noted in our listings, colors can vary from computer monitor to computer monitor depending on settings. We would be happy to assist you in finding another color that will meet your needs.

Please let us know how we can be of assistance.

We look forward to hearing from you,

(Name/Name of Business)

Here you can see how two very different responses that say the same thing can present a very different tone. Reply #1 can be read as defensive, harsh, and abrupt. It sets an antagonistic tone for future communication. The customer may react negatively, and the situation could be escalated further.

Reply #2 is helpful and encourages an open and understanding dialogue with your customer. Think about what you want to say and be sure to edit so that when a customer is reading your message they will see it as helpful and open to communication. It will take time and practice to develop these skills.

Do not be in such a rush to respond to your customer that you don't take the time to read and edit for tone. Try to read your message as if you are the person receiving it. Even if you feel you have received a correspondence that is harsh or rude, you will always want to put aside your feelings and be as professional and courteous as possible.

Of course, not all situations can be resolved by the methods discussed in this article. Occasionally, customers can be very difficult regardless of your actions or demeanor. These situations are even more frustrating when you have done everything in your power to assist the customer and de-escalate the situation.

Just remember to stay calm, firm, and never lose your composure—treat each message as if it is the first message with a new customer (even if it is actually tenth message), and never allow your emotions or nerves to dictate your responses, even under the most trying circumstances.

Implementing these tips may seem like a lot of work, but remember poor customer service can only makes your job harder. We hope these tried-and-true tips help you to best serve your business and streamline your customer communications.

JOHN AND ELIZABETH RAPPA

John and Elizabeth are the creative team behind Wyoming-based ForgottenCotton, which focuses on high-quality handmade women's accessories. With more than five years of business experience, they have grown their online business into a full-time venture, selling to customers all over the world.

www.forgottencotton.com

[CRAFTING A WORKSPACE FOR YOUR BUSINESS]

....

by Lisa Chamoff

People who are passionate about crafting can always find room to create. When you turn your passion into a business, however, a key part of success is creating a workspace that works for you.

Whether you have a corner of your home or an outside studio, it's important for a workspace to be multifunctional, well organized, inspiring, and set up in a way to prevent injuries that can easily impact makers who perform repetitive movements.

Especially when you're just getting started, working from home may be the best option. Melissa Stahl, who sells handmade porcelain buttons and also designs knitting patterns, runs her business, Melissa Jean Design, out of a large space in her home in upstate New York that doubles as a playroom for her kids.

Stahl keeps her kiln in the basement, away from the play area, and her main crafting space is a draftsman's table that once belonged to her father-in-law, which she uses to make and paint her buttons. Stahl does her computer work at a separate desk— something that is recommended by ergonomics experts—and has another large table for miscellaneous tasks.

For storage, Stahl decided against ubiquitous IKEA shelving and scoured Craigslist for antique and vintage furniture to fit her aesthetic and her home décor. She stores her ceramic, art, and sewing supplies in an oak armoire she bought for $250, and she recently found an inexpensive cedar armoire for storing her yarn.

"When (my kids) have friends over, I like my tools and supplies behind closed doors," Stahl says. "By using antique and vintage furniture for storage, my space can feel like a family room when needed."

If you have the luxury of a workspace outside of the home, keep an eye out for flexible space that will allow your business to expand.

Laura Lundy of Slipped Stitch Studios, who creates project bags, notions pouches, and other accessories for knitters and crocheters, rents a small four-room office in downtown Huntington Beach, California. The rooms provide separate areas for work and product storage—Lundy uses the largest part of the studio for production, which has a worktable and shelving with rods to holds fabric rolls; pieces custom built by her brother—but the small team started to outgrow the space after less than three years.

"We are in a constant shuffle here," Lundy says, "always looking for the best way to keep things organized."

Organization can be a challenge for most people, but crafting often necessitates some specialized tactics. Beth Penn, who runs organizing business BNeato, recommends, if possible, having separate zones for projects that are completed and that are in progress, and cleaning up your workspace after each crafting session.

"A lot of (organization) is just the habit of putting everything back where it belongs," Penn says. "Crafting is going to make a bigger mess than most people's work. [Keeping it under control] should be a priority."

Penn also recommends getting rid of supplies or equipment you no longer use, something Stahl can relate to.

"I have had fabric kicking around for twenty years," Stahl says. "Some things that I am afraid of getting rid of entirely—for example, I have a whole 24" x 18" bin full of embroidery thread—I store in my basement."

It's also important to make sure your workspace is set up as ergonomically as possible, to prevent repetitive stress injuries common among crafters.

Karen Jacobs, an occupational therapist and certified professional ergonomist, with an expertise in ergonomics and workplace issues, recommends having a crafting area that's separate from where you work on the computer.

Before she became an OT, Jacobs ran a leather-crafting business and fashioned her work area out of a metal garbage can topped with a round piece of marble, which she used while standing.

"It put me in good position for hammering," Jacobs says. "I was a poor student, so that was the best I could do, but it was fabulous."

If you're standing on hard floors while crafting, Jacobs recommends using an anti-fatigue mat to support your feet while you work.

Computer workstations should ideally be set up differently from where you do your crafting, Jacobs says. When working at a computer, it's best to have an adjustable chair with lumbar support that allows you to sit with your feet flat on the floor and your knees at 90 degrees. If your feet don't reach the floor, get a footrest.

Photo by Melissa Stahl

While laptops are popular because they're portable, they're not ideal for everyday use, Jacobs says. If you work on a laptop, she suggests getting separate keyboard and mouse and bringing the laptop up to eye level to use the screen like a monitor, which should sit at arm's length. One of Jacobs's clients used old hatboxes to raise her computer screen.

"Artisans are creative people," Jacobs says. "Just look at what you have in the house or go to the recycling center and see what you can use."

LISA CHAMOFF

Lisa Chamoff is a freelance journalist in the New York Metro area who specializes in home design, real estate, and healthcare. When she's not writing or knitting shawls and sweaters, Lisa runs *Indie Untangled* (www.indieuntangled. com), a marketplace and blog that promotes the work of yarn dyers, pattern designers, and crafters of knitting-related accessories.

[THE ART AND CRAFT OF THE CLASS]

....

by Becka Rahn

I often call myself a teaching artist because that is a significant part of what I do to support my artistic business. I teach. A lot. For me, hearing a student gleefully say "I get it!" and knowing that I helped them get there is the best part of my job.

If you haven't taught before, it can be overwhelming, but there are things you can do to make sure you have a class that both you and the students love. Just like there are classical design principles that apply to making art, I think there are key principles to crafting a great class.

A GREAT CLASS STARTS WITH A GREAT PLAN.

First, decide what you want to teach. Think "What would I have loved to have someone show me when I was learning my craft?" or "What was the magic thing I learned that helped everything fall into place?" This gives you a built-in way to relate to students; you've been in their shoes, and this was how you moved forward.

Next, write a plan. I use a timeline with bullet points. For instance, for a dye class I might say: intros (5 min); vocabulary and tools (10 min); dye safety (20 min); and so on. With the timeline, I write specific learning goals, which helps me decide how to break up and focus the class time. My goals are usually three or four sentences that start with phrases such as:

Students will learn . . .

Students will understand . . .

Students will practice . . .

For the dye class, for example, my goals might be:

Students will learn to dye cotton fabric using low immersion techniques.

Students will understand how to mix and use dyes safely.

Students will practice dyeing fat quarters layering three basic dye colors.

Finally, think about the supplies you need and whether you or the students will provide them. If you are teaching a knitting class, your students probably don't have the information they need to get "a skein of worsted-weight yarn and size 7 needles." That's what they are expecting to learn in class. Are there shared materials, such as sticky notes or masking tape, that you can provide for a small fee?

EVERY CLASS IS FUN, CREATIVE, AND INSPIRING.

The goals and timeline you've written for your class will next help you to write the description, which is the most important part of your teaching plan. You, or the venue where you are teaching, will use this description to advertise your class, so it needs to catch everyone's attention, as well as provide a summary of your class.

The description should mention your teaching goals: skills learned, projects completed, or knowledge gained. Be specific about any prerequisite skills students need to be successful in your class. Think about the physical tasks that are part of your class. Will students be standing a lot? Will they need an apron because it will be messy?

Nothing can make a workshop go downhill faster than students who aren't getting what they anticipated when they signed up. Even though you know your class will be "fun, creative, and inspiring," using only splashy or superficial phrases like that in your description doesn't let students know what to expect, and the resulting disappointment can make it a lot less fun for everyone.

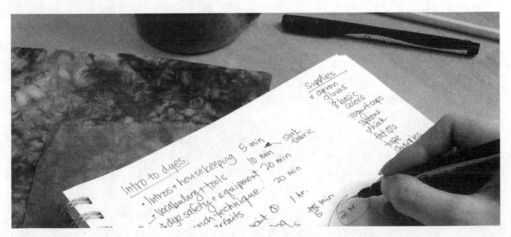

Photo by Becka Rahn

"THE DIFFERENCE BETWEEN ORDINARY AND EXTRAORDINARY IS PRACTICE."

- Vladimir Horowitz, conductor

You can learn a lot by running a practice session, so gather a group of friends and teach it. First, make sure that your timeline works. A class that gets done early or runs over time will make you look like you are unprepared and unprofessional. I plan a "time adjuster" for every class so that I can speed up or slow down on the fly. If we are ahead of schedule, we do the bonus material, such as an advanced embroidery stitch. If we are behind, I can drop it and move on.

As you practice, think about whether you had everything that you needed. Was there a step that would be easier with a handout? Did you have enough tools and materials for everyone to work comfortably? Were your friends successful and excited about their finished product?

YOU HAVE A CLASS, NOW ALL YOU NEED IS THE STUDENTS.

Once you have an amazing class put together, it's time to start teaching. The reality is that you probably aren't going to make much money the first time you teach this class. New classes take time to design and prepare, and usually that is time for which you aren't getting paid. Time spent getting started is an investment. But by designing a fantastic class from the start, I can teach it many times, and each time it will be easier and will take less time to prepare.

You can teach on your own or as a contractor for a shop, art center, museum, or library. The organization may advertise and register students for you, which is an easy way to get established. Do some research in your area to find out the typical cost and teaching rate for classes like yours. As a new teacher, expect your class to fall in this range. Be realistic about how many students you can work with per class and what the space can accommodate.

TAKE A DEEP BREATH.

The best way to calm the first-day-of-class jitters is to be prepared. Visit the classroom ahead of time so you can think through where you should stand so everyone can see you and where materials should go. If you are using technology, test it, check all of the adaptors you need, and bring a backup on a thumb drive.

For a class with eight students, bring enough materials and handouts for ten, in case an extra person shows up or someone spills coffee on their supplies. Bring a clock so you can stay on schedule. Bring water. Get to class early. Turn off your cell phone. All of these are things I have learned "the hard way."

In the end, there will be some part of your class that won't go as planned. Someone will ask you a question that you won't know the answer to. There will be a student who doesn't follow your instructions. But those can be some of the best parts of a class; where you learn something from the students or they all learn something from each other.

Photo by Jennifer Nicklay

BECKA RAHN

Becka Rahn is a fabric designer and teacher from Minneapolis, Minnesota. She is the co-author of *The Spoonflower Handbook* and a member of the 2016 Etsy Sellers Advisory Board.

www.beckarahn.com

[RETAIL READINESS FOR CRAFTERS]

by Talia Halliday

One day in 2009, I walked into an art gallery. I had my baby in a sling, leather tote on one arm, my own handmade products in the other, and a big dream. "Today is going to be the day I get my products into a store," I thought to myself. I had a smile on my face and good intentions in my heart, but a moment later I was turned away and felt only red-hot humiliation. In that moment, I learned a really important lesson: getting your crafts ready for retail isn't as easy as it might seem.

Eventually, my dream did come true, and today I sell my work to over seventy stores. I also own a shop featuring other makers' goods and run an indie craft show where I work with hundreds of artists each year. Over the past six years I've learned a lot about how to go about getting your work ready to be sold in retail stores.

If selling your goods in shops is one of your goals, I suggest beginning by creating a strong, cohesive product line. I've seen so many makers rush past this part too quickly, only to be stopped in their tracks when a shop is confused by their application or line sheet.

Your products should also be priced properly. It's vital to set a price for your goods that takes into account material costs, hourly wage, profit, and overhead. This price is your wholesale cost; retail will be double or sometimes triple this amount. I've seen so many crafters get stuck not making any money because they didn't take this into account. Although at first it can feel hard to sell your goods to a store at 50 percent off retail, remember that the store will be handling all of the marketing and customer service for your goods. Once you set your retail price, stick to it even in your own online shop on Etsy or elsewhere so that you're not inadvertently competing with the stores that sell your work.

And lastly, your product line should evolve over time. You need to add new products and styles to your line to keep it current so that you have new work to show stores on a regular basis.

Now it's time to package the work you've toiled away at for so long. When it comes to packaging handmade work we want to keep four things in mind: the recognizability of your brand, the consistency between your product and it's packaging, proper display tactics, and what I like to call the "tossability" factor.

In order to make your product recognizable, you'll need to include your logo, signature colors, and signature fonts on your packaging. Those brand attributes should be consistent with the look and feel of your product. For example, don't use a brightly colored hangtag on your otherwise earth-tone product. Simple packaging, such as a paper tag or a paper belt to wrap around, is perfect for some products. Other products might require a special container, box, or jar. When designing your hangtags keep in mind that retailers will need to affix their own barcode to your product's tag, so leave some room.

Clear containers allow customers to see what's inside, and I recommend them for products such as food, crayons, liquid soap, or lotions. When applicable include a photo or illustration of your item in use. A photo of a model wearing your handmade infinity scarf is much more convincing to customers than just a photo of the scarf on a hanger, for example. When it comes to display, you know your product best, and you know how best to present it. Share this knowledge with your retailers. In fact, if you happen to know the exact display that will work great for your product, include that as an option for purchase on your line sheet. Your retailers will be appreciative!

"Tossability" refers to packaging that a customer is going to throw away after purchase. Once they do, will they still be able to identify the product as having been made by you? To ensure that they will, include your branding physically on your product. For example, if your product is made from fabric, include a fabric tag in addition to the paper tag. Think Hermes bags or Christian-Louboutin shoes. Brand it baby!

Once your product is properly packaged and tagged you're ready to begin approaching shops. To start, I suggest identifying stores in your local area that reach your target customers. Go online to see if they accept submissions. Follow those stores on social media and interact with them. Then, make the jump. Sometimes that means filling out an online submission form, and other times it means e-mailing the store with an inquiry. I will venture to say that nine times out of ten it does not mean walking into their store unannounced with your wares in hand.

Once you've made contact with a store, be sure to follow up, just like any job interview. And then, when it's time to meet in person, dress the part. You're creating a relationship here, one that will hopefully last for years to come, so you want to make a good first impression.

Getting your products ready for retail takes careful planning and a lot of hard work, but retail partners can be great ambassadors for your products. It's worth the time and effort to learn what they need to make your products sell successfully.

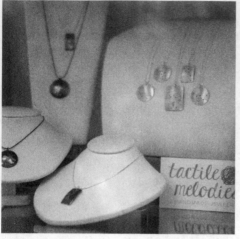

Photos by Melissa Laster

TALIA HALLIDAY

Talia Halliday lives in Bloomington, Indiana, with her three children and husband in a home filled with handcrafted treasures. Talia runs her studio, Conduit Press, out of the back of her brick-and-mortar store, Gather, where she sells the work of over 250 other makers from the Midwest. In her spare time, she organizes events such as the Bloomington Handmade Market, where she continues her promotion of indie craft.

www.Gathershoppe.com

[STYLING YOUR PHOTOS FOR SALES SUCCESS]

by Nissa Brehmer

Well-styled photography elevates your product and helps it sell. No matter what kind of product you have or how you might be selling it, it's vital to take your time and plan your photographs. And yet it can feel overwhelming to imagine how to accomplish professional-level photographs with limited resources.

Kristy Zacharias and I are the co-founders of Page + Pixel, a design and photography packaging service for the craft publishing industry. Combined, Kristy and I have eighteen years, experience in this sector, and we've styled and shot the covers and interior photographs for hundreds of books and patterns. We've got some tips that will make a photo shoot run smoothly, no matter what your budget. We think you'll be pleasantly surprised at how just a little extra planning and patience can pay off.

SHOT PLANNING—IT'S A MUST

Once you've got a location secured, take the time to plan out your shots the old-fashioned way—with pencil and paper. Writing down your goals and sketching out basic composition and shot angles will save you time and energy on the shoot day. Planning ahead what is most crucial to your project also allows you to feel better prepared when styling the rest of the photo and gathering all your props.

BE TREND-FORWARD AND TIMELESS

Kristy has a knack for being ahead of the times. She keeps herself up to speed with current and upcoming trends in a wide range of creative industries, so our projects are on trend when they're published, sometimes more than a year in the future.

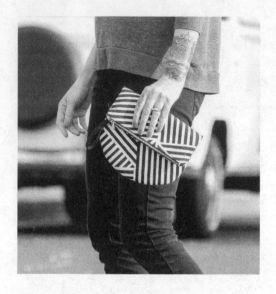

It's easy to jump on a trend while it's happening, but not as easy to create trend-forward images that remain relevant even years later. The goal is to be cutting edge and classic, a difficult balance to maintain, but one that will elevate your images to a higer level.

DON'T OVER STYLE—YOUR PROJECT IS THE STAR

I know—we've all done it. Your finished image features props from West Elm so well that it would fit perfectly in their next catalog. But wait! You aren't shooting for West Elm—you're shooting for you!

Your project should be the star of your photo. Any props or styling that outshines the project or confuses the message must be ditched. A good stylist knows how to find pieces that elevate projects, not overtake them. Steer clear of props that imitate your techniques, match too perfectly, or that pull the eye away from the project. Effective styling can make a so-so project look like a million bucks, which means more cash in your pocket. Eye on the prize!

HAVE A ROBUST TOOLBOX

I cannot emphasize enough the importance of a well-stocked toolbox when you're prepping a photo shoot. There's nothing worse than having a styling idea that goes down in flames because you're missing a roll of gaffer tape, clothespins, or Command strips. I recommend keeping the toolbox items separate from your personal home collection, so if you need a pair of scissors or a lint roller—two things that live permanently in our box—you don't need to remember to grab them from a drawer or a desk.

A few other things we can't live without: a good iron, a very long extension cord, fishing wire, safety and sewing pins, pen and paper, and bubble wrap.

SHOOT WITH PURPOSE

Think through the specific purpose you have for your photos. How will you use your photos? If you're shooting for Instagram, for example, you'll need square images. If you're shooting a sewing pattern cover, you'll need to leave some space for type.

I almost always tether my camera to the computer for shoots using a good old USB cord and the fabulous Adobe software, Lightroom. Tethering means that Kristy and I can see the images as they are taken and play with styling and composition changes on the fly so we are sure to accomplish our shot as planned. For example, we can put a temporary "crop" on the image to show Kristy what an 8"×10" cover will look like. Since we're testing these parameters while shooting, we can make adjustments as we shoot, thus avoiding unnecessary reshoots. Patience and planning can help eliminate silly mistakes and save valuable time.

DON'T FORCE A LOCATION IF SOMETHING ISN'T RIGHT

I can't tell you how many times Kristy or I have sketched out a brilliant shot plan that, once we arrive at the location, doesn't pan out or that doesn't meet the styling criteria we thought it would. The lighting might be poor or the fabric on the couch doesn't work with a project, for example.

It's OK to say, "This isn't working," and find a new location. Follow your gut and remember your key points. If bad lighting turns a beautiful, vibrant quilt into a dingy gray rectangle, you need to bail. The pre-planning you did will help you figure out an even better idea quickly and efficiently.

KEEP PHOTO EDITING SIMPLE

As trends in styling come and go, so do trends in photo editing. We recommend steering clear of gimmicky stuff such as light filters and instead sticking with a timeless, color-true editing style. Let your project and your styling speak for themselves.

Even if you can't hire a professional photographer to shoot your work, a little planning and creative thinking will help you set up a photo shoot that will give you the best results. You'll be so proud to present your beautifully styled and photographed products to the world.

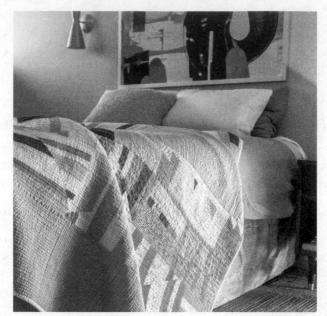

Photos by Nissa Brehmer

PAGE + PIXEL

Page + Pixel is a design and photography-packaging service for the craft publishing industry, co-founded by designer Kristy Zacharias and photographer Nissa Brehmer. With a combined eighteen years of experience and hundreds of books, patterns, and products under their belts, Kristy and Nissa have collaborated with the industry's most prominent quilters, fabric, and garment designers.

www.pageandpixel.net

[WRITING STYLE FOR THE HANDMADE MARKETPLACE]

by Lauren Lang

The maker movement has continued to expand online at full speed, making the art of effective writing more important than ever. Writing is now a central method for many creative entrepreneurs to reach out to their clients, particularly when the overhead costs of brick-and-mortar retail just aren't feasible.

Like it or not, you probably write regularly in at least several contexts: e-commerce platforms, newsletter blasts to followers, social media, and more. It's tempting to adopt a "one size fits all" approach (especially when writing competes with precious time spent in the studio), and many artisan sellers tend to not adapt their writing styles for the various forms of communications they use. The problem? It's a missed opportunity to boost their impact! Here's how to adjust your technique for the most common forms of writing in the handmade sector.

NEWSLETTERS

Promotional e-mails can entertain and motivate clients, but they are usually most persuasive when they're short and sweet. One important strategy for writing effective newsletters is to get to the point quickly. If you're hosting a sale or highlighting a specific product, a relevant headline should appear in the subject line of your newsletter and at the top of the body of your e-mail. Burying the lead and making readers wait for the good stuff means that they're likely to click away before they get your message.

Newsletters should also convey only the information that is absolutely necessary for readers to act. This may include quirky content fitting for a crafty audience, but now is probably not the time to wax poetic about a new supplier or explain your philosophy of process in detail. You'll have other opportunities (blog posts, profile pages, social media, etc.) to get chatty; instead, maximize the precious time you have your buyers' attention with two or three brief topics at most. Clearly displayed links and an encouraging call to action should make it easy for customers to engage.

SHOP AND MAKER PROFILES

The handmade movement strongly values makers and techniques and so do customers. Unlike the competitive, rapid-fire setting of promotional e-mails, profile pages (such as those on e-commerce platforms and retail websites) open up space for creative entrepreneurs to delve into the story behind their business and what drives it, thereby establishing trust with clients.

The key to a successful profile page is telling the story that your customers truly want to hear. They're less interested in your personal life (your kids, your spouse, your religious affiliation) than your creative life. How did you learn your craft? What inspired your best-selling product? What differentiates your work from others on the market? Unlike targeted newsletters to your followers, Web content extends to a much larger audience: new clients, investors, wholesalers, and the media. Consider how the persona you craft might affect new sales and opportunities. Coming across as friendly yet professional may open more doors than sounding too informal or sharing too much.

PRODUCT LISTINGS

Whether on a business website or on a platform such as Etsy, product listings require specific conventions to be successful. Search engine optimization (SEO) is a key feature of successful product listings because it increases page views. There are many SEO strategies floating in the ether, both online and in print. I strongly recommend taking the time to research and employ these methods.

Once you've identified your ideal SEO keywords, write original content for each listing that efficiently describes your item and its relevant benefits. Don't feel like you need to get super fancy and bombard your client with details about your vision or your process here; I've seen sellers ramble on about the virtues of olive wood or turmeric but forget to include salient details that buyers need to confidently close the sale (size, variation, care method, production time, etc.). It's a quick way to lose customers at the most important point in the selling process.

As you write your description, do consider choosing a voice, tone, and language that will best entice your specific audience. Who is most likely to shop from you, and what's the best way to appeal to them? A business that sells high-value jewelry to a sophisticated client base, for example, will likely adopt a refined tone; a maker of hip baby accessories might use humor to appeal to young parents.

Photo by Lauren Lang

While it may seem that varying your writing style will result in more work and time, that's not always the case. Many business owners compose newsletters and product listings three times longer than they should be, announcing what they did over the weekend and choosing ten words to say what three would accomplish. No matter your craft or brand identity, clean writing is always preferable to complicated. Keep it simple, keep it informative, and keep it engaging. When you tailor your writing to each situation, you'll give your readers exactly what they hope for.

LAUREN LANG

Lauren Lang is a freelance writer and editor working in the handmade industry. Her business, Wordcraft, provides copyediting services to both large companies and independent designers and artists. A former college English instructor, Lauren has more than thirteen years of experience writing, editing, and teaching people of all ages to communicate effectively.

www.wordcraft-editorial.com

WHEN YOUR SPOUSE JOINS YOUR BUSINESS

....

by Abby Glassenberg

This article originally appeared in the Craft Industry Alliance Journal.

In 2008, Liesl Gibson launched a sewing pattern company for kids called Oliver + S. She'd recently left her job as a designer for a large fashion brand and was enjoying working by herself out of the home she shared with her husband, Todd, and their young daughter.

"Originally, the business was to be a part-time thing for Liesl," Todd recalls. "She thought maybe she'd hire an assistant at some point, but that was about it."

It turned out that Gibson had great timing. She'd entered the market at the moment when home sewing was having resurgence. Consumers were eager to get their hands on patterns by independent designers and Oliver + S products were in high demand. Soon, so was Gibson.

"Opportunities began to come in and she couldn't take advantage of them by herself. She was being asked to travel and teach, to write a book and do fabric collections," Todd says of his wife's early days at Oliver + S. "She needed a growth path for the business and we had to make a decision—do we want to grow this or keep it an extremely small, part-time hobby?"

The couple chose growth.

A former college professor with a PhD in literature, Todd was working at an investment bank after a ten-year stretch in management consulting. Not entirely happy with his current job, Todd decided to quit and come to work for Oliver + S full-time. With their combined skills and work experience, the Gibsons were able to grow the company into a mainstay on the home sewing market.

One of the first things Liesl and Todd considered when discussing Todd's move to full-time, was whether they could afford it.

"Hiring someone else with my skills and level of experience would mean paying a salary and providing benefits that would have been way too expensive," Todd explains.

"Fortunately, we had built up a financial cushion that allowed us to live for a while without a salary, which was a good thing because neither of us drew a salary that first year," he said.

Pattern designer Jen Beeman found herself in a similar position when her women's sewing pattern business, Grainline, began to grow. Beeman began asking her partner, Jon Krohn, to help her during his off-hours. A graphic designer by training with experience in laying out books, Krohn was able to help Beeman create her first print patterns.

"I'd be so stressed about creating stuff for print and he'd take one look at it and say, 'Oh, this is easy. Let me do it.' He'd lay it out and call the printer and set it all up. It was great," Beeman says of Krohn's contributions.

In May of 2015, Krohn began working for Grainline full-time, taking over all of the graphic design work and managing shipping and distribution — a time-consuming task that Beeman desperately needed help with.

"I'm not even allowed to do the shipping anymore," Beeman jokes. "I made too many mistakes. [My employee] Kendra and I were spending two to three hours a day on shipping. Now Jon does it. He's better at it and he loves it."

For other creative business owners, bringing their spouse on full-time is a future goal.

Right out of art school, Jordan Perme started making faux taxidermy creatures by carving foam and covering it in felt shapes. She called them Horrible Adorables and took them to a craft show in Philadelphia to see if they might sell. Her husband, Chris Lees, came along to help out.

"For the first show I just did the logistical stuff," Lees recalls. "I booked the hotel room and helped her pack the car."

Shoppers loved Perme's quirky critters, and she felt encouraged to continue making them, but cutting the felt shapes that covered each animal was labor intensive. Lees, a mechanical engineer and artist, helped to streamline production in a way that would allow Perme to create a Horrible Adorables creature quickly and efficiently enough to sell in a retail setting.

"I sourced custom dies Jordan could use to cut felt faster and I learned about how to create foam molds. Now we cast forms for her pieces — we can cast ten pieces in an hour, which allows us to make so many more than before," Lees says.

Nowadays, Lees spends ten to twenty hours a week working for Horrible Adorables, in addition to his full-time job. He's taken over the bookkeeping, and he manages the production schedule and has recently helped Perme trademark Horrible Adorables.

"He's really good at spreadsheets," Perme laughs.

Lees also makes much of the product that goes to retail stores they stock around the country, while Perme focuses on more intricate fine art pieces for gallery shows.

Until now, Lees has kept his engineering job because the couple needs the income and health benefits, but in 2016, they're hoping that Lees will come to work for the business full-time.

"It's a leap of faith," Lees says. "But we've put money aside in savings so that even if we don't make any profit in 2016 we can still live."

"I'm a little nervous about having us both home all day," Perme says. "I think it's going to be important to be respectful of how each other work."

Todd Gibson, of Oliver + S, agrees: "Working together will have an impact on your relationship. You're going to be spending a lot more time with that person. You're raising kids together, living together and now working together, so any disagreements in any sphere are going to spill over."

Gibson recommends setting boundaries and deciding when you'll talk about work and when you'll leave work behind.

Lees and Perme say they talk about the business almost all the time, but it works for them.

"I work at home and I really don't have anything else to talk about," Perme says. "This is all I do. Well, this summer we got beehives, so sometimes we talk about the bees."

For some couples, the dynamic of their personal relationship helps them manage the stresses of owning a business. Beeman says Krohn is a good balance for her emotionally and that plays out in their business in a positive way.

"We get stressed out in opposite ways and he's great at calming me down," Beeman says.

Before bringing your spouse on full-time, consider whether their skills complement yours and are a match for what the business needs. For the Gibsons, Todd's skills were a perfect fit.

"I'm a business person. I know how to do strategic and financial planning. I know how to do forecasting and how to focus on process. And I have the skills to build the technology we needed to grow," he explains, adding that Liesl wouldn't have been able to afford to hire someone at his level otherwise.

"It's just too easy for your work to become all encompassing when your work and life partner are the same," Gibson says. "We have a strict 'no discussion about the business and no technology at the dinner table' rule."

Krohn also brings skills to Grainline that Beeman needed and couldn't have afforded otherwise.

"When Jon works a design job it's $100 per page," Beeman explains. "I can't afford to pay that. But he said, 'Yes, let's build this thing together.' If you hire someone they're never going to say that."

Photo by Jordan Perme

It's also important to think through how you'll define your spouse's work status for legal, payroll, and tax purposes; will they be a contractor, an employee, or a partner?

The Gibsons own Oliver + S as an equal partnership, while Krohn is an employee of Grainline, with Beeman retaining sole ownership of the company.

"He feels like, 'You built this company. You can own it.'" Beeman explains. "He's not a person who feels he needs to be in charge. As a graphic designer, he was used to taking assignments from clients. Then again, we don't really have typical gender roles. Jon does all the grocery shopping and all the cooking for us."

Permes still has her business registered as a sole proprietorship LLC, but plans to amend that to bring Lees on as an equal partner in the coming year.

Owning a business that you both work for can give couples a level of flexibility in their work lives that can feel very freeing. Beeman says: "I set our schedule so if we want to go on vacation we can go on vacation."

The Gibsons have rented their home in New York City to spend this year in Spain with their daughter, an experience that would have likely been impossible if they didn't own their own business.

Being in business together doesn't come without risk, though. When both partners' financial futures are tied to a single business, the stakes are high. Beeman says Krohn helps her relax when she begins to worry about the risks involved.

"Jon tells me, 'We can always go and get jobs if everything fails,'" she says.

And the Gibsons say the trade-off has been worth it. "Even now, we both make less money than we did when we were working corporate jobs, but it's really about how you define success. If success means owning a second home and a big boat and two or three cars this wouldn't be success, but we feel we've been able to use this business to escape from working for the man and being tied to an office cubicle in midtown Manhattan. This business gives us the lifestyle we want."

ABBY GLASSENBERG

Abby Glassenberg is a sewing pattern designer, craft book author, teacher, and writer. On her blog, WhileSheNaps.com, she writes about the sewing industry, running a creative business and the online culture of craft. She is the co-founder of Craft Industry Alliance. Abby has an undergraduate degree in history from Johns Hopkins and a master's degree in education from Harvard. She taught middle school social studies in Mississippi through Teach For America, and sixth grade in the Newton, Massachusetts, Public Schools before becoming a textile artist. She's the author of three sewing books. Abby lives in Wellesley, Massachusetts, with her husband and three daughters.

www.whileshenaps.com

[LICENSING YOUR ART FOR PRODUCTS]

....

by Bari J. Ackerman

If you'd like to get started licensing your art for products, there are several things you will want to know. For starters, you need to figure out if licensing is truly the route you'd like to take to get your designs onto products. And I recommend thoroughly reviewing your options to figure that out.

First, it's important to understand what licensing is. When you license your art, you give a company permission to produce your art on products. This is usually for a limited amount of time and often in just a particular category, such as bolt fabric, for instance. In return, the company pays you a royalty. You can license the same piece of art for multiple categories, which means that piece of art you created one time can bring you multiple streams of income. This likely sounds like a great deal, and often it is.

It may sound like you're "one and done" here. But the truth is, there's likely more work ahead. Often times you will have to alter artwork for different products, create additional pieces, change colors.

In addition, you'll want to think about what you will be paid. Generally, royalties range from 1 percent to 10 percent or more, depending on the market the product goes into. If it's going to mass market (think Target, Walmart, Kohls, etc.), you'll likely be offered a lower royalty. In other words: more products produced, lower royalty rate; less products produced, higher royalty rate. The trade-offs may lead you to wonder: "Do I possibly want to produce this product myself?" And truly, that's something you'll need to figure out for yourself. Producing your own products presents it's own challenges. But in the end, if you decide to go ahead and get into licensing your art, it's a doable task.

The most important part of creating art for products is to first create a lot of art. It sounds obvious, but it's important to note that you're not just creating art with the end game of licensing in mind. Creating a lot of art will help you define your style, and in today's market, having a unique voice is imperative. There's lots of competition out there, and you want to stand out. The only way to develop a voice is to create and then create some more.

Once you understand your own unique style, you'll want to start thinking about what kinds of products you'd like to see your art on. Think about these categories: home décor, wall art, bolt fabric, fashion, stationery, and gifts. Go to stores and look at these products. How do you see your art fitting into the market?

Now build your portfolio. Your art should be created in collections. You'll probably have a focal piece and then several pieces that go with it. Create collection sheets for your portfolio. Within the collections, mock up your art on products. Create a line of dishes or bedding, home décor, and more. You'll want to show potential companies exactly how you envision your art being used.

Next, you'll want to think about how to get your art in front of art directors. You can, of course, do trade shows such as Surtex and Printsource. And that works for a lot of people. Talk to people who have done trade shows and be sure to do your research well. Get to know all of the costs and benefits before you do any trade shows.

You can also get an art agent or a rep; there is a resource list at artlicensingblog.com. For some people, this is the best answer. Are you willing to do research and follow up? Can you sell yourself? If the answer is no, you might want to seek an agent.

However, if you have the time, energy, and where-with-all, you might also think about this: with Internet access, you have the world at your fingertips. Because we live in the age we do, we are able to search for all of the information we need in an instant. I have won many contracts by simply finding and e-mailing the right art directors a targeted pitch for their company.

Here's how: Find the companies you are most interested in by looking in shops and turning over the product to see who made it. Follow other artists on social media and make note of who they license to. Manufacturer's websites are usually easy to find and are always the first place to look. If they license art, sometimes they have a specific submission process to follow. You will find it there. If not, simply call the company and ask for the name and e-mail of art directors. Once you have a contact (unless they have another specific submission process outlined), send a targeted, beautiful pitch. A one sheet PDF with art, mocked-up products, and a short introduction is often enough to get you noticed. (Make sure your contact info and logo is on the PDF, too!)

However, be ready. Often you won't hear back. And often the answer will be "no thank you." That's tough. But you need to be tough, too. Get used to hearing "no" and get used to following up. I'm not suggesting that you be a nag about it, but do send follow up e-mails. Several weeks later, it's not a bad idea to write back and simply check in. You'll also want to send new art every quarter—even where you've been rejected before. You never know.

Photo by Jessica Downey Photo

Photo by Bari Ackerman

The timing may have been not quite right before, and the next time you may hit the nail on the head.

In the end, art licensing is a game of numbers. Oftentimes, you'll have to hear many "no's" before you hear a "yes." The more art you make and the more you put yourself out there, the more likely you will find success. The best advice I can give is to create more than you ever thought you could, submit the best of that art, and be prepared to be patient and persistent.

BARI J. ACKERMAN

Bari is a self-described maximalist and has coined the term "Curated Maximalism" to describe her "more is more" style. Her painterly art and design, bursting with color and expression, are instantly recognizable. While likely best known for her art on fabric, the Bari J. brand spans many categories including wall art, fabric, home décor, stationery, cards, wall murals, wall paper, stencils, and more.

www.barijdesigns.com

[GETTING PRESS COVERAGE]

....

by Mei Pak

Do you ever wonder how magazines and blogs find all of the products that they feature in their articles? Some of them come from the research efforts of the writers and bloggers. But a lot of those ideas come from business owners pitching their products. You, too, can pitch the media and see your products featured in magazines and blogs!

BEFORE YOU PITCH: BUILD A MEDIA LIST

While you could run out and start e-mailing any blogger or magazine editor you can find, the best approach to pitching the media is a planned one. Read on to learn how to find the right places to pitch your product.

KNOW YOUR CUSTOMER

The best place to start is with a clear understanding of your customer. Who is she? What other similar products or brands does she love? Knowing the answer to these questions can help you determine which magazines or blogs she's reading.

There are several ways to find this information:

- Look at your Google or social media analytics for demographic information.
- When someone favorites an item in your Etsy shop, check to see what other types of items she's favoriting.
- After a customer makes a purchase from your Etsy shop, look to see what other types of activity she's had on Etsy.
- Search for similar items on Pinterest and see what types of boards they're grouped on.

CREATE A LIST OF IDEAL MEDIA OUTLETS

Google your target customer's favorite brands to see where they've been featured. Major brands will likely be featured in national magazines and big blogs; smaller competitors will probably be in local or online magazines and blogs with smaller followings. You'll want to keep a list of these media outlets because you'll be pitching to them!

Your list can be anywhere: in a notebook, in a text file, or in a spreadsheet. I like the spreadsheet approach because I can easily track extra information, such as the dates I pitched and followed up and whether I received a response.

IDENTIFY SPECIFIC CONTACTS

Now that you know which magazines and blogs you want to pitch, you should also know that blindly sending an e-mail to a generic e-mail such as "contact@domain.com" is unlikely to generate a response. The best approach is to find a specific editor's contact information.

A magazine has a masthead that lists all of the staff roles and names. It can usually be found somewhere within the first few pages of the print issue or online. If you're selling clothing, jewelry, or something similar, look for fashion or accessories editors. Record their names in your list.

Most blogs have an about or contact page with e-mail information. Many even include a "how to pitch" page. Read these instructions and make some notes about them in your files. They are unlikely to respond if you don't use the format they prefer. If more than one person runs the blog, pinpoint the most relevant editor for your product.

LOCATE E-MAIL ADDRESSES

There are several ways to find e-mail addresses online. Try these:

1. **Google the editor's name and workplace.** For example, "Jane Doe Vogue magazine" or "Jane Doe Vogue magazine e-mail."
2. **Search LinkedIn or Twitter for the editor's name.** If you receive too many results, include the publication name or city. You can send a direct message to the person asking for their e-mail address.
3. **Some people are harder to find than others.** If it's taking you too long, take a break and try searching for another person.

WRITE AND SEND YOUR PITCH

Now it's time to create your pitch! Pitches are like resumes and cover letters. The "guts" can remain the same, but you should tailor each one to the specific recipient. Take into consideration a blogger's specific rules for receiving pitches or a magazine's timeline. Don't pitch beach accessories in June because a magazine's lead-time is three to six months—they've already got your product covered!

WRITE AN OPEN-WORTHY SUBJECT LINE

Your subject line should be descriptive and explain exactly what you're pitching. Keep it concise and compelling so the recipient knows what you're pitching and wants to read the message.

CREATE THE PITCH

It goes without saying that your pitch should have perfect spelling, grammar, and punctuation. If writing's not your strong suit, you should ask someone to proofread your pitch.

A good pitch has several components:

- **Fewer than ten sentences total**
- **Salutation that addresses the editor by name**
- **One or two sentences introducing yourself and your brand**
- **A specific explanation of how your product is a good fit for the editor's magazine or blog.** If they've featured something similar in the past, mention that! It'll help spark interest.
- **A call to action to encourage the editor to respond to you.** This could be a question or a personal note.

Remember that editors and bloggers are sometimes pitched to hundreds of times a day and are super busy, so your pitch needs to stand out! I once found that the editor of a magazine I was pitching was a big fan of Bon Iver, a band that went to the same college that I did. I made sure to mention that coincidence! Doing something like this makes the editor open up a bit more and increases the likelihood of them taking the time to check out your website.

AFTER THE PITCH: FOLLOWING UP

If you haven't heard back from the editor after a week, you MUST follow up. The secret sauce of pitching is the follow-up.

SEND A FOLLOW-UP MESSAGE

Oftentimes editors and bloggers have already decided in their minds that they would like to work with you, but they don't have the time to respond to your e-mail and they forget! Your prompt follow-up gives them a gentle reminder. You're also giving the ones who are on the fence a chance to look over your website again.

Remember, this is an essential step that most people don't do. Make sure you do it! You'll stand out.

IF AT FIRST YOU DON'T SUCCEED, TRY AGAIN

If you still don't hear back, it's OK to move on to the next editor or blogger. Sometimes they simply aren't working on any articles where your product would be a good fit.

RESPONDING TO AN EDITOR

If you do hear back, you'll want to answer any of the editor's questions quickly. Editors and bloggers work on tight deadlines!

SENDING SAMPLES

Some editors may require samples, and if it's within your budget to give away a couple of products, do it! Shipping with USPS is fine.

If your product is expensive, you can mention to the editor that you'll be including a prepaid return label and packaging that they can use to send the item back to you. Few magazines will not return items, but you will know this ahead of time and can make a decision if you want to pursue the opportunity further.

SUBMITTING IMAGES AND DETAILS

Editors may want high-resolution images that are suitable for printing. This usually means a quality of 300 dpi or better, but the editor will be specific about what she wants. You can usually e-mail digital files.

Other requested information may include pricing details and where to buy your product. Provide all the information they need in a timely manner, and editors will love you! They'll also be more likely to work with you again in the future.

WAIT TO SEE IF YOU'LL BE FEATURED—AND SEND A BIG THANK-YOU!

After sending the samples it may take a few weeks to hear the editor's decision on whether they'll feature your product or not. Sometimes they'll decide to hold off on featuring your product until another time.

More often than not, though, they'll mention which magazine issue your products will be featured in and thank you for your submission! Remember that editors and bloggers are always in need of content to feed to their readers. In a way, you're helping them do their job!

WHEN YOUR FEATURE IS PUBLISHED

The waiting game begins when the editor says your product will be featured. Hopefully, the issue or blog post arrives soon! Once it's been published, scan it into your computer or take a screenshot of it.

Be sure to:

- Share the feature with your existing customers via social media or your e-mail newsletter.
- Store a copy of the feature for your portfolio.
- Include the feature on your website for building credibility and trust.

Being featured in a magazine or on a blog will help build trust and desire in your brand. Keep at it and you'll be well-known before you know it!

Photos by Eric Sorensen

MEI PAK

Mei Pak is a marketing mentor helping makers, artists, and designers create a consistent income with their businesses. Mei also runs Tiny Hands, a line of handmade scented food jewelry, with her small team of assistants. She sells in more than 100 stores across the U.S., has been featured on major TV shows and in glossy print magazines.

www.creativehiveco.com

[THE VALUE OF IN-PERSON EVENTS]

by Nicole Stevenson

Like most creative business owners, I work alone. Although I've done my best to build my creative community online and at short in-person events such as craft shows and workshops, I ultimately found my main creative support system at conferences.

There's something about meeting in person that speeds up the get-to-know-you process and creates a nearly instant intimacy. Through meeting fellow creative entrepreneurs at conferences I began what I believe will be life-long friendships. What started as carpooling to the conference, hanging out in each other's hotel rooms, and attending workshops together, became friendships that we nurtured from afar. We developed lasting bonds, some of which are as strong as those with my close friends from high school who I've known for nearly twenty years.

My business partner, Delilah Snell, and I co-produce a craft and business conference each year called Craftcation. Our hope is to foster strong connections among fellow crafters in our community through a weekend of workshops on craft and entrepreneurship.

Part of our driving force for creating a conference was our positive experience with an in-person community. This community not only lends support and provides a sense of belonging, it also encourages a spirit of generosity through sharing tips, tricks, and new technologies. This sort of info sharing has helped me run every aspect of my business more efficiently, from social media to accounting to marketing. The noisy online world especially can feel overwhelming if you're trying to keep up with and sift through every blog, social media outlet, webinar, and newsletter for the advice that you need. Figuring out if a particular social-media scheduling platform is right for you can feel frustrating as you weigh the choices, trying to understand interfaces, or evaluate reviews. Being able to talk in person about the pros and cons with someone who has actually used it and is willing to share their experience is priceless.

GET FRESH PERSPECTIVE

Connecting with other craft entrepreneurs is not just about gaining tools. It's also about a fresh perspective. Sometimes we're too close to our business to see how to grow it. Or we may have an inkling of what we need to do but require a second opinion or reassurance from someone who knows the ins and outs of our industry.

After several years of juggling three websites and eight social media accounts representing different aspects of our business, my business partner and I decided to attend a branding workshop at a conference. Based on what we learned there, we decided to merge everything under one umbrella business. The amount of time (and money) we've saved just from this one adjustment made the trip to the conference more than worth it.

REGROUP AND RECHARGE

Conferences have not only helped me see my business methodology in a new light but have also recharged my creativity and helped me rediscover the love for making. I often forget that the whole reason that I'm in this industry is because of a deep passion for making things. It's also hard to push through feelings of imposter syndrome or that your to-do list will never get done. Conferences provide a space where the daily distractions of juggling your business and personal life are lessened so you can be present and focus on what you're learning. At a conference I allow myself the luxury of making just to make.

Photo by Laurie Wilson

EASE INTO NETWORKING

Escaping my cozy craft bubble isn't the only way experiences at conferences have helped me step out of my comfort zone. Although Craftcation attendees who see me leading workshops and giving speeches to hundreds of people probably wouldn't guess it, starting a conversation with a stranger is one of the most anxiety-inducing social situations I can imagine. Yet, when I'm at a conference, being the first person to say "hello" is easier because I'm among a community of people who share my interests. Taking that initial risk and turning to the person next to me and telling them that I like the way the terrarium they're making is turning out or asking them what they thought about a presenter's take on building a brand feels so much more natural and less scary than approaching a stranger at a party or networking event. If you're at a conference, the chances are extremely high that you're surrounded by like-minded individuals. Plus, you already have at least one thing in common—you're all attending that conference!

MAKE BUSINESS CONNECTIONS

At conferences it's not only easier to talk to your peers, it's also easier to make connections with brands or media that can become an integral part of building your business. When we planned the first Craftcation no one (and I mean NO ONE) had heard of it. I was desperate to spread the word. After I reached out to all the connections I already had (ahem … "Hi Auntie, will you share about Craftcation on your Facebook page?"), I went rogue and wrote more than 800 personalized e-mails to bloggers about Craftcation. Many of my e-mails went unanswered.

In the years since, I've met dozens of the influencers at in-person events that I had e-mailed. Those personal connections have done way more for our business than those 800 e-mails. Craftcation has been featured on some of our favorite blogs and media outlets, and we now have good relationships with brands that align with our vision. Nurturing these connections with more established brands as well as your community creates a network of relationships that pushes your business to the next level.

GET FOCUSED

And yet, when you're embroiled in the day-to-day of being the head of pretty much every department in your business, it's tough dedicating time to figure out what "the next level" looks like. Long-term planning gets lost as you prioritize the things that you have to do over the things that you should do. Conferences offer a focused opportunity to ask yourself the big questions that normally get pushed to the bottom of your daily to-do list (i.e., What's working in my business and what isn't? What is my long-term vision and idea of success, and how can I make it happen?).

Photos by Laurie Wilson

Aside from Craftcation, my business partner and I made a promise to attend at least one conference every year. I encourage you to do the same. This commitment requires serious planning, research, and saving. However, if you choose carefully, push yourself, and set intentions for your time, you open yourself to new connections and friends as well as insight into and renewed excitement for your business. You will inspire your creativity and stay on track to meet your goals. As much as I love talking shop with my family, something magical happens when I'm at a conference, surrounded by a community of creatives in my industry. I get to have wondrous 'ah-ha' moments that alter my creativity and business in ways I never could have imagined otherwise.

NICOLE STEVENSON

Nicole Stevenson is a writer and illustrator at Show and Tell Design Studio and a creative business consultant. She's also the co-owner of Dear Handmade Life, which produces Patchwork Show: Modern Makers Festival and Craftcation: Business and Makers Conference as well as the *Dear Handmade Life* blog and podcast. When she's not working you may find her breaking up scuffles between her dog and three chickens, couch crafting while watching a film she's seen too many times to count, playing guitar with her husband, sitting in her backyard with good friends and a margarita while playing Cards vs. Humanity, or squeezing in time for a quick trip to a lovely place where people are scarce and trees are not.

www.showandtelldesignstudio.com/
www.dearhandmadelife.com/

[SHOWS AND FAIRS]

What better way to sell your handmade wares than to attend a craft or art fair? Craft fairs are found in most cities throughout the year. Some are specifically geared toward holiday handmades, while others are indie shows that tend to have a hip/trendy vibe. From traditional to modern, yarn to paper, and quilting to woodworking, crafts of all kinds can find a home at a craft fair. The listings in the following pages are for craft and art fairs that might be a good fit for you and your artisan product.

Peruse the listings in the following pages to find the fairs that are most interesting to you. Perhaps there's a show that takes place just a few miles away from your home, or perhaps there's a show dedicated to your style of craft. After selling at a few fairs, you will learn even more about which type of show is best suited to your craft, attracts your demographic, and is most valuable for you to attend.

Each listing includes the basic information about the show, but visiting the show will always give you a better sense of the market, and if your wares fit in that particular venue. Over time, you'll develop an instinct for knowing what market will work for your business. Selling in person at craft shows is not only a way to make money, but it provides invaluable firsthand contact with your customer. That firsthand feedback is key to developing your brand and your business. Are certain colors more popular? Do you need to expand the sizes you have on offer? Do attendees at different markets want different things, and how can that help you develop your focus?

Attending craft shows can also be a way of marketing your online store. Many exhibitors note that, while they may see only a handful of sales at a particular show, they'll often see a spike in orders through their online shop from that area. That being the case, make a point to advertise your online shop. Print your website name on your packaging, of course, and have business cards and brochures available. See Talia Halliday's article "Retail Readiness for Crafters" for more ideas on how to present and pacakge your work.

Whether you focus on in-person selling at craft fairs or online through sites such as Etsy.com, you will find benefits to both. Meeting your customers face-to-face is invaluable for building lifelong customers, and creating a beautiful online shop allows you to craft a story through photos that your customers will want to come back to time and again.

As you become a regular exhibitor at craft shows, you'll develop a schedule, your booth's look and feel, a set plan for handling payment, and a routine for setting up and breaking down. If this is your first time out, check out the regional craft show index in order to focus on shows nearby. Over time you can consider expanding your reach to markets in other regions.

Key to Symbols & Abbreviations

◑	Canadian market
◔	market located outside of the U.S. and Canada
⌂	market prefers to work with local artists/ designers
b&w	black & white (photo or illustration)
SASE	self-addressed, stamped envelope
SAE	self-addressed envelope
IRC	International Reply Coupon, for use when mailing to countries other than your own

3RD ANNUAL CABIN FEVER

2901 Key St., Maumee OH 43537. (419)436-1457. E-mail: cloudpro@tds.net. Website: www.cloudshows.biz. **Contact:** Judy Cloud, promoter. Estab. 2015.

ADDITIONAL INFORMATION Event held annually in end of February. Event held indoors. Accepts handmade crafts. Accepts 15% of total exhbits retail/direct sales. Not juried. Prizes given: Customer and exhibitor drawings. Average number of exhibitors: 100. Average number of attendees: 2,500. Admission fee for the public: $5, kinds under 12 are free (coupons available). Artisans should apply via e-mail or inquire via website. Deadline: Until full. Application fee: 0. Space fee: $140–185. Square footage of the space: 10x8, 10x10, 12x10. Average gross sales: n/a. For more information, e-mail, visit website, or call. Help promote and talk with customers.

3RD ANNUAL MISTLETOE MAGIC HOLIDAY MARKETPLACE

22 E. 5th St., Dayton OH 45402, U.S.. (419)436-1457. E-mail: cloudproctds.net. Website: www.cloudshows.biz. **Contact:** Judy Cloud, producer. Estab. 2015.

ADDITIONAL INFORMATION Event held annually, in mid-December. Held indoors. Accepts handmade crafts. Accepts 15% total exhibitors' retail/direct sales. Not juried. We do require photos and visually check. Prizes given: exhibitor drawing. Average number of exhibitors: 100+. Average number of attendees: n/a. Admission fee for public: $5, 12 and under free (coupon available). Artisans should apply via e-mail or inquire via website. Deadline: Until full. Application fee: 0. Space fee: $225. Square footage of the space: 10x10, backdrop and signage provided. Average gross sales for a typical exhibitor: n/a. E-mail, visit website, or call. Help promote and talk with customers.

4 BRIDGES ARTS FESTIVAL

30 Frazier Ave., Chattanooga TN 37405. (423)265-4282 ext. 3. Fax: (423)265-5233. E-mail: katdunn@avarts.org. Website: www.4bridgesartsfestival.org. **Contact:** Kat Dunn. Estab. 2000.

ADDITIONAL INFORMATION 2-day fine arts and crafts show held annually in mid-April. Held in a covered, open-air pavilion. Accepts photography and 24 different mediums. Juried by 3 different art professionals each year. Awards: $10,000 in artist merit awards; the on-site jurying for merit awards will take place Saturday morning. Number of exhibitors: 150. Public attendance: 13,000. Public admission: $7/day or a 2-day pass for $10; children under 18 are free. Apply at www.zapplication.org. Deadline for entry: early November (see website for details). Application fee: $40. Space fee: $450-550 for 10×12 ft.; $900–1,000 for 20×12. Average gross sales/exhibitor: $2,923. For more information, e-mail, call, or visit website. The event is held at First Tennessee Pavilion.

6TH STREET FAIR

Bellevue Downtown Association, 400 108th Ave. NE, Suite 110, Bellevue WA 98004. (425)453-1223. E-mail: tyler@bellevuedowntown.org. Website: www.bellevuedowntown.org.

ADDITIONAL INFORMATION Art and crafts fair held annually in July. Outdoors. Accepts sculpture, jewelry, home décor, wood, glass, fabrics and more. Juried. Awards/prizes: Best in Show, Best Booth, Best Newbie. Exhibitors: 120. Number of attendees: 45,000. Free to public. Apply online. Deadline for entry: March 18. Application fee: $25. Space fee: varies. Exhibition space: varies. For more information, call, e-mail, or visit website.

TIPS "Sales are best for items under $100."

22ND ANNUAL HOLIDAY CRAFT AND GIFT MARKETPLACE

2901 Key St., Maumee OH 43537. (419)436-1457. E-mail: cloudpro@tds.net. Website: www.cloudshows.biz. **Contact:** Judy Cloud, promoter. Estab. 1995.

ADDITIONAL INFORMATION Event held annually, beginning of November. Held indoors. Accepts handmade crafts.Not juried. We do require photos and visually make decisions. Prizes given: exhibitor drawing. Average number of exhibitors: 100+. Average number of attendees: 3,500. Admission fee for public: $5, children 12 and under are free (coupons available). Artisans should apply via e-mail or inquire via website. Deadline: Until full. Application fee: 0. Space fee: $155–195. Square footage of the space: 10x8, 10x10, 12x10. Average gross sales for a typical exhibitor: n/a. For more information, e-mail, visit website, or call. Promote and talk with customers.

29TH ANNUAL HOLIDAY HANDCRAFTERS SHOWCASE AND MARKETPLACE

1210 N. Wheeling Ave., Muncie IN 47303, U.S.. (419)436-1457. E-mail: cloudpro@tds.net. Website: www.cloudshows.biz. **Contact:** Judy Cloud, promoter. Estab. 1988.

ADDITIONAL INFORMATION Event held annually in November, the Friday and Saturday before Thanksgiving. Event held indoors. Accepts handmade crafts. Accepts 15% of total exhibits' retail/direct sales. Not juried. Prizes given: exhibitor drawing. Average number of exhibitors: 100+. Average number of attendees: 3,500. Admission fee for pubic: $4, children under 12 are free (coupon available). Artisans should apply via e-mail or inquire via website. Deadline: Until full. Application fee: 0. Space fee: $45–155. Square footage of the space: 10x10, 9x12. Average gross sales: n/a. For more information, e-mail, visit webslte, or call. Help promote and talk with customers.

29TH ANNUAL SPRINGTIME IN OHIO

1017 E. Sandusky St., Findlay OH 45840, U.S.. (419)436-1457. E-mail: cloudpro@tds.net. Website: www.cloudshows.biz. **Contact:** Judy Cloud, promoter. Estab. 1988.

ADDITIONAL INFORMATION Event held annually, 1st Saturday/Sunday of May. Held indoors and outdoors. Not juried. Average number of exhibitors: 280. Average number of attendees: 4,000–6,000. Admission fee for public: 5.00, children 12 and under are free (coupons available). Artisans should apply via e-mail or inquire via website. Deadline: Until full. Application fee: 0. Space fee: $90–185. Square footage of spaces: 10x8, 10x10, 10x20, 12x15. Average gross sales for typical exhibitor: n/a. For more information, e-mail, visit website, or call. Use provided promotional material to help advertise, use social media avenues, and talk with customers.

30TH ANNUAL CHRISTMAS IN OCTOBER

1017 E. Sandusky St., Findlay OH 45840, U.S.. (419)436-1457. E-mail: cloudpro@tds.net. Website: www.cloudshows.biz. **Contact:** Judy Cloud, promoter. Estab. 1988.

ADDITIONAL INFORMATION Event held annually, 1st Saturday and Sunday of October. Event held indoors and outdoors. Accepts handmade crafts. Not juried. Prizes given: exhibitor drawing at end. Average number of exhibitors: 300+. Average number of attendees: 6,000–8,000. Admission fee for public: $5, kids under 12 are free (coupon available). Artisans should apply e-mail, inquire via website. Deadline: Until full. Application fee: 0. Space fee: $90–225. Square footage of space: 10x8, 10x10, 10x20, 12x15. Average gross sales for typical exhibitor: n/a. For more information, e-mail, visit website, or call. Help promote, talk with customers.

57TH STREET ART FAIR

1507 E. 53rd St., PMB 296, Chicago IL 60615. (773)234-3247. E-mail: info@57thstartfair.org. Website: www.57thstreetartfair.org. **Contact:** Linda or Ron Mulick, owners/promoters. Estab. 1948.

ADDITIONAL INFORMATION Fine art and craft show held annually in June. Outdoors. Accepts painting, sculpture, photography, glass, jewelry, leather, wood, ceramics, fiber, printmaking. Juried. Free to public. Apply via www. zapplication.org. Deadline for entry: January 15. Application fee: $35. Space fee: $300. Exhibition space: 10×10. For more information, e-mail, or visit website.

ART FAIR AT LAUMEIER SCULPTURE PARK

Laumeier Sculpture Park, 12580 Rott Rd., St. Louis MO 63127. E-mail: smatthew@laumeier. org. Website: www.laumeiersculpturepark.org/art-fair/. **Contact:** Sara Matthew, special events manager. Estab. 1987.

ADDITIONAL INFORMATION More than 15,000 patrons attend this annual 3-day event on Mother's Day weekend, featuring local food vendors, a wine garden, live music and 150 juried artists from across the country exhibiting work in ten media categories: ceramics, fiber/textiles, glass, jewelry, mixed media 2D, painting, photography/digital, printmaking/drawing, sculpture and wood. Founded in 1976, Laumeier Sculpture Park is1 of the first and largest dedicated sculpture parks in the country, making it an institution of international significance as well as a unique complement to the cultural landscape of the St. Louis region. Laumeier is a nonprofit, accredited art museum that operates in partnership with St. Louis County Parks. Laumeier presents 60 works of large-scale outdoor sculpture in a 105-acre park available Free to public year-round. Eligibility: All artists ages 18 and up who exhibit work of original concept, design and execution are eligible to apply. Artists may apply in more than1 category; however, a separate application and jury fee must be submitted for each category. Artists may not apply more than once in the same category. Total event participation is limited to 150 artists. Apply via www.zapplication.org. Required images: 5 (booth shot required).

ADDITIONAL INFORMATION Laumeier Sculpture Park is a living laboratory where artists and audiences explore the relationship between contemporary art and the natural environment.

AFFORDABLE ARTS FESTIVAL

P.O. Box 1743, Berthoud CO 80513. (303)330-8237. E-mail: jdphotos@earthlink.net. Website: www.affordableartsfestival.com. **Contact:** Jim DeLutes, director.

ADDITIONAL INFORMATION Fine art and craft show held annually in August. Outdoors. Accepts painting, jewelry, glass, sculpture, photography, wood, fiber, pottery, mixed media, drawing, pastels, and more. Juried. Admission: $5. Apply via www.zapplication.org. Deadline for entry: see website. Application fee: $30. Space fee: $225. Exhibition space: 10×15. For more information, e-mail, call, or visit website.

AIKEN'S MAKIN'

Greater Aiken Chamber of Commerce, 121 Richland Ave. E, Aiken SC 29801. (803) 649-1200 ext. 224. Fax: (803) 641-4174. E-mail: dphillips@aikenchamber.net. Website: www.aikensmakin.net. **Contact:** Dianne Phillips, vice president administration. Estab. 1976.

ADDITIONAL INFORMATION Annual arts and crafts show held in September the Friday and Saturday after Labor Day. Outdoors. Accepts handmade crafts, photography, art, needle crafts, pottery, wood. Juried. exhibitors: 205. Number of attendees: 30,000. Free to public. See website for application. Deadline for entry: February 28. Space fee: $200–225. Exhibition space: 13×10. For more information, e-mail, call, or see website or Facebook page.

AKRON ARTS EXPO

220 Balch St., Akron OH 44302. (330)375-2836. Fax: (330)375-2883. E-mail: PBomba@akronohio.gov. Website: www.akronartsexpo.org. **Contact:** Penny Bomba, artist coordinator. Estab. 1979.

ADDITIONAL INFORMATION Held in late July. "The Akron Arts Expo is a nationally recognized juried fine arts and crafts show held outside with over 160 artists, ribbon and cash awards, great food, an interactive children's area, and entertainment for the entire family. Participants in this festival present quality fine arts and crafts that are offered for sale at reasonable prices. For more information, see the website." Application fee $10. Booth fee: $200. Event held in Hardesty Park.

ALASKA-JUNEAU PUBLIC MARKET

P.O. Box 021145, Juneau AK 99802. (907)586-4072. Fax: (907)586-1166. E-mail: metcom@gci.net. Website: www.juneaupublicmarket.com. **Contact:** Peter Metcalfe, owner/manager. Estab. 2010.

ADDITIONAL INFORMATION Seasonal/holiday show held annually Thanksgiving weekend (November). Indoors. Accepts handmade crafts. Exhibitors: 175. Number of attendees: 10,000 (all 3 days). Admission: $7 for weekend pass. Apply via website. Deadline for entry: July 31. Space fee: $125–980. Exhibition space: 8×8. Average sales: $5,000. For more information, see website.

TIPS "Basic salesmanship: look the customer in the eye and draw them in."

ALEXANDRIA KING STREET ART FESTIVAL

270 Central Blvd., Suite 107B, Jupiter FL 33458. (561)746-6615. Fax: (561)746-6528. E-mail: info@artfestival.com. Website: www.artfestival.com. **Contact:** Malinda Ratliff, communications manager. Estab. 2003.

ADDITIONAL INFORMATION Fine art and craft fair held annually in late September. Outdoors. Accepts photography, jewelry, mixed media, sculpture, wood, ceramic, glass, painting, digital, fiber, metal. Juried. Number of exhibitors: 230. Number of attendees: 150,000. Free to public. Apply online via www.zapplication.org. Deadline: see website. Application fee: $35. Space fee: $575. Exhibition space: 10×10 and 10×20. For more information, e-mail, call, or visit website.

TIPS "You have to start somewhere. First, assess where you are, and what you'll need to get things off the ground. Next, make a plan of action. Outdoor street art shows are a great way to begin your career and lifetime as a working artist. You'll meet a lot of other artists who have been where you are now. Network with them!"

ALLEN PARK ARTS & CRAFTS STREET FAIR

City of Allen Park, P.O. Box 70, Allen Park MI 48101. (734)258-7720. E-mail: applications@allenparkstreetfair.org. Website: www.allenparkstreetfair.org. **Contact:** Allen Park Festivities Commission. Estab. 1981.

ADDITIONAL INFORMATION Arts and crafts show held annually the 1st Friday and Saturday in August. Outdoors. Accepts photography, sculpture, ceramics, jewelry, glass, wood, prints, drawings, paintings. All work must be of fine quality and original work of entrant. Such items as imports, velvet paintings, manufactured or kit jewelry and any commercially produced merchandise are not eligible for exhibit or sale. Juried by 5 photos of work. Number of exhibitors: 200. Free to public. Deadline: March 15 (first review) and May 13 (second review). Application fee: $25. Space fee: $175–200. Exhibition space: 10×10. Apply via www.zapplication.org. Call or For more information, visit website.

ALLENTOWN ART FESTIVAL

P.O. Box 1566, Buffalo NY 14205. (716)881-4269. E-mail: allentownartfestival@verizon.net. Website: www.allentownartfestival.com. **Contact:** Mary Myszkiewicz, president. Estab. 1958.

ADDITIONAL INFORMATION Fine arts and crafts show held annually 2nd full weekend in June. Outdoors. Accepts photography, painting, watercolor, drawing, graphics, sculpture, mixed media, clay, glass, acrylic, jewelry, creative craft (hard/soft). Slides juried by hired professionals that change yearly. Awards/prizes: 41 cash prizes totaling over $20,000; includes Best of Show awarding $1,000. Number of exhibitors: 450. Public attendance: 300,000. Free to public. Apply by downloading application from website. Deadline for entry: late January. Exhibition space: 10×13. Application fee: $15. Booth fee $275. For more information, e-mail, visit website, call or send SASE. Show held in Allentown Historic Preservation District.

TIPS "Artists must have attractive booth and interact with the public."

ALLEY ART FESTIVAL

Water Street Mall, Aurora IL 60506. E-mail: downtownauroran@gmail.com. Website: www.facebook.com/pages/Alley-Art-Festival/107654222593659; www.downtownauroran.com/alley-art-festival/. Estab. 2010.

ADDITIONAL INFORMATION Art and craft show held annually the last Saturday in August. Outdoors. Apply via e-mail. Deadline for entry: July 1. Application fee: none. Space fee: see website. Exhibition space: 10×10. For more information, e-mail or visit website.

ALTON ARTS & CRAFTS EXPRESSIONS

P.O. Box 1326, Palatine IL 60078. (312)751-2500; (847)991-4748. E-mail: asoaartists@aol.com. Website: www.americansocietyofartists.org. **Contact:** ASA Office. Estab. 1979.

ADDITIONAL INFORMATION Fine arts and crafts show held annually indoors in Alton, Illinois, in spring and fall, usually March and September. Accepts quilting, fabric crafts, artwear, photography, sculpture, jewelry, glass works, woodworking and more. Please submit 4 images representative of your work you wish to exhibit, 1 of your display setup, your first/last name, physical address, daytime telephone number—résumé/show listing helpful. "See our website for online jury information." Number of exhibitors: 50. Free to public. Apply by submitting jury materials. Submit to: asoartists@aol.com. If juried in, you will receive a jury/approval number. Deadline for entry: 2 months prior to show or earlier if spaces fill. Space fee: to be announced. Exhibition space: approximately 100 sq. ft. for single space; other sizes available. For more information, artisits should send SASE and submit jury material to ASA, P.O. Box 1326, Palatine IL 60078.

AMAGANSETT FINE ARTS FESTIVAL

David Oleski Events, 977 Broad Run Rd., West Chester PA 19380. (610)864-3500. E-mail: davidoleski@gmail.com. Website: www. amagansettfinearts.com.

ADDITIONAL INFORMATION The cutting edge of individual artistic expression and the communities of the Hamptons go hand in hand, and this festival will provide a rare opportunity for the public to meet these talented visonaries in an up close and personal experience for1 remarkable weekend. For more information, visit website.

AMERICAN ARTISAN FESTIVAL

P.O. Box 41743, Nashville TN 37204. (615)429-7708. E-mail: americanartisanfestival@ gmail.com. Website: www.facebook.com/ theamericanartisanfestival. Estab. 1971.

ADDITIONAL INFORMATION Fine arts and crafts show held annually mid-June, Father's Day weekend. Outdoors. Accepts photography and 21 different medium categories. Juried by 3 different art professionals each year. Three cash awards presented. Number of exhibitors: 165. Public attendance: 30,000. No admission fee for the public. Apply online at www.zapplication. org. Deadline for entry: early March (see website for details). For more information, e-mail or visit the website. Festival held at Centennial Park, Nashville, Tennessee.

AMERICAN CRAFT ATLANTA SHOW

American Craft Council, 1224 Marshall St. NE, Suite 200, Minneapolis MN 55413. E-mail: shows@craftcouncil.org. Website: www. craftcouncil.org. Estab. 1990.

ADDITIONAL INFORMATION Annual juried indoor marketplace in Atlanta featuring original work by more than 230 of the nation's premier, jury-selected artists. You'll find a wide variety of fine craft: jewelry, wearable art, quilts, baskets, toys, and furniture, as well as sculptural and functional works of glass, ceramics, metal, wood, paper and decorative fiber. Deadline for entry: August 1. Application fee: $30 + $10 handling/ processing fee for each set of images. Space fee: varies. Exhibition space: varies. For more information, E-mail or visit website.

AMERICAN CRAFT SHOW BALTIMORE

American Craft Shows, 155 Water St., 4th Floor, Unit 5, Brooklyn NY 11201. E-mail: shows@ craftcouncil.org. Website: www.craftcouncil.org.

ADDITIONAL INFORMATION Art and craft show held annually in February. Indoors. Accepts handmade crafts, ceramics, fiber, metal, and other mediums. Juried. Awards/prizes: Awards of Excellence. Number of exhibitors: 300. Number attendees: varies. Apply online. Deadline for entry: August 1. Application fee: $30 + $10 handling/processing fee for each set of images. Space fee: varies. Exhibition space: varies. For more information, e-mail or visit website.

AMERICAN CRAFT ST. PAUL SHOW

American Craft Council, 1224 Marshall St. NE, Suite 200, Minneapolis MN 55413. E-mail: shows@ craftcouncil.org. Website: www.craftcouncil.org. **Contact:** Shows Office. Estab. 1987.

ADDITIONAL INFORMATION Annual juried indoor marketplace in St. Paul featuring original work by more than 240 of the nation's premier, jury-selected artists. You'll find a wide variety of fine craft: jewelry, wearable art, quilts, baskets, toys and furniture, as well as sculptural and functional works of glass, ceramics, metal, wood, paper and decorative fiber. Deadline for entry: August 1st. Application fee: $30 + $10 handling/processing fee for each set of images. Space fee: varies. Exhibition space: varies. For more information, e-mail or visit website.

AMERICAN FINE CRAFT SHOW NYC
P.O. Box 480, Slate Hill NY 10973. (845)355-2400; (845)661-1221. Fax: (845)355-2444. E-mail: show.director@americanartmarketing.com; hello@americanartmarketing.com. Website: www.americanfinecraftshownyc.com. **Contact:** Richard Rothbard, director.
ADDITIONAL INFORMATION Fine art and craft show held annually in October. Indoors. Accepts handmade crafts, basketry, ceramics, decorative fiber, furniture, glass, jewelry, leather, metal, mixed media, paper, wearable art, wood. Juried. Apply online. Deadline for entry: April 30. Application fee: $35. Space fee: $200. Exhibition space: varies. For more information, e-mail or visit website.

AMERICAN FOLK ART FESTIVAL
(707)246-2460. E-mail: gavitee@aol.com. Website: www.americanfolkartfestival.com. **Contact:** Susan Bartolucci.
ADDITIONAL INFORMATION Arts and Antiques show held annually in September. Under a tent handmade1-of-a-kind folk art, Americana, and folk art antiques. Admission: $10. Invitation only; see website. For more information, e-mail or visit website.
TIPS "We are looking for outside of the norm, so feel free to experiment."

AMISH ACRES ARTS & CRAFTS FESTIVAL
1600 W. Market St., Nappanee IN 46550. (574)773-4188 or (800)800-4942. E-mail: amishacres@amishacres.com; beckymaust@amishacres.com. Website: www.amishacres.com. **Contact:** Becky Cappert, marketplace coordinator. Estab. 1962.

ADDITIONAL INFORMATION Arts and crafts show held annually first weekend in August. Outdoors. Accepts photography, crafts, floral, folk, jewelry, oil, acrylic, sculpture, textiles, watercolors, wearable, wood. Juried by 5 images, either 35mm slides or e-mailed digital images. Awards/prizes: $5,000 cash including Best of Show and $1,000 purchase prizes. Number of exhibitors: 300. Public attendance: 50,000. Admission: $7; $6 seniors; Children under 12 free. Apply by sending SASE or printing application from website. Deadline for entry: April 1. Exhibition space: 10×12, 15×12, 20×12 or 30×12; optional stable fee, with tent, also available. For more information, e-mail, call, visit website, or send SASE.
TIPS "Create a vibrant, open display that beckons to passing customers. Interact with potential buyers. Sell the romance of the purchase."

ANACORTES ARTS FESTIVAL
505 O Ave., Anacortes WA 98221. (360)293-6211. Fax: (360)299-0722. E-mail: staff@anacortesartsfestival.com. Website: www.anacortesartsfestival.com.
ADDITIONAL INFORMATION Fine arts and crafts show held annually 1st full weekend in August. Accepts photography, painting, drawings, prints, ceramics, fiber art, paper art, glass, jewelry, sculpture, yard art, woodworking. Juried by projecting 3 images on a large screen. Works are evaluated on originality, quality, and marketability. Each applicant must provide 5 high-quality digital images, including a booth shot. Awards/prizes: festival offers awards totaling $3,500. Number of exhibitors: 270. Apply via www.zapplication.org. Application fee: $30. Deadline for entry: early March. Space fee: $325. Exhibition space: 10×10. For more information, see website. Show is located on Commercial Ave. from 4th to 10th St.

ANDERSON ORCHARD APPLE FESTIVAL & CRAFT FAIR
369 E. Greencastle Rd., Mooresville IN 46158. (317)831-4181. E-mail: erin@andersonorchard.com. Website: www.andersonorchards.com/apple_festival.php. **Contact:** Erin.

ADDITIONAL INFORMATION Arts and crafts show held annually in September. Indoors and outdoors. Accepts handmade crafts and other items. Apply online. Deadline for entry: see website. Application fee: none. Space fee: $100. Exhibition space: varies. For more information, e-mail, visit website, or call.

ANNA MARIA ISLAND ARTS & CRAFTS FESTIVAL, THE

270 Central Blvd., Suite 107B, Jupiter FL 33458. (561)746-6615. Fax: (561)746-6528. E-mail: info@artfestival.com. Website: www.artfestival. com. **Contact:** Malinda Ratliff, communications manager.

ADDITIONAL INFORMATION Fine art and craft fair held annually in mid-November. Outdoors. Accepts photography, jewelry, mixed media, sculpture, wood, ceramic, glass, painting, digital, fiber, metal. Juried. Number of exhibitors: 106. Number of attendees: 10,000. Free to public. Apply online via www.zapplication.org. Deadline: see website. Application fee: $15; free to mail in paper application. Space fee: $250. Exhibition space: 10×10 and 10×20. For more information, e-mail, call, or visit website.

ANN ARBOR STREET ART FAIR, THE ORIGINAL

721 E. Huron, Suite 200, Ann Arbor MI 48104. (734)994-5260. Fax: (734)994-0504. E-mail: production@artfair.org; mriley@artfair.org. Website: www.artfair.org. Estab. 1958.

ADDITIONAL INFORMATION Fine arts and crafts show held annually beginning the 3rd Thursday in July. Outdoors. Accepts photography, fiber, glass, digital art, jewelry, metals, 2D and 3D mixed media, sculpture, clay, painting, drawing, printmaking, pastels, wood. Juried based on originality, creativity, technique, craftsmanship, and production. Awards/prizes: cash prizes for outstanding work in any media. Number of exhibitors: 200. Public attendance: 500,000. Free to public. Apply through www.zapplication. org. Application fee: $35/40. Space fee: $650. Exhibition space: 10×12. Average gross sales/exhibitor: $7,000. For more information, e-mail, visit website, or call.

ANN ARBOR SUMMER ART FAIR

118 N.4th Ave., Ann Arbor MI 48104. (734)662-3382. Fax: (734)662-0339. E-mail: info@theguild. org. Website: www.theguild.org. Estab. 1970.

ADDITIONAL INFORMATION Fine arts and craft show held annually on the third Wednesday through Saturday in July. Outdoors. Accepts all fine art categories. Juried. Number of exhibitors: 325. Attendance: 500,000–750,000. Free to public. Deadline for entry is January; enter online at www. juriedartservices.com. Exhibition space: 10×10, 10×13, 10×17. For information, visit the website, call, or e-mail. Show is located on University of Michigan campus and in downtown Ann Arbor.

ANNUAL ARTS & CRAFTS ADVENTURE

American Society of Artists, P.O. Box 1326, Palatine IL 60078. (847)991-4748. E-mail: asoaartists@aol.com. Website: www. americansocietyofartists.org. **Contact:** ASA Office. Estab. 1991.

ADDITIONAL INFORMATION Fine arts and crafts show held annually in May the Saturday before Mother's Day. Outdoors. Accepts fine art and handmade crafts. Juried. Number of exhibitors: 55. Free to public. Apply be e-mailing asoaartists@ aol.com or via mail with SASE. Send 4 images representative of your work you wish to exhibit, 1 of your display setup, your first/last name, physical address, daytime phone number, and résumé/show listing. Deadline for entry: varies. Space fee: $95 (price less or more for smaller or larger space). Exhibition space: 10×10 (smaller and larger spaces also available upon request). For more information, visit website.

TIPS "Remember to present your work in a professional manner."

ANNUAL ARTS AND CRAFTS FESTIVAL— FAIRHOPE

(251)928-6387. E-mail: lroberts@ eschamber.com. Website: www. annualartsandcraftsfestivalfairhope.com. **Contact:** Liz R. Thomson, director of tourism and special events. Estab. 1952. Arts and crafts show held annually in March. Outdoors. Accepts handmade crafts, fine art, painting, sculpture, jewelry, watercolor, graphics and drawing, woodworking, pottery and ceramics, photography. Juried. Awards/prizes: $10,750 in prize money. Number of exhibitors: 200+. Number of attendees: 300,000. Festival located in downtown Fairhope on Fairhope Ave. Free to public. Apply online. **ADDITIONAL INFORMATION** Deadline for entry: September 30. Application fee: $30. Space fee: $300 (single); $600 (double). Exhibition space: 10×10. For more information, visit website, e-mail, or call.

ANNUAL BOCA FEST

270 Central Blvd., Suite 107B, Jupiter FL 33458. (561)746-6615. Fax: (561)746-6528. E-mail: info@artfestival.com. Website: www.artfestival. com. **Contact:** Malinda Ratliff, communications manager.

ADDITIONAL INFORMATION "Boca Fest is the longest running show presented by Howard Alan Events and has become considered Boca's #1 event to attend. Over 2 decades since it's inception, this esteemed community art festival continues to highlight the talents of more than 150 exhibitors displaying a wide range of works from life-size sculptures to photography, paintings, and jewelry. The festival offers many opportunities to appreciate—and purchase— art during this weekend of visual inspiration. This phenomenal art festival brings together an affluent customer base with an exceptional eye for great art, the aesthetic beauty of Boca Raton, and an abundant mix of fine art." For more information, visit website.

ANNUAL DOWNTOWN HYATTSVILLE ART FESTIVAL

(301)683-8267. E-mail: jfair@hyattsvillecdc. org. Website: www.hyattsvilleartsfestival.com. **Contact:** Stuart Eisenberg, executive director.

ADDITIONAL INFORMATION "See over 70 exhibiting and performing artists, enjoy live entertainment, and eat some great food on the happening streets of Hyattsville, in the Gateway Arts District of Prince George's County." For more information, visit website.

ANNUAL HERITAGE FESTIVAL & CRAFT SHOW

Attn: Heritage Festival, P.O. Box 6015, Columbia MO 65205. (573)874-7460. E-mail: klr@gocolumbiamo.com. Website: www. gocolumbiamo.com. **Contact:** Karen Chandler, director. Estab. 1976.

ADDITIONAL INFORMATION Arts and crafts show held annually in September. Outdoors. Festival located in Nifong Park. Accepts handmade crafts and fine art. Juried. Number of exhibitors: 80. Number of attendees: 20,000. Free to public. Apply online. Deadline for entry: September 1. Application fee: none. Space fee: $80; $85 after Sept. 1. Exhibition space: 12×12. For more information, visit website, e-mail, or call.

ANNUAL SHADYSIDE—THE ART FESTIVAL ON WALNUT ST.

270 Central Blvd., Suite 107B, Jupiter FL 33458. (561)746-6615. Fax: (561)746-6528. E-mail: info@artfestival.com. Website: www.artfestival. com. **Contact:** Malinda Ratliff, communications manager.

ADDITIONAL INFORMATION "The annual Shadyside—The Art Festival on Walnut Street, which started out as a neighborhood street fair, is now regarded as 1 of the top shows in Pittsburgh. Shadyside features boutiques, shops and galleries mingled with national retailers in a neighborhood of tree-lined streets, historic homes, hip events, and distinctive restaurants." For more information, visit website.

ANNUAL SIESTA FIESTA

270 Central Blvd., Suite 107B, Jupiter FL 33458. (561)746-6615. Fax: (561)746-6528. E-mail: info@artfestival.com. Website: www.artfestival. com. **Contact:** Malinda Ratliff, communications manager.

ADDITIONAL INFORMATION "Hosted in an exquisite venue seated along the beautifully lush Ocean Boulevard and BeachRd., you can stroll along the beach as you take in art from 250 of the nation's most talented artists and crafters out there. Showcasing an extensive collection of work ranging from life-size sculptures, spectacular paintings,1-of-a-kind jewels, photography, ceramics and much, much more, this show truly has something for anyone. Complete with an additional green market, this spectacular show also features plants, orchids, body products, and tasty dips." For more information, visit website.

ANNUAL ST. ARMANDS CIRCLE FESTIVAL

270 Central Blvd., Suite 107B, Jupiter FL 33458. (561)746-6615. Fax: (561)746-6528. E-mail: info@artfestival.com. Website: www.artfestival. com. **Contact:** Malinda Ratliff, communications manager.

ADDITIONAL INFORMATION "Year after year, the Annual St. Armands Circle Art Festival makes the list of *Sunshine Artist Magazine*'s top art shows in the country. For 2 days, festival-goers will enjoy works from the nation's best talent and long-time festival favorites, along with the newest names on the contemporary art scene. Come see some of America's best artists displaying 1-of-a-kind jewelry, pottery, paintings, and much, much more. Festival patrons and art collectors alike can meet and visit with their favorite artists—having the opportunity to view and purchase original art." For more information, visit website.

APPLE ANNIE CRAFTS & ARTS SHOW

4905 Roswell Rd., Marietta GA 30062. (770)552-6400, ext. 6110. Fax: (770)552-6420. E-mail: sagw4905@gmail.com. Website: www.st-ann. org/womens-guild/apple-annie. Estab. 1981.

ADDITIONAL INFORMATION Handmade arts and crafts show held annually the 1st weekend in December. Juried. Indoors. Accepts handmade arts and crafts such as photography, woodworking, ceramics, pottery, painting, fabrics, glass, etc. Number of exhibitors: 120. Public attendance: 4,000. Apply by visiting website to print application form. Deadline: March 1 (see website for details). Application fee: $20, nonrefundable. Booth fee $200. Exhibition space: 80 sq. ft. minimum, may be more. For more information, visit website.

TIPS "We are looking for vendors with an open, welcoming booth, who are accessible and friendly to customers."

APPLE COUNTRY CRAFT FAIR

St. Peter's Episcopal Church, 3 Peabody Row, Londonderry NH 03052. (603)437-8333. E-mail: saintpeterscraftfair@gmail.com. Website: www.stpeterslondonderry.org. **Contact:** Diana LaGasse. Estab. 1999.

ADDITIONAL INFORMATION Arts and crafts show held annually in May. Outdoors. Accepts handmade crafts. Juried. Number of exhibitors: 50. Number of attendees: varies. Free to public. Apply online. Deadline for entry: early May. Application fee: none. Space fee: $65. Exhibition space: 10×10. For more information, visit website, e-mail, or call.

TIPS High-quality, unique crafts are bestsellers.

⊕ APPLEWOOD ARTS

12897 W. 78th Cir., Arvada CO (303)797-9656. Fax: (303)797-9656. E-mail: kness50@gmail. com. Website: www.applewoodartsandcrafts. com. **Contact:** Kathleen Ness. Estab. 1977.

ADDITIONAL INFORMATION Arts and crafts show held annually 3 times in November. Indoors. Accepts original fine art and handmade crafts. Juried. Awards/prizes: 9 Most Original Booth prizes. Number of exhibitors: 100. Number of attendees: 4,000. Admission: $4. Apply via website. Deadline for entry: mid-June. Application fee: none. Space fee: $300. Exhibition space: 10×10; 12×12. For more information, visit website. Festival takes place at 3 locations: Highlands Ranch; Standley Lake; The Ranch—Loveland, Larimer Co. Fairgrounds.

TIPS Present a creative, well-done booth.

⊕ APPLEWOOD ARTS

3300 S. Platte River Dr., Englewood CO 80110. (303)797-9656. Website: www. applewoodartsandcrafts.com. **Contact:** Kathleen and Peggy, Owners. Estab. 1977.

ADDITIONAL INFORMATION Held annually in November. Event held indoors. Accepts handmade crafts. Accepts some gift items. Juried event. Prizes given: booth, advertising, promotion. Average number of exhibitors: 110. Average number of attendees: 4,000. Admission fee for public: $4. Deadline for entry: TBA. Application fee: $0. Space fee: $300. Square footage of the space: 10x10 and 12x12. Visit website for more information.

ARLINGTON FESTIVAL OF THE ARTS

270 Central Blvd., Suite 107B, Jupiter FL 33458. (561)746-6615. Fax: (561)746-6528. E-mail: info@artfestival.com. Website: www.artfestival. com. **Contact:** Malinda Ratliff, communications manager. Estab. 2013.

ADDITIONAL INFORMATION Fine art and craft fair held annually in mid-April. Outdoors. Accepts photography, jewelry, mixed media, sculpture, wood, ceramic, glass, painting, digital, fiber, metal. Juried. Number of exhibitors: 140. Number of attendees: 50,000. Free to public. Apply online via www.zapplication.org. Deadline: see website. Application fee: $25. Space fee: $395. Exhibition space: 10×10 and 10×20. For more information, e-mail, call, or visit the website. Festival located at Highland St. in the Clarendon district of Arlington, Virginia.

ART & APPLES FESTIVAL®

Presented by Paint Creek Center for the Arts, 407 Pine St., Rochester MI 48307. (248)651-4110. Fax: (248)651-4757. E-mail: general@pccart. org. Website: www.pccart.org. **Contact:** Tami Salisbury, executive director. Estab. 1965.

ADDITIONAL INFORMATION Fine art festival held annually the weekend after Labor Day in Rochester, Michigan. Outdoors. Accepts handmade fine art. Juried. Exhibitors: 290. Number of attendees: 200,000. Admission: $5 donation. Apply online. Deadline for entry: see website. Application fee: see website. Space fee: see website. Exhibition space: see website. For more information, e-mail or visit website.

ART & CRAFT MARKETPLACE AT THE COLUMBUS OKTOBERFEST

4275 Fulton Rd. NW, Canton OH 44718. (330)493-4130. Fax: (330)493-7607. E-mail: shows@huffspromo.com. Website: www. huffspromo.com. Estab. 1965.

ADDITIONAL INFORMATION Arts and crafts show held annually in September. Outdoors (covered). Accepts handmade crafts and other items. Juried. Number of exhibitors: varies. Number of attendees: 30,000. Free to public. Apply online. Deadline for entry: see website. Application fee: none. Space fee: $190 (single); $380 (double). Exhibition space: 10×14. For more information, e-mail, visit website, or call.

ART & CRAFT SHOWCASE AT THE AKRON HOME & FLOWER SHOW

4275 Fulton Rd. NW, Canton OH 44718. (330)493-4130. Fax: (330)493-7607. E-mail: shows@huffspromo.com. Website: www. huffspromo.com. Estab. 1965.

ADDITIONAL INFORMATION Arts and crafts show held annually in February. Indoors. Accepts handmade crafts. Juried. Exhibitors: varies. Number of attendees: 30,000. Free to public. Apply online. Deadline for entry: see website. Application fee: none; $100 space deposit required at time of application. Space fee: $395. Exhibition space: 8×12. For more information, e-mail, visit website, or call.

ART-A-FAIR

P.O. Box 547, Laguna Beach CA 92652. (949)494-4514. E-mail: marketing@art-a-fair. com. Website: www.art-a-fair.com. Estab. 1967.

ADDITIONAL INFORMATION Fine arts show held annually in June–August. Outoors. Accepts painting, sculpture, ceramics, jewelry, printmaking, photography, master crafts, digital art, fiber, glass, pencil, wood. Juried. Exhibitors: 125. Number of attendees: see website. Admission: $7.50 adults; $4.50 seniors; children 12 and under free. Apply online. Deadline for entry: see website. Application fee: $40 (per medium). Space fee: $200 + $35 membership fee. Exhibition space: see website. For more information, e-mail, call, or visit website.

ART AT THE GLEN

P.O. Box 550, Highland Park IL 60035. (847)926-4300. Fax: (847)926-4330. E-mail: info@amdurproductions.com. Website: www. amdurproductions.com. Estab. 1967.

ADDITIONAL INFORMATION Arts and crafts show held annually in August. Outoors. Accepts handmade crafts, ceramics, fiber, furniture, glass, jewelry, metal, mixed media, paintings, drawings, photography and wood. Juried. Exhibitors: 185. Number of attendees: 50,000. Free to public. Apply online. Deadline for entry: see website. Application fee: $35. Space fee: $525. Exhibition space: see website. For more information, e-mail, visit website, or call.

ART BIRMINGHAM

118 N.4th Ave., Ann Arbor MI 48104. (734)662-3382. Fax: (734)662-0339. E-mail: info@theguild. org. Website: www.theguild.org. Estab. 1981.

ADDITIONAL INFORMATION Arts and crafts show held annually in May. Outoors. Accepts handmade crafts painting, ceramics, photography, jewelry, glass, wood, sculpture, mixed media, fiber, metal, and more. Juried. Exhibitors: 150. Number of attendees: see website. Free to public. Apply online. Deadline for entry: see website. Application fee: see website. Space fee: see website. Exhibition space: see website. For more information, call or visit website.

ART CENTER'S ARTSPLASH

Sioux City Art Center, 225 Nebraska St., Sioux City IA 51101-1712. (712)279-6272 ext. 232. Fax: (712)255-2921. E-mail: ewebber@sioux-city.org. Website: www.siouxcityartcenter.org/artsplash. **Contact:** Erin Webber-Dreeszen, development coordinator. Estab. 1984.

ADDITIONAL INFORMATION Fine arts and crafts fair held annually over Labor Day weekend. Outdoors. Accepts handmade fine art and fine craft. Juried. Exhibitors: see website. Number of attendees: see website. Admission: $5; kids 11 and under free. Apply online. Deadline for entry: see website. Application fee: see website. Space fee: see website. Exhibition space: see website. For more information, e-mail, visit website, or call.

ART FAIR AT JUNCTION CITY

4275 Fulton Rd. NW, Canton OH 44718. (330)493-4130. Fax: (330)493-7607. E-mail: shows@huffspromo.com. Website: www. huffspromo.com. Estab. 1965.

ADDITIONAL INFORMATION Arts and crafts show held annually in September. Outoors (covered). Accepts handmade crafts and other items. Juried. Exhibitors: varies. Number of attendees: 30,000. Free to public. Apply online. Deadline for entry: see website. Application fee: none. Space fee: $190 (single); $380 (double). Exhibition space: 10×14. For more information, e-mail, visit website, or call.

ART FAIR AT QUEENY PARK

GSLAA-Vic Barr, 1668 Rishon Hill Dr., St. Louis MO 63146. (636)724-5968. Website: www. artfairatqueenypark.com.

ADDITIONAL INFORMATION Arts and crafts show held annually in August. Indoors. Accepts handmade crafts, clay, digital (computer) art, drawing/print, fiber (basketry, paper, wearable, woven), glass, jewelry, 2D/3D mixed media, oil/acrylic, photography, sculpture, water media, wood. Juried. Exhibitors: 140. Number of attendees: see website. Free to public. Apply online. Deadline for entry: see website. Application fee: $25; $50 for late application. Space fee: $225. Exhibition space: 10×8. For more information, call or visit website.

ART FAIR JACKSON HOLE

Art Association of Jackson Hole, P.O. Box 1248, Jackson WY 83001. (307)733-6379. Fax: (307)733-6694. E-mail: artistinfo@jhartfair.org. Website: www.jhartfair.org. **Contact:** Elisse La May, events director. Estab. 1965.

ADDITIONAL INFORMATION Arts and crafts show held annually the second weekends of July & August in Miller Park, Jackson Hole, Wyoming. Outdoors. Accepts handmade crafts, ceramic, drawing, fiber, furniture, glass, graphics & printmaking, jewelry, leather, metalwork, 2D/3D mixed media, painting, photography, sculpture, toys & games, wearable fiber, wood. Juried. Exhibitors: 145. Number of attendees: 12,000. Free for art association members; $5 per day for non-members. Apply via www.zapplication. org. Deadline for entry: see website. Application fee: $35. Space fee: standard booth space is 10X10. Other booth options vary. Exhibition space: varies. For more information, e-mail, visit website, or call.

ART FAIR OFF THE SQUARE

P.O. Box 1791, Madison WI 53701-1791. (262)537-4610. E-mail: wiartcraft@gmail.com. Website: www.artcraftwis.org/AFOS.html. Estab. 1965.

ADDITIONAL INFORMATION Arts and crafts show held annually in July. Outoors. Accepts handmade crafts ceramics, art glass, painting, fiber, sculpture, jewelry, graphics, papermaking, photography, wood and more. Juried. Awards/prizes: Best of Category. Exhibitors: 140. Number of attendees: see website. Free to public. Apply via www.zapplication.org. Deadline for entry: see website. Application fee: $25. Space fee: $300. Exhibition space: 10×10. For more information, e-mail, visit website or call.

ART FAIR ON THE COURTHOUSE LAWN

P.O. Box 795, Rhinelander WI 54501. (715)365-7464. E-mail: assistant@rhinelanderchamber.com. Website: www.explorerhinelander.com. **Contact:** events coordinator. Estab. 1985.

ADDITIONAL INFORMATION Arts and crafts show held annually in June. Outoors. Accepts woodworking (includes furniture), jewelry, glass items, metal, paintings and photography. Number of exhibitors: 150. Public attendance: 3,000. Free to public. Space fee: $75–300. Exhibit space: 10×10 to 10×30. For more information, e-mail, call, or visit website. Show located at1ida County Courthouse.

TIPS "We accept only items handmade by the exhibitor."

ART FAIR ON THE SQUARE

July 9–10, 2016, Madison Museum of Contemporary Art, 227 State St., Madison WI 53703. (608)257-0158, ext 229. Fax: (608)257-5722. E-mail: artfair@mmoca.org. Website: www.mmoca.org/events/special-events/art-fair-square/art-fair-square. **Contact:** Annik Dupaty. Estab. 1958.

ADDITIONAL INFORMATION Arts and crafts show held annually in July. Outoors. Accepts handmade crafts, ceramics, fiber, leather, furniture, jewelry, glass, digital art, metal, sculpture, 2D/3D mixed media, painting, photography, printmaking/graphics/drawing, wood. Juried. Awards/prizes: Best of Show; Invitational Award. Exhibitors: varies. Number of attendees: 150,000+. Free to public. Apply via www.zapplication.org. Deadline for entry: see website. Application fee: $35. Space fee: $520

(single); $1,075 (double). Exhibition space: 10×10 (single); 20×10 (double). For more information, e-mail, call, or visit website.

ART FEST BY THE SEA

270 Central Blvd., Suite 107B, Jupiter FL 33458. (561)746-6615. Fax: (561)746-6528. E-mail: info@artfestival.com. Website: www.artfestival.com. **Contact:** Malinda Ratliff, communications manager. Estab. 1958.

ADDITIONAL INFORMATION Fine art and craft fair held annually in early March. Outoors. Accepts photography, jewelry, mixed media, sculpture, wood, ceramic, glass, painting, digital, fiber, metal. Juried. Number of exhibitors: 340. Number of attendees: 125,000. Free to public. Apply online via www.zapplication.org. Deadline: see website. Application fee: $25. Space fee: $415. Exhibition space: 10×10 and 10×20. For more information, e-mail, call, or visit website. Fair located along A1A between Donald Ross Rd. and Marcinski in Juno Beach, Florida.

ARTFEST FORT MYERS

1375 Jackson St., Suite 401, Fort Myers FL 33901. (239)768-3602. E-mail: info@artfestfortmyers.com. Website: www.artfestfortmyers.com.

ADDITIONAL INFORMATION Fine arts and crafts fair held annually in February. Outoors. Accepts handmade crafts, ceramics, digital, drawing/graphics, fiber, glass, jewelry, metal, 2D/3D mixed media, painting, photography, printmaking, sculpture, wearable, wood. Juried. Awards/prizes: $5,000 in cash. Exhibitors: 200. Number of attendees: 85,000. Free to public. Apply online. Deadline for entry: September 15. Application fee: $35. Space fee: $460.50. Exhibition space: 10×10. For more information, e-mail, call, or visit website.

ART FESTIVAL BETH-EL

400 Pasadena Ave. S, St. Petersburg FL 33707. (727)347-6136. Fax: (727)343-8982. E-mail: annsoble@gmail.com. Website: www.artfestivalbethel.com. Estab. 1972.

ADDITIONAL INFORMATION Fine arts and crafts show held annually the last weekend in January. Indoors. Accepts photography, painting, jewelry, sculpture, woodworking, glass. Juried by special committee on-site or through slides. Awards/prizes: over $7,000 prize money. Number of exhibitors: over 170. Public attendance: 8,000–10,000. Free to public. Apply by application with photos or slides; show is invitational. Deadline for entry: September. For more information, call or visit website. A commission is taken.

TIPS "Don't crowd display panels with artwork. Make sure your prices are on your pictures. Speak to customers about your work."

ART FESTIVAL OF HENDERSON

P.O. Box 95050, Henderson NV 89009-5050. (702)267-2171. E-mail: info@artfestival.com.

ADDITIONAL INFORMATION Arts and crafts show held annually in May. Outdoors. Accepts handmade crafts, paintings, pottery, jewelry, photography, and much more. Juried. Exhibitors: varies. Number of attendees: 25,000. Free to public. Apply online. Deadline for entry: see website. Application fee: see website. Space fee: see website. Exhibition space: see website. For more information, call or visit website.

ARTFEST MIDWEST—"THE OTHER ART SHOW"

Stookey Companies, P.O. Box 31083, Des Moines IA 50310. (515)278-6200. Fax: (515)276-7513. E-mail: suestookey@att.net. Website: www.artfestmidwest.com.

ADDITIONAL INFORMATION Fine art fair held annually in June. Indoors and outdoors. Accepts handmade fine art, ceramic, fiber, drawing, glass, jewelry, metal, 2D/3D mixed media, painting, photography, wood. Juried. Exhibitors: 240. Number of attendees: 30,000. Free to public. Apply via www.zapplication.org. Deadline for entry: March. Application fee: $30. Space fee: varies. Exhibition space: see website. For more information, visit website, or call.

ARTIGRAS FINE ARTS FESTIVAL

5520 PGA Blvd., Suite 200, Palm Beach Gardens FL 33418. (561)746-7111. E-mail: info@artigras. org. Website: www.artigras.org. **Contact:** Hannah Sosa, director of special events. Estab. 2008.

ADDITIONAL INFORMATION Annual fine arts festival held in February during Presidents' Day weekend. Outdoors. Accepts all fine art (including photography). Juried. $17,000 in cash awards and prizes. Average number of exhibitors: 300. Average number of attendees: 85,000. Admission: $10. Apply by enclosing a copy of prospectus or by application form, if available; can also apply via www.zapplication. org. Deadline: September. Application fee: $40. Space fee: $450. Space is 12×12. For more information, e-mail, or visit website.

ART IN BLOOM—CANTIGNY PARK

(630)668.5161. E-mail: info@cantigny.org. Website: www.cantigny.org/calendar/signature-events/art-in-bloom.

ADDITIONAL INFORMATION Fine arts and crafts show held annually in June. Outdoors. Accepts handmade crafts, ceramics, drawing, fiber nonfunctional, fiber wearable, paper nonfunctional, furniture, glass, jewelry, acrylic, oil, watercolor, pastel, sculpture, wood, mixed media, collage, photography, and printmaking. Juried. Exhibitors: 80. Number of attendees: 8,000. Free to public. Apply online. Deadline for entry: see website. Application fee: $10. Space fee: $300. Exhibition space: 10×10. For more information, e-mail, call, or visit website.

ART IN THE BARN—BARRINGTON

Advocate Good Shepherd Hospital, Art in the Barn Artist Committee, 450 W. Hwy. 22, Barrington IL 60010. (847)842-4496. E-mail: artinthebarn.barrington@gmail.com. Website: www.artinthebarn-barrington.com. Estab. 1974.

ADDITIONAL INFORMATION Fine arts and crafts show held annually in September. Indoors and outdoors. Accepts handmade crafts, ceramics, painting, jewelry, glass, sculpture, fiber, drawing, photography, digital media, printmaking, scratchboard, mixed media, wood. Juried. Awards/prizes: Best of Show; Best of Medium; Purchase Awards. Exhibitors: 185.

Number of attendees: 8,500. Admission: $5; children 12 and under free. Apply online. Deadline for entry: see website. Application fee: $20. Space fee: $100 (indoors); $85 (outdoors). Exhibition space: varies. For more information, e-mail, call, or visit website.

ART IN THE BARN—FITCHBURG

5927 Adams Rd., Fitchburg WI 53575. (608)835-0454. E-mail: artinthebarn@comcast.net. Website: www.site.artinthebarnwi.org. Estab. 1974.

ADDITIONAL INFORMATION "Art in the Barn is dedicated to bringing quality visual and performing arts for people of all ages, in a serene and natural rural setting for life enriching experiences and pure enjoyment. Art in the Barn is a series of performances featuring local, national and international performers, and visual artists. The series takes place in an 1870s restored barn in a rural setting outside of Madison, Wisconsin."

ART IN THE GARDENS

9400 Boerner Dr., Hales Corners WI 53130. (414)525-5656. Fax: (414)525-5668. E-mail: jschmitz@fbbg.org. Website: www. boernerbotanicalgardens.org. **Contact:** Jennifer Schmitz, gift shop manager. Estab. 2009.

ADDITIONAL INFORMATION Arts and crafts show held annually in May. Indoors and outdoors. Accepts handmade crafts, photography, painting. Juried. Number of exhibitors: 40. Number of attendees: 1,000. Free to public. Apply online. Deadline for entry: April 3. Application fee: $5 before February 3; $10 after February 3. Space fee: $75. Exhibition space: 8×8 inside; 10×10 outside. Average sales: $500–2,000. For more information, e-mail or visit website.

ART IN THE PARK (ARIZONA)

P.O. Box 748, Sierra Vista AZ 85636-0247. (520)803-0584. E-mail: Libravo@live.com. Website: www.artintheparksierravista.com. Estab. 1972.

ADDITIONAL INFORMATION Oldest, longest running arts and crafts fair in Southern Arizona. Fine arts and crafts show held annually 1st full weekend in October. Outdoors. Accepts photography, all fine arts and crafts created by vendor. No resale retail strictly applied. Juried by Huachaca Art Association Board. Artists submit 5 photos. Returnable with SASE. Number of exhibitors: 203. Public attendance: 15,000. Free to public. Apply by downloading the application www.artintheparksierravista.com. Deadline for entry: postmarked by late June. Last minute/late entries always considered. No application fee. Space fee: $200–275, includes jury fee. Exhibition space: 15×30. Some electrical; additional cost of $25. Some RV space available at $15/night. For more information, visit website, e-mail, call, or send SASE. Show located in Veteran's Memorial Park.

ART IN THE PARK (VIRGINIA)

20 S. New St., Staunton VA 24401. (540)885-2028. E-mail: director@saartcenter.org. Website: www.saartcenter.org. **Contact:** Beth Hodges, executive director. Estab. 1961.

ADDITIONAL INFORMATION Fine arts and crafts show held annually every Memorial Day weekend. Outdoors. Juried by submitting 4 photos representative of the work to be sold. Award/prizes: $1,500. Number of exhibitors: 60. Public attendance: 3,000–4,000. Free to public. Apply by sending in application. Exhibition space: 10×10. For more information, e-mail, call or visit website. Show located at Gypsy Hill Park.

ART IN THE PARK (ELMHURST)

(630)712-6541. E-mail: roz@rglmarketingforthearts.com. Website: www.rglmarketingforthearts.com/elmhurst-art-in-the-park. Estab. 1996.

ADDITIONAL INFORMATION Fine arts and crafts show held annually in May. Outdoors. Accepts handmade crafts and other items. Juried. Exhibitors: varies. Number of attendees: 10,000. Free to public. Apply online. Deadline for entry: see website. Application fee: see website. Space fee: see website. Exhibition space: see website. For more information, visit website.

ART IN THE PARK FALL FOLIAGE FESTIVAL

Rutland Area Art Association, P.O. Box 1447, Rutland VT 05701. (802)775-0356. E-mail: info@chaffeeartcenter.org; artinthapark@chaffeeartcenter.org. Website: www.chaffeeartcenter.org. **Contact:** Meg Barros. Estab. 1961.

ADDITIONAL INFORMATION A fine arts and crafts show held at Main Street Park in Rutland Vermont, annually in October over Columbus Day weekend. Accepts fine art, specialty foods, fiber, jewelry, glass, metal, wood, photography, clay, floral, etc. All applications will be juried by a panel of experts. The Art in the Park Festivals are dedicated to high-quality art and craft products. Number of exhibitors: 100. Public attendance: 9,000–10,000. Public admission: voluntary donation. Apply online and either e-mail or submit a CD with 3 photos of work and 1 of booth (photos upon preapproval). Deadline for entry: early bird discount of $25 per show for applications received by March 31. Space fee: $200–350. Exhibit space: 10×12 or 20×12. For more information, e-mail, visit website, or call. Show located in Main Street Park.

TIPS "Have a good presentation, variety, if possible (in pricing also), to appeal to a large group of people. Apply early, as there are a limited amount of accepted vendors per category. Applications will be juried on a first come, first served basis until the category is determined to be filled."

ART IN THE PARK (HOLLAND)

Holland Friends of Art, P.O. Box 1052, Holland MI 49422. E-mail: info@hollandfriendsofart.com. Website: www.hollandfriendsofart.com. **Contact:** Beth Canaan, art fair chairperson. Estab. 1969.

ADDITIONAL INFORMATION This annual fine arts and crafts fair is held on the first Saturday of August in Holland. The event draws one of the largest influx of visitors to the city on a single day, second only to Tulip Time. More than 300 fine artists and artisans from 8 states will be on hand to display and sell their work. Juried. All items for sale must be original. Public attendance: 10,000+. Entry fee: $90 includes a $20 application fee. Deadline: late March. Space fee: $160 for a double-wide space. Exhibition space:

12×12. Details of the jury and entry process are explained on the application. Application available online. E-mail or visit website for more information. Event held in Centennial Park.

TIPS "Create an inviting and neat booth. Offer well-made quality artwork and crafts at a variety of prices."

ART IN THE PARK (KEARNY)

Kearney Artist Guild, P.O. Box 1368, Kearney NE 68848-1368. (308)708-0510. E-mail: artintheparkkearney@charter.net. Website: www.kearneyartistsguild.com. **Contact:** Daniel Garringer (308)708 0510. Estab. 1971. Fine arts held annually in July. Outdoors. Accepts handmade fine crafts, ceramics, drawing, fiber, mixed media, glass, jewelry, painting, photography, sculpture. Juried. Exhibitors: 90. Number of attendees: estimated 7,000. Free to public. Apply online. Deadline for entry: early June. Application fee: $10. Space fee: $50–100. Exhibition space: 12×12 or 12×24 . For more information, e-mail, visit website, or call.

ART IN THE PARK (PLYMOUTH)

P.O. Box 702490, Plymouth MI 48170. (734)454-1314. Fax: (734)454-3670. E-mail: info@artinthepark.com. Website: www.artinthepark.com. Estab. 1979.

ADDITIONAL INFORMATION Arts and crafts show held annually in July. Outdoors. Accepts handmade crafts, paintings, sculpture, ceramics, jewelry, fiber, fine glass, woodwork, mixed media, photography, and folk art. Juried. Exhibitors: 400. Number of attendees: 300,000. Free to public. Apply online. Deadline for entry: see website. Application fee: $20. Space fee: $580. Exhibition space: 10×10. For more information, e-mail, visit website, or call.

ART IN THE PEARL FINE ARTS & CRAFTS FESTIVAL

P.O. Box 5906, Portland OR 97228-5906. (503)722-9017. E-mail: info@artinthepearl.com. Website: www.artinthepearl.com. Estab. 1996.

ADDITIONAL INFORMATION Arts and crafts show held annually Labor Day weekend. Outdoors. Accepts handmade crafts, fine art, ceramics, fiber, glass, drawings, computer-generated media, 2D/3D mixed media, jewelry, metal, painting, photography, printmaking, sculpture, wood. Juried. Exhibitors: 130. Number of attendees: varies. Free to public. Apply online at www.zapplication.org. Deadline for entry: February 15; late deadline: February 28. Application fee: $35; late fee $45. Space fee: varies. Exhibition space: varies. For more information, visit www.artinthepearl.com or www.zapplication.org.

ART IN THE VILLAGE WITH CRAFT MARKETPLACE

270 Central Blvd., Suite 107B, Jupiter FL 33458. (561)746-6615. Fax: (561)746-6528. E-mail: info@artfestival.com. Website: www.artfestival.com. **Contact:** Malinda Ratliff, communications manager. Estab. 1991.

ADDITIONAL INFORMATION Fine art and craft fair held annually in early June. Outdoors. Accepts photography, jewelry, mixed media, sculpture, wood, ceramic, glass, painting, digital, fiber, metal. Juried. Number of exhibitors: 150. Number of attendees: 70,000. Free to public. Apply online via www.zapplication.org. Deadline: see website. Application fee: $25. Space fee: $450. Exhibition space: 10×10 and 10×20. For more information, e-mail, call, or visit website. Show located at Legacy Village in Cleveland, Ohio.

ARTISPHERE

101B Augusta St., Greenville SC 29601. (864)412-1040. Fax: (864)283-6580. E-mail: polly@artisphere.org. Website: www.artisphere.org. **Contact:** Polly Gaillard.

ADDITIONAL INFORMATION Fine arts and crafts art festival held annually second weekend in May (see website for details). Showcases local and national fine art and fine craft artists on Artist Row along South Main Street. Accepts digital art and photography. Apply via www.zapplication.org. Free to public. For more information, e-mail, visit website, or call.

ARTMARKET SAN FRANCISCO

109 S. Fifth St., Suite 407, Brooklyn NY 11249. (212)518-6912. Fax: (212)518-7142. E-mail: info@art-mrkt.com. Website: www.artmarketsf.com. Estab. 2011.

ADDITIONAL INFORMATION "Since 2011, Art Market Productions has produced a different type of art fair that focuses on creating the highest-quality fair experience by connecting collectors with dealers in the most optimal settings and contexts. Art Market Productions is dedicated to improving the art world by creating platforms and expanding networks of connection."

ART ON THE CHATTAHOOCHEE

(678)277-0920. E-mail: brian.r.bentley@gwinnettcounty.com. Website: www.gwinnettcounty.com.

ADDITIONAL INFORMATION "Art on the Chattahoochee is a delightful, fine art event at a unique venue along the Chattahoochee River in Jones Bridge Park. The event brings together outstanding artists throughout North Georgia in a fine art market highlighting their talent. The event also features a shaded food court area, a fun, interactive kids craft corner, as well as all the park amenities!"

ART ON THE LAWN

Village Artisans, 100 Corry St., Yellow Springs OH 45387. (937)767-1209. E-mail: villageartisans.e-mail@yahoo.com. Website: www.villageartisans.blogspot.com. **Contact:** Village Artisans. Estab. 1983.

ADDITIONAL INFORMATION Fine arts and crafts show held annually the 2nd Saturday in August. Outdoors. Accepts photography, all hand-made media and original artwork. Juried, as received, from photos accompanying the application. Awards: Best of Show receives a free booth space at next year's event. Number of exhibitors: 90–100. Free to public. Request an application by calling or e-mailing, or download an application from the website. Deadline for entry: July 31; however, the sooner received, the better the chances of acceptance. Jury fee: $15. Space fee: $75 before May; $85 until late

July; $105 thereafter. Exhibition space: 10×10. Average gross sales vary. For more information, visit website, e-mail, call, send SASE or stop by Village Artisans at above address.

⊕ ART ON THE MALL

The University of Toledo, Office of Alumni Relations, 2801 W. Bancroft St., Mail Stop 301, Toledo OH 43606-3390. (419)530-2586. Fax: (419)530-4994. E-mail: artonthemall@utoledo. edu; ansley.abrams@utoledo.edu. Website: www.toledoalumni.org. Shirley Grzecki. **Contact:** Ansley Abrams-Frederick. Estab. 1992.

ADDITIONAL INFORMATION Art show held annually on the last Sunday in July in Centennial Mall in the heart of the main campus of the University of Toledo. Outdoor juried art show. This show accepts submissions in the following categories: acrylic, glass, jewelry, mixed media, pen and ink, photography, pottery, oil, textiles/fibers/basketry, watercolors, wood and other. Awards/prizes: UT Best of Show (has to have a UT connection), 1st place, 2nd place, 3rd place, Purchase Award. Number of exhibitors: 105–115. Number of attendees: 12,000. Free to public. Apply online or call the office to have an application mailed to you. Deadline for entry: April 30. Application fee: $25. Space fee: $100. Exhibition space: 10×10. For more information, e-mail, call, or visit website.

"The purpose of the University of Toledo Alumni Association shall be to support the University by fostering a spirit of loyalty to the university among its alumni. This is accomplished by providing a communications link between alumni and the university, encouraging and establishing activities for alumni and promoting programs to assist int he academic and cultural development of the University of Toledo."

ART ON THE SQUARE

P.O. Box 23561, Belleville IL 62223. (618)233-6769. E-mail: clindauer@bellevillechamber.org. Website: www.artonthesquare.com. Estab. 2002.
ADDITIONAL INFORMATION Fine arts and crafts show held annually in May. Outdoors. Accepts handmade crafts, photography, glass, jewelry, clay, sculpture, fine craft, mixed media, wood, and digital art. Juried. Awards/prizes:

over $30,000 in cash. Exhibitors: 105. Number of attendees: varies. Free to public. Apply online. Deadline for entry: see website. Application fee: see website. Space fee: see website. Exhibition space: see website. For more information, e-mail, visit website, or call.

ART RAPIDS!

P.O. Box 301, Elk Rapids MI 49629. (231)264-6660. E-mail: art@mullalys128.com. Website: www.artrapids.org. **Contact:** Barb Mullaly.
ADDITIONAL INFORMATION Art fair held annually last Saturday in June. Outdoors. Accepts handmade crafts, ceramic, drawing, fiber, glass, jewelry, painting, photography, printmaking, sculpture, wood, metal, paper, or mixed media. Juried. Awards/prizes: Best of Show, Honorable Mention, People's Choice. Exhibitors: 70. Number of attendees: 4,000. Free to public. Apply online. Deadline for entry: early April. Application fee: $20. Space fee: varies. Exhibition space: 10×10. For more information, e-mail, visit website, or call.

⊙ ARTS & CRAFTS ADVENTURE

American Society of Artists, P.O. Box 1326, Palatine IL 60078. (312)751-2500. E-mail: asoaartists@aol.com. Website: www.americansocietyofartists.org. **Contact:** ASA Office. Estab. 1991.
ADDITIONAL INFORMATION Fine arts and crafts show held annually in early May and mid-September. Outdoors. Event held in Park Ridge, Illinois. Accepts photography, pottery, paintings, sculpture, glass, wood, woodcarving, and more. Juried by 4 slides or photos of work and 1 slide or photo of display; a résumé or show listing is helpful. See our website for online jury. To jury via e-mail: asoaartists@aol.com. Number of exhibitors: 60. Free to public. Apply by submitting jury materials. Submit to asoaartists@aol.com. If juried in, you will receive a jury/approval number. Deadline for entry: 2 months prior to show or earlier if spaces fill. Space fee: to be announced. Exhibition space: about 100 sq. ft. for single space; other sizes available. For more information, send SASE, submit jury material. Show located in Hodges Park.

AN ARTS & CRAFTS AFFAIR, AUTUMN & SPRING TOURS

P.O. Box 655, Antioch IL 60002. (402)331-2889. E-mail: hpifestivals@cox.net. Website: www.hpifestivals.com. **Contact:** Huffman Productions. Estab. 1983.

ADDITIONAL INFORMATION An arts and crafts show that tours different cities and states. Autumn Festival tours annually October-November; Spring Festival tours annually in March and April. Visit website to see list of states and schedule. Indoors. Accepts photography, pottery, stained glass, jewelry, clothing, wood, baskets. All artwork must be handcrafted by the actual artist exhibiting at the show. Juried by sending in 2 photos of work and 1 of display. Awards/prizes: 4 $30 show gift certificates; $50, $100, and $150 certificates off future booth fees. Number of exhibitors: 300–500 depending on location. Public attendance: 15,000–35,000. Public admission: $8–9/adults; $7–8/seniors; 10 and under, free. Apply by calling to request an application. Deadline for entry: varies for date and location. Space fee: $350–1,350. Exhibition space: 8×11. up to 8×22. For more information, e-mail, call, or visit website.

TIPS "Have a nice display, make sure business name is visible, dress professionally, have different price points, and be willing to talk to your customers."

ARTS & CRAFTS FESTIVAL

Simsbury Woman's Club, P.O. Box 903, Simsbury CT 06070. (860)658-2684. E-mail: simsburywomansclub@hotmail.com; swc_artsandcrafts@yahoo.com. Website: www.simsburywomansclub.org. **Contact:** Shirley Barsness, co-chairman. Estab. 1978.

ADDITIONAL INFORMATION Arts and crafts show held in mid-September. Juried event. Outdoors rain or shine. Original artwork, photography, clothing, accessories, jewelry, toys, wood objects, and floral arrangements accepted. Manufactured items or items made from kits not accepted. Individuals should apply by submitting completed application, 4 photos or JPEG files, including 1 of display booth. Exhibition space: 11×14. or 15×14. frontage. Space fee: $160–175; late applications $170–185. Number of exhibitors: 120. Public attendance: 5,000–7,000. Free to public. Deadline for entry: August 15. For more information, e-mail swc_artsandcrafts@yahoo.com or call Jean at (860)658-4490 or Shirley at (860)658-2684. Applications available on website. Show located in Simsbury Center.

TIPS "Display artwork in an attractive setting."

ARTS & WINE FESTIVAL AT LOCUST GROVE

P.O. Box 156, Walkerton VA 23177. (804)769-8201. E-mail: ftmattaponi@aol.com. Website: www.locustgrove1665.com. **Contact:** Cecky Ropelewski, promoter. Estab. 2005.

ADDITIONAL INFORMATION Arts and Crafts Show. Event held outdoors. Accepts handmade crafts. Accepts art, pottery, glass, wood, photography, fiber, jewelry, and metal. Juried committee event. No awards or prizes given. Average number of exhibitors: 60. Average number of attendees: 1,000. Admission fee: $5. Wine tasters: $10 in advance/$15 at door. Children 12 and under are free. Artisans should apply via phone or e-mail. Deadline for entry applications is April 15. No application fee. Space fee: $100—10×10; $160—10×20. Event size: 3 acres. Average gross sales for typical exhibitor: $700. For more information, e-mail, visit website or call. Make your craft—"Be friendly and fun or you can't come."

ARTS, BEATS & EATS

301 W.4th St., Suite LL-150, Royal Oak MI 48067. (248)541-7550. Fax: (248)541-7560. E-mail: lisa@artsbeatseats.com. Website: www.artsbeatseats.com. **Contact:** Lisa Konikow, art director. Estab. 1997.

ADDITIONAL INFORMATION Fine arts and crafts fair held annually in September. Outdoors. Accepts handmade crafts, ceramic, digital art, fiber, drawing, glass, jewelry, metal, 2D/3D mixed media, painting, photography, printmaking, wood. Juried. Awards/prizes: $7,500 in cash awards. Exhibitors: 145. Number of attendees: 400,000. Free to public. Apply online. Deadline for entry: March. Application fee: $25. Space fee: $490. Exhibition space: 10×10. For more information, e-mail, call, or visit website.

⊕ ARTS ADVENTURE

P.O. Box 1326, Palatine IL 60078. (312)571-2500 or (847)991-4748. E-mail: asoaartists@aol.com. Website: www.americansocietyofartists.org. Estab. 2001. American Society of Artists.

ADDITIONAL INFORMATION Fine arts and crafts show held annually the end of July. Event held in Chicago. Outdoors. Accepts photography, paintings, pottery, sculpture, jewelry and more. Juried. Please submit 4 images representative of your work you wish to exhibit,1 of your display setup, your first/last name, physical address, daytime telephone number (résumé/show listing helpful). See our website for online jury. To jury: submit via e-mail to asoaartists@aol.com or to the above address. Include a business-size (#10) SASE please. Number of exhibitors: 50. Free to public. If juried in, you will receive a jury/approval number. Deadline for entry: 2 months prior to show or earlier if spaces fill. Entry fee: TBA. Exhibition space: about 100 sq. ft. for single space; other sizes available. For more information, send SASE.

TIPS "Remember that when you are at work in your studio, you are an artist. But when you are at a show, you are a business person selling your work."

ART'S ALIVE

200 125th St., Ocean City MD 21842. (410)250-0125. Website: www.oceancitymd.gov/recreation_and_parks/specialevents.html. **Contact:** Brenda Moore, event coordinator. Estab. 2000.

ADDITIONAL INFORMATION Fine art show held annually in mid-June. Outdoors. Accepts photography, ceramics, drawing, fiber, furniture, glass, printmaking, jewelry, mixed media, painting, sculpture, fine wood. Juried. Awards/prizes: $5,250 in cash prizes. Number of exhibitors: 100. Public attendance: 10,000. Free to public. Apply by downloading application from website or call. Deadline for entry: February 28. Space fee: $200. Jury Fee: $25. Exhibition space: 10×10. For more information, visit website, call or send SASE. Show located in Northside Park.

TIPS Apply early.

ARTSCAPE

Dallas Arboretum, 8525 Garland Rd., Dallas TX 75218. (214)515-6615. Website: www.dallasarboretum.org/visit/seasonal-festivals-events/artscape.

ADDITIONAL INFORMATION Arts and crafts show held annually in April. "The beauty of art meets the beauty of nature at the Dallas Arboretum's annual fine art and fine craft show and sale in the garden. This juried art fair features art that is of or about nature by artists from around the country. Guests will also enjoy artist demonstrations, entertainment, food, and fun for all ages! Don't miss the chance to see and buy from your favorite artists set amid a garden that has been listed as1 of the top3 most beautiful display gardens in the nation." For more information, visit website.

ARTS COUNCIL FOR WYOMING COUNTY'S LETCHWORTH ARTS & CRAFTS SHOW

P.O. Box 249, Perry NY 14530. (585)237-3517. **Fax:** (585)237-6385. E-mail: info@artswyco.org. Website: www.artswyco.org. **Contact:** Sunny Simmons, show coordinator. Estab. 1975.

ADDITIONAL INFORMATION Event held annually in mid-October on Columbus Day weekend and Canadian Thanksgiving. Arts and craft show. Event held Outdoors. Accepts handmade crafts. Accepts paintings, fiber, pottery, toys, mixed media, and jewelry. Juried event, viewed by 6 professional artists. Prizes given: Cash plus free booth for next show. Average number of exhibitors: 320. Average number of attendees: 90,000. Admission fee for public: $8 park admission fee. Deadline: March 15. Application fee: $35. Space fee: $295. Square footage of space: 12×12. Average gross sales for a typical exhibitor: unknown. For more information, e-mail, visit website, or call.

ARTS EXPERIENCE

P.O. Box 1326, Palatine IL 60078. (312)751-2500 or (847)991-4748. E-mail: asoaartists@aol.com. Website: www.americansocietyofartists.org. Estab. 1979.

ADDITIONAL INFORMATION Fine arts and crafts show held in summer in Chicago. Outdoors. Accepts photography, paintings, graphics, sculpture, quilting, woodworking, fiber art, hand-crafted candles, glass work, jewelry, and more. Juried by 4 images representative of work being exhibited; 1 image of display setup, résumé with show listings helpful. Submit to asoaartists@aol.com. Number of exhibitors: 50. Free to public. Apply by submitting jury material and indicate you are interested in this particular show. When you pass the jury, you will receive jury approval number and application you requested. You may also submit to ASA, P.O. Box 1326, Palatine IL 60078. Include a SASE (business size, #10). Deadline for entry: 2 months prior to show or earlier if space is filled. Space fee: to be announced. Exhibition space: 100 sq. ft. for single space; other sizes are available. For more information, send SASE to submit jury material.

ARTSFEST
P.O. Box 99, 13480 Dowell Rd., Dowell MD 20629. (410)326-4640. Fax: (410)326-4887. E-mail: info@annmariegarden.org. Website: www.annmariegarden.org. Estab. 1984.
ADDITIONAL INFORMATION Fine arts and crafts fair held annually in September. Indoors and outdoors. Accepts handmade crafts, ceramic, digital art, fiber, drawing, furniture, glass, jewelry, metal, 2D/3D mixed media, painting, photography, printmaking, wood. Juried. Awards/prizes: Best of Show, Best Demonstration, Wooded Path Award, Best New Artsfest Artist Award. Exhibitors: 170. Number of attendees: varies. Admission: $6 adults; children 11 & under free; members free. Apply online. Deadline for entry: March. Application fee: $25. Space fee: varies. Exhibition space: varies. For more information, e-mail, visit website, or call.

ARTS IN THE PARK
302 Second Ave. E., Kalispell MT 59901. (406)755-5268. E-mail: information@hockadaymuseum.com. Website: www.hockadaymuseum.org. Estab. 1968.
ADDITIONAL INFORMATION Fine arts and crafts show held annually 4th weekend in July (see website for details). Outdoors. Accepts photography, jewelry, clothing, paintings, pottery, glass, wood, furniture, baskets. Juried by a panel of five members. Artwork is evaluated for quality, creativity, and originality. Jurors attempt to achieve a balance of mediums in the show. Number of exhibitors: 100. Public attendance: 10,000. Apply by completing the online application form and sending 5 images in JPEG format; 4 images of work and 1 of booth. Application fee: $25. Exhibition space: 10×10 or 10×20. Booth fees: $170−435. For more information, e-mail, call, or visit website. Show located in Depot Park.

ARTS ON THE GREEN
Arts Association of Oldham County, 104 E. Main St., LaGrange KY 40031. (502)222-3822;. E-mail: maryklausing@bellsouth.net. Website: www.aaooc.org. **Contact:** Mary Klausing, director. Estab. 1999.
ADDITIONAL INFORMATION Fine arts and crafts festival held annually 1st weekend in June. Outdoors. Accepts photography, painting, clay, sculpture, metal, wood, fabric, glass, jewelry. Juried by a panel. Awards/prizes: cash prizes for Best of Show and category awards. Number of exhibitors: 130. Public attendance: 10,000. Free to public. Apply online with website, call or visit www.zapplication.org. Deadline for entry: April 15. Jury fee: $25. Space fee: $200. Electricity fee: $20. Exhibition space: 10×10 or 10×12. For more information, e-mail, visit website, call. Show located on the lawn of the Oldham County Courthouse Square.
TIPS "Make potential customers feel welcome in your space. Don't overcrowd your work. Smile!"

ARTSPLOSURE
313 S. Blount St., #200B, Raleigh NC 27601. (919)832-8699. Fax: (919)832-0890. E-mail: sarah@artsplosure.org. Website: www.artsplosure.org. **Contact:** Sarah Wolfe, art market coordinator. Estab. 1979.
ADDITIONAL INFORMATION Annual outdoor art/craft fair held the 3rd weekend of May. Accepts ceramics, glass, fiber art, jewelry, metal, painting, photography, wood, 2D, and 3D

artwork. Juried event. Awards: 6 totaling $3,500 cash. Number of exhibitors: up to 170. Public attendance: 75,000. Free admission to the public. Applications available in October, deadline is late January. Application fee: $32. Space fee: $330 for 12×12.; $660 for a double space. Average sales: $2,500. To apply, visit website.

⊕ ARTSPLOSURE — THE RALEIGH ART FESTIVAL

313 W. Blount St., Suite 200B, Raleigh NC 27601. (919)832-8699. Fax: (919)832-0890. E-mail: info@artsplosure.org; sarah@artsplosure.org. Website: www.artsplosure.org. **Contact:** Sarah Wolfe, art market coordinator. Estab. 1979.

ADDITIONAL INFORMATION Arts and craft show held annually 3rd weekend of May. Outdoors. Accepts handmade crafts, 2D/3D, glass, jewelry, ceramics, wood, metal, fiber, photography, painting. Juried. Awards/prizes: $3,500 in cash. Exhibitors: 175. Number of attendees: 75,000. Free to public. Apply via www.application.org. Deadline for entry: January 16.

TIPS "We use entrythingy.com for processing applications."

ARTSQUEST FINE ARTS FESTIVAL

Cultural Arts Alliance of Walton County, Bayou Arts Center, 105 Hogtown Bayou Lane, Santa Rosa Beach FL 32459. (850)622-5970. E-mail: info@culturalartsalliance.com; jennifersmith@culturalartsalliance.com. Website: www.artsquestflorida.com. **Contact:** Jennifer Smith. Estab. 1988.

ADDITIONAL INFORMATION Fine arts and crafts fair held anually in May. Outdoors. Accepts handmade crafts, ceramic, digital art, fiber, drawing, glass, jewelry, metal, 2D/3D mixed media, painting, photography, printmaking, sculpture, wood. Juried. Awards/prizes: Best in Show, Awards of Excellence, and Awards of Merit. Exhibitors: 125. Number of attendees: varies. Free to public. Apply online. Deadline for entry: February. Application fee: $40. Space fee: $300. Exhibition space: 10×10. For more information, e-mail, call, or visit website.

ART STAR CRAFT BAZAAR

(231)264-6660. E-mail: info@artstarphilly.com. Website: www.artstarcraftbazaar.com. Estab. 2003.

ADDITIONAL INFORMATION Arts and crafts fair held annually in May. Outdoors. Accepts handmade crafts, fabric, clay, glass, wood, paper, paintings/drawings, sculpture, and more. Juried. Exhibitors: varies. Number of attendees: varies. Free to public. Apply online. Deadline for entry: see website. Application fee: see website. Space fee: see website. Exhibition space: see website. For more information, e-mail or visit website.

ARTSTREET

130 E Walnut St., Suite 509, Green Bay WI 54115. (920)435-5220. Fax: (920)435-2787. E-mail: info@mosaicartsinc.org. Website: www.mosaicartsinc.org/artstreet. **Contact:** Staci Thompson. Estab. 1981.

ADDITIONAL INFORMATION Fine arts and crafts fair held annually in August. Outdoors. Accepts handmade crafts and other mediums. Juried. Awards/prizes: $5,000 in cash awards. Exhibitors: 200. Number of attendees: 80,000. Free to public. Apply online. Deadline for entry: March. Application fee: $35. Space fee: $225. Exhibition space: 10×10. For more information, e-mail, visit website, or call.

ART UNDER THE ELMS

415 Main St., Lewiston ID 83501. (208)792-2447. Fax: (208)792-2850. E-mail: aue@lcsc.edu. Website: www.lcsc.edu/ce/aue/. **Contact:** Amanda Coleman. Estab. 1984.

ADDITIONAL INFORMATION Fine arts and crafts fair held annually in April. Outdoors. Accepts handmade crafts, ceramic, digital art, fiber, drawing, furniture, glass, jewelry, metal, 2D/3D mixed media, painting, photography, pre-packaged food, printmaking, wood. Juried. Awards/prizes: announced after jury. Exhibitors: 100. Number of attendees: varies. Free to public. Apply online. Deadline for entry: early January. Application fee: $20. Space fee: varies. Exhibition space: 10×10. For more information, e-mail, visit website, or call.

ARVADA CENTER FOR THE ARTS HOLIDAY CRAFT FAIR

(720)763-9013. E-mail: misty@eventsetc.net. Website: www.arvadacenter.org/galleries/special-events/call-for-entries. Estab. 1979.

ADDITIONAL INFORMATION Fine arts and crafts fair held annually in November. Indoors. Accepts handmade crafts and other mediums. Juried. Exhibitors: see website. Number of attendees: varies. Free to public. Apply online. Deadline for entry: August. Application fee: $35. Space fee: varies. Exhibition space: varies. For more information, e-mail, visit website, or call.

ATLANTA ARTS FESTIVAL

P.O. Box 724694, Atlanta GA 31139. (770)941-9660. Fax: (866)519-2918. E-mail: info@atlantaartsfestival.com. Website: www.atlantaartsfestival.com. Estab. 2006.

ADDITIONAL INFORMATION Fine arts and crafts fair held annually in September. Outdoors. Accepts handmade crafts, ceramic, digital art, fiber, drawing, glass, jewelry, metal, 2D/3D mixed media, painting, photography, printmaking, wood. Juried. Awards/prizes: Best in Category, Best in Show. Exhibitors: 200. Number of attendees: varies. Free to public. Apply online. Deadline for entry: April. Application fee: $25. Space fee: varies. Exhibition space: 10×10. For more information, e-mail, visit website, or call.

ATOMIC HOLIDAY BAZAAR

801 N. Tamiami Trail, Sarasota FL 34236. E-mail: atomicholidaybazaar@gmail.com. Website: www.atomicholidaybazaar.com. **Contact:** Adrien Lucas, event producer. Estab. 2006.

ADDITIONAL INFORMATION Arts and crafts show held annually the 1st or 2nd weekend of December. Indoors. Accepts handmade crafts, vintage clothing, kitsch, vintage jewelry, art, paper products, body products and makeup, homemade canned goods, fine jewelry, silversmiths, shoe cobblers, T-shirt screen printing, artists, and plushie makers. Exhibitors: 200. Number of attendees: 1,200. Admission: $5 adults; 12 and under free. Apply via website. Deadline for entry: mid-September. Space fee: $90 for full table or $45 for half-table; $280 booth; $80 stage;

Bay Front room tables $75; Street Fair $300, $200, $160, $100. Exhibition space: Main Room tables—8×3 (table); 12×8 (booth); Bay Front tables 6×3, street fair spaces vary but begin at 10×10. Average gross sales for typical exhibitor: n/a. For more information, e-mail AND visit website to view vendor pictures of past shows.

TIPS Atomic is an indie-craft show representing a wide spectrum of hand made arts and crafts, not interested in mass-production products, think of off the beaten path, from rock n roll to whimsy, affordable, quality, amusing and colorful, punk to feminine. Atomic is not your typical craft show. Think of modern words such as upcycle, DIY, repurposed, vintage, or just plain beautiful to the darker nods of adult-tattoo,art. Atomic is family friendly, but there are mature themes and words/images accepted if the style suits the Atomic show.

AUSTIN CRAFT RIOT

E-mail: austincraftriot@gmail.com. Website: www.austincraftriot.com. Estab. 2011.

ADDITIONAL INFORMATION Arts and crafts show held annually in August. Indoors. Accepts handmade crafts and vintage items. Exhibitors: see website. Number of attendees: varies. Admission: $2 adults; children free. Apply online. Deadline for entry: June. Application fee: $25. Space fee: varies. Exhibition space: 8×8. For more information, e-mail or visit website.

AUTUMN CRAFTS FESTIVAL AT LINCOLN CENTER FOR THE PERFORMING ARTS

American Concern for Artistry and Craftsmanship, P.O. Box 650, Montclair NJ 7042. (973)746-0091. Fax: (973)509-7739. E-mail: acacinfo@gmail.com. Website: www.craftsatlincoln.org.

ADDITIONAL INFORMATION Fine art and craft show held annually in October. Outdoors. Accepts handmade crafts. Juried. Number of exhibitors: 250. Number of attendees: varies. Free to public. Apply online or via www.zapplication.org. Deadline for entry: June. Application fee: none. Space fee: varies. Exhibition space: varies. For more information, call, e-mail, or visit website.

AUTUMN FESTIVAL: AN ARTS & CRAFTS AFFAIR

P.O. Box 655, Antioch IL 60002. (402)331-2889. E-mail: hpifestivals@cox.net. Website: www.hpifestivals.com. Estab. 1985.

ADDITIONAL INFORMATION Fine arts and crafts fair held annually in November. Indoors. Accepts handmade crafts and other mediums. Juried. Exhibitors: 500. Number of attendees: 60,000. Admission: $9 adults; $8 seniors; children 10 & under free. Apply online. Deadline for entry: see website. Application fee: none. Space fee: see website. Exhibition space: 10×10. For more information, e-mail, visit website, or call.

AVANT-GARDE ART & CRAFT SHOWS

Avant-Garde Art & Craft Shows, Rebecca Adele Events, Solon OH 44139. (440)227-8794. E-mail: becki@ag-shows.com. Website: www.avantgardeshows.com.

ADDITIONAL INFORMATION The Avant-Garde Art & Craft Shows are based around Ohio year-round. They feature an eclectic selection of the area's most talented handmade artisans and crafters. For more information, visit website.

BARRINGTON ART FESTIVAL

Amdur Productions, P.O. Box 550, Highland Park IL 60035. (847)926-4300. Fax: (847)926-4330. E-mail: info@amdurproductions.com. Website: www.amdurproductions.com. Estab. 2009.

ADDITIONAL INFORMATION Fine arts and crafts fair held annually in May. Outdoors. Accepts handmade crafts, ceramics, fiber, glass, jewelry, metal, photography, watercolors, and wood. Juried. Awards/prizes: announced at awards party. Exhibitors: 125. Number of attendees: 122,000. Free to public. Apply online. Deadline for entry: early January. Application fee: $25. Space fee: $415. Exhibition space: see website. For more information, e-mail, call, or visit website.

BARTLETT FESTIVAL OF THE ARTS

118 W. Bartlett Ave., Suite 2, Bartlett IL 60103. (630) 372-4152. E-mail: art@artsinbartlett.org. Website: www.artsinbartlett.org. Estab. 2002.

ADDITIONAL INFORMATION Fine arts and crafts fair held annually in June. Outdoors. Accepts handmade crafts, paintings, photography, fiber, sculpture, glass, jewelry, wood, and more. Juried. Exhibitors: see website. Number of attendees: 3,000. Free to public. Apply online. Deadline for entry: April. Application fee: see website. Space fee: $150. Exhibition space: 10×10. For more information, e-mail, call, or visit website.

BASS RIVER ARTS AND CRAFTS FESTIVAL

38 Charles St., Rochester NH 03867. (603)332-2616. E-mail: info@castleberryfairs.com. Website: www.castleberryfairs.com.

ADDITIONAL INFORMATION Fine arts and crafts fair held annually in July. Outdoors. Accepts handmade crafts and other mediums. Juried. Exhibitors: see website. Number of attendees: varies. Free to public. Apply online. Deadline for entry: see website. Application fee: see website. Space fee: $225. Exhibition space: 10×10. For more information, e-mail, visit website, or call.

BAYOU CITY ART FESTIVAL

38 Charles St., Rochester NH 03867. (713) 521-0133. E-mail: info@bayoucityartfestival.com; carrie@bayoucityartfestival.com. Website: www.artcolonyassociation.org/bayou-city-art-festival-memorial-park.

ADDITIONAL INFORMATION Fine arts and crafts fair held annually in March. Outdoors. Accepts handmade crafts, ceramic, digital art, fiber, drawing, furniture, glass, jewelry, metal, 2D/3D mixed media, painting, photography, printmaking, sculpture, wood. Juried. Awards/prizes: Best of Show, 2nd place, 3rd place, Best Booth, Award of Excellence. Exhibitors: see website. Number of attendees: varies. Admission: $15 adults; $3 children 4–12; children 3 and under free. Apply online. Deadline for entry: November. Application fee: see website. Space fee: varies. Exhibition space: varies. For more information, e-mail, call, or visit website.

BEAVER CREEK ART FESTIVAL

270 Central Blvd., Suite 107B, Jupiter FL 33458. (561)746-6615. Fax: (561)746-6528. E-mail: info@artfestival.com. Website: www. artfestival.com. **Contact:** Malinda Ratliff, communications manager.

ADDITIONAL INFORMATION Fine arts and crafts fair held annually in August. Outdoors. Accepts handmade crafts, clay, digital, fiber, glass, jewelry, mixed media, painting, photography, printmaking/drawing, sculpture, wood. Juried. Awards/prizes: announced after jury. Exhibitors: 150. Number of attendees: varies. Free to public. Apply online. Deadline for entry: see website. Application fee: $35. Space fee: $475. Exhibition space: 10×10 and 10×20. For more information, e-mail, call or visit website. Festival located at Beaver Creek Village in Avon, Colorado.

🎧 BELLEVUE ARTS MUSEUM ARTSFAIR

(928)284-9627. E-mail: meredithl@bellevuearts. org. Website: www.bellevuearts.org.

ADDITIONAL INFORMATION "For more than 60 years, BAM ARTSfair has been celebrating the connection between our community and the world of art, craft, and design. Devoted to bringing some of the nation's most talented artists to our region, the Fair features thousands of original artworks, including painting, sculpture, fashion, and jewelry. With over 300 exhibiting artists, both emerging and well-known, BAM ARTSfair is1 the region's largest gatherings and a unique opportunity to acquire art directly from the makers. Also join us for live music, artist demonstrations, community art projects, KIDSfair, and complimentary admission to BAM. See more at: http://www.bellevuearts.org/fair/index.html#sthash.2lzYtAjm.dpuf."

BELLEVUE FESTIVAL OF THE ARTS

Craft Cooperative of the Northwest, 1916 Pike Place, Suite 146, Seattle WA 98101-1013. (206)363-2048. E-mail: info@bellevuefest.org. Website: www.bellevuefest.org. **Contact:** Ann Sutherland, fair coordinator. Estab. 1984.

ADDITIONAL INFORMATION Fine arts and crafts fair held annually in June. Outdoors. Accepts handmade crafts, and other mediums. Juried. Exhibitors: 150-200. Number of attendees:

75,000. Free to public. Apply online. bellevuefest. org and www.zapplication.org. Applications open Feb 1 and close March 31st. Application fee: $40. Space fee: varies. Exhibition space: varies. For more information, e-mail, visit website, or call.

BELL ROCK PLAZA ART & CRAFT SHOW

Donna Campbell, P.O. Box 20039, Sedona AZ 86341. (928)284-9627. E-mail: ohdarnitall@yahoo.com. Website: www.bellrockartshows.com. **Contact:** Donna Campbell.

ADDITIONAL INFORMATION Fine arts and crafts fair held annually several times a year. Outdoors. Accepts handmade crafts and other mediums. Juried. Exhibitors: see website. Number of attendees: varies. Free to public. Apply online. Deadline for entry: varies per show. Application fee: see website. Space fee: $125. Exhibition space: 10×10. For more information, e-mail, visit website, or call.

BERKELEY ARTS FESTIVAL

E-mail: fabarts@silcon.com. Website: www. berkeleyartsfestival.com.

ADDITIONAL INFORMATION Month-long arts festival in Berkeley. See website for details.

BERKSHIRE CRAFTS FAIR

E-mail: paulgib@mapinternet.com. Website: www.berkshirecraftsfair.org. **Contact:** Paul Gibbons. Estab. 1974.

ADDITIONAL INFORMATION Fine arts and crafts fair held annually in August. Indoors. Accepts handmade crafts, jewelry, furniture, ceramics, textiles, glassware, woodwork, and more. Juried. Exhibitors: 90. Number of attendees: varies. Admission: $7; children 12 and under free. Apply online. Deadline for entry: April. Application fee: $25. Space fee: $450. Exhibition space: 10×6. For more information, e-mail or visit website.

BEST OF THE NORTHWEST FALL ART & FINE CRAFT SHOW

Northwest Art Alliance, 7777 62nd Ave., NE, Suite 103, Seattle WA 98115. (206) 525-5926. E-mail: info@nwartalliance.com. Website: www. nwartalliance.com.

ADDITIONAL INFORMATION Fine art and craft show held annually in October and November. Indoors. Accepts handmade crafts, ceramics, paintings, jewelry, glass, photography, wearable art, and other mediums. Juried. Number of exhibitors: 110. Number of attendees: varies. Admission: $5 online; $6 at door; children 12 and under free. Apply via www.zapplication.org. Deadline for entry: May. Application fee: $35. Space fee: varies. Exhibition space: varies. For more information, call, e-mail, or visit website.

BEST OF THE NORTHWEST SPRING ART & FINE CRAFT SHOW

Northwest Art Alliance, 7777 62nd Ave., NE, Suite 103, Seattle WA 98115. (206)525-5926. E-mail: info@nwartalliance.com. Website: www. nwartalliance.com.

ADDITIONAL INFORMATION Fine art and craft show held annually in March. Indoors. Accepts handmade crafts, ceramics, paintings, jewelry, glass, photography, wearable art, and other mediums. Juried. Number of exhibitors: 110. Number of attendees: varies. Admission: $5 online; $6 at door; children 12 and under free. Apply via www.zapplication.org. Deadline for entry: January. Application fee: $35. Space fee: varies. Exhibition space: varies. For more information, call, e-mail, or visit website.

BEVERLY HILLS ART SHOW

(310)285-6836. E-mail: kmclean@beverlyhills. org; artshow@beverlyhills.org. Website: www. beverlyhills.org/artshow. **Contact:** Karen Fitch McLean. Estab. 1973.

ADDITIONAL INFORMATION Fine arts and crafts show held biannually 3rd weekend in May and 3rd weekend in October. Outdoors, 4 blocks in the center of Beverly Hills. Accepts photography, painting, sculpture, ceramics, jewelry, glass, traditional printmaking and digital media. Juried. Awards/prizes: 1st place in category, cash awards, Best in Show cash award; Mayor's Purchase Award in May show. Number of exhibitors: 230–250. Public attendance: 30,000–50,000. Free to public. Deadline for entry: mid-February for the May show; mid-July for the October show. For more information, e-mail, call, or visit website or send SASE. Show located at historic Beverly Gardens.

TIPS "Art fairs tend to be commercially oriented. It usually pays off to think in somewhat commercial terms. Personally, I like risky and unusual art, but the artists who produce esoteric art sometimes go hungry! Be nice and have a clean presentation."

BIG CRAFTY, THE

E-mail: crafty@thebigcrafty.com. Website: www. thebigcrafty.com.

ADDITIONAL INFORMATION "The Big Crafty revives the tradition of the community bazaar, a lively celebration of handmade commerce, featuring local food, beer, music, and fine wares from a juried group of select indie artists and crafters. Our free and fun-for-all-ages events are held semiannually in the heart of beautiful Asheville, NC." For more information, visit website.

BIG HEAP VINTAGE & HANDMADE FESTIVAL, THE

(480)329-6118. Fax: (800)846-8552. E-mail: info@thievesmarketvintageflea.com. Website: www.thebigheap.com. **Contact:** Mickey.

ADDITIONAL INFORMATION "The Big Heap Vintage & Handmade Festival, a juried event featuring the most exciting vintage furniture and decor, fashion, adornment, and hand-wrought and hand-rendered items in the West. Our focus is beyond avoiding tetanus and lead poisoning, our focus is on style. The Big Heap will support you with the raw elements to make your own unique statement in your home, your garden, and in the way you express yourself. We are not a flea market, not an antiques show, and we sure as he** aren't a craft show. Come see us. Gon' be good." For more information, visit website.

THE BIG1 ART & CRAFT FAIRS

The Big1 Art & Craft Fair LLC, 101 22nd Street SW, P.O. Box 1276, Minot ND 58701. (701)837-6059. Fax: (701)839-0874. E-mail: info@ thebigone.biz. Website: www.thebigone.biz.

ADDITIONAL INFORMATION The Big1 Art and Craft Fair consists of4 shows in North Dakota with over 350 different exhibitors showcasing their handmade items to thousands of consumers. Items you will see at each show are handcrafted wood furniture and decorative pieces; photography; pottery; jewelry; variety of floral arrangements to accommodate all tastes; flavorful foods including baked goods, soups, dips, jams, jellies, breads, salsa, spices, candies, and wonderful desserts; creative and comfortable clothing pieces for all ages; handmade soaps and lotions made from various natural resources; unlimited baby items from blankets to bibs and everything in between; hand woven rugs; home-sewn quilts and blankets; wind chimes; photography and artwork; and handmade toys. For more information, visit website.

BITCHCRAFT TRADING POST

E-mail: btchcrafttradingpost@gmail.com. Website: www.bitchcrafttradingpost.com.

ADDITIONAL INFORMATION Bitchcraft Trading Post is a vintage and art collective event. We host a variety of vendors who sell hand-made goods, vintage items, jewelry, artwork, records, food, beverages, and more. For more information, visit website.

BLACK SWAMP ARTS FESTIVAL

P.O. Box 532, Bowling Green OH 43402. E-mail: info@blackswamparts.org. Website: www.blackswamparts.org.

ADDITIONAL INFORMATION The Black Swamp Arts Festival (BSAF), held early September, connects art and the community by presenting an annual arts festival and by promoting the arts in the Bowling Green community. Awards: Best in Show ($1,500); Best 2D ($1,000); Best 3D ($1,000); 2nd place ($750); 3rd place ($500); honorable mentions (3 awards, $200 each). Apply online at www.zapplication.org. Call, e-mail, or visit website for more information. Application fee: $35. Single booth fee: $275. Double booth fee: $550. Show located in downtown Bowling Green. For more information, e-mail, visit website, or call.

BLISSFEST MUSIC FESTIVAL

(231)348-7047. E-mail: jennifer@blissfest.org. Website: www.blissfest.org. **Contact:** Jennifer Ferguson.

ADDITIONAL INFORMATION The arts and craft fair is open to amateur and professional artists and craftspeople who create their own works of arts/crafts. Our goal is to provide opportunities for these creators and innovators of traditional and contemporary arts and crafts to present their respective talents in a festival atmosphere of music and dance that affirms and honors our shared cultural heritage and diversity. For more information, visit website to apply.

BOCA FEST

270 Central Blvd., Suite 107B, Jupiter FL 33458. (561)746-6615. Fax: (561)746-6528. E-mail: info@artfestival.com. Website: www.artfestival.com. **Contact:** Malinda Ratliff, communications manager. Estab. 1988.

ADDITIONAL INFORMATION Fine art and craft fair held annually in January. Outdoors. Accepts photography, jewelry, mixed media, sculpture, wood, ceramic, glass, painting, digital, fiber, metal. Juried. Number of exhibitors: 210. Number of attendees: 80,000. Free to public. Apply online via www.zapplication.org. Deadline: see website. Application fee: $25. Space fee: $395. Exhibition space: 10×10 and 10×20. For more information, e-mail, call, or visit website. Festival located at The Shops at Boca Center in Boca Raton, Florida.

BOCA RATON FINE ART SHOW

Hot Works, P.O. Box 1425, Sarasota FL 34230. (248)684-2613. E-mail: info@hotworks.org; patty@hotworks.org. Website: www.hotworks.org. **Contact:** Patty Naronzny. Estab. 2008.

ADDITIONAL INFORMATION The annual Boca Raton Fine Art Show brings high-quality juried artists to sell their artworks in the heart of downtown Boca Raton. "The event takes place in a premium location on Federal Highway/US-1 at Palmetto ParkRd.. In its 3rd year, the Boca Raton Fine Art Show was voted no. 68 in the country by *Art Fair Source Book*." All work is original and personally handmade by the artist. "We offer awards to attract the nation's best artists. Our goal is to create an atmosphere that enhances the artwork and creates a relaxing environment for art lovers." All types of disciplines for sale including sculpture, paintings, clay, glass, printmaking, fiber, wood, jewelry, photography, and more. Art show also has artist demonstrations, live entertainment, and food. Awards: two $500 Juror's Awards, five $100 Awards of Excellence. "In addition to the professional artists, as part of our commitment to bring art education into the event, there is a Budding Artists Art Competition, sponsored by the Institute for the Arts & Education, Inc., the 501(c)(3) nonprofit organization behind the event." For more information, visit www.hotworks.org.

BOCA RATON MUSEUM OF ART OUTDOOR JURIED ART FESTIVAL

Boca Museum of Art, 501 Plaza Real, Mizner Park, Boca Raton FL 33432. (561)392-2500. Fax: (561)391-6410. E-mail: info@bocamuseum.org. Website: www.bocamuseum.org. Estab. 1986.

ADDITIONAL INFORMATION Fine arts and crafts fair held annually in February. Outdoors. Accepts handmade crafts and other mediums. Juried. Awards/prizes: Best in Show, Merit Awards. Exhibitors: 200. Number of attendees: varies. Free to public. Apply online. Deadline for entry: see website. Application fee: see website. Space fee: see website. Exhibition space: see website. For more information, e-mail, visit website, or call.

BONITA SPRINGS NATIONAL ART FESTIVAL

P.O. Box 367465, Bonita Springs FL 34136-7465. (239)992-1213. Fax: (239)495-3999. E-mail: artfest@artinusa.com. Website: www.artinusa.com/bonita. **Contact:** Barry Witt, director.

ADDITIONAL INFORMATION Fine arts and crafts fair held annually 3 times a year. Outdoors. Accepts handmade crafts, paintings, glass, jewelry, clay works, photography, sculpture, wood, and more. Juried. Awards/prizes: Best of Show, Best 2D, Best 3D, Distinction Award. Exhibitors: see website. Number of attendees: varies. Free to public. Apply online. Deadline for entry: early January. Application fee: $30. Space fee: $400. Exhibition space: 10×12. For more information, e-mail, call, or visit website.

BOSTON MILLS ARTFEST

(330)467-2242. Website: www.bmbw.com.

ADDITIONAL INFORMATION Fine arts and crafts fair held annually in June and July. Outdoors. Accepts handmade crafts, ceramic, digital art, fiber, drawing, furniture, glass, jewelry, metal, 2D/3D mixed media, painting, photography, printmaking, wood. Juried. Awards/prizes: First in Category, Award of Excellence. Exhibitors:

see website. Number of attendees: varies. Free to public. Apply online. Deadline for entry: see website. Application fee: see website. Space fee: see website. Exhibition space: see website. For more information, e-mail, call, or visit website.

BOULDER MOUNTAIN HANDMADE

1905 Linden Dr., Boulder CO 80304. (303)997-8319. E-mail: bmhart@bouldermountainhandmade.com. Website: www.bouldermountainhandmade.com. Estab. 1973.

ADDITIONAL INFORMATION "Boulder Mountain Handmade is a fine art, craft, and baked goods tradition since 1973. We invite you to sip complimentary cider, chat with the artists, and browse unique creations in all price ranges."

BRECKENRIDGE MAIN STREET ART FESTIVAL

Mountain Art Festivals, P.O. Box 3578, Breckenridge CO 80424. (970)547-9326. E-mail: info@mountainartfestivals.com. Website: www.mountainartfestivals.com. Estab. 2001.

ADDITIONAL INFORMATION Fine arts and crafts fair held annually in July. Outdoors. Accepts handmade crafts and other mediums. Juried. Exhibitors: 120. Number of attendees: varies. Free to public. Apply online. Deadline for entry: April. Application fee: $35. Space fee: $500. Exhibition space: 10×10. For more information, e-mail, visit website, or call.

BRICK STREET MARKET

E-mail: info@zionsvillechamber.org. Website: www.zionsvillechamber.org. **Contact:** Diane Schultz. Estab. 1985.

ADDITIONAL INFORMATION Fine art, antique and craft show held annually the Saturday after Mother's Day. Outdoors. In collaboration with area merchants, this annual event is held on Main Street in the Historic Downtown of Zionsville, Indiana. Please submit application found online at www.zionsvillechamber.org and 3 JPEG images. All mediums are welcome. Artists are encouraged to perform demonstrations of their work and talk with visitors during the event. Tents will be provided. Artists may use their own white 10×10. tents if space is available. Artists must supply display equipment. Committee will not accept catalog or mass-produced products. Number of exhibitors: 150–180. Public attendance: 8,000–10,000. Free to public. Space fee: see website.

BROAD RIPPLE ART FAIR

Indianapolis Art Center, Marilyn K. Glick School of Art, 820 E. 67th St., Indianapolis IN 46220. (317)255-2464. E-mail: pflaherty@indplsartcenter.org. Website: www.indplsartcenter.org/events/braf. Estab. 1971.

ADDITIONAL INFORMATION Fine arts and crafts fair held annually in May. Outdoors. Accepts handmade crafts and other mediums. Juried. Exhibitors: 225. Number of attendees: varies. Admission: $13 adult presale; $15 adult day of; $3 children. Apply online. Deadline for entry: see website. Application fee: see website. Space fee: varies. Exhibition space: see website. For more information, visit website or call.

BROOKINGS SUMMER ARTS FESTIVAL

Brookings Summer Arts Festival, P.O. Box 4, Brookings ND 57006. (605)692-2787. E-mail: generalinfo@bsaf.com or artbooths@bsaf.com. Website: www.bsaf.com. Estab. 1972.

ADDITIONAL INFORMATION Fine arts and skilled crafts festival held annually in July. Outdoors. Accepts original art and handcrafted work. Juried. Exhibitors: 200 art booths. Number of attendees: 75,000. Free to public. Apply online. Festival held in historic Pioneer Park. Features free entertainment, children's art area, over 40 food booths, regional, and historic areas. Vendor social the Friday evening before festival. Free vendor parking. Deadline for entry: March 1. Application fee: $25. Space fee: $200. Exhibition space: 12×12. For more information, e-mail, visit website, or call.

BROOKSIDE ART ANNUAL

Brookside Business Association, 6814 Troost Ave., Kansas City MO 64131-1509. (816)523-5553. Fax: (816)333-1022. E-mail: brooksideartannualkc@gmail.com. Website: www.brooksidekc.org. Estab. 1984.

ADDITIONAL INFORMATION Fine arts and crafts fair held annually in May. Outdoors. Accepts handmade crafts and other mediums. Juried. Awards/prizes: Best of Show, Best in Category. Exhibitors: 180. Number of attendees: 70,000. Free to public. Apply online. Deadline for entry: see website. Application fee: see website. Space fee: see website. Exhibition space: see website. For more information, e-mail, visit website, or call.

BROWNWOOD PADDOCK SQUARE ART & CRAFT FESTIVAL

270 Central Blvd., Suite 107B, Jupiter FL 33458. (561)746-6615. Fax: (561)746-6528. E-mail: info@artfestival.com. Website: www.artfestival.com. **Contact:** Malinda Ratliff, communications manager. Estab. 1997.

ADDITIONAL INFORMATION Fine art and craft fair held annually in mid-April. Outdoors. Accepts photography, jewelry, mixed media, sculpture, wood, ceramic, glass, painting, digital, fiber, metal. Juried. Number of exhibitors: 205. Number of attendees: 20,000. Free to public. Apply online via www.zapplication.org or visit website for paper application. Deadline: see website. Application fee: $15. Space fee: $265. Exhibition space: 10×10 and 10×20. For more information, e-mail, call or visit website. Festival located at Brownwood in The Villages, FL.

TIPS "You have to start somewhere. First, assess where you are, and what you'll need to get things off the ground. Next, make a plan of action. Outdoor street art shows are a great way to begin your career and lifetime as a working artist. You'll meet a lot of other artists who have been where you are now. Network with them!"

BRUCE MUSEUM OUTDOOR ARTS FESTIVAL

1 Museum Dr., Greenwich CT 06830-7157. (203) 869-0376, ext. 336. E-mail: cynthiae@brucemuseum.org; sue@brucemuseum.org. Website: www.brucemuseum.org. **Contact:** Sue Brown Gordon, festival director. Estab. 1981.

ADDITIONAL INFORMATION Fine arts fair held annually in October and fine crafts fair in May. Outdoors. Accepts handmade crafts, painting, sculpture, mixed media, graphics/drawing (including computer-generated works), photography. Juried. Exhibitors: see website. Number of attendees: varies. Free/$8 to public. Apply online. Deadline for entry: June for October; November for May. Application fee: $25. Space fee: $370. Exhibition space: 10×12. For more information, e-mail, call, or visit website.

BUCKTOWN ARTS FEST

Bucktown Arts Fest, C/O Holstein Park, 2200 N. Oakley Ave., Chicago IL 60647. E-mail: inquiries@bucktownartsfest.com. Website: www. bucktownartsfest.com. Estab. 1984.

ADDITIONAL INFORMATION Fine arts and crafts fair held annually in August. Outdoors. Accepts handmade crafts and other mediums. Juried. Exhibitors: 200. Number of attendees: 40,000. Free to public. Apply online. Deadline for entry: March. Application fee: $45. Space fee: $300; $200 (seniors 60 and over). Exhibition space: 10×10. For more information, e-mail, visit website, or call.

BUFFALO GROVE INVITATIONAL FINE ART FESTIVAL

Amdur Productions, P.O. Box 550, Highland Park IL 60035. (847)926-4300. Fax: (847)926-4330. E-mail: info@amdurproductions.com. Website: www.amdurproductions.com. Estab. 2002. Fine arts and crafts fair held annually in July. Outdoors. Accepts handmade crafts, ceramic, digital art, fiber, drawing, furniture, glass, jewelry, metal, 2D/3D mixed media, painting, photography, printmaking, wood. Juried. Exhibitors: 120. Number of attendees: 20,000. Free to public. Apply online.

ADDITIONAL INFORMATION Deadline for entry: see website. Application fee: $25. Space fee: $450. Exhibition space: 10×10. For more information, e-mail, call, or visit website.

BUFFALO RIVER ELK FESTIVAL

Jasper AR 72641. (870)446-2455. E-mail: chamber@ritternet.com. Website: www. theozarkmountains.com. **Contact:** Patti or Nancy, vendor coordinators. Estab. 1997. Arts and crafts show held annually in June. Outdoors. Accepts fine art and handmade crafts, photography, on-site design. Exhibitors: 60. Number of attendees: 6,000. Free to public. Apply via website.

ADDITIONAL INFORMATION Deadline for entry: June 1. Application fee: none. Space fee: $75. Exhibition space: 10×10. For more information, visit website.

BUST MAGAZINE'S HOLIDAY CRAFTACULAR

(212)675-1707, ext. 104. E-mail: craftacular@bust.com. Website: www.bust.com. Fine arts and crafts fair held annually in June. Indoors. Accepts handmade crafts and other mediums. Exhibitors: see website. Number of attendees: varies. Admission: $3 adults; children 12 and under free. Apply online.

ADDITIONAL INFORMATION Deadline for entry: May. Application fee: $20. Space fee: see website. Exhibition space: see website. For more information, e-mail, visit website, or call.

BY HAND FINE ART & CRAFT FAIR

One I-X Center Dr., Cleveland OH 44135. (216)265-2663. E-mail: rattewell@ixcenter.com. Website: www.clevelandbyhand.com. **Contact:** Rob Attewell, show manager. Estab. 2004. Fine arts and crafts show held annually in November. Indoors. Accepts photography, 2D, 3D, clay, digital, fiber, furniture, glass, jewelry, leather, metal, oil/acrylics, printmaking, sculpture, watercolor, wood, wearable art. Juried; group reviews applications and photos. Awards/prizes: ribbons, booths. Number of exhibitors: 150–200. Number of attendees: 20,000. Admission: free. Apply via www.zapplication.org.

ADDITIONAL INFORMATION Deadline: June 15. Application fee: $25. Space fee: $399 (8×10); $425 (10×10). Exhibition space: 10×10, 15×10, 20×10. For more information, e-mail or go to www.zapplication.org.

CABIN FEVER CRAFT SHOW

1641 Old York Rd, Hartsville/Warminster Pa 18974, USA. (215)850-1888. E-mail: frommyhand@gmail.com. Website: www.craftsatmolandhouse.com. **Contact:** Gwyn Duffy.

ADDITIONAL INFORMATION "Chase away the winter blahs! We have gathered over 50 talented local crafters to lift your spirits with their creativity.

Find the perfect gift, tasty treat, or decoration for your home and leave here knowing that spring is just around the corner. Spend some time wandering around the beautiful historic setting that was once the headquarters for General George Washington. $1 admission benefits the Moland House Restoration Project."

CAIN PARK ARTS FESTIVAL

City of Cleveland Heights, 40 Severance Circle, Cleveland Heights OH 44118-9988. (216)291-3669. Fax: (216)291-3705. E-mail: jhoffman@clvhts.com; artsfestival@clvhts.com. Website: www.cainpark.com. Estab. 1976. Fine arts and crafts show held annually 2nd weekend in July (3-day event). Outdoors. Accepts photography, painting, clay, sculpture, wood, jewelry, leather, glass, ceramics, clothes and other fiber, paper, block printing. Juried by a panel of professional artists; submit digital images online or mail CD. Awards/prizes: Artist to Artist Award, $450; also Judges' Selection, Director's Choice, and Artists' Award. Number of exhibitors: 150. Public attendance: 15,000. Fee for public: $5; Free on Friday. "Applications are available online at our website www.cainpark.com." apply by requesting an application by mail, visiting website to download application or by calling.

ADDITIONAL INFORMATION Deadline for entry: early March. Application fee: $40. Space fee: $450. Exhibition space: 10×10. Average gross sales/exhibitor: $4,000. For more information, e-mail, call, or visit website. Show located in Cain Park.

TIPS "Have an attractive booth to display your work. Have a variety of prices. Be available to answer questions about your work."

CANTIGNY PARK JEWELRY & ACCESSORIES SHOW

1s151 Winfield Rd., Wheaton IL 60189. (630)260-8216. Fax: (630)260-8284. E-mail: aanderson@cantigny.org. Website: www.cantigny.org. **Contact:** Alicia Anderson, Membership and Retail Operations Manager. Estab. 2011. Arts and crafts/jewelry show held in September. Indoors. Accepts handmade crafts. Exhibitors: 30. Number of attendees: 1,200. Admission: price per car. Apply online.

ADDITIONAL INFORMATION Deadline for entry: August 31. Application fee: $50. Space fee: see website. Exhibition space: 8ft. table. For more information, e-mail or visit website. Show located in Cantigny Park

CANTIGNY PARK MISTLETOE MARKET

1s151 Winfield Rd., Wheaton IL 60189. (630)260-8216. Fax: (630)260-8284. E-mail: aanderson@cantigny.org. Website: www.cantigny.org. **Contact:** Alicia Anderson, membership and retail operations manager. Estab. 2012. Arts and crafts/holiday show held in December. Indoors. Accepts handmade crafts. Exhibitors: 30. Number of attendees: 2,500. Admission: $5. Apply online.

ADDITIONAL INFORMATION Deadline for entry: mid-November. Space fee: see website. Exhibition space: 8 ft. table. For more information, e-mail or visit website. Show located in Cantigny Park.

CAPE CORAL FESTIVAL OF THE ARTS

Cape Coral Festival of the Arts Committee, P.O. Box 101346, Cape Coral FL 33910. (239)699-7942. E-mail: info@capecoralfestival.com. Website: www.capecoralfestival.com. Estab. 1985.

Fine arts and crafts fair held annually in January. Outdoors. Accepts handmade crafts and other mediums. Juried. Exhibitors: see website. Number of attendees: see website. Free to public. Apply online.

ADDITIONAL INFORMATION Deadline for entry: October 1. Application fee: $20. Space fee: $306. Exhibition space: see website. For more information, e-mail, visit website, or call.

CAREFREE FINE ART & WINE FESTIVAL

101 Easy St., Carefree AZ 85377. (480)837-5637. Fax: (480)837-2355. E-mail: info@thunderbirdartists.com. Website: www.thunderbirdartists.com. **Contact:** Denise Colter, president. Estab. 1993. This award-winning, spring Carefree Fine Art and Wine Festival is produced by Thunderbird Artists, in conjunction with the Carefree/Cave Creek Chamber of Commerce and officially named a 'Signature

Event' by the Town of Carefree. This nationally acclaimed fine art festival in Carefree is widely known as "...a collector's paradise." Thunderbird Artists' mission is to promote fine art and fine crafts, paralleled with the ambiance of unique wines and fine music, while supporting the artists, merchants, and surrounding communities.

ADDITIONAL INFORMATION It is the mission of Thunderbird Artists to further enhance the art culture with the local communities by producing award-winning, sophisticated fine art festivals throughout the Phoenix metro area. Thunderbird Artists has played an important role in uniting nationally recognized and award-winning artists with patrons from across the globe."

TIPS "A clean gallery-type presentation is very important."

CAROLINA1 STOP SHOP HOP

Hubbard Dr., Lancaster SC 29720. (803)273-3834. E-mail: dusawyer@comporium.net. Website: www.carolinaonestopshophop. blogspot.com. **Contact:** Donna Sawyer, co-chair. Estab. 2005. Annual shop hop held last Saturday in February. Indoors. Accepts handmade crafts, fabric, yarns, thread, patterns, quilting tools and gadgets, vintage linens, buttons, quilting supplies. Awards/prizes: door prizes. Exhibitors: 25. Number of attendees: 300. Admission: $3. See website for application.

ADDITIONAL INFORMATION Deadline for entry: February . Space fee: $60–200. Exhibition space: classroom, 10×10. For more information, e-mail.

CAROUSEL FINE CRAFT SHOW

City of Kingsport, Kingsport Farmer's Market, 308 Clinchfield St., Kingsport TN 37660, USA. (423)392-8415. E-mail: stephanos@kingsporttn. gov. Website: www.engagekingsport.com. **Contact:** William Kai Stephanos, show director. Estab. 2013. Arts & crafts show held annually in November. Indoors. Accepts fine art and handmade crafts. Juried. Exhibitors: 42. Number of attendees: 10,000. Free to public. Apply online.

ADDITIONAL INFORMATION Deadline for entry: December 2. Application fee: none. Space fee: $250. Exhibition space: 10×10. For more information, e-mail, visit website, or call.

The highest quality fine craft exhibited in East Tennessee.

TIPS Start with good work, photos, display, and personal connections.

☺ CASA GRANDE HOLIDAY ARTS & CRAFTS FESTIVAL

7225 N. Oracle Rd., Suite 112, Tucson AZ 85704. (520)797-3959, ext. 0. Fax: (520)531-9225. E-mail: lauren@saaca.org. Website: www.saaca. org. Fine arts and crafts fair held annually in December. Outdoors. Accepts handmade crafts and other mediums. Exhibitors: 60. Number of attendees: see website. Free to public. Apply online.

ADDITIONAL INFORMATION Deadline for entry: December. Application fee: see website. Space fee: $185 (single); $310 (double). Exhibition space: 12×12 (single); 12×24 (double). For more information, e-mail, visit website, or call.

CASTLEBERRY FAIRE

38 Charles St., Rochester NH 03867. (603)332-2616. E-mail: terry@castleberryfairs.com. Website: www.castleberryfairs.com. **Contact:** Terry and Chris Mullen. Estab. 1995. Fine arts and crafts fair held annually in November on Thanksgiving weekend. Indoors. Accepts handmade crafts and other mediums. Juried. Exhibitors: see website. Number of attendees: see website. Admission: $8 adults; children 12 and under free. Apply online.

ADDITIONAL INFORMATION Deadline for entry: see website. Application fee: see website. Space fee: $375 (10×6); $475 (10×10). Exhibition space: 10×6; 10×10. For more information, e-mail, visit website, or call.

CEDARHURST ART & CRAFT FAIR

P.O. Box 923, 2600 Richview Rd., Mt. Vernon IL 62864. (618)242-1236, ext. 234. Fax: (618)242-9530. E-mail: linda@cedarhurst.org; sarah@cedarhurst.org. Website: www.cedarhurst.org. **Contact:** Linda Wheeler, staff coordinator. Estab. 1977. Arts and crafts show held annually on the 1st weekend after Labor Day each September. Outdoors. Accepts photography, paper, glass, metal, clay, wood, leather, jewelry, fiber, baskets, 2D art. Juried. Awards/prizes: Best of most category. Number of exhibitors: 125+. Public attendance: 8,000. Public admission: $5. pply by filling out online application form.

ADDITIONAL INFORMATION Deadline for entry: March. Application fee: $25. Exhibition space: 10×15. For more information, e-mail, call, or visit website.

CENTERFEST: THE ART LOVERS FESTIVAL

Durham Arts Council, 120 Morris St., Durham NC 27701. (919)560-2722. E-mail: centerfest@ durhamarts.org. Website: www.centerfest. durhamarts.org. Estab. 1974. Fine arts and crafts fair held annually in September. Outdoors. Accepts handmade crafts, clay, drawing, fibers, glass, painting, photography, printmaking, wood, jewelry, mixed media, sculpture. Juried. Awards/ prizes: Best in Show, 1st place, 2nd place, 3rd place. Exhibitors: 140. Number of attendees: see website. Admission: $5 donation accepted at gate. Apply online.

ADDITIONAL INFORMATION Deadline for entry: May. Application fee: see website. Space fee: $195 (single); $390 (double). Exhibition space: 10×10 (single); 10×20 (double). For more information, e-mail, call, or visit website.

CENTERVILLE–WASHINGTON TOWNSHIP AMERICANA FESTIVAL

P.O. Box 41794, Centerville OH 45441-0794. (937) 433-5898. Fax: (937)433-5898. E-mail: americanafestival@sbcglobal.net. Website: www.americanafestival.org. Estab. 1972. Arts, crafts, and antiques show held annually on the 4th of July, except when the 4th falls on a Sunday and then festival is held on Monday the 5th. Festival includes entertainment, parade, food, car show, and other activities. Accepts arts, crafts, antiques, photography, and all mediums. "No factory-made items accepted." Awards/ prizes: 1st, 2nd, 3rd places; certificates and ribbons for most attractive displays. Number of exhibitors: 275-300. Public attendance: 75,000. Free to public. Exhibitors should send SASE for application form, or apply online.

ADDITIONAL INFORMATION Deadline for entry: early June (see website for details). Space fee: $40–55 site specific. Exhibition space: 12×10. For more information, e-mail, call or visit website. Arts & crafts booths located on N. Main St., in Benham's Grove and limited spots in the Children's Activity area.

TIPS "Moderately priced products sell best. Bring business cards and have an eye-catching display."

CENTRAL OREGON WILD WEST SHOW

Central Oregon Shows, P.O. Box 1555, Sisters OR 97759. (541) 420-0279. E-mail: centraloregonshows@gmail.com. Website: www. centraloregonshows.com. **Contact:** Richard. August 7, Deschutes County Fair and Rodeo. This event is a theatrical production similar to the famous Buffalo Bill Wild West Show. It is part of the Deschutes County Fair & Rodeo. For more information, visit website.

CENTRAL PENNSYLVANIA FESTIVAL OF THE ARTS

403 S. Allen St., Suite 205A, P.O. Box 1023, State College PA 16804. (814)237-3682. Website: www.arts-festival.com. Estab. 1966. Fine arts and crafts fair held annually in July. Outdoors. Accepts handmade crafts and other mediums. Exhibitors: see website. Number of attendees: see website. Admission: Free to public. Apply online.

ADDITIONAL INFORMATION Deadline for entry: June. Application fee: see website. Space fee: see website. Exhibition space: see website. For more information, visit website or call.

CHAMBER SOUTH'S ANNUAL SOUTH MIAMI ART FESTIVAL

Sunset Dr. (SW 72nd St.) from US 1 to Red Rd. (SW 57th Ave.), South Miami FL 33143. (305)661-1621. Fax: (305)666-0508. E-mail: art@chambersouth.com. Website: www. chambersouth.com/events/south-miami-art-festival. **Contact:** Robin Stieglitz, art festival coordinator. Estab. 1971. Annual. Fine art and craft show held the 1st weekend in November. Outdoors. Accepts 2D and 3D mixed media, ceramics, clay, digital art, glass, jewelry, metalwork, painting (oil, acrylic, watercolor), printmaking, drawing, sculpture, textiles, wood. Juried by panel of jurors who meet to review work; includes artists and board members. Cash prizes, ribbons to display during event, exemption from jury in the following year's show. Average number of exhibitors: 130. Average number of attendees: 50,000. Admission: free. Apply by www.zapplication.org.

ADDITIONAL INFORMATION Deadline: July 31. Application fee: $25. Space fee: standard, $325; corner $375. Space is 10×10 (10×20 also available). For more information, e-mail, call, or visit the website.

TIPS "Good, clean displays; interact with customers without hounding."

CHARDON SQUARE ARTS FESTIVAL
Chardon Square Association, P.O. Box 1063, Chardon OH 44024. (440)285-4548. E-mail: sgipson@aol.com. Website: www. chardonsquareassociation.org. **Contact:** Mariann Goodwin and Jan Gipson. Estab. 1980. Fine arts & crafts show held annually in early August (see website for details). Outdoors. Accepts photography, pottery, weaving, wood, paintings, jewelry. Juried. Number of exhibitors: 110. Public attendance: 4,000. Free to public. Artists can find application on website. Exhibition space: 12×12. For more information, call or visit website.

TIPS "Make your booth attractive; be friendly and offer quality work."

CHARLEVOIX WATERFRONT ART FAIR
P.O. Box 57, Charlevoix MI 49720. (231)547-2675. E-mail: cwaf14@gmail.com. Website: www.charlevoixwaterfrontartfair.org. "The Annual Charlevoix Waterfront Art Fair is a juried and invitational show and sale. Categories are: ceramics, glass, fiber; drawing; wood; painting; mixed media 2D and 3D; jewelry, fine and other; printmaking; photography; sculpture. To apply, each entrant must submit 4 digital images (3 images of your art work and 1 booth image) sized 1920 x 1920 pixels at 72 dpi for consideration

by the jury (ZAPP images are acceptable). A nonrefundable processing fee of $25, plus $15 for each additional category entered, must accompany the artist's application."

CHASTAIN PARK FESTIVAL
4469 Stella Dr., Atlanta GA 30327. (404)873-1222. E-mail: info@affps.com. Website: www. chastainparkartsfestival.com. **Contact:** Randall Fox. Estab. 2008. Arts and crafts show held annually early November. Outdoors. Accepts handmade crafts, painting, photography, sculpture, leather, metal, glass, jewelry. Juried by a panel. Awards/prizes: ribbons. Number of exhibitors: 175. Number of attendees: 45,000. Free to public. Apply online at www.zapplication.org.

ADDITIONAL INFORMATION Deadline for entry: August 26. Application fee: $25. Space fee: $300. Exhibition space: 10×10. For more information, e-mail or visit website.

CHEERFULLY MADE MARKETS
(Formerly Handmade Harvest Craft Show, Cheerfully Made, 72 Mill Street, Almonte, Ontario K0A 1A0, Canada. (613)461-6233. E-mail: hello@cheerfullymade.com. Website: www. cheerfullymade.com. **Contact:** Emily Arbour. Estab. 2010.

ADDITIONAL INFORMATION "Cheerfully Made Markets take place in Ottawa and the surrounding area. Founded in 2010, the show is organized by local Almonte business owner Emily Arbour."

CHEROKEE TRIANGLE ART FAIR
Cherokee Triangle Association, P.O. Box 4306, Louisville KY 40204. (502)459-0256. E-mail: cherokeetriangle@bellsouth.net. Website: www. cherokeetriangleartfair.org. **Contact:** Antonia.

ADDITIONAL INFORMATION "The Cherokee Triangle Art Fair is a juried fair with more than 200 artists' booths. The outdoor event is in Louisville's historic Cherokee Triangle neighborhood on tree-lined Cherokee Pkwy. between Willow Ave. and Cherokee Rd. adjacent to the Gen. John Breckinridge Castleman statue." For more information, visit website.

CHERRY CREEK ARTS FESTIVAL

2 Steele Street, Suite B-100, Denver CO 80206. (303)355-2787. E-mail: management@cherryarts.org. Website: www.cherrycreekartsfestival.org.

ADDITIONAL INFORMATION "The Cherry Creek Arts Festival (CCAF) weekend event is a world-class and award-winning celebration of the visual, culinary, and performing arts, and enjoys an attendance of 350,000 visitors over the course of the 3-day event. The Arts Festival features artists in 14 different media categories including: ceramics, digital art, drawing, fiber, glass, jewelry, metalworks, mixed media, new media, painting, photography, printmaking, sculpture, and wood. The CCAF's year-round 501c3 non-profit mission is to provide access to art experiences and to support education."

CHERRYWOOD ART FAIR

Cherrywood Art Fair, P.O. Box 4283, Austin TX 78765. E-mail: cherrywoodartfair@gmail.com. Website: www.cherrywoodartfair.org. Estab. 2001.

ADDITIONAL INFORMATION Cherrywood Art Fair is an art-filled 2-day event showcasing local artists, live music, kids activities, and great food in a free, family-friendly environment. More than 8,000 visitors stroll through the fairgrounds looking at art, listening to beautiful music, and sampling some of Austin's finest food-trailer cuisine. Since its inception, the Fair has served as a destination for discerning holiday shoppers seeking unique and artful items from Texas artists.

CHESTER CRAFT SHOWS

P.O. Box 613, Madison NJ 07940. (973)377-6600. Website: www.chestercraftshow.com.

ADDITIONAL INFORMATION "Rated No. 1 in New Jersey and1 of the Top 50 "Best Crafts Show in the Nation" by America's Premier Art and Craft Show Magazine, *Sunshine Artist*, previous shows have set all-time attendance records, with crafters and artisans from throughout the region offering an array of select, handcrafted furniture, jewelry, apparel, ornaments, home accessories, and more."

CHESTERTON ART FAIR

The Chesterton Art Fair, P.O. Box 783, Chesterton IN 46304. (219)926-4711. E-mail: gallery@chestertonart.com. Website: www.chestertonart.com. Fine arts and crafts fair held annually. Outdoors. Accepts handmade crafts and other mediums. Exhibitors: see website. Number of attendees: see website. Admission: Free to public. Apply online.

ADDITIONAL INFORMATION Deadline for entry: July. Application fee: $25. Space fee: single- $190.00 (non AACPC member); $180.00 (member); double- $350.00 (nonmember); $295.00 (member). Exhibition space: see website. For more information, visit website or call.

CHICAGO BOTANIC ART FESTIVAL

E-mail: info@amdurproductions.com. Website: www.amdurproductions.com. Fine arts and crafts fair held in July. Outdoors. Accepts handmade crafts and other mediums. Exhibitors: 95. Number of attendees: 30,000. Free to public. Apply online.

ADDITIONAL INFORMATION Deadline for entry: January. Application fee: $35. Space fee: $625. Exhibition space: see website. For more information, e-mail, visit website, or call.

CHRISTKINDL MARKT

Canton Museum of Art, 1001 Market Ave. N., Canton OH 44702. (330)453-7666, ext. 105. E-mail: carol@cantonart.org. Website: www.cantonart.org/christkindl. **Contact:** Carol Paris, assistant. Estab. 1972. Fine arts and crafts show held annually in November. Indoors. Accepts handmade crafts, ceramics, drawing, pastel, fiber, leather, glass, graphics, printmaking, jewelry, metalwork, mixed media, painting, photography, sculpture, wearable art, wood. Juried. Awards/prizes: Best in Show; 1st Place Fine Art; 1st Place Fine Craft; 2nd Place Fine Art; 2nd Place Fine Craft; Best Booth; honorable mentions, ribbons. Exhibitors: 106. Number of attendees: 4,500. Admission: $6 advance; $7 at the door. Apply online.

ADDITIONAL INFORMATION Deadline for entry: June 15. Application fee: $25. Space fee: $300 (single); $550 (double). Exhibition space: 8×10 (single); 8×20 (double). For more information, visit website.

TIPS All work must be original and handcrafted by the artist. No buy/sell or imports. The artist must be present during the show.

CHRISTMAS IN SEATTLE GIFT & GOURMET FOOD SHOW

Washington State Convention Center, 800 Convention Place, Seattle WA 98101. (800)521-7469. Fax: (425)889-8165. E-mail: seattle@showcaseevents.org. Website: www. showcaseevents.org. Estab. 1992. Seasonal holiday show held annually in November. Indoors. Accepts handmade crafts, art, photography, pottery, glass, jewelry, clothing, fiber. Juried. Exhibitors: 300. Number of attendees: 15,000. Admission: $14.50 (for all 3 days); 12 and under free. Apply via website or call or e-mail for application.

ADDITIONAL INFORMATION Deadline for entry: October 31. Space fee: see website. Exhibition space: 10×10. For more information, e-mail, call, send SASE, or visit website.

TIPS "Competitive pricing, attractive booth display, quality product, something unique for sale, friendly and outgoing personality."

CHRISTMAS IN THE COUNTRY ARTISAN MARKET

(910)799-9424. E-mail: wnypremier@ec.rr.com. Website: www.wnypremierpromotions.com/ christmas-in-the-country.

ADDITIONAL INFORMATION Christmas in the Country has been recognized as the No. 2 Contemporary and Classic Artisan Market in the nation by *Sunshine Artist*, the leading publication in the art and craft event industry. The event has been ranked either No. 1 or No. 2 in the nation for the past 10 years. Now, drawing almost 60,000 visitors over 4 days, the event is widely recognized as the preeminent holiday artisan market in the United States. Christmas in the Country is held in November at the Hamburg Fairgrounds. Christmas in the Country will welcome over 400 artisans spread out over 5 buildings. Attendees to Christmas in the Country will find unique and only handcrafted creations including home décor, gourmet foods and wine, original music, trendsetting jewelry, handpoured aromatic candles, children's toys and clothing, stylish pottery, original wall art, gifts for pets, and holiday gift items galore.

CHUN CAPITOL HILL PEOPLE'S FAIR

1290 Williams St., Suite 102, Denver CO 80218. (303)830-1651. Fax: (303)830-1782. E-mail: andreafurness@chundenver.org. Website: www. peoplesfair.com; www.chundenver.org. **Contact:** Andrea Furness, assistant director. Estab. 1972. Arts and music festival held annually 1st full weekend in June. Outdoors. Accepts photography, ceramics, jewelry, paintings, wearable art, glass, sculpture, wood, paper, fiber, children's items, and more. Juried by professional artisans representing a variety of mediums and selected members of fair management. The jury process is based on originality, quality, and expression. Awards/prizes: Best of Show. Number of exhibitors: 300. Public attendance: 200,000. Free to public. Apply by downloading application from website.

ADDITIONAL INFORMATION Deadline for entry: March. Application fee: $35. Space fee: $350-400, depending on type of art. Exhibition space: 10×10. For more information, e-mail, visit website or call. Festival located at Civic Center Park.

CHURCH ON THE HILL ANNUAL FINE ARTS AND HANDMADE CRAFTS FAIR

55 Main St., Lenox MA 01240. (413)637-1001. Fax: (413)637-3395. E-mail: ucclenox@verizon. net. Website: www.churchonthehilllenox.org. Arts and crafts show held annually in July. Outdoors. Accepts handmade crafts and other mediums. Juried. Exhibitors: 60. Number of attendees: 800. Free to public. Apply online.

ADDITIONAL INFORMATION Deadline for entry: mid-April. Application fee: none. Space fee: $250. Exhibition space: 11×11. For more information, e-mail, or visit website.

CHURCH STREET ART & CRAFT SHOW

Downtown Waynesville Association, P.O. Box 1409, Waynesville NC 28786. (828)456-3517. E-mail: info@downtownwaynesville.com.

Website: www.downtownwaynesville.com. Estab. 1983. Fine arts and crafts show held annually 2nd Saturday in October. Outdoors. Accepts photography, paintings, fiber, pottery, wood, jewelry. Juried by committee: submit 4 slides or digital photos of work and 1 of booth display. Number of exhibitors: 110. Public attendance: 15,000-18,000. Free to public. Entry fee: $25. Space fee: $110 ($200 for 2 booths). Exhibition space: 10×12. (option of 2 booths for 12×20 space). For more information, and application, visit website.

ADDITIONAL INFORMATION Deadline: mid-August. Show located in downtown Waynesville, North Carolina, on Main St.

TIPS Recommends "quality in work and display."

CITY OF FAIRFAX FALL FESTIVAL

10455 Armstrong St., Fairfax VA 22030. (703)385-7800. Fax: (703)246-6321. E-mail: leslie.herman@fairfaxva.gov; mitzi.taylor@fairfaxva.gov. Website: www.fairfaxva.gov. **Contact:** Mitzi Taylor, special event coordinator. Estab. 1985. Arts and crafts festival held annually the 2nd weekend in October. Outdoors. Accepts photography, jewelry, glass, pottery, clay, wood, mixed media. Juried by a panel of 5 independent jurors. Number of exhibitors: 400. Public attendance: 25,000. Free to public.

ADDITIONAL INFORMATION Deadline for entry: mid-March. Apply by contacting Mitzi Taylor for an application. Application fee: $12. Space fee: $160 10×10. For more information, e-mail. Festival located in historic downtown Fairfax.

CITY OF FAIRFAX HOLIDAY CRAFT SHOW

10455 Armstrong St., Fairfax VA 22030. (703)385-1710. Fax: (703)246-6321. E-mail: katherine.maccammon@fairfaxva.gov. Website: www.fairfaxva.gov. **Contact:** Katherine MacCammon. Estab. 1985. Arts and crafts show held annually 3rd weekend in November. Indoors. Accepts photography, jewelry, glass, pottery, clay, wood, mixed media. Juried by a panel of 5 independent jurors. Number of exhibitors: 247. Public attendance: 5,000. Public admission: $5 for age 18 and older. $8 for 2 day pass. Apply by contacting Katie MacCammon for an application.

ADDITIONAL INFORMATION Deadline for entry: early March (visit website for details). Application fee: $15. Space fee: 10×6. $195; 11×9. $245; 10×10. $270. For more information, e-mail.

CITYPLACE ART FAIR

270 Central Blvd., Suite 107B, Jupiter FL 33458. (561)746-6615. Fax: (561)746-6528. E-mail: info@artfestival.com. Website: www.artfestival. com. **Contact:** Malinda Ratliff, communications manager. Fine art and craft fair held annually in early March. Outdoors. Accepts photography, jewelry, mixed media, sculpture, wood, ceramic, glass, painting, digital, fiber, metal. Juried. Number of exhibitors: 200. Number of attendees: 40,000. Free to public. Apply online via www. zapplication.org.

ADDITIONAL INFORMATION Deadline: see website. Application fee: $25. Space fee: $395. Exhibition space: 10×10 and 10×20. For more information, e-mail, call, or visit website. Fair located in CityPlace in downtown West Palm Beach, Florida.

⊕ CLEVELAND HANDMADE

E-mail: info@clevelandhandmade.com. Website: www.clevelandhandmade.com. **Contact:** Lori Paximadis, co-founder/membership director.

ADDITIONAL INFORMATION "Cleveland Handmade brings together artists and craftspeople from northeast Ohio and promotes the value of buying and selling handmade goods. We foster relationships and provide opportunities for education, socializing, and networking among creators. We bring together resources that benefit our members and share our members' stories with the public."

COARSEGOLD CHRISTMAS FAIRE

P.O. Box 1514, Coarsegold CA 93614. (559)683-3900. E-mail: events@coarsegoldhistoricvillage. com. Website: www.coarsegoldhistoricvillage.com.

ADDITIONAL INFORMATION "Get into the Christmas Spirit mountain style. Listen to carolers, visit with Father Christmas, and do some Christmas shopping at the craft booths in the park." For more information, visit website and to apply.

COCONUT GROVE ARTS FESTIVAL

3390 Mary St., Suite 128, Coconut Grove FL 33133. (305)447-0401. E-mail: katrina@cgaf. com. Website: www.coconutgroveartsfest. com. **Contact:** Katrina Delgado. The Coconut Grove Arts Festival showcases the works of 360 internationally recognized artists who are selected from nearly 1,300 applicants. Jurors evaluate the artist's work and displays to select participants in such categories as mixed media, painting, photography, digital art, printmaking and drawing, watercolor, clay work, glass, fiber, jewelry and metalwork, sculpture, and wood.

COCONUT POINT ART FESTIVAL

270 Central Blvd., Suite 107B, Jupiter FL 33458. (561)746-6615. Fax: (561)746-6528. E-mail: info@artfestival.com. Website: www.artfestival. com. **Contact:** Malinda Ratliff, communications manager. Estab. 2007. Fine art and craft fair held annually in late December/early January and February. Outdoors. Accepts photography, jewelry, mixed media, sculpture, wood, ceramic, glass, painting, digital, fiber, metal. Juried. Number of exhibitors: 200-280. Number of attendees: 90,000. Free to public. Apply online via www.zapplication.org.

ADDITIONAL INFORMATION Deadline: see website. Application fee: $25. Space fee: $395–425. Exhibition space: 10×10 and 10×20. For more information, e-mail, call, or visit website. Festival held at Coconut Point in Estero, Florida.

COLLEGE HILL ARTS FESTIVAL

College Hill Arts Festival, P.O. Box 544, Cedar Falls IA 50613. (559)683-3900. E-mail: mary-suebartlett@cfu.net. Website: www. collegehillartsfestival.com.

ADDITIONAL INFORMATION The College Hill Arts Festival is a juried art show held on the campus of the University of Northern Iowa featuring 75 artists in a variety of media.

COLORADO COUNTRY CHRISTMAS GIFT SHOW

Denver Mart, 451 E. 58th Ave., Denver CO , 80216. (800)521-7469. **Fax:** (425)889-8165.

E-mail: denver@showcase.events.org. **Website:** www.showcaseevents.org. **Contact:** Kim Peck, show manager. Estab. 2003. Annual holiday show held early November. Indoors. Accepts handmade crafts, art, photography, pottery, glass, jewelry, fiber, clothing. Juried. Exhibitors: 400. Number of attendees: 25,000. Admission: see website. Apply by e-mail, call, or see website.

ADDITIONAL INFORMATION Deadline for entry: see website. Space fee: see website. Exhibition space: 10×10. For more information, e-mail, call, send SASE, or visit website.

COLUMBIANA ARTIST MARKET

104 Mildred St., P.O. Box 624, Columbiana AL 35051. (205) 669-0044. E-mail: info@ shelbycountyartscouncil.com. Website: www. shelbycountyartscouncil.com. Member artists gather to offer their original artwork. Work available includes oil paintings, acrylic paintings, photography, jewelry, fabric arts, printmaking, pottery, and more.

COMMONWHEEL ARTISTS ANNUAL LABOR DAY ARTS & CRAFTS FESTIVAL

Memorial Park in Manitou Springs Colorado, Manitou Springs CO 80829. (719)577-7700. E-mail: festival@commonwheel.com. Website: www.commonwheel.com/festival. **Contact:** Festival Committee (by e-mail). Estab. 1975. Arts and crafts show held annually on Labor Day weekend. Outdoors. Accepts original fine art & handmade crafts in all mediums. Juried. Awards/prizes: ribbons in all categories and free booth for following year. Exhibitors: 110. Number of attendees: 15,000. Free to public. Use the application found on the website to apply.

ADDITIONAL INFORMATION Commonwheel Artists is an artist co-op that has existed since 1974 in Manitou Springs, Colorado. About 37 members belong to the co-op. The Art Festival has been hosted by Commonwheel since 1975 and is the premiere outdoor art event in the Pikes Peak Region.

CONYERS CHERRY BLOSSOM FESTIVAL

1996 Centennial Olympic Pkwy., Conyers GA 30013. (770)860-4190; (770)860-4194. E-mail:

rebecca.hill@conyersga.com. Website: www.conyerscherryblossomfest.com. **Contact:** Jill Miller. Estab. 1981. Arts and crafts show held annually in late March (visit website for details). Outdoors. The festival is held at the Georgia International Horse Park at the Grand Prix Plaza overlooking the Grand Prix Stadium used during the 1996 Centennial Olympic Games. Accepts photography, paintings, and any other handmade or original art. Juried. Submit 5 images: 1 picture must represent your work as it is displayed; 1 must represent a workshop photo of the artist creating their work; the other 3 need to represent your items as an accurate representation in size, style, and quality of work. Number of exhibitors: 300. Public attendance: 40,000. Free to public. Space fee: $135. Exhibition space: 10×10. Electricity fee: $30. Application fee: $10; apply online.

ADDITIONAL INFORMATION For more information, e-mail, call, or visit website. Show located at the Georgia International Horse Park.

CORAL SPRINGS FESTIVAL OF THE ARTS

270 Central Blvd., Suite 107B, Jupiter FL 33458. (561)746-6615. Fax: (561)746-6528. E-mail: info@artfestival.com. Website: www.artfestival.com. **Contact:** Malinda Ratliff, communications manager. "The Coral Springs Festival of the Arts has grown considerably over the years into a 2-day celebration of arts and culture with a fine art show, contemporary craft festival, theatrical performances, and full lineup of live music. Held in conjunction with the Coral Springs Art Festival Committee and the City, this event brings 250 of the nation's best artists and crafters to south Florida. Stroll amidst life-size sculptures, spectacular paintings, 1-of-a-kind jewels, photography, ceramics, a separate craft festival, Green Market, and much more. No matter what you're looking for, you'll be sure to find it among the array of various artists and crafters participating in this arts and crafts fair."

CORN HILL ARTS FESTIVAL

Corn Hill Neighbors Association, 133 S. Fitzhugh St., Rochester NY 14608-9956. (585)262-3142. E-mail: chna@cornhill.org. Website: www.cornhillartsfestival.com. **Contact:** Joanie Fraver, 2016 festival chair. Estab. 1969. Juried fine arts and crafts festival. Outdoors. Handmade only, no buy/sell. $8000 in prize money. Exhibitors: about 380; Number of attendees: 125,000; Free to public. Apply online through website.

ADDITIONAL INFORMATION Deadline for entry: March 20. Application fee: $35. Space fee: $275 (single); $530 (double). Exhibition space: 10×10 (single); 10×20 (double). For more information, visit website, e-mail, or call.

CORVALLIS FALL FESTIVAL

133 S. Fitzhugh St., Rochester NY 14608-9956. (541)752-9655. E-mail: director@corvallisfallfestival.com. Website: www.corvallisfallfestival.org.

ADDITIONAL INFORMATION Corvallis Fall Festival is a not-for-profit event with the mission to help sustain local arts and crafts while serving, supporting, and showcasing the Corvallis community.

COTTONWOOD ART FESTIVAL

2100 E. Campbell Rd., Suite 100, Richardson TX 75081. (972)744-458. E-mail: serri.ayers@cor.gov. Website: www.cottonwoodartfestival.com. **Contact:** Serri Ayers. The semiannual Cottonwood Art Festival is a juried show. Jurors have selected over 240 artists from 800 submissions to exhibit their museum-quality work at the festival. The artists compete in 14 categories: 2D mixed media, 3D mixed media, ceramics, digital, drawings/pastels, fiber, glass, jewelry, leather, metalwork, painting, photography, sculpture, and wood. Rated as one of the top art festivals in the United States, the prestigious show is the premier fine art event in north Texas.

COUNTRY FOLK ARTS AND CRAFTS SHOW

(248)634-4151, ext. 631. E-mail: shows@countryfolkart.com; Karen1@countryfolkart.com. Website: www.countryfolkart.com. **Contact:** Karen Kiley. Country Folk Art Shows has grown to 17 shows in 5 states. Every participant is juried and hand selected for their outstanding workmanship and integrity of creative design. Some of the more popular decorating items found at our shows are handcrafted furniture, home and garden décor, jewelry, textiles, holiday décor, wearable art, handmade candles and soaps, quilts, paintings, framed art, florals, iron work, wood carvings, baskets, stained glass, and much more.

COUNTRYSIDE VILLAGE ART FAIR

Countryside Village Art Fair, 11004 Prairie Brook Rd., Omaha NE 68144. (402)391-2200. E-mail: mgmt@countryside-village.com. Website: www.countryside-village.com. **Contact:** Juanita Galvan. Estab. 1969.

ADDITIONAL INFORMATION "A mix of styles, perspectives, and media, the Countryside Village Art Fair takes place the first Saturday and Sunday in June. The incredible array of artwork inspires casual visitors to start art collections, and connoisseurs to add to existing collections."

COVINGTON ART FAIR

The Covington Art Fair, C/O Asher Agency, 535 W. Wayne St., Ft. Wayne IN 46802. (800)900-7031. E-mail: covingtonartfair@asheragency.com. Website: www.facebook.com/CovingtonArtFair.

ADDITIONAL INFORMATION The Covington Art Fair is a high-quality 2-day community event featuring fine arts. The fair is located at Covington Plaza, Fort Wayne's most prestigious shopping plaza, featuring high fashion, specialty large shops, gourmet restaurants, a spa, and much, much more.

CRAFT & FINE ART FESTIVAL AT THE NASSAU COUNTY MUSEUM OF ART

American Concern for Artistry and Craftsmanship, P.O. Box 650, Montclair NJ 7042. (973)746-0091. Fax: (973)509-7739. E-mail: acacinfo@gmail.com. Website: www.craftsatlincoln.org. Fine art and craft show held annually in September. Outdoors. Accepts handmade crafts. Juried. Number of exhibitors: 90. Number of attendees: varies. Free to public. Apply online or via www.zapplication.org.

ADDITIONAL INFORMATION Deadline for entry: June. Application fee: none. Space fee: varies. Exhibition space: varies. For more information, call, e-mail, or visit website.

CRAFT & SPECIALTY FOOD FAIR (NEW HAMPSHIRE)

38 Charles St., Rochester NH 03867. (603)332-2616. E-mail: info@castleberryfairs.com. Website: www.castleberryfairs.com. **Contact:** Terry and Chris Mullen. Art and craft show held annually in November. Indoors. Accepts handmade crafts and other mediums. Juried. Number of exhibitors: see website. Number of attendees: varies. Admission: $7 adults; children 12 and under free. Apply online.

ADDITIONAL INFORMATION Deadline for entry: see website. Application fee: see website. Space fee: $350 (10×6); $450 (10×10). Exhibition space: 10×6; 10×10. For more information, e-mail, call, or visit website.

🎧 CRAFT ALASKA ARTS AND CRAFTS SHOW

Website: www.yelp.com/events/anchorage-craft-alaska-arts-and-crafts-show.

ADDITIONAL INFORMATION CraftAlaska features live entertainment and dozens of Alaska-made arts and crafts vendors.

CRAFTAPALOOZA & FABULOUS VINTAGE MARKET—ABILENE

E-mail: montagefestivals@earthlink.net. Website: www.montagefestivals.com. **Contact:** Serra Ferguson, organizer. Arts and Crafts show held twice a year (visit website for dates). Indoors. Accepts handmade crafts, artisan designs, antique and vintage, home décor and inspiration, and more. Exhibitors: varies. Number of attendees: varies. Admission: $3 adults; under 12 free. Apply via website.

ADDITIONAL INFORMATION Deadline for entry: see website. Application fee: see website. Space fee: $95 (10×10); $165 (10×20). Exhibition space: 10×10; 10×20. For more information, e-mail or visit website.

CRAFTAPALOOZA & FABULOUS VINTAGE MARKET—SALINA

E-mail: montagefestivals@earthlink.net. Website: www.montagefestivals.com. **Contact:** Serra Ferguson, organizer. Arts and Crafts show held in March. Indoors. Accepts handmade crafts, artisan designs, antique and vintage, home décor & inspiration, and more. Exhibitors: varies. Number of attendees: varies. Admission: $3 adults; under 12 free. Apply via website.

ADDITIONAL INFORMATION Deadline for entry: see website. Application fee: see website. Space fee: $70 (10×10); $105 (10×20). Exhibition space: 10×10; 10×20. For more information, e-mail or visit website.

CRAFTAPALOOZA & FABULOUS VINTAGE MARKET—WICHITA

E-mail: montagefestivals@earthlink.net. Website: www.montagefestivals.com. **Contact:** Serra Ferguson, organizer. Arts and Crafts show held twice a year (see website for dates). Indoors. Accepts handmade crafts, artisan designs, antique and vintage, home décor and inspiration, and more. Exhibitors: varies. Number of attendees: varies. Admission: $3 adults; under 12 free. Apply via website.

ADDITIONAL INFORMATION Deadline for entry: see website. Application fee: see website. Space fee: $95 (8×10); $165 (8×20). Exhibition space: 8×10; 8×20. For more information, e-mail or visit website.

CRAFTBOSTON

The Society of Arts & Crafts, 175 Newbury St., Boston MA 02116. (617)266-1810. Fax: (617)266-5654. E-mail: CraftBoston@societyofcrafts.org. Website: www.societyofcrafts.org.

ADDITIONAL INFORMATION "Presented by The Society of Arts and Crafts, CraftBoston Spring and Holiday are New England's premier juried exhibitions and sales of contemporary craft. This twice annual, well-established show features the most outstanding artists of our time, showcasing 1-of-a-kind and limited-edition pieces in baskets, ceramics, decorative fiber, wearables, furniture, glass, jewelry, leather, metal, mixed media, paper, and wood."

CRAFT FAIR AT THE BAY

38 Charles St., Rochester NH 03867. (603)332-2616. Fax: (603)332-8413. E-mail: info@castleberryfairs.com. Website: www.castleberryfairs.com. Estab. 1988. Arts and crafts show held annually in July in Alton Bay NH. Outdoors. Accepts photography and all other mediums. Juried by photo, slide, or sample. Number of exhibitors: 85. Public attendance: 7,500. Free to public. Apply by downloading application from website.

ADDITIONAL INFORMATION Deadline for entry: until full. Exhibition space: 100 sq. ft. For more information, visit, call, e-mail or visit website.

TIPS "Do not bring a book; do not bring a chair. Smile and make eye contact with everyone who enters your booth. Have them sign your guest book; get their e-mail address so you can let them know when you are in the area again. And, finally, make the sale—they are at the fair to shop, after all."

CRAFT FAIR OF THE SOUTHERN HIGHLANDS

(828)298-7928. Website: www.southernhighlandguild.org.

ADDITIONAL INFORMATION Nearly 200 juried artists of the Southern Highland Craft Guild will be selling works of clay, metal, wood, jewelry, fiber, paper, natural materials, leather, and mixed media. With styles ranging from traditional to contemporary, the Fairs showcase the rich talent, diversity, and craft mastery of Guild members.

CRAFT LAKE CITY DIY FESTIVAL

351 Pierpont Ave., 4B, Salt Lake City UT 84101. (801)487-9221. Fax: (801)487-1359. Website: www.craftlakecity.com. Fine arts & crafts fair held annually in June. Outdoors. Accepts handmade crafts and other mediums. Exhibitors: 200. Number of attendees: see website. Admission: Free to public. Apply online.

ADDITIONAL INFORMATION Deadline for entry: early May. Application fee: $15. Space fee: varies. Exhibition space: varies. For more information, visit website or call.

CRAFT LAKE CITY DIY FESTIVAL

351 Pierpont Ave. 4B, Salt Lake City UT 84101. (801)906-8521. Fax: (801)487-1359. E-mail: craftlakecity@gmail.com. Website: www. craftlakecity.com. **Contact:** Crafters/Artisans should contact website.. Estab. 2008. Event held annually. Customarily held in 2nd weekend of August. Fine art show. Arts and crafts show. Held outdoors. Accepts DIY electronics, craft food, and vintage items. Artisans are juried to keep selection fresh and to limit amount of artisans within categories. No prizes given. Average number of exhibitors: 200+. Average number of attendees: 30,000. Admission fee for public: $5. **ADDITIONAL INFORMATION** Application open in February and stays open until mid-April. Application fee: $20. Space fee: $200: 6x3 table; $300: 10x10 tent; $450: 10x10 tent with walls. For more information, e-mail, visit website or call.

CRAFTLAND

235 Westminster St., Providence RI 02903. (401)272-4285. E-mail: info@craftlandshop.com. Website: www.craftlandshop.com/pages/show. **ADDITIONAL INFORMATION** Craftland Show is an annual holiday craft show featuring the work of 170 artists from Rhode Island and nationwide. It celebrates all kinds of handmade objects and the people who make them.

CRAFTOBERFEST

E-mail: chelsiehellige@gmail.com. Website: www.craftoberfest.com. **ADDITIONAL INFORMATION** "Craftoberfest is St. Louis's first lantern-lit outdoor night market featuring local beer, live music, and some of the best handmade and vintage finds our fair city has to offer."

CRAFTS AT MOLAND HOUSE

1641 Old York Rd., Warminter/Hartsville PA 18974. (215)850-1888. E-mail: frommyhand@ gmail.com. Website: www.craftsatmolandhouse. com. **Contact:** Gwyn Duffy, show coordinator. Estab. 2010. Arts and crafts show held biannually in March and November. Indoors. Accepts handmade crafts. Juried. Exhibitors: 55.

Number of attendees: 5,000. Admission: $1. E-mail for application. **ADDITIONAL INFORMATION** Deadline for entry: rolling. Application fee: $50. Space fee: 25% of sales. Exhibition space: varies. For more information, e-mail or visit website.

CRAFTS AT PURCHASE

P.O. Box 28, Woodstock NY 12498. (845)331-7900. Fax: (845)331-7484. E-mail: crafts@ artrider.com. Website: www.artrider.com. **Contact:** Laura Kandel, assistant director. Estab. 2012. Boutique show of fine contemporary craft held annually in late October or early November. Indoors. Accepts photography, fine art, ceramics, wood, mixed media, leather, glass, metal, fiber, jewelry. Juried. Submit 5 images of work and 1 of booth. Exhibitors: 100. Number of attendess: 3,500. Admission: $10. Apply online at www. artrider.com or www.zapplication.org. **ADDITIONAL INFORMATION** Deadline for entry: end of May. Application fee: $45. Space fee: $545. Exhibition space: 10×10. For more information, e-mail, call, or visit website.

CRAFTS IN THE BARN

4130 Thistlewood Rd., Hatboro PA 19040. (215)850-1888. E-mail: frommyhand@gmail.com. Website: www.craftsinthebarn.com. **Contact:** Gwyn Duffy, show coordinator. Estab. 1985. Arts and crafts show held semiannually in May and October. Indoors. Accepts handmade crafts. Exhibitors: 75. Number of attendees: 6,000. Free to public. E-mail for application. **ADDITIONAL INFORMATION** Deadline for entry: rolling. Application fee: $50. Space fee: 25% of sales. Exhibition space: varies. For more information, e-mail or visit website.

CRAFTWESTPORT

P.O. Box 28, Woodstock NY 12498. (845)331-7484. Fax: (845)331-7484. E-mail: crafts@ artrider.com. Website: www.artrider.com. Estab. 1975. Fine arts and craft show held annually in the 3rd weekend before Thanksgiving. Indoors. Accepts photography, wearable and nonwearable fiber, jewelry, clay, leather, wood, glass, painting, drawing, prints, mixed media. Juried by 5 images of work and 1 of booth, viewed sequentially. Number of exhibitors: 160. Public attendance: 5,000. Public admission: $10. Apply online at www.artrider.com or at www.zapplication.org.

ADDITIONAL INFORMATION Deadline for entry: end of May. Application fee: $45. Space fee: $525. Exhibition space: 10×10. For more information, e-mail, call, or visit website.

CRAFTY BASTARDS ARTS & CRAFTS FAIR

E-mail: craftybastards@washingtoncitypaper.com. Website: www.washingtoncitypaper.com/craftybastards.

ADDITIONAL INFORMATION Crafty Bastards Arts & Crafts Fair is an exhibition and sale of handmade goods from independent artists presented by the *Washington City Paper*. Crafty Bastards is held outdoors at Union Market and features 175+ vendors.

CRAFTY SUPERMARKET

Cincinnati OH. E-mail: craftysupermarket@gmail.com. Website: www.craftysupermarket.com. **Contact:** Chris Salley Davis and Grace Dobush, co-organizers. Estab. 2009. Semiannual indie arts and crafts show held late spring and late November. Indoors. Accepts handmade crafts, art and design, occasionally accepts edible gifts. Juried. Exhibitors: spring show 50; holiday show 90. Number of attendees: spring show, 2,000; holiday show 6,500. Free to public. Apply online.

ADDITIONAL INFORMATION Deadline for entry: check website. Application fee: $10. Space fee: $100 (spring); $140 (holiday). Exhibition space: varies. For more information, visit website.

CRAFTY WONDERLAND

E-mail: craftywonderland@yahoo.com. Website: www.craftywonderland.com.

ADDITIONAL INFORMATION "Crafty Wonderland is the place to go to find the best handmade goods in the NW, as well as affordable work from talented visual artists. It's an event meant to bring together crafty people with those who appreciate cool handmade items, to support artists, and to spread the joy of craft throughout our community. The show even offers a kids' area where budding young artists can set up and sell their work! Each Crafty Wonderland features a free DIY area where local artists share their talent and teach visitors how to make a craft of their own to take home."

CREATIVE HAND

E-mail: info@creativehandkc.org. Website: www.creativehandkc.org.

ADDITIONAL INFORMATION "Handcrafted fiber show sponsored by the Kansas City Fiber Guild and the Kansas City Weavers Guild. Artists from both groups come together for the Creative Hand Show and Sale. The show is both exhibition and sale of art-to-wear that members of both groups have created by hand."

CRESTED BUTTE ARTS FESTIVAL

P.O. Box 324, Crested Butte CO 81224. (970)349-1184. E-mail: juliette@crestedbutteartsfestival.com. Website: www.crestedbutteartsfestival.com. Estab. 1972.

ADDITIONAL INFORMATION The Crested Butte Arts Festival, Crested Butte's signature cultural event and1 of Colorado's top 5 fine art and fine craft shows, features 175 well-known, established artists from around the world and is recognized as a top-quality, juried show. For more information, visit website.

CROCKER PARK FINE ART FAIR WITH CRAFT MARKETPLACE

270 Central Blvd., Suite 107B, Jupiter FL 33458. (561)746-6615. Fax: (561)746-6528. E-mail: info@artfestival.com. Website: www.artfestival.com. **Contact:** Malinda Ratliff, communications manager. Estab. 2006. Fine art and craft fair held annually in mid-June. Outdoors. Accepts photography, jewelry, mixed media, sculpture, wood, ceramic, glass, painting, digital, fiber, metal. Juried. Number of exhibitors: 125. Number of attendees: 50,000. Free to public. Apply online via www.zapplication.org.

ADDITIONAL INFORMATION Deadline: see website. Application fee: $25. Space fee: $395.

Exhibition space: 10×10 and 10×20. For more information, e-mail, call or visit website. Fair located in Crocker Park in Westlake/Cleveland, Ohio.

CROSBY FESTIVAL OF THE ARTS
(419)536-5588. E-mail: info@toledogarden. org. Website: www.toledogarden.org. Fine arts and crafts fair held annually in June. Outdoors. Accepts handmade crafts and other mediums. Exhibitors: 200. Number of attendees: see website. Admission: $8, general admission; free Toledo Botanical Gardens Members, children 12 and under. Apply via www.zapplication.org.

ADDITIONAL INFORMATION Deadline for entry: late February. Application fee: $25. Space fee: varies. Exhibition space: 10×10, $250 (standard); 10×10, $400 (corner); 10×20, $500 (double); 10×20, $650 (corner). For more information, visit website or call.

CUSTER FAIR
Piccolo Theatre Inc., P.O. Box 6013, Evanston IL 60204. (847)328-2204. E-mail: office@custerfair. com. Website: www.custerfair.com. **Contact:** Amanda Kulczewski. Estab. 1972. Outdoor fine art craft show held in June. Accepts photography and all mediums. Number of exhibitors: 400. Public attendance: 60,000. Free to public. Application fee: $10. Booth fee: $250–400.

ADDITIONAL INFORMATION Deadline for entry: mid-June. Space fee varies, e-mail, call or visit website for more details.

TIPS "Turn your hobbies into profits! Be prepared to speak with patrons; invite them to look at your work and broaden your patron base!"

A DAY IN TOWNE
Boalsburg Village Conservancy, 230 W. Main St., Boalsburg PA 16827. (814) 466 7813. E-mail: mgjohn@comcast.net. Website: www. boalsburgvillage.com. fisherjeff13@gmail.com. **Contact:** John Wainright; Jeff Fisher. Estab. 1976. Arts and crafts show held annually on Memorial Day, the last Monday in May. Outdoors. Accepts photography, clothes, wood, wool knit, soap, jewelry, dried flowers, children's toys, pottery, blown glass, other crafts. Vendors must

make their own work. Number of exhibitors: 125–135. Public attendance: 20,000+. Apply by sending an e-mail message to the above e-mail address.

ADDITIONAL INFORMATION Deadline for application is Feb. 1 each year. Space fee: $75. Exhibition space: 10×15.

TIPS "Please do not send fees until you receive an official contract. Have a neat booth and nice smile. Have fair prices—if too high, product will not sell here."

DEERFIELD FINE ARTS FESTIVAL
3417 R.F.D., Long Grove IL 60047. (847)726-8669. E-mail: dwevents@comcast.net. Website: www.dwevents.org. **Contact:** D&W Events, Inc. Estab. 2003. Fine art show held annually end of May/beginning of June. Outdoors. Accepts photography, fiber, oil, acrylic, watercolor, mixed media, jewelry, sculpture, metal, paper, ceramics, painting. Juried by 3 jurors. Awards/prizes: Best of Show; 1st place, awards of excellence. Number of exhibitors: 120–150. Public attendance: 20,000. Free to public. Free parking. Apply via www.zapplication.com or our promoter website: www.dwevents.org. Exhibition space: 100 sq. ft.

ADDITIONAL INFORMATION For more information, e-mail, call or visit website. Show located at Park Ave. and Deerfield Rd. adjacent to Jewett Park in Deerfield, Illinois.

TIPS "Display professionally and attractively, and interact positively with everyone."

DELAND OUTDOOR ART FESTIVAL
(386)717-1888. E-mail: delandoutdoorartfestival@ cfl.rr.com. Website: www.delandoutdoorartfest.com.

ADDITIONAL INFORMATION "This annual festival is held in March. Admission is free. Fine artists from throughout the Southeast will be competing for thousands of dollars in cash prizes and awards. The DOAF attracts 95 juried artists and 70 traditional crafters. The festival offers a craft section with items for sale ranging from handmade jewelry, carved wooden toys to Adirondack lawn furniture. More than 5,000 spectators visit the festival." Appy online. For more information, contact Martie Cox (386)736-7855) or Patty Clausen (386)717-1888.

DELAWARE ARTS FESTIVAL

P.O. Box 589, Delaware OH 43015. E-mail: info@delawareartsfestival.org. Website: www.delawareartsfestival.org. Estab. 1973. Fine arts and crafts show held annually the Saturday and Sunday after Mother's Day. Outdoors. Accepts photography; all mediums, but no buy/sell. Juried by category panels who are also artists. Awards/prizes: Ribbons, cash awards, free booth for Best of Show the following year. Number of exhibitors: 160. Public attendance: 50,000. Free to public. Submit 3 photographs per category that best represent your work. Your work will be juried in accordance with our guidelines. Photos (no slides) will be returned only if you provide a SASE. Apply by visiting website for application. Jury fee: $10 per category, payable to the Delaware Arts Festival. Space fee: $140. Exhibition space: 120 sq. ft.

ADDITIONAL INFORMATION For more information, e-mail or visit website. Show located in historic downtown Delaware, Ohio, just 2 blocks from the heart of Ohio Wesleyan University Campus.

TIPS "Have high-quality, original stuff. Engage the public. Applications will be screened according to originality, technique, craftsmanship, and design. Unaffiliated professional judges are hired to make all prize award decisions. The Delaware Arts Festival, Inc. will exercise the right to reject items during the show that are not the quality of the media submitted with the applications. No commercial buy and resell merchandise permitted. Set up a good booth."

DELRAY MARKETPLACE ART & CRAFT FESTIVAL

270 Central Blvd., Suite 107B, Jupiter FL 33458. (561)746-6615. Fax: (561)746-6528. E-mail: info@artfestival.com. Website: www.artfestival.com. **Contact:** Malinda Ratliff, communications manager. Estab. 2013. Fine art and craft fair held annually in November. Outdoors. Accepts photography, jewelry, mixed media, sculpture, wood, ceramic, glass, painting, digital, fiber, metal. Juried. Number of exhibitors: 100. Number of attendees: 40,000. Free to public. Apply online via www.zapplication.org.

ADDITIONAL INFORMATION Deadline: see website. Application fee: $25. Space fee: $350. Exhibition space: 10×10 and 10×20. For more information, e-mail, call, or visit website. Festival located at Delray Marketplace off West Atlantic Ave. in Delray Beach, Florida.

DES MOINES ARTS FESTIVAL

601 Locust St., Suite 700, Des Moines IA 50309. (951)735-4751. Website: www.desmoinesartsfestival.org.

ADDITIONAL INFORMATION "The Des Moines Arts Festival features the nation's top professional artists and emerging Iowa artists in a juried exhibition of artwork in a variety of mediums. Providing guests with the unique opportunity to meet artists from around the world and purchase their artwork, the Des Moines Arts Festival has become a signature event for the community."

DETROIT LAKE STREET FESTIVAL

Central Oregon Shows, P.O. Box 1555, Sisters OR 97759. (541)420-0279. E-mail: centraloregonshows@gmail.com. Website: www.centraloregonshows.com. **Contact:** Richard. July 16 and 17 Downtown Detroit. Detroit Lake is a resort area which attracts thousands of visitors year after year. There will be a variety of arts, crafts, antiques, food, and entertainment with a special fund-raiser benefiting the local Fire Department. For more information, visit website.

DETROIT URBAN CRAFT FAIR

E-mail: vendors@detroiturbancraftfair.com. Website: www.detroiturbancraftfair.com.

ADDITIONAL INFORMATION "The Detroit Urban Craft Fair (DUCF) is a 2 day alternative craft fair held annually in the city of Detroit. The fair features 100 handmade crafters and indie artists. DUCF is a community market that encourages the interaction of maker and buyer. It is unique opportunity for shoppers to find1-of-a-kind items and meet the people who made them. Participating crafters have the chance to connect with a large, supportive audience. The Detroit Urban Craft Fair's mission is to elevate handmade goods as an alternative to mass-produced items, support and elevate small craft business by providing a place for them to sell during the busy holiday shopping season, and raise awareness of handmade craft." For more information, visit website.

DICKENS HOLIDAY CRAFTS FAIR
Finley Community Center, Attn: Crafts Fair, 2060 W. College Ave., Santa Rosa CA 95401. (707)543-3755. E-mail: craftsfair@srcity. org. Website: www.http://ci.santa-rosa.ca.us/ departments/recreationandparks/programs/ specialevents/craftfair/Pages/default.aspx. Craft fair held annually in December. Indoors. Accepts handmade crafts. Exhibitors: 70. Number of attendees: see website. Admission: $2; children 12 and under free. Apply online.

ADDITIONAL INFORMATION Deadline for entry: July. Application fee: $25. Space fee: varies. Exhibition space: varies. For more information, visit website or call.

DILLON ART FESTIVAL
CCM Events, 4214 E. Colfax Ave., Denver CO 80220. (720)941-6088. Website: www. summitcountyartfestival.com. Fine arts and crafts fair held annually in July. Outdoors. Accepts handmade crafts and other mediums. Exhibitors: see website. Number of attendees: see website. Free to public. Apply online.

ADDITIONAL INFORMATION Deadline for entry: mid-April. Application fee: $35. Space fee: see website. Exhibition space: see website. For more information, visit website or call.

DIYPSI — AN INDIE ART FAIR
Website: www.diypsi.com.

ADDITIONAL INFORMATION Indie art fair. For more information, visit website and to apply.

DIY STREET FAIR
E-mail: info@diystreetfair.com. Website: www. diystreetfair.com.

ADDITIONAL INFORMATION "The DIY Street Fair is a free 2-day, 3-night event in Ferndale, Michigan, where local artists, crafters, businesses, groups and organizations, musicians, restaurants, food trucks, brewers,

and others whose lives and work adhere to do-it-yourself ethic converge for1 big celebration. The event, which launched its first weekend fair in 2008, showcases the immense creative energy, independent spirit, and innovative talent that can be found throughout the area. Open to the public, free to attend, and all are welcome." For more information, visit website and to apply.

✚ ☺ DOLLAR BANK3 RIVERS ARTS FESTIVAL
803 Liberty Ave., Pittsburgh PA 15222. (412)471-6070. E-mail: trafmarket@trustarts.org. Website: www.trustarts.org/traf. **Contact:** Melissa Franko, artist market manager. Estab. 1960. Fine art show held annually in June. Outdoors. Accepts fine art and handmade crafts, photography, clay, ceramics, fiber, paintings, furniture, wood, metal, leather, mixed media, jewelry, glass, sculpture, drawing, digital art, printmaking. Juried. Awards/ prizes: $10,000. Exhibitors: 360. Number of attendees: 600,000. Free to public. Apply via www.zapplication.org.

ADDITIONAL INFORMATION Deadline for entry: February 1. Application fee: $35. Space fee: $360–485. Exhibition space: 10×10. For more information, visit website. Event located at Gateway Center, Pittsburgh, Pennsylvania.

TIPS "The only way to participate is to apply!"

ALDEN B. DOW MUSEUM SUMMER ART FAIR
Alden B. Dow Museum of Science & Art, Midland Center for the Arts, 1801 W. St. Andrews Rd., Midland MI 48640. Fax: (989)631-7890. E-mail: mills@mcfta.org. Website: www.mcfta.org. **Contact:** Emmy Mills, executive assistant/ special events manager. Estab. 1966. Fine art and crafts show held annually in early June. Outdoors. Accepts photography, ceramics, fibers, jewelry, mixed media 3D, painting, wood, drawing, glass, leather, sculpture, basket, furniture. Juried by a panel. Awards: $1,000 1st place, $750 2nd place, $500 3rd place. Average number of exhibitors: 150. Public attendance: 5,000–8,000. Free to public. Apply at www. mcfta.org/specialevents.html.

ADDITIONAL INFORMATION Deadline for entry: late March; see website for details. Application fee: jury $35, second medium $5/each. Space fee: $195/single booth, $365/double booth. Exhibition space: approximately 12×12. Average gross sales/exhibitor: $1,500. E-mail or visit website for more information. Event takes place at Midland Center for the Arts.

DOWNTOWN ASPEN ART FESTIVAL

270 Central Blvd., Suite 107B, Jupiter FL 33458. (561)746-6615. Fax: (561)746-6528. E-mail: info@artfestival.com. Website: www.artfestival. com. **Contact:** Malinda Ratliff, communications manager. Estab. 2003. Fine art and craft fair held annually in July. Outdoors. Accepts photography, jewelry, mixed media, sculpture, wood, ceramic, glass, painting, digital, fiber, metal. Juried. Number of exhibitors: 150. Number of attendees: 80,000. Free to public. Apply online via www. wwww.zapplication.org. Deadline: see website. Application fee: $35. Space fee: $475. Exhibition space: 10×10 and 10×20. For more information, e-mail, call, or visit website. Festival located at Monarch Street in Aspen, Colorado.

DOWNTOWN DELRAY BEACH FESTIVAL OF THE ARTS

270 Central Blvd., Suite 107B, Jupiter FL 33458. (561)746-6615. Fax: (561)746-6528. E-mail: info@artfestival.com. Website: www.artfestival. com. **Contact:** Malinda Ratliff, communications manager. Estab. 2000. Fine art and craft fair held annually in mid-January. Outdoors. Accepts photography, jewelry, mixed media, sculpture, wood, ceramic, glass, painting, digital, fiber, metal. Juried. Number of exhibitors: 305. Number of attendees: 100,000. Free to public. Apply online via www.zapplication.org.

ADDITIONAL INFORMATION Deadline: see website. Application fee: $25. Space fee: $395. Exhibition space: 10×10 and 10×20. For more information, e-mail, call, or visit website. Festival located at Atlantic Ave. in downtown Delray Beach, Florida.

DOWNTOWN DELRAY BEACH THANKSGIVING WEEKEND ART FESTIVAL

270 Central Blvd., Suite 107B, Jupiter FL 33458. (561)746-6615. Fax: (561)746-6528. E-mail: info@artfestival.com. Website: www.artfestival. com. **Contact:** Malinda Ratliff, communications manager. Estab. 2000. Fine art and craft fair held annually in November. Outdoors. Accepts photography, jewelry, mixed media, sculpture, wood, ceramic, glass, painting, digital, fiber, metal. Juried. Number of exhibitors: 150. Number of attendees: 80,000. Free to public. Apply online via www.zapplication.org.

ADDITIONAL INFORMATION Deadline: see website. Application fee: $25. Space fee: $395. Exhibition space: 10×10 and 10×20. For more information, e-mail, call or visit website. Festival located at 4th Ave. & Atlantic Ave. in downtown Delray Beach FL.

DOWNTOWN DOWNERS GROVE FESTIVAL

Downers Grove Downtown Management Corp., Attn: Fine Arts Festival, 933A Curtiss St., Downers Grove IL 60515. (630)725-0991. Website: www.juriedartservices.com/index. php?content=event_info&event_id=903. Fine arts and crafts fair held annually In September. Outdoors. Accepts handmade crafts and other mediums. Exhibitors: see website. Number of attendees: 10,000. Admission: Free to public. Apply online.

ADDITIONAL INFORMATION Deadline for entry: mid-March. Application fee: $20. Space fee: $200 (single); $400 (double). Exhibition space: 10×10 (single); 10×20 (double). For more information, visit website or call.

DOWNTOWN DOWNERS GROVE FESTIVAL (ILLINOIS)

Amdur Productions, P.O. Box 550, Highland Park IL 60035. (847)926-4300. Fax: (847)926-4330. E-mail: info@amdurproductions.com. Website: www.amdurproductions.com. Art and craft show held annually in September. Outdoors. Accepts handmade crafts and other mediums. Juried. Awards/prizes: given at festival. Number of exhibitors: 100. Number of attendees: 30,000. Free to public. Apply online.

ADDITIONAL INFORMATION Deadline for entry: early January. Application fee: $20. Space fee: $335. Exhibition space: 10×10. For more information, e-mail, call, or visit website.

DOWNTOWN DUNEDIN ART FESTIVAL

270 Central Blvd., Suite 107B, Jupiter FL 33458. (561)746-6615. Fax: (561)746-6528. E-mail: info@artfestival.com. Website: www.artfestival. com. **Contact:** Malinda Ratliff, communications manager. Estab. 1997. Fine art and craft fair held annually in January. Outdoors. Accepts photography, jewelry, mixed media, sculpture, wood, ceramic, glass, painting, digital, fiber, metal. Juried. Number of exhibitors: 130. Number of attendees: 40,000. Free to public. Apply online via www.zapplication.org.

ADDITIONAL INFORMATION Deadline: see website. Application fee: $25. Space fee: $395. Exhibition space: 10×10 and 10×20. For more information, e-mail, call, or visit website. Festival located at Main St. in downtown Dunedin, Florida.

DOWNTOWN DUNEDIN CRAFT FESTIVAL

270 Central Blvd., Suite 107B, Jupiter FL 33458. (561)746-6615. Fax: (561)746-6528. E-mail: info@artfestival.com. Website: www.artfestival. com. **Contact:** Malinda Ratliff, communications manager.

ADDITIONAL INFORMATION "If Tampa is on your travel agenda this June, you can't miss out on this terrific craft event in the city's most desirable suburb of Dunedin. It is here, a short drive from Tampa, along Dunedin's Main Street, you will meet some of the country's finest crafters with products all handmade in the USA. Botanical hotplates, ceramic planters, functional pottery, hair accessories, handmade1-of-a-kind jewelry pieces, and an expansive Green Market offers something for every taste and budget."

DOWNTOWN FESTIVAL & ART SHOW

City of Gainesville, P.O. Box 490, Gainesville FL 32627. (352)393-8536. Fax: (352)334-2249. E-mail: piperlr@cityofgainesville.org. Website: www.gainesvilledowntownartfest.org. **Contact:** Linda Piper, events coordinator. Estab. 1981. Fine arts and crafts show held annually in November (For more information, visit website). Outdoors. Accepts photography, wood, ceramic, fiber, glass, and all mediums. Juried by 3 digital images of artwork and 1 digital image of booth. Awards/prizes: $20,000 in cash awards; $2,000 in purchase awards. Number of exhibitors: 240. Public attendance: 100,000. Free to public. Apply by mailing 4 digital images.

ADDITIONAL INFORMATION Deadline for entry: May. Space fee: $285, competitive, $260 non-competitive. Exhibition space: 12×12. Average gross sales/exhibitor: $6,000. For more information, e-mail, visit website, call.

TIPS "Submit the highest quality digital images. A proper booth image is very important."

DOWNTOWN SARASOTA CRAFT FAIR

270 Central Blvd., Suite 107B, Jupiter FL 33458. (561)746-6615. Fax: (561)746-6528. E-mail: info@artfestival.com. Website: www.artfestival. com. **Contact:** Malinda Ratliff, communications manager.

ADDITIONAL INFORMATION "This popular annual craft festival has garnered crowds of fine craft lovers each year. Behold contemporary crafts from more than 100 of the nation's most talented artisans. A variety of jewelry, pottery, ceramics, photography, painting, clothing, and much more—all handmade in America—will be on display, ranging from $15 to $3,000. An expansive Green Market with plants, orchids, exotic flora, handmade soaps, gourmet spices, and freshly popped kettle corn further complements the weekend, blending nature with nurture."

DOWNTOWN SARASOTA FESTIVAL OF THE ARTS

270 Central Blvd., Suite 107B, Jupiter FL 33458. (561)746-6615. Fax: (561)746-6528. E-mail: info@artfestival.com. Website: www.artfestival. com. **Contact:** Malinda Ratliff, communications manager. Fine art and craft fair held annually in mid-February. Outdoors. Accepts photography, jewelry, mixed media, sculpture, wood, ceramic, glass, painting, digital, fiber, metal. Juried. Number of exhibitors: 305. Number of attendees: 80,000. Free to public. Apply online via www. zapplication.org.

ADDITIONAL INFORMATION Deadline: see website. Application fee: $25. Space fee: $395. Exhibition space: 10×10 and 10×20. For more information, e-mail, call, or visit website. Festival located at Main St. at Orange Ave. heading east and ending at Links Ave. in downtown Sarasota, Florida.

DOWNTOWN STEAMBOAT SPRINGS ART FESTIVAL ON YAMPA STREET, THE YAMPA ART STROLL

270 Central Blvd., Suite 107B, Jupiter FL 33458. (561)746-6615. Fax: (561)746-6528. E-mail: info@artfestival.com. Website: www.artfestival. com. **Contact:** Malinda Ratliff, communications manager. Estab. 2015. Fine art and craft fair held annually in August. Outdoors. Accepts photography, jewelry, mixed media, sculpture, wood, ceramic, glass, painting, digital, fiber, metal. Juried. Number of exhibitors: see website. Number of attendees: see website. Free to public. Apply online via www.zapplication.org.

ADDITIONAL INFORMATION Deadline: see website. Application fee: $35. Space fee: $350. Exhibition space: 10×10 and 10×20. For more information, e-mail, call or visit website. Festival located at Yampa Ave. in Steamboat Springs, Colorado.

DOWNTOWN STUART ART FESTIVAL

270 Central Blvd., Suite 107B, Jupiter FL 33458. (561)746-6615. Fax: (561)746-6528. E-mail: info@artfestival.com. Website: www.artfestival. com. **Contact:** Malinda Ratliff, communications manager. Estab. 1991. Fine art and craft fair held annually in February. Outdoors. Accepts photography, jewelry, mixed media, sculpture, wood, ceramic, glass, painting, digital, fiber, metal. Juried. Number of exhibitors: 200. Number of attendees: 50,000. Free to public. Apply online via www.zapplication.org.

ADDITIONAL INFORMATION Deadline: see website. Application fee: $25. Space fee: $395. Exhibition space: 10×10 and 10×20. For more information, e-mail, call or visit website. Festival located at Osceola St. in Stuart, FL.

DOWNTOWN VENICE ART FESTIVAL

270 Central Blvd., Suite 107B, Jupiter FL 33458. (561)746-6615. Fax: (561)746-6528. E-mail: info@artfestival.com. Website: www.artfestival. com. **Contact:** Malinda Ratliff, communications manager. Estab. 1987. Fine art and craft fair held semiannually in early March and mid-November. Outdoors. Accepts photography, jewelry, mixed media, sculpture, wood, ceramic, glass, painting, digital, fiber, metal. Juried. Number of exhibitors: 130-200. Number of attendees: 50,000. Free to public. Apply online via www.zapplication.org.

ADDITIONAL INFORMATION Deadline: see website. Application fee: $25. Space fee: $350-395. Exhibition space: 10×10 and 10×20. For more information, e-mail, call, or visit website. Festival located at W. Venice Ave. in downtown Venice, Florida.

DOYLESTOWN ARTS FESTIVAL

E-mail: info@doylestownalliance.org. Website: www.doylestownartsfestival.com.

ADDITIONAL INFORMATION "This 2 day festival is the largest event of the year in the heart of beautiful Doylestown Borough in Bucks County, Pennsylvania. This annual festival has grown to include more than 160 exhibitors and a food court. Diverse activities are available at numerous locations throughout the downtown area. Live music features solo acts as well as rock, pop, folk, big band, and music for kids. The festival is a free event for the community."

DRIFTLESS AREA ART FESTIVAL

E-mail: info@driftlessareaartfestival.com. Website: www.driftlessareaartfestival.com.

ADDITIONAL INFORMATION The Driftless Area Art Festival celebrates the visual, performing, and culinary arts of the Driftless Area.

DUBUQUEFEST FINE ARTS FESTIVAL

C/O Paula Neuhaus, 8 Lindberg Terrace, Dubuque IA 52001. (563)564-5290. E-mail: paula@dubuquefest.org. Website: www. dubuquefest.org. **Contact:** Paula Neuhaus, art fair director. Estab. 1977. Fine arts and crafts fair held annually in May. Outdoors.

Accepts handmade crafts and other mediums. Juried. Awards/prizes: 1st place, 2nd place, 3rd place. Exhibitors: 70. Number of attendees: varies. Admission: Free to public. Apply online.

ADDITIONAL INFORMATION Deadline for entry: see website. Application fee: $15. Space fee: $110. Exhibition space: 12×12. For more information, e-mail, visit website, or call.

DURANGO AUTUMN ARTS FESTIVAL

802 E. Second Ave., Durango CO 81301. (970)422-8566. Fax: (970)259-6571. E-mail: daaf@durangoarts.org. Website: durangoarts. org/events/daaf. **Contact:** Jules Masterjohn. Estab. 1994. Fine arts and fine crafts show. September 17 & 18, 2016. Outdoors. Accepts photography and all mediums. Juried. Number of exhibitors: 90. Public attendance: 6,500. Free to public. Exhibition space: 10×10. & 10×20. Space fee $325 & $650. Application fee of $30. Apply via www.zapplication.org. For more information, visit the website.

EAGLE RIVER WATERMELON DAYS CRAFT & GIFT FESTIVAL

705 Bugbee Ave., Wausau WI 54401. (715)675-6201. Fax: (715)675-7649. E-mail: mac@macproductionllc.com. Website: www. macproductionllc.com. **Contact:** Mac and Bonnie McCallin. Fine arts and crafts fair held annually in July. Outdoors. Accepts handmade crafts and other mediums. Juried. Exhibitors: see website. Number of attendees: varies. Free to public. Apply online.

ADDITIONAL INFORMATION Deadline for entry: see website. Application fee: see website. Space fee: varies. Exhibition space: 12×10. For more information, e-mail, visit website, or call.

EAST LANSING ART FESTIVAL

410 Abbot Rd., East Lansing MI 48823. (517)319-6804. E-mail: info@elartfest.com. Website: www. elartfest.com. **Contact:** Michelle Carlson, festival director. Estab. 1963. Fine arts and crafts fair held annually in May. Outdoors. Accepts handmade crafts and other mediums. Juried. Awards/prizes: over $5,500 in cash awards. Exhibitors: see

website. Number of attendees: varies. Free to public. Apply online.

ADDITIONAL INFORMATION Deadline for entry: November. Application fee: $25. Space fee: $300 (single); $600 (double). Exhibition space: 10×10 (single); 10×10 (double). For more information, e-mail, visit website, or call.

EASTON ART AFFAIR

(330)284-1082. Fax: (330)494-0578. E-mail: bhuff@eastonartaffair.com. Website: www. eastonartaffair.com. **Contact:** Barb Huff. Estab. 1999. Fine arts and crafts fair held annually in June. Outdoors. Accepts handmade crafts, ceramics, digital art, drawing, glass, jewelry, metalwork, mixed media, painting, photography, printmaking and graphics, sculpture, wearable art, wood. Juried. Awards/prizes: Best of Show, Honorable Mention. Exhibitors: 105. Number of attendees: varies. Free to public. Apply via www. zapplication.org.

ADDITIONAL INFORMATION Deadline for entry: March 1. Application fee: $25. Space fee: $300 (single); $600 (double). Exhibition space: 10×10 (single); 10×20 (double). For more information, e-mail, visit website, or call.

ECHO PARK CRAFT FAIR

Website: www.echoparkcraftfair.com.

ADDITIONAL INFORMATION "The EPCF is a biannual design event in Silver Lake featuring over 70 artists and designers. Beatrice Valenzuela and Rachel Craven founded the Echo Park Craft Fair (EPCF) in 2009. The pair visualized a space that would showcase and nurture the many talented artisans, designers, and craftspeople living in their inspired community on the east side of Los Angeles. Originally held in Valenzuela's backyard featuring just a handful of friends, The Echo Park Craft Fair has grown into a highly anticipated biannual arts event, attracting thousands of visitors from around Los Angeles...and beyond."

EDENS ART FAIR

P.O. Box 1326, Palatine IL 60078. (312)751-2500. (847)991-4748. E-mail: asoaartists@aol. com. Website: www.americansocietyofartists.

com. **Contact:** ASA Office. Estab. 1995 (after renovation of location; held many years prior to renovation). American Society of Artists. Fine arts and fine selected crafts show held annually in mid-July. Outdoors. Event held in Wilmette, Illinois. Accepts photography, paintings, sculpture, glass works, jewelry, and more. Juried. Send 4 slides or photos of your work and 1 slide or photo of your display; #10 SASE; a résumé or show listing is helpful. Number of exhibitors: 50. Free to public. Apply by submitting jury materials. Please jury by submitting4 images representative of your work you wish to exhibit,1 of your display setup, your first/last name, physical address, daytime telephone number—résumé/show listing helpful. Submit to: asoaartists@aol.com. If you pass jury, you will receive a nonmember jury approval number. If juried in, you will receive a jury/approval number.

ADDITIONAL INFORMATION Deadline for entry: 2 months prior to show or earlier if spaces fill. Entry fee: to be announced. Exhibition space: about 100 sq. ft. for single space; other sizes available. For more information, send SASE, submit jury material.

TIPS "Remember that when you are at work in your studio, you are an artist. But when you are at a show, you are a business person selling your work."

EDINA ART FAIR

(952)922-1524. Fax: (952)922-4413. E-mail: info@50thandfrance.com. Website: www. edinaartfair.com. Fine arts and crafts fair held annually in June. Outdoors. Accepts handmade crafts, ceramics, enamel, fiber, glass, jewelry, mixed media, photography, sculpture, wearable art, wood. Juried. Awards/prizes: Best of Show, Best Display, awards of excellence, merit awards. Number of exhibitors: 300. Number of attendees: 165,000. Free to public. Apply online.

ADDITIONAL INFORMATION Deadline for entry: February. Application fee: $35. Space fee: $425 (single); $850 (double). Exhibition space: 10×10 (single); 10×20 (double). For more information, visit website or call.

EDMOND QUILT FESTIVAL

Alice Kellog, 2805 Old Farm Rd., Edmond OK 73013. (405)348-2233. E-mail: edmondquiltguild@yahoo.com. Website: www. edmondquiltguild.us. **Contact:** Alice Kellog. Quilt show held annually in July. Indoors. Accepts handmade quilts. Entry only open to Edmond Quilt Guild members. Juried. Awards/prizes: Founder's Award, Best Hand Quilting, Best of Show, Judges' Choice, Viewers' Choice. Number of exhibitors: see website. Number of attendees: see website. Free to public. Apply online.

ADDITIONAL INFORMATION Deadline for entry: mid-July. Application fee: see website. Space fee: see website. Exhibition space: see website. For more information, e-mail, visit website, or call.

EL DORADO COUNTY FAIR

100 Placerville Dr., Placerville CA 95667. (530)621-5860. Fax: (530)295-2566. E-mail: fair@eldoradocountyfair.org. Website: www. eldoradocountyfair.org. Estab. 1859. County fair held annually in June. Indoors. Accepts photography, fine arts, and handcrafts. Awards/prizes given, see entry guide on website for details. Number of exhibitors: 350-450. Average number of attendees: 55,000. Admission fee: $9.

ADDITIONAL INFORMATION Deadline: mid-May. Application fee: varies by class, see entry guide. For more information, visit website. Fair held at El Dorado County Fairgrounds in Placerville, California.

TIPS "Not a lot of selling at fair shows, competition mostly."

ELK RIVER ARENA'S FALL CRAFT SHOW

1000 School St., Elk River MN 55330. (763)635-1145. Fax: (763)635-1144. Email: lestby@elkrivermn.gov. Website: www.elkriverarena.com. Contact: Laura Estby, office assistant. Estab. 1997. Annual fine arts and crafts show held mid-September. Indoors and outdoors. Accepts handmade crafts, paintings, ceramics, photography, woodwork. Juried. Exhibitors: 85+. Number of attendees: 1,500. Free to public.

ADDITIONAL INFORMATION Deadline for entry: until filled. Space fee: $53–78. Exhibition space: 90–126 sq. ft. For more information email or see website.

ELMWOOD AVE. FESTIVAL OF THE ARTS, INC.

P.O. Box 786, Buffalo NY 14213-0786. (716)830-2484. E-mail: directoreafa@aol.com. Website: www.elmwoodartfest.org. Estab. 2000. Arts and crafts show held annually in late August, the weekend before Labor Day weekend. Outdoors. Accepts photography, metal, fiber, ceramics, glass, wood, jewelry, basketry, 2D media. Juried. Awards/prizes: to be determined. Number of exhibitors: 170. Public attendance: 80,000–120,000. Free to public. Apply by e-mailing their contact information or by downloading application from website.

ADDITIONAL INFORMATION Deadline for entry: April. Application fee: $25. Space fee: $295. Exhibition space: 10×15. Average gross sales/exhibitor: $3,000. For more information, e-mail, call, or visit website. Show located on Elmwood Ave.

TIPS "Make sure your display is well designed, with clean lines that highlight your work. Have a variety of price points—even wealthy people don't always want to spend $500 at a booth where they may like the work."

ESSEX FALL CRAFT SHOW

Vermont Craft Workers, Inc., P.O. Box 8139, Essex VT 05451. (802)879-6837. E-mail: info@vtcrafts.com. Website: www.vtcrafts.com. **Contact:** Kathy Rose, owner. Estab. 1981. Arts and crafts show held annually in October. Indoors. Accepts fine art and handmade crafts.

Number of exhibitors: 200. Number of attendees: 10,000. Admission: $8. Apply via website.

ADDITIONAL INFORMATION Deadline for entry: see website. Application fee: none. Space fee: $525. Exhibition space: 10×10. For more information, visit website. Event held at Champlain Valley Exposition, 105 Pearl St., Essex Junction, Vermont.

ESSEX SPRING CRAFT SHOW

P.O. Box 8139, Essex VT 5451. (802)879-6837. E-mail: info@vtcrafts.com. Website: www.vtcrafts.com. **Contact:** Kathy Rose, owner. Estab. 1997. Arts and crafts show held annually in May. Indoors. Accepts fine art and handmade crafts. Juried. Number of exhibitors: 120. Number of attendees: 8,000. Admission: $7. Apply via website.

ADDITIONAL INFORMATION Deadline for entry: see website. Application fee: none. Space fee: $350. Exhibition space: 10×10. For more information, visit website. Event held at Champlain Valley Exposition, 105 Pearl St., Essex Junction. Vermont.

EVANSTON ART & BIG FORK FESTIVAL

Amdur Productions, P.O. Box 550, Highland Park IL 60035. (847)926-4300. Fax: (847)926-4330. E-mail: info@amdurproductions.com. Website: www.amdurproductions.com. Art and craft show held annually in September. Outdoors. Accepts handmade crafts and other mediums. Juried. Awards/prizes: given at artist breakfast. Number of exhibitors: 30. Number of attendees: varies. Free to public. Apply online.

ADDITIONAL INFORMATION Deadline for entry: early May. Application fee: $25. Space fee: $430. Exhibition space: 10×10. For more information, e-mail, call, or visit website.

EVANSTON ETHNIC ARTS FAIR

Evanston Cultural Arts Programs, Morton Civic Center, Parks, Recreation and Community Services, 2100 Ridge Ave., Room 1116, Evanston IL 60201. (847)448-8260. Fax: (847)448-8051. E-mail: pbattaglia@cityofevanston.org. Website: www.cityofevanston.org/festivals-concerts/ethnic-arts-festival. **Contact**: Patricia Battaglia. Estab. 1984. Fine arts and crafts fair held annually in July. Outdoors. Accepts handmade crafts and other media. Juried. Awards/prizes: see website. Number of exhibitors: see website. Number of attendees: varies. Free to public. Apply online.

ADDITIONAL INFORMATION Deadline for entry: see website. Application fee: see website. Space fee: see website. Exhibition space: see website. For more information, e-mail, visit website, or call.

EVERGREEN FINE ARTS FESTIVAL

Evergreen Artists Association, 22528 Blue Jay Rd., Morrison CO 80465. (303) 349-3464. E-mail: director@evergreenfineartsfestival.com. Website: www.evergreenfineartsfestival.com; www.evergreenartists.org. **Contact:** Josh Trefethen, festival director. Estab. 1966. Fine arts show held annually the 4th weekend in August. Outdoors in Historic Heritage Grove Venue, next to Hiwan Homestead. Accepts both 2D and 3D media, including photography, fiber, oil, acrylic, pottery, jewelry, mixed media, ceramics, wood, watercolor. Juried event with jurors that change yearly. Submit online 3 views of work and 1 of booth display by digital photograph high-res. Awards/prizes: Best of Show in 2D and 3D and 6 awards of excellence, monetary plus jury exempt next year. Number of exhibitors: 100. Public attendance: 6,000–8,000. Free to public.

ADDITIONAL INFORMATION Deadline for entry: March 15. Application fee: $30. Space: $350 (upon acceptance). Exhibition space: 10×10. Submissions only on www.zapplication.org begin in December and jurying completed in early April. "Currently ranked in the top 100 by *Art Fair Source Book*." For more information, call or send SASE.

FAIRE ON THE SQUARE

117 W. Goodwin St., Prescott AZ 86303. (928)445-2000, ext. 112. Fax: (928)445-0068. E-mail: scott@prescott.org. Website: www.prescott.org. Estab. 1985. Arts and crafts show held annually Labor Day weekend. Outdoors. Accepts photography, ceramics, painting, sculpture, clothing, woodworking, metal art, glass, floral, home décor. No resale. Juried. Photos of work and artist creating work are required. Number of exhibitors: 160. Public attendance: 6,000–7,000. Free to public. Application can be printed from website or obtained by phone request.

ADDITIONAL INFORMATION Deadline: spaces are sold until show is full. Exhibition space: $425; $460 for food booth; 10×15. For more information, e-mail, visit website, or call.

A FAIR IN THE PARK

6300 Fifth Ave., Pittsburgh PA 15232. E-mail: fairdirector@craftsmensguild.org. Website: www.afairinthepark.org. Estab. 1969. Contemporary fine arts and crafts show held annually the weekend after Labor Day. Outdoors. Accepts photography, clay, fiber, jewelry, metal, mixed media, wood, glass, 2D visual arts. Juried. Awards/prizes: 1 Best of Show and 4 Craftsmen's Guild Awards. Number of exhibitors: 105. Public attendance: 25,000+. Free to public. Submit 5 JPEG images; 4 of artwork, 1 of booth display. Application fee: $25. Booth fee: $350 or $400 for corner booth.

ADDITIONAL INFORMATION Deadline for entry: see website. Exhibition space: 10×10. Average gross sales/exhibitor: $1,000 and up. For more information, e-mail or visit website. Show located in Mellon Park.

TIPS "It is very important for artists to present their work to the public, to concentrate on the business aspect of their artist career. They will find that they can build a strong customer/collector base by exhibiting their work and by educating the public about their artistic process and passion for creativity."

FALL CRAFT FEST

(479)756-6954. E-mail: info@craftfairsnwa.com. Website: www.ozarkregionalartsandcrafts.com.

ADDITIONAL INFORMATION Art and craft show held annually in October. Indoors. Accepts handmade crafts and other mediums. Juried. Number of exhibitors: see website. Number of attendees: varies. Free to public. Apply online.

FALL CRAFTS AT LYNDHURST

P.O. Box 28, Woodstock NY 12498. (845)331-7900. Fax: (845)331-7484. E-mail: crafts@artrider.com. Website: www.artrider.com. Estab. 1984. Fine arts and crafts show held annually in early to mid-September. Outdoors. Accepts photography, wearable and nonwearable fiber, jewelry, clay, leather, wood, glass, painting, drawing, prints, mixed media. Juried by 5 images of work and 1 of booth, viewed sequentially. Number of exhibitors: 275. Number of attendees: 14,000. Admission: $10. Apply at www.artrider.com or www.zapplication.org.

ADDITIONAL INFORMATION Deadline for entry: end of May. Application fee: $45. Space fee: $795–895. Exhibition space: 10×10. For more information, e-mail, call, or visit website.

FALL FEST IN THE PARK

117 W. Goodwin St., Prescott AZ 86303. (928)445-2000 or (800)266-7534. E-mail: chamber@prescott.org; scott@prescott.org. Website: www.prescott.org. Estab. 1981. Arts and crafts show held annually in mid-October. Outdoors. Accepts photography, ceramics, painting, sculpture, clothing, woodworking, metal art, glass, floral, home décor. No resale. Juried. Photos of work, booth, and artist creating work are required. Number of exhibitors: 150. Public attendance: 6,000–7,000. Free to public. Application can be printed from website or obtained by phone request. Deposit: $50, nonrefundable. Electricity is limited and has a fee of $15.

ADDITIONAL INFORMATION Deadline: Spaces are sold until show is full. Exhibition space: $250; $275 for food booth; 10×15. For more information, e-mail, call, or visit website.

FALL FESTIVAL OF ART AT QUEENY PARK

P.O. Box 31265, St. Louis MO 63131. (314)889-0433. E-mail: info@gslaa.org. Website: artfairatqueenypark.com. Estab. 1976. Fine arts and crafts show held annually Labor Day weekend at Queeny Park. Indoors. Accepts photography, all fine art and fine craft categories. Juried by 4 jurors; 5 slides shown simultaneously. Awards/prizes: 3 levels, ribbons, $4,000+ total prizes. Number of exhibitors: 130–140. Public attendance: 4,000–6,000. Admission: $5. Apply online. Application fee: $25. Booth fee: $225; $250 for corner booth.

ADDITIONAL INFORMATION Deadline for entry: mid-June, see website for specific date. Exhibition space: 80 sq. ft. (8×10) For more information, e-mail or visit website.

TIPS "Excellent, professional slides; neat, interesting booth. But most important—exciting, vibrant, eye-catching artwork."

FALL FESTIVAL OF THE ARTS OAKBROOK CENTER

Amdur Productions, P.O. Box 550, Highland Park IL 60035. (847)926-4300. Fax: (847)926-4330. E-mail: info@amdurproductions.com. Website: www.amdurproductions.com. Estab. 1962. Fine arts and crafts fair held annually in September. Outdoors. Accepts handmade crafts, jewelry, ceramics, painting, photography, digital, printmaking, and more. Juried. Number of exhibitors: see website. Number of attendees: varies. Admission: Free to public. Apply online.

ADDITIONAL INFORMATION Deadline for entry: see website. Application fee: $25. Space fee: $460. Exhibition space: 10×10. For more information, e-mail, call, or visit website.

FALL FESTIVAL ON PONCE

Olmstead Park, N. Druid Hills, 1451 Ponce de Leon, Atlanta GA 30307. (404)873-1222. E-mail: lisa@affps.com. Website: www.festivalonponce.com. **Contact:** Lisa Windle, festival director. Estab. 2010. Arts and crafts show held annually mid-October. Outdoors. Accepts handmade crafts, painting, photography, sculpture, leather, metal, glass, jewelry. Juried by a panel. Awards/prizes: ribbons. Number of exhibitors: 125.

Number of attendees: 45,000. Free to public. Apply online at www.zapplication.org.

ADDITIONAL INFORMATION Application fee: $25. Space fee: $275. Exhibition space: 10×10. For more information, e-mail or see website.

FALL FINE ART & CRAFTS AT BROOKDALE PARK

Rose Squared Productions, Inc., 473 Watchung Ave., Bloomfield NJ 07003. (908)874-5247. Fax: (908)874-7098. E-mail: info@rosesquared.com. Website: www.rosesquared.com. **Contact:** Howard Rose, vice president. Estab. 1998. Fine arts and crafts show held annually in mid-October. Outdoors. Accepts photography and all other mediums. Juried. Number of exhibitors: 160. Public attendance: 12,000. Free to public. Apply on the website.

ADDITIONAL INFORMATION Deadline for entry: mid-September. Application fee: $30. Space fee: varies by booth size. Exhibitor space: 120 sq. ft. See application form on website for details. For more information, visit website. Promoters of fine art and craft shows that are successful for the exhibitors and enjoyable, tantalizing, satisfying artistic buying experiences for the supportive public.

TIPS "Have a range of products and prices."

FARGO'S DOWNTOWN STREET FAIR

Downtown Community Partnership, 210 Broadway N. #202, Fargo ND 58102. (701)241-1570; (701)451-9062. Fax: (701)241-8275. E-mail: fargostreetfair@downtownfargo.com. Website: www.downtownfargo.com. **Contact:** Stephanie Holland, street fair consultant. Estab. 1975. "This juried event is located in historic downtown Fargo on Broadway in July. It is a street fair that successfully combines arts and crafts, food, marketplace, music and entertainment. It attracts a large number of visitors from the tri-state region/Winnepeg and many vacationers. The locals also look forward to it every year! The show is largely made up of traditional crafts, jewelry, clothing and is focused on increasing its fine arts entries each year." Outdoors. Accepts food/culinary, mixed media, pottery/ceramic, wood furniture, glass, music, printmaking, wood other, jewelry, naturals/floral, recycled/found object/green, leather, painting, sculpture, metal, photography, textiles/fibers/clothing. Number of exhibitors: 300. Public attendance: 130,000–150,000. Free to public. "Apply online and submit 3 photos for the jury: 3 images of your work, 1 image of booth, and 4 images of process." All JPEG photos must be 300 dpi and be at least 1,800×1,200 pixels.

ADDITIONAL INFORMATION Deadline for entry: mid-February. Space fee: $325–700 depending on size and/or corner. Exhibition space: 11×11. For more information, visit website. Fair located in downtown Fargo.

FESTIVAL FETE

Festival Fete, P.O. Box 2552, Newport RI 2840. (401)207-9729. E-mail: pilar@festivalfete.com. Website: www.festivalfete.com. Fine arts and crafts fair held annually in July. Outdoors. Accepts handmade crafts, painting, sculpture, photography, drawing, fabric, crafts, ceramics, glass, and jewelry. Juried. Awards/prizes: see website. Number of exhibitors: 150. Number of attendees: varies. Free to public. Apply online.

ADDITIONAL INFORMATION Deadline for entry: see website. Application fee: see website. Space fee: $175. Exhibition space: 10×10. For more information, e-mail, call, or visit website.

⌂ FESTIVAL FOR THE ENO

(919)620-9099 ext. 203. E-mail: crafts@enoriver.org. Website: www.enoriver.org/festival. The Festival for the Eno is presented by the Eno River Association to celebrate and preserve the natural, cultural, and historic resources of the Eno River Valley. All participants must recognize that the Festival is a combined effort toward this specific goal. As1 of its chief attractions, the Festival features the excellence and diversity of the region's arts and crafts. The Festival is held at West Point on the Eno, a Durham City Park on Roxboro Rd. Open to residents of the Carolinas, Virginia, Georgia, and Tennessee only, and all items must be the handiwork of the participant, who must be present. For more information, visit website.

FESTIVAL IN THE PARK

1409 East Blvd., Charlotte NC 28203. (704)338-1060. E-mail: festival@festivalinthepark.org. Website: www.festivalinthepark.org. **Contact:** Julie Whitney Austin. Estab. 1964. Fine arts and crafts show held annually in late September (3rd Friday after Labor Day). Outdoors. Accepts photography and all arts mediums. Awards/prizes: $4,000 in cash awards. Number of exhibitors: 180. Public attendance: 100,000. Free to public. Apply by visiting website for application. Application fee: $45. Space fee: $345. Exhibition space: 10×10. For more information, e-mail, call, or visit website.

FESTIVAL OF THE VINE

Geneva Chamber of Commerce, 8 S. Third St., Geneva IL 60134. (630)232-6060. Fax: (630)232-6083. E-mail: kandersen@genevachamber.com. Website: www.genevachamber.com. **Contact:** Krista Andersen, volunteer coordinator. Estab. 1981. Arts and crafts show held annually in mid-September. Outdoors. Accepts handmade crafts. Juried. Number of exhibitors: 100. Number of attendees: 200,000. Free to public. Apply online. **ADDITIONAL INFORMATION** Deadline for entry: June 1. Application fee: none. Space fee: $175. Exhibition space: 10×10. For more information, e-mail, visit website, or call.

FESTIVAL OF TREES CRAFT & GIFT SHOW

The Family Tree Center, 2520 Fifth Ave. S., Billings MT 59101-4342. (406)252-9799. Fax: (406)256-3014. Website: www.familytreecenterbillings.org. Estab. 1985. **ADDITIONAL INFORMATION** "Begun in 1985, the Festival of Trees has become synonymous with the holiday season in Billings. For many residents and visitors, the holidays would not be complete without at least1 visit to view the trees or participate in the weekend activities. Each year, the Festival of Trees provides an opportunity for community members to help prevent child abuse and neglect in Yellowstone County and the surrounding area. Donating or buying a tree, sponsoring the event, or participating in1 of the many weekend activities during the Festival helps raise money and awareness; both help The Family Tree Center. Over the course of this 4-day event, over 10,000 people pass through the doors to view the unique Holiday Trees and participate in the assortment of activities. All dollars raised at the Festival go where they are needed most—toward the many child abuse prevention programs in place at The Family Tree Center. Referrals are increasing, and the number of families that we serve continues to grow. Now more than ever, the Family Tree Center needs your support." For more information, visit website.

FIESTA ARTS FAIR

Southwest School of Art, 300 Augusta St., San Antonio TX 78205. (210)224-1848. Fax: (210)224-9337. Website: www.swschool.org/fiestaartsfair. Art and craft market/show held annually in April. Outdoors. Accepts handmade crafts, ceramics, paintings, jewelry, glass, photography, wearable art, and other mediums. Juried. Number of exhibitors: 125. Number of attendees: 12,000. Admission: $16 weekend pass; $10 daily adult pass; $5 daily children pass; children 5 and under free. Apply via www.zapplication.org. **ADDITIONAL INFORMATION** Deadline for entry: November. Application fee: none. Space fee: varies. Exhibition space: varies. For more information, should call or visit website.

FILLMORE JAZZ FESTIVAL

Steven Restivo Event Services, LLC, P.O. Box 151017, San Rafael CA 94915. (800)310-6563. Fax: (415)456-6436. Website: www.fillmorejazzfestival.com. Estab. 1984. Fine arts and crafts show and jazz festival held annually 1st weekend of July in San Francisco, between Jackson and Eddy St. Outdoors. Accepts photography, ceramics, glass, jewelry, paintings, sculpture, metal clay, wood, clothing. Juried by prescreened panel. Number of exhibitors: 250. Public attendance: 100,000. Free to public. **ADDITIONAL INFORMATION** Deadline for entry: ongoing; apply online. Exhibition space: 8×10. or 10×10. Average gross sales/exhibitor: $800–11,000. For more information, visit website or call.

FINE ART & CRAFTS AT ANDERSON PARK

274 Bellevue Ave., Upper Montclair NJ 07043. (908)874-5247. Fax: (908)874-7098. E-mail: info@rosesquared.com. Website: www.rosesquared.com. **Contact:** Howard and Janet Rose. Estab. 1984. Fine art and craft show held annually in mid-September. Outdoors. Accepts photography and all other mediums. Juried. Number of exhibitors: 160. Public attendance: 12,000. Free to public. Apply on the website.

ADDITIONAL INFORMATION Deadline for entry: mid-August. Application fee: $30. Space fee varies by booth size; see application form on website for details. For more information, visit the website.Promoters of fine art and craft shows that are successful for the exhibitors and enjoyable, tantalizing, satisfying artistic buying experiences for the supportive public.

TIPS "Create a range of sizes and prices."

FINE ART & CRAFTS AT VERONA PARK

Rose Squared Productions, Inc., 542 Bloomfield Ave., Verona NJ 07044. (908)874-5247. Fax: (908)874-7098. E-mail: info@rosesquared.com. Website: www.rosesquared.com. **Contact:** Howard Rose, vice president. Estab. 1986. Fine arts and crafts show held annually in mid-May. Outdoors. Accepts photography and all other mediums. Juried. Number of exhibitors: 140. Public attendance: 10,000. Free to public. Apply on the website.

ADDITIONAL INFORMATION Deadline for entry: mid-April. Application fee: $25. Space fee varies by booth size; see application form on website for details. For more information, visit the website.

TIPS "Have a range of sizes and price ranges."

FINE ART FAIR

Foster Arts Center, 203 Harrison St., Peoria IL 61602. (309)637-2787. E-mail: fineartfair@peoriaartguild.org. Website: www.peoriaartguild.org. **Contact:** fine art fair coordinator. Estab. 1962. Fine art and fine craft fair held annually the last full weekend in September. Outdoors. Accepts handmade crafts, painting, sculpture, photography, drawing, fabric, ceramics, glass, and jewelry. Juried. Number of exhibitors: 150. Number of attendees: 25,000. Admission: $5 adults; children 12 and under free; Peoria Art Guild members free. Apply online.

ADDITIONAL INFORMATION Deadline for entry: see website. Application fee: see website. Space fee: see website. Exhibition space: see website. For more information, e-mail, call, or visit website.

FINE CRAFT SHOW

Memorial Art Gallery of the University of Rochester, 500 University Ave., Rochester NY 14607. (585)276-8900. Fax: (585)473-6266. E-mail: maginfo@mag.rochester.edu. Website: www.mag.rochester.edu/events/fine-craft-show/. Estab. 2000. Fine arts and crafts fair held annually in October. Indoors. Accepts handmade crafts, ceramics, glass, jewelry, metal, leather, wood, wearable art, and more. Juried. Number of exhibitors: 40. Number of attendees: varies. Admission: $12; $5 college students w/ID. Apply online.

ADDITIONAL INFORMATION Deadline for entry: see website. Application fee: see website. Space fee: see website. Exhibition space: see website. For more information, e-mail, visit website or call.

FINE CRAFT SHOW AND SALE — MEMORIAL ART GALLERY

500 University Ave., Rochester NY 14607. (585)276-8910. E-mail: smcnamee@mag. rochester.edu. Website: www.magrochester. edu. Contact: Sharon McNamee, gallery council assistant. Fine craft show held annually early November. Indoors. Accepts handmade crafts, glass, ceramics, leather, wearables, jewelry, wood, furniture, metal. Juried. Awards/prizes: Best in Show; Award of Excellence (2). Number of exhibitors: 40. Number of attendees: 2,000. Admission: $10–12. Apply online.

ADDITIONAL INFORMATION Deadline for entry: March 31. Application fee: $35. Space fee: $525. Exhibition space: 10×10. Average sales: $1,500–6,000. For more information, e-mail or visit website.

TIPS "One of a kind or limited edition."

FIREFLY ART FAIR

Wauwatosa Historical Society, 7406 Hillcrest Dr., Wauwatosa WI 53213. (414)774-8672. E-mail: staff@wauwatosahistoricalsociety.org. Website: www.wauwatosahistoricalsociety. org. **Contact:** Janel Ruzicka. Estab. 1985. Fine arts and crafts fair held annually 1st weekend in August. Outdoors. Accepts painting, sculpture, photography, ceramics, jewelry, fiber, printmaking, glass, paper, leather, wood. Juried. Number of exhibitors: 90. Number of attendees: 4,000–5,000. $5 public admission. Apply online.

ADDITIONAL INFORMATION Deadline for entry: March 15. Application fee: $15. Space fee: $140. Exhibition space: 10×10. For more information, e-mail, visit website, or call.

FIREFLY HANDMADE MARKET

Firefly Handmade Markets, P.O. Box 3195, Boulder CO 80307. E-mail: fireflyhandmade@ gmail.com. Website: www.fireflyhandmade.com. Estab. 2010. Fine crafts fair held annually 3 times a year. Outdoors. Accepts handmade crafts. Juried. Number of exhibitors: 100. Number of attendees: 6,000. Free to public. Apply online.

ADDITIONAL INFORMATION Deadline for entry: May. Application fee: $25. Space fee: varies. Exhibition space: varies. For more information, e-mail or visit website.

FLINT ART FAIR

(810)695-0604. E-mail: committee@flintartfair. org. Website: www.flintartfair.org.

ADDITIONAL INFORMATION Fine arts and crafts fair held annually in June. Outdoors. Accepts handmade crafts and other mediums. Juried. Number of exhibitors: see website. Number of attendees: varies. Admission: $5 adults; $3 children 12 and under, seniors, and FOMA members. Apply online.

ADDITIONAL INFORMATION Deadline for entry: see website. Application fee: see website. Space fee: see website. Exhibition space: see website. For more information, e-mail, visit website, or call.

FOOTHILLS ARTS & CRAFTS FAIR

2753 Lynn Rd., Suite A, Tryon NC 28782-7870. (828)859-7427. Fax: 888-296-0711. E-mail: info@blueridgebbqfestival.com. Website: www. blueridgebbqfestival.com. Estab. 1994. Fine arts and crafts show and Blue Ridge BBQ Festival/Championship held annually the 2nd Friday and Saturday in June. Outdoors. Accepts contemporary, traditional and fine art by artist only; nothing manufactured or imported. Juried. Number of exhibitors: 50. Public attendance: 15,000+. Public admission: $8; 12 and under free. Apply by downloading application from website or sending personal information to e-mail or mailing address.

ADDITIONAL INFORMATION See website for deadline for entry. Jury fee: $25, nonrefundable. Space fee: $175. Exhibition space: 10×10. For more information, e-mail or visit website.

TIPS "Have an attractive booth, unique items, and reasonable prices."

FOUNTAIN HILLS FINE ART & WINE AFFAIRE

16810 E. Ave. of the Fountains, Fountain Hills AZ 85268. (480)837-5637. Fax: (480)837-2355. E-mail: info@thunderbirdartists.com. Website: www.thunderbirdartists.com. **Contact:** Denise Colter, president. Estab. 2005. "The 12th Annual Fountain Hills Fine Art and Wine Affaire is produced by Thunderbird Artists, in conjunction with Sunset Kiwanis and the town of Fountain Hills. Thunderbird Artists again unite with Sunset Kiwanis of Fountain Hills to celebrate 12 years!

Held on the picturesque Ave. of the Fountains, the signature fountain attracts thousands of visitors every year and runs at the top of each hour for 15 minutes 9 a.m.–9 p.m. daily. Thunderbird Artists Mission is to promote fine art and fine crafts (through an extensive and dedicated advertising campaign) paralleled with the ambiance of unique wines and fine music, while supporting the artists, merchants and surrounding communities.."

TIPS "A clean, gallery-type presentation is very important."

FOUNTAIN HILLS GREAT FAIR

P.O. Box 17598, Fountain Hills AZ 85269. E-mail: sharon@fountainhillschamber.com. Website: www.fountainhillschamber.com/the-great-fair. asp. **Contact:** Sharon Morgan.

ADDITIONAL INFORMATION "This 3-day juried art fair features nearly 500 artists and artisans from across the United States and around the globe and attracts 200,000+ visitors. Food booths, beer garden, and seating areas abound throughout the venue, with great breakfast, lunch, and rest stops situated at locations in the middle and at both ends of the festival area. Live musical entertainment." For more information, visit website.

FOURTH AVE. STREET FAIR

434 E. Ninth St., Tucson AZ 85705. (520)624-5004 or (800)933-2477. Fax: (520)624-5933. E-mail: kurt@fourthAve..org. Website: www.fourthAve..org. **Contact:** Kurt. Estab. 1970. Arts and crafts fair held annually in late March/early April and December (see website for details). Outdoors. Accepts photography, drawing, painting, sculpture, arts and crafts. Juried by five jurors. Awards/prizes: Best of Show. Number of exhibitors: 400. Public attendance: 300,000. Free to public. Apply by completing the online application at www.zapplication.org. Requires 4 photos of art/craft and 1 booth photo. $35 application fee. Booth fee $505, additional $150 for corner booth.

ADDITIONAL INFORMATION Deadline for entry: see website for details. Exhibition space: 10×10. Average gross sales/exhibitor: $3,000. For more information, e-mail, visit website, call, send SASE. Fair located on 4th Ave., between 9th St. and University Ave.

FOURTH STREET FESTIVAL FOR THE ARTS & CRAFTS

P.O. Box 1257, Bloomington IN 47402. (812)575-0484; (812)335-3814. E-mail: info@4thstreet.org. Website: www.4thstreet.org. Estab. 1976. Fine arts and crafts show held annually Labor Day weekend. Outdoors. Accepts photography, clay, glass, fiber, jewelry, painting, graphic, mixed media, wood. Juried by a4-member panel. Awards/prizes: Best of Show ($750), 1st, 2nd, 3rd in 2D and 3D. Number of exhibitors: 105. Public attendance: 25,000. Free to public. Apply by sending requests by mail, e-mail or download application from website at www.zapplication.org. Exhibition space: 10×10. Average gross sales/exhibitor: $2,700.

ADDITIONAL INFORMATION For more information, e-mail, visit website, call or send for information with SASE. Show located at 4th St. and Grant St. adjacent to Indiana University.

TIPS Be professional.

FREDERICK FESTIVAL OF THE ARTS

11 W. Patrick St., Suite 201, Frederick MD 21701. (301)662-4190. E-mail: info@fredericksartcouncil.org. Website: www.frederickartscouncil.org. Estab. 1993. Fine arts and crafts fair held annually in June. Outdoors. Accepts handmade crafts, jewelry, photography, painting, glass, wood, metal, drawing, digital, sculpture, fiber, and other forms of mixed media. Juried. Number of exhibitors: 110. Number of attendees: varies. Free to public. Apply online.

ADDITIONAL INFORMATION Deadline for entry: see website. Application fee: see website. Space fee: see website. Exhibition space: see website. For more information, e-mail, call or visit website.

FREDERICKSBURG FALL HOME & CRAFTS FESTIVAL

Ballantine Management Group of Virginia, 2371 Carl D. Silver Pkwy., Fredericksburg VA 22401. (540)548-5555, ext.108. Fax: (540)548-5577.

E-mail: csilversmith@bmg1.com. Website: www. fredericksburgartsandcraftsfaire.com. **Contact:** Casey Silversmith. Estab. 2006. Handmade-only crafts fair held annually in October. Indoors. Accepts handmade arts and crafts only. Number of exhibitors: see website. Number of attendees: varies. Admission: $8 at door; $7 online and seniors 60+; children 12 and under free. Apply online.

ADDITIONAL INFORMATION Deadline for entry: see website. Application fee: see website. Space fee: varies. Exhibition space: varies. For more information, e-mail, visit website, or call.

FREDERICKSBURG HOLIDAY CRAFT SHOW

Ballantine Management Group of Virginia, 2371 Carl D. Silver Pkwy., Fredericksburg VA 22401. (540)548-5555, ext. 108. Fax: (540)548-5577. E-mail: csilversmith@bmg1.com. Website: www. fredericksburgholidaycraftshow.com. **Contact:** Casey Silversmith. Estab. 2006. Check your list and see who has been naughty or nice before you head over to the Holiday Craft Show. The Fredericksburg Holiday Craft Show is the largest Craft Show ever held at the Expo Center. Vendors will showcase1-of-a-kind handmade arts and crafts that will make wonderful gifts for your family, friends, and even your pets. Browse through aisles filled with holiday ornaments, knickknacks and wreaths, jewelry, soaps and lotions, gourmet foods, glassware, artwork, organic dog treats, clothing, candles, and much more.

ADDITIONAL INFORMATION For more information, visit website. Show located at Fredericksburg Expo & Conference Center

FREDERICKSBURG SPRING ARTS & CRAFTS FAIRE

Ballantine Management Group of Virginia, 2371 Carl D. Silver Pkwy., Fredericksburg VA 22401. (540)548-5555, ext. 108. Fax: (540)548-5577. E-mail: csilversmith@bmg1.com. Website: www. fredericksburgholidaycraftshow.com. **Contact:** Casey Silversmith. Estab. 2007. Handmade arts and crafts fair held annually in March. Indoors. Accepts handmade crafts and other mediums. Number of exhibitors: see website. Number of attendees: varies. Admission: $8 at door; $7 online and seniors 60+; children 12 and under free. Apply online.

ADDITIONAL INFORMATION Deadline for entry: see website. Application fee: see website. Space fee: varies. Exhibition space: varies. For more information, e-mail, visit website, or call.

FRIENDS OF THE KENOSHA PUBLIC MUSEUMS ART FAIR

5500 First Ave., Kenosha WI 53140. (262)653-4140. Fax: (262)653-4437. E-mail: pgregorski@kenosha.org. Website: www. kenoshapublicmuseum.org. **Contact:** Peggy Gregorski, deputy director. Estab. 1964. Fine arts and crafts show held annually 3rd Sunday of July. Indoors and outdoors. Accepts handmade crafts. Juried. Awards/prizes: Five awards totaling $2,000. Number of exhibitors: 125. Number of attendees: 7,000. Free to public. Apply online.

ADDITIONAL INFORMATION Deadline for entry: May 1. Application fee: none. Space fee: $125–200. Exhibition space: 10×10 (indoors); 15×15 (outdoors). For more information, e-mail or visit website.

FUNKY FERNDALE ART SHOW

Integrity Shows, P.O. Box 1070, Ann Arbor MI 48106. E-mail: info@integrityshows.com. Website: www.funkyferndaleartfair.com. **Contact:** Mark Loeb. Estab. 2004. Fine arts and crafts show held annually in September. Outdoors. Accepts photography and all fine art and craft mediums; emphasis on fun, funky work. Juried by 3 independent jurors. Awards/prizes: purchase and merit awards. Number of exhibitors: 120. Public attendance: 30,000. Free to public. Application fee: $25. Booth fee: $295. Electricity limited; fee: $100. For more information, visit our website.

TIPS "Show enthusiasm. Keep a mailing list. Develop collectors."

FUNKY JUNK ROUNDUP

E-mail: montagefestivals@earthlink.net.
Website: www.montagefestivals.com.1-day
shopping extravaganza held in May. Indoors.
Accepts handmade crafts, junktiques, artisan
designs, antique and vintage, home decor and
inspiration, and more. Exhibitors: varies. Number
of attendees: varies. Admission: $3 adults; under
12 free. Apply via website.

ADDITIONAL INFORMATION Deadline for entry:
see website. Application fee: see website. Space
fee: $95 (10×10); $165 (10×20). Exhibition space:
10×10; 10×20. For more information, e-mail or
visit website.

GAITHERSBURG-KENTLANDS DOWNTOWN ART FESTIVAL

270 Central Blvd., Suite 107B, Jupiter FL 33458.
(561)746-6615. Fax: (561)746-6528. E-mail:
info@artfestival.com. Website: www.artfestival.
com. **Contact:** Malinda Ratliff, communications
manager. Estab. 2015. Fine art and craft fair
held annually in September. Outdoors. Accepts
photography, jewelry, mixed media, sculpture,
wood, ceramic, glass, painting, digital, fiber,
metal. Juried. Number of exhibitors: see website.
Number of attendees: see website. Free to public.
Apply online via www.zapplication.org.

ADDITIONAL INFORMATION Deadline: see
website. Application fee: $25. Space fee: $450.
Exhibition space: 10×10 and 10×20. For more
information, e-mail, call, or visit website. Festival
located at The Streets of Market and Main at
Kentlands Downtown.

GARAGE SALE ART FAIR

E-mail: bonnie@garagesaleartfair.com. Website:
www.garagesaleartfair.com. Fine arts and crafts
fair held annually in February. Indoors. Accepts
handmade crafts and other mediums. Juried.
Number of exhibitors: 125. Number of attendees:
3,500. Free to public. Apply online.

ADDITIONAL INFORMATION Deadline for entry:
see website. Application fee: see website. Space
fee: varies. Exhibition space: varies. For more
information, e-mail, visit website.

GARRISON ART CENTER'S JURIED FINE CRAFTS FAIR

23 Garrison's Landing, P.O. Box 4, Garrison
NY 10524. (845)424-3960. Fax: 845-424-4711.
E-mail: info@garrisonartcenter.org. Website:
www.garrisonartcenter.org. Outdoor, riverside
fine crafts show held annually on the 3rd weekend
in August. Eighty-five exhibitors are selected to
exhibit and sell handmade original work. Entries
are judged based on creativity, originality, and
quality. Annual visitors 4,000–5,000.

ADDITIONAL INFORMATION Visit our website
for information, prospectus, and application. Fair
located at Garrison's Landing.

TIPS "Have an inviting booth and be pleasant and
accessible. Don't hide behind your product—
engage the audience."

GASLIGHT CRAFT FAIR

7010 E. Broadway Blvd., Tucson AZ 85710.
(520)886-4116. Fax: (520)722-6232. E-mail: glt@
qwestoffice.net. **Contact:** Teresa, bookkeeper.
Estab. 2012. Art and craft show/seasonal/holiday
show held every Saturday (weather permitting);
Friday–Sunday in November and December.
Outdoors. Accepts handmade crafts. ENumber
of exhibitors: 30. Number of attendees: 300. Free
to public. Apply online.

ADDITIONAL INFORMATION Deadline for entry:
1 week before event. Application fee: none.
Space fee: $10/space per day; $30 in November
and December. Exhibition space: 8×10 (under
tent); 12×12 (in parking lot). For more information,
e-mail, call, or visit Facebook page.

GASPARILLA FESTIVAL OF THE ARTS

P.O. Box 10591, Tampa FL 33679. (813)876-
1747. E-mail: info@gasparillaarts.com. Website:
www.gasparilla-arts.com. Estab. 1970. Fine arts
and crafts fair held annually in March. Outdoors.
Accepts handmade crafts, ceramic, digital,
drawing, fiber, glass, jewelry, mixed media,
painting, photography, printmaking, sculpture,
watercolor, and wood. Juried. Awards/prizes:
$74,500 in cash awards. Number of exhibitors:

300. Number of attendees: 250,000. Free to public. Apply online.

ADDITIONAL INFORMATION Deadline for entry: September. Application fee: $40. Space fee: $375. Exhibition space: 10×10. For more information, e-mail, visit website, or call.

GATHERING AT THE GREAT DIVIDE

Mountain Art Festivals, P.O. Box 3578, Breckenridge CO 80424. (970)547-9326. E-mail: info@mountainartfestivals.com. Website: www.mountainartfestivals.com. Estab. 1975. Fine arts and crafts fair held annually in August. Outdoors. Accepts handmade crafts, painting, sculpture, photography, drawing, fabric, crafts, ceramics, glass, and jewelry. Juried. Number of exhibitors: see website. Number of attendees: varies. Free to public. Apply online.

ADDITIONAL INFORMATION Deadline for entry: March 31. Application fee: $35. Space fee: $500. Exhibition space: 10×10. For more information, e-mail, visit website, or call.

GENEVA ARTS FAIR

8 S. Third St., Geneva IL 60134. (630)232-6060. E-mail: chamberinfo@genevachamber.com; lrush@genevachamber.com. Website: www.genevachamber.com. Fine arts show held annually in late-July (see website for details). Outdoors. Juried. "The unprecedented Geneva Arts Fair transforms downtown Geneva into a venue for over 150 esteemed artists and draws a crowd of more than 20,000. The juried show was voted a Top 200 Fine Craft Fair by *Art Fair SourceBook* and a previous winner of 'Best Craft or Art Show' by *West Suburban Living* magazine." Accepts photography, ceramics, fiber, printmaking, mixed media, watercolor, wood, sculpture, and jewelry.

ADDITIONAL INFORMATION Application deadline: early February. Please visit www.emevents.com to apply.

GERMANTOWN FESTIVAL

P.O. Box 381741, Germantown TN 38183. (901)757-9212. E-mail: gtownfestival@aol.com. Website: www.germantownfest.com. **Contact:** Melba Fristick, coordinator. Estab. 1971. Arts and crafts show held annually the weekend after Labor Day. Outdoors. Accepts photography, all arts and crafts mediums. Number of exhibitors: 400+. Public attendance: 65,000. Free to public. Apply by sending applications by mail.

ADDITIONAL INFORMATION Deadline for entry: until filled. Application/space fee: $200–250. Exhibition space: 10×10. For more information, e-mail, call, or send SASE. Show located at Germantown Civic Club Complex, 7745 Poplar Pike.

TIPS "Display and promote to the public. Price attractively."

GERMANTOWN FRIENDS SCHOOL JURIED CRAFT SHOW

31 W. Coulter St., Philadelphia PA 19144. (215)900-7734. E-mail: craftshow@gfsnet.org. Website: www.germantownfriends.org/parents/parents-association/craft-show/index.aspx. This jewel of a show, located on the GFS campus, has been ranked among the top 10% of the nation's craft shows by the authoritative *ArtFair SourceBook*.

GLAM INDIE CRAFT SHOW

E-mail: glamcraftshow@gmail.com. Website: www.glamcraftshow.com. Fine arts and crafts fair held annually in December. Outdoors. Accepts handmade crafts, painting, sculpture, photography, drawing, fabric, crafts, ceramics, glass, and jewelry. Juried. Number of exhibitors: varies. Number of attendees: varies. Admission: $3 adults; children 10 and under free. Apply online.

ADDITIONAL INFORMATION Deadline for entry: September. Application fee: see website. Space fee: varies. Exhibition space: varies. For more information, e-mail or visit website.

GLENCOE FESTIVAL OF ART

Amdur Productions, P.O. Box 550, Highland Park IL 60035. (847)926-4300. Fax: (847)926-4330. E-mail: info@amdurproductions.com. Website: www.amdurproductions.com. Fine arts and crafts fair held annually in August. Outdoors. Accepts handmade crafts, painting, sculpture, photography, drawing, fabric, crafts, ceramics, glass, and jewelry. Juried. Number of exhibitors: 120. Number of attendees: 35,000. Free to public. Apply online.

ADDITIONAL INFORMATION Deadline for entry: see website. Application fee: $25. Space fee: varies. Exhibition space: varies. For more information, e-mail or visit website.

GLENVIEW OUTDOOR ART FAIR

Glenview Art League, P.O. Box 463, Glenview IL 60025-0463. (847)724-4007. E-mail: glenviewartleague@att.net. Website: www.glenviewartleague.org. Fine arts and crafts fair held annually in July. Outdoors. Accepts handmade crafts, paintings, sculpture, hand-pulled artist's prints (e.g., etchings), drawings, mixed media, ceramics, photography, and jewelry. Juried. Awards/prizes: Best of Show, awards of excellence, merit awards. Number of exhibitors: see website. Number of attendees: varies. Free to public. Apply online.

ADDITIONAL INFORMATION Deadline for entry: May. Application fee: $10. Space fee: varies. Exhibition space: 12×12. For more information, e-mail, call, or visit website.

GLENWOOD AVE. ARTS FEST

E-mail: info@glenwoodave.org. Website: www.glenwoodave.org.

ADDITIONAL INFORMATION "The Glenwood Ave. Arts Fest (GAAF) is a free weekend-long event that features artists, open studios, and live entertainment on 3 outdoor stages. Experience art, theater, music, as well as food and drink, on the brick-laid streets of the Glenwood Ave. Arts District in Chicago's historic Rogers Park neighborhood." For more information, visit website.

GLOUCESTER COUNTY SPRING CRAFT & HOME SHOW

B&K Enterprise, P.O. Box 925, Millville NJ 08332. (856)765-0118. Fax: (856)765-9050. E-mail: bkenterprisenj@aol.com. Website: www.gloucestercraftfair.com. **Contact:** Kathy Wright, organizer. Estab. 2010. Arts and crafts show held annually 1st Saturday in May. Indoors and outdoors. Accepts fine art and handmade crafts, home and garden, food. Awards/prizes: $100 for Best Spring Booth. Exhibitors: 150. Number of attendees: 2,500. Free to public. Apply via website. Application fee: none. Space fee: $40 (1 day) $75.00 (2 days). Exhibition space: 10×10. For more information, e-mail, visit website, or call. Event held at Gloucester Co. Fairgrounds, 275 Bridgeton Pike, Mullica Hill NJ 08098.

GLOUCESTER WATERFRONT FESTIVAL

38 Charles St., Rochester NH 03867. (603)332-2616. E-mail: info@castleberryfairs.com; terrym@worldpath.net. Website: www.castleberryfairs.com. **Contact:** Terry Mullen, events coordinator. Estab. 1971.

ADDITIONAL INFORMATION Arts and crafts show held the 3rd weekend in August in Gloucester, Massachusetts. Outdoors in Stage Fort Park. Accepts photography and all other mediums. Juried by photo, slide, or sample. Number of exhibitors: 225. Public attendance: 50,000. Free to public.

ADDITIONAL INFORMATION Deadline for entry: until full. Space fee: $375. Exhibition space: 10×10 . Average gross sales/exhibitor: "Generally, this is considered an 'excellent' show, so I would guess most exhibitors sell ten times their booth fee, or in this case, at least $3,500 in sales." For more information, visit website. Show located in Stage Fort Park, Hough Ave., Gloucester, New Hampshire.

TIPS "Do not bring a book; do not bring a chair. Smile and make eye contact with everyone who enters your booth. Have them sign your guest book; get their e-mail address so you can let them know when you are in the area again. And, finally, make the sale—they are at the fair to shop, after all."

GOLD CANYON ARTS FESTIVAL

5301 S. Superstition Mountain Dr., Suite 104, #183, Gold Canyon AZ 85118. E-mail: info. gcartsfest@gmail.com. Website: www.gcartsfest. com. Juried fine arts and fine crafts fair held annually the 4th Saturday in January. Outdoors. Accepts handmade crafts and other mediums. Juried. Number of exhibitors: 85. Number of attendees: 4,000. Free to public. Applications accepted after September 1.

ADDITIONAL INFORMATION Deadline for entry: November. Application fee: none. Space fee: $75. Exhibition space: 10×10. For more information, or application, visit website, or e-mail.

GOLD COAST ART FAIR

Amdur Productions, P.O. Box 550, Highland Park IL 60035. (847)926-4300. Fax: (847)926-4330. E-mail: info@amdurproductions.com. Website: www.amdurproductions.com. Fine arts and crafts fair held annually in June. Outdoors. Accepts handmade crafts and other mediums. Juried. Awards: announced at festival. Number of exhibitors: 300. Number of attendees: 100,000. Free to public. Apply online.

ADDITIONAL INFORMATION Deadline for entry: see website. Application fee: $35. Space fee: $595. Exhibition space: see website. For more information, e-mail, call, or visit website.

GOLDEN FINE ARTS FESTIVAL

1010 Washington Ave., Golden CO 80401. (303)279-3113. E-mail: info@goldencochamber. org. Website: www.goldenfineartsfestival.org. Fine arts and crafts fair held annually in August. Outdoors. Accepts handmade crafts, ceramics, fiber, glass, jewelry, mixed media, 2D, painting, photography, and sculpture. Juried. Number of exhibitors: see website. Number of attendees: 40,000. Free to public. Apply online.

ADDITIONAL INFORMATION Deadline for entry: April. Application fee: $25. Space fee: $350. Exhibition space: 10×10. For more information, e-mail, call, or visit website.

GOLD RUSH DAYS

Dahlonega Jaycees, P.O. Box 774, Dahlonega GA 30533. E-mail: info@dahlonegajaycees.com.

Website: www.dahlonegajaycees.com. Estab. 1954. Arts and crafts show held annually the 3rd full week in October. Accepts photography, paintings, and homemade, handcrafted items. No digitally originated artwork. Outdoors. Number of exhibitors: 300. Public attendance: 200,000. Free to public. Apply online at dahlonegajaycees.com.

ADDITIONAL INFORMATION Deadline: June 1. Exhibition space: 10×10. Show located at the public square and historic district.

TIPS "Talk to other artists who have done other shows and festivals. Get tips and advice from those in the same line of work."

GOT CRAFT?

5301 S. Superstition Mountain Dr., Suite 104, #183, Gold Canyon AZ 85118. E-mail: info@ gotcraft.com. Website: www.gotcraft.com.

ADDITIONAL INFORMATION "Founded in 2007, Got Craft? is held twice a year in May and December featuring 75+ handmade designers, craft workshops, tasty treats, music, FREE swag bags, and an average attendance of 6,000 a year." See website for more info.

GRAND LAKE FESTIVAL OF THE ARTS & CRAFTS

P.O. Box 429, Grand Lake CO 80447-0429. (970)627-3402. Fax: (970)627-8007. E-mail: glinfo@grandlakechamber.com. Website: www. grandlakechamber.com. Fine arts and crafts show held annually in June, July, and August. Outdoors. Accepts photography, jewelry, leather, mixed media, painting, paper, sculpture, wearable art. Juried by chamber committee. Awards/prizes: Best in Show and People's Choice. Number of exhibitors: 50–75. Public attendance: 1,000+. Free to public. Apply by submitting slides or photos.

ADDITIONAL INFORMATION Deadline for entry: early June, July, and August. Application fee: $190; includes space fee and business license. No electricity available. Exhibition space: 12x12. For more information, e-mail or call. Show held at Town Square Park on Grand Ave. in Grand Lake, Colorado.

GRAND LAKE STREAM FOLK ART FESTIVAL

P.O. Box 465, Princeton ME 04668-0465. (207)796-8199. E-mail: grandlakestreamfolkartfestival@gmail.com. **Contact:** Cathy or Bill Shamel. Estab. 1994. Arts and crafts show held annually last full weekend in July. Outdoors. Accepts handmade crafts, canoe building. Juried. Exhibitors: 60. Number of attendees: 3,000. Admission: $8. Apply via e-mail or call.

ADDITIONAL INFORMATION Deadline for entry: none. Application fee: none. Space fee: $300 (10×10); $450 (10×15); $600 (10×20). Exhibition space: 10×10; 10×15; 10×20. For more information, e-mail or call.

TIPS "Upscale display and good lighting."

GREAT GULFCOAST ARTS FESTIVAL

Website: www.ggaf.org.

ADDITIONAL INFORMATION "The Great Gulfcoast Arts Festival is a juried art show. Each year, we receive more than 600 applications for the festival. Each applicant is required to submit 3 images of their work and 1 image of their display area along with their application. Qualified jurors are shown each artist's images simultaneously and anonymously, and collectively choose more than 200 artists who will be invited to exhibit their work. Best of Show, Awards of Distinction, Awards of Excellence, Awards of Honor, and Awards of Merit winners from the previous year's festival are exempt from the jurying process." For moreinformation, visit website.

GREAT LAKES ART FAIR

46100 Grand River Ave., Novi MI 48374. (248) 486-3424. Fax: (248)347-7720. E-mail: info@greatlakesartfair.com. Website: www.greatlakesartfair.com. **Contact:** Andrea Picklo, event manager. Estab. 2009. Held in April. Accepts paintings, sculptures, metal and fiber work, jewelry, 2D and 3D art, ceramics, and glass. Cash prizes are given. Number of exhibitors: 150–200. Public attendance: 12,000–15,000. Application fee: $30. Space fee: $400–800. Exhibition space: 10×12. For more information, e-mail, visit website, or call.

GREAT MIDWEST ART FEST, THE

Amdur Productions, P.O. Box 550, Highland Park IL 60035. (847)926-4300. Fax: (847)926-4330. E-mail: info@amdurproductions.com. Website: www.amdurproductions.com. Estab. 2014. Art and craft show held annually in July. Outdoors. Accepts handmade crafts and other mediums. Juried. Number of exhibitors: 50. Number of attendees: varies. Free to public. Apply online.

ADDITIONAL INFORMATION Deadline for entry: early May. Application fee: $25. Space fee: $230. Exhibition space: 10×10. For more information, e-mail, call, or visit website.

TIPS "Visit our website! We have many tips for how to succeed as an artist!"

GREAT NECK STREET FAIR

Showtiques Crafts, Inc., 1 Orient Wy., Suite F, #127, Rutherford NJ 07070. (201)869-0406. E-mail: showtiques@gmail.com. Website: www.showtiques.com. Estab. 1978. Fine arts and crafts show held annually in early May (see website for details) in the Village of Great Neck. "Welcomes professional artists, craftspeople, and vendors of upscale giftware." Outdoors. Accepts photography, all arts and crafts made by the exhibitor. Juried. Number of exhibitors: 250. Public attendance: 50,000. Free to public.

ADDITIONAL INFORMATION Deadline for entry: until full. Space fee: $150–250. Exhibition space: 10×10. For more information, e-mail, call, or visit website.

GREEN VALLEY ART FESTIVAL

2050 W. State Route 89A, Lot 237, Cottonwood AZ 86326. (928)300-4711. E-mail: alan@runningbearproductions.net. Website: www.runningbearproductions.net. **Contact:** Alan Smith.

ADDITIONAL INFORMATION Fine art and craft show held 3 times a year. For more information, e-mail or visit website.

GREEN WITH INDIE

St. Louis Craft Mafia, St. Louis MO 63139. E-mail: stlouiscraftmafia@gmail.com. Website: www.greenwithindiecraftshow.com. **Contact:** Holly Schroeder. Fine arts and crafts fair held annually in March. Indoors. Accepts handmade crafts and vintage items. Emphasis on sustainable and "green" items. Juried. Number of exhibitors: 70. Number of attendees: 2,000+. Free to public. Apply online.

ADDITIONAL INFORMATION Deadline for entry: January. Application fee: $10. Space fee: varies $65–95. Exhibition space: 6×6 to 9×9. For more information, e-mail or visit website.

GUILFORD ART CENTER'S CRAFT EXPO

Guilford Art Center, P.O. Box 589, Guilford CT 06437. (203)453-5947. E-mail: expo@guilfordartcenter.org. Website: www.guilfordartcenter.org. Estab. 1957. Fine craft and art show held annually in mid-July. Outdoors. Accepts photography, wearable and nonwearable fiber, metal and nonmetal jewelry, clay, leather, wood, glass, painting, drawing, prints, mixed media, sculpture. Juried by 5 images of work, viewed sequentially. Number of exhibitors: 180. Public attendance: 8,000. Public admission: $7 and $9. Apply online at www.zapplication.org (preferred) or by downloading an application at www.guilfordartcenter.org.

ADDITIONAL INFORMATION Deadline for entry: early January. Application fee: $40. Space fee: $680. Exhibition space: 10×10. For more information, e-mail, visit website, or call.

GUMTREE FESTIVAL

GumTree Festival, P.O. Box 786, Tupelo MS 38802. (662)844-2787. Website: www.gumtreefestival.com.

ADDITIONAL INFORMATION "The Festival is highly respected, and brings an influx of 30,000 people to downtown Tupelo the actual weekend of the Festival. GumTree Festival showcases the artwork of around 100 artists from all over the South and beyond. GumTree Festival is an iconic institution for the fine arts." For more information, visit website.

HALIFAX ART FESTIVAL

P.O. Box 2038, Ormond Beach FL 32175-2038. (386)304-7247 or (407)701-1184. E-mail: patabernathy2012@hotmail.com. Website: www.halifaxartfestival.com. Estab. 1962. Fine arts and crafts fair held annually in November. Outdoors.

Accepts handmade crafts, ceramics, fiber, glass, jewelry, mixed media, 2D, painting, photography, and sculpture. Juried. Awards/prizes: Best of Show, Judges' Choice, Awards of Excellence, Awards of Distinction, Awards of Honor, Awards of Merit, Student Art Awards, Purchase Award, Patron Purchase Award. Number of exhibitors: 200. Number of attendees: 45,000. Free to public. Apply online.

ADDITIONAL INFORMATION Deadline for entry: August. Application fee: $30. Space fee: $225 (competitive); $125 (noncompetitive). Exhibition space: see website. For more information, e-mail, call, or visit website.

HAMPTON FALLS CRAFT FESTIVAL

38 Charles St., Rochester NH 03867. (603)332-2616. E-mail: info@castleberryfairs.com. Website: www.castleberryfairs.com. **Contact:** Terry and Chris Mullen. Estab. 2008. Fine arts and crafts fair held annually in September. Outdoors. Accepts handmade crafts and other mediums. Juried. Number of exhibitors: see website. Number of attendees: varies. Free to public. Apply online.

ADDITIONAL INFORMATION Deadline for entry: see website. Application fee: see website. Space fee: $225. Exhibition space: 10×10. For more information, e-mail, call, or visit website.

HANDMADE ARCADE

(412)654-3889. E-mail: info@handmadearcade.com. Website: www.handmadearcade.com; www.facebook.com/handmadearcade.

ADDITIONAL INFORMATION "Handmade Arcade (HA), founded in 2004, is Pittsburgh's first and largest independent craft fair. HA brings young, innovative crafters and progressive do-it-yourself designers to the David L. Lawrence Convention Center to sell their handmade, locally produced, and offbeat wares at a bustling marketplace. A highly anticipated annual event, HA attracts more than 8,000 attendees in 1 day. Spaces are $150. HA provides craft artists working outside mainstream and fine arts sectors with a grassroots, high-visibility venue to sell wares, build community, network, and share their artistic practice." For more information, visit website.

TIPS "Carefully planning your display for the space and following our guidelines that we put forth online every year. Consider your pricing carefully. We are happy to help newer vendors with this challenge. In the past, we have had vendors overprice and not do well and conversely underprice and sell out too quickly."

HANDMADE BABY FAIR
Om Baby, 2201 Rear Market St., Camp Hill PA 17011. (717)761-4975. E-mail: holly@ombabycenter.com. Website: www.ombabycenter.com/Handmade_Baby.html. Fine craft fair featuring local, handmade, natural, and sustainable baby products.
ADDITIONAL INFORMATION "If you are seeking unique, handmade, local baby and children's items, then this is the event to attend! You'll find everything from bibs to diapers, clothing and nursery décor for your special little1!" For more information, visit website.

HAND MADE CHICAGO
Plumbers Hall 1340 W. Washington Blvd., Chicago IL 60607. (847)926-4300. E-mail: caitlin@amdurproductions.com. Website: www.amdurproductions.com. **Contact:** Caitlin Pfleger, director of artists relations. Estab. 2016. Outdoors. Accepts handmade crafts, paintings, ceramics, fiber, glass, jewelry, and wood. Juried. Prizes awarded. Average number of exhibitors: 100. Average number of attendees: 15,000. Free to public.
ADDITIONAL INFORMATION Deadline: rolling admission. Application fee: $35. Space fee: $350. Square footage of the space: 10×10. Average gross sales for a typical exhibitor: Depends on the piece being sold. For more information, e-mail, visit website, or call.

HANDMADE CITY SPRING FAIR
E-mail: handmadecityinfo@gmail.com. Website: www.handmade-city.com. Fine arts and crafts fair held annually in December. Indoors. Accepts handmade crafts and other mediums. Juried. Number of exhibitors: see website. Number of attendees: varies. Free to public. Apply online.

ADDITIONAL INFORMATION Deadline for entry: October. Application fee: none. Space fee: $40. Exhibition space: 6×10. For more information, e-mail or visit website.

HANDMADE MARKET CHICAGO
Website: www.handmadechicago.com.
ADDITIONAL INFORMATION "Handmade Market is a unique event to connect the makers of beautiful things to people who appreciate the unique and handmade." For more information, visit website.

HANDMADE TOLEDO MAKER'S MART
Website: www.handmadetoledo.com.
ADDITIONAL INFORMATION "45+ handmade vendors from all over the Midwest will showcase their wares for a 1-day pop-up shop. Grab some grub from local food trucks and bakeries, sip on some locally roasted coffee, enjoy the sounds of some of Toledo's talented buskers, shop handmade, and celebrate 419 Day with us! Handmade fun for the whole family! There will be kid-friendly activities, crafty make and takes, and much more!" For more information, visit website.

HANDWEAVERS GUILD OF BOULDER ANNUAL SALE
Barbara Olson, 2111 Hermosa Dr., Boulder CO 80304. (303)444-1010. E-mail: frey.barb@gmail.com. Website: www.handweaversofboulder.org. Fine arts and crafts fair held annually in October. Accepts handmade crafts. Juried. Open to members only. Awards/prizes: Juror's Award, People's Choice Award. Number of exhibitors: see website. Number of attendees: varies. Free to public. Apply online.
ADDITIONAL INFORMATION Deadline for entry: October. Application fee: $15. Space fee: see website. Exhibition space: see website. For more information, e-mail, call, or visit website.

HARD CANDY CHRISTMAS ART/CRAFT SHOW
92 Catamount Dr., Cullowhee NC 28763. (828)524-3405. E-mail: djhunter@dnet.net. Website: www.mountainartisans.net. **Contact:**

Doris Hunter, owner. Estab. 1987. Annual event. Held Friday and Saturday after Thanksgiving. Indoors. Accepts handmade crafts, fine art/folk art. Juried. 3 photos of work, 1 of display. No prizes given. Average number of exhibitors: 100. Average number of attendees: 2,800. Admission fee for public: $4.50 for adults, children under 12 free.

ADDITIONAL INFORMATION Deadline for applications: September 15, 2015. Application fee: $0. Space fee: $180. Square footage of space: 10×10. Average gross sales for typical exhibitor: $750. For more information, e-mail, visit website, or call.

TIPS Be original and cover your tables to the floor!

⊕ HARVEST FESTIVAL ORIGINAL ART & CRAFT SHOW

1145 Second St., Ste. A332, Brentwood CA 94513. (925) 392-7300. Fax: (925)-392-7303. E-mail: info@harvestfestival.com. Website: www.harvestfestival.com. **Contact:** Tony Glenn. Arts and crafts show held annually September–December. Indoors. Accepts handmade crafts. Juried. Number of exhibitors: varies. Number of attendees: 12,000+. Admission fee: $9 adults; $7 seniors; $4 youth; 12 and under free. Apply online.

ADDITIONAL INFORMATION Deadline for entry: until filled. Space fee: 10×10, $795; 10×15, $1192.50; 10×20, $1590 ($7.95/sq.ft.). Exhibition space: varies by location and size; corners additional $125. For more information, e-mail or visit website.

HEARTFEST: A FINE ART SHOW

Stookey Companies, P.O. Box 31083, Des Moines IA 50310. (515)278-6200. Fax: (515)276-7513. E-mail: suestookey@att.net. Website: www.stookeyshows.com. Fine art and fine crafts fair held annually in February on the weekend before Valentine's Day. Indoors. Accepts handmade artwork. Juried. Number of exhibitors: see website. Number of attendees: see website. Free to public. Apply online at www.zapplication.org.

ADDITIONAL INFORMATION Deadline for entry: January. Application fee: $25. Space fee: $185. Exhibition space: varies. For more information, e-mail, call, or visit website.

HERKIMER COUNTY ARTS & CRAFTS FAIR

100 Reservoir Rd., Herkimer NY 13350. (315)866-0300, ext. 8459. Fax: (315)866-1706. E-mail: fuhrerjm@herkimer.edu. Website: www.herkimer.edu/ac. **Contact:** Jan Fuhrer, coordinator. Estab. 1976. Fine art and craft show held annually in mid-November on Veterans Day weekend. Indoors. Accepts photography and all handcrafted artwork. Juried by a committee. Awards/prizes: ribbons. Number of exhibitors: 120+. Public attendance: 4,000. Admission: $4.

ADDITIONAL INFORMATION Deadline: May 1 or until filled. Application fee: $10. Exhibition space: 10×6. Space fee: $155. For more information, call, e-mail, or send SASE.

HIGHLAND MAPLE FESTIVAL

P.O. Box 223, Monterey VA 24465. (540)468-2550. Fax: (540)468-2551. E-mail: findyourescape@highlandcounty.org. Website: www.highlandcounty.org. Estab. 1958. Fine arts and crafts show held annually the 2nd and 3rd weekends in March. Indoors and outdoors. Accepts photography, pottery, weaving, jewelry, painting, wood crafts, furniture. Juried by 5 photos or slides. Photos need to include 1 of setup and your workshop. Number of exhibitors: 150. Public attendance: 35,000–50,000.

ADDITIONAL INFORMATION "Vendors accepted until show is full." Exhibition space: 10×10. For more information, e-mail, call, or visit website.

TIPS "Have quality work and good salesmanship."

HIGHLAND PARK FESTIVAL OF FINE CRAFT

Amdur Productions, P.O. Box 550, Highland Park IL 60035. (847)926-4300. Fax: (847)926-4330. E-mail: info@amdurproductions.com. Website: www.amdurproductions.com. Fine arts and crafts fair held annually in June. Outdoors. Accepts handmade crafts, ceramics, fiber, glass, jewelry, wood, and more. Juried. Number of exhibitors: 130. Number of attendees: varies. Free to public. Apply online.

ADDITIONAL INFORMATION Deadline for entry: April. Application fee: $35. Space fee: $455. Exhibition space: 10×10. For more information, e-mail, call, or visit website.

HIGHLANDS ART LEAGUE'S ANNUAL FINE ARTS & CRAFTS FESTIVAL

1989 Lakeview Dr., Sebring FL 33870. (863)385-6682. E-mail: director@highlandsartleague.org. Website: www.highlandsartleague.org. **Contact:** Martile Blackman, festival director. Estab. 1966. Fine arts and crafts show held annually 1st Saturday in November. Outdoors. Accepts photography, pottery, painting, jewelry, fabric. Juried based on quality of work. Awards/prizes: monetary awards. Number of exhibitors: 100+. Public attendance: more than 15,000. Free to public. Apply by calling or visiting website for application form.

ADDITIONAL INFORMATION Deadline for entry: September 1. Exhibition space: 10×14 and 10×28. For more information, e-mail, or visit website. Festival held in Circle Park in downtown Sebring.

HIGHWOOD LAST CALL ART FAIR

Amdur Productions, P.O. Box 550, Highland Park IL 60035. (847)926-4300. Fax: (847)926-4330. E-mail: info@amdurproductions.com. Website: www.amdurproductions.com.

ADDITIONAL INFORMATION "The Highwood Last Call Art Fair features great art at great prices. The show gives the public the chance to buy end-of-the-season original art, leftover inventory, slightly damaged, bruised, and odd pieces at discounted prices. Artists decide how much to discount their work and can use festival stickers to mark work at 10% to 50% off." For more information, visit website.

HILTON HEAD ISLAND ART FESTIVAL WITH CRAFT MARKETPLACE

270 Central Blvd., Suite 107B, Jupiter FL 33458. (561)746-6615. Fax: (561)746-6528. E-mail: info@artfestival.com. Website: www.artfestival.com. **Contact:** Malinda Ratliff, communications manager. Estab. 2009. Fine art and craft fair held annually in late May. Outdoors. Accepts photography, jewelry, mixed media, sculpture, wood, ceramic, glass, painting, digital, fiber, metal. Juried. Number of exhibitors: 100. Number of attendees: 60,000. Free to public. Apply online via www.zapplication.org.

ADDITIONAL INFORMATION Deadline: see website. Application fee: $25. Space fee: $375. Exhibition space: 10×10 and 10×20. For more information, e-mail, call, or visit website. Festival located at Shelter Cove Harbour and Marina on Hilton Head Island.

HINSDALE FINE ARTS FESTIVAL

22 E. First St., Hinsdale IL 60521. (630)323-3952. Fax: (630)323-3953. E-mail: info@hinsdalechamber.com. Website: www.hinsdalechamber.com. Fine arts show held annually in mid-June. Outdoors. Accepts photography, ceramics, painting, sculpture, fiber arts, mixed media, jewelry. Juried by 3 images. Awards/prizes: Best in Show, President's Award and 1st, 2nd, and 3rd place in 2D and 3D categories. Number of exhibitors: 140. Public attendance: 2,000–3,000. Free to public. Apply online at www.zapplication.org.

ADDITIONAL INFORMATION Deadline for entry: 1st week in March. Application fee: $30. Space fee: $275. Exhibition space: 10×10. For more information, E-mail or visit website.

TIPS "Original artwork sold by artist."

HISTORIC SHAW ART FAIR

(314)771-3101. E-mail: greg@gobdesign.com. Website: www.shawartfair.org. **Contact:** Greg Gobberdiel, coordinator. Fine arts and crafts fair held annually in October. Outdoors. Accepts handmade crafts, ceramics, fiber, glass, jewelry, mixed media, painting, photography, and sculpture. Juried. Number of exhibitors: see website. Number of attendees: varies. Free to public. Apply online.

ADDITIONAL INFORMATION Deadline for entry: April. Application fee: $25. Space fee: $280. Exhibition space: 10×10. For more information, e-mail, call, or visit website.

HOBE SOUND FESTIVAL OF THE ARTS & CRAFT SHOW

270 Central Blvd., Suite 107B, Jupiter FL 33458. (561)746-6615. Fax: (561)746-6528. E-mail: info@artfestival.com. Website: www.artfestival.com. **Contact:** Malinda Ratliff, communications

manager. Estab. 2006. Fine art and craft fair held annually in February. Outdoors. Accepts photography, jewelry, mixed media, sculpture, wood, ceramic, glass, painting, digital, fiber, metal. Juried. Number of exhibitors: 130. Number of attendees: 70,000. Free to public. Apply online via www.zapplication.org.

ADDITIONAL INFORMATION Deadline: see website. Application fee: $25. Space fee: $395. Exhibition space: 10×10 and 10×20. For more information, e-mail, call, or visit website. Show located at A1A/Dixie Hwy. where the street intersects with Bridge Rd., in Hobe Sound, Florida.

HOLIDAY CRAFT & VENDOR SHOW

140 Oak St., Frankfort IL 60423. (815)469-9400. **Fax:** (815)469-9275. E-mail: cdebella@frankfortparks.org. Website: www.frankfortparks.org. **Contact:** Cali DeBella, special events coordinator. Estab. 1993. Arts and crafts/holiday show held annually in November. Indoors. Accepts handmade crafts. Exhibitors: 65. Number of attendees: 500–700. Free to public. Apply online.

ADDITIONAL INFORMATION Deadline for entry: early October. Application fee: $45. Space fee: $45. Exhibition space: 10×6. For more information, e-mail, or visit website.

HOLIDAY CRAFTMORRISTOWN

P.O. Box 28, Woodstock NY 12498. (845)331-7900. Fax: (845)331-7484. E-mail: crafts@artrider.com. Website: www.artrider.com. Estab. 1990. Fine arts and crafts show held annually in early December. Indoors. Accepts photography, wearable and nonwearable fiber, jewelry, clay, leather, wood, glass, painting, drawing, prints, mixed media. Juried by 5 images of work and 1 of booth, viewed sequentially. Number of exhibitors: 165. Public attendance: 5,000. Public admission: $9. Apply online at www.artrider.com or www.zapplication.org.

ADDITIONAL INFORMATION Deadline for entry: end of May. Application fee: $45. Space fee: $545. Exhibition space: 10×10. For more information, e-mail, call, or visit website.

HOLIDAY FINE ARTS & CRAFTS SHOW

60 Ida Lee Dr., Leesburg VA 20176. (703)777-1368. Fax: (703)737-7165. E-mail: lfountain@leesburgva.gov. Website: www.idalee.org. **Contact:** Linda Fountain. Estab. 1990. Fine arts and crafts show held annually the 1st full weekend in December. Indoors. Accepts handcrafted items only, including but not limited to: photography, jewelry, pottery, baskets, clothing, gourmet food products, wood work, fine art, accessories, pet items, soaps/lotions, and florals. Juried. Number of exhibitors: 99. Public attendance: 2,500+. Free to public. Apply by downloading application from website.

ADDITIONAL INFORMATION Deadline for entry: August 18. Space fee: $110–150. Exhibition space: 10×7. and 10×10. For more information, e-mail or visit website.

HOLIDAY HANDMADE CAVALCADE

Website: www.handmadecavalcade.com.

ADDITIONAL INFORMATION "The Handmade Cavalcade is a biannual craft fair in NYC, put together by the dedication and DIY drive of Etsy New York and local New York metro area Etsy sellers. Come out and shop the unique handmade gifts of your local Etsy Shops while snacking on locally made sweets and connecting with other small crafty businesses." For more information, visit website.

HOLIDAY SIZZLE — POTOMAC FIBER ARTS GALLERY

Website: www.potomacfiberartsgallery.com.

ADDITIONAL INFORMATION "Potomac Fiber Arts Gallery (Studio 18) announces the opening of the juried show 'Holiday Sizzle.' In this show, our artists excel in holiday spirit and sparkle. Whether for self or gifts, jewelry, sculpture, clothing, and wall pieces are some of the items that will be exhibited." For more information, visit website.

HOLLY ARTS & CRAFTS FESTIVAL

P.O. Box 64, Pinehurst NC 28370. (910)295-7462. E-mail: info@pinehurstbusinessguild.com. Website: www.pinehurstbusinessguild.com. Estab. 1978. Annual arts and crafts show held 3rd Saturday in October. Outdoors. Accepts quality photography, arts, and crafts. Juried based on uniqueness, quality of product, and overall display. Number of exhibitors: 200. Public attendance: 7,000. Free to public. Submit 3 color photos, 2 of work to be exhibited, 1 of booth.

ADDITIONAL INFORMATION Deadline: late March. Application fee: $25 by separate check. Space fee: $75. Electricity fee: $5 Exhibition space: 10×10. For more information, call or visit website.

HOME DECORATING & REMODELING SHOW

P.O. Box 230699, Las Vegas NV 89105-0699. (702)450-7984; (800)343-8344. Fax: (702)451-7305. E-mail: showprosadmin@cox.net. Website: www.nashvillehomeshow.com. Estab. 1983. Home show held annually in early September (see website for details). Indoors. Accepts photography, sculpture, watercolor, oils, mixed media, pottery. Awards/prizes: Outstanding Booth Award. Number of exhibitors: 350–400. Public attendance: 15,000. Public admission: $10 (discount coupon available on website); Seniors 62+ free on Friday; children 12 and under free with adult. Apply by calling. Marketing is directed to middle-and-above income brackets.

ADDITIONAL INFORMATION Deadline for entry: open until filled. Space fee: starts at $950. Exhibition space: 10×10. or complements of 10×10. For more information, call or visit website.

HOMEWOOD FINE ARTS & CRAFTS FESTIVAL

Pacific Fine Arts Festivals, P.O. Box 280, Pine Grove CA 95665. (209)267-4394. Fax: (209)267-4395. E-mail: pfa@pacificfinearts.com. Website: www.pacificfinearts.com. This free event brings together an exciting group of more than 50 artists showcasing an assortment of collectible arts and crafts in a variety of media including paintings, ceramics, jewelry, woodwork, photography, and much more. For more information, visit website.

HONOLULU GLASS ART & BEAD FESTIVAL

Soft Flex Company, Attn: Sara Oehler/Scott Clark, P.O. Box 80, Sonoma CA 95476. (707)732-3513. Fax: (707)938-3097. E-mail: thomas@softflexcompany.com; sara@softflexcompany.com. Website: www.softflexcompany.com/WSWrapper.jsp?mypage=FestivalHI_Main.html. Beading event held semiannually in March and September. Indoors. Accepts beads, gemstones, findings, collectible glass art, and jewelry. Juried. Number of exhibitors: see website. Number of attendees: see website. Free to public. Apply online.

ADDITIONAL INFORMATION Deadline for entry: March. Application fee: see website. Space fee: varies. Exhibition space: varies. For more information, e-mail, call, or visit website.

HOPI FESTIVAL OF ARTS & CULTURE

(928)774-5213. Website: www.musnaz.org/hp/hopi_fest.shtml. A4th of July tradition since the 1930s, the Hopi Festival of Arts and Culture is the oldest Hopi show in the world. Attendees will enjoy 2 days of authentic food, artist demonstrations, musical performances, dancing, and a not-to-be missed children's area that will entertain the young at heart with take-home crafts related to Hopi culture. For more information, visit website.

HOT SPRINGS ARTS & CRAFTS FAIR

308 Pullman, Hot Springs AR 71901. (501)623-9592. E-mail: sephpipkin@aol.com. Website: www.hotspringsartsandcraftsfair.com. **Contact:** Peggy Barnett. Estab. 1968. Fine arts and crafts show held annually the 1st full weekend in October at the Garland County Fairgrounds. Indoors and outdoors. Accepts photography and varied mediums ranging from heritage, crafts, jewelry, furniture. Juried by a committee of 12 volunteers. Number of exhibitors: 350+. Public attendance: 50,000+. Free to public.

ADDITIONAL INFORMATION Deadline for entry: August. Space fee: $125 (single); $250 (double). Exhibition space: 10×10 or 10×20. For more information,and to apply, e-mail, call, or visit website. Fair located at Garland County Fairgrounds.

HUDSON MOHAWK WEAVERS GUILD ANNUAL SHOW & SALE

Website: www.hmwg.org/showandsale.html.

ADDITIONAL INFORMATION "For 4 days each November, the Guild takes over the historic Pruyn House and turns it into a showcase for the best of modern handweaving, from traditional to contemporary. Guild members work all year to produce a tremendous variety of handwoven items, from rugs and other home goods to clothing pieces such as scarves, shawls, and jackets. Holiday gifts such as cards and ornaments are also available. Each room in the Pruyn House is devoted to a particular class of items such as linens or scarves and staffed with an accomplished local weaver to assist and answer questions. Admission is free, and visitors can watch fashion shows featuring woven goods or take in demonstrations of handweaving and spinning." For more information, visit website.

HUNGRY MOTHER ARTS & CRAFTS FESTIVAL

Website: www.hungrymotherfestival.com. Every summer the Hungry Mother State Park, in Marion, Virginia, opens its doors to visitors and artisans from all over the country.3 days of art, entertainment, food, and fun are guaranteed. For more information, and to apply, visit website.

HYDE PARK ARTS & CRAFTS ADVENTURE

P.O. Box 1326, Palatine IL 60078. (312)751-2500, (847)991-4748. E-mail: asoaartists@aol.com. Website: www.americansocietyofartists.org. Estab. 2006. Arts and crafts show held once a year in late September. Event held in Chicago. Outdoors. Accepts photography, painting, glass, wood, fiber arts, handcrafted candles, quilts, sculpture, and more. Juried. Please submit 4 images representative of your work you wish to exhibit, 1 of your display setup, your first/last name, physical address, daytime telephone number—résumé/show listings helpful. Number of exhibitors: 50. Free to public. Apply by submitting jury materials to asoaartists@aol.com. If juried in, you will receive a jury/approval number. For more information, visit website.

ADDITIONAL INFORMATION Deadline for entry: 2 months prior to show or earlier if available. Entry fee: to be announced. Exhibition space: about 100 sq.. for single space; other sizes available. For more information, send SASE, submit jury material. Show located at University of Chicago's Hyde Park Shopping Center.

TIPS "Remember that when you are at work in your studio, you are an artist. But when you are at a show, you are a business person selling your work."

HYDE PARK SQUARE ART SHOW

P.O. Box 8402, Cincinnati OH 45208. E-mail: hpartshowinfo@aol.com. Website: www.hydeparksquare.org. Fine arts and crafts fair held annually in October. Outdoors. Accepts handmade crafts, ceramics, fiber, glass, jewelry, mixed media, 2D, painting, photography, and sculpture. Juried. Awards/prizes: Best of Show, 1st, 2nd, 3rd, honorable mention. Number of exhibitors: see website. Number of attendees: see website. Free to public. Apply online.

ADDITIONAL INFORMATION Deadline for entry: March. Application fee: $40. Space fee: $130. Exhibition space: see website. For more information, and to apply, visit website.

IMAGES — A FESTIVAL OF THE ARTS

(386)423-4733. E-mail: images@imagesartfestival.org. Website: www.imagesartfestival.org. Fine arts and crafts fair held annually in January. Outdoors. Accepts handmade crafts, ceramics, fiber, glass, jewelry, mixed media, 2D, painting, photography, and sculpture. Juried. Awards/prizes: $100,000 in awards and prizes. Number of exhibitors: 225. Number of attendees: 45,000. Free to public. Apply online.

ADDITIONAL INFORMATION Deadline for entry: October. Application fee: $40. Space fee: $250. Exhibition space: 11×12. For more information, e-mail, call, or visit website.

INDIANA ART FAIR

650 W. Washington St., Indianapolis IN 46204. (317)233-9348. Fax: (317)233-8268. E-mail: cmiller@indianamuseum.org. Website: www. indianamuseum.org. Estab. 2004. Annual art/craft show held the 2nd weekend of February. Indoors. Juried; 5–6 judges award points in 3 categories. Number of exhibitors: 60. Number of attendees: 3,000. $13 admission for the public. Application fee $25. Space fee $165; 80 sq. ft. Accepts ceramics, glass, fiber, jewelry, painting, sculpture, mixed media, drawing/pastels, garden, leather, surface decoration, wood, metal, printmaking, and photography.

TIPS "Make sure that your booth space complements your product and presents well. Good photography can be key for juried shows."

INDIAN WELLS ARTS FESTIVAL

78-200 Miles Ave., Indian Wells CA 92210. (760)346-0042. Fax: (760)346-0042. E-mail: info@indianwellsartsfestival.com. Website: www. indianwellsartsfestival.com. **Contact:** Dianne Funk, producer.

ADDITIONAL INFORMATION "A premier fine arts festival attracting thousands annually. The Indian Wells Arts Festival brings a splash of color to the beautiful grass concourse of the Indian Wells Tennis Garden. This spectacular venue transforms into an artisan village featuring 200 judged and juried artists and hundreds of pieces of 1-of-a-kind artwork available for sale. Enjoy special exhibits and demonstrations. Watch glassblowing, monumental rock sculpting, wood carving, pottery wheel, weaving and painting. Wine tasting, gourmet market, children's activities, entertainment and refreshments add to the festival atmosphere." Apply online at indianwellsartsfestival.com/artists.html. For more information, visit website.

INDIE CRAFT BAZAAR

E-mail: indiecraftbazaar@gmail.com. Website: www.getupandcraft.com/Indie_Craft_Bazaar.html.

ADDITIONAL INFORMATION "Indie Craft Bazaar is your local source for orginal art, handmade items, vintage, recycled, and vegan goods! These 'ain't your grandma's crafts!" ICB is a pop-up shop filled with all sorts of imaginative, impressive and, oftentimes quirky, handmade curiosities! Support our community, small business, and the arts by joining us at the next show! Admission is $5." See website for more info.

INDIE CRAFT EXPERIENCE

E-mail: craft@ice-atlanta.com. Website: www. ice-atlanta.com.

ADDITIONAL INFORMATION "The Indie Craft Experience was founded in January 2005. With a vision to provide indie crafters an opportunity to sell and promote their creations in Atlanta, ICE quickly caught on as a favorite event for participants and attendees alike. ICE is a grassroots effort, organized by 2 Atlanta crafters—Christy Petterson and Shannon Mulkey. Inspired by indie craft markets in Chicago and Austin, the Indie Craft Experience was founded in order to provide Atlanta with a major indie craft event. In addition to craft markets, ICE also organizes a vintage market called Salvage and an annual Pop-Up Shop during the holiday season." For more information, visit website.

INDIE CRAFT PARADE

E-mail: info@makerscollective.org. Website: www.indiecraftparade.com. **Contact:** Elizabeth Ramos. Estab. 2010. Annual arts & crafts show held annually in Greenville, South Carolina, in September 2 weekends after Labor Day. Indoors. Accepts handmade crafts, 2D/3D fine art, fiber art, paper goods, handmade wearables, and toys, home and garden, artisan food, supplies, etc. Juried. Awards/prizes: small cash prize for best booth display. Exhibitors: 80. Number of attendees: 7,000. Admission: $2; children free. Apply via website.

ADDITIONAL INFORMATION Deadline for entry: June 25. Application fee: $20. Space fee: $95 and $125. Exhibition space: 32 sq. ft.; 16 sq. ft. Average sales: $3,000. For more information, e-mail or visit website.

TIPS "To sell successfully, understand your market. Attendees at Indie Craft include a vast range from high school/college students to well-established families to retired adults. Have products that fit within a variety of price ranges;

make a well-built display that prominently shows your products; be engaging with your potential customers."

INDIEMADE CRAFT MARKET

P.O. Box 3204, Allentown PA 18106. (610)703-8004. E-mail: ann@indiemadecraftmarket.com. Website: www.indiemadecraftmarket.com. **Contact:** Ann Biernat-Rucker, co-producer. Estab. 2007. Arts and craft show held annually the 1st Saturday in December. Indoors. Accepts handmade crafts. Juried. Exhibitors: see website. Number of attendees: see website. Admission: $3. Apply online.

ADDITIONAL INFORMATION Deadline for entry: April 1. Application fee: none. Space fee: $50. Exhibition space: 8. table. For more information, visit website.

INDIE SOUTH FAIR

660 N. Chase St., Athens GA 30601. E-mail: indiesouthfair@gmail.com. Website: www.indiesouthfair.com. **Contact:** Serra Ferguson, organizer. Estab. 2007. Arts and Crafts show held semiannually the 1st weekends of May and December. Outdoors. Accepts handmade crafts and all other mediums. Exhibitors: 100. Number of attendees: 5,000. Free to public. Apply via website.

ADDITIONAL INFORMATION Deadline for entry: March for spring show; September 28 for holiday market. Application fee: $15. Space fee: $175 (10×10). Exhibition space: 10×10. Average sales: $800–1,200. For more information, e-mail.

TIPS "Create beautiful and functional art, present it well, and have a friendly, outgoing demeanor."

INGLE FEST HANDMADE CRAFT FAIR

Website: www.eventcalifornia.com.

ADDITIONAL INFORMATION "One of the largest handmade tabletop craft fair events in San Jose and in the San Francisco Bay Area. Jingle Fest Craft Fair is a curated handmade craft marketplace showcasing the best Bay Area talents in contemporary craft and artwork. Our show brings the best local artists and designers out of their studios and workshops and into the spotlight for a festive 1-day celebration of everything handmade." For more information, visit website.

ISLE OF EIGHT FLAGS SHRIMP FESTIVAL

P.O. Box 17251, Fernandina Beach FL 32035. (904)701-2786; (904) 261-7020. Website: www.islandart.org. Estab. 1963. Fine arts and crafts show and community celebration held annually the 1st weekend in May. Outdoors. Accepts all mediums. Juried. Awards: $9,000 in cash prizes. Number of exhibitors: 300. Public attendance: 150,000. Free to public. Apply by downloading application from website. Slides are not accepted. Digital images in JPEG format only must be submitted on a CD/DVD with application.

ADDITIONAL INFORMATION Deadline for entry: January 31. Application fee: $30 (nonrefundable). Space fee: $225. Exhibition space: 10×12. Average gross sales/exhibitor: $1,500+. For more information, visit website.

ITASCA ART & WINE FESTIVAL

Village of Itasca, 550 W. Irving Park Rd., Itasca IL 60143-1795. (630)773-0835. Fax: (630)773-2505. Website: www.itasca.com.

ADDITIONAL INFORMATION "Annual juried Fine Arts and Wine Festival, Benches on Parade, takes place in historic downtown Itasca, located in scenic Usher Park near the gateway to the newly created River Walk. There will be live music in the gazebo, a backdrop for meandering through the winding walkways of the park with wine tasting and painted iron benches (up for silent auction) on display throughout." For more information, visit website or call.

JACKSON HOLE FALL ARTS FESTIVAL

(307)733-3316. Website: www.jacksonholechamber.com/fall_arts_festival.

ADDITIONAL INFORMATION "The Jackson Hole Fall Arts Festival is widely recognized as 1 of the premier cultural events in the Rocky Mountain West. Thousands of art enthusiasts are drawn each year to experience the diverse artwork and breathtaking natural surroundings that make Jackson Hole a leading cultural center. Experience the world-class installments of contemporary, culinary, landscape, Native American, wildlife, and Western arts. Visitors will appreciate the works of nationally and internationally acclaimed artists along with an exceptional array of art, music, cuisine, and wine. More than 50 events round out our 11-day festival." For more information, visit website.

JAMAICA PLAIN OPEN STUDIOS

Jamaica Plain Arts Council, JPAC, P.O. Box 300222, Jamaica Plain MA 02130. (617)855-5767. E-mail: coordinator@jpopenstudios.com. Website: www.jpopenstudios.com.

ADDITIONAL INFORMATION "Jamaica Plain Open Studios is the premier annual arts event in1 of Boston's most eclectic neighborhoods. JPOS is an opportunity to take a rare public peek at some private spaces. The free event showcases the artwork of over 200 artists at dozens of sites including artists' studios, the historic Eliot School, the Sam Adams brewery complex, the Arnold Arboretum, and more." For more information, visit website.

JEFFERSON QUILT SHOW QUILTS ON THE BAYOU

120 E. Austin St., Jefferson TX 75657. (903)926-6695. E-mail: jqshow@yahoo.com. Website: www.jeffersonquiltshow.com. Contact: Edris McCrary. Estab. 2002. Quilt show held annually in January. Indoors. Accepts handmade crafts. Juried. Exhibitors: 150. Number of attendees: 1,200–1,500. Admission: $5 adults; $4 children. Apply online.

ADDITIONAL INFORMATION Deadline for entry: until full. Application fee: $5 per item. Space fee: varies. Exhibition space: varies. For more information, ,e-mail or visit website.

JOHNS HOPKINS UNIVERSITY SPRING FAIR

3400 N. Charles St., Mattin, Suite 210, Baltimore MD 21218. (410)516-7692. Fax: (410)516-6185. E-mail: springfair@gmail.com. Website: www.jhuspringfair.com. Estab. 1972. Fine arts and crafts, campus-wide festival held annually in April. Outdoors. Accepts photography and all mediums. Juried. Number of exhibitors: 80. Public attendance: 20,000+. Free to public. Apply via website.

ADDITIONAL INFORMATION Deadline for entry: early March. Application and space fee: $200. Exhibition space: 10×10. For more information, e-mail, call, or visit website. Fair located on Johns Hopkins Homewood Campus.
TIPS "Artists should have fun displays, good prices, good variety, and quality pieces."

JUBILEE FESTIVAL

Eastern Shore Chamber of Commerce, Olde Towne Daphne, P.O. Drawer 310, Daphne AL 36526. (251)621-8222; (251)928-6387. Fax: (251)621-8001. E-mail: lroberts@eschamber.com; office@eschamber.com. Website: www.eschamber.com. **Contact:** Liz R. Thomson. Estab. 1952. Fine arts and crafts show held in late September in Olde Towne of Daphne, Alabama. Outdoors. Accepts photography and fine arts and crafts. Juried. Awards/prizes: ribbons and cash prizes total $4,300 with Best of Show $750. Number of exhibitors: 258. Free to public. Jury fee: $20. Space fee: $100 for single; $200 for double. Exhibition space: 10×10. or 10×20. For more information, and application form, e-mail, call, or visit website. Festival located in "Olde Towne" Daphne on Main St.

JUNO BEACH CRAFT FESTIVAL ON THE OCEAN

270 Central Blvd., Suite 107B, Jupiter FL 33458. (561)746-6615. Fax: (561)746-6528. E-mail: info@artfestival.com. Website: www.artfestival.com. **Contact:** Malinda Ratliff, communications manager.

ADDITIONAL INFORMATION "Join us in Jupiter for another fantastic weekend craft festival. Shop handcrafted leather goods, paintings, photography, personalized products, glassworks, and much more—all made in the USA! A Palm Beach favorite, this craft festival is not to be missed! Stroll along the scenic A1A and shop handmade fine crafts that suit every budget, while visiting with some of the nation's best crafters. Get a jumpstart on holiday gifts at this fabulous free craft event." For more information, visit website.

KEEPSAKE COLLECTION ART & CRAFT SHOWS

(989)681-4023 or (989)781-9165. E-mail: craftpeddler@nethawk.com; bonnmur9@aol.com. Website: www.keepsakecollectionshows.com. **Contact:** Leslie Needham or Bonnie Murin.

ADDITIONAL INFORMATION "The Keepsake Collection endeavors to connect quality artists and craftspeople with interested buyers of unique and desirable workmanship. To ensure this goal, categories are limited both in scope and number. You'll always find professional-quality exhibitors and merchandise at our shows, as all are juried. Advertising is extensive; including direct mail, postcards, flyers, radio advertising, newspaper ads, in-ground signs, billboards, etc." For more information, visit website.

KENTUCK FESTIVAL OF THE ARTS

503 Main Ave., Northport AL 35476. (205)758-1257. Fax: (205)758-1258. E-mail: kentuck@kentuck.org. Website: www.kentuck.org. **Contact:** Amy Echols, executive director. For more information, e-mail or visit website.

ADDITIONAL INFORMATION "Celebrates a variety of artistic styles ranging from folk to contemporary arts as well as traditional crafts. Each of the 250+ artists participating in the festival is either invited as a guest artist or is juried based on the quality and originality of their work. The guest artists are nationally recognized folk and visionary artists whose powerful visual images continue to capture national and international acclaim." Festival held at Kentuck Park.

KENTUCKY CRAFTED

Capital Plaza Tower, 500 Mero St., 21st Floor, Frankfort KY 40601-1987. (502)564-3757 or (888)833-2787. Fax: (502)564-2839. E-mail: Ed.Lawrence@ky.gov. Website: www.artscouncil.ky.gov/KentuckyArt/Event_Market.htm. Art and craft market/show held annually in March. Indoors. Accepts handmade crafts, ceramics, fiber, metal, and other mediums. Juried. Number of exhibitors: 200. Number of attendees: varies. Admission: $10, 1-day ticket; $15, 2-day ticket; children 15 and under free. Apply online.

ADDITIONAL INFORMATION Deadline for entry: see website. Application fee: see website. Space fee: varies. Exhibition space: varies. For more information, e-mail, call, or visit website.

KETNER'S MILL COUNTY ARTS FAIR

P.O. Box 322, Lookout Mountain TN 37350. (423)267-5702. E-mail: contact@ketnersmill.org. Website: www.ketnersmill.org. **Contact:** Dee Nash, event coordinator. Estab. 1977. Arts and crafts show held annually the 3rd weekend in October held on the grounds of the historic Ketner's Mill, in Whitwell, Tennessee, and the banks of the Sequatchie River. Outdoors. Accepts photography, painting, prints, dolls, fiber arts, baskets, folk art, wood crafts, jewelry, musical instruments, sculpture, pottery, glass. Juried. Number of exhibitors: 170. Number of attendees: 10,000/day, depending on weather. Apply online.

ADDITIONAL INFORMATION Space fee: $125. Electricity: $10 limited to light use. Exhibition space: 15×15. Average gross sales/exhibitor: $1,500. Fair held at Ketner's Mill.

TIPS "Display your best and most expensive work, framed. But also have smaller unframed items to sell. Never underestimate a show: Someone may come forward and buy a large item."

KEY BISCAYNE ART FESTIVAL

270 Central Blvd., Suite 107B, Jupiter FL 33458. (561)746-6615. Fax: (561)746-6528. E-mail: info@artfestival.com. Website: www.artfestival.com. **Contact:** Malinda Ratliff, communications manager. Estab. 1964. Fine art and craft fair held annually in March. Outdoors. Accepts photography, jewelry, mixed media, sculpture, wood, ceramic, glass, painting, digital, fiber, metal. Juried. Number of exhibitors: 125. Number of attendees: 50,000. Free to public. Apply online via www.zapplication.org.

ADDITIONAL INFORMATION Deadline: see website. Application fee: $25. Space fee: $395. Exhibition space: 10×10 and 10×20. For more information, e-mail, call, or visit website. Festival located at Village Green Park in Key Biscayne, Florida.

KEY WEST CRAFT SHOW

301 Front St., Key West FL 33040. (305)294-1243. E-mail: kwcraftshow@earthlink.net. Website: www.keywestartcenter.com/craft.html. Fine arts and crafts fair held annually in January. Outdoors. Accepts handmade crafts and other mediums. Juried. Number of exhibitors: 100. Number of attendees: 25,000. Free to public. Apply online.

ADDITIONAL INFORMATION Deadline for entry: September. Application fee: $25. Space fee: $225; $340. Exhibition space: 10×10; 10×15. For more information, e-mail, call, or visit website.

KINGS BEACH FINE ARTS & CRAFTS ON THE SHORE

Pacific Fine Arts Festivals, P.O. Box 280, Pine Grove CA 95665. (209)267-4394. Fax: (209)267-4395. E-mail: pfa@pacificfinearts.com. Website: www.pacificfinearts.com. The annual Fine Arts and Crafts on the Shore at Kings Beach is 1 of Lake Tahoe's must-attend events, showcasing an outstanding array of creations that capture the imagination and inspire the heart. Set among the towering pine trees along the shores of Lake Tahoe at Kings Beach State Park, this free outdoor festival is sponsored by the North Tahoe Business Association and features original collectibles including watercolor and oil paintings, glasswork, sculptures, photography, fine crafts, jewelry, and much more. For more information, visit website.

KINGS DRIVE ART WALK

Festival in the Park, Little Sugar Creek Greenway, 600 South Kings Dr., Charlotte NC 28203. (704)338-1060. E-mail: festival@festivalinthepark.org. E-mail: festival@festivalinthepark.org. Website: www.festivalinthepark.org. **Contact:** Julie Whitney Austin, executive director. Estab. 1964. Fine art and craft show held annually the 1st weekend of May. Outdoors. Accepts photography. Juried. Number of exhibitors: 85. Public attendance: 35,000+. Free to public. Apply online at www.festivalinthepark.org/kingsdrive.asp.

ADDITIONAL INFORMATION Deadline for entry: March 1. Application fee: $25. Space fee: $235. Exhibition space: 10×10. For more information, e-mail, call, or visit website.

KINGS MOUNTAIN ART FAIR

13106 Skyline Blvd., Woodside CA 94062. (650)851-2710. E-mail: kmafsecty@aol.com. Website: www.kingsmountainartfair.org. **Contact:** Carrie German, administrative assistant. Estab. 1963. Fine arts and crafts show held annually Labor Day weekend. Fund-raiser for volunteer fire dept. Accepts photography, ceramics, clothing, 2D, painting, glass, jewelry, leather, sculpture, textile/fiber, wood. Juried. Number of exhibitors: 138. Public attendance: 10,000. Free to public.

ADDITIONAL INFORMATION Deadline for entry: January 30. Application fee: $20 (online). Exhibition space: 10×10. Average gross sales/exhibitor: $3,500. For more information, e-mail or visit website.

TIPS "Located in Redwood Forest South of San Francisco. Keep an open mind and be flexible."

KPFA WINTER CRAFTS FAIR

1929 MLK Jr. Wy, Berkeley CA 94704. (510)848-6767, ext. 243. E-mail: jan@kpfa.org. Website: www.kpfa.org/craftsfair/winter. **Contact:** Jan Etre, coordinator. Estab. 1970. Fine arts and crafts fair held annually in December. Indoors. Accepts handmade crafts, ceramics, fiber, glass, jewelry, mixed media, 2D, painting, photography, and sculpture. Juried. Number of exhibitors: 200. Number of attendees: see website. Admission: $12; disabled, 65+: $8, and children under 17 free. Apply online.

ADDITIONAL INFORMATION Deadline for entry: see website. Application fee: $25. Space fee: varies. Exhibition space: 10×6, 10×10. For more information, e-mail, call, or visit website. Show located at: Craneway Pavilion at the Richmond Waterfront, 1414 Harbour Way S., Richmond CA 94804

KRASL ART FAIR ON THE BLUFF

707 Lake Blvd., St. Joseph MI 49085. (269) 983-0271. Fax: (269)983-0275. E-mail: info1@krasl.org. Website: www.krasl.org. **Contact:** Julia Gourley. Estab. 1962. Fine arts and fine craft show held annually the 2nd weekend of July (see website for details). Outdoors. Accepts art in 19 media categories including photography, painting (oils, acrylics, and watercolors), digital

art, drawing, pastels, fibers (wearable and decorative), clay (functional and nonfunctional), glass, jewelry (precious and nonprecious), sculpture, printmaking and graphics, metals (mixedmedia 2D and 3D), and woods. Number of exhibitors: 200. Number of attendees: thousands. Free to public. Application fee: $30. Applications are available online through www.zapplication.org.

ADDITIONAL INFORMATION Deadline for entry: early January. There is on-site jurying the same day of the fair and about 30% are invited back without having to pay the $30 application fee. Space fee: $275. Exhibition space: 10×10 to 15×15. or $300 for 20×20. (limited). "Krasl Art Fair on the Bluff is ranked #10 in the *Sunshine Artist Magazine's* 200 Best for 2014; #8 on the Art Fair Calendar's new Best Art Shows List from their 2014 survey; #48 in the *Art Fair Sourcebook's* Top 100 shows." For more information, e-mail or visit website.

KRIS KRINGLE HOLIDAY CRAFT SHOW

Linda Williams, 14735 National Pike, Clear Springs MD 21722. (301)582-1233. E-mail: brianpitsnogle@gmail.com. Website: www.kriskringlecraftshow.com. Fine arts and crafts fair held annually in November. Indoors. Accepts handmade crafts and other mediums. Juried. Number of exhibitors: see website. Number of attendees: see website. Free to public. Apply online.

ADDITIONAL INFORMATION Deadline for entry: see website. Application fee: see website. Space fee: varies. Exhibition space: varies. For more information, call or visit website.

LABOR DAY WEEKEND CRAFT FAIR AT THE BAY

38 Charles St., Rochester NH 03867. (603)332-2616. E-mail: info@castleberryfairs.com. Website: www.castleberryfairs.com. **Contact:** Terry and Chris Mullen. Fine arts and crafts fair held annually in August. Indoors and outdoors. Accepts handmade crafts and other items. Juried. Number of exhibitors: see website. Number of attendees: see website. Free to public. Apply online.

ADDITIONAL INFORMATION Deadline for entry: see website. Application fee: see website. Space fee: $350. Exhibition space: varies. For more information, e-mail, call, or visit website.

LAKE CABLE WOMAN'S CLUB CRAFT SHOW

5725 Fulton Dr. NW, Canton OH 44718. (330)323-3202. E-mail: lcwccraftshow@gmail.com. **Contact:** Connie Little, chairman. Estab. 1982. Craft show held semiannually the 1st Sunday in March and November. Indoors. Accepts handmade crafts. Juried. Number of exhibitors: 60. Number of attendees: 500–800. Free to public. Call or e-mail for application.

ADDITIONAL INFORMATION Deadline for entry: varies. Space fee: Starting at $35. Exhibition space: 8×5. For more information, call or e-mail.

LAKE CITY ARTS & CRAFTS FESTIVAL

P.O. Box 1147, Lake City CO 81235. (817)343-3305. E-mail: info@lakecityarts.org; kerrycoy@aol.com. Website: www.lakecityarts.org. Estab. 1975. Fine arts/arts and craft show held annually 3rd Tuesday in July.1-day event. Outdoors. Accepts photography, jewelry, metal work, woodworking, painting, handmade items. Juried by 3–5 undisclosed jurors. Prize: Winners are entered in a drawing for a free booth space in the following year's show. Number of exhibitors: 85. Public attendance: 500. Free to public. Space fee: $85. Jury fee: $10. Exhibition space: 12×12.

ADDITIONAL INFORMATION Deadline for submission: mid April. Average gross sales/exhibitor: $500–$1,000. For more information, and application form, visit website. Festival located at the Lake City Town Park and along Silver St.

TIPS "Repeat vendors draw repeat customers. People like to see their favorite vendors each year or every other year. If you come every year, have new things as well as your best-selling products."

LAKEFRONT FESTIVAL OF ART

700 N. Art Museum Dr., Milwaukee WI 53202. (414)224-3853. E-mail: lfoa@mam.org. Website:

www.mam.org/lfoa. **Contact:** Krista Renfrew, festival director. Estab. 1963. Fine art show held annually the 3rd week in June. Indoors and outdoors. Accepts printmaking, sculpture, wood, painting, jewelry, ceramics, digital, drawing/pastel, MM2, non-wearable fiber, glass, photography, metal, NM. Juried. Awards/prizes: Artist Awards (10), Honorable Mention (10), Sculpture Garden. Exhibitors: 176. Number of attendees: 25,000. Admission: $17 general; $10 members and advance; 12 and under free. Apply via www.zapplication.org.

ADDITIONAL INFORMATION Deadline for entry: November 25. Application fee: $35. Space fee: $500; $600 corner. Exhibition space: 10×10. For more information, e-mail or visit website.

LAKELAND CRAFT FESTIVAL, THE

270 Central Blvd., Suite 107B, Jupiter FL 33458. (561)746-6615. Fax: (561)746-6528. E-mail: info@artfestival.com. Website: www.artfestival.com. **Contact:** Malinda Ratliff, communications manager. Estab. 2013. Fine art and craft fair held annually in late March. Outdoors. Accepts photography, jewelry, mixed media, sculpture, wood, ceramic, glass, painting, digital, fiber, metal. Juried. Number of exhibitors: 110. Number of attendees: 18,000. Free to public. Apply online via www.zapplication.org or visit website for paper application.

ADDITIONAL INFORMATION Deadline: see website. Application fee: $15. Space fee: $250. Exhibition space: 10×10 and 10×20. For more information, e-mail, call, or visit website. Festival located at Lakeside Village in Lakeland, Florida.

LAKE NORMAN FOLK ART FESTIVAL

Hickory Museum of Art, Attn: Lake Norman Folk Art Festival, 243 Third Ave. NE, Hickory NC 28601. (828)327-8576. E-mail: blohr@hickorymuseumofart.org. Website: www.lakenormanfolkartfestival.com. Fine arts and crafts fair held annually in October. Outdoors. Accepts handmade crafts and other mediums. Juried. Number of exhibitors: see website. Number of attendees: see website. Free to public. Apply online.

ADDITIONAL INFORMATION Deadline for entry: July. Application fee: none. Space fee: $75. Exhibition space: see website. For more information, e-mail, call, or visit website.

LAKESHORE ART FESTIVAL

380 W. Western, Suite 202, Muskegon MI 49440. (231)724-3176. Fax: (231)728-7281. E-mail: artfest@muskegon.org. Website: www.lakeshoreartfestival.org. Estab. 2013. Fine arts and crafts show held annually the first Friday and Saturday in July. Outdoors. Accepts handmade crafts. Juried. Awards/prizes: First place/Best in Show, $1,000; 2nd place, $800; 3rd place, $600; Honorable Mention, $400; Committee's Choice, $200. Exhibitors: 300. Number of attendees: 50,000. Free to public. Apply via website or www.zaplication.org

ADDITIONAL INFORMATION Deadline for entry: March. Application fee: $30. Space fee: $250 fine art/craft; $180 craft, Children's Lane, Artisan Food Market. Exhibition space: 12×12. Average sales: $800–1,200. For more information, e-mail, call, or visit website.

LAKE ST LOUIS FARMERS AND ARTISTS MARKET

P.O. Box 91, Warrenton MO 63383-0091. (314)495-2531. E-mail: lakestlouisfarmersmarket@gmail.com. Website: www.themeadowsatlsl.com. Farmer and craft market held annually every Saturday, April–October. Outdoors. Accepts handmade crafts, jewelry, art, pottery, soap, candles, clothing, wood crafts, and other crafts. Exhibitors: varies. Number of attendees: varies. Free to public. Apply online.

ADDITIONAL INFORMATION Deadline for entry: see website. Application fee: none. Space fee: $325 (full season); $25 (daily vendor). Exhibition space: 10×10. For more information, e-mail, visit website, or call.

LAKE SUMTER ART & CRAFT FESTIVAL

270 Central Blvd., Suite 107B, Jupiter FL 33458. (561)746-6615. Fax: (561)746-6528. E-mail: info@artfestival.com. Website: www.artfestival.com. **Contact:** Malinda Ratliff, communications

manager. Estab. 2010. Fine art and craft fair held annually in mid-February. Outdoors. Accepts photography, jewelry, mixed media, sculpture, wood, ceramic, glass, painting, digital, fiber, metal. Juried. Number of exhibitors: 205. Number of attendees: 20,000. Free to public. Apply online via www.zapplication.org or visit website for paper application.

ADDITIONAL INFORMATION Deadline: see website. Application fee: $15. Space fee: $265. Exhibition space: 10×10 and 10×20. For more information, e-mail, call, or visit website. Festival located at Lake Sumter Landing in The Villages, Florida.

LAKEVIEW EAST FESTIVAL OF THE ARTS
(773)348-8608. Website: www. lakevieweastfestivalofthearts.com.

ADDITIONAL INFORMATION "The Lakeview East Festival of the Arts showcases more than 150 juried artists featuring paintings, sculpture, photography, furniture, jewelry, and more. These original pieces are for sale in a wide range of prices. In addition to the art, the Festival has become a center of activity for the weekend with live demonstrations, entertainment stages, family activities, and a garden oasis. Lakeview East is a dynamic and diversified neighborhood community rich in culture, history, and the arts. The Lakeview East Chamber of Commerce works hand in hand with their local residents and business owners and is pleased to offer its neighbors and the Chicagoland area1 of the premier fine art outdoor festivals." For more information, sponsorship, and volunteer opportunities, call.

LAKEWOOD ARTS FESTIVAL
The Lakewood Arts Festival, P.O. Box 771288, Lakewood OH 44107. (216)529-6651. Website: www.lakewoodartsfest.org. Fine arts and crafts fair held annually in August. Outdoors. Accepts handmade crafts and other mediums. Juried. Number of exhibitors: 164. Number of attendees: 10,000. Free to public. Apply online.

ADDITIONAL INFORMATION Deadline for entry: March. Application fee: $10. Space fee: $100. Exhibition space: 10×10. For more information, call, or visit website.

LAMKT
Los Angeles Convention Center, Los Angeles CA 90015, (800)318-2238. Website: www.la-mkt. com. **Contact:** Chris Menefee, sales manager. Semiannual. Cash and carry show. Wholesale show. Indoors. Not for general public. Accepts handmade craft merchants. Accepts pattern/ magazine/book publishers. Select sections are juried. No prizes given. Admission fee: n/a. Application fee: n/a. Space fee: See prospectus for booth rates. Square footage of the space: varies. For more information, e-mail, visit website, or call.

LANSDOWNE ARTS FESTIVAL
E-mail: events@lansdownesfuture.org. Website: www.lansdowneartsfestival.com.

ADDITIONAL INFORMATION "The Lansdowne Arts Festival is a weekend-long event featuring an array of creative and performing arts, including painting, crafts, sculpture, jewelry, live music, demonstrations, and children's events. Set in the historic suburb of Lansdowne, Pennsylvania, the festival has grown to include over 50 exhibiting artists and musical acts. All festival events will be held at the historic Twentieth Century Club at 84 S. Lansdowne Ave." For more information, visit website.

LA QUINTA ARTS FESTIVAL
78150 Calle Tampico #215, La Quinta CA 92253. (760)564-1244. Fax: (760)564-6884. E-mail: helpline@lqaf.com. Website: www.lqaf. com. **Contact:** artists: Kathleen Hughes, events manager; photographers: Christi Salamone, executive director. Estab. 1983. Fine arts and crafts festival held annually. Outdoors. Accepts mixed-media 2D/3D, printmaking, photography, drawing and pastel, painting, jewelry, ceramics, fiber, sculpture, glass, wood. Juried over 3 days online by 5 jury members per each of the 11 media categories. Awards/prizes: cash, automatic acceptance into future show, gift cards from premier local restaurants, hotel package, ad in *SW Art*. Number of exhibitors: 230. Public attendance: 28,000+. Admission: $15-day pass; $20 multiday pass. Apply via www.zapplication.org only.

ADDITIONAL INFORMATION Deadline for entry: September 30. Jury fee: $50. Space fee: $275. Exhibition space: 12×12. Average exhibitor sales: $13,450. For more information, visit website.

TIPS "Make sure that booth image looks like an art gallery! Less is more."

LAS OLAS ART FAIR

270 Central Blvd., Suite 107B, Jupiter FL 33458. (561)746-6615. Fax: (561)746-6528. E-mail: info@artfestival.com. Website: www.artfestival. com. **Contact:** Malinda Ratliff, communications manager. Fine art and craft fair held annually in January, March, and mid-October. Outdoors. Accepts photography, jewelry, mixed media, sculpture, wood, ceramic, glass, painting, digital, fiber, metal. Juried. Number of exhibitors: 280/January, 260/March, 150/October. Number of attendees: 100,000/January, 100,000/March, 70,000/October. Free to public. Apply online via www.zapplication.org.

ADDITIONAL INFORMATION Deadline: see website. Application fee: $25. Space fee: $400/January, $400/March, $395/October. Exhibition space: 10×10 and 10×20. For more information, e-mail, call, or visit website. Fair located on Las Olas Blvd. in Ft. Lauderdale, Florida.

LATIMER HALL ARTS & CRAFT SHOW

103 Towne Lake Pkwy. Woodstock GA 30188. (347)216-4691. E-mail: mainstreetcraftshow@yahoo.com. Website: www.mainstreetcraftshow.com. **Contact:** Deb Skroce, director. Estab. 2013. Monthly arts and crafts. Indoors and outdoors. Accepts handmade crafts, repurposed items. Exhibitors: 50. Number of attendees: 1,000. Free to public. Apply via e-mail or website.

ADDITIONAL INFORMATION Deadline for entry: see website or contact by e-mail. Space fee: $50 and $30. Exhibition space: 10×10, 10×9, 9×6. For more information, e-mail or visit website.

LAUDERDALE BY THE SEA CRAFT FESTIVAL

270 Central Blvd., Suite 107B, Jupiter FL 33458. (561)746-6615. Fax: (561)746-6528. E-mail: info@artfestival.com. Website: www.artfestival.com. **Contact:** Malinda Ratliff, communications manager.

ADDITIONAL INFORMATION "Come visit with more than 100 crafters exhibiting and selling their work in an outdoor gallery. From photography, paintings, sculpture, jewelry, and more showcased from local and traveling crafters, your visit to Lauderdale By the Sea is promised to be a feast for the senses. This spectacular weekend festival is not to be missed. Spanning along A1A and Commercial Blvd., the venue is right off the beach and is set up amongst the restaurants and retailers." For more information, visit website.

LEAGUE OF NH CRAFTSMEN ANNUAL FAIR

League of NH Craftsmen, 49 S. Main St., Suite 100, Concord NH 03301-5080. (603)224-3375. **Fax:** (603)225-8452. **E-mail:** twiltse@nhcrafts.org. **Website:** www.nhcrafts.org/craftsmens-fair-overview.php. **Contact:** Susie Lowe-Stockwell, executive director. The Lansdowne Arts Festival is a weekend-long event featuring an array of creative and performing arts, including painting, crafts, sculpture, jewelry, live music, demonstrations, and children's events. Set in the historic suburb of Lansdowne, Pennsylvania, the festival has grown to include dozens of exhibiting artists and musical acts. All festival events will be held at the historic Twentieth Century Club at 84 S. Lansdowne Ave. For more information, visit website.

LEEPER PARK ART FAIR

22180 Sundancer Court, #504, Estero FL 33928. (574) 276-2942. E-mail: Studio266@aol.com. Website: www.leeperparkartfair.org. **Contact:** Judy Ladd, director. Estab. 1968. Fine arts and crafts show held annually in June. Outdoors. Accepts photography and all areas of fine art. Juried. Awards/prizes: $3,700. Number of exhibitors: 120. Public attendance: 10,000. Free to public. Apply by going to the website and clicking on "To Apply."

ADDITIONAL INFORMATION Deadline for entry: early March. Space fee: $340. Exhibition space: 12×12. Average gross sales/exhibitor: $5,000. For more information, e-mail, call, or visit website.

TIPS "Make sure your booth display is well presented and, when applying, slides are top notch!"

LEESBURG FINE ART FESTIVAL

Paragon Fine Art Festivals, 8258 Midnight Pass Rd., Sarasota FL 34242. (941)487-8061. Fax: (941)346-0302. E-mail: admin@paragonartfest. com; spadagraphix@yahoo.com. Website: www.paragonartevents.com/lee. **Contact:** Bill Kinney. Fine arts and crafts fair held annually in September. Outdoors. Accepts handmade crafts, ceramics, fiber, glass, jewelry, mixed media, painting, photography, and sculpture. Juried. Number of exhibitors: 115. Number of attendees: varies. Free to public. Apply online.

ADDITIONAL INFORMATION Deadline for entry: July. Application fee: $30. Space fee: $395. Exhibition space: see website. For more information, e-mail, call, or visit website.

LEVIS COMMONS FINE ART FAIR

The Guild of Artists and Artisans, 118 N.4th Ave., Ann Arbor MI 48104. (734)662-3382, ext. 101. E-mail: info@theguild.org; nicole@theguild.org. Website: www.theguild.org. **Contact:** Nicole McKay, artist relations director. Fine arts and crafts fair held annually in September. Outdoors. Accepts handmade crafts, jewelry, ceramics, painting, glass, photography, fiber, and more. Juried. Number of exhibitors: 130. Number of attendees: 35,000. Free to public. Apply online.

ADDITIONAL INFORMATION Deadline for entry: April. Application fee: $25 members; $30 nonmembers. Space fee: varies. Exhibition space: varies. For more information, e-mail, call, or visit website.

LEWISTON ART FESTIVAL

P.O. Box 1, Lewiston NY 14092. (716)754-0166. **Fax:** (716)754-9166. E-mail: director@artcouncil. org. Website: www.artcouncil.org. **Contact:** Irene Rykaszewski, executive director. Arts and crafts show held annually in August. Outdoors. Accepts handmade crafts, drawing, printmaking, computer-generated art, 2D/3D mixed media, photography, ceramics, fiber, glass, jewelry, sculpture, wood. Juried. Number of exhibitors: 175. Number of attendees: 35,000. Free to public. Apply online.

ADDITIONAL INFORMATION Deadline for entry: early May. Application fee: $15. Space fee: $175. Exhibition space: 10×10. For more information, e-mail, or visit website.

LIBERTY ARTS SQUARED

P.O. Box 302, Liberty MO 64069. E-mail: staff@libertyartssquared.org. Website: www.libertyartssquared.org. Estab. 2010. Outdoor fine art/craft show held annually. Accepts all mediums. Awards: prizes totaling $4,000; Visual Arts for Awards $1,500; Folk Art for Awards $1,500; Overall Best of Show Award $500. Free admission to the public; free parking. Application fee: $25. Space fee: $200. Exhibition space: 10×10. For more information, e-mail or visit website.

LILAC FESTIVAL ARTS & CRAFTS SHOWS

26 Goodman St., Rochester NY 14607. (585)244-0951; (585)473-4482. E-mail: lyn@rochesterevents.com. Website: www.rochesterevents.com. Estab. 1985. Arts and crafts shows held annually in mid-May (see website for details). Outdoors. Accepts photography, painting, ceramics, woodworking, metal sculpture, fiber. Juried by a panel. Number of exhibitors: 120. Public attendance: 25,000. Free to public. Exhibition space: 10×10. Space fee: $200. For more information, and to apply, e-mail or visit website. Festival held at Highland Park in Rochester, New York.

LINCOLN ARTS FESTIVAL

(402)434-2787. E-mail: lori@artscene.org. Website: artscene.org/events/lincoln-arts-festival/. Fine arts and crafts fair held annually in September. Outdoors. Accepts handmade crafts, jewelry, ceramics, painting, glass, photography, fiber, and more. Juried. Awards/prizes: $6,000. Number of exhibitors: see website. Number of attendees: varies. Free to public. Apply online.

ADDITIONAL INFORMATION Deadline for entry: May. Application fee: $25. Space fee: $190 (10×10); $310 (10×20). Exhibition space: 10×10; 10×20. For more information, e-mail or visit website.

LINCOLNSHIRE ART FESTIVAL

Amdur Productions, P.O. Box 550, Highland Park IL 60035. (847)926-4300. Fax: (847)926-4330. E-mail: info@amdurproductions.com. Website: www.amdurproductions.com. Fine arts and crafts fair held annually in August. Outdoors. Accepts handmade crafts, jewelry, ceramics, painting, glass, photography, fiber, and more.

Juried. Awards/prizes: given at festival. Number of exhibitors: 130. Number of attendees: 30,000. Free to public. Apply online.

ADDITIONAL INFORMATION Deadline for entry: January. Application fee: $25. Space fee: $430. Exhibition space: 10×10. For more information, e-mail or visit website.

LIONS CLUB ARTS & CRAFTS FESTIVAL

Henderson Lions Club, P.O. Box 842, Henderson KY 42419. E-mail: lionsartsandcrafts@gmail.com. Website: www.lionsartsandcrafts.com. Estab. 1972. Formerly Gradd Arts and Crafts Festival. Arts and crafts show held annually 1st full weekend in October. Outdoors. Accepts photography taken by crafter only. Number of of exhibitors: 100–150. Public attendance: 10,000+. Apply by calling to be put on mailing list. Space fee: $100. Exhibition space: 15×15. For more Information, e-mail, visit website, or call. Festival located at John James Audubon State Park.

TIPS "Be sure that only hand-crafted items are sold. No buy/sell items will be allowed."

LITTLE FALLS ARTS & CRAFTS FAIR

200 First St. NW, Little Falls MN 56345-1365. (320)632-5155. Fax: (320)632-2122. E-mail: artsandcrafts@littlefallsmnchamber.com. Website: www.littlefallsmnchamber.com. **Contact:** Mary Bednarek, registrar. Estab. 1972. Arts and crafts show held annually the 1st weekend after Labor Day in September. Outdoors. Accepts handmade crafts. Juried. Number of exhibitors: 600. Number of attendees: 125,000. Free to public. Apply online.

ADDITIONAL INFORMATION Deadline for entry: March 31. Application fee: $10. Space fee: $195. Exhibition space: 10×10. Average sales: $5,000. For more information, e-mail, call, or visit website.

TIPS "Have quality product that is reasonably priced!"

LOMPOC FLOWER FESTIVAL

414 W. Ocean Ave., Lompoc CA 93436. (805)735-8511. Fax: (805)7359228. E-mail: lompocvalle1@verizon.net. Website: lompocvalleyartassociation.com/. **Contact:** Kathy Badrak. Estab. 1942. Sponsored by Lompoc Valley Art Association, Cyprus Gallery. Show held annually last week in June. Festival event includes a parade, food booths, entertainment, beer garden, and commercial center, which is not located near arts and crafts area. Outdoors. Accepts photography, fine art, woodworking, pottery, stained glass, fine jewelry. Juried by 5 members of the LVAA. Vendor must submit 3 photos of their work and a description on how they make their art. Apply by downloading application from website.

ADDITIONAL INFORMATION Deadline for entry: early May. Space fee: $375 (single); $575 (double); $100 cleaning deposit (to be refunded after show—see application for details). Exhibition space: 12×16. For more information, visit website.

LONG ISLAND STREET FAIRS

(516)442-6000. Fax: (516)543-5170. E-mail: alan@nassaucountycraftshows.com. Website: www.longislandstreetfairs.com. **Contact:** Alan Finchley, owner. Estab. 2008. Art and craft shows, seasonal/holiday and street fairs held year-round on Long Island. Indoors and outdoors. Accepts handmade crafts and other mediums. Juried. Exhibitors: 100. Number of attendees: varies by event. Most events free to public. Apply online.

ADDITIONAL INFORMATION Deadline for entry: when events are sold out. Application fee: none. Space fee: $175. Exhibition space: 10×10. Average sales: $1,000. For more information, e-mail, call, send SASE, or visit website.

LONG'S PARK ART & CRAFT FESTIVAL

Long's Park Amphitheater Foundation, 630 Janet Ave., Suite A-111, Lancaster PA 17601-4541. (717)735-8883. Website: www.longspark.org. Fine arts and crafts fair held annually Labor Day weekend. Outdoors. Accepts handmade crafts, jewelry, ceramics, painting, glass, photography, fiber, and more. Juried. Number of exhibitors: 200. Number of attendees: varies. Admission: see website. Apply online.

ADDITIONAL INFORMATION Deadline for entry: February. Application fee: see website. Space fee: $510 (single); $645 (double). Exhibition space: 10×10 (single); 10×20 (double) . For more information, call or visit website.

LORING PARK ART FESTIVAL

Minneapolis Minnesota (612) 203-9911. E-mail: info@loringparkartfestival.com. Website: www. loringparkartfestival.com. **Contact:** Pat Parnow.

ADDITIONAL INFORMATION "The Loring Park Art Festival is produced by Artists for Artists LLP, an organization of experienced artists. The juried festival is a 2-day event on July 30 and 31 in Loring Park near downtown Minneapolis. The hours are Saturday, 10 a.m.–6 p.m. and Sunday, 10 a.m.–5 p.m..The Festival consists of 140 visual artists displaying their original work in 12x12 booths, strolling musicians, scheduled stage performances, children's activities, and food booths. The artwork presented will be from a variety of media including painting, photography, printmaking, handmade paper, wood, jewelry, clay, sculpture, fiber, mixed media, and glass. Within these categories will be a variety of styles from traditional to abstract in a variety of price ranges with the goal being 'something for everyone.'" For more information, visit website.

LOS ALTOS ROTARY FINE ART SHOW

Website: www.rotaryartshow.com.

ADDITIONAL INFORMATION "Each year, the Los Altos Rotary Club presents Fine Art in the Park—one of the Bay Area's premier open-air art shows, featuring original, juried works by some 170 artists. Fine art pieces range from paintings and sculpture to ceramics, jewelry, and unique gifts. Entertainment, food, and beverages make this an ideal occasion for shopping and family fun. As you stroll through the lovely park viewing first-rate art, you'll take comfort knowing that your purchase goes to support a great cause. All proceeds of the Rotary Fine Art in the Park show go to support a wide range of community service agencies in the Bay Area, and support international development projects in places such as Nepal, Mexico, Malaysia, and Afghanistan. Come for a day of fun and great art. There is free parking at Los Altos High School, with shuttles to the park." For more information, visit website.

LOUISVILLE FESTIVAL OF THE ARTS WITH CRAFT MARKETPLACE AT PADDOCK SHOPS

270 Central Blvd., Suite 107B, Jupiter FL 33458. (561)746-6615. Fax: (561)746-6528. E-mail: info@artfestival.com. Website: www.artfestival. com. **Contact:** Malinda Ratliff, communications manager. Estab. 2008. Fine art and craft fair held annually in mid-June. Outdoors. Accepts photography, jewelry, mixed media, sculpture, wood, ceramic, glass, painting, digital, fiber, metal. Juried. Number of exhibitors: 130. Number of attendees: 50,000. Free to public. Apply online via www.zapplication.org.

ADDITIONAL INFORMATION Deadline: see website. Application fee: $25. Space fee: $375. Exhibition space: 10×10 and 10×20. For more information, e-mail, call or visit website. Show located at Paddock Shops on Summit Plaza Dr. in Louisville, KY.

LUTZ ARTS & CRAFTS FESTIVAL

18105 Gunn Hwy, Odessa FL 33556. Estab. 1979. Fine arts and crafts show held annually in December in Odessa, FL. Outdoor and indoor spaces available. Accepts fine arts, jewelry, painting, photography, sculpture, crafts. Juried.

Number of exhibitors: 250+. Public attendance: 35,000. Admission fee: $3 per car (for parking).
ADDITIONAL INFORMATION Deadline for entry: September 1 or until category is full. Exhibition space: 12×12. For more information, e-mail fsincich@gmail.com or call. Festival takes place at Lake Park.

LVCRAFTSHOWS CRAFT + GIFT SHOW

8265 Harvest Spring Place, Las Vegas NV 89143, U.S.. (702)339-6689. E-mail: info@lvcraftshows.com. Website: lvcraftshows.com. **Contact:** Susi Engl, promoter/owner. Estab. 1999. Held monthly. Arts and crafts show. Event held indoors and outdoors. Accepts handmade crafts. Accepts various other mediums. Not juried. No prizes given. Average number of exhibitors: 90. Average number of attendees: 900-1200. Admission fee for public: Free. Artisans should apply via website. No application fee. Space fee: Table—$85, Booth—$125. Square footage of space: 32ft, 64ft. Average gross sales for typical exhibitor: Unknown. For more information, e-mail or visit website.

MADEIRA BEACH CRAFT FESTIVAL

270 Central Blvd., Suite 107B, Jupiter FL 33458. (561)746-6615. Fax: (561)746-6528. E-mail: info@artfestival.com. Website: www.artfestival.com. **Contact:** Malinda Ratliff, communications manager.
ADDITIONAL INFORMATION "Join us in Madeira Beach to browse and purchase a wide variety of ceramics, jewelry, stained glass, metalworks, and much more. Our Green Market offers live flora, freshly popped kettle corn, gourmet spices, and sauces. Come meet and visit with some of the nation's best crafters at this free, weekend event, where you are sure to find something for everyone on your gift list."

MADEIRA BEACH THANKSGIVING WEEKEND CRAFT FESTIVAL

270 Central Blvd., Suite 107B, Jupiter FL 33458. (561)746-6615. Fax: (561)746-6528. E-mail: info@artfestival.com. Website: www.artfestival.com. **Contact:** Malinda Ratliff, communications manager. Estab. 2012. Fine art and craft fair held annually in November. Outdoors. Accepts photography, jewelry, mixed media, sculpture, wood, ceramic, glass, painting, digital, fiber, metal. Juried. Number of exhibitors: 80. Number of attendees: 13,000. Free to public. Apply online via www.zapplication.org or visit website for paper application.
ADDITIONAL INFORMATION Deadline: see website. Application fee: $15. Space fee: $250. Exhibition space: 10×10 and 10×20. For more information, e-mail, call, or visit website. Festival located at Madeira Way between Gulf Blvd. and 150th Ave.

MADISON CHAUTAUQUA FESTIVAL OF ART

601 W. First St., Madison IN 47250. (812)571-2752. Fax: (812)273-3694. E-mail: info@madisonchautauqua.com. Website: www.madisonchautauqua.com. **Contact:** Amy Fischmer and Jenny Youngblood, coordinators. Estab. 1971. Premier juried fine arts and crafts show, featuring painting, photography, stained glass, jewelry, textiles pottery and more, amid the tree-lined streets of Madison's historic district. Held annually the last weekend in September. Stop by the Riverfront FoodFest for a variety of foods to enjoy. Relax and listen to the live performances on the Lanier Mansion lawn, on the plaza and along the riverfront. Painting (2D artists may sell prints, but must include originals as well), photography, pottery, sculpture, wearable, jewelry, fiber, wood, baskets, glass, paper, leather.
ADDITIONAL INFORMATION The number of artists in each category is limited to protect the integrity of the show. Festival held in Madison's National Landmark Historic District.

MAGNOLIA BLOSSOM FESTIVAL

Magnolia/Columbia County Chamber of Commerce, P.O. Box 866, Magnolia AR 71754. (870)901-2216 or (870)693-5265; 870-234-4352. E-mail: jpate006@centurytel.net; jpate002@centurytel.net. Website: www.blossomfestival.org. Craft show held annually in May. Outdoors. Accepts handmade crafts, ceramics, paintings, jewelry, glass, photography, wearable art, and other mediums. Juried. Number of exhibitors: see website. Number of attendees: varies. Free to public. Apply online.

ADDITIONAL INFORMATION Deadline for entry: late March. Application fee: none. Space fee: varies. Exhibition space: varies. For more information, e-mail, call or visit website.

MAINE CRAFTS GUILD ANNUAL DIRECTIONS SHOW

The Maine Crafts Guild, 369 Old Union Rd., Washington ME 04574. (207)557-3276. E-mail: mdi.show@mainecraftsguild.com. Website: www.mainecraftsguild.com/shows.

ADDITIONAL INFORMATION "The Maine Craft Guild's Mount Desert Island Directions Show is often referred to as the most outstanding, most successful, and longest running craft show in Maine. At the annual Show, 80 of Maine's finest craftspeople will fill the newly renovated gymnasium and cafeteria at the Mount Desert Island High School with their work, transforming the space into a gallery-like setting of carefully designed individual displays. Come and meet extraordinary artisans and purchase work of heirloom quality handmade here in Maine. Admission: $6 adults; children under 18 free."

MAINSAIL ARTS FESTIVAL

E-mail: artist@mainsailart.org. Website: www.mainsailart.org. Fine arts and crafts fair held annually in April. Outdoors. Accepts handmade crafts, ceramics, digital art, fibers, glass, graphics, jewelry, metal, mixed media, oil/acrylic, photography, sculpture, watercolor, and wood . Juried. Awards/prizes: $60,000 in cash awards. Number of exhibitors: 270. Number of attendees: 100,000. Free to public. Apply online.

ADDITIONAL INFORMATION Deadline for entry: December. Application fee: $35. Space fee: $275. Exhibition space: 10×10. For more information, e-mail or visit website.

⊙ MAIN STREET FORT WORTH ARTS FESTIVAL

777 Taylor St., Suite 100, Fort Worth TX 76102. (817)336-2787. Fax: (817)335-3113. E-mail: festivalinfo@dfwi.org. Website: www.mainstreetartsfest.org.

ADDITIONAL INFORMATION "Presented by Downtown Fort Worth Initiatives, Inc., MAIN ST. has a history of attracting tens of thousands of people annually during the 4 day visual arts, entertainment, and cultural event. MAIN ST. showcases a nationally recognized fine art and fine craft juried art fair, live concerts, performance artists, and street performers on the streets of downtown Fort Worth. We invite a total of 223 artists to the show (including 12 Emerging Artists), which includes approximately 26 award artists from the previous year's event. We project our images at our jury using state-of-the-art projectors direct from the exact electronic files submitted by the artists." For more information, visit website.

MAIN STREET TO THE ROCKIES ART FESTIVAL

270 Central Blvd., Suite 107B, Jupiter FL 33458. (561)746-6615. Fax: (561)746-6528. E-mail: info@artfestival.com. Website: www.artfestival.com. **Contact:** Malinda Ratliff, communications manager. Estab. 2007. Fine art and craft fair held annually in mid-August. Outdoors. Accepts photography, jewelry, mixed media, sculpture, wood, ceramic, glass, painting, digital, fiber, metal. Juried. Number of exhibitors: 100. Number of attendees: 60,000. Free to public. Apply online via www.zapplication.org.

ADDITIONAL INFORMATION Deadline: see website. Application fee: $35. Space fee: $475. Exhibition space: 10×10 and 10×20. For more information, e-mail, call, or visit website. Festival located at Main St. in downtown Frisco, Colorado.

MAKER FAIRE—BAY AREA

E-mail: makers@makerfaire.com. Website: www.makerfaire.com.

ADDITIONAL INFORMATION "Part science fair, part county fair, and part something entirely new, Maker Faire is an all-ages gathering of tech enthusiasts, crafters, educators, tinkerers, hobbyists, engineers, science clubs, authors, artists, students, and commercial exhibitors. All of these 'makers' come to Maker Faire to show what they have made and to share what they have learned. The launch of Maker Faire in the Bay Area in 2006 demonstrated the popularity of making and interest among legions of aspiring makers to participate in hands-on activities and learn new skills at the event. A record 195,000 people attended the 2 flagship Maker Faires in the Bay Area and New York in 2013, with 44% of attendees first-timers at the Bay Area event, and 61% in New York. A family event, 50% attend the event with children. Maker Faire is primarily designed to be forward-looking, showcasing makers who are exploring new forms and new technologies. But it's not just for the novel in technical fields; Maker Faire features innovation and experimentation across the spectrum of science, engineering, art, performance, and craft." For more information, visit website.

MAKER FAIRE—NEW YORK

E-mail: makers@makerfaire.com. Website: www.makerfaire.com.

ADDITIONAL INFORMATION "Part science fair, part county fair, and part something entirely new, Maker Faire is an all-ages gathering of tech enthusiasts, crafters, educators, tinkerers, hobbyists, engineers, science clubs, authors, artists, students, and commercial exhibitors. All of these 'makers' come to Maker Faire to show what they have made and to share what they have learned. The launch of Maker Faire in the Bay Area in 2006 demonstrated the popularity of making and interest among legions of aspiring makers to participate in hands-on activities and learn new skills at the event. A record 195,000 people attended the 2 flagship Maker Faires in the Bay Area and New York in 2013, with 44% of attendees first-timers at the Bay Area event, and 61% in New York. A family event, 50% attend the event with children. Maker Faire is primarily designed to be forward-looking, showcasing makers who are exploring new forms and new technologies. But it's not just for the novel in technical fields; Maker Faire features innovation and experimentation across the spectrum of science, engineering, art, performance, and craft." For more information, visit website.

MAMMOTH LAKES FINE ARTS & CRAFTS FESTIVAL

Pacific Fine Arts Festivals, P.O. Box 280, Pine Grove CA 95665. (209)267-4394. Fax: (209)267-4395. E-mail: pfa@pacificfinearts.com. Website: www.pacificfinearts.com. This free event, which runs from 10 a.m.–5 p.m. each day, will give attendees the opportunity to meet with talented artists and artisans from throughout the western United States as they present their original works against the majestic background of the Sierra Nevada mountains. On display will be a wide variety of arts and crafts including photography, watercolor and oil paintings, ceramics, jewelry, woodwork, and much more. For more information, visit website.

MANAYUNK ARTS FESTIVAL

4312 Main St., Philadelphia PA 19127. (215)482-9565. E-mail: info@manayunk.org; cmaloney@manayunk.org. Website: manayunk.com/signature-events/manayunk-arts-festival/. **Contact:** Caitlin Maloney, director of marketing and events. Estab. 1990. Arts and crafts show held annually late June. Outdoors. Accepts handmade crafts, fiber, glass, ceramics, jewelry, mixed media, painting, photography, wood, sculpture. Juried. Awards/prizes: Best in each category; Best in Show. Exhibitors: 300. Number of attendees: 200,000. Free to public. Apply via www.zapplication.org.

ADDITIONAL INFORMATION Deadline for entry: March 1. Application fee: $30. Space fee: $450. Exhibition space: 10×10. Average sales: $2,000–7,000. For more information, e-mail or call.

TIPS "Displaying your work in a professional manner and offering items at a variety of price points always benefits the artist."

MARCO ISLAND FESTIVAL OF THE ARTS

270 Central Blvd., Suite 107B, Jupiter FL 33458. (561)746-6615. Fax: (561)746-6528. E-mail: info@artfestival.com. Website: www.artfestival. com. **Contact:** Malinda Ratliff, communications manager. Estab. 2014. Fine art and craft fair held annually in mid-March. Outdoors. Accepts photography, jewelry, mixed media, sculpture, wood, ceramic, glass, painting, digital, fiber, metal. Juried. Number of exhibitors: 175. Number of attendees: 40,000. Free to public. Apply online via www.zapplication.org.

ADDITIONAL INFORMATION Deadline: see website. Application fee: $25. Space fee: $415. Exhibition space: 10×10 and 10×20. For more information, e-mail, call, or visit website. Festival located at Veteran's Park off N. Collier Blvd. in Marco Island, Florida.

MARION ARTS FESTIVAL

1225 Sixth Ave., Suite 100, Marion IA 52302. E-mail: mafdirector@marioncc.org. Website: www.marionartsfestival.com. Fine arts and crafts fair held annually in May. Outdoors. Accepts handmade crafts, jewelry, ceramics, painting, photography, digital, printmaking, and more. Juried. Awards/prizes: Best of Show, IDEA Award. Number of exhibitors: 50. Number of attendees: 14,000. Free to public. Apply via www.zapplication.org.

ADDITIONAL INFORMATION Deadline for entry: January. Application fee: $25. Space fee: $225. Exhibition space: 10×10. For more information, visit website.

MARITIME MAGIC ARTS & CRAFTS SHOW

107 S. Harrison St., Ludington MI 49431. (231)845-2787. E-mail: artcraftshows@ ludingtonartscenter.org. Website: www. ludingtonartscenter.org. **Contact:** Marion Riedl, show chair. Estab. 2012. Arts and crafts show held annually 1st Saturday in June. Indoors. Accepts handmade arts and crafts items. Exhibitors: 30. Number of attendees: 500. Admission: $1 suggested donation. Apply by calling, e-mailing, or visiting www.ludingtonartscenter.org.

ADDITIONAL INFORMATION Deadline for entry: April 1. Application fee: none. Space fee: varies. Exhibition space: varies. For more information, e-mail or visit website.

TIPS Remember, this is an arts/crafts show; items selling for a reasonable price are more successful.

MARKET ON THE GREEN ARTS & CRAFTS FAIR

(203)333-0506. E-mail: crdraw9@aol.com.

ADDITIONAL INFORMATION Outdoor show featuring 70 quality artisans, food vendors, bake booth, flowers, and raffle booth. Held annually in May. For more information, e-mail.

MARSHFIELD ART FAIR

New Visions Gallery, 1000 N. Oak Ave., Marshfield WI 54449. (715)387-5562. E-mail: newvisions.gallery@frontier.com. Website: www.newvisionsgallery.org. Share a Marshfield tradition with family and friends at this FREE community celebration of the arts, held each year on Mother's Day. Marshfield Art Fair offers a wide variety of fine art and craft by more than 100 Midwestern artists. Musicians and performers entertain throughout the day. Hands-On-Art activities are available for kids. For more information, visit website.

MASON ARTS FESTIVAL

Mason-Deerfield Arts Alliance, P.O. Box 381, Mason OH 45040. (513)309-8585. E-mail: masonarts@gmail.com; info@the-arts-alliance. org; mraffel@the-arts-alliance.org. Website: www.masonarts.org. Fine arts and crafts show held annually in mid-September (see website for details). Indoors and outdoors. Accepts photography, graphics, printmaking, mixed media; painting and drawing; ceramics, metal sculpture; fiber, glass, jewelry, wood, leather. Awards/prizes: $3,000+. Number of exhibitors: 75-100. Public attendance: 3,000-5,000. Free to public. Apply by visiting website for application, e-mailing, or calling.

ADDITIONAL INFORMATION Deadline for entry: see website. Jury fee: $25. Space fee: $75. Exhibition space: 12×12.; artist must provide 10×10. pop-up tent.City Gallery show is held indoors; these artists are not permitted to participate outdoors and vice versa.

MCGREGOR SPRING ARTS & CRAFTS FESTIVAL

McGregor-Marquette Chamber of Commerce, P.O. Box 105, McGregor IA 52157. (800)896-0910 or (563)873-2186. E-mail: mcgregormarquettechamber@gmail.com. Website: www.mcgreg-marq.org. Fine arts and crafts fair held annually in May and October. Indoors and outdoors. Accepts handmade crafts, jewelry, ceramics, painting, photography, digital, printmaking, and more. Number of exhibitors: see website. Number of attendees: varies. Free to public. Apply via online.

ADDITIONAL INFORMATION Deadline for entry: see website. Application fee: none. Space fee: $75 outdoor; $100 indoor. Exhibition space: 10×10. For more information, e-mail, call, or visit website.

MEMORIAL WEEKEND ARTS & CRAFTS FESTIVAL

38 Charles St., Rochester NH 03867. (603)332-2616. Fax: (603)332-8413. E-mail: info@castleberryfairs.com. Website: www.castleberryfairs.com. **Contact:** Sherry Mullen. Estab. 1989. Arts and crafts show held annually on Memorial Day weekend in Meredith, New Hampshire. Outdoors. Accepts photography and all other mediums. Juried by photo, slide, or sample. Number of exhibitors: 85. Public attendance: 7,500. Free to public. Apply by downloading application from website.

ADDITIONAL INFORMATION Deadline for entry: until full. Space fee: $225. Exhibition space: 10×10. For more information, visit website. Festival held at Mill Falls Marketplace.

TIPS "Do not bring a book; do not bring a chair. Smile and make eye contact with everyone who enters your booth. Have them sign your guest book; get their e-mail address so you can let them know when you are in the area again. And, finally, make the sale—they are at the fair to shop, after all."

MENDOTA SWEET CORN FESTIVAL CRAFTERS MARKET PLACE & FLEA MARKET

Mendota Area Chamber of Commerce, P.O. Box 620, Mendota IL 61342. (815)539-6507. Fax: (815)539-6025. E-mail: rfriedlein@mendotachamber.com. Website: www.sweetcornfestival.com. **Contact:** Roberta Friedlein, administrative assistant. Estab. 1979. Arts and crafts show held annually in August. Outdoors. Accepts handmade crafts, fine art, antiques, flea market items. Exhibitors: 200. Number of attendees: 55,000. Free to public. Apply by calling or sending e-mail.

ADDITIONAL INFORMATION Deadline for entry: until full. Application fee: none. Space fee: $70. Exhibition space: 10×10. For more information, e-mail, call, or visit website.

MESA ARTS FESTIVAL

Mesa Arts Center,1 E. Main St., Mesa AZ 85201. (480)644-6627. Fax: (480)644-6503. E-mail: shawn.lawson@mesaartscenter.com. Website: www.mesaartscenter.com. Fine arts and crafts fair held annually in December. Outdoors. Accepts handmade crafts, jewelry, ceramics, painting, photography, digital, printmaking, and more. Number of exhibitors: see website. Number of attendees: varies. Free to public. Apply online.

ADDITIONAL INFORMATION Deadline for entry: see website. Application fee: $25. Space fee: $250. Exhibition space: 10×10. For more information, e-mail, call, or visit website.

MESA MACFEST

E-mail: info@macfestmesa.com. Website: www.macfestmesa.com.

ADDITIONAL INFORMATION "The Mission of Mesa Arts and Crafts Festival (MACFest) is to provide an environment that encourages the economic and artistic growth of emerging and established artists and crafters while revitalizing downtown Mesa and building a sense of community. MACFest is a free event featuring unique artist creations, music, and fun for the whole family." For more information, visit website.

MESQUITE QUILT SHOW

Rutherford Recreation Center, 900 Rutherford Dr., P.O. Box 850137, Mesquite TX 75185-0137. (972)523-7672. Website: www.mesquitequiltguildinc.com.

ADDITIONAL INFORMATION Juried quilt show. For more information, visit website.

MIAMI PROJECT, THE

(212)518-6912. Fax: (212)518-7142. E-mail: info@art-mrkt.com. Website: www.miami-project.com. **ADDITIONAL INFORMATION** "Miami Project is a contemporary and modern art fair that takes place during Miami's art fair week. Working with a focused selection of galleries from around the globe, Miami Project presents a diverse selection of work by today's leading artists. What sets Miami Project apart is its unique venue that is constructed for the most optimal viewing experience for both dealers and collectors alike." For more information, visit website.

MICHIGAN FIRST SUMMER IN THE VILLAGE

City of Lathrup Village, 27400 Southfield Rd., Lathrup Village MI 48076. (248)557-2600 ext. 224. E-mail: recreation@lathrupvillage.org. Website: www.summerinthevillage.com. Estab. 1979. Arts and crafts show held annually in June. Outdoors. Accepts handmade crafts, ceramics, fiber, glass, jewelry, metal, mixed media, painting, photography, printmaking, sculpture, wood. Juried. Exhibitors: varies. Number of attendees: varies. Free to public. Apply online.

ADDITIONAL INFORMATION Deadline for entry: see website. Application fee: $20. Space fee: $85. Exhibition space: 10×10. For more information, e-mail, visit website, or call.

MICHIGAN STATE UNIVERSITY HOLIDAY ARTS & CRAFTS SHOW

49 Abbot Rd., Room 26, MSU Union, East Lansing MI 48824. (517)355-3354. E-mail: uab@rhs.msu.edu; artsandcrafts@uabevents.com. Website: www.uabevents.com. **Contact:** Brian D. Proffer. Estab. 1963. Arts and crafts show held annually the 1st weekend in December. Indoors. Accepts photography, basketry, candles, ceramics, clothing, sculpture, soaps, drawings, floral, fibers, glass, jewelry, metals, painting, graphics, pottery, wood. Selected by a committee using photographs submitted by each vendor to eliminate commercial products. They will evaluate on quality, creativity, and crowd appeal. Number of exhibitors: 139. Public attendance: 15,000. Free to public. Apply online. Exhibition space: 8×5. For more information, visit website or call.

MICHIGAN STATE UNIVERSITY SPRING ARTS & CRAFTS SHOW

49 Abbot Rd., Room 26, MSU Union, East Lansing MI 48824. (517)355-3354. E-mail: artsandcrafts@uabevents.com. Website: www.uabevents.com. **Contact:** Brian Proffer, (517) 884-3338. Estab. 1963. In its 52nd year, the Spring Arts and Crafts show will take place, once again, on the grounds of the MSU Union, which is located on the corner of Grand River Ave. and Abbot Rd. in East Lansing, Michigan. This year's show is going to host more than 300 artisans with many new vendors as well as include many returning favorites! There will be a broad range of handmade items including candles, furniture, jewelry, home and yard décor, aromatherapy, clothing, children's toys, paintings, graphics, pottery, sculpture, photography, and much more! **ADDITIONAL INFORMATION** For more information, visit uabevents.com/retailad/arts-and-crafts-show.

MID-MISSOURI ARTISTS CHRISTMAS ARTS & CRAFTS SALE

P.O. Box 116, Warrensburg MO 64093. (660)441-5075. E-mail: mbush22@yahoo.com. Website: www.midmissouriartists.webs.com. **Contact:** Pam Comer. Estab. 1970. Holiday arts and crafts show held annually in November. Indoors. Accepts photography and all artist/crater made arts and crafts (no resale items). Juried by 3 good-quality color photos (2 of the artwork, 1 of the display). Number of exhibitors: 60. Public attendance: 1,200. Free to public. Apply by e-mailing or calling for an application form. Entry form also available at www.midmissouriartists. webs.com.

ADDITIONAL INFORMATION Deadline for entry: early November. Space fee: $50. Exhibition space: 10×10. For more information, e-mail or call.1-day show 9 a.m. Saturday., Warrensburg Community Center, 445 E. Gay St.

TIPS "Items under $100 are most popular."

MIDSUMMER ARTS FAIRE

1515 Jersey St., Quincy IL 62301. (217)779-2285. Fax: (217)223-6950. E-mail: info@artsfaire.org. Website: www.artsfaire.org. **Contact:** Kayla Obert, coordinator. Fine art show held annually in

June. Outdoors. Accepts photography, paintings, pottery, jewelry. Juried. Awards/prizes: various totaling $5,000. Exhibitors: 60. Number of attendees: 7,000. Free to public. Apply via www.zapplication.org.

ADDITIONAL INFORMATION Deadline for entry: February 5. Application fee: $20. Space fee: $100. Exhibition space: 10×10. Average sales: $2,500. For more information, e-mail, call, visit Facebook or website.

TIPS "Variety of price points with several options at a lower price point as well."

MIDWEST FIBER & FOLK ART FAIR

P.O. Box 754, Crystal Lake IL 60039-0754. (815)276-2537. E-mail: carol@fiberandfolk.com. Website: www.fiberandfolk.com.

ADDITIONAL INFORMATION "The Midwest Fiber and Folk Art Fair held annually on the 1st weekend of August. Come on out for shopping in the Marketplace, featuring both supplies and finished goods (wearable art), take a workshop, watch the demonstrations, listen to the music, pet an alpaca, or enjoy the food." For more information, visit website.

MILLENIUM ART FESTIVAL

Amdur Productions, P.O. Box 550, Highland Park IL 60035. (847)926-4300. Fax: (847)926-4330. E-mail: info@amdurproductions.com. Website: www.amdurproductions.com. Estab. 2002. Fine arts and crafts fair held annually in May. Outdoors. Accepts handmade crafts and other mediums. Juried. Exhibitors: 110. Number of attendees: varies. Admission: Free to public. Apply online.

ADDITIONAL INFORMATION Deadline for entry: see website. Application fee: see website. Space fee: $495. Exhibition space: see website. For more information, e-mail, visit website, or call.

MILL VALLEY FALL ARTS FESTIVAL

P.O. Box 300, Mill Valley CA 94942. (415) 381-8090. E-mail: mvfafartists@gmail.com. Website: www.mvfaf.org. **Contact:** Steve Bajor. Estab. 1955. The Mill Valley Fall Arts Festival has been recognized as a fine art and craft show of high-quality original artwork for 60 years. The festival draws well-educated buyers from nearby affluent neighborhoods of Marin County and the greater San Francisco Bay Area. The event provides an exceptional opportunity for the sale of unique, creative, and high-end work. Artists interested in participating must apply via www.zapplication.org.

ADDITIONAL INFORMATION Applications open mid-January and close mid-April. For more information, visit website.

MILWAUKEE DOMES ART FESTIVAL

Website: www.milwaukeedomeartsfestival.com. Fine arts and crafts fair held annually in August. Indoors and outdoors. Accepts handmade crafts, jewelry, ceramics, painting, photography, digital, printmaking, and more. Juried. Awards/prizes: $10,500 in awards and prizes. Number of exhibitors: see website. Number of attendees: varies. Free to public. Apply online.

ADDITIONAL INFORMATION Deadline for entry: see website. Application fee: $35. Space fee: $250 outdoor; $450 indoor. Exhibition space: 10×10. For more information, visit website.

MINNE-FAIRE: A MAKER AND DIY EXPOSITION

3119 E. 26th St., Minneapolis Minnesota 55409. E-mail: fair@tcmaker.org. Website: www.tcmaker.org.

ADDITIONAL INFORMATION "This 2-day event will be returning to its roots. Admission will be free, though we'll happily accept donations to keep it running. We'll be showing off our expanded space and capabilities and celebrating all things Maker—that is after all what this is all about. If you're interested in participating, feel free to e-mail us at fair@tcmaker.org." For more information, visit website.

MINNESOTA WOMEN'S ART FESTIVAL

2924 Fourth Ave S., Minneapolis MN 55408. E-mail: naomiotr@aol.com. Website: www.womensartfestival.com. The mission of the Women's Art Festival is to provide a welcoming place for women artists to show and sell their creations and to provide a fun and festive atmosphere for guests to shop, gather, and enjoy community. Supporting local women artists of all experience levels, from first-time exhibitors to experienced professionals, we are a non-juried show with the expectation that all goods are of excellent quality, made and sold by local women. We do not accept dealers or importers and define local as any woman who wants to travel to Minneapolis for a day of fun, camaraderie, community, and creativity. Now held at the Colin Powell Youth Leadership Center, 29244th Ave. S., in Minneapolis, the event has grown to include over 130 women artists working in a large variety of media. There is live music by women performers throughout the day and a women-owned coffee shop providing food, beverages, and treats. Artists and guests alike comment on the quality of the artistic work, the fun and comfortable atmosphere, the caliber of the music, and the wonderful addition of good food, good coffee, and the chance to see good friends. For more information, visit website.

MISSION FEDERAL ARTWALK

2210 Columbia St., San Diego CA 92101. (619)615-1090. Fax: (619)615-1099. E-mail: info@artwalksandiego.org. Website: www.artwalksandiego.org. Fine arts and crafts fair held annually in April. Outdoors. Accepts handmade crafts, jewelry, ceramics, painting, photography, digital, printmaking, and more. Juried. Number of exhibitors: 350. Number of attendees: 90,000. Free to public. Apply online.

ADDITIONAL INFORMATION Deadline for entry: January. Application fee: none. Space fee: varies. Exhibition space: varies. For more information, e-mail, call ,or visit website.

MOLLIE MCGEE'S HOLIDAY MARKET

Mollie McGee's Market, P.O. BOX 6324, Longmont CO 80501. (303)772-0649. E-mail: mollie@molliemcgee.com. Website: www.molliemcgee.com. Fine arts and crafts fair held annually in October and November. Outdoors. Accepts handmade crafts and other mediums. Juried. Number of exhibitors: see website. Number of attendees: varies. Free to public. Apply online.

ADDITIONAL INFORMATION Deadline for entry: see website. Application fee: none. Space fee: varies. Exhibition space: varies. For more information, e-mail, call, or visit website.

MONTAUK ARTISTS' ASSOCIATION, INC.

P.O. Box 2751, Montauk NY 11954. (631)668-5336. E-mail: montaukart@aol.com. Website: www.montaukartistsassociation.org; www.montaukchamber.com. **Contact:** Anne Weissman. Estab. 1970. Arts and crafts show held annually Memorial Day weekend; 3rd weekend in August. Outdoors. Accepts photography, paintings, prints (numbered and signed, in bins), sculpture, limited fine art, jewelry, and ceramics. Number of exhibitors: 90. Public attendance: 8–10,000. Free to public. Exhibition space: 12×12. For more information, call or visit website.

MONTE SANO ART FESTIVAL

706 Randolph Ave., Huntsville AL 35801. (256)519-2787. E-mail: amayfield@artshuntsville.org. Website: www.montesanoartfestival.com. Estab. 1987. Annual fine art show held the 3rd weekend in June. Outdoors. Accepts handmade crafts, sculpture, glass, ceramics, paper, wood, paint, mix, fiber/textile, photography, jewelry. Juried. Awards/prizes: Best of Show in each category. Exhibitors: 195. Number of attendees: 7,000. Admission: $9–$16. Apply via www.zapplication.org.

ADDITIONAL INFORMATION Deadline for entry: March 1. Application fee: $25 Space fee: $500–$800. Exhibition space: 10×10, 10×20. For more information, visit website.

☺ MONUMENT SQUARE ART FESTIVAL

Monument Square Art Festival, C/O The Racine Arts Council, 316 Sixth St., Racine WI 53403. Website: www.monumentsquareartfest.com.

ADDITIONAL INFORMATION Fine arts and crafts fair held annually in May. Outdoors. Accepts handmade crafts and other mediums. Juried. Number of exhibitors: see website. Number of attendees: varies. Free to public. Apply online.

ADDITIONAL INFORMATION Deadline for entry: April. Application fee: none. Space fee: varies. Exhibition space: varies. For more information, e-mail or visit website.

MORNING GLORY FINE CRAFT FAIR

E-mail: info@www.wdcc.org. Website: www.wdcc.org. **Contact:** Beth Hoffman. Fine craft fair held annually in August. Outdoors (on the grounds of the Marcus; enter at Red Arrow Park). Accepts fine crafts. Juried. Awards/prizes: $3,000 in cash and prizes. Number of exhibitors: 135. Number of attendees: 7,000. Free to public. Apply via www.zapplication.org.

ADDITIONAL INFORMATION Deadline for entry: March. Application fee: $35. Space fee: $300–650. Exhibition space: 10×10; limited number of double booths available. For more information, e-mail, call, or visit website.

MOUNTAIN STATE FOREST FESTIVAL

P.O. Box 388, 101 Lough St., Elkins WV 26241. (304)636-1824. Fax: (304)636-4020. E-mail: msff@forestfestival.com. Website: www.forestfestival.com. **Contact:** Cindy Nucilli, executive director. Estab. 1930. Arts, crafts, and photography show held annually in early October. Accepts photography and homemade crafts. Awards/prizes: cash awards for photography only. Number of exhibitors: 50+. Public attendance: 75,000. Free to public. Apply by requesting an application form.

ADDITIONAL INFORMATION For more information, visit website, call, or visit Facebook page (search "Mountain State Forest Festival").

MOUNT DORA ARTS FESTIVAL

Mount Dora Center for the Arts, 138 E. Fifth Ave., Mount Dora FL 32757. (352)383-0880. Fax: (352)383-7753. E-mail: nancy@mountdoracenterforthearts.org or kristina@mountdoracenterforthearts.org. Website: www.mountdoracenterforthearts.org/arts-festival. **Contact:** Nancy Zinkofsky, artist/vendor submissions; Kristina Rosenburg, sponsors and marketing. Held the 1st weekend of February. "Join us for the upcoming 42nd Annual Mount Dora Arts Festival on Saturday and Sunday, February 4–5, 2017, from 9 a.m.–5 p.m." A juried fine arts festival for art lovers, casual festival-goers, and families. In addition to the endless rows of fine art, including oil paintings, watercolors, acrylics, clay, sculpture, and photography, the festival features local and regional musical entertainment at a main stage in Donnelly Park. For more information, visit website.

MOUNT GRETNA OUTDOOR ART SHOW

P.O. Box 637, Mount Gretna PA 17064. (717)964-3270. Fax: (717)964-3054. E-mail: mtgretnaart@comcast.net. Website: www.mtgretnaarts.com. Estab. 1974. Fine arts and crafts show held annually 3rd full weekend in August. Outdoors. Accepts photography, oils, acrylics, watercolors, mixed media, jewelry, wood, paper, graphics, sculpture, leather, clay/porcelain. Juried by 4 professional artists who assign each applicant a numeric score. The highest scores in each medium are accepted. Awards/prizes: Judges' Choice Awards: 30 artists are invited to return the following year, jury exempt; the top 10 are given a monetary award of $250. Number of exhibitors: 250. Public attendance: 15,000–19,000. Public admission: $10; children under 12 free. Apply via www.zapplication.org.

ADDITIONAL INFORMATION Deadline for entry: April 1. Application fee: $25. Space fee: $350 per 10×12. space; $700 per 10×24. double space. For more information, e-mail, visit website, or call.

MOUNT MARY STARVING ARTIST SHOW

(414)930-3000. Website: www.mtmary.edu/alumnae/events/starving-artists-show.html. **Contact:** Alumnae and Parent Engagement Office.

ADDITIONAL INFORMATION "Always the Sunday after Labor Day! This annual outdoor art show features local and national artists that work in all mediums and sell original artwork for $100 or less." For more information, visit website.

MULLICA HILL ARTS AND CRAFTS FESTIVAL

50 S. Main St., Mullica Hill NJ 08062. (856)418-1135. E-mail: mullicahillartcenter@gmail.com. Website: www.mullicahillartcenter.com. **Contact:** Lynne Perez or Chelsea Hagerty. Estab. 2011. Fine arts and crafts show held annually in May. Outdoors. Accepts handmade crafts and original art. Exhibitors: 100. Number of attendees: 3,000. Free to public. Apply online.

ADDITIONAL INFORMATION Deadline for entry: April 15. Application and Space fee: $40. Exhibition space: 15 ft. For more information, e-mail.

TIPS Register early and stay for the day.

MYSTIC OUTDOOR ART FESTIVAL

E-mail: Cherielin@MysticChamber.org. Website: www.mysticchamber.org/?sec=sec&s=44. The annual Mystic Outdoor Art Festival has evolved in many ways from its humble beginnings. In 1957, Milton Baline and several other local business owners and art lovers proposed that Mystic pattern a festival after the famous Washington Square Festival in New York. That first show featured 105 artists and 500 paintings. Between 4,000 and 6,000 visitors came to admire and purchase art. Today, the Mystic Outdoor Art Festival stretches over 2 miles and is the oldest of its kind in the Northeast. The Mystic Outdoor Art Festival has grown to over 250 artists who come from all corners of the United States and bring more than 100,000 works of art. For more information, visit website.

NAMPA FESTIVAL OF ARTS

131 Constitution Wy., Nampa ID 83686. (208)468-5858. Fax: (208)465-2282. E-mail: burkeyj@cityofnampa.us. Website: www.nampaparksandrecreation.org. **Contact:** Wendy Davis, program director. Estab. 1986. Fine art and craft show held annually mid-August. Outdoors. Accepts handmade crafts, fine art, photography, metal, anything handmade. Juried. Awards/prizes: cash. Exhibitors: 180. Number of attendees: 15,000. Free to public. See website for application.

ADDITIONAL INFORMATION Deadline for entry: July 10. Space fee: $40–90. Exhibition space: 10×10, 15×15, 20×20. For more information, e-mail, call, or visit website.

TIPS "Price things reasonably and have products displayed attractively."

NAPERVILLE WOMAN'S CLUB ART FAIR

(630)803-9171. E-mail: naperartfair@yahoo.com. Website: www.napervillewomansclub.org. **Contact:** Marie Gnesda. Over 100 local and national artists will be displaying original artwork in clay, fiber, glass, jewelry, mixed media, metal, painting, photography, sculpture, and wood. Ribbons and cash prizes are awarded to winning artists by local judges and NWC. The Naperville Woman's Club Art Fair is the longest continuously running art fair in Illinois. Activities at this event include entertainment, a silent auction, artist demonstrations, the Empty Bowl Fund-raiser to benefit local food pantries, and the Petite Picassos children's activities tent. This is the largest fund-raiser of the year for the Naperville Woman's Club. Proceeds from the event help fund a local art scholarship and local charities. Admission and parking are free. For more information, e-mail.

NAPLES NATIONAL ART FESTIVAL

(239)262-6517. Website: www.naplesart.org.

ADDITIONAL INFORMATION "The annual Naples National Art Festival is consistently voted among the top 10 art festivals in the country by *Sunshine Artist Magazine*, and the local community continues to count the Naples National Art Festival among its premier, must-see events. This festival features the talents of more than 260 artists from around the country and awards $5,000 in cash to top artists. The festival draws crowds in excess of 22,000. Don't miss it!" For more information, visit website.

NATIVE AMERICAN FINE ART FESTIVAL

(623)935-5033. E-mail: tkramer@litchfield-park. org. Website: www.litchfield-park.org. **Contact:** Tricia Kramer.

ADDITIONAL INFORMATION "The Native American Arts Festival highlights the finest Southwest Native American artists including traditional and contemporary Native American jewelry, pottery, basketry, weaving, katsinas, painting, and beadwork. The event includes a variety of Native American art, entertainment, and learning opportunities. Admission fee is $5 per person, $3 students with I.D., children 12 and under admitted free. For more information, call (623)935-9040."

NEACA'S FALL CRAFT SHOW

NEACA Fall Show, Attn: Annie Hannah, 2100 Mythewood Dr., Huntsville AL 35803. (256)859-0511 or (256)883-4028. Website: www.neaca. org. Craft show held annually in September. Indoors. Accepts handmade crafts, ceramics, paintings, jewelry, glass, photography, wearable art, and other mediums. Juried. Number of exhibitors: 150. Number of attendees: 25,000. Free to public. Apply online.

ADDITIONAL INFORMATION Deadline for entry: August. Application fee: none. Space fee: $225. Exhibition space: 10×12. For more information, call, e-mail, or visit website.

NEPTUNE ART AND CRAFT SHOW

(757)425-0000. E-mail: christie@virginiamoca. org. Website: www.virginiamoca.org/outdoor-art-shows/neptune-arts-craft-show.

ADDITIONAL INFORMATION "The Neptune Festival Art and Craft Show is part of a citywide festival at the Virginia Beach oceanfront. The Art and Craft Show portion is produced by The Virginia Museum of Contemporary Art and showcases 250 artists and crafters." For more information, visit website.

NEW ENGLAND CRAFT & SPECIALTY FOOD FAIR

38 Charles St., Rochester NH 03867. (603)332-2616. Fax: (603)332-8413. E-mail: info@castleberryfairs.com. Website: www. castleberryfairs.com. Estab. 1995. Arts and crafts show held annually on Veterans Day weekend in Salem, New Hampshire. Indoors. Accepts photography and all other mediums. Juried by photo, slide, or sample. Number of exhibitors: 200. Public attendance: 15,000. Apply by downloading application from website.

ADDITIONAL INFORMATION Deadline for entry: until full. Space fee: $350–450. Exhibition space: 10×6 or 10×10. Average gross sales/exhibitor: "Generally, this is considered an 'excellent' show, so I would guess most exhibitors sell 10 times their booth fee, or in this case, at least $3,000 in sales." For more information, visit website. Fair is held at Rockingham Park Racetrack.

NEW ENGLAND HOLIDAY CRAFT SPECTACULAR

38 Charles St., Rochester NH 03867. (603)332-2616. E-mail: info@castleberryfairs.com. Website: www.castleberryfairs.com. **Contact:** Terry and Chris Mullen. Fine arts and crafts fair held annually in December. Indoors. Accepts handmade crafts, jewelry, ceramics, painting, photography, digital, printmaking, and more. Juried. Number of exhibitors: see website. Number of attendees: varies. Admission: $7 adults; children 12 and under free. Apply online.

ADDITIONAL INFORMATION Deadline for entry: see website. Application fee: see website. Space fee: varies. Exhibition space: varies. For more information, e-mail, call, or visit website.

⬁ NEW MEXICO ARTS AND CRAFTS FAIR

2501 San Pedro St. NE, Suite 110, Albuquerque NM 87110. (505)884-9043. E-mail: info@ nmartsandcraftsfair.org. Website: www. nmartsandcraftsfair.org. Estab. 1962. Fine arts and craft show held annually in June.

Indoors. Accepts decorative and functional ceramics, digital art, drawing, fiber, precious and nonprecious jewelry, photography, paintings, printmaking, mixed media, metal, sculpture, and wood. *Only New Mexico residents 18 years and older are eligible.* For more information, visit website.

NEW SMYRNA BEACH ART FIESTA
City of New Smyrna Beach, 210 Sams Ave., New Smyrna Beach FL 32168. (386)424-2175. Fax: (386)424-2177. E-mail: kshelton@cityofnsb.com. Website: www.cityofnsb.com. **Contact:** Kimla Shelton. Estab. 1952. Arts and crafts show held annually in February. Outdoors. Accepts photography, oil, acrylics, pastel, drawings, graphics, sculpture, crafts, watercolor. Awards/prizes: $15,000 prize money; $1,600/category; Best of Show. Number of exhibitors: 250. Public attendance: 14,000. Free to public. Apply by calling to get on mailing list. Applications are always mailed out the day before Thanksgiving. **ADDITIONAL INFORMATION** Deadline for entry: until full. Exhibition space: 10×10. For more information, call. Show held in the Old Fort Park area.

NEWTON ARTS FESTIVAL
Piper Promotions, 4 Old Green Rd., Sandy Hook CT 6482. (203)512-9100. E-mail: staceyolszewski@yahoo.com. Website: www.newtownartsfestival.com. **Contact:** Stacey Olszewski. Fine arts and crafts fair held annually in September. Outdoors. Accepts handmade crafts, jewelry, ceramics, painting, photography, digital, printmaking, and more. Juried. Number of exhibitors: see website. Number of attendees: varies. Admission: $5; children 12 and under free. Apply online. **ADDITIONAL INFORMATION** Deadline for entry: August. Application fee: none. Space fee: $105 (booth); $225 (festival tent). Exhibition space: 10×10. For more information, e-mail, call, or visit website.

NEW WORLD FESTIVAL OF THE ARTS
P.O. Box 2300, Manteo NC 27954. (252) 473-5558. E-mail: dareartsinfo@gmail.com. Website: darearts.org. **Contact:** Louise Sanderlin. Estab. 1963. Fine arts and crafts show held annually in mid-August. Outdoors. Juried. Location is the Waterfront in downtown Manteo. Features 80 selected artists from Vermont to Florida exhibiting and selling their works. Application fee: $15. Space fee: $85. For more information, visit website.

NIANTIC OUTDOOR ART & CRAFT SHOW
P.O. Box 227, Niantic CT 6357. (860)705-7800. E-mail: artshowwoody@yahoo.com. Website: www.nianticartsandcraftshow.com. **Contact:** Craig Woody. Estab. 1960. Fine art and craft show held annually in July. Outdoors. Accepts handmade crafts, ceramics, fiber, glass, graphics, jewelry, leather, metal, mixed media, painting, photography, printmaking, sculpture, woodworking. Juried. Number of exhibitors: 142. Number of attendees: varies. Free to public. Apply online. **ADDITIONAL INFORMATION** Deadline for entry: March. Application fee: $20. Space fee: varies. Exhibition space: varies. For more information, e-mail, call, or visit website.

NORTH CHARLESTON ARTS FESTIVAL
P.O. Box 190016, North Charleston SC 29419-9016. (843)740-5854. E-mail: culturalarts@northcharleston.org. Website: www.northcharlestonartsfest.com. Fine arts and crafts fair held annually in May. Outdoors. Accepts handmade crafts, jewelry, ceramics, painting, photography, digital, printmaking, and more. Juried. Number of exhibitors: see website. Number of attendees: 30,000. Admission: see website. Apply online. **ADDITIONAL INFORMATION** Deadline for entry: January. Application fee: see website. Space fee: see website. Exhibition space: see website. For more information, e-mail, call, or visit website.

NORTH CONGREGATIONAL PEACH & CRAFT FAIR
17 Church St., New Hartford CT 06057. (860)379-2466. Website: www.northchurchucc.com. **Contact:** K.T. "Sully" Sullivan. Estab. 1966. Arts and crafts show held annually in mid-August. Outdoors on the Green at Pine Meadow. Accepts photography, most arts and crafts. Number of exhibitors: 50. Public attendance: 500–2,000. Free to public. Call for application form.

ADDITIONAL INFORMATION Deadline for entry: August. Application fee: $60. Exhibition space: 11×11.

TIPS "Be prepared for all kinds of weather."

NORTHERN ILLINOIS ART SHOW

E-mail: info@kval.us. Website: www.kval.us. Held annually in June in Sycamore, Illinois, on the DeKalb County Courthouse Lawn, the Northern Illinois Art Show features the work of 70 artists from across the Midwest. For more information, visit website or call Tamara Shriver at (815)758-2606.

TIPS All work must be original and handcrafted by the artist. No buy/sell or imports. The artist must be present during the show.

NORTHERN VIRGINIA FINE ARTS FESTIVAL

(703)471-9242. E-mail: info@restonarts.org. Website: www.northernvirginiafineartsfestival. org. Fine arts and crafts fair held annually in May. Outdoors. Accepts handmade crafts, jewelry, ceramics, painting, photography, digital, printmaking, and more. Juried. Number of exhibitors: 200. Number of attendees: varies. Admission: $5; children 18 and under free. Apply online.

ADDITIONAL INFORMATION Deadline for entry: see website. Application fee: see website. Space fee: see website. Exhibition space: see website. For more information, e-mail, call, or visit website.

🎧 NORTH IOWA EVENT CENTER'S SPRING EXTRAVAGANZA

Mason City Iowa 50401. (641)529-3003. E-mail: craftsunlted@gmall.com. Webslte: North Iowa Events Center. **Contact:** Jennifer Martin.

ADDITIONAL INFORMATION Annual indoor craft show at the North Iowa Events Center in Mason City, Iowa. Hourly door prizes given away. Admission is free—will donation to an Autism Support Group in the area. Handcrafted items, hand-baked goods, and home-based businesses allowed. A local Special Olympics group "Team Abilities" will be providing a lunch and bake sale as their fund-raiser. This year the show will be a day event in conjunction with the North Iowa Home Show. For more information, e-mail or call.

NORTH SHORE FESTIVAL OF ART

Amdur Productions, P.O. Box 550, Highland Park IL 60035. (847)926-4300. Fax: (847)926-4330. E-mail: info@amdurproductions.com. Website: www.amdurproductions.com. Fine arts and crafts fair held annually in July. Outdoors. Accepts handmade crafts, jewelry, ceramics, painting, photography, digital, printmaking, and more. Juried. Number of exhibitors: 100. Number of attendees: 84,000. Free to public. Apply online.

ADDITIONAL INFORMATION Deadline for entry: see website. Application fee: $25. Space fee: $445. Exhibition space: 10×10. For more information, e-mail, call, or visit website.

NORWALK ART FESTIVAL

(518)488-4907. E-mail: gordonfinearts@aol.com. Website: gordonfinearts.org. Estab. 2012. Arts and crafts show held annually in June. Outdoors. Accepts handmade crafts and fine art. Juried. Awards/prizes: cash and ribbons. Exhibitors: 150. Number of attendees: 7,000–10,000. Free to public. Apply online.

ADDITIONAL INFORMATION Deadline for entry: April 1. Application fee: $25. Space fee: $350. Exhibition space: 10×12. For more information, visit website, e-mail, or call. Event located at Mathews Park on West Ave.

TIPS Display your best works.

NORWAY ARTS FESTIVAL

Irina Kahn, Western Maine Art Group, P.O. Box 122, Norway ME 4268. (207)890-3649. E-mail: judywestschneider@gmail.com. Website: www. norwayartsfestival.org. Norway Arts Festival is a 4-day event held in Norway, Maine. The Festival starts on Thursday evening with a focus feature and continues Friday evening with music. Saturday is the Art Show and myriad events and performances that are held along Norway's historic Main Street. All events are free and open to all ages. For more information, visit website.

NOT YO MAMA'S CRAFT FAIR

E-mail: notyomamajc@gmail.com. Website: www.notyomamasaffairs.com.

ADDITIONAL INFORMATION "Not Yo Mama's Craft Fair is an exclusive and unique event where the best and brightest creatives from the Jersey

City metro area can hock their DIY wares to the coolest cats in Chill Town." For more information, visit website.

NUTS ABOUT ART
(815)285-4924. E-mail: nps@grics.net. Website: www.thenextpictureshow.com/pdf/NAA2014.pdf. Fine art show sponsored by The Next Picture Show at John Dixon Park. Free Admission. For more information, visit website.

OAK PARK AVE.—LAKE ARTS & CRAFTS SHOW
P.O. Box 1326, Palatine, Illinois 60078. (312)751-2500; (847)991-4748. E-mail: asoaartists@aol.com. Website: www.americansocietyofartists.org. **Contact:** ASA Office. Estab. 1974. Fine arts and crafts show held annually in mid-August. Event held in Oak Park, Illinois. Outdoors. Accepts photography, painting, graphics, sculpture, glass, wood, paper, fiber arts, mosaics, and more. Juried. Please submit 4 images representative of your work you wish to exhibit, 1 of your display setup, your first/last name, physical address, daytime telephone number—résumé/show listings helpful. Number of exhibitors: 150. Free to public. Apply by submitting jury materials. To jury online, submit to: asoaartists@aol.com. If juried in, you will receive a jury/approval number.

ADDITIONAL INFORMATION Deadline for entry: 2 months prior to show or earlier if spaces fill. Entry fee: $195. Exhibition space: about 100 sq. ft. for single space; other sizes available. For more information, send SASE with jury material to the above address. Show takes place in Scoville Park (located in Oak Park).

TIPS "Remember that when you are at work in your studio, you are an artist. But when you are at a show, you are a business person selling your work."

OCONOMOWOC FESTIVAL OF THE ARTS
P.O. Box 651, Oconomowoc WI 53066. Website: www.oconomowocarts.org. Estab. 1970. Fine arts and crafts fair held annually in August. Outdoors. Accepts handmade crafts, jewelry, ceramics, painting, photography, digital, printmaking, and more. Juried. Awards/prizes: $3,500. Number of exhibitors: 140. Number of attendees: varies. Admission: Free to public. Apply online. Deadline for entry: March. Application fee: $40. Space fee: $250. Exhibition space: 10×10. For more information, visit website.

ODD DUCK BAZAAR
P.O. Box 813045, Hollywood FL 33081. (954)243-9856. Fax: (954)243-9856. E-mail: info@oddduckbazaar.com. Website: www.oddduckbazaar.com. **Contact:** Shelley Mitchell, co-producer. Estab. 2010. Arts and crafts show (specializes in "odd" or unusual) held annually in late March or early April. Indoors. Accepts handmade crafts, vintage, antique. Juried. Exhibitors: 65. Number of attendees: 3,000. Admission: $5. Apply online.

ADDITIONAL INFORMATION Deadline for entry: see website. Application fee: $3. Space fee: $75–100. Exhibition space: 36–72 sq. ft. For more information, e-mail, visit website, or see social media.

TIPS "We are looking for outside of the norm, so feel free to experiment."

OHIO MART
Stan Hywet Hall and Gardens, 714 N. Portage Path, Akron OH 44303. (330)836-5533 or (888)836-5533. E-mail: info@stanhywet.org. Website: www.stanhywet.org. Estab. 1966. Fine arts and crafts fair held annually in October. Outdoors. Accepts handmade crafts, jewelry, ceramics, painting, photography, digital, printmaking, and more. Juried. Number of exhibitors: see website. Number of attendees: varies. Admission: $9 adults; $2 youth. Apply online.

ADDITIONAL INFORMATION Deadline for entry: see website. Application fee: see website. Space fee: see website. Exhibition space: see website. For more information, call, e-mail, or visit website.

OHIO SAUERKRAUT FESTIVAL
P.O. Box 281, Waynesville OH 45068. (513)897-8855, ext. 2. Fax: (513)897-9833. E-mail: barb@waynesvilleohio.com. Website: www.sauerkrautfestival.com. **Contact:** Barb Lindsay, office and event coordinator. Estab. 1969. Arts and crafts show held annually 2nd full weekend

in October. Outdoors. Accepts photography and handcrafted items only. Juried by jury team. Number of exhibitors: 458. Public attendance: 350,000. Jury fee: $20. Space fee: $200 + $25 processing fee. Exhibition space: 10×10. For more information, visit website or call.

TIPS "Have reasonably priced items."

OKLAHOMA CITY FESTIVAL OF THE ARTS

Arts Council of Oklahoma City, 400 W. California, Oklahoma City OK 73102. (405)270-4848. Fax: (405)270-4888. E-mail: info@artscouncilokc. com. Website: www.artscouncilokc.com. Estab. 1967. Fine arts and crafts fair held annually in April. Outdoors. Accepts handmade crafts, jewelry, ceramics, painting, photography, digital, printmaking, and more. Juried. Number of exhibitors: 144. Number of attendees: varies. Free to public. Apply online.

ADDITIONAL INFORMATION Deadline for entry: see website. Application fee: see website. Space fee: see website. Exhibition space: see website. For more information, call, e-mail, or visit website.

OLD CAPITOL ART FAIR

P.O. Box 5701, Springfield IL 62705. (405)270-4848. Fax: (405)270-4888. E-mail: artistinfo@yahoo.com. Website: www.socaf.org. **Contact:** Kate Baima. Estab. 1961. Fine arts and crafts fair held annually in May. Outdoors. Accepts handmade crafts, jewelry, ceramics, painting, photography, digital, printmaking, and more. Juried. Awards/prizes: 1st, 2nd, and 3rd, awards of merit. Number of exhibitors: see website. Number of attendees: varies. Free to public. Apply online.

ADDITIONAL INFORMATION Deadline for entry: November. Application fee: $35. Space fee: $300 (single); $550 (double). Exhibition space: 10×10 (single); 10×10 (double). For more information, call, e-mail, or visit website.

OLD FASHIONED CHRISTMAS—REDMOND

Central Oregon Shows, P.O. Box 1555, Sisters OR 97759. (541)420-0279. E-mail: centraloregonshows@gmail.com. Website: www.centraloregonshows.com. The theme is an old-fashioned atmosphere, with dimmed lighting to set the buying mood for the variety of arts, crafts, antiques, and entertainment. There will be a candy-land maze leading to Santa, 3 resting stations with flat-screen televisions playing classic holiday movies, and a festive entrance lined with Christmas trees, garland, Chanukah, and Kwanzaa displays. Free parking for customers and exhibitors. The entrance fee is $4 with a canned food for a local charity. For more information, visit website. Event located at the Deschutes Co. Fair and Expo.

● OLD FASHIONED CHRISTMAS—SALEM

Central Oregon Shows, P.O. Box 1555, Sisters OR 97759. (541) 420-0279. E-mail: centraloregonshows@gmail.com. Website: www.centraloregonshows.com. **Contact:** Richard. Estab. 2015. November 19 and 20 Jackman-Long Building Salem Fairgrounds. The theme is an old-fashioned atmosphere, with dimmed lighting to set the buying mood of the variety of arts, crafts, antiques, and entertainment. There will be a candy-land maze leading to Santa, 2 resting stations with flat-screen televisions playing classic holiday movies, and a festive entrance lined with Christmas trees, garland. Free parking for customers and exhibitors. The entrance fee is $5 with a canned food for a local charity. For more information, visit website. Event located at the Oregon State Fair and Exposition Center.

OLD FOURTH WARD PARK ARTS FESTIVAL

592 N. Angier Ave. NE, Atlanta GA 30308. (404)873-1222. E-mail: info@affps.com. Website: www.oldfourthwardparkartsfestival. com/. **Contact:** Randall Fox, festival director. Estab. 2013. Arts and crafts show held annually late June. Outdoors. Accepts handmade crafts, painting, photography, sculpture, leather, metal, glass, jewelry. Juried by a panel. Awards/prizes: ribbons. Number of of exhibitors: 130. Number of of attendees: 25,000. Free to public. Apply online at www.zapplication.com.

ADDITIONAL INFORMATION Deadline for entry: late April. Application fee: $25. Space fee: $225. Exhibition space: 10×10. For more information, e-mail or visit website.

OLD SAYBROOK ARTS & CRAFTS SHOW

Website: www.oldsaybrookchamber.com/pages/ArtsCraftsFestival/. From acrylics to photography, jewelry and oil painting, wood sculptures and glass creations, the 51st annual juried show will feature fine art and handmade crafts sure to please a wide array of tastes and interests. Admission and ample parking are free. For more information, and to apply, visit website.

OLD TOWN ART FAIR

1763 N. North Park Ave., Chicago IL 60614. (312)337-1938. E-mail: info@oldtowntriangle.com. Website: www.oldtownartfair.com. Estab. 1950. Fine art festival held annually in early June (see website for details). Located in the city's historic Old Town Triangle District. Artists featured are chosen by an independent jury of professional artists, gallery owners, and museum curators. Features a wide range of art mediums, including 2D and 3D mixed media, drawing, painting, photography, printmaking, ceramics, fiber, glass, jewelry and works in metal, stone, and wood. Apply online at www.zappplication.org. For more information, call, e-mail, or visit website. Fair located in Old Town Triangle District.

OLD TOWN ART FESTIVAL

Old Town San Diego Chamber of Commerce, P.O. Box 82686, San Diego CA 92138. (619)233-5008. **Fax:** (619)233-0898. E-mail: robvslmedia@cox.net; otsd@aol.com. Website: www.oldtownartfestival.org. Fine arts and crafts fair held annually in September. Outdoors. Accepts handmade crafts, jewelry, ceramics, painting, photography, digital, printmaking, and more. Juried. Number of exhibitors: see website. Number of attendees: 15,000. Free to public. Apply online.

ADDITIONAL INFORMATION Deadline for entry: September 1. Application fee: $25. Space fee: varies. Exhibition space: varies. For more information, call, e-mail, or visit website.

✚ ❂ OMAHA SUMMER ARTS FESTIVAL

P.O. Box 31036, Omaha NE 68131-0036. (402)345-5401. Fax: (402)342-4114. E-mail: ebalazs@vgagroup.com. Website: www.summerarts.org. **Contact:** Emily Peklo. Estab. 1975. Fine arts and crafts fair held annually in June. Outdoors. Accepts handmade crafts, jewelry, ceramics, painting, photography, digital, printmaking, and more. Juried. Number of exhibitors: 135. Number of attendees: varies. Free to public. Apply online.

ADDITIONAL INFORMATION Deadline for entry: see website. Application fee: see website. Space fee: varies. Exhibition space: varies. For more information, call, e-mail, or visit website.

❂ ONE OF A KIND CRAFT SHOW (ONTARIO)

10 Alcorn Ave., Suite 100, Toronto, Ontario M4V 3A9 Canada. (416)960-5399. Fax: (416)923-5624. E-mail: jill@oneofakindshow.com. Website: www.oneofakindshow.com. **Contact:** Jill Benson. Estab. 1975. Fine arts and crafts fair held annually 3 times a year. Outdoors. Accepts handmade crafts, jewelry, ceramics, painting, photography, digital, printmaking, and more. Juried. Number of exhibitors: varies per show. Number of attendees: varies per show. Free to public. Apply online.

ADDITIONAL INFORMATION Deadline for entry: see website. Application fee: see website. Space fee: varies. Exhibition space: varies. For more information, call, e-mail, or visit website.

ON THE GREEN FINE ART & CRAFT SHOW

P.O. Box 304, Glastonbury CT 06033. (860)659-1196. Fax: (860)633-4301. E-mail: info@glastonburyarts.org. Website: www.glastonburyarts.org. **Contact:** Jane Fox, administrator. Estab. 1961. Fine art and craft show held annually 2nd week of September. Outdoors. Accepts photography, pastel, prints, pottery, jewelry, drawing, sculpture, mixed media, oil, acrylic, glass, watercolor, graphic, wood, fiber, etc. Juried (with 3 photos of work, 1 photo of booth). Awards/prizes: $3,000 total prize money in different categories. Number of of exhibitors: 200. Public attendance: 15,000. Free to public. Apply online.

ADDITIONAL INFORMATION Deadline for entry: early June. Jury fee: $15. Space fee: $275. Exhibition space: 12×15. Average gross sales/exhibitor: varies. For more information, visit website. Show located at Hubbard Green.

ORANGE BEACH FESTIVAL OF ART

26389 CanalRd., Orange Beach AL 36561. (251)981-2787. Fax: (251)981-6981. E-mail: helpdesk@orangebeachartcenter.com. Website: www.orangebeachartsfestival.com. Fine art and craft show held annually in March. Outdoors. Accepts handmade crafts, ceramics, paintings, jewelry, glass, photography, wearable art, and other mediums. Juried. Number of exhibitors: 90. Number of attendees: varies. Free to public. Apply online.

ADDITIONAL INFORMATION Deadline for entry: see website. Application fee: see website. Space fee: varies. Exhibition space: varies. For more information, call, e-mail, or visit website.

ORCHARD LAKE FINE ART SHOW

P.O. Box 79, Milford MI 48381-0079. (248)684-2613. E-mail: info@hotworks.org. Website: www.hotworks.org. **Contact:** Patty Narozny, executive director and producer. Estab. 2003. Voted in the top 100 art fairs nationwide the last eight years in the row by *Sunshine Artists Magazine* out of more than 4,000 art fairs. "The Orchard Lake Fine Art Show takes place in the heart of West Bloomfield, located on a street with high visibility from Orchard Lake Rd., south of Maple Rd., in an area that provides plenty of free parking for patrons and weekend access for local businesses. West Bloomfield, Michigan, is located adjacent to Bloomfiled Hills, listed as the #2 highest income city in the US, according to Wikipedia.org, and home of Cranbrook Art Institute. West Bloomfield has been voted1 of *Money Magazine*'s 'Best Places to Live,' and is an upscale community with rolilng hills that provide a tranquil setting for beautiful and lavish homes. $5 admission helps support the Institute for the Arts and Education, Inc., a 501(c)(3) nonprofit organization whose focus is visual arts and community enrichment. 12 and under free. This event follows Ann Arbor, has great event hours, and provides ease of move-in and move-out. All work must be original and personally handmade by the artist. There is $2,500 in professional artist awards. We accept all disciplines including sculpture, paintings, clay, glass, wood, fiber, jewelry, photography, and more." Professional applications are accepted "manual" or via www.zapplication.org. Please include3 images of your most compelling work, plus1 of your booth presentation as you would set up at the show. Space fee: $375, 10×10; 10×15, $525; 10×20, $650; add $75 for corner. "Generators are permitted as long as they do not bother anyone for any reason."

ADDITIONAL INFORMATION Deadline to apply: March 15. "No buy/sell/import permitted. As part of our commitment to bring art education into the community, there is the Chadwick Accounting Group's Youth Art Competition for grades K–8 or ages 5–12, in which we encourage budding artists to create their original and personally handmade artwork that is publicly displayed in the show the entire weekend." $250 in youth art awards. The deadline to apply for youth art is July 1. More information can be found on the web at www.hotworks.org.

ORIGINAL VINTAGE & HANDMADE FAIR, THE

E-mail: info@cowboysandcustard.com. Website: www.vintageandhandmade.co.uk.

ADDITIONAL INFORMATION "This popular event is always a joy to attend with 40 stalls brimming with scrumptious vintage goodies and divine handmade lovelies. Showcasing some of the best vintage dealers, artists and creative designer-makers from the southwest and beyond, it is a day not to be missed. With everything from vintage china and glass, toys and games, books and ephemera, fabrics and haberdashery, homewares, handmade hats, quilts, notebooks, cards, purses, bags and so much more, you will find much to inspire and delight you!" For more information, visit website.

OUTDOOR ART FESTIVAL OF THE BRUCE MUSEUM

(518)852-6478. E-mail: sue@brucemuseum.org. Website: www.brucemuseum.org. Estab. 1979. Arts and crafts show held annually in October. Outdoors. Accepts handmade crafts and fine art. Juried. Awards/prizes: cash and ribbons. Exhibitors: 90. Number of attendees: 7,000–10,000. Admission: $8; free for members. Apply online.

ADDITIONAL INFORMATION Deadline for entry: December 1. Application fee: $25. Space fee: $360. Exhibition space: 10×12. For more information, visit website, e-mail, or call. Event located at the Bruce Museum, 1 Museum Dr., Greenwich, Connecticut.

OUTDOOR CRAFTS FESTIVAL OF THE BRUCE MUSEUM

(518)852-6478. E-mail: sue@brucemuseum. org. Website: www.brucemuseum.org. Estab. 1985. Arts and crafts show held annually in May. Outdoors. Accepts handmade crafts and fine art. Juried. Awards/prizes: cash and ribbons. Exhibitors: 85. Number of attendees: 7,000–10,000. Admission: $8; free for members. Apply online.

ADDITIONAL INFORMATION Deadline for entry: December 1. Application fee: $25. Space fee: $360. Exhibition space: 10×12. For more information, visit website, e-mail, or call. Event located at the Bruce Museum, 1 Museum Dr., Greenwich, Connecticut.

PACIFIC CITY ART ON THE BEACH

Central Oregon Shows, P.O. Box 1555, Sisters OR 97759. (541)420-0279. E-mail: centraloregonshows@gmail.com. Website: www.centraloregonshows.com. This event features a variety of arts, crafts, antiques, food, and entertainment with a special fund-raiser benefiting a local charity. For more information, visit website.

⊙ PACIFIC INTERNATIONAL QUILT FESTIVAL

Mancuso Show Management, P.O. Box 667, New Hope PA 18938. (215)862-5828. Fax: (215)862-9753. E-mail: mancuso@quiltfest.com. Website: www.quiltfest.com.

ADDITIONAL INFORMATION "This well-recognized and largest quilt show on the West Coast, known to quilters as P.I.Q.F., is held at the Santa Clara Convention Center in the greater San Francisco Bay Area. Not only does this incredible event feature astounding works of quilt art, it also offers a wide array of workshops and lectures presented by world-renowned instructors. A 300-booth Merchants Mall can be found with the best in fabrics, notions, machines, wearable art, and *everything* for the quilter, artist, and home sewer." For more information, visit website.

PALM BEACH FINE CRAFT SHOW

Crafts America, LLC, P.O. Box 603, Green Farms CT 06838. (203)254-0486. Fax: (203)254-9672. E-mail: info@craftsamericashows.com. Website: www.craftsamericashows.com. Fine crafts fair held annually in February. Indoors. Accepts handmade crafts, basketry, ceramics, fiber, furniture, glass, jewelry, leather, metal, mixed media, paper, wood. Juried. Number of exhibitors: 125. Number of attendees: varies. Admission: $15 general; $14 senior citizens; children 12 and under free. Apply online.

ADDITIONAL INFORMATION Deadline for entry: October. Application fee: $45. Space fee: varies. Exhibition space: varies. For more information, e-mail, call, or visit website.

PALMER PARK ART FAIR

E-mail: info@integrityshows.com. Website: www.palmerparkartfair.com. **Contact:** Mark Loeb. Estab. 2014. Fine arts and crafts show held annually in May. Outdoors. Accepts photography and all fine art and craft mediums. Juried by3 independent jurors. Awards/prizes: purchase and merit awards. Number of exhibitors: 80. Public attendance: 7,000. Free to public. Apply online.

ADDITIONAL INFORMATION Deadline for entry: see website. Application fee: $25. Booth fee: $295. Electricity limited; fee: $100. For more information, visit website.

PALM SPRINGS ARTS FESTIVAL

Palm Springs Arts Festival, 78206 Varner Rd., Ste D-114, Palm Desert CA 92211-4136. Website: www.palmspringsartsfestival.com.

ADDITIONAL INFORMATION "In the birthplace of Western Chic, Palm Springs Arts Festivals is pleased to present 175 of the finest traditional and contemporary artists from throughout the West, Southwest, and the World to dazzle your eyes." For more information, visit website.

PALM SPRINGS DESERT ART FESTIVAL

West Coast Artists, P.O. Box 750, Acton CA 93510. (818)813-4478. E-mail: info@westcoastartists. com. Website: www.westcoastartists.com. Fine arts and crafts fair held annually several times a year. Outdoors. Accepts handmade crafts and other mediums. Juried. Number of exhibitors: varies. Number of attendees: varies. Free to public. Apply online.

ADDITIONAL INFORMATION Deadline for entry: varies. Application fee: see website. Space fee: varies. Exhibition space: varies. For more information, e-mail, call, or visit website.

⊕ ∩ PALM SPRINGS FINE ART FAIR

HEG—Hamptons Expo Group, 223 Hampton Rd., Southampton NY 11968. (631)283-5505. Fax: (631)702-2141. E-mail: info@hegshows.com. Website: www.palmspringsfineartfair.com. Fine art fair held annually in February. Indoors. Accepts fine art from galleries. Juried. Number of exhibitors: 60. Number of attendees: 12,000. Admission: see website. Apply online.

ADDITIONAL INFORMATION Deadline for entry: see website. Application fee: none. Space fee: varies. Exhibition space: varies. For more information, e-mail, call, or visit website.

PALO ALTO FESTIVAL OF THE ARTS

MLA Productions, 1384 Weston Rd., Scotts Valley CA 95066. (831)438-4751. E-mail: marylou@mlaproductions.com. Website: www.mlaproductions.com/PaloAlto/index.html.

ADDITIONAL INFORMATION "This high-quality, community-friendly event is sponsored by the Palo Alto Chamber of Commerce and the City of Palo Alto. In the past, it has attracted over 150,000 people every year from throughout California and the West Coast. The festival takes place on tree-lined University Ave. in beautiful downtown Palo Alto, a vital economic area 35 miles south of San Francisco." For more information, visit website.

PARADISE CITY ARTS FESTIVALS

30 Industrial Dr. E. Northampton MA 01060. (413)587-0772. Fax: (413)587-0966. E-mail: artist@paradisecityarts.com. Website: www.paradisecityarts.com. Estab. 1995. Four fine arts and crafts shows held annually in March, May, October, and November. Indoors. Accepts photography, all original art and fine craft media. Juried by 5 digital images of work and an independent board of jury advisors. Number of exhibitors: 150–275. Public attendance: 5,000–20,000. Public admission: $12. Spply by submitting name and address to be added to mailing list or print application from website.

ADDITIONAL INFORMATION Deadlines for entry: April 1 (fall shows); September 9 (spring shows). Application fee: $30–45. Space fee: $855–1,365. Exhibition space varies by show, For more information, visit website. For more information, e-mail, visit website, or call.

∩ PARK CITY KIMBALL ARTS FESTIVAL

638 Park Ave., P.O. Box 1478, Park City UT 84060. (435)649-8882. E-mail: artsfest@kimballartcenter.org. Website: www.parkcitykimballartsfestival.org. Estab. 1970. Fine art show held annually 1st weekend in August. Outdoors. Accepts ceramics, drawing, fiber, glass, jewelry, metalwork, mixed media, painting, photography, printmaking, sculpture, wood. Juried. Awards/prizes: Best in Show. Exhibitors: 210. Number of attendees: 55,000. Admission: see website. Apply online.

ADDITIONAL INFORMATION Deadline for entry: March 1. Application fee: $50. Space fee: $550–1,500. Exhibition space: 100 sq.ft.–200 sq. ft. For more information, visit website.

PARK FOREST ART FAIR

367 Artists Walk, Park Forest IL 60466. (708)748-3377. Fax: (708)748-9132. E-mail: tallgrass367@sbcglobal.net; jmuchnik@sbcglobal.net. Website: www.tallgrassarts.org. **Contact:** Janet Muchnik, president. Estab. 1955. Fine arts and crafts festival held annually 3rd weekend in September. Outdoors. Accepts photography and any media that would fit the criteria and meet the standards of fine art or craft. Juried by professional artists (representing several media). Jurying opens in January when "call for artists" is posted on website; closes at end of June. Jurying is done on a monthly basis so successful applicants can make plans to participate. Juried artists may also exhibit in the Tall Grass Gallery and Gift Shop. Awards/prizes: Best 2D work: $750; Best 3D work: $750; Best Jewelry: $750; 2 director's prizes: $100 each; Judge's Choice (any media); several purchase awards and1 Purchase Prize for the Tall Grass Permanent Collection. Number of exhibitors: 70–100. Public attendance: 3,000–4,000. Free to public. Apply online. Submit six photographs of work by CD or e-mail. Deadline for entry: June 28. Jury fee: $35. Space fee:

$175. Exhibition space: 12×10. tent with space around it. "Some spaces are under an awning and do not require the use of a tent but should be requested early." For more information, e-mail or visit website.

TIPS "A good display is a large key to sales; however, in recent years, fair attendees have also looked for a range of prices. This includes prints or smaller-size artworks. Exhibitors should be prepared (and willing) to talk about their artworks and techniques."

PARK POINT ART FAIR

(218)428-1916. E-mail: coordinator@parkpointartfair.org. Website: www.parkpointartfair.org. **Contact:** Carla Tamburro, art fair coordinator. Estab. 1970. Fine arts and crafts fair held annually the last full weekend in June. Outdoors. Accepts handmade crafts, jewelry, ceramics, painting, photography, digital, printmaking, and more. Juried. Awards/prizes: $1,300 in awards. Number of exhibitors: 120. Number of attendees: 10,000. Free to public. Apply online.

ADDITIONAL INFORMATION Deadline for entry: March. Application fee: $15. Space fee: $185. Exhibition space: 10×10. For more information, e-mail, call, or visit website.

☺ PATCHWORK SHOW

E-mail: hello@patchworkshow.com. Website: www.patchworkshow.com.

ADDITIONAL INFORMATION Fine handmade fair held biannually in spring and fall in 4 locations. Outdoors. Accepts handmade crafts and other mediums. Juried. Number of exhibitors: see website. Number of attendees: varies. Free to public. Apply online.

ADDITIONAL INFORMATION Deadline for entry: see website. Application fee: $10. Space fee: varies. Exhibition space: varies. For more information, e-mail or visit website.

PATTERSON APRICOT FIESTA

P.O. Box 442, Patterson CA 95363. (209)892-3118. Fax: (209)892-3388. E-mail: patterson_apricot_fiesta@hotmail.com. Website: www.apricotfiesta.com. **Contact:** Jaclyn Camara, chairperson. Estab. 1984. Arts and crafts show held annually in May/June. Outdoors. Accepts photography, oils, leather, various handcrafts. Juried by type of product. Number of exhibitors: 140–150. Public attendance: 30,000. Free to public.

ADDITIONAL INFORMATION Deadline for entry: mid-April. Application fee/space fee: $225/craft, $275/commerical. Exhibition space: 12×12. For more information, call, or send SASE. Event held at Center Circle Plaza in downtown Patterson.

TIPS "Please get your applications in early!"

PEMBROKE ARTS FESTIVAL

Website: www.pembrokeartsfestival.org. Fine Arts and Crafts Fair held annually in August. For more information, visit website.

PEND OREILLE ARTS COUNCIL

P.O. Box 1694, Sandpoint ID 83864. (208)263-6139. E-mail: poactivities@gmail.com. Website: www.artinsandpoint.org. Estab. 1978. Arts and crafts show held annually, 2nd week in August. Outdoors. Accepts photography and all handmade, noncommercial works. Juried by 8-member jury. Number of exhibitors: 120. Public attendance: 5,000. Free to public. Apply by sending in application, available in February, along with4 images (three of your work,1 of your booth space).

ADDITIONAL INFORMATION Deadline for entry: April. Application fee: $25. Space fee: $185–280, no commission taken. Electricity: $50. Exhibition space: 10×10. or 10×15. (shared booths available). For more information, e-mail, call, or visit website. Show located in downtown Sandpoint.

PENNSYLVANIA GUILD OF CRAFTSMEN FINE CRAFT FAIRS

Center of American Craft, 335 N. Queen St., Lancaster PA 17603. (717)431-8706. E-mail: nick@pacrafts.org; handmade@pacrafts.org. Website: www.pacrafts.org/fine-craft-fairs. **Contact:** Nick Mohler. Fine arts and crafts fair held annually 5 times a year. Outdoors. Accepts handmade crafts, jewelry, ceramics, painting, photography, digital, printmaking, and more. Juried. Number of exhibitors: varies per show. Number of attendees: varies per show. Free to public. Apply online.

ADDITIONAL INFORMATION Deadline for entry: January. Application fee: $25. Space fee: varies. Exhibition space: 10×10. For more information, call, e-mail, or visit website.

🎧 PENROD ARTS FAIR

The Penrod Society, P.O. Box 40817, Indianapolis IN 46240. E-mail: artists@penrod.org. Website: www.penrod.org. Fine handmade fair held annually in September. Outdoors. Accepts handmade crafts and other mediums. Juried. Awards/prizes: Best in Show. Number of exhibitors: 350. Number of attendees: varies. Admission: see website. Apply via www.zapplication.org.

ADDITIONAL INFORMATION Deadline for entry: April. Application fee: see website. Space fee: varies. Exhibition space: varies. For more information, e-mail or visit website.

PENTWATER FINE ARTS & CRAFT FAIR

Pentwater Jr. Women's Club, P.O. Box 357, Pentwater MI 49449. E-mail: pentwaterjuniorwomensclub@yahoo.com. Website: www.pentwaterjuniorwomensclub.com. Always the 2nd Saturday in July, the fair is held on the beautiful Village Green located in downtown Pentwater, Michigan, during the height of the summer resort season. The fair is held regardless of the weather, and space is limited for this juried show. Artists can apply via www.zapplication.org. For more information, visit website.

PETERS VALLEY FINE CRAFT FAIR

19 Kuhn Rd., Layton NJ 07851. (973)948-5200. E-mail: craftfair@petersvalley.org; info@petersvalley.org. Website: www.petersvalley.org. Estab. 1970. Fine craft show held annually in late September at the Sussex County Fairgrounds in Augusta, New Jersey. Indoors/enclosed spaces. Accepts photography, ceramics, fiber, glass, basketry, metal, jewelry, sculpture, printmaking, paper, drawing, painting. Juried. Awards. Number of exhibitors: 150. Public attendance: 7,000–8,000. Public admission: $9. Apply via www.juriedartservices.com.

ADDITIONAL INFORMATION Deadline for entry: April 1. Application fee: $35. Space fee: $455 (includes electricity). Exhibition space: 10×10. Average gross sales/exhibitor: $2,000–5,000. For more information, e-mail, visit website, or call.

PHILADELPHIA GIFT SHOW

Greater Philadelphia Expo Center, Oaks PA 19456. (800)318-2238. Website: www.philadelphiagiftshow.com. **Contact:** Russ Turner, sales manager. Semiannual event. Wholesale show. Indoors. Accepts handmade craft merchants. Not for general public. Accepts pattern/magazine/book publishers. Select sections are juried. No prizes given. Admission fee: n/a.

ADDITIONAL INFORMATION Deadline for entry applications: n/a. Application fee: n/a. Space fee: See prospectus for booth rates. For more information, e-mail, visit Web site or call.

PHILADELPHIA MUSEUM OF ART CONTEMPORARY CRAFT SHOW

P.O. Box 7646, Philadelphia PA 19101-7646. (215)684-7930. E-mail: info@twcpma.org. Website: www.pmacraftshow.org. Estab. 1977. Fine craft show (specializes in "odd" or unusual) held annually 2nd weekend in November. Indoors. Accepts handmade crafts, clay, glass, wood, fiber, metal. Juried. Exhibitors: 195. Number of attendees: 18,000. Admission: $15. Apply online.

ADDITIONAL INFORMATION Deadline for entry: April 1. Application fee: $50. Space fee: $1,200+. Exhibition space: see website. For more information, visit website.

PICCOLO SPOLETO FINE CRAFTS SHOW

Fine Craft Shows Charleston, Fine Craft Shows Charleston, P.O. Box 22152, Charleston SC 29413-2152. (843)364-0421. E-mail: piccolo@finecraftshowscharleston.com. Website: www.finecraftshowscharleston.com. Estab. 1979. Fine handmade fair held annually in Memorial Day weekend and the following weekend. Outdoors. Accepts handmade crafts and other mediums. Juried. Awards/prizes: $5–6,000 in cash awards. Number of exhibitors: 95. Number of attendees: 9,000. Admission: $3 adults; children 18 and under free. Apply via www.zapplication.org.

ADDITIONAL INFORMATION Deadline for entry: February. Application fee: $30. Space fee: $250. Exhibition space: 10×10. For more information, e-mail, call, or visit website.

PICNIC MUSIC & ARTS FESTIVAL

E-mail: picnicportland@gmail.com. Website: www.picnicportland.com. Estab. 2008. Indie craft fair and music festival held twice a year in August and December. Outdoors (August); Indoors (December). Accepts handmade crafts and other mediums. Juried. Number of exhibitors: 100. Number of attendees: varies. Free to public. Apply online.

ADDITIONAL INFORMATION Deadline for entry: mid-May. Application fee: $10. Space fee: $125. Exhibition space: 10×10 (August show); 8×4 (December show). For more information, e-mail or visit website.

PIEDMONT PARK ARTS FESTIVAL

1701 Piedmont Ave., Atlanta GA 30306. (404)873-1222. E-mail: Info@affps.com. Website: www.piedmontparkartsfestival.com. **Contact:** Randall Fox. Estab. 2011. Arts and crafts show held annually in mid-August. Outdoors. Accepts handmade crafts, painting, photography, sculpture, leather, metal, glass, jewelry. Juried by a panel. Awards/prizes: ribbons. Number of exhibitors: 250. Number of attendees: 60,000. Free to public. Apply online at www.zapplication. com.

ADDITIONAL INFORMATION Deadline for entry: June 3. Application fee: $25. Space fee: $300. Exhibition space: 10×10. For more information, visit website.

PITTSBURGH ART, CRAFT & LIFESTYLE SHOW

Huff's Promotions, Inc., 4275 Fulton Rd. NW, Akron OH 44718. (330)493-4130. Fax: (330)493-7607. E-mail: shows@huffspromo.com. Website: www.huffspromo.com. Art and craft show held

annually several times a year. Indoors. Accepts handmade crafts and other mediums. Juried. Number of exhibitors: see website. Number of attendees: varies. Free to public. Apply online.

ADDITIONAL INFORMATION Deadline for entry: varies. Application fee: see website. Space fee: varies. Exhibition space: see website. For more information, e-mail, call, or visit website.

PLAZA ART FAIR

Plaza Art Fair, C/O Melissa Anderson, Highwoods Properties, 4706 Broadway, Suite 260, Kansas City MO 64112. (816)753-0100. Fax: (816)753-4625. E-mail: countryclubplaza@highwoods. com. Website: www.countryclubplaza.com. Estab. 1931. Art and craft show held annually in September. Outdoors. Accepts handmade crafts and other mediums. Juried. Awards/prizes: $10,000 in cash awards. Number of exhibitors: 240. Number of attendees: 300,000. Free to public. Apply via www.zapplication.org.

ADDITIONAL INFORMATION Deadline for entry: May. Application fee: $35. Space fee: $425. Exhibition space: 12×12. For more information, e-mail, call, or visit website.

PORT CLINTON ART FESTIVAL

Amdur Productions, P.O. Box 550, Highland Park IL 60035. (847)926-4300. Fax: (847)926-4330. E-mail: info@amdurproductions.com. Website: www.amdurproductions.com. Art and craft show held annually in August. Outdoors. Accepts handmade crafts and other mediums. Juried. Awards/prizes: bestowed at artist breakfast. Number of exhibitors: 260. Number of attendees: 250,000. Free to public. Apply online.

ADDITIONAL INFORMATION Deadline for entry: early January. Application fee: $50. Space fee: $765. Exhibition space: 10×10. For more information, e-mail, call, or visit website.

POWDERHORN ART FAIR

Powderhorn Art Fair C/O PPNA, 821 E. 35th St., Minneapolis MN 55407. (612)767-3515. E-mail: dixie@powderhornartfair.org. Website: www. powderhornartfair.com. **Contact:** Dixie Treichel. Estab. 1991. Fine arts and fine crafts show held annually in August. Outdoors. Accepts handmade crafts and other mediums. Juried. Awards/prizes:

Best in Show, 2nd Place, 3rd Place, Merit Award, Spirit of Powderhorn. Number of exhibitors: 184. Number of attendees: 20,000. Free to public. Apply via www.zapplication.org.

ADDITIONAL INFORMATION Deadline for entry: early March. Application fee: $35. Space fee: $240. Exhibition space: 11×11. For more information, e-mail, call, or visit website.

PRAIRIE ARTS FESTIVAL
201 Schaumburg Court, Schaumburg IL 60193. (847)923-3605. Fax: (847)923-2458. E-mail: rbenvenuti@villageofschaumburg.com. Website: www.prairiecenter.org. **Contact:** Roxane Benvenuti, special events coordinator. Estab. 1988. Outdoor fine art and fine craft exhibition and sale featuring artists, food truck vendors, live entertainment, and children's activities. Held over Saturday–Sunday of Memorial Day weekend. Located in the Robert O. Atcher Municipal Center grounds, adjacent to the Schaumburg Prairie Center for the Arts. Artist applications available in mid-January; due online or postmarked by March 4. 150 spaces available. Application fee: $110 (15×10); $220 (30×10). No jury fee. "With thousands of patrons in attendance, an ad in the Prairie Arts Festival program is a great way to get your business noticed. Rates are reasonable, and an ad in the program gives you access to a select regional market. Sponsorship opportunities are also available." For more information, e-mail, call, or visit the website.

TIPS "Submit your best work for the jury since these images are selling your work."

PRAIRIE VILLAGE ART FAIR
(913)362-9668. Website: www.prairievillageshops.com. Annual art fair held in May. For more information, visit website.

PROMENADE OF ART
Amdur Productions, P.O. Box 550, Highland Park IL 60035. (847)926-4300. Fax: (847)926-4330. E-mail: info@amdurproductions.com. Website: www.amdurproductions.com. Art and craft show held annually in June. Outdoors. Accepts handmade crafts and other mediums. Juried. Awards/prizes: given at festival. Number

of exhibitors: 125. Number of attendees: 35,000. Free to public. Apply online.

ADDITIONAL INFORMATION Deadline for entry: early January. Application fee: $25. Space fee: $460. Exhibition space: 10×10. For more information, e-mail, call, or visit website.

PUNGO STRAWBERRY FESTIVAL
P.O. Box 6158, Virginia Beach VA 23456. (757)721-6001. Fax: (757)721-9335. E-mail: pungofestival@aol.com; leebackbay@gmail.com; robinwlee23@gmail.com. Website: www.pungostrawberryfestival.info. Estab. 1983. Arts and crafts show held annually on Memorial Day weekend. Outdoors. Accepts photography and all media. Number of exhibitors: 60. Public attendance: 120,000. Free to public; $5 parking fee. Apply by calling for application or downloading a copy from the website and mailing.

ADDITIONAL INFORMATION Deadline for entry: early March; applications accepted from that point until all spaces are full. Notice of acceptance or denial by early April. Application fee: $50 refundable deposit. Space fee: $200 (offRd. location); $500 (onRd. location). Exhibition space: 10×10. For more information, e-mail, call, or visit website.

PUNTA GORDA SULLIVAN STREET CRAFT FESTIVAL
270 Central Blvd., Suite 107B, Jupiter FL 33458. (561)746-6615. Fax: (561)746-6528. E-mail: info@artfestival.com. Website: www.artfestival.com. **Contact:** Malinda Ratliff, communications manager.

ADDITIONAL INFORMATION "Since it's inception, the Punta Gorda Craft Fair continues to grow and highlight the talents of many unique crafters, providing the area with1 of its most enjoyable summer traditions. Come meet and visit with some of the nation's best crafters while enjoying the charming streets of Punta Gorda."

PYRAMID HILL ANNUAL ART FAIR
1763 Hamilton Cleves Rd., Hamilton OH 45013. (513)868-8336. Fax: (513)868-3585. E-mail: pyramid@pyramidhill.org. Website: www.pyramidhill.org. Art fair held the last Saturday

and Sunday of September. Application fee: $25. Booth fee: $100 for a single, $200 for a double. For more information, call, e-mail, or visit website. Fair located at Pyramid Hill Sculpture Park and Museum.

TIPS "Make items affordable! Quality work at affordable prices will produce profit." For more information and to apply, visit website.

QUAKER ARTS FESTIVAL

P.O. Box 202, Orchard Park NY 14127. (716)667-2787. E-mail: opjaycees@aol.com; kelly@opjaycees.com. Website: www.opjaycees.com. Estab. 1961. Fine arts and crafts show held annually in mid-September (see website for details). 80% outdoors, 20% indoors. Accepts photography, painting, graphics, sculpture, crafts. Juried by 4 panelists during event. Awards/prizes: over $10,000 total cash prizes, ribbons, and trophies. Number of exhibitors: up to 300. Public attendance: 75,000. Free to public. Artists can obtain applications online or by sending SASE.

ADDITIONAL INFORMATION Deadline for entry: May 31 for returning exhibitors and then first come, first serve up to festival date (see website for details). Space fee: Before September 1: $185 (single) or $370 (double); after September 1: $210 (single) or $420 (double). Exhibition space: 10×12. (outdoor), 10×6. (indoor). For more information, visit website or e-mail.

TIPS "Have an inviting booth with a variety of work at various price levels."

QUILT, CRAFT & SEWING FESTIVAL

Website: www.quiltcraftsew.com/phoenix.html.

ADDITIONAL INFORMATION "At the Quilt, Craft and Sewing Festival you will find a wide variety of Sewing, Quilting, Needle-Art, and Craft supply exhibits from many quality companies." For more information, visit website.

RATTLESNAKE AND WILDLIFE FESTIVAL

P.O. Box 292, Claxton GA 30417. (912)739-3820. E-mail: rattlesnakewildlifefestival@yahoo.com. Website: www.evanscountywildlifeclub.com; Facebook page: Rattlesnake and Wildlife Festival. **Contact:** Heather Dykes. Estab. 1968.

Arts and crafts show held annually 2nd weekend in March. Outdoors. Accepts photography and various mediums. Number of exhibitors: 150–200. Public attendance: 15,000–20,000. Apply by filling out an application. Click on the "Registration Tab" located on the Rattlesnake and Wildlife Festival home page.

ADDITIONAL INFORMATION Deadline for entry: late February/early March (see website for details). Space fee: $100 (outdoor); $200 (indoor). Exhibition space: 10×16 (indoor); 10×10 (outdoor). For more information, e-mail, call, or visit website.

TIPS "Your display is a major factor in whether people will stop to browse when passing by. Offer a variety."

REDMOND STREET FESTIVAL

Central Oregon Shows, P.O. Box 1555, Sisters OR 97759. (541)420-0279. E-mail: centraloregonshows@gmail.com. Website: www.centraloregonshows.com. This event caters to a variety of arts, crafts, antiques, food, entertainment, with a small section for a limited amount of commercial booths. The booths will run down the center of street leaving room on the sidewalks for storefronts to have sidewalk sales. For more information, visit website. This event is located in in downtown Redmond on 6th St.

RED RIVER QUILTERS ANNUAL QUILT SHOW

Website: www.redriverquilters.com. Judged quilt show held annually in October. For more information, visit website.

⌂ RENEGADE CRAFT FAIR—AUSTIN, THE

Renegade Craft Fair, 1910 S. Halsted St., Suite #2, Chicago IL 60608. E-mail: rachel@renegadecraft.com. Website: www.renegadecraft.com.

ADDITIONAL INFORMATION "Renegade Craft Fair is the world's premier network of events serving the DIY craft community. RCF was the first event of its kind when it was founded in 2003, and we are still the largest and most far-reaching with 14 annual events in Chicago; New York; San Francisco; Los Angeles; Austin, Texas; Portland, Oregon; London. On average, our events are attended by over 250,000 people annually, and hundreds of craft-based businesses have been launched successfully out of the fairs." For more information and to apply, visit website.

RENEGADE CRAFT FAIR —BROOKLYN, THE

Renegade Craft Fair, 1910 S. Halsted St., Suite #2, Chicago IL 60608. E-mail: rachel@renegadecraft.com. Website: www. renegadecraft.com.

ADDITIONAL INFORMATION "Renegade Craft Fair is the world's premier network of events serving the DIY craft community. RCF was the first event of its kind when it was founded in 2003, and we are still the largest and most far-reaching with 14 annual events in Chicago; New York; San Francisco; Los Angeles; Austin, Texas; Portland, Oregon; London. On average, our events are attended by over 250,000 people annually, and hundreds of craft-based businesses have been launched successfully out of the fairs." For more information and to apply, visit website.

RENEGADE CRAFT FAIR—CHICAGO, THE

Renegade Craft Fair, 1910 S. Halsted St., Suite #2, Chicago IL 60608. E-mail: rachel@renegadecraft.com. Website: www. renegadecraft.com.

ADDITIONAL INFORMATION "Renegade Craft Fair is the world's premier network of events serving the DIY craft community. RCF was the first event of its kind when it was founded in 2003, and we are still the largest and most far-reaching with 14 annual events in Chicago; New York; San Francisco; Los Angeles; Austin, Texas; Portland, Oregon; London. On average, our events are attended by over 250,000 people annually, and hundreds of craft-based businesses have been launched successfully out of the fairs." For more information and to apply, visit website.

RENEGADE CRAFT FAIR—LONDON, THE

Renegade Craft Fair, 1910 S. Halsted St., Suite #2, Chicago IL 60608. E-mail: rachel@renegadecraft.com. Website: www. renegadecraft.com.

ADDITIONAL INFORMATION "Renegade Craft Fair is the world's premier network of events serving the DIY craft community. RCF was the first event of its kind when it was founded in 2003, and we are still the largest and most far-reaching with 14 annual events in Chicago; New York; San Francisco; Los Angeles; Austin, Texas; Portland, Oregon; London. On average, our events are attended by over 250,000 people annually, and hundreds of craft-based businesses have been launched successfully out of the fairs." For more information and to apply, visit website.

RENEGADE CRAFT FAIR—LOS ANGELES, THE

Renegade Craft Fair, 1910 S. Halsted St., Suite #2, Chicago IL 60608. E-mail: rachel@renegadecraft.com. Website: www. renegadecraft.com.

ADDITIONAL INFORMATION "Renegade Craft Fair is the world's premier network of events serving the DIY craft community. RCF was the first event of its kind when it was founded in 2003, and we are still the largest and most far-reaching with 14 annual events in Chicago; New York; San Francisco; Los Angeles; Austin, Texas; Portland, Oregon; London. On average, our events are attended by over 250,000 people annually, and hundreds of craft-based businesses have been launched successfully out of the fairs." For more information and to apply, visit website.

RENEGADE CRAFT FAIR—SAN FRANCISCO, THE

Renegade Craft Fair, 1910 S. Halsted St., Suite #2, Chicago IL 60608. E-mail: rachel@renegadecraft.com. Website: www. renegadecraft.com.

ADDITIONAL INFORMATION "Renegade Craft Fair is the world's premier network of events serving the DIY craft community. RCF was the first event of its kind when it was founded in 2003, and we are still the largest and most far-reaching with 14 annual events in Chicago; New York; San Francisco; Los Angeles; Austin, Texas; Portland, Oregon; London. On average, our events are attended by over 250,000 people annually, and hundreds of craft-based businesses have been launched successfully out of the fairs." For more information and to apply, visit website.

🎧 RHINEBECK ARTS FESTIVAL

P.O. Box 28, Woodstock NY 12498. (845)331-7900. Fax: (845)331-7484. E-mail: crafts@artrider.com. Website: www.artrider.com. **Contact:** Stacey Jarit. Estab. 2013. Festival of fine contemporary craft and art held annually in late September or early October. 150 indoors and 40 outdoors. Accepts photography, fine art, ceramics, wood, mixed media, leather, glass, metal, fiber, jewelry, sculpture. Juried. Submit 5 images of your work and 1 of your booth. Public attendance: 10,000. Public admission: $10. Apply online at www.artrider.com or www.zapplication.org.

ADDITIONAL INFORMATION Deadline for entry: first Monday in January. Application fee: $45. For more information, e-mail, visit website, or call. Application fees: $0 first time Artrider applicant, $40 mailed in or online, $65 late. Space fee: $495–545. Exhibition space: 10×10 and 10×20. For more information, e-mail, call or visit website.

RIDGELAND FINE ARTS FESTIVAL

(253)344-1058. E-mail: bobmcfarland2@hotmail.com. Website: www.ridgelandartsfest.com.

ADDITIONAL INFORMATION Fine art and craft show held annually in April. Outdoors. Accepts handmade crafts and other mediums. Juried. Awards/prizes: $7,500 in awards. Number of exhibitors: 80. Number of attendees: varies. Free to public. Apply via Www.zapplication.org.

ADDITIONAL INFORMATION Deadline for entry: November. Application fee: see website. Space fee: varies. Exhibition space: varies. For more information, e-mail, call, or visit website.

RILEY FESTIVAL

312 E. Main St., Suite C, Greenfield IN 46140. (317)462-2141. Fax: (317)467-1449. E-mail: info@rileyfestival.com. Website: www.rileyfestival.com. **Contact:** Sarah Kesterson, public relations. Estab. 1970. Fine arts and crafts festival held in October. Outdoors. Accepts photography, fine arts, home arts, quilts. Juried. Awards/prizes: small monetary awards and ribbons. Number of exhibitors: 450. Public attendance: 75,000. Free to public. Apply by downloading application on website.

ADDITIONAL INFORMATION Deadline for entry: mid-September. Space fee: $185. Exhibition space: 10×10. For more information, visit website. **TIPS** "Keep arts priced for middle-class viewers."

RISING SUN FESTIVAL OF FINE ARTS & CRAFTS

(812)438-4933. E-mail: andrea@enjoyrisingsun.com. Website: www.enjoyrisingsun.com. Fine arts and craft show held annually in September. Outdoors. Accepts handmade crafts and other mediums. Juried. Awards/prizes: $8,000 in awards. Number of exhibitors: see website. Number of attendees: varies. Free to public. Apply via www.zapplication.org.

ADDITIONAL INFORMATION Deadline for entry: July. Application fee: $15. Space fee: $100 (single); $200 (double). Exhibition space: 10×10 (single); 10×10 (double). For more information, e-mail or visit website.

RIVERWALK FINE ART FAIR

Naperville Art League, 508 N. Center St., Naperville IL 60563. (630)355-2530. Fax: (630)355-3071. E-mail: naperartleague@aol.com. Website: www.napervilleartleague.com. Estab. 1984. Fine art and fine craft show held annually the 3rd weekend in September. Outdoors. Accepts handmade fine crafts and other mediums. Juried. Awards/prizes: Best of Show, 1st Place, Honorable Mentions, Purchase Awards. Number of exhibitors: 130. Number of attendees: 76,000. Free to public. Apply via www.zapplication.org.

ADDITIONAL INFORMATION Deadline for entry: March 30. Application fee: $35. Space fee: $400. Exhibition space: 10×12. For more information, e-mail, call, or visit website.

TIPS "No reproductions; artists sell well to an affluent and appreciative crowd."

ROCK 'N ROLL CRAFT SHOW

(314)649-7727. E-mail: info@rocknrollcraftshow. com. Website: www.rocknrollcraftshow.com.

ADDITIONAL INFORMATION "RockN Roll Craft Show is St. Louis's original alternative art, craft, and music event! RRCS showcases unique items handcrafted from new and recycled materials by talented artisans, as well as locally and nationally acclaimed bands!" For more information, visit website.

ROCKPORT ART FESTIVAL

Rockport Center for the Arts, 902 Navigation Circle, Rockport TX 78382. (361)729-5519. E-mail: info@rockportartcenter.com. Website: www.rockportartcenter.com. Over 120 artists, live music and food, and A/C party tent, kids' activities, and more just steps away from Aransas Bay and Rockport Beach Park! For more information, visit website.

ROTARY KEY BISCAYNE ART FESTIVAL

270 Central Blvd., Suite 107B, Jupiter FL 33458. (561)746-6615. Fax: (561)746-6528. E-mail: info@artfestival.com. Website: www. artfestival.com. **Contact:** Malinda Ratliff, communications manager. Estab. 1963. "The annual Key Biscayne Art Fair benefits our partner and co-producer, the Rotary Club of Key Biscayne. Held in Key Biscayne, an affluent island community in Miami-Dade County, just south of downtown Miami, the annual Key Biscayne Art Festival is1 not to be missed! In fact, visitors plan their springtime vacations to South Florida around this terrific outdoor festival that brings together longtime favorites and the newest names in the contemporary art scene. Life-size sculptures, spectacular paintings,1-of-a-kind jewels, photography, ceramics, and much more make for1 fabulous weekend." For more information, visit website.

ROUND THE FOUNTAIN ART FAIR

Round The Fountain Art, P.O. Box 1134, Lafayette IN 47902. (765)491-6298. Website: www.roundthefountain.org. Estab. 1973. Art and craft show held annually in May. Outdoors. Accepts handmade crafts and other mediums. Juried. Awards/prizes: Best of Show, 2nd Place, 3rd Place, Merit Awards, Aldo Award. Number of exhibitors: 100. Number of attendees: varies. Free to public. Apply via www.zapplication.org.

ADDITIONAL INFORMATION Deadline for entry: early April. Application fee: $35. Space fee: $150 (single); $300 (double). Exhibition space: 10×10 (single); 10×20 (double). For more information, call or visit website.

ROYAL OAK CLAY GLASS AND METAL SHOW

(734)216-3958. E-mail: info@integrityshows. com. Website: www.clayglassandmetal.com. **Contact:** Mark Loeb. Estab. 1994. Art show featuring works made of clay, glass, or metal only held annually in June. Outdoors. Accepts clay, glass and metal only. We encourage demonstrations. Juried by 3 independent jurors. Awards/prizes: purchase and merit awards. Number of exhibitors: 120. Public attendance: 35,000. Free to public. Apply online.

ADDITIONAL INFORMATION Deadline for entry: see website. Application fee: $25. Booth fee: $295. Electricity limited; fee: $100. For more information, visit website.

ROYAL OAK OUTDOOR ART FAIR

211 Williams St., P.O. Box 64, Royal Oak MI 48068. (248)246-3180. E-mail: artfair@ci.royal-oak.mi.us. Website: www.romi.gov. **Contact:** recreation office staff. Estab. 1970. Fine arts and crafts show held annually in July. Outdoors. Accepts photography, collage, jewelry, clay, drawing, painting, glass, fiber, wood, metal, leather, soft sculpture. Juried. Number of exhibitors: 125. Public attendance: 25,000. Free to public. Free adjacent parking. Apply with online application form at www.royaloakarts. com and 3 images of current work. Space fee: $260 (plus a $20 nonrefundable processing fee per medium). Exhibition space: 15×15. For more

information, e-mail, call or visit website. Fair located at Memorial Park.

TIPS "Be sure to label your images on the front with name, size of work and 'top.'"

RUBBER STAMP & PAPER ARTS FESTIVALS
(541)574-8000. E-mail: info@heirloompro.com. Website: www.heirloompro.com. Estab. 1993.

ADDITIONAL INFORMATION "Retail Consumer Events featuring Art Stamps, Cardmaking, Scrapbooking and Paper Arts. You will find art stamps, paper, cardstock and envelopes, inks and pads, die-cuts, brass stencils, glitter, embossing powder, tools, pencils, pens and markers, embellishments, and more. Classes, workshops, Design and Treasure, make 'n takes, demonstrrations. Learn, become inspired, and shop." For more information, visit website.

SACO SIDEWALK ART FESTIVAL
P.O. Box 336, 12½ Pepperell Square, Suite 2A, Saco ME 04072. (207)286-3546. E-mail: sacospirit@hotmail.com. Website: www. sacospirit.com. Estab. 1970. Event held in late June. Annual event organized and managed by Saco Spirit, Inc., a nonprofit organization committed to making Saco a better place to live and work by enhancing the vitality of our downtown. Dedicated to promoting art and culture in our community. Space fee: $75. Exhibition space: 10×10. For more information, visit website. Festival located in historic downtown Saco.

TIPS "Offer a variety of pieces priced at various levels."

➕ SACRAMENTO ARTS FESTIVAL
Sacramento Convention Center, Sacramento CA. (805)667-9290. Fax: (844)272-2796. E-mail: americanartfestival@yahoo.com. Website: www.sacartsfest.com. **Contact:** Warren Cook, producer. Estab. 1998. Event held annually in early November. Indoors. Accepts handmade crafts. Accepts fine arts. Juried event. No prizes given. Average number of exhibitors: 225. Average number of attendees: 10,000. Admission fee for public: $8 for adults, $7 for seniors, free for kids.

ADDITIONAL INFORMATION Deadline: April 30, 2017. Application fee: $10 or ZAPP. Space fee: $590 for 8×10, $730 for 10×10. Average gross sales for typical exhibitor: $4,000. For more information, e-mail, visit website, or call.

SACRAMENTO ARTS FESTIVAL
(805)461-6700. E-mail: americanartfestivals@yahoo.com. Website: www.sacartsfest.com. Art and craft show held annually in November. Outdoors. Accepts handmade crafts and other mediums. Juried. Number of exhibitors: see website. Number of attendees: 10,000. Free to public. Apply via www.zapplication.org.

ADDITIONAL INFORMATION Deadline for entry: April. Application fee: $10. Space fee: varies. Exhibition space: varies. For more information, e-mail, call, or visit website.

ST. ARMANDS CIRCLE CRAFT FESTIVAL
270 Central Blvd., Suite 107B, Jupiter FL 33458. (561)746-6615. Fax: (561)746-6528. E-mail: info@artfestival.com. Website: www.artfestival. com. **Contact:** Malinda Ratliff, communications manager. Estab. 2004. Fine art and craft fair held biannually in January and November. Outdoors. Accepts photography, jewelry, mixed media, sculpture, wood, ceramic, glass, painting, digital, fiber, metal. Juried. Number of exhibitors: 180–210. Number of attendees: 80,000–100,000. Free to public. Apply online via www.zapplication.org.

ADDITIONAL INFORMATION Deadline: see website. Application fee: $25. Space fee: $415–435. Exhibition space: 10×10 and 10×20. For more information, e-mail, call, or visit website. Fair held in St. Armands Circle in Sarasota, Florida.

ST. CHARLES FINE ART SHOW
2 E. Main St., St. Charles IL 60174. (630)443-3967. E-mail: info@downtownstcharles. org. Website: www.downtownstcharles.org/fineartshow. **Contact:** Jamie Blair. Fine art show held annually in May during Memorial Day weekend. Outdoors. Accepts photography, painting, sculpture, glass, ceramics, jewelry, nonwearable fiber art. Juried by committee: submit 4 slides of art and 1 slide of booth/

display. Awards/prizes: Cash awards in several categories. Free to public. Artists can apply via website.

ADDITIONAL INFORMATION Deadline for entry: early January. Jury fee: $35. Space fee: $375. Exhibition space: 10×10. For more information, e-mail or visit website.

ST. CLAIR ART FAIR

(810)329-9576. Fax: (810)329-9464. Website: www.stclairart.org.

ADDITIONAL INFORMATION The annual St. Clair Art Fair is1 of the oldest art fairs in eastern Michigan. This juried Art Fair is traditionally the last full weekend in June, Saturday and Sunday. For more information, visit website.

ST. GEORGE ART FESTIVAL

50 S. Main, St. George UT 84770. (435)627-4500. E-mail: artadmn@sgcity.org; gary.sanders@sgcity.org; leisure@sgcity.org. Website: www.sgcity.org/artfestival. **Contact:** Gary Sanders. Estab. 1979. Fine arts and crafts show held annually Easter weekend in either March or April. Outdoors. Accepts photography, painting, wood, jewelry, ceramics, sculpture, drawing, 3D mixed media, glass, metal, digital. Juried from digital submissions. Awards/prizes: $5,000 Purchase Awards. Art pieces selected will be placed in the city's permanent collections. Number of exhibitors: 110. Public attendance: 20,000/day. Free to public. Apply by completing application form via EntryThingy, nonrefundable application fee, slides or digital format of 4 current works in each category and 1 of booth, and SASE.

ADDITIONAL INFORMATION Deadline for entry: January 11. Exhibition space: 10×11. For more information, visit website or e-mail.

TIPS "Have more than 50% originals. Have quality booths and setup to display art in best possible manner. Be outgoing and friendly with buyers."

ST. JOHN MEDICAL CENTER FESTIVAL OF THE ARTS

(440)808-9201. E-mail: ardis.radak@csauh. com. Website: www.sjws.net/festival_of_arts. aspx. **Contact:** Ardis Radak. Art and craft show held annually in July. Outdoors. Accepts handmade crafts, ceramics, glass, fiber, glass, graphics, jewelry, leather, metal, mixed media, painting, photography, printmaking, sculpture, woodworking. Juried. Awards/prizes: Best of Show, 1st place, 2nd place, honorable mention. Number of exhibitors: 200. Number of attendees: 15,000. Free to public. Apply via www.zapplication.org.

ADDITIONAL INFORMATION Deadline for entry: May. Application fee: $15. Space fee: $300 (single); $600 (double). Exhibition space: 10×10 (single); 10×20 (double). For more information, e-mail, call, or visit website.

ST. JOHN'S CHRISTMAS CRAFT SHOW

St. John's Catholic School, 37 Pleasant St, Brunswick Maine 04011. (207)725-5507. E-mail: craftshow@sjcsbme.org. Website: www.sjcsbme.org; Facebook.com/sjcscraftshow. **Contact:** Amy Pelletier, show director. Estab. 1973. Arts and crafts/holiday show held in December. Indoors. Accepts handmade crafts, art, photography, packaged artisan foods. Juried. Exhibitors: 30+. Number of attendees: 600–700. Free to public. Apply by phone or e-mail.

ADDITIONAL INFORMATION Deadline for entry: July 1. Application fee: none. Space fee: varies. Exhibition space: varies. For more information, e-mail, call, or visit website.

TIPS Local artisans should submit completed application with clear focused photos of product and display by deadline for best chance of acceptance. Incomplete applications will be rejected. This is a school fund-raiser and is less than 2 weeks before Christmas.

ST. LOUIS ART FAIR

225 S. Meramec Ave., Suite 105, St. Louis MO 63105. E-mail: info@culturalfestivals.com. Website: www.culturalfestivals.com. **Contact:** Laura Miller, director of operations. Estab. 1994. Fine art/craft show held annually in September, the weekend after Labor Day. Outdoors. Accepts photography, ceramics, drawings, digital, glass, fiber, jewelry, mixed media, metalwork, printmaking, paintings, sculpture, and wood. Juried event, uses 5 jurors using 3 rounds, digital

app. Total prize money available: $21,000—26 awards ranging from $500–1,000. Number of exhibitors: 180. Average attendance: 130,000. Free to public. $40 application fee. Space fee: $625–725. 100 sq. ft. Average gross sales for exhibitor: $8,500. Apply at www.zapplication. org. For more information, call, e-mail, or visit website. Fair held in the central business district of Clayton Missouri.

TIPS "Look at shows and get a feel for what it is."

ST. PATRICK'S DAY CRAFT SALE & FALL CRAFT SALE

P.O. Box 461, Maple Lake MN 55358-0461. Website: www.maplelakechamber.com. **Contact:** Kathy. Estab. 1988. Arts and crafts show held biannually in March and early November. Indoors. Number of exhibitors: 30–40. Public attendance: 300–600. Free to public.

ADDITIONAL INFORMATION Deadline for entry: 2 weeks before the event. Exhibition space: 10×10. For more information, or an application, visit website.

TIPS "Don't charge an arm and a leg for the items. Don't overcrowd your items. Be helpful, but not pushy."

ST. PETE BEACH COREY AREA CRAFT FESTIVAL

270 Central Blvd., Suite 107B, Jupiter FL 33458. (561)746-6615. Fax: (561)746-6528. E-mail: info@artfestival.com. Website: www.artfestival. com. **Contact:** Malinda Ratliff, communications manager.

ADDITIONAL INFORMATION "Corey Ave. in St. Pete Beach comes alive with the nation's best crafters displaying their handmade pottery, jewelry, paintings, and so much more! This open-air craft festival also includes a Green Market featuring exotic live plants, handmade soaps, savory dips, and gourmet sauces. Join us for a fun, free event in the heart of St. Pete Beach."

SALEM ART FAIR & FESTIVAL

(503)581-2228. Fax: (503)371-3342. Website: www.salemart.org.

ADDITIONAL INFORMATION "SAA is the proud organization behind the nationally ranked Salem Art Fair and Festival, which is both our largest annual fund-raiser and the largest festival of its kind in Oregon. Each year, the SAF&F attracts about 35,000 visitors from all over the nation and is committed to upholding the importance of fine arts and crafts by providing access to a range of artistic mediums appealing to both art appreciators and art collectors alike. With a variety of different activities and offerings, the art fair is an experience the whole family can enjoy." For more information, visit website.

SALEM ARTS FESTIVAL

Salem MA 01970. (978)744-0004 ext.15. Fax: (978)745-3855. E-mail: kylie@salemmainstreets. org. Website: www.salemartsfestival.com. **Contact:** Kylie Sullivan.

ADDITIONAL INFORMATION "The Salem Arts Festival promotes the arts in downtown Salem through a collaborative festival for residents and visitors providing opportunities to highlight the existing artist community and encourage general community participation in the arts. The festival regularly draws over 5,000 visitors. The festival is looking for art and performance for the sophisticated art patron as well as for the art novice including interactive events for children. It will engage participants of diverse backgrounds and ages by reaching out to current art patrons, local students, and the community at large." For more information, visit website.

SALT FORK ARTS & CRAFTS FESTIVAL

P.O. Box 250, Cambridge OH 43725. (740)439-9379; 740-732-2259. E-mail: director@saltforkfestival.org. Website: www. saltforkfestival.org. The Salt Fork Arts & Crafts Festival (SFACF) is a juried festival that showcases high-quality art in a variety of mediums, painting, pottery, ceramics, fiber art, metalwork, jewelry, acrylics, mixed media, photography, and more. Between 90 and 100 artists come from all over the US, for this 3-day event. In addition, the festival heralds Heritage of the Arts. This program offers a look at Early American and Appalachian arts and crafts, many of which are demonstrated by craftsmen practicing arts such as basket weaving, flint knapping, spindling, flute making, quilting, blacksmithing, and more. Area students are given the opportunity to display their work , visitors are entertained throughout the weekend by a variety of talented performing artists, concessionaires offer satisfying foods, and there are crafts for kids and adults. For more information, visit website.

SALT LAKE'S FAMILY CHRISTMAS GIFT SHOW

South Towne Exposition Center, 9575 S. State St., Sandy UT 84070. (800)521-7469. Fax: (425)889-8165. E-mail: saltlake@showcaseevents.org. Website: www.showcaseevents.org. **Contact:** Dena Sablan, show manager. Estab. 1999. Seasonal holiday show held annually in November. Indoors. Accepts gifts, handmade crafts, art, photography, pottery, glass, jewelry, clothing, fiber. Juried. Exhibitors: 450. Number of attendees: 25,000. Admission: $12.50 (for all 3 days); 13 and under free. Apply via website or call or e-mail for application.

ADDITIONAL INFORMATION Deadline for entry: October 31. Space fee: contact via website, phone, e-mail. Exhibition space: 10×10. For more information, e-mail, call, send SASE, or visit website.

TIPS "Competitive pricing, attractive booth display, quality product, something unique for sale, friendly and outgoing personality."

SAN DIEGO FESTIVAL OF THE ARTS

1600 Pacific Hwy, San Diego CA 92101. (619)744-0534. E-mail: info@sdfestivalofthearts.org. Website: www.sdfestivalofthearts.org. **Contact:** Kaylie Rolin. Estab. 1987. Annual fine art show held in early June. Outdoors. Accepts handmade crafts, sculpture, glass, ceramics, paper, wood, paint, mix, fiber/textile, photography, jewelry. Juried. Awards/prizes: Best of Show in each category. Exhibitors: 195. Number of attendees: 7,000. Admission: $9–16. Apply via www.zapplication.org.

ADDITIONAL INFORMATION Deadline for entry: March 1. Application fee: $25 Space fee: $500–$800. Exhibition space: 10×10, 10×20. For more information, visit website.

SANDY SPRINGS ARTSAPALOOZA

6100 Lake Forrest Dr. NE, Sand Springs GA 30328. (404)873-1222. E-mail: info@affps.com. Website: www.sandyspringsartsapalooza.com. **Contact:** Randall Fox, festival director. Estab. 2011. Arts and crafts show held annually mid-April. Outdoors. Accepts handmade crafts, painting, photography, sculpture, leather, metal, glass, jewelry. Juried by a panel. Awards/prizes: ribbons. Number of exhibitors: 150. Number of attendees: 25,000. Free to public. Apply online at www.zapplication.org.

ADDITIONAL INFORMATION Deadline for entry: February 2. Application fee: $25. Space fee: $225. Exhibition space: 10×10. For more information, see website.

SANDY SPRINGS FESTIVAL & ARTISTS MARKET

6075 Sandy Springs Circle, Sandy Springs GA 30328. (404)873-1222. E-mail: info@affps.com. Website: www.sandyspringsartsapalooza.com. **Contact:** Randall Fox, festival director. Estab. 1986. Arts and crafts show held annually late June. Outdoors. Accepts handmade crafts, painting, photography, sculpture, leather, metal, glass, jewelry. Juried by a panel. Awards/prizes: ribbons. Number of exhibitors: 120. Number of attendees: 40,000. Free to public. Apply online at www.zapplication.com.

ADDITIONAL INFORMATION Deadline for entry: July 26. Application fee: $25. Space fee: $250. Exhibition space: 10×10. For more information, visit website.

☻ SAN FRANCISCO FINE CRAFT SHOW

American Craft Council Shows, 155 Water St., 4th Floor, Unit 5, Brooklyn NY 11201. (612) 206-3100. E-mail: council@craftcouncil.org. Website: www.craftcouncil.org. Art and craft show held annually in August. Indoors. Accepts handmade crafts, ceramics, fiber, metal, and other mediums. Juried. Awards/prizes: Awards of Excellence.

Number of exhibitors: 225. Number of attendees: varies. Free to public. Apply online.

ADDITIONAL INFORMATION Deadline for entry: August. Application fee: $30 + $10 handling/ processing fee for each set of images. Space fee: varies. Exhibition space: varies. For more information, e-mail, call, or visit website.

SAN MARCO ART FESTIVAL

270 Central Blvd., Suite 107B, Jupiter FL 33458. (561)746-6615. Fax: (561)746-6528. E-mail: info@artfestival.com. Website: www.artfestival. com. **Contact:** Malinda Ratliff, communications manager.

ADDITIONAL INFORMATION "Browse and purchase original handmade works including: glass, photography, painting, mixed media, fiber, jewelry, and much more. Artists will be on hand all weekend to share their inspirations for each uniquely crafted piece. No matter what you're looking for, you'll be sure to find it among the numerous artisans participating in this greatly anticipated, juried, community art fair."

SANTA CALI GON DAYS FESTIVAL

210 W. Truman Rd., Independence MO 64050. (816)252-4745. E-mail: lois@ichamber.biz. Website: www.santacaligon.com. Estab. 1973. Market vendors 4-day show held annually Labor Day weekend. Outdoors. Ranked in top 20 for vendor profitability. Accepts handmade arts and crafts, photography, and other mediums. Juried by committee. Number of exhibitors: 250. Public attendance: 300,000. Free to public. Apply online. Application requirements include completed application, full booth fee, $20 jury fee (via seperate check), 4 photos of product/art and 1 photo of display. Exhibition space: 10×10. For more information, e-mail, call, or visit website.

SANTA CRUZ COUNTY HERITAGE FOUNDATION HOLIDAY CRAFT & GIFT FAIR

(831)612-9118. E-mail: heritageholidayfair@ gmail.com. Website: www.sccfheritage.org/ heritage-holiday-craft-fair.

ADDITIONAL INFORMATION "This festive event full of holiday cheer includes crafts, folk art, antiques, collectibles, gift foods, delicious refreshments at the food courts, and free parking. The 25-foot Christmas tree will light up your child's eyes! The Agricultural History Project will host a County Christmas. Children under 5 are free." For more information, visit website.

SANTA FE COLLEGE SPRING ARTS FESTIVAL

3000 NW 83rd St., Gainesville FL 32606. (352)395-5355. Fax: (352)336-2715. E-mail: kathryn.lehman@sfcollege.edu. Website: www. sfspringarts.com. **Contact:** Kathryn Lehman, cultural programs coordinator. Estab. 1969. Fine arts and crafts festival held in mid-April (see website for details).

ADDITIONAL INFORMATION "The festival is1 of the 3 largest annual events in Gainesville and is known for its high-quality, unique artwork." Held in the downtown historic district. Public attendance: 130,000+. For more information, e-mail, call, or visit website.

SARASOTA CRAFT FAIR

270 Central Blvd., Suite 107B, Jupiter FL 33458. (561)746-6615. Fax: (561)746-6528. E-mail: info@artfestival.com. Website: www.artfestival. com. Contact: Malinda Ratliff, communications manager. "Behold contemporary crafts from more than 100 of the nation's most talented artisans. A variety of jewelry, pottery, ceramics, photography, painting, clothing, and much more—all handmade in America—will be on display, ranging from $15–3,000. An expansive Green Market with plants, orchids, exotic flora, handmade soaps, gourmet spices, and freshly popped kettle corn further complements the weekend, blending nature with nurture." For more information, visit website.

SARATOGA ARTS CELEBRATION

(518)852-6478. E-mail: suebg.art@gmail. com. Website: www.saratogaartscelebration. org; gordonfinearts.org. Estab. 2008. Arts and crafts show held annually in August. Outdoors. Accepts handmade crafts and fine art. Juried.

Awards/prizes: cash and ribbons. Exhibitors: 100. Number of attendees: 7,000–10,000. Free to public. Apply online.

ADDITIONAL INFORMATION Deadline for entry: April 1. Application fee: $25. Space fee: $350–450. Exhibition space: 10×12. For more information, visit website, e-mail, or call. Event located at Harbor Point Park, Stamford, Connecticut.

SAULT SAINTE MARIE ART, CRAFT & FAMILY FUN FAIR

(906)253-9840. Fax: (888)664-6402. E-mail: coordinator@saultcraftfair.org. Website: www. saultcraftfair.org.

ADDITIONAL INFORMATION "This event is held annually on the last Friday of June. Please join us on the lawn of Historic City Hall, overlooking the east end of the Sault Locks and the St. Mary's River." For more information, visit website.

SAUSALITO ART FESTIVAL

P.O. Box 10, Sausalito CA 94966. (415)332-3555. Fax: (415)331-1340. E-mail: info@ sausalitoartfestival.org. Website: www. sausalitoartfestival.org. **Contact:** Paul Anderson, managing director; Lexi Matthews, operations coordinator. Estab. 1952. Premiere fine art festival held annually Labor Day weekend. Outdoors. Accepts painting, photography, 2D and 3D mixed media, ceramics, drawing, fiber, functional art, glass, jewelry, printmaking, sculpture, watercolor, woodwork. Juried. Jurors are elected by their peers from the previous year's show (1 from each category). They meet for a weekend at the end of March and give scores of 1, 2, 4, or 5 to each applicant (5 being the highest). Five images must be submitted, 4 of art and 1 of booth. Number of exhibitors: 280. Public attendance: 40,000. Apply by visiting website for instructions and application. Applications are through Juried Art Services.

ADDITIONAL INFORMATION Deadline for entry: March. Exhibition space: 100 or 200 sq. ft. Application fee: $50; $100 for late applications. Booth fees range from $1,425–3,125. Average gross sales/exhibitor: $7,700. For more information, visit website. Festival located in Marinship Park.

SAWDUST ART FESTIVAL

935 Laguna Canyon Rd., Laguna Beach CA 92651. (949)494-3030. Fax: (949)494-7390. E-mail: info@sawdustartfestival.org; tkling@sawdustartfestival.org. Website: www. sawdustartfestival.org. Estab. 1967. Annual arts and crafts show held annually June–August (see website for dates; also has winter shows). Outdoors. Accepts handmade crafts, all art mediums. Awards/prizes: peer awards. Exhibitors: 210 (summer); 175 (winter). Number of attendees: 300,000 (summer); 20,000 (winter). Admission: $8.50, adults; $7, seniors; $4 children ages 6–12; children 5 and under free. Application release date varies (see website).

ADDITIONAL INFORMATION Deadline for entry: varies (see website). Application fee: $30 per show. Space fee: $1,250+ (summer). Exhibition space: 10×8. For more information, call, e-mail, or see website.

SAWTOOTH MOUNTAIN MAMAS ARTS & CRAFTS FAIR

P.O. Box 33, Stanley ID 83278. (208)781-0889. E-mail: stanleymountainmamas@gmail.com. Website: www.sawtoothmountainmamas.org. **Contact:** Kay Davies, fair chair. Estab. 1976. Event held annually, always the 3rd weekend in July. Outdoors. Accepts handmade crafts. Juried. Jewelry is pre-juried. All others juried at fair. No prizes given. Average number of exhibitors: 140. Average number of attendees: 5,000–8,000. Free admission.

ADDITIONAL INFORMATION Deadline for applications: June 15, 2016. No application fee. Space fee: $125 for 10×10; $175 for 10×15; $225 for 10×20; additional $50 for corners. For more information, e-mail, visit website, or call. Must be original and handmade by vendor.

SCOTTSDALE ARTS FESTIVAL

7380 E. Second St., Scottsdale AZ 85251, USA. (480)874-4671. Fax: (480)874-4699. E-mail: festival@sccarts.org. Website: www. scottsdaleartsfestival.org. Estab. 1970. Fine arts and crafts show held annually, this year March 10–12, 2017. Outdoors at the Scottsdale Civic Center Park. Accepts photography, jewelry, ceramics, digital art, sculpture, metal, glass, drawings, fiber, paintings, printmaking, mixed media, wood. Juried. Awards/prizes: 1st in each category and Best of Show. Number of exhibitors: 170. Public attendance: 25,000. Public admission: $10/single day; $15/2-day pass. Apply through www.zapplication.org.

ADDITIONAL INFORMATION Exhibition space: 100–200 sq. ft. For more information, visit website www.scottsdaleartsfestival.org.

SCOTTSDALE CELEBRATION OF FINE ART

Celebration of Fine Art, 7900 E. Greenway Rd., Suite 101, Scottsdale AZ 85260-1714. (480)443-7695. Fax: (480)596-8179. E-mail: info@celebrateart.com. Website: www.celebrateart.com. The Celebration of Fine Art™ is a 10-week long, juried show taking place from mid-January through mid-March in Scottsdale, Arizona. We jury not only for quality but variety. This helps ensure that direct competition is minimized and that you will have the best opportunity for success. All styles of art in all mediums are welcome. In addition to painting and sculpture we also have fine crafts such as furniture, jewelry, ceramics, basketry, and weaving. Only work created by the artist and handmade work is accepted. We do not allow manufactured goods of any kind. Artists who have previously been selected for the show will be juried in the2 months following the current exhibit.

ADDITIONAL INFORMATION Additional details, prices, and other information are contained in the artist application packet. For more information, visit website.

SCRAPBOOK EXPO

(951)734-4307. Fax: (951)848-0711. E-mail: exhibitors@scrapbookexpo.com. Website: www.scrapbookexpo.com.

ADDITIONAL INFORMATION "Scrapbook Expo combines Scrapbooking, Paper Crafting, and Stamping and offers YOU the crafter the most amazing crafting experience you'll ever find." For dates and more information, visit website.

SEASONS OF THE HEART CRAFT, DECOR & GIFT FAIRE

P.O. Box 191, Ramona CA 92064. (760)445-1330. E-mail: seasonsoftheheart@cox.net. Website: seasonsoftheheartcraftfaire.com. **Contact:** Linda or Ron Mulick, owners/promoters. Estab. 1988. Arts and crafts show, seasonal/holiday show held annually in November. Indoors. Accepts handmade crafts, collectibles, gourmet foods. Exhibitors: 100. Number of attendees: 6,000. Free to public. Apply online.

ADDITIONAL INFORMATION Deadline for entry: October 1. Application fee: none. Space fee: $225 + 15% of sales. Exhibition space: 10×10. Average sales: $2,000. For more information, e-mail, visit website, or call.

TIPS "Do quality work and price your items reasonably."

SEATTLE GIFT SHOW

Washington State Convention Center, Seattle WA , U.S. (800)318-2238. Website: www.seattlegiftshow.com. **Contact:** April Turner, sales manager. Semiannual event. Wholesale show. Indoors. Not for general public. Accepts handmade craft merchants. Accepts pattern/magazine/book publishers. Select sections are juried. No prizes given. Admission fee: n/a.

ADDITIONAL INFORMATION Deadline for entry applications: n/a. Application fee: n/a. Space fee: See prospectus for booth rates. For more information, exhibitors should e-mail, visit web site, or call.

SEATTLE HANDMADE

Alice Kellog, 2805 Old Farm Rd., Edmond OK 73013. Website: www.seattlehandmade.com.

ADDITIONAL INFORMATION "Enjoy the official beginning of the Holiday gift-shopping season and find the perfect gifts for the loved1s on your list at the Seattle Handmade Holiday Show (formerly etsyRAIN Handmade Holiday Show). Celebrating many fabulous years of supporting the handmade community of Seattle and the greater Pacific Northwest." For more information, visit website.

SEATTLE'S HOLIDAY DIY FAIR

E-mail: katherineh@theveraproject.org. Website: www.theveraproject.org.

ADDITIONAL INFORMATION "This extravaganza features several independent Northwest record and cassette labels, musicians, silk-screened show posters, vintage record dealers, local artists, craft makers, and designers selling their wares throughout Vera's venue. This is the perfect opportunity to find a1-of-a-kind gift just in time for the holidays. Interactive entertainments will take place throughout the day, including the Surrealist Songwriting Project and live silk-screening lessons, and the event will also include Hollow Earth DJs spinning on-site, a bake sale, and a raffle for rare posters, records, and more!" For more information, visit website.

SEATTLE WEAVERS GUILD ANNUAL SHOW & SALE

E-mail: sale@seattleweaversguild.com. Website: www.seattleweaversguild.com/sale.asp.

ADDITIONAL INFORMATION "The annual sale showcases1-of-a-kind handcrafted items, including towels, rugs, blankets, tapestries, exquisite jewelry, accessories for pets, children's items, handmade cards, household goods, hats, bags, wall art, jackets, scarves, wraps, sculptural basketry, liturgical weaving, handspun and/or hand-dyed yarns along with weaving and spinning tools. There will also be demonstrations of spinning, weaving and other fiber crafts during the sale. Proceeds from the sale are used to fund the guild's volunteer outreach program and to bring talented practicing artists to Seattle Weavers' Guild to educate both its members and the public. Parking and entrance to the sale are free." Open to members only. For more information, visit website.

SELL-A-RAMA

Tyson Wells Sell-A-Rama, P.O. Box 60, Quartzsite AZ 85346. (928)927-6364. E-mail: tysonwells@tds.net. Website: www.tysonwells.com. Arts and craft show held annually in January. Outdoors and indoors. Accepts handmade crafts, ceramics, paintings, jewelry, glass, photography, wearable art, and other mediums. Juried.

Number of exhibitors: see website. Number of attendees: varies. Free to public. Apply online.

ADDITIONAL INFORMATION Deadline for entry: see website for dates. Application fee: none. Space fee: varies. Exhibition space: varies. For more information, e-mail, call, or visit website.

SFUSD ART'S FESTIVAL

(415)695-2441. Fax: (415)695-2496. E-mail: sfusdaf2014@gmail.com. Website: sfusdartsfestival.org.

ADDITIONAL INFORMATION "The San Francisco Unified School District proudly presents the SFUSD Arts Festival; a celebration of student creativity in visual, literary, media, and performing arts. This unique San Francisco event, (formerly Young at Art), has been a point of destination for families, teachers, artists, and community members from San Francisco and beyond. The promise of equity and access in arts education for all students K–12 during the curricular day, made real by the SFUSD's groundbreaking Arts Education Master Plan, finds its point of destination in this festival, where all who attend may see for themselves the inspiration and creativity inherent in all of our youngest San Franciscans!" For more information, visit website.

SHADYSIDE ART & CRAFT FESTIVAL

270 Central Blvd., Suite 107B, Jupiter FL 33458. (561)746-6615. Fax: (561)746-6528. E-mail: info@artfestival.com. Website: www.artfestival.com. **Contact:** Malinda Ratliff, communications manager. Estab. 1996. Fine art and craft fair held annually in late May. Outdoors. Accepts photography, jewelry, mixed media, sculpture, wood, ceramic, glass, painting, digital, fiber, metal. Juried. Number of exhibitors: 125. Number of attendees: 60,000. Free to public. Apply online via www.zapplication.org.

ADDITIONAL INFORMATION Deadline: see website. Application fee: $25. Space fee: $395. Exhibition space: 10×10 and 10×20. For more information, e-mail, call, or visit website. Festival located at Walnut St. in Shadyside (Pittsburgh, Pennsylvania).

SHADYSIDE: THE ART FESTIVAL ON WALNUT STREET

270 Central Blvd., Suite 107B, Jupiter FL 33458. (561)746-6615. Fax: (561)746-6528. E-mail: info@artfestival.com. Website: www.artfestival.com. **Contact:** Malinda Ratliff, communications manager. Estab. 1996. Fine art and craft fair held annually in late August. Outdoors. Accepts photography, jewelry, mixed media, sculpture, wood, ceramic, glass, painting, digital, fiber, metal. Juried. Number of exhibitors: 125. Number of attendees: 100,000. Free to public. Apply online via www.zapplication.org.

ADDITIONAL INFORMATION Deadline: see website. Application fee: $25. Space fee: $450. Exhibition space: 10×10 and 10×20. For more information, e-mail, call, or visit website. Festival located at Walnut St. in Shadyside (Pittsburgh, Pennsylvania).

SHIPSHEWANA QUILT FESTIVAL

P.O. Box 245, Shipshewana IN 46565. (260)768-4887. E-mail: info@shipshewanaquiltfest.com. Website: www.shipshewanaquiltfest.com. **Contact:** Nancy Troyer, show organizer. Estab. 2009. Quilt and vendor show held annually in late June. Indoors. Accepts handmade crafts and other mediums. Juried. Awards/prizes: cash. Exhibitors: 20. Number of attendees: 4,000. Admission: $8/day; $12/week. Apply online.

ADDITIONAL INFORMATION Deadline for entry: see website. Application fee: none. Space fee: varies. Exhibition space: varies. Average sales: $5,000–10,000. For more information, e-mail, call, or visit website.

SIDEWALK ART MART

Downtown Helena, Inc., Mount Helena Music Festival, 225 Cruse Ave., Suite B, Helena MT 59601. (406)447-1535. Fax: (406)447-1533. E-mail: jmchugh@mt.net. Website: www.downtownhelena.com. **Contact:** Jim McHugh. Estab. 1974. Arts, crafts and music festival held annually in June. Outdoors. Accepts photography. No restrictions except to display appropriate work for all ages. Number of exhibitors: 50+. Public attendance: 5,000. Free to public. Apply by visiting website to download application. Space fee: $100–125. Exhibition space: 10×10. For more information, e-mail, call, or visit website. Festival held at Women's Park in Helena, Montana.

TIPS "Greet people walking by and have an eye-catching product in front of booth. We have found that high-end artists or expensively priced art booths that had business cards with e-mail or website information received many contacts after the festival."

SIERRA MADRE WISTARIA FESTIVAL

19 Suffolk Ave., Unit A, Sierra Madre CA 91024. (626)355-5111; (626)233-5524. Fax: (626)306-1150. E-mail: smadrecc@gmail.com. Website: www.sierramadrechamber.com/wistaria/photos.htm. Fine arts, crafts and garden show held annually in March. Outdoors. Accepts photography, anything handcrafted. Juried. Craft vendors send in application and photos to be juried. Most appropriate are selected. Awards/prizes: Number of exhibitors: 175. Public attendance: 12,000. Free to public. Apply by sending completed and signed application, 3–5 photographs of their work, application fee, license application, space fee, and 2 SASEs.

ADDITIONAL INFORMATION Deadline for entry: late December. Application fee: $25. Public Safety Fee (nonrefundable) $25. Space fee: $185. Exhibition space: 10×10. For more information, e-mail, visit website, or call. Applications can be found on chamber website.

TIPS "Have a clear and simple application. Be nice."

SIESTA FIESTA

270 Central Blvd., Suite 107B, Jupiter FL 33458. (561)746-6615. Fax: (561)746-6528. E-mail: info@artfestival.com. Website: www.artfestival.com. **Contact:** Malinda Ratliff, communications manager. Estab. 1978. Fine art and craft fair held annually in April. Outdoors. Accepts photography, jewelry, mixed media, sculpture, wood, ceramic, glass, painting, digital, fiber, metal. Juried. Number of exhibitors: 85. Number of attendees: 40,000. Free to public. Apply online via www.zapplication.org.

ADDITIONAL INFORMATION Deadline: see website. Application fee: $25. Space fee: $350. Exhibition space: 10×10 and 10×20. For more information, e-mail, call, or visit website. Festival located at Ocean Blvd. in Siesta Key Village.

SIESTA KEY CRAFT FESTIVAL
270 Central Blvd., Suite 107B, Jupiter FL 33458. (561)746-6615. Fax: (561)746-6528. E-mail: info@artfestival.com. Website: www.artfestival.com. **Contact:** Malinda Ratliff, communications manager.

ADDITIONAL INFORMATION "Join us at the annual Siesta Key Craft Festival and take in the sand and the sea along Ocean Boulevard and Beach Rd. as you discover wonderful creations from more than 100 crafters exhibiting and selling their work in an outdoor gallery. From photography, paintings, sculpture, jewelry, and more showcased from local and traveling crafters, your visit to Siesta Key is promised to be a feast for the senses. This spectacular weekend festival is not to be missed." For more information, visit website.

SISTERS ANTIQUES IN THE PARK
Central Oregon Shows, P.O. Box 1555, Sisters OR 97759. (541)420-0279. E-mail: centraloregonshows@gmail.com. Website: www.centraloregonshows.com. This event features antiques, collectibles, some crafts, food, and entertainment. This event runs the same time as the Sisters Chamber of Commerce annual Classic Car Show. This is a Friday and Saturday event. For more information, visit website. Event takes place at the Sisters Creekside Park (Hwy. 20 and Jefferson St.).

SISTERS ART IN THE PARK
Central Oregon Shows, P.O. Box 1555, Sisters OR 97759. (541)420-0279. E-mail: centraloregonshows@gmail.com. Website: www.centraloregonshows.com. This annual event features a variety of arts, crafts, food, entertainment, and a special fund-raiser benefiting the Make-A-Wish Foundation of Oregon. This event runs the same time as the Sisters Rodeo and is located in the Sisters Creekside Park (Hwy. 20 and Jefferson Street).

SISTERS ARTIST MARKETPLACE
Central Oregon Shows, P.O. Box 1555, Sisters OR 97759. (541)420-0279. E-mail: centraloregonshows@gmail.com. Website: www.centraloregonshows.com. There will be a variety of arts, crafts, food, and entertainment. This event is on a Friday and Saturday only and requires a city business license for each vendor (see online application). For more information, visit website.

SISTERS ARTS & CRAFTS FESTIVAL
Central Oregon Shows, P.O. Box 1555, Sisters OR 97759. (541)420-0279. E-mail: centraloregonshows@gmail.com. Website: www.centraloregonshows.com. It is an annual event that featuresa variety of arts, crafts, food, entertainment, with a special fund-raiser benefiting the Make-A-Wish Foundation of Oregon. For more information, visit website. Event takes place at the Sisters Creekside Park (Highway 20 and Jefferson St.).

SISTERS FALL STREET FESTIVAL
Central Oregon Shows, P.O. Box 1555, Sisters OR 97759. (541)420-0279. E-mail: centraloregonshows@gmail.com. Website: www.centraloregonshows.com. This annual event features a variety of arts, crafts, food, and entertainment with a special fund-raiser benefiting the Sisters High School Visual Arts Department. For more information, visit website. Show takes place in downtown Sister on Oak St. and Main St.

SISTERS OUTDOOR QUILT SHOW
220 S. Ash St. #4, Sisters OR 97759. (541)549-0989. E-mail: info@soqs.org. Website: www.sistersoutdoorquiltshow.org. **Contact:** Jeanette Pilak, executive director. Estab. 1975. Quilt show held in July. Outdoors. Accepts handmade and machine-made quilts. Exhibitors: 600. Number of attendees: 12,000. Free to public. Apply online. Deadline for entry: May 31 (or when filled). Application fee: $10. Space fee: none. Exhibition space: quilts are hung. For more information, visit website. Show located on Cascade Ave. in Sisters, Oregon.

TIPS Watch the video on the home page of our website, then read the submission information on the registration page.

⊕ SISTERS WILD WEST SHOW

Central Oregon Shows, P.O. Box 1555, Sisters OR 97759. (541)420-0279. E-mail: centraloregonshows@gmail.com. Website: www.centraloregonshows.com. There will be a variety of arts, crafts, antiques, and food. Entertainment will be 6 western skits with a western front town and demonstrations. For more information, visit website. Show takes place at Bend/Sisters Garden RV Resort, 67667 Hwy. 20 (next to Sisters Rodeo grounds).

SKOKIE ART GUILD FINE ART EXPO

Devonshire Cultural Center, 4400 Greenwood St., Skokie IL 60077. (847)677-8163. E-mail: info@skokieartguild.org; skokieart@aol.com. Website: www.skokieartguild.org. Outdoor fine art/craft show open to all artists (18+) in the Chicagoland area. Held in mid-May. Entrance fee: $20 (members); $30 (nonmembers). Awards: 1st, 2nd, 3rd place ribbons, Purchase Awards.

ADDITIONAL INFORMATION Deadline for application: early May. Event held at Oakton Park.

TIPS Display your work in a professional manner: matted, framed, etc.

SLIDELL NEWCOMERS SELL-A-BRATION ARTS & CRAFTS SHOW

Slidell Newcomers Club, P.O. Box 2681, Slidell LA 70459. (985)641-2021. E-mail: ncsellabration@aol.com. Website: www.sell-a-brationcraftshow.webs.com. **Contact:** Linda Tate, show chair. Estab. 1982. Arts and crafts show held annually in October. Indoors. Accepts handmade crafts, original artwork, original photography. Number of exhibitors: 70–80. Number of attendees: 2,200–2,300. Free to public. Apply online.

ADDITIONAL INFORMATION Deadline for entry: October 5. Space fee: Starting at $110. Exhibition space: 10×10; 10×15; 10×20. For more information, see website.

SMITHSONIAN CRAFT SHOW

(202)633-5069. E-mail: joneshl@smithsonian.si.edu. Website: www.smithsoniancraftshow.org. **Contact:** Hannah Jones, administrative assistant. Art and craft show held annually in April. Indoors. Accepts handmade crafts, basketry, ceramics, decorative fiber, furniture, glass, jewelry, leather, metal, mixed media, paper, wearable art, and wood. Juried. Awards/prizes: Gold Award, Silver Award, Bronze Award, Excellence Awards, Exhibitor's Choice Awards. Number of exhibitors: 125. Number of attendees: 8,000. Admission: see website for rates. Apply online.

ADDITIONAL INFORMATION Deadline for entry: September. Application fee: $50. Space fee: varies. Exhibition space: varies. For more information, e-mail or visit website.

SMITHVILLE FIDDLERS' JAMBOREE AND CRAFT FESTIVAL

P.O. Box 83, Smithville TN 37166. (615)597-8500. E-mail: eadkins@smithvillejamboree.com. Website: www.smithvillejamboree.com. **Contact:** Emma Adkins, craft coordinator. Estab. 1971. Arts and crafts show held annually the weekend nearest the 4th of July holiday. Indoors. Juried by photos and personally talking with crafters. Awards/prizes: ribbons and free booth for following year for Best of Show, Best of Appalachian Craft, Best Display, Best New Comer. Number of exhibitors: 235. Public attendance: 130,000. Free to public. Apply online.

ADDITIONAL INFORMATION Deadline: May 1. Space fee: $125. Exhibition space: 12×12. Average gross sales/exhibitors: $1,200+. For more information, call or visit website. Festival held in downtown Smithville.

SMOKY HILL RIVER FESTIVAL FINE ART SHOW

(785)309-5770. E-mail: sahc@salina.org. Website: www.riverfestival.com. Fine art and craft show held annually in June. Outdoors. Accepts handmade crafts, ceramics, jewelry, fiber, mixed media, painting, drawing/pastels, glass, metal, wood, graphics/printmaking, digital, paper, sculpture, and photography. Juried.

Awards/prizes: Jurors' Merit Awards, Purchase Awards. Number of exhibitors: 90. Number of attendees: 60,000. Admission: $10 in advance; $15 at gate; children 11 and under free. Apply via www.zapplication.org.

ADDITIONAL INFORMATION Deadline for entry: February. Application fee: $30. Space fee: $275. Exhibition space: 10×10. For more information, e-mail or visit website.

SMOKY HILL RIVER FESTIVAL4 RIVERS CRAFT SHOW

(785)309-5770. E-mail: sahc@salina.org. Website: www.riverfestival.com. Fine art and craft show held annually in June. Outdoors. Accepts handmade crafts, ceramics, folk art, leather, paper, clothing, glass, metal, herbal/soaps, basketry, wood, mixed media, jewelry, fiber, and more. Juried. Awards/prizes: Jurors' Merit Awards. Number of exhibitors: 50. Number of attendees: 60,000. Admission: $10 in advance; $15 at gate; children 11 and under free. Apply via www.zapplication.org.

ADDITIONAL INFORMATION Deadline for entry: February. Application fee: $30. Space fee: $325. Exhibition space: 10×10. For more information, e-mail or visit website.

SNAKE ALLEY ART FAIR

E-mail: Contact form on website. Website: www.snakealley.com/artfair.html.

ADDITIONAL INFORMATION Art fair held annually on Father's Day. Features 104 selected artists from throughout the Midwest. For more information, visit website.

SOFA

(800)563-7632. Fax: (773)326-0660. E-mail: info@sofaexpo.com. Website: www.sofaexpo.com.

ADDITIONAL INFORMATION The annual Exposition of Sculpture Objects & Functional Art + Design Fair (SOFA) is a gallery-presented, international art exposition dedicated to bridging the worlds of design, decorative, and fine art. Works by emerging and established artists and designers are available for sale by premier galleries and dealers. For more information, visit website.

SOLANO AVE. STROLL

1563 Solano Ave., #101, Berkeley CA 94707. (510)527-5358. E-mail: info@solanostroll.org. Website: www.solanostroll.org. **Contact:** Allen Cain. Estab. 1974. Fine arts and crafts show held annually 2nd Sunday in September. Outdoors. "Since 1974, the merchants, restaurants, and professionals, as well as the twin cities of Albany and Berkeley have hosted the Solano Ave. Stroll, the East Bay's largest street festival." Accepts photography and all other mediums. Juried by board of directors. Number of exhibitors: 150 spaces for crafts; 600 spaces total. Public attendance: 250,000. Free to public.

ADDITIONAL INFORMATION Apply online in April or send SASE. Space fee: $150. Exhibition space: 10×10. For more information, e-mail, visit website, or send SASE. Event takes place on Solano Ave. in Berkeley and Albany, California.

TIPS "Have a clean presentation; small-ticket items as well as large-ticket items; great customer service; enjoy themselves."

SONORAN FESTIVAL OF FINE ART

(623)734-6526; (623)386-2269. E-mail: cvermillion12@cox.net; info@sonoranartsleague.com. Website: www.vermillionpromotions.com. **Contact:** Candy Vermillion.

ADDITIONAL INFORMATION "The prestigious Sonoron Arts Festival is1 of the largest open-air fine art venues in the Southwest featuring more than 125 local and nationally acclaimed artists. Sponsored each year by the Sonoran Arts League, the Festival is a juried show open to artists from around the country. With more than 400 members, the Arts League is a vital contributor to the cultural life in the Foothills and a focal point for artists and art patrons." For more information, visit website.

SOUTHERN WOMEN'S SHOW— BIRMINGHAM, ALABAMA

Southern Shows, Inc., Southern Shows, Inc., P.O. Box 36859, Charlotte NC 28236. (800)849-0248, ext. 107. E-mail: banderson@southernshows.com. Website: www.southernshows.com. **Contact:** Beth Anderson, show manager. Exhibitor fair held annually in October. Indoors.

Accepts handmade crafts and other items. Exhibitors: see website. Number of attendees: varies. Admission: $10 adults; $5 youth; children 6 and under free. Apply online.

ADDITIONAL INFORMATION Deadline for entry: see website. Application fee: see website. Space fee: varies. Exhibition space: varies. For more information, e-mail, visit website, or call.

⊕ SOUTH JERSEY PUMPKIN SHOW

B&K Enterprise, P.O. Box 925, Millville NJ 8332. (856)765-0118. Fax: (856)765-9050. E-mail: sjpumpkinshow@aol.com; bkenterprisenj@aol.com. Website: www.sjpumpkinshow.com. **Contact:** Kathy Wright, organizer. Estab. 2003. Arts and crafts show held annually 2nd weekend in October. Indoors and outdoors. Accepts fine art and handmade crafts, wood, metal, pottery, glass, quilts. Awards/prizes: $100 for Fall Booth. Exhibitors: 175. Number of attendees: 10,500. Admission: $5/car (good all 3 days). Apply via website.

ADDITIONAL INFORMATION Deadline for entry: late September. Application fee: none. Space fee: $40 (one day); $100 (weekend). Exhibition space: 10×10. For more information, e-mail, visit website, or call. Event held at Salem Co. Fairgrounds, 760 Harding Hwy., Woodstown, NJ.

THE SOUTHWEST ARTS FESTIVAL

Indio Chamber of Commerce, 82921 Indio Blvd., Indio CA 92201. (760)347-0676. Fax: (763)347-6069. E-mail: jonathan@indiochamber.org;swaf@indiochamber.org. Website: www.southwestartsfest.com. Estab. 1986.

ADDITIONAL INFORMATION Featuring over 275 acclaimed artists showing traditional, contemporary and abstract fine works of art and quality crafts, the festival is a major, internationally recognized cultural event attended by nearly 10,000 people. The event features a wide selection of clay, crafts, drawings, glasswork, jewelry, metalworks, paintings, photographs, printmaking, sculpture, and textiles. Application fee: $55. Easy check-in and check-out procedures with safe and secure access to festival grounds for setup and breakdown. Allow advance setup for artists with special requirements (very large art requiring the use of cranes, forklifts, etc., or artists with special needs). Artist parking is free. Disabled artist parking is available. Apply online. For more information, call, e-mail, or visit website. Show takes place in January.

SPACE COAST ART FESTIVAL

(321)784-3322. Fax: (866)815-3322. E-mail: info@spacecoastartfestival.com. Website: www.spacecoastartfestival.com. Art and craft show held annually in November. Outdoors. Accepts handmade crafts and other mediums. Juried. Awards/prizes: up to $50,000 in awards. Number of exhibitors: 250. Number of attendees: varies. Admission: see website. Apply online.

ADDITIONAL INFORMATION Deadline for entry: early July. Application fee: $40. Space fee: $300. Exhibition space: 12×12. For more information, e-mail, call, or visit website.

SPANISH SPRINGS ART & CRAFT FESTIVAL

270 Central Blvd., Suite 107B, Jupiter FL 33458. (561)746-6615. Fax: (561)746-6528. E-mail: info@artfestival.com. Website: www.artfestival.com. **Contact:** Malinda Ratliff, communications manager. Estab. 1997. Fine art and craft fair held biannually in January and November. Outdoors. Accepts photography, jewelry, mixed media, sculpture, wood, ceramic, glass, painting, digital, fiber, metal. Juried. Number of exhibitors: 210. Number of attendees: 20,000. Free to public. Apply online via www.zapplication.org or visit website for paper application.

ADDITIONAL INFORMATION Deadline: see website. Application fee: $15. Space fee: $265. Exhibition space: 10×10 and 10×20. For more information, e-mail, call, or visit website. Festival located at Spanish Springs, The Villages, Florida.

SPANKER CREEK FARM ARTS & CRAFTS FAIR

P.O. Box 5644, Bella Vista AR 72714. (479)685-5655. E-mail: info@spankercreekfarm.com. Website: www.spankercreekfarm.com. Arts and crafts show held biannually in the spring and fall. Outdoors and indoors. Accepts handmade crafts, ceramics, paintings, jewelry, glass, photography, wearable art, and other mediums. Juried. Number of exhibitors: see website. Number of attendees: varies. Free to public. Apply online.

ADDITIONAL INFORMATION Deadline for entry: see website for dates. Application fee: none. Space fee: varies. Exhibition space: varies. For more information, call, e-mail, or visit website.

SPRING CRAFT & VENDOR SHOW

140 Oak St., Frankfort IL 60423. (815)469-9400. Fax: (815)469-9275. E-mail: cdebella@frankfortparks.org. Website: www.frankfortparks.org. **Contact:** Cali DeBella, special events coordinator. Estab. 1999. Arts and crafts show held annually in March. Indoors. Accepts handmade crafts. Exhibitors: 65. Number of attendees: 500–700. Free to public. Apply online.

ADDITIONAL INFORMATION Deadline for entry: early October. Application fee: $45. Space fee: $45. Exhibition space: 10×6. For more information, e-mail or visit website.

TIPS Keep prices reasonable.

SPRING CRAFT FEST

(479)756-6954. E-mail: info@craftfairsnwa.com. Website: www.craftfairsnwa.com. Art and craft show held annually in May. Indoors. Accepts handmade crafts and other mediums. Juried. Number of exhibitors: see website. Number of attendees: varies. Free to public. Apply online.

ADDITIONAL INFORMATION Deadline for entry: March. Application fee: none. Space fee: varies. Exhibition space: varies. For more information, e-mail, call, or visit website.

SPRING CRAFTMORRISTOWN

P.O. Box 28, Woodstock NY 12498. (845)331-7900. Fax: (845)331-7484. E-mail: crafts@artrider.com. Website: www.artrider.com. Estab. 1990. Fine arts and crafts show held annually in March. Indoors. Accepts photography, wearable and nonwearable fiber, jewelry, clay, leather, wood, glass, painting, drawing, prints, mixed media. Juried by 5 images of work and 1 of booth, viewed sequentially. Number of exhibitors: 150. Public attendance: 5,000. Public admission: $9. Apply at www.artrider.com or www.zapplication.org.

ADDITIONAL INFORMATION Deadline for entry: January 1. Application fee: $45. Space fee: $495. Exhibition space: 10×10. For more information, e-mail, call, or visit website.

SPRING CRAFTS AT LYNDHURST

P.O. Box 28, Woodstock NY 12498. (845)331-7900. Fax: (845)331-7484. E-mail: crafts@artrider.com. Website: www.artrider.com. Estab. 1984. Fine arts and crafts show held annually in early May. Outdoors. Accepts photography, wearable and nonwearable fiber, jewelry, clay, leather, wood, glass, painting, drawing, prints, mixed media. Juried by 5 images of work and 1 of booth, viewed sequentially. Number of exhibitors: 275. Public attendance: 14,000. Public admission: $10. Apply at www.artrider.com or www.zapplication.org.

ADDITIONAL INFORMATION Deadline for entry: January 1. Application fee: $45. Space fee: $775–875. Exhibition space: 10×10. For more information, e-mail, call, or visit website.

SPRINGFEST

Southern Pines Business Association, P.O. Box 831, Southern Pines NC 28388. (910)315-6508. E-mail: spbainfo@southernpines.biz. Website: www.southernpines.biz. **Contact:** Susan Harris. Estab. 1979. Arts and crafts show held annually last Saturday in April. Outdoors. Accepts photography and crafts. We host over 160 vendors from all around North Carolina and the country. Enjoy beautiful artwork and crafts including paintings, jewelry, metal art, photography, woodwork, designs from nature, and other amazing creations. Event is held in conjunction with Tour de Moore, an annual bicycle race in Moore County, and is co-sponsored by the town of Southern Pines. Public attendance: 8,000. Free to public.

ADDITIONAL INFORMATION Deadline: March (For more information, visit website). Space fee: $75. Exhibition space: 10×12. For more information, e-mail, call, visit website, or send SASE. Apply online. Event held in historic downtown Southern Pines on Broad St.

SPRING FESTIVAL, AN ARTS & CRAFTS AFFAIR

P.O. Box 655, Antioch IL 60002. (402)331-2889. E-mail: hpifestivals@cox.net. Website: www.hpifestivals.com. Annual tour takes place in Omaha (March and April), Minneapolis (March and April) and Chicago (April). Application available online. For more information, visit website or e-mail.

SPRING FESTIVAL OF THE ARTS OAKBROOK CENTER

Amdur Productions, P.O. Box 550, Highland Park IL 60035. (847)926-4300. Fax: (847)926-4330. E-mail: info@amdurproductions.com. Website: www.amdurproductions.com. Art and craft show held annually in May. Outdoors. Accepts handmade crafts and other mediums. Juried. Number of exhibitors: see website. Number of attendees: varies. Free to public. Apply online.

ADDITIONAL INFORMATION Deadline for entry: early April. Application fee: $25. Space fee: $460. Exhibition space: 10×10. For more information, e-mail, call, or visit website.

SPRING FESTIVAL ON PONCE

Olmstead Park, North Druid Hills, 1451 Ponce de Leon, Atlanta GA 30307. (404)873-1222. E-mail: info@affps.com. Website: www.festivalonponce.com. **Contact:** Randall Fox, festival director. Estab. 2011. Arts and crafts show held annually early April. Outdoors. Accepts handmade crafts, painting, photography, sculpture, leather, metal, glass, jewelry. Juried by a panel. Awards/prizes: ribbons. Number of exhibitors: 125. Number of attendees: 40,000. Free to public. Apply online at www.zapplication.org.

ADDITIONAL INFORMATION Deadline for entry: February 6. Application fee: $25. Space fee: $275. Exhibition space: 10×10. For more information, see website.

SPRING FINE ART & CRAFTS AT BROOKDALE PARK

Rose Squared Productions, Inc., 473 Watchung Ave., Bloomfield NJ 07003. (908)874-5247. Fax: (908)874-7098. E-mail: info@rosesquared.com.

Website: www.rosesquared.com. **Contact:** Howard and Janet Rose. Estab. 1988. Fine arts and crafts show held annually at Brookdale Park on the border of Bloomfield and Montclair, New Jersey. Event takes place in mid-June on Father's Day weekend. Outdoors. Accepts photography and all other mediums. Juried. Number of exhibitors: 180. Public attendance: 16,000. Free to public. Apply by downloading application from website or call for application.

ADDITIONAL INFORMATION Deadline: 1 month before show date. Application fee: $30. Space fee: varies by booth size. Exhibition space: 120 sq. ft. For more information, e-mail, call, or visit website.

TIPS "Create a professional booth that is comfortable for the customer to enter. Be informative, friendly, and outgoing. People come to meet the artist."

SPRING GREEN ARTS & CRAFTS FAIR

P.O. Box 96, Spring Green WI 53588. E-mail: springgreenartfair@gmail.com. Website: www.springgreenartfair.com. Fine arts and crafts fair held annually in June. Indoors. Accepts handmade crafts, glass, wood, painting, fiber, graphics, pottery, sculpture, jewelry, photography. Juried. Awards/prizes: Best of Show, Award of Excellence. Number of exhibitors: see website. Number of attendees: varies per show. Admission: varies per show. Apply online.

ADDITIONAL INFORMATION Deadline for entry: mid-February. Application fee: $10–20. Space fee: $150. Exhibition space: 10×10. For more information, e-mail or visit website.

KIRK SCHOOL SPRING SHOWCASE OF ARTS & CRAFTS

NSSEO Foundation, Inc., NSSEO Foundation Inc, 799 W. Kensington Rd., Mt. Prospect IL 60056. (847)463-8155. E-mail: showcase@nsseo.org. Website: www.nsseo.org/nsseo-foundation/. **Contact:** Lynn Davis. Estab. 1972. Fine arts and crafts fair held annually during the 1st weekend in March. Indoors. Accepts handmade crafts and other items. Juried. Number of exhibitors: 90. Number of attendees: 1,600. $3 donation admission suggested. Apply online.

ADDITIONAL INFORMATION Deadline for entry: January. Application fee: none. Space fee: $75. Exhibition space: 10×5. For more information, e-mail, call, or visit website.

SPRINGTIME IN OHIO

P.O. Box 586, Findlay OH 45839-0586. (419)436-1457. Fax: (419)435-5035. E-mail: cloudpro@tds.net. Website: www.cloudshows.biz. Estab. 1988. Arts and crafts show held annually in May. Indoors and outdoors. Accepts handmade crafts and other items. Exhibitors: 280. Admission: $5; children 12 and under free. Apply online.

ADDITIONAL INFORMATION Deadline for entry: see website. Application fee: see website. Space fee: see website. Exhibition space: see website. For more information, e-mail, or visit website.

SQUARE TOMATOES CRAFT FAIR

Davis, CA 95616. (530)758-4903. E-mail: squaretcrafts@gmail.com. Website: www.squaretomatoescrafts.com. **Contact:** Sally Parker. Estab. 2012. Fine arts and crafts fair held annually in July. Outdoors. Accepts handmade crafts and other mediums. Juried. Number of exhibitors: see website. Number of attendees: varies. Free to public. Apply online. Fine arts and crafts fair held annually July. Outdoors. Accepts handmade crafts and other mediums. Juried. Number of exhibitors: see website. Number of attendees: varies. Free to public. Apply online.

STAMFORD ART FESTIVAL

(518)852-6478. E-mail: suebg.art@gmail.com. Website: www.stamfordartfestival.org; gordonfinearts.org. Estab. 2015. Arts and crafts show held annually in July. Outdoors. Accepts handmade crafts and fine art. Juried. Awards/prizes: cash and ribbons. Exhibitors: 150. Number of attendees: 3,000–7,000. Free to public. Apply online.

ADDITIONAL INFORMATION Deadline for entry: April 1. Application fee: $25. Space fee: $350. Exhibition space: 10×12. For more information, visit website, e-mail, or call. Event located at Harbor Point Park, Stamford, Connecticut.

STAN HYWET HALL & GARDENS OHIO MART

714 N. Portage Path, Akron OH 44303. (330)315-3255. E-mail: ohiomart@stanhywet.org. Website: www.stanhywet.org. Estab. 1966. Artisan crafts show held annually 1st full weekend in October. Outdoors. Accepts photography and all mediums. Juried via mail application. Awards/prizes: Best Booth Display. Number of exhibitors: 150. Public attendance: 15,000–20,000.

ADDITIONAL INFORMATION Deadline for entry varies. Application fee: $25, nonrefundable. Application available online. Exhibition space: 10×10 or 10×15. For more information, visit website or call.

STEPPIN' OUT

Downtown Blacksburg, Inc., P.O. Box 233, Blacksburg VA 24063. (540)951-0454. E-mail: dbi@downtownblacksburg.com; events@downtownblacksburg.com. Website: www.blacksburgsteppinout.com. **Contact:** Laureen Blakemore. Estab. 1980. Arts and crafts show held annually 1st Friday and Saturday in August. Outdoors. Accepts photography, pottery, painting, drawing, fiber arts, jewelry, general crafts. All arts and crafts must be handmade. Number of exhibitors: 230. Public attendance: 40,000. Free to public. Space fee: $200. An additional $10 is required for electricity. Exhibition space: 10×16. Apply by e-mailing, calling or downloading an application on website.

ADDITIONAL INFORMATION Deadline for entry: May 1. Downtown Blacksburg, Inc. (DBI) is a nonprofit (501c6) association of merchants, property owners, and downtown advocates whose mission is to sustain a dynamic, vital, and diverse community through marketing, events, economic development, and leadership.

TIPS "Visit shows and consider the booth aesthetic—what appeals to you. Put the time, thought, energy, and money into your booth to draw people in to see your work."

STILLWATER ARTS FESTIVAL

P.O. Box 1449, Stillwater OK 74076. (405)747-8070. E-mail: stillwaterartsfestival@stillwater.org; rjanway@stillwater.org. **Contact:** Rachel Janway. Estab. 1977. Fine art show held annually in April. Outdoors. Accepts photography, oil, acrylic, watercolor and multimedia paintings, pottery, pastel work, fiber arts, jewelry, sculpture, glass art, wood, and other. Juried. Awards are based on entry acceptance on quality, distribution, and various media entries. Awards/prizes: Best of Show, $500; 1st place, $200; 2nd place, $150; 3rd place, $100. Number of exhibitors: 80. Public attendance: 7,500–10,000. Free to public. Apply via www.zapplication.org. Deadline for entry: early spring (visit website for details). Jury fee: $20. Booth fee $140; $240 for 2 booths. Exhibition space: 10×10. For more information, e-mail or call. Festival held at 8th and Husband Sts.

STITCHES IN BLOOM QUILT SHOW AT THE OREGON GARDEN

879 W. Main St., Silverton OR 97381. (503)874-8100. E-mail: info@oregongarden.org. Website: www.oregongarden.org. **Contact:** Mary Ridderbusch, events coordinator. Estab. 2005. Arts and crafts/quilt show held annually in late January. Indoors. Accepts handmade crafts and quilts. Awards/prizes: Peoples Choice; Challenge Quilt. Exhibitors: 20. Number of attendees: 2,300. Admission: $11. Apply online at www.oregongarden.org/events/quiltshow.

ADDITIONAL INFORMATION Deadline for entry: January 9. Application fee: $10. Space fee: $150–260. Exhibition space: 9,000 sq. ft. For more information, e-mail or visit website.

STITCH ROCK

E-mail: info@rockthestitch.com. Website: www.rockthestitch.com.

ADDITIONAL INFORMATION "Stitch Rock is South Florida's largest annual indie craft fair and bazaar bringing back old- school crafting techniques with new-school flair! With over 80 vendors, the show is full of uncommon handmade goods such as DIY fashion, funky home décor items, adorable plushies, natural bath and body goodies, vintage finds, hot rod paintings, pinup photography, and much more!" For more information, visit website.

STONE ARCH BRIDGE FESTIVAL

(651)398-0590. E-mail: stacy@weimarketing.com; heatherwmpls@gmail.com. Website: www.stonearchbridgefestival.com. **Contact:** Sara Collins, manager. Estab. 1994. Fine arts and crafts and culinary arts show held annually on Father's Day weekend in the Riverfront District of Minneapolis. Outdoors. Accepts drawing/pastels, printmaking, ceramics, jewelry (metals/stone), mixed media, painting, photography, sculpture metalwork, beadwork (jewelry or sculpture), glass, fine craft, special consideration. Juried by committee. Awards/prizes: free booth the following year; $100 cash prize. Number of exhibitors: 250+. Public attendance: 80,000. Free to public. Apply by application found on website or through www.zapplication.org. Application fee: $25.

ADDITIONAL INFORMATION Deadline for entry: early April. Space fee: depends on booth location (see website for details). Exhibition space: 10×10. For more information, call (651)228-1664 or e-mail Stacy De Young at stacy@weimarketing.com.

TIPS "Have an attractive display and variety of prices."

STRAWBERRY FESTIVAL

Downtown Billings Alliance, 2815 Second Ave. N., Billings MT 59101. (406)294-5060. Fax: (406)294-5061. E-mail: inatashap@downtownbillings.com. Website: www.downtownbillings.com. **Contact:** Natasha. Estab. 1991. Fine arts and crafts show held annually 2nd Saturday in June. Outdoors. Accepts photography and only finely crafted work. Handcrafted works by the selling artist will be given priority. Requires photographs of booth setup and 2–3 of work. Juried. Public attendance: 15,000. Free to public. Apply online.

ADDITIONAL INFORMATION Deadline for entry: April. Space fee: $160–195. Exhibition space: 10×10. For more information, e-mail or visit website. Show located at N. Broadway and 2nd Ave. N in downtown Billings.

SUGARLOAF CRAFT FESTIVALS

(301)990-1400; (800)210-9900. Fax: (301)253-9620. E-mail: sugarloafinfo@sugarloaffest.com. Website: www.sugarloafcrafts.com.

ADDITIONAL INFORMATION "For over 30 years, the nation's most talented artisans have personally sold their contemporary crafts and fine art at Sugarloaf Craft Festivals. You will find Sugarloaf Craft Festivals in 5 great locations in the Mid-Atlantic area. Sugarloaf art fairs and craft festivals are among the nation's best and largest shows of their kind. Each show features a variety of work by the most talented craft designers and fine artists. From blown glass and sculpture to fine art and designer clothing, you'll find the handcrafted creations you're looking for at Sugarloaf!" For more information, visit website.

SUGAR PLUM BAZAAR
E-mail: sugarplumbazaar@yahoo.com. Website: www.sugarplumbazaar.com.

ADDITIONAL INFORMATION Handmade and vintage event. Juried. Apply online. For more information, visit website.

SUMMER ART IN THE PARK FESTIVAL
16 S. Main St., Rutland VT 05701. (802)775-0356. E-mail: info@chaffeeartcenter.org. Website: www.chaffeeartcenter.org. Estab. 1961. A fine arts and crafts show held at Main Street Park in Rutland, Vermont, annually in mid-August. Accepts fine art, specialty foods, fiber, jewelry, glass, metal, wood, photography, clay, floral, etc. All applications will be juried by a panel of experts. The Art in the Park Festivals are dedicated to high-quality art and craft products. Number of exhibitors: 100. Public attendance: 9,000–10,000. Public admission: voluntary donation. Apply online and either e-mail or submit a CD with 3 photos of work and 1 of booth (photos upon preapproval).

ADDITIONAL INFORMATION Deadline for entry: early bird discount of $25 per show for applications received by March 31. Space fee: $200–350. Exhibit space: 10×12 or 20×12. For more information, e-mail, call, or visit website. Festival held in Main Street Park.

TIPS "Have a good presentation, variety if possible (in price ranges, too) to appeal to a large group of people. Apply early as there may be a limited amount of accepted vendors per category. Applications will be juried on a first come, first served basis until the category is determined to be filled."

SUMMER ARTS & CRAFTS FESTIVAL
38 Charles St., Rochester NH 03867. E-mail: info@castleberryfairs.com. Website: www.castleberryfairs.com. Estab. 1992. Arts and crafts show held annually 2nd weekend in August in Lincoln, New Hampshire. Outdoors. Accepts photography and all other mediums. Juried by photo, slide, or sample. Number of exhibitors: 100. Public attendance: 7,500. Free to public. Apply by downloading application from website. Application fee: $50. Space fee: $225. Exhibition space: 10×10. For more information, visit website. Festival held at Village Shops and Town Green, Main St.

SUMMERFAIR
7850 Five Mile Rd., Cincinnati OH 45230. (513)531-0050. E-mail: exhibitors@summerfair.org. Website: www.summerfair.org. Estab. 1968. Fine arts and crafts show held annually the weekend after Memorial Day. Outdoors. Accepts photography, ceramics, drawing, printmaking, fiber, leather, glass, jewelry, painting, sculpture, metal, wood and mixed media. Juried by a panel of judges selected by Summerfair, including artists and art educators with expertise in the categories offered at Summerfair. Submit application with 5 digital images (no booth image) through www.zapplication.org. Awards/prizes: $18,000 in cash awards. Number of exhibitors: 300. Public attendance: 20,000. Public admission: $10.

ADDITIONAL INFORMATION Deadline: February. Application fee: $35. Space fee: $450, single; $900, double space; $125 canopy fee (optional—exhibitors can rent a canopy for all days of the fair). Exhibition space: 10×10. for single space; 10×20. for double space. For more information, e-mail, visit website, or call. Fair held at Cincinnati's historic Coney Island.

SUMMER ON SOUTHPORT
Amdur Productions, P.O. Box 550, Highland Park IL 60035. (847)926-4300. Fax: (847)926-4330. E-mail: info@amdurproductions.com. Website: www.amdurproductions.com. Art and craft show held annually in July. Outdoors. Accepts handmade crafts and other mediums. Juried. Number of exhibitors: 100. Number of attendees:

varies. Admission: $5 donation to Southport Neighbors Association. Apply online.

ADDITIONAL INFORMATION Deadline for entry: early January. Application fee: $25. Space fee: $335. Exhibition space: 10×10. For more information, e-mail, call, or visit website.

SUMMIT ART FESTIVAL

Website: www.summitartfest.org. Fine arts and crafts fair held annually in October. Outdoors. Accepts handmade crafts, jewelry, ceramics, painting, glass, photography, fiber, and more. Juried. Awards/prizes: Best of Show, 2nd place, 3rd place, Mayor's Award, Jurors' Merit Award. Number of exhibitors: see website. Number of attendees: varies. Free to public. Apply online.

ADDITIONAL INFORMATION Deadline for entry: July. Application fee: $25. Space fee: $255. Exhibition space: 10×10. For more information, visit website.

SUNCOAST ARTS FESTIVAL

E-mail: info@suncoastartsfest.com. Website: www.suncoastartsfest.com.

ADDITIONAL INFORMATION "The Suncoast Arts Fest (SAF) has brought together quality fine artists and craftspeople with area art lovers who are motivated to buy. The event takes place in the heart of the Tampa Bay area, convenient to major interstates. SAF is a family-oriented cultural event. Artwork exhibited must be appropriate for viewers of all ages. The SAF committee has the sole exclusive and final authority to determine if any work is not acceptable for display." For more information, visit website.

SUN FEST, INC.

P.O. Box 2404, Bartlesville OK 74005. (918)331-0456. Fax: (918)331-3217. E-mail: sunfestbville@gmail.com. Website: www.bartlesvillesunfest.org. Estab. 1982. Fine arts and crafts show held annually in early June. Outdoors. Accepts photography, painting, and other arts and crafts. Juried. Awards: $2,000 in cash awards along with a ribbon/award to be displayed. Number of exhibitors: 95–100. Number of attendees: 25,000–30,000. Free to public. Apply by e-mailing

or calling for an entry form or completing online, along with 3–5 photos showing your work and booth display.

ADDITIONAL INFORMATION Deadline: April. Space fee: $125. An extra $20 is charged for use of electricity. Exhibition space: 10×10. For more information, e-mail, call, or visit website.

SUN VALLEY CENTER ARTS & CRAFTS FESTIVAL

Sun Valley Center for the Arts, P.O. Box 656, Sun Valley ID 83353. (208)726-9491. Fax: (208)726-2344. E-mail: festival@sunvalleycenter.org. Website: www.sunvalleycenter.org. **Contact:** Sarah Kolash, festival director. Estab. 1968. Annual fine art and craft show held 2nd weekend in August. Outdoors. Accepts handmade crafts, ceramics, drawing, fiber, glass, jewelry, metalwork, mixed media, painting, photography, printmaking, sculpture, woodwork. Juried. Exhibitors: 140. Number of attendees: 10,000. Free to public. Apply via www.zapplication.org.

ADDITIONAL INFORMATION Application fee: $35. Space fee: $450 and $900; $500 or $1000 for corner spaces. Exhibition space: 10×10 and 10×20. Average sales: $3,700. For more information, e-mail or visit website.

SURPRISE FINE ART & WINE FESTIVAL

15940 N. Bullard Ave., Surprise AZ 85374. (480)837-5637. Fax: (480)837-2355. E-mail: info@thunderbirdartists.com. Website: www.thunderbirdartists.com. **Contact:** Denise Colter, president. Estab. 2012. "The Surprise Fine Art & Wine Festival, produced by Thunderbird Artists and in conjunction with the City of Surprise and Surprise Sundancers, is back by popular demand! The sales, attendance, and support were spectacular for a newer event and the most popular quote used by vendors: "What a wonderful surprise!" This event will receive an extensive and dedicated advertising campaign, like all events produced by Thunderbird Artists. The Thunderbird Artists Mission is to promote fine art and fine crafts, paralleled with the ambiance of unique wines and fine music, while supporting the artists, merchants, and surrounding community."

ADDITIONAL INFORMATION It is the mission of Thunderbird Artists to further enhance the art culture with the local communities by producing award-winning, sophisticated fine art festivals throughout the Phoenix metro area. Thunderbird Artists has played an important role in uniting nationally recognized and award-winning artists with patrons from across the globe.

TIPS "A clean, gallery-type presentation is very important."

SWEET PEA, A FESTIVAL OF THE ARTS

424 E. Main St., Suite 203B, Bozeman MT 59715. (406)586-4003. Fax: (406)586-5523. E-mail: admin@sweetpeafestival.com. E-mail: spartscrafts@sweetpeafestival.org. Website: www.sweetpeafestival.org. **Contact:** arts and crafts chair. Estab. 1978. Arts and crafts show held annually in August. Outdoors. Accepts handmade crafts and other mediums. Juried. Exhibitors: 110. Number of attendees: 14,000. Admission: $10/day; $15, 3-day pass. Apply via www.zapplication.org.

ADDITIONAL INFORMATION Deadline for entry: early April. Application fee: $40. Space fee: $345 (10×10); $495 (10×20). Exhibition space: 10×10; 10×20. For more information, e-mail, call, or visit website.

SYRACUSE ARTS & CRAFTS FESTIVAL

115 W. Fayette St., Syracuse NY 13202. (315)422-8284. Fax: (315)471-4503. E-mail: mail@downtownsyracuse.com. Website: www.syracuseartsandcraftsfestival.com. **Contact:** Laurie Reed, director. Estab. 1970. Fine arts and crafts show held annually in late July. Outdoors. Accepts photography, ceramics, fabric/fiber, glass, jewelry, leather, metal, wood, computer art, drawing, printmaking, painting. Juried by 4 independent jurors. Jurors review 4 digital images of work and 1 digital image of booth display. Number of exhibitors: 165. Public attendance: 50,000. Free to public. Apply online through www.zapplication.org.

ADDITIONAL INFORMATION Application fee: $25. Space fee: $280. Exhibition space: 10×10. For more information, e-mail, call, or visit website.

TACOMA HOLIDAY FOOD & GIFT FESTIVAL

Tacoma Dome, 2727 E. D St., Tacoma WA 98421. (800)521-7469. Fax: (425)889-8165. E-mail: tacoma@showcaseevents.org. Website: www.showcaseevents.org. Estab. 1982. Seasonal holiday show held annually in October. Indoors. Accepts handmade crafts, art, photography, pottery, glass, jewelry, clothing, fiber, seasonal food. Juried. Exhibitors: 500. Number of attendees: 40,000. Admission: $14.50 (for all 5 days)—a $1 off coupon online at holidaygiftshows.com; 12 and under free. Apply via website or call or e-mail for application.

ADDITIONAL INFORMATION Deadline for entry: until full. Space fee: see website. Exhibition space: 6×10, 10×10. For more information, e-mail, call, send SASE, or visit website.

TAHOE ARTS PROJECT ART FAIR

(530)542-3632. E-mail: tahoearts@aol.com. Website: www.tahoeartsproject.org.

ADDITIONAL INFORMATION "Tahoe Arts Project Art Festival is an art show nestled in a pine forest in the heart of South Lake Tahoe. Festival admission and parking will be free for artists." For more information, visit website.

TAHOE CITY FINE ARTS & CRAFTS FESTIVAL

Pacific Fine Arts Festivals, P.O. Box 280, Pine Grove CA 95665. (209)267-4394. Fax: (209)267-4395. E-mail: pfa@pacificfinearts.com. Website: www.pacificfinearts.com. The annual Tahoe City Fine Arts and Crafts Festival will give visitors a special opportunity to meet with more than 45 artisans and craftspeople showcasing a wide variety of arts and crafts including photography, oil paintings, ceramic vessels, jewelry, and much more. For more information, visit website.

TALBOT STREET ART FAIR

(317)745-6479. E-mail: talbotstreetartfair@hotmail.com. Website: www.talbotstreet.org.

ADDITIONAL INFORMATION "With over 270 artists from across the nation, this juried art fair continues to be ranked as1 of the finest fairs in the country. Talbot Street Art Fair is located between

16th and 20th Delaware and Pennsylvania —Indianapolis in the historic Herron-Morton neighborhood. This is a family-friendly event with plenty to see and do for everyone." For more information, visit website.

TAOS FALL ARTS FESTIVAL
P.O. Box 675, Taos NM 87571. (575)758-4648. E-mail: tfafvolunteer@gmail.com. Website: www.taosfallarts.com. **Contact:** Patsy S. Wright. Estab. 1974. This festival is the oldest art festival in Taos, premiering in 1974 and only showcasing artists that reside in Taos County. It includes 3 major art shows: the curated exhibit titled "Distinguished Achievement Award Series," a juried exhibit titled Taos Select, and the Taos Open, as its name implies, an exhibit open to all artists working in Taos County. The festival represents over 250 Taos County artists working in a variety of mediums. Each year a limited-edition poster is printed to commemorate the arts festival. The proceeds from the shows will benefit art programs for Taos County children. For more information, visit website.

TARPON SPRINGS FINE ARTS FESTIVAL
111 E. Tarpon Ave., Tarpon Springs FL 34689. (727)937-6109. Fax: (727)937-2879. E-mail: reggie@tarponspringschamber.org. Website: www.tarponspringschamber.com. Estab. 1974. Fine arts and crafts show held annually in late March. Outdoors. Accepts photography, acrylic, oil, ceramics, digital, fiber, glass, graphics, drawings, pastels, jewelry, leather, metal, mixed media, sculpture, watercolor, wood. Juried by CD or images e-mailed. Awards/prizes: cash, ribbons, and Patron Awards. Number of exhibitors: 200. Public attendance: 20,000. Public admission: $5 (includes free drink ticket: wine, beer, soda, or water); age 12 and under and active duty military free. Apply by submitting signed application, CD or e-mailed images, fees, and SASE.

ADDITIONAL INFORMATION Deadline for entry: late December. Jury fee: $30. Space fee: $230. Exhibition space: 10×12. For more information, e-mail, call, or send SASE.

TIPS "Produce good CDs for jurors."

THIRD WARD ART FESTIVAL
Amdur Productions, P.O. Box 550, Highland Park IL 60035. (847)926-4300. Fax: (847)926-4330. E-mail: info@amdurproductions.com. Website: www.amdurproductions.com. Art and craft show held annually in August. Outdoors. Accepts handmade crafts and other mediums. Juried. Awards/prizes: given at festival. Number of exhibitors: 135. Number of attendees: 30,000. Free to public. Apply online.

ADDITIONAL INFORMATION Deadline for entry: early January. Application fee: $25. Space fee: $450. Exhibition space: 10×10. For more information, e-mail, call, or visit website.

THOUSAND OAKS ART FESTIVAL
(805)498-6591. E-mail: richardswilliams@roadrunner.com. Website: www.toartsfestival.com. Estab. 2004.

ADDITIONAL INFORMATION "2-Day Festival with more than 60 visual art exhibitors. Continuous live performances, children's hands-on artistic and interactive art exhibits, and over 12,000 visitors. FREE admission and parking. Smoke-Free Premises. Wine Tasting at THE LAKES." For more information, visit website.

THREE RIVERS ART FESTIVAL
(985)327-9797. E-mail: info@threeriversartfestival.com. Website: www.threeriversartfestival.com.

ADDITIONAL INFORMATION "With 200 artists from more than 20 states. A juried show of original works. Tent after colorful tent ranged along the streets of historic downtown Covington, Louisiana. Arts and fine crafts demonstrations. Music. Food. 3 Rivers Run. And lots of activities just for kids. It's the Covington Three Rivers Art Festival. Where the fun starts with art and goes on for 2 wonderful days." For more information, visit website.

THREE RIVERS ARTS FESTIVAL
803 Liberty Ave., Pittsburgh PA 15222. (412)456-6666. Fax: (412)471-6917. Website: www.3riversartsfest.org. **Contact:** Sonja Sweterlitsch, director. Estab. 1960. "Three

Rivers Arts Festival has presented, during its vast and varied history, more than 10,000 visual and performing artists and entertained millions of residents and visitors.3 Rivers Arts Festival faces a new turning point in its history as a division of the Pittsburgh Cultural Trust, further advancing the shared mission of each organization to foster economic development through the arts and to enhance the quality of life in the region." Application fee: $35. Booth fee: $340–410. For more information, visit website. Festival located at Point State Park in downtown Pittsburgh.

TILLAMOOK FREEDOM FESTIVAL

Central Oregon Shows, P.O. Box 1555, Sisters OR 97759. (541)420-0279. E-mail: centraloregonshows@gmail.com. Website: www.centraloregonshows.com. **Contact:** Richard. Estab. 2015. At the Blue Heron off 101. This event features a variety of arts, crafts, antiques, food, and entertainment with a special fund-raiser benefiting the Tillamook Animal Shelter. For more information, visit website.

TALUCA LAKE FINE ARTS FESTIVAL

West Coast Artists, P.O. Box 750, Acton CA 93510. (818)813-4478. Fax: (661)526-4575. E-mail: info@westcoastartists.com. Website: www.westcoastartists.com. Open to all media of original fine art and fine crafts. All work will be juried. Categories will be limited. No commercial, manufactured, imported, mass-produced or purchased for resale items will be accepted. No clothing. No representatives. For more information, visit website.

TORRIANO CRAFT & HANDMADE FAIR

E-mail: torrianoparents@gmail.com. Website: www.facebook.com/TorrianoCraftMarket/info. **ADDITIONAL INFORMATION** "Biannual pop-up market selling affordable and original creations. Have-a-go craft demos, portraits, and face painting for children." For more information, visit website.

TRENTON AVENUE ARTS FESTIVAL

E-mail: info@trentonaveartsfest.org. Website: www.trentonaveartsfest.org.

ADDITIONAL INFORMATION "Free and open to the public, the Trenton Ave. Arts Festival celebrates East Kensington's incredible mix of local artists, musicians, and eateries. Organized by the dedicated volunteers of the East Kensington Neighbors Association and featuring over 200 local arts and food vendors, TAAF attracts 10k+ attendees to raise funds for neighborhood projects and revitalization. The festival is held on Trenton Ave., a wide cobblestone street that has been part of Kensington's rich creative history for over a hundred years. By hosting the Trenton Ave. Arts Festival, EKNA continues that tradition." For more information, visit website.

TRUMBULL ARTS FESTIVAL

Trumbull Arts Commission, 23 Priscilla Place, Trumbull CT 06611. (203)452-5065. Fax: (203)452-3853. E-mail: arts@trumbull-ct.gov. Website: www.trumbull-ct.gov. **Contact:** Emily Areson, arts coordinator. Estab. 1978. Arts and crafts show held annually in September. Outdoors. Accepts handmade crafts and fine art. Juried. Awards/prizes: cash and ribbons. Exhibitors: 75. Number of attendees: 3,500. Free to public. Apply by calling or sending e-mail.

ADDITIONAL INFORMATION Deadline for entry: early April. Application fee: none. Space fee: varies. Exhibition space: 10×10. For more information, e-mail, send SASE, or call.

TIPS Display your best works.

TUBAC FESTIVAL OF THE ARTS

P.O. Box 1866, Tubac AZ 85646. (520)398-2704. Fax: (520)398-3287. E-mail: assistance@tubacaz.com. Website: www.tubacaz.com. Estab. 1959. Fine arts and crafts show held annually in early February (see website for details). Outdoors. Accepts photography and considers all fine arts and crafts. Juried. A 7-member panel reviews digital images and artist statement. Names are withheld from the jurists. Number of exhibitors: 170. Public attendance: 65,000. Free to public; parking: $6.

ADDITIONAL INFORMATION Deadline for entry: late October (see website for details). Application fee: $30. Apply online and provide images on a labeled CD (see website for requirements). Space fee: $575. Electrical fee: $50. Exhibition space: 10×10. (a limited number of double booths are available). For more information, e-mail, call, or visit website.

☺ TULSA INTERNATIONAL MAYFEST

2210 S. Main St., Tulsa OK 74114. (918)582-6435. Fax: (918)517-3518. E-mail: comments@ tulsamayfest.org. Website: www.tulsamayfest. org. Estab. 1972. Fine arts and crafts show annually held in May. Outdoors. Accepts photography, clay, leather/fiber, mixed media, drawing, pastels, graphics, printmaking, jewelry, glass, metal, wood, painting. Juried by a blind-jurying process. Apply online at www. zapplication.org and submit 4 images of work and 1 photo of booth setup. Awards/prizes: Best in Category and Best in Show. Number of exhibitors: 125. Public attendance: 350,000. Free to public. Apply by downloading application in the fall.

ADDITIONAL INFORMATION See website for deadline entry. Application fee: $35. Space fee: $350. Exhibition space: 10×10. For more information, e-mail or visit website.

UC SPRING ART FAIR

32 Campus Dr., UC Room 232, Missoula MT 59812-0012. (406)243-5622. E-mail: ucartfair. student@mso.umt.edu. Website: www.umt.edu/ uc/Arts-Entertainment/uc-art-fairs. **Contact:** Brianna McLean, art fair coordinator. Estab. 1970s. Arts and crafts show held 3 times/ year in April (spring show), September, and December. Indoors. Accepts handmade crafts, photography, jewelry, prints, painting, pottery. Juried. Exhibitors: 60. Number of attendees: 20,000. Free to public. Apply online.

ADDITIONAL INFORMATION Deadline for entry: March 20. Application fee: $10. Space fee: varies. Exhibition space: varies. For more information, visit website, e-mail, or call. Show located on the University of Montanna campus on the 1st floor of the University Center.

UNPLAZA ART FAIR

Peace Works Kansas City, 4509 Walnut, Kansas City Missouri 64111. E-mail: PeaceWorksKC@ gmail.com. Website: www.peaceworkskc.org/ unplaza.html. **Contact:** Debbie Wallin. Estab. 1975.

ADDITIONAL INFORMATION Art fair. Annual fund-raiser for Peace Works Kansas City. For more information, visit website and to apply.

UPPER ARLINGTON LABOR DAY ARTS FESTIVAL

(614)583-5310. Fax: (614)437-8656. E-mail: arts@uaoh.net. Website: www.uaoh.net/ department/index.php?structureid=101. Fine art and craft show held annually in September. Outdoors. Accepts handmade crafts, ceramics, fiber, glass, graphics, jewelry, leather, metal, mixed media, painting, photography, printmaking, sculpture, woodworking. Juried. Awards/prizes: $1,350 in awards. Number of exhibitors: 200. Number of attendees: 25,000. Free to public. Apply via www.zapplication.org.

ADDITIONAL INFORMATION Deadline for entry: February. Application fee: see website. Space fee: varies. Exhibition space: varies. For more information, call or visit website.

UPTOWN ART FAIR

1406 W. Lake St., Lower Level C, Minneapolis MN 55408. (612)823-4581. Fax: (612)823-3158. E-mail: maude@uptownminneapolis. com; info@uptownminneapolis.com; jessica@uptownminneapolis.com; hannah@ uptownminneapolis.com. Website: www. uptownartfair.com. **Contact:** Maude Lovelle. Estab. 1963. Fine arts and crafts show held annually 1st full weekend in August. Outdoors. Accepts photography, painting, printmaking, drawing, 2D and 3D mixed media, ceramics, fiber, sculpture, jewelry, wood, and glass. Juried by 4 images of artwork and 1 of booth display. Awards/prizes: Best in Show in each category; Best Artist. Number of exhibitors: 350. Public attendance: 375,000. Free to public. The Uptown Art Fair uses www.zapplication.org. Each artist must submit 5 images of his or her work. All artwork must be in a high-quality digital format. Five highly qualified artists, instructors, and critics handpick Uptown Art Fair exhibitors after previewing projections of the images on 6-ft. screens. The identities of the artists remain anonymous during the entire review process. All submitted images must be free of signatures, headshots, or other identifying marks. 3 rounds of scoring determine the final selection and waitlist for the show. Artists will be notified shortly after of their acceptance. For additional information, see the links on website.

ADDITIONAL INFORMATION Deadline for entry: early March. Application fee: $40. Space fee: $550 for 10×10 space; $1,100 for 10×20 space. For more information, call or visit website. Fair located at Lake St. and Hennepin Ave. and "The Mall" in southwest Minneapolis.

URBAN CRAFT UPRISING

(206)728-8008. E-mail: info@urbancraftuprising. com. Website: www.urbancraftuprising.com. **Contact:** Kristen Rask, president.

ADDITIONAL INFORMATION "Urban Craft Uprising is Seattle's largest indie craft show! At UCU, now in its 11th year, fans can choose from a wide variety of handcrafted goods, including clothing of all types, jewelry, gifts, bags, wallets, buttons, accessories, aprons, children's goods, toys, housewares, paper goods, candles, kits, art, food, and much, much more. Each show is carefully curated and juried to ensure the best mix of crafts and arts, along with quality and originality. This biannual show showcases over 100 vendors excelling in the world of craft, art, and design." For more information, visit website.

UTAH ARTS FESTIVAL

(801)322-2428. E-mail: lisa@uaf.org. Website: www.uaf.org.

ADDITIONAL INFORMATION "The annual Festival takes place the 4th weekend of June each summer and is held downtown in Salt Lake City at Library and Washington Squares. A full-time staff of 4 and 1 part-time person work year-round to produce the Festival. In addition, we engage seasonal coordinators to help plan and implement artistic programs each year. A technical staff, stage and production crews, along with more than 1,000 volunteers round out the personnel needed to produce the annual event. The Utah Arts Festival is the largest outdoor multi-disciplinary arts event in Utah with attendance hovering over 80,000 each summer. Having garnered numerous awards internationally, nationally, and locally, the event remains 1 of the premiere events that kicks off the summer in Utah each June." For more information, visit website.

VAGABOND INDIE CRAFT FAIR

E-mail: info@urbanbazaarsf.com. Website: www. urbanbazaarsf.com.

ADDITIONAL INFORMATION "This event, which includes more than 20 talented local artists and craftspeople selling their work over 2 days (different vendors each day!), takes place in the back garden of Urban Bazaar. The merchandise offered at Vagabond will include all manner of gifts, with a focus on jewelry, accessories, and affordable artwork." For more information, visit website.

VERMONT MAPLE FESTIVAL

(802)524-5800. E-mail: info@vtmaplefestival.org. Website: www.vtmaplefestival.org.

ADDITIONAL INFORMATION "Glittery jewelry, taste-tempting specialty foods, classy clothing, assorted artwork, wooden things, fine photographs, and so much more! Now enlarged to more than 60 vendors, the show offers both traditional and the latest in craft innovations, AS WELL AS the fine specialty foods for which Vermont is famous! It's 1 of the first LARGE craft shows of the year, and it's ADMISSION FREE—a show that folks who delight in creativity have on their 'don't miss' list." For more information, visit website.

A VICTORIAN CHAUTAUQUA

1101 E. Market St., Jeffersonville IN 47130. (812)283-3728 or (888)472-0606. Fax: (812)283-6049. E-mail: hsmsteam@aol.com. Website: www.steamboatmuseum.org. **Contact:** Roger

Fisher, festival chairman. Estab. 1993. Fine arts and crafts show held annually 3rd weekend in May. Outdoors. Accepts photography, all mediums. Juried by a committee of 5. Number of exhibitors: 80. Public attendance: 3,000. Exhibition space: 12×12. For more information, e-mail, call, or visit website.

VILLAGES CRAFT FESTIVAL AT COLONY PLAZA, THE

270 Central Blvd., Suite 107B, Jupiter FL 33458. (561)746-6615. Fax: (561)746-6528. E-mail: info@artfestival.com. Website: www.artfestival. com. **Contact:** Malinda Ratliff, communications manager.

ADDITIONAL INFORMATION "There's something for everyone at this craft festival, featuring arts and crafts all created in the USA. Handmade1-of-a-kind jewelry pieces you will not find anywhere else, personalized wall hangings, art for your pets, ceramics—functional and decorative, and much, much more. An expansive Green Market lends plants, exotic flora, and homemade soaps. Come find that unique gift and we will see you there!"

VILLAGES CRAFT FESTIVAL AT LA PLAZA GRANDE, THE

270 Central Blvd., Suite 107B, Jupiter FL 33458. (561)746-6615. Fax: (561)746-6528. E-mail: info@artfestival.com. Website: www.artfestival. com. **Contact:** Malinda Ratliff, communications manager. Arts and crafts show held annually in January. Outdoors. Accepts handmade crafts and other items. Juried. Exhibitors: see website. Number of attendees: varies. Admission: see website. Apply online.

ADDITIONAL INFORMATION Deadline for entry: see website. Application fee: see website. Space fee: see website. Exhibition space: see website. For more information, e-mail, visit website, or call.

VILLAGE SQUARE ARTS & CRAFTS FAIR

P.O. Box 176, Saugatuck MI 49453. E-mail: artclub@saugatuckdouglasartclub.org. Website: www.saugatuckdouglasartclub.org. Estab. 2004. The art club offers 2 fairs each summer. See website for upcoming dates. This fair has some fine artists as well as crafters. Both fairs take place on the 2 busiest weekends in the resort town of Saugatuck's summer season. Both are extremely well attended. Generally the vendors do very well. Booth fee: $95–140. Fair located at corner of Butler and Main streets, Saugatuck, Michigan.

TIPS "Create an inviting booth. Offer well-made artwork and crafts for a variety of prices."

VINTAGE DAYS CRAFTS FAIRE

5280 N. Jackson Ave., M/S SU 36, Fresno CA 93740. (559)278-2741. Fax: 559-278-7786. E-mail: vintagecraftsfaire@gmail.com. Website: www.fresnostate.edu/craftsfaire. Sherri Fisk. **Contact:** Breanne Scogin. The Vintage Days Crafts Faire is a marketplace for over 100 exhibitors specializing in handmade items including jewelry, children's toys, home décor, and more. To ensure high quality and innovative items, all applications are juried. For more information, visit website.

VIRGINIA BEACH DOWNTOWN ART FAIR

270 Central Blvd., Suite 107B, Jupiter FL 33458. (561)746-6615. Fax: (561)746-6528. E-mail: info@artfestival.com. Website: www.artfestival. com. **Contact:** Malinda Ratliff, communications manager. Estab. 2015. Fine art and craft fair held annually in April. Outdoors. Accepts photography, jewelry, mixed media, sculpture, wood, ceramic, glass, painting, digital, fiber, metal. Juried. Number of exhibitors: 80. Number of attendees: see website. Free to public. Apply online via www.zapplication.org.

ADDITIONAL INFORMATION Deadline: see website. Application fee: $25. Space fee: $395. Exhibition space: 10×10 and 10×20. For more information, e-mail, call, or visit website. Festival located Main St. between Central Park Ave. and Constitution Dr.

VIRGINIA CHRISTMAS MARKET

The Exhibition Center at Meadow Event Park, 13111 Dawn Blvd., Doswell VA 23047. (804)253-6284. **Fax:** (804)253-6285. E-mail: bill.wagstaff@ virginiashows.com. Website: www.virginiashows. com. Indoors. Virginia Christmas Market is held the last weekend in October at the Exhibition Center at Meadow Event Park. Virginia Christmas Market will showcase up to 300 quality artisans, crafters, boutiques, and specialty food shops.

Features porcelain, pottery, quilts, folk art, fine art, reproduction furniture, flags, ironwork, carvings, leather, toys, tinware, candles, doll craft, woven wares, book authors, musicians, jewelry, basketry, gourmet foods—all set amid festive Christmas displays. Accepts photography and other arts and crafts. Juried by 3 photos of artwork and 1 of display. Attendance: 15,000. Public admission: $7; children free (under 10). Apply by calling, e-mailing or downloading application from website.

ADDITIONAL INFORMATION Space fee: $335. Exhibit spaces: 10×10. For more information, e-mail, call, or visit website.

TIPS If possible, attend the show before you apply.

VIRGINIA SPRING MARKET

11050 Branch Rd., Glen Allen VA 23059. (804)253-6284. Fax: (804)253-6285. E-mail: bill.wagstaff@virginiashows.com. Website: www.virginiashows.com. **Contact:** Bill Wagstaff. Estab. 1988. Holiday arts and crafts show held annually 1st weekend in March at the Exhibition Center at Meadow Event Park, 13111 Dawn Blvd., Doswell VA. Virginia Spring Market will showcase up to 300 quality artisans, crafters, boutiques, and specialty food shops. Features porcelain, pottery, quilts, folk art, fine art, reproduction furniture, flags, ironwork, carvings, leather, toys, tinware, candles, doll craft, woven wares, book authors, musicians, jewelry, basketry and gourmet foods, all set amid festive spring displays. Accepts photography and other arts and crafts. Juried by 3 images of artwork and 1 of display. Public attendance: 12,000. Public admission: $7; children free (under 10). Apply by calling, e-mailing, or downloading application from website.

ADDITIONAL INFORMATION Space fee: $335. Exhibition space: 10×10. For more information, e-mail, call or visit website.

TIPS "If possible, attend the show before you apply."

VIRTU ART FESTIVAL

45 Broad St., Westerly RI 2891. (401)596-7761. Fax: (401)596-2190. E-mail: lkonicki@oceanchamber.org. Website: www.oceanchamber.org. **Contact:** Lisa Konicki, executive director. Estab. 1996. Arts and crafts show held annually in May. Outdoors.

Accepts original fine art and handmade crafts, oils, acrylics, prints, wood, watercolor, pottery, glass, jewelry, sculpture. Juried. Exhibitors: 150. Number of attendees: 20,000. Free to public. Apply via website.

ADDITIONAL INFORMATION Deadline for entry: February 20. Application fee: none. Space fee: $200. Exhibition space: 12×12. For more information, e-mail. Event located in Wilcox Park in downtown Westerly.

WALK IN THE WOODS ART FAIR

Hawthorn Hollow, 880 Green Bay Rd., Kenosha WI 53144. (334)794-3452. E-mail: hawthornhollow@wi.rr.com. Website: www.hawthornhollow.org/events/art-fair. The Walk in the Woods Art Fair has grown to be 1 of the more popular and well respected in southeastern Wisconsin, where over 60 artists display their creations along the wooded trails and gardens of Hawthorn Hollow. Fine art ranging from jewelry to acrylic and watercolor paintings, from photography to wood sculpting, glass and garden art will all be available for purchase. We also feature live entertainment throughout the day, face painting, food/beverages for sale, and a Silent Auction. A $5 donation per vehicle is requested. Come and enjoy a beautiful day combining fine art with music and nature. For more information, visit website.

WALNUT CREEK SIDEWALK FINE ARTS & CRAFTS FESTIVAL

Pacific Fine Arts Festivals, P.O. Box 280, Pine Grove CA 95665. (209)267-4394. Fax: (209)267-4395. E-mail: pfa@pacificfinearts.com. Website: www.pacificfinearts.com. The annual Fine Arts and Crafts Festival is Free to public and will feature more than 150 professional artists traveling from throughout California and the Western United States to showcase original paintings, sculpture, photography, jewelry, clothing, and other fine works. For more information, visit website.

WASHINGTON SQUARE OUTDOOR ART EXHIBIT

P.O. Box 1045, New York NY 10276. (212)982-6255. Fax: (212)982-6256. E-mail: jrm.wsoae@gmail.com. Website: www.wsoae.org.

Estab. 1931. Fine arts and crafts show held semiannually Memorial Day weekend and Labor Day weekend. Outdoors. Accepts photography, oil, watercolor, graphics, mixed media, sculpture, crafts. Juried by submitting five slides of work and 1 of booth. Awards/prizes: certificates, ribbons, and cash prizes. Number of exhibitors: 150. Public attendance: 100,000. Free to public. Apply by sending a SASE or downloading application from website.

ADDITIONAL INFORMATION Deadline for entry: March, spring show; July, fall show. Exhibition space: 5×10. up to 10×10., double spaces available. Jury fee of $20. First show weekend (3 days) fee of $410. Second show weekend (2 days) $310. Both weekends (all 5 days) fee of $525. For more information, call or send SASE.

TIPS "Price work sensibly."

WATERFRONT FINE ART & WINE FESTIVAL

7135 E Camelback Rd., Scottsdale AZ 85251. (480)837-5637. Fax: (480)837-2355. E-mail: info@thunderbirdartists.com. Website: www.thunderbirdartists.com. **Contact:** Denise Colter, president. Estab. 2011. 125 juried fine artists will line the banks of Scottsdale Waterfront's pedestrian walkway, along with wineries, chocolate vendors, and musicians. The Waterfront is an elegant backdrop for this event, adding romantic reflections across the waters—mirroring tents, art, and patrons. Thunderbird Artists Mission is to promote fine arts and fine crafts, paralleled with the ambiance of unique wines and festive music, through a dedicated, extensive advertising campaign.

TIPS "A clean, gallery-type presentation is very important."

WATERFRONT INVITATIONAL ART FAIR

Saugatuck Douglas Art Club, Box 176, Saugatuck MI 49453-0176. (334)794-3452. E-mail: artclub@saugatuckdouglasartclub.org. Website: www.saugatuckdouglasartclub.org. Juried art and craft fair. For more information, visit website.

WAUSAU FESTIVAL OF ARTS

P.O. Box 1763, Wausau WI 54402. (715)842-1676. E-mail: info@wausaufoa. Website: www.wausaufoa.org. Since its inception in 1965, this outdoor celebration of the arts has become an annual event in the heart of Wausau's historic downtown and an integral part of Wausau's Artrageous weekend. Patrons can enjoy and purchase artwork in a variety of styles and price ranges from over 120 juried, professional artists from all over the United States. For more information, visit website.

⌂ WEDGWOOD ART FESTIVAL

Wedgwood Art Festival, P.O. Box 15246, Seattle WA 98115. E-mail: wafestival@gmail.com. E-mail: wafestival@gmail.com. Website: www.wedgwoodfestival.com. **Contact:** Alex Strazzanti and Nancy Reed. Estab. 2005. The Wedgwood Art Festival is a 2-day event supporting and celebrating arts for the community of Wedgwood, Seattle. Most participating artists reside in Seattle and the Puget Sound area. A few guest Northwest artists who live outside the Puget Sound area are also included to add variety to the show. For more information, visit website.

☊ WELLS STREET ART FESTIVAL

E-mail: rrobinson@chicagoevents.com. Website: www.chicagoevents.com.1 of the city's largest and most acclaimed fine arts happenings, it's held in the heart of Chicago's historic Old Town neighborhood. The annual art extravaganza features the works of more than 250 juried artists, with the eclectic mix running the gamut from paintings, sculptures, and glasswork to photography, ceramics, woodwork, and much more. It also features the tasty cuisine of Old Town restaurants, the always-hoppin' music stage, and a silent auction. For more information, visit website.

WESTMORELAND ARTS & HERITAGE FESTIVAL

252 Twin Lakes Rd., Latrobe PA 15650-3554. (724)834-7474. E-mail: info@artsandheritage.com; diane@artsandheritage.com. Website: www.artsandheritage.com. **Contact:** Diane Shrader, executive director. Estab. 1975. Juried fine art exhibition and crafts show held annually in early July (see website for details). Juried art exhibition is indoors. Photography displays are indoors. Accepts photography, all handmade

mediums. Juried by 2 jurors. Awards/prizes: $3,400 in prizes. Number of exhibitors: 190. Public attendance: 125,000. Free to public. Apply by downloading application from website. Application fee: $25/craft show vendors; $35/art nationals exhibitors.

ADDITIONAL INFORMATION Deadline for entry: early March. Space fee: $375–750. Artist Market exhibition space: 10×10 or 10×20. For more information, visit e-mail, call, or visit website. Please direct questions to our executive director.

❸❓ WEST SHORE ART FAIR

The Ludington Area Center for the Arts, 107 S. Harrison St., Ludington MI 49431. (231)845-2787. E-mail: wsaf@ludingtonartscenter.org. Website: www.ludingtonartscenter.org. **Contact:** Christine Plummer, WSAF coordinator. Estab. 1968. The 2016 West Shore Art Fair was recognized as1 of *Sunshine Artist Magazine*'s 200 Best Fine Art and Fine Craft Fairs. It takes place July 2-3, at Rotary Park (formerly City Park) in the beautiful Lake Michigan resort community of Ludington, Michigan, featuring 100 plus jury-selected fine artists across a variety of media, including clay, fiber, glass, jewelry, painting, photography, sculpture, and more. In its 48th year, the open-air, juried fine art and fine crafts show is managed by the Ludington Area Center for the Arts, a community arts organization that cultivates access to arts and culture in west Michigan. In addition to original, jury-selected art, the show features live performances, food stations, and a children's art activity area. For more information, visit www.ludingtonartscenter.org or facebook.com/WestShoreArtFair.

WHITEFISH ARTS FESTIVAL

P.O. Box 131, Whitefish MT 59937. (406)862-5875. E-mail: wafdirector@gmail.com. Website: www.whitefishartsfestival.org. **Contact:** Clark Berg; Angie Scott. Estab. 1979. High-quality art show held annually the 1st full weekend in July. Outdoors. Accepts photography, pottery, jewelry, sculpture, paintings, woodworking. Art must be original and handcrafted. Work is evaluated for creativity, quality, and originality.120 booths. Public attendance: 3,000–5,000. Free to public. Juried entry fee: $35.

ADDITIONAL INFORMATION Deadline: see website. Space fee: $230. Exhibition space: 10×10. For more information, and to apply, visit website.

TIPS Recommends "variety of price range, professional display, early application for special requests."

WHITE OAK CRAFTS FAIR

1424 John Bragg Hwy., Woodbury TN 37190. (615)563-2787. E-mail: mary@artscenterofcc.com; artscenter@artscenterofcc.com; carol@artscenterofcc.com. Website: www.artscenterofcc.com. Estab. 1985. Arts and crafts show held annually in early September (see website for details) featuring the traditional and contemporary craft arts of Cannon County and Middle Tennessee. Outdoors. Accepts photography; all handmade crafts, traditional and contemporary. Must be handcrafted displaying excellence in concept and technique. Juried by committee. Send 3 slides or photos. Awards/prizes: more than $1,000 cash in merit awards. Number of exhibitors: 80. Public attendance: 6,000. Free to public. Applications can be downloaded from website.

ADDITIONAL INFORMATION Deadline: early July. Space fee: $120 ($90 for artisan member) for a 10×10. under tent; $95 ($65 for artisan member) for a 12×12. outside. For more information, e-mail, call, or visit website. Fair takes place along the banks of the East Fork Stones River just down from the Arts Center.

WICKFORD ART FESTIVAL

Wickford Art Association, 36 Beach St., North Kingstown RI 2852. (401)294-6840. E-mail: festivaldirector@wickfordart.org. Website: www.wickfordart.org. **Contact:** Judy Salvadore, director. Estab. 1962. Fine art show held annually in July. Outdoors. Accepts fine art, painting, jewelry, drawing, photography. Juried. Exhibitors: 250. Number of attendees: 50,000. Free to public. Apply online.

ADDITIONAL INFORMATION Deadline for entry: April 1. Application fee: $35. Space fee: $200 (members); $240 (nonmembers). Exhibition space: 10×10. For more information, visit website, e-mail, or call.

TIPS Fine artists only should apply—no functional art accepted. Rhode Island does not collect sales tax on fine art. Festival is outdoors, rain or shine so be prepared for New England weather, which could be hot and humid, rainy, or gorgeous! Festival has a long history in coastal Wickford Village and is a summer highlight in southern New England.

WILD WIND FOLK ART & CRAFT FESTIVAL

P.O. Box 719, Long Lake NY 12847. (207) 479-9867 (814)688-1516. E-mail: wildwindcraftshow@yahoo.com; info@wildwindfestival.com. Website: www.wildwindfestival.com. **Contact:** Liz Allen and Carol Jilk, directors. Estab. 1979. Traditional crafts show held annually the weekend after Labor Day at the Warren County Fairgrounds in Pittsfield, Pennsylvania. Barn locations and outdoors. Accepts traditional country crafts, photography, paintings, pottery, jewelry, traditional crafts, prints, stained glass. Juried by promoters. Need 3 photos or slides of work plus 1 of booth, if available. Number of exhibitors: 160. Public attendance: 9,000. Apply by visiting website and filling out application request, calling, or sending a written request. Request application form on website page or by phone.

WILLOUGHBY ARTSFEST

WWLCC ArtsFest, 28 Public Square, Willoughby OH 44094. (440)942-1632. E-mail: info@wwlcchamber.com. Website: www.wwlcchamber.com. **Contact:** Donna Swan. Estab. 1991. Historical Downtown Willoughby, in the hub of Lake County, is located 20 miles east of Cleveland and easily accessible from both Interstate 2 and 90. Featuring over 150 artists, entertainment, and food, this show welcomes over 10,000 people. Willoughby ArtsFest—you won't want to miss it! For more information, visit website.

WINNEBAGOLAND ART FAIR

South Park Ave., Oshkosh WI 54902. E-mail: oshkoshfaa@gmail.com. **Contact:** Kathy Murphy. Estab. 1957. Fine arts show held annually the 2nd Sunday in June. Outdoors. Accepts painting, wood or stone, ceramics, metal sculpture, jewelry, glass, fabric, drawing, photography, wall hangings, basketry. Artwork must be the original work of the artist in concept and execution. Juried. Applicants send in photographs to be reviewed. Awards/prizes: monetary awards, purchase, merit, and Best of Show awards. Number of exhibitors: 125–160. Public attendance: 5,000–8,000. Free to public.

ADDITIONAL INFORMATION Deadline for entry: Previous exhibitors due mid-March; new exhibitors due late March. $25 late entry fee after March. Exhibition space: 20×20. For more information, e-mail or visit website. The updated entry form will be added to the website in early January.

TIPS "Artists should send clear, uncluttered photos of their current work that they intend to show in their booth as well as a photo of their booth setup."

☺ WINNIPEG FOLK FESTIVAL HANDMADE VILLAGE

Winnipeg Folk Festival, 203-211 Bannatyne Ave. Winnipeg, Manitoba R3B 3P2 Canada. (204)231-0096; (866)301-3823. Fax: (204)231-0076. E-mail: info@winnipegfolkfestival.ca. Website: www.winnipegfolkfestival.ca. The Hand-Made Village celebrates the long-standing history that folk art shares with folk music festivals. Our village features the handmade work of up to 50 artisans from across Canada. For more information, visit website.

WINTER PARK SIDEWALK ART FESTIVAL

Winter Park Sidewalk Art Festival, P.O. Box 597, Winter Park FL 32790-0597. (407)644-7207. E-mail: wpsaf@yahoo.com. Website: www.wpsaf.org. The Winter Park Sidewalk Art Festival is 1 of the nation's oldest, largest, and most prestigious juried outdoor art festivals, consistently rated among the top shows by *Sunshine Artist* and *American Style* magazines. Each year more than 350,000 visitors enjoy the show. For more information, visit website.

☺ WOODLANDS WATERWAY ARTS FESTIVAL

The Woodlands Waterway Arts Festival, P.O. Box 8184, The Woodlands TX 77387. (832)745-3560. E-mail: info@woodlandsartsfestival.com. Website:

www.woodlandsartsfestival.com. The Woodlands Waterway Arts Festival (WWAF) weekend event is a celebration of visual, culinary, and performing arts. The Festival gives patrons the rare and special opportunity to meet and talk with artists from around the country, sample great food, watch the Art of Food demos, enjoy live music, and entertain their families at our interactive 'ARTOPOLY' area. Adult tickets are $12/day; weekend pass is $15; children 12 and under are admitted free. Cash ONLY at all gates and food vendors. For more information, visit website.

WOODSSTOCK MUSIC & ARTS FESTIVAL

(419)862-3182. Fine art and craft show held annually in August. Outdoors. Accepts handmade crafts, ceramics, drawing, fiber, glass, jewelry, leather, metal, mixed media, painting, photography, sculpture, wood. Juried. Awards/prizes: Best of Show, honorable mention. Number of exhibitors: see website. Number of attendees: varies. Admission: $25 general; $45 VIP. Apply via www.zapplication.org.

ADDITIONAL INFORMATION Deadline for entry: June. Application fee: $20. Space fee: $100 (single); $150 (double). Exhibition space: 10×10 (single); 10×20 (double). For more information, visit website.

WYANDOTTE STREET ART FAIR

2624 Biddle Ave., Wyandotte MI 48192. (734)324-4502. Fax: (734)324-7283. E-mail: hthiede@wyan.org. Website: www.wyandottestreetartfair.org. **Contact:** Heather Thiede, special events coordinator. Estab. 1961. Fine arts and crafts show held annually 2nd week in July. Outdoors. Accepts photography, 2D and 3D mixed media, painting, pottery, basketry, sculpture, fiber, leather, digital cartoons, clothing, stitchery, metal, glass, wood, toys, prints, drawing. Juried. Awards/prizes: Best New Artist $500; Best Booth Design Award $500; Best of Show $1,200. Number of exhibitors: 300. Public attendance: 200,000. Free to public. Artists may apply online or request application.

ADDITIONAL INFORMATION Deadline for entry: early February. Application fee: $20 jury fee. Space fee: $250/single space; $475/double space. Exhibition space: 10×12 ft. Average gross sales/exhibitor: $2,000–4,000. For more information, and to apply, artists should call, e-mail, visit website, or send SASE.

YELLOW DAISY FESTIVAL

E-mail: ydf@stonemountainpark.com. Website: www.stonemountainpark.com/events/Yellow-Daisy-Festival.aspx. More than 400 artists and crafters from 38 states and 2 countries display their works for your appreciation and purchase. Daily live entertainment, Children's Corner activities, and crafter demonstrations throughout the event as well as fabulous festival foods. Yellow Daisy Festival is free with paid parking admission. Vehicle entry to the park is $15 for a 1-day permit or $40 for an annual permit. For more information, visit website.

[ONLINE MARKETPLACES]

Most crafters are aware of Etsy, but there are other online marketplaces that provide support for craft artisans. Whether you choose to diversify your online presence by selling across multiple platforms, or choose to focus on one or 2 sites, you need to be aware of the ever-changing landscape of online sales. Visit their website and take a look around. Do they offer a functionality that would be helpful to your online sales? Do you recognize anyone who is selling on that site? What is the competition? How do images appear? What is the site's financial take of your sales, or do they charge a flat fee per listing? Consider all of your options and do your research to make sure you are maximizing your online opportunities. Also, be sure to read Isaac Watson's article "Choosing an Online Marketplace."

The listings here are only the tip of the iceberg. More and more online venues sprout up every day. As a crafter and business person, get to know the venues that apply to you as they become available. If you can, order from a vendor to gain a firsthand understanding of the user's experience. Try to talk with someone who has a shop on the site—or sites—you're interested in.

KEY TO SYMBOLS AND ABBREVIATIONS

✹	Canadian market
◗	market located outside of the U.S. and Canada
⌂	market prefers to work with local artists/ designers
bandw	black and white (photo or illustration)
SASE	self-addressed, stamped envelope
SAE	self-addressed envelope
IRC	International Reply Coupon, for use when mailing to countries other than your own

COMPLAINT PROCEDURE

If you feel you have not been treated fairly by a company listed in Crafter's Market, we advise you to take the following steps:

- First, try to contact the company. Sometimes one e-mail or letter can quickly clear up the matter.
- Document all your correspondence with the company. If you write to us with a complaint, provide the details of your submission, the date of your first contact with the company, and the nature of your subsequent correspondence.
- We will enter your complaint into our files.
- The number and severity of complaints will be considered in our decision whether to delete the listing from the next edition.
- We reserve the right to not list any company for any reason.

ARTFIRE

E-mail: service@artfire.com. Website: www.artfire.com. Geared toward handmade items. Provides shopping cart checkout feature. Products sold: handmade items, vintage, supplies, PDF downloads, patterns/books. Setup costs: $12.95/month. Accepted payment methods: Visa, MasterCard, American Express, PayPal, Bill Me Later, ProPay, Amazon Payments. Sales disputes: dedicated customer service team to resolve disputes and answer queries. Provided to sellers: community forums/chats, additional free marketing opportunities, groups.

ARTFUL HOME

E-mail: artists@artfulhome.com. Website: www.artfulhome.com. Geared toward handmade items and other merchandise. Provides shopping cart checkout feature. Products sold: handmade, craft, art, vintage. Provided to sellers: community forums/chats, additional free marketing opportunities, groups.

ARTULIS

E-mail: help@artulis.com. Website: www.artulis.com. Artulis is an online marketplace for artists, makers, and crafts people to showcase their work and find new buyers for their talents. We provide an online shop as well as a range of tools to help keep track of sales and messages from buyers.

BONANZA

109 W. Denny Wy. #312, Seattle WA , 98119. E-mail: support@bonanza.com. Website: www.bonanza.com. Products sold: handmade items, vintage, supplies, art, crafts, accessories, apparel. Setup costs: free. Accepted payment methods: see website. Sales disputes: dedicated customer service team to resolve disputes and answer queries. Provided to sellers: community forums/chats.

CAFEPRESS

Website: www.cafepress.com. "CafePress is where the world's creative minds join forces to provide an unparalleled marketplace. We give you the power to create custom products and personalized gifts on a variety of high-quality items such as T-shirts, hoodies, posters, bumper stickers, and mugs. CafePress also allows you to set up online shops where you can design and sell your own unique merchandise. Our design tools make it easy to add photos, text, images, and even create cool designs or logos from scratch. As if it couldn't get any better, you can even find content from major entertainment partners such as *The Hunger Games*, *Big Bang Theory*, and *Star Trek* as well as products dedicated to hobbies, birthdays, the military, and more. At CafePress we print each item as it's ordered and many products ship within 24 hours."

CORIANDR

Mookle Studios Limited, 12 Parklands Close, Chandlers Ford, Eastleigh Hants SO53 2EQ, UK. E-mail: support@coriandr.com. Website: www.coriandr.com. Geared toward handmade items. Setup costs: see website. Accepted payment methods: credit card, PayPal. Provided to sellers: community forums/chats, groups.

CRAFT IS ART

Las Vegas NV Website: www.craftisart.com. Estab. 2009. Geared toward handmade items. Provides shopping cart checkout feature. Setup costs: free option; premium option $79.99/yr. Accepted payment methods: Visa, MasterCard, American Express, PayPal, Amazon Payments, Google Checkout. Provided to sellers: community forums/chats, Facebook integration, customizable store, coupons, business cards, postcards.

CRAFTSY

999 18th St., Suite 240, Denver CO 80202. Website: www.craftsy.com. Estab. 2010. "Craftsy provides education and tools to help you bring your creativity to life. Our hundreds of classes in quilting, sewing, knitting, cake decorating, art, photography, cooking, and many more categories, bring the world's best instructors to you. Learn at your pace with easy-to-follow HD video lessons you can access on your computer and mobile device anytime, anywhere, forever. Craftsy's Supplies Shop is carefully curated to bring you the best brands at incredible values, ensuring you always have exactly what you need for your next project. Find your new favorite fabric collections, designer yarns, art supplies, books, class materials, and more. Find your next project

in Craftsy's Pattern Marketplace, featuring thousands of beautiful patterns from the world's best independent designers. All proceeds go directly to supporting passionate designers, and you can instantly download high-quality patterns for chic shawls, adorable baby booties, couture dresses, scalloped lace hats, and so much more!"

DAWANDA

Windscheidstr 18, Berlin 10627, Germany. (44)20 3608 1414. E-mail: english@dawanda. com. Website: en.dawanda.com. Estab. 2006. Geared toward handmade items. Provides shopping cart checkout feature. Products sold: handmade items, vintage, supplies, PDF downloads, patterns/books. Setup costs: free; 10% commission on successful sales. Handling and tax should be included by seller in item price; shipping is added automatically at checkout. Accepted payment methods: Visa, MasterCard, American Express, PayPal, checking account, Wirecard, voucher, cash on collection. Sales disputes: dedicated customer service team to resolve disputes and answer queries within 24 hours. Standard listings: 4 photos and 5,000 characters. Other listing features: detailed product description, size/dimensions/weight, materials utilized, production method, customization options, keywords. Site statistics: 340,000 designers, 5.7 million products, 6.2 million members, over 200 million page impressions a month, 20 million page visits per month, strong social media presence. Provided to sellers: community forums/chats, additional marketing opportunities, groups.

TIPS "As an international community, we would recommend sellers translate their listings into a selection of our 7 languages available. In addition, we would recommend uploading high-quality photos with your product on a light, neutral background—DaWanda is a very visual community. Don't forget to tell the story behind your products, too! DaWanda is the online marketplace for unique and handmade products and gives creatives and designers the opportunity to offer their one-of-a-kind and limited-edition products for sale. DaWanda centers around the idea of 'social commerce,' allowing customers to interact with designers, comment on favorite products, and pass on recommendations. Our lively and passionate community allows buyers and sellers to interact and personalize the shopping experience—going against the grain of mass-produced products. DaWanda is an international community available in 7 languages and offers a space for designers and creatives to develop their business, talents, and success, in turn allowing them to make a living from doing what they love."

ELECTRONIC COTTAGE

Website: www.electroniccottage.com. Estab. 2010. "This arts portal is first and foremost a direct connection between those individuals who enjoy purchasing originally created handmade art and craftwork and those professionals who enjoy creating that work. The extent of this connection is only made possible through the use of computers and the World Wide Web, exactly as Joseph Deken predicted decades ago. At EC Gallery, there is no need to join a club, become a member, make up a user name, remember a password, leave us your e-mail, or jump through any other hoops. All we ask is that you sit back and enjoy your visits to the studio websites of the immensely talented people from around the world who exhibit via this online gallery. At EC Gallery you can connect directly to make purchases from the distinct websites of over 2,000 contemporary and traditional artists and craftspeople. Each cyberstudio is a truly unique experience, so explore and have fun. You will find much amazing work throughout our community of talented professionals."

ETSY

Website: www.etsy.com. Geared toward handmade items. Shopping cart checkout feature. Products sold: handmade items, vintage, craft supplies. Setup costs: $0.20 to list an item; 3.5% fee on sale price. Listing features: user profiles, photos, shop banner.

FOLKSY

Harland Works, 72 John St. Sheffield S2 4QU, UK. Website: www.folksy.com. Geared toward handmade items. Setup costs: see website. Folksy currently only supports sellers who are living and working in the UK.

GLC CRAFT MALL
(604)946-8041. E-mail: info@glcmall.com. Website: www.glccraftmall.com. Geared toward handmade items. Setup costs: see website. Provides shopping cart checkout feature. Shipping and handling handled by individual shops. Payments accepted: credit cards, PayPal.

GOODSMITHS
218½ Fifth St., West Des Moines IA 50265. Website: www.goodsmiths.com. Geared toward handmade items. Setup costs: see website. Provides shopping cart checkout feature. Payments accepted: MasterCard, Visa, PayPal.

HANDMADE ARTISTS' SHOP
Website: www.handmadeartists.com. Geared toward handmade items. Setup costs: must have a subscription to the Handmade Artists' Shop ($5/month; $50/year). Provides shopping cart checkout feature. Payments accepted: MasterCard, Visa, Discover, American Express, PayPal. Provided to sellers: items added to Google Product Search and The Find, search engine optimization (SEO), internal PM system, coupons, forums, community.

HANDMADE CATALOG
(800)851-0183. E-mail: pam@handmadecatalog.com. Website: www.handmadecatalog.com. Estab. 2002. Geared toward handmade items. Setup costs: see website. Provides shopping cart checkout feature. Provided to sellers: website maintenance, marketing, feature in weekly e-mail newsletter, no contracts, and cancel anytime.

ICRAFT
Website: www.icraftgifts.com. Geared toward handmade items. Setup costs: $25 + monthly subscription fee. Provides shopping cart checkout feature. Provided to sellers: search engine optimization (SEO), Facebook and Twitter integration, free Seller's Bootcamp, free blogging software, iCraft community.

I MADE IT! MARKETPLACE
P.O. Box 9613, Pittsburgh PA 15226. (412)254-4464. Website: www.imadeitmarket.com. Contact: Carrie Nardini, director. Estab. 2007. Geared toward handmade items. Products sold: handmade items. Setup costs: currently no online for sales. Ongoing fees: see website. Provided to sellers: community forums/chats, additional paid marketing opportunities, additional free marketing opportunities, seminars, social events, workshops. **TIPS** "We have built a reputation for fun, unique, high-quality handmade wares including a wide variety of work that is ideal for anyone on a shopper's list."

MADE IT MYSELF
P.O. Box 888, Fresno California 93714. E-mail: support@madeitmyself.com. Website: www.madeitmyself.com. Geared toward handmade items. Setup costs: none; 3% fee for every item sold.

MAIN ST. REVOLUTION
Website: www.overstock.com/Main-St.-Revolution/39/store.html. "Main St. Revolution is Overstock.com showing its commitment to small businesses across the US. By giving local shopkeepers a broader audience, we're supporting the American Dream."

MELA ARTISANS
Website: www.melaartisans.com. "Mela Artisans is a luxury lifestyle brand that combines traditional handcrafting techniques with the freshness and functionality of contemporary design. Our distinctive and original collections fuse modern designs with enduring techniques passed down through generations in artisan communities."

MISI
27 Old Gloucester St. London WC1N 3AX, England. E-mail: admin@misi.co.uk. Website: www.misi.co.uk. Estab. 2008. Geared toward handmade items. Setup costs: none; 3% fee for every item sold. Provided to sellers: crafter's blog, free domain, 12-month listing, forum.

NOT MASS PRODUCED
Orchard Cottage, Station Rd. Longstanton, Cambridge, Cambridgeshire CB24 3DS, England. 01954 261066. E-mail: enquiries@notmassproduced.com. Website: www.notmassproduced.com. Estab. 2008. Geared toward handmade items. All artisans are vetted. "Designers are from the UK and no farther than Europe."

REDBUBBLE

650 Castro St., Suite 120-275, Mountain View California , 94041. Website: www.redbubble. com. "Redbubble is a free marketplace that helps thousands of artists reach new audiences and sell their work more easily. RB gives you access to a wide range of high-quality products, just waiting for your designs to make them more amazing. We coordinate everything from printing and shipping through to ongoing customer service, giving you more time to focus on creating great art and design (and occasionally watching cat videos on the Internet)."

SHOP HANDMADE

11901 137th Ave. Ct. KPN, Gig Harbor WA , 98329-6617. E-mail: Service@ShopHandmade. com. Website: www.shophandmade.com. Geared toward handmade items. Setup fee: none. Payments accepted: PayPal.

SILK FAIR

Website: www.silkfair.com. Geared toward handmade items and other merchandise. Setup fee: see website.

SPOONFLOWER

2810 Meridian Pkwy. Suite 176, Durham NC 27713. (919)886-7885. Website: www.spoonflower.com. Geared toward handmade items. Products sold: fabric, wallpaper, decals, and gift wrap. Setup fee: see website. "At Spoonflower we make it possible for individuals to design, print, and sell their own fabric, wallpaper, decals, and gift wrap. It was founded in May 2008 by 2 Internet geeks who had crafty wives but who knew nothing about textiles. The company came about because Stephen's wife, Kim, persuaded him that being able to print her own fabric for curtains was a really cool idea. She wasn't alone. The Spoonflower community now numbers over a million individuals who use their own fabric to make curtains, quilts, clothes, bags, furniture, dolls, pillows, framed artwork, costumes, banners, and much, much more. The Spoonflower marketplace offers the largest collection of independent fabric designers in the world."

STORENVY

Website: www.storenvy.com. Geared toward handmade items. Setup costs: none. Payments accepted: all major credit cards, PayPal. Provided to sellers: customizable options, Facebook integration, visitor stats, mobile- and tablet-friendly sites, custom domain option, inventory, and order tracking.

SUPERMARKET

E-mail: help@supermarket.com. Website: www. supermarkethq.com. Geared toward handmade items. "Supermarket is a curated collection of awesome designed products."

TOPHATTER

292 Lambert Ave., Palo Alto, California 94306. Website: www.tophatter.com. "Tophatter is a virtual auction house. It also happens to be the world's most entertaining live marketplace. Tophatter conducts live online auctions every day where buyers and sellers can interact, chat, and transact in a wide variety of categories. Tophatter is based in Palo Alto, California, and backed by leading venture capital firms."

ZIBBET

Website: www.zibbet.com. Geared toward handmade items. Products sold: handmade goods, fine art, vintage, craft supplies. Setup costs: see website. Provided to sellers: search engine optimization (SEO), Etsy importer, business cards, and more.

[BOOK PUBLISHERS]

Seeing your name on the cover of a book is both a dream and a goal for many professional crafters. This section of listings is dedicated to book publishers that publish craft books of some kind. Keep in mind that a large publisher may have many different imprints, or trade names, under that books for a more specific demographic are published. For example, F+W Media, Inc., publishes mixed-media craft books under the North Light imprint and quilting books under the Fons and Porter imprint. Where appropriate, we have included different imprints in order to specify the type of craft that imprint publishes.

Before sending off queries to book publishers, make sure you have a strong idea with industry research to back it up. Just like you, publishers are trying to generate a profit, so make sure your idea is well thought out and is unique but relevant. Most successful book proposals will be accompanied by photos of potential projects. However, until they are specifically requested by an editor, never send physical materials to a publisher; it is possible you will never see those samples again. Instead, take some simple but beautiful photos of your samples for inclusion in your proposal.

Each publisher is different in the way they accept submissions and draft proposals, so read the instructions for each publisher's information to understand their process. Also, do further research on any company in that you are interested in submitting a proposal. Visit the company's website, look at books they have published and where those books are sold. Do you respect the authors they have worked with previously? Do you like the content they produce? What is the reputation of the company or of their books? Do you like the photography and design? Although each book is different, keep in mind that similarities amongst an entire publisher's line of books will likely impact yours as well.

- Mass-market paperbacks are sold at supermarkets, newsstands, drugstores, etc. They include romance novels, diet books, mysteries, and novels by popular authors such as Stephen King.
- Trade books are the hardcovers and paperbacks found only in bookstores and libraries. The paperbacks are larger than those on the mass-market racks and are printed on higher-quality paper and often feature matte-paper jackets.
- Textbooks contain plenty of illustrations, photographs, and charts to explain their subjects.
- Small-press books are produced by small independent publishers. Many are literary or scholarly in theme and often feature fine art on their covers.
- Backlist titles or reprints refer to publishers' titles from past seasons that continue to sell year after year. These books are often updated and republished with freshly designed covers to keep them up to date and attractive to readers.

Before signing a contract, identify your goals for writing a book and make sure that your contract is meeting those expectations. Where will your book be sold? What kind of marketing and promotional assistance will the publisher give you? Will you receive an advance and royalty on book sales, or will you receive one flat fee for the book, regardless of sales? Is it important for you to have a say in the photography or not? Don't sign a contract before making sure that your goals are in line with your publisher and specified in the contract.

Writing a book is a lot of hard work, but sharing your craft with the world through a published book will provide you with a strong foothold in the professional craft world. Good luck with your book proposal!

4TH LEVEL INDIE

E-mail: 4thlevelindie@gmail.com. Website: www.4thlevelindie.com. Estab. 2012. Types of books published: alternative craft and hobby. A small book publishing company based in San Francisco, California. Currently publishes 1–2 titles per year.

ADAMS MEDIA

Division of F+W Media, Inc., 57 Littlefield St., Avon MA 02322. (508)427-7100. Fax: (800)872-5628. E-mail: adamsmediasubmissions@fwmedia. com. Website: www.adamsmedia.com. **Contact:** Acquisitions Editor. Estab. 1980. Publishes hardcover originals, trade paperback, e-book originals, and reprints. Adams Media publishes commercial nonfiction, including self-help, women's issues, pop psychology, relationships, business, careers, pets, parenting, New Age, gift books, cookbooks, how-to, reference, and humor. Does not return unsolicited materials. Publishes **more than 250** titles/year.

RECENT TITLE(S) *Oh Boy, You're Having a Girl*, by Brian A. Klems; *Graphic the Valley*, by Peter Hoffmeister.

AMERICAN QUILTER'S SOCIETY

5801 Kentucky Dam Rd., Paducah KY 42003. (270)898-7903. Fax: (270)898-1173. E-mail: editor@aqsquilt.com. Website: www. americanquilter.com. **Contact:** Elaine Brelsford, executive book editor (primarily how-to and patterns, but other quilting books sometimes published, including quilt-related fiction). Estab. 1984. Publishes trade paperbacks. "American Quilter's Society publishes how-to and pattern books for quilters (beginners through intermediate skill level). We are not the publisher for non-quilters writing about quilts. We now publish quilt-related craft cozy romance and mystery titles, series only. Humor is good. Graphic depictions and curse words are bad." Publishes **20–24** titles/year.

RECENT TITLE(S) *Liberated Quiltmaking II*, by Gwen Marston; *T-Shirt Quilts Made Easy*, by Martha Deleonardis; *Decorate Your Shoes*, by Annemart Berendse.

ANDREWS MCMEEL PUBLISHING

1130 Walnut St., Kansas City MO 64106. (816)581-8921 or (800) 851-8923. E-mail: tlynch@ amuniversal.com; marketing@amuniversal.com. Website: www.andrewsmcmeel.com. **Contact:** Tim Lynch, creative director. Estab. 1972. Our company's core publication categories include: cook books, comics and humor, puzzles andgames, and illustrated middle grade. We're always looking for new authors and new book ideas.

TIPS "We want designers who can read a manuscript and design a concept for the best possible cover. Communicate well and be flexible with design."

❂ ANNESS PUBLISHING LTD./ SOUTHWATER

Anness Publishing Ltd. Book Trade Services, 108 Great Russell St. London WC1B 3NA, UK. 0116 275 9060. Fax: 0116 275 9090. E-mail: info@ anness.com. Website: www.annesspublishing. com. Estab. 1999.

BLACK DOG AND LEVENTHAL PUBLISHERS

1290 Ave. of the Americas, New York NY 10104. (212)364-1100. E-mail: info@ blackdogandleventhal.com. Website: www. blackdogandleventhal.com. "Black Dog and Leventhal books represent hours of reading and visual pleasure for book lovers of all types. We publish strikingly original books of light reference, humor, cooking, sports, music, film and entertainment, mysteries, history and biography, and much, much more. Many of them are in unusual formats and many are rich with color and imagery. Some are just for curling up with, some sharpen your mind, some teach valuable skills, while others are just pure pleasure."

C&T PUBLISHING

1651 Challenge Dr., Concord California 94520. (925)677-0377. Fax: (925)677-0373. E-mail: ctinfo@ctpub.com. E-mail: ctinfo@ctpub.com. Website: www.ctpub.com. **Contact:** Roxane Cerda, acquisitions editor. Estab. 1983. C&T Publishing releases a variety of quilting, sewing, needle art, and mixed-media books and patterns. In addition, C&T releases related gift and notions products for the quilting and sewing enthusiast. C&T Publishing has become the industry leader for providing exceptional books and products to the quilting, sewing, needle arts, and fiber art markets throughout the United States and internationally. Publishes **50+** titles/year. Available online.

HOW TO CONTACT Accepts unsolicited proposals and manuscripts; guidelines available on website at www.ctpub.com/client_pages/submissions.cfm. Keeps information on file. Samples not filed are returned. Considers simultaneous submissions.

NEEDS Buys all rights. Finds authors through submissions. Works with never-before-published authors frequently. Look for original concept, popluar concept, on-trend concept, large following on social media, existing fan base. Average book has 60–144 pages. Average craft/DIY book contains 6–20+ projects/patterns. Provides print-ready illustrations in-house. Provides photography.

TERMS Books undergo technical edit prior to publication. Payment based on royalty/advance and royalty only.

TIPS Provide a lot of visual imagery with your proposal. Try to really show me what you envision for your book and what makes your work special. Be sure to provide ample information regarding your author biography and the extent of your current outreach and audience size. I want to know how you reach your audience and how strong the number of followers you enjoy. It is crucial that an author is able to summarize in one sentence what makes their book stand out from the crowd. If a book's topic and uniqueness cannot be explained in a sentence (long sentences are okay), the resulting book will be hard to sell.

CHRONICLE BOOKS

680 Second St., San Francisco California 94107. E-mail: submissions@chroniclebooks.com. Website: www.chroniclebooks.com. "We publish an exciting range of books, stationery, kits, calendars, and novelty formats. Our list includes children's books and interactive formats; young adult books; cookbooks; fine art, design, and photography; pop culture; craft, fashion, beauty, and home décor; relationships, mind-body-spirit; innovative formats such as interactive journals, kits, decks, and stationery; and much, much more." Publishes **90** titles/year. Book catalog for 9x12 SAE and 8 first-class stamps.

HOW TO CONTACT Submit via mail only. Children's submissions only. Submit proposal (guidelines online) and allow up to 3 months for editors to review. If submitting by mail, do not include SASE since our staff will not return materials.

TERMS Generally pays authors in royalties based on retail price, "though we do occasionally work on a flat-fee basis." Advance varies. Illustrators paid royalty based on retail price or flat-fee.

DAVID AND CHARLES

E-mail: james.woollam@fwcommunity.com. Website: www.fwcommunity.com/uk. Publishes craft books.

DK PUBLISHING

Penguin Random House, 80 Strand, London WC2R 0RL, UK. Website: www.dk.com. "DK publishes photographically illustrated nonfiction for children of all ages." *DK Publishing does not accept unagented mss or proposals.*

DORLING KINDERSLEY (DK PUBLISHING)

345 Hudson St., 4th Floor, New York NY 10014. E-mail: ecustomerservice@randomhouse.com.. Website: www.dk.com/us. "DK produces content for consumers in over 87 countries and 62 languages, with offices in Delhi, London, Melbourne, Munich, New York, and Toronto. DK's aim is to inform, enrich, and entertain readers of all ages and everything DK publishes, whether print or digital, embodies the unique DK design approach. DK brings unrivaled clarity to a wide range of topics with a unique combination of words and pictures, put together to spectacular effect. We have a reputation for innovation in design for both print and digital products."

DOVER PUBLICATIONS, INC.

31 E. Second St., Mineola NY 11501. (516)294-7000. Fax: (516)873-1401. Website: www.doverpublications.com. Estab. 1941. Publishes trade paperback originals and reprints. Publishes **660** titles/year. Book catalog online.

HOW TO CONTACT Query with SASE.

TERMS Makes outright purchase.

FIREFLY BOOKS

50 Staples Ave., Unit 1, Richmond Hill Ontario, L4B 0A7 Canada. (416)499-8412. E-mail: service@fireflybooks.com. E-mail: valerie@fireflybooks.com. Website: www.fireflybooks.com. Estab. 1974. Publishes high-quality nonfiction.

HOW TO CONTACT Prefers images in digital format, but will accept 35mm transparencies.

NEEDS "We're looking for book-length ideas, not stock. We pay a royalty on books sold, plus advance."

TERMS Send query letter with résumé of credits. Does not keep samples on file; include SAE/IRC for return of material. Simultaneous submissions OK. Payment negotiated with contract. Credit line given.

WALTER FOSTER PUBLISHING, INC.

3 Wrigley, Suite A, Irvine California 92618. (800)426-0099. Fax: (949)380-7575. E-mail: walterfoster@quartous.com. Website: www.walterfoster.com. **Contact:** Submissions. Estab. 1922. Publishes trade paperback originals. "Walter Foster publishes instructional how-to/craft instruction as well as licensed products."

FOX CHAPEL PUBLISHING

1970 Broad St., East Petersburg PA 17520. (800)457-9112. Fax: (717)560-4702. E-mail: acquisitions@foxchapelpublishing.com. Website: www.foxchapelpublishing.com. Publishes hardcover and trade paperback originals and trade paperback reprints. Fox Chapel publishes craft, lifestyle, and woodworking titles for professionals and hobbyists. Publishes **90–150** titles/year.

RECENT TITLE(S) *Creative Coloring Inspirations; Zen Drawing for a Calm and Focused Mind; Zenspirations.*

TIPS "We're looking for knowledgeable artists, craftspeople, and woodworkers, all experts in their fields, to write books of lasting value."

GUILD OF MASTER CRAFTSMAN PUBLICATIONS

166 High St., Lewes East Sussex BN7 1XU, UK. 44 01273 477374. E-mail: helen.chrystie@thegmcgroup.com. Website: www.thegmcgroup.com. Types of books published: photography, woodworking, DIY, gardening, cookery, art, puzzles, all manner of craft subjects, from knitting and sewing to jewelrymaking, dolls' house, upholstery, paper crafts, and more. "Publishes and distributes over 3,000 books and magazines that are both valued by professional craftsmen/women and enjoyed by keen amateurs." Available online.

INTERWEAVE

4868 Innovation Dr., Fort Collins CO 80525. (970)669-7672. Fax: (970)667-8317. E-mail: Kerry.bogert@fwcommunity.com. Website: www.interweave.com. **Contact:** Kerry Bogert, editorial director. Estab. 1975. Publishes hardcover and trade paperback originals. Interweave publishes instructive titles relating to the fiber arts and beadwork topics. Publishes **40–45** titles/year. Book catalog and guidelines online.

HOW TO CONTACT Submit outline, sample chapters. Accepts simultaneous submissions if informed of non-exclusivity.

NEEDS Subjects limited to fiber arts (spinning, knitting, dyeing, weaving, sewing/stiching, art quilting, mixed-media/collage) and jewelry making (beadwork, stringing, wireworking, metalsmithing).

RECENT TITLE(S) *Beastly Crochet*, by Brenda K.B. Anderson; *Jewelry Maker's Field Guide*, by Helen Driggs.

TIPS "We are looking for very clear, informally written, technically correct manuscripts, generally of a how-to nature, in our specific fiber and beadwork fields only. Our audience includes a variety of creative self-starters who appreciate inspiration and clear instruction. They are often well educated and skillful in many areas."

KALMBACH PUBLISHING CO.

21027 Crossroads Circle, P.O. Box 1612, Waukesha WI 53186. (262)796-8776. Fax: (262)798-6468. Website: www.kalmbach.com. Estab. 1934. Publishes paperback originals and reprints. Publishes **40–50** titles/year.

NEEDS 10–20% require freelance illustration; 10-20% require freelance design. Book catalog free upon request. Approached by 25 freelancers/year. Prefers freelancers with experience in the hobby field. Uses freelance artists mainly for book layout/design and line art illustrations. Freelancers should have the most recent versions of Adobe InDesign, Photoshop, and Illustrator. Projects by assignment only.

TERMS Send query letter with résumé, tearsheets, and photocopies. No phone calls, please. Samples are filed and will not be returned. Art director will contact artist for portfolio review. Finds artists through word-of-mouth, submissions. Assigns 10–12 freelance design jobs/year. Pays by the project. Assigns 3–5 freelance illustration jobs/year. Pays by the project.

TIPS "Our how-to books are highly visual in their presentation. Any author who wants to publish with us must be able to furnish good photographs and rough drawings before we'll consider his or her book."

KANSAS CITY STAR QUILTS

The Kansas City Star, 1729 Grand Blvd., Kansas City MO 64108. E-mail: info@kansascitystarquilts.com. Website: www.kansascitystarquilts.com. Types of books published: quilt books.

KNOPF

Imprint of Random House, 1745 Broadway, New York NY 10019. Fax: (212)940-7390. Website: knopfdoubleday.com/imprint/knopf. Estab. 1915. Publishes hardcover and paperback originals. Publishes **200** titles/year.

KRAUSE PUBLICATIONS

A Division of F+W Media, Inc., 700 E. State St., Iola WI 54990. (715)445-2214. Fax: (715)445-4087. E-mail: paul.kennedy@fwcommunity.com. Website: www.krausebooks.com. **Contact:** Paul Kennedy (antiques and collectibles, rocks, gems and minerals, music, sports, militaria, numismatics); Corrina Peterson (firearms); Chris Berens (outdoors); Brian Earnest (automotive). Publishes hardcover and trade paperback originals. "We are the world's largest hobby and collectibles publisher." Publishes **60** titles/year.

HOW TO CONTACT Submit proposal package, including outline, TOC, a sample chapter, and letter explaining your project's unique contributions. Reviews artwork/photos. Accepts only digital photography. Send sample photos.

RECENT TITLE(S) *Antique Trader Antiques and Collectibles 2016*; *The Ultimate Guide to Vintage Star Wars Action Figues*, by Mark Bellomo; *Standard Catalog of Firearms*, by Jerry Lee; *Collecting Rocks, Gems and Minerals*, by Patti Polk.

TIPS Audience consists of serious hobbyists. "Your work should provide a unique contribution to the special interest."

LANDAUER PUBLISHING

3100 101st St., Suite A, Urbandale IA 50322. (800)557-2144 or (515)287-2144. Fax: (515)276-5102. E-mail: info@landauercorp.com. E-mail: jeramy@landauercorp.com; info@landauercorp.com. Website: www.landauerpub.com. **Contact:** Jeramy Landauer. Estab. 1991.

HOW TO CONTACT In preparing a book proposal for review/discussion, please include the following: 1. Author Profile and The Book Concept: a brief paragraph about the author followed by the concept, namely, the vision for the book, the intended audience, and why the book is needed/different from what is currently available. Please include tentative specs for the book: projects (how many/range), special features (e. g., an essay promoting/romancing the history/concept/author, unique teaching section, video, location photography, special needs such as full-size patterns). Also, please include author website. 2. A Table of Contents: the TOC gives the preliminary project list and shows project variety/balance. 3. Sample projects showing the quality of your work (at least 1 or 2 completed projects must accompany the proposal along with photo samples or printouts of your work). 4. A sample of how-to instructions, diagrams, and illustrations (can be rough or finished). 5. Author expectations from the publisher re: guarantees, royalty rates, etc. 6. Timing.

NEEDS "Landauer strives to publish books that are more than project books. We require quality. We look for clear concepts. Books often include a technique section or other features enabling us to enhance the book and expand the audience. Most importantly, we prefer to publish works that will sell for many seasons and lend themselves to add-on product and new editions."

TERMS Authors are expected to take an active role in promoting their books such as attending and introducing their book at Quilt Market, engaging in teaching, maintaining a website/blog, creating a promotional project pattern for social media and/or magazines.

LARK CRAFTS

166 Ave. of the Americas, 17th Floor, New York NY 10036. (212)532-7160. E-mail: info@larkbooks.com. E-mail: jewelryteam@larkcrafts.com; needleartsteam@larkcrafts.com; craftyourlifeteam@larkcrafts.com. Website: www.larkcrafts.com. Estab. 1979.

HOW TO CONTACT Send query letter via e-mail or mail (with information on your skills and qualifications in the subject area of your submission), résumé, and images of your work or a link to your website. Include SASE if you would like materials returned to you. Submissions should be sent to the attention of the category editor, e.g., the material on a ceramics book should be addressed to the Ceramics Editor; a craft book proposal should be addressed to the Craft Acquisitions Editor; and so on.

TERMS "Please note that, due to the volume of mail received, we cannot guarantee the return of unsolicited material. Please do not send original art or irreplaceable work of any kind; while we will make every effort to return your submissions, we are not responsible for any loss or damage."

LAURENCE KING PUBLISHING LTD.

361–373 City Rd., London EC1V 1LR, UK. 44 (0)20 7841 6900. Fax: 44 (0)20 7841 6910. E-mail: commissioning@laurenceking.com. Website: www.laurenceking.com.

HOW TO CONTACT See website for details.

LEISURE ARTS

104 Champs Blvd., Suite 100, Maumelle AR. E-mail: submissions@leisurearts.com. Website: www.leisurearts.com. **Contact:** Tona Jolly, editorial production director. Estab. 1971. Leisure Arts is a leading publisher of lifestyle and instructional craft publications. In addition to printed publications, the Leisure Arts product line also includes e-books, digital downloads, and DVDs.

HOW TO CONTACT Submit an e-mail letter with a PDF file or JPEG attachments to: submissions@leisurearts.com. Please do not send the actual designs or instructions unless asked to do so.

MACMILLAN

175 Fifth Ave., New York NY 10010. (646)307-5151. Website: www.us.macmillan.com. Publishes hardcover, trade paperback, and paperback books.

MARTINGALE PUBLISHING

19021 120th Ave. NE, Suite 102, Bothell WA 98011. (800)426-3126 or (425)483-3313. Fax: (425)486-7596. E-mail: creitan@martingale-pub.com. Website: www.shopmartingale.com. **Contact:** Cathy Reitan, editorial author liaison. Estab. 1976. Types of books published: quilting, sewing, knitting, and crochet. Publishes books and e-books.

HOW TO CONTACT Please e-mail your submission to Cathy Reitan, editorial author liaison, at creitan@martingale-pub.com.

TERMS "Manuscript proposals are reviewed on a monthly basis. Editorial, marketing, and production personnel are involved in the review. The final decision will be based on your proposal, your work sample, your completed Author Questionnaire, and our feasibility analysis. The feasibility analysis investigates such basics as our cost of producing the book and our ability to market your work successfully and competitively. Part of this process may also include a customer survey to test the concept. If your proposal is approved for publication, you will receive a call from one of the editors regarding a publishing contract. We pay quarterly royalty based on net sales of your book, as spelled out in the publishing contract that you will be asked to sign. As a service to you, Martingale applies for the copyright on your book in your name. After you have signed your contract, you will receive detailed guidelines for preparing your manuscript. You are responsible for sending the completed manuscript and projects for photography to us at your own expense by the due date specified in the contract. From then on, Martingale pays all expenses for book production, shipping, and handling. These expenses include editing, design, layout, illustration, and photography."

MEREDITH BOOKS

1716 Locust St., Des Moines IA 50309-3023. (515)284-3000. Website: www.meredith.com. Types of books published: food, home, family. "Meredith Books feature more than 300 titles focusing on food, home, and family."

NEW HOLLAND PUBLISHERS

The Chandlery, Unit 009, 50 Westminster Bridge Rd., London SE1 7QY, UK. 44(0) 207 953 75 65. Fax: 44(0) 207 953 76 05. E-mail: enquiries@nhpub.co.uk. Website: www.newhollandpublishers.com. "New Holland is a publishing house dedicated to the highest editorial and design standards."

NORTH LIGHT BOOKS

F+W, a Content + eCommerce Company, 10151 Carver Rd., Suite 200, Blue Ash OH 45242. Fax: (513)891-7153. E-mail: mona.clough@fwcommunity.com. Website: www.fwcommunity.com; www.artistsnetwork.com; www.createmixedmedia.com. **Contact:** Mona Clough, content director art and mixed-media. Publishes hardcover and trade paperback how-to books. "North Light Books publishes art books, including watercolor, drawing, mixed-media, acrylic that emphasize illustrated how-to art instruction. Currently emphasizing drawing including traditional, zen, doodle, and creativity and inspiration." Publishes **50** titles/year. Visit www.northlightshop.com. Does not return submissions.

HOW TO CONTACT Send query letter with photographs, digital images. Accepts e-mail submissions. Samples are not filed and are returned. Responds only if interested. Company will contact artist for portfolio review if interested.

NEEDS Buys all rights. Finds freelancers through art competitions, art exhibits, submissions, Internet, and word-of-mouth.

PAGE STREET PUBLISHING

27 Congress St., Suite 103, Salem MA 01970. (978)594-8295. E-mail: info@pagestreetpublishing.com. Website: www.pagestreetpublishing.com. Publishes paperback originals. Publishes **20+** titles/year.

PENGUIN/PERIGEE TRADE

Website: www.penguin.com/meet/publishers/perigee.

HOW TO CONTACT "Due to the high volume of manuscripts received, most Penguin Group (USA) imprints do not normally accept unsolicited manuscripts. Neither the corporation nor its imprints assume responsibility for any unsolicited manuscripts that we may receive. As such, it is recommended that sole original copies of any manuscript not be submitted, as the corporation is not responsible for the return of any manuscript (whether sent electronically or by mail), nor do we guarantee a response. Further, in receiving a submission, we do not assume any duty not to publish a book based on a similar idea, concept, or story."

POTTER CRAFT/RANDOM HOUSE

1745 Broadway, New York NY 10019. Website: www.crownpublishing.com/imprint/potter-craft. Estab. 2006. Types of books published: knitting, crochet, sewing, paper crafts, jewelry making.

HOW TO CONTACT Random House LLC does not accept unsolicited submissions, proposals, manuscripts, or submission queries via e-mail at this time.

🌑 PRACTICAL PUBLISHING INTERNATIONAL

0844 561 1202. E-mail: customerservice@ practicalpublishing.co.uk. Website: www. practicalpublishing.co.uk. "Practical holds market-leading positions within several craft sectors internationally. It has comprehensive global distribution of its key brands and distributes over 3 million magazines and books a year. It is also the UK's only specialist publisher to produce and directly distribute titles specifically for the independent craft retail channel."

QUARTO PUBLISHING GROUP USA

400 First Ave. N., Suite 400, Minneapolis MN 55401. E-mail: customerservice@quartous. com. Website: www.quartoknows.com. Types of books published: general craft, art, design, sewing, crochet, knitting, quilting, paper craft, scrapbooking, mixed-media art. Publishes hardcover originals, trade paperback originals, trade paperback reprints. Titles can be found at Amazon, Barnes and Noble, craft chains, independents, and internationally. Publishes **100** titles/year. Available online or free on request

HOW TO CONTACT Accepts unsolicited proposals and manuscripts; guidelines available on website. Does not keep information on file. If not filed, returned by SASE. Responds only if interested. Considers simultaneous submissions and previously published work.

NEEDS Rights purchased vary according to project. Will negotiate with those unwilling to sell rights. Finds authors through agents/reps, submissions, word-of-mouth, magazines, Internet. Works with never-before-published authors frequently. Looks for original concept, popular concept, on-trend concept, large following on social media, existing fan base. Average book has 128–160 pages. Average craft/DIY book contains 20–52 projects/patterns. Author provides print-ready illustrations when possible.

TERMS Some books undergo technical edits. Typical time frame from contract to manuscript due date is 4–6 months. Payment based on project. First-time authors typically paid $5,000–6,000.

RECENT TITLE(S) *One Zentangle a Day,* by Beckah Krahula; *3D Art Lab for Kids,* by Susan Schwake; *20 Ways to Draw a Cat,* by Julia Kuo

TIPS "Do your research. Be familiar with the other competitive books on your topic. Think about how your book is better and different."

QUIRK BOOKS

215 Church St. Philadelphia PA 19106. (215)627-3581. Fax: (215)627-5220. E-mail: tiffany@ quirkbooks.com. Website: www.quirkbooks. com. **Contact:** Tiffany Hill. Estab. 2002. Types of books published: unconventional, cookbooks, craft books, children's books, and nonfiction. Publishes books and e-books. Publishes **25** titles/year. Available online

HOW TO CONTACT "E-mail a query letter to one of our editors. The query letter should be a short description of your project. Try to limit your letter to a single page. If you have sample chapters, go ahead and include them. You can also mail materials directly to our office. If you would like a reply, please include a self-addressed stamped envelope. If you want your materials returned, please include adequate postage."

RODALE BOOKS

400 S. Tenth St., Emmaus PA 18098. (610)967-5171. Fax: (610)967-8961. Website: www.rodaleinc. com. Estab. 1932. "Rodale Books publishes adult trade titles in categories such health and fitness, cooking, spirituality, and pet care."

RUNNING PRESS BOOK PUBLISHERS

2300 Chestnut St., Suite 200, Philadelphia PA 19103. (215)567-5080. Fax: (215)568-2919. E-mail: frances.soopingchow@perseusbooks.com; perseus.promos@perseusbooks.com. Website: www.runningpress.com. **Contact:** Frances Soo Ping Chow, design director. Estab. 1972. Publishes hardcover originals, trade paperback originals. Subjects include adult and children's fiction and nonfiction; cooking; crafts, lifestyle, kits; miniature editions used for text illustrations, promotional materials, book covers, dust jackets.

HOW TO CONTACT Prefers images in digital format. Send via CD/DVD, via FTP/e-mail as TIFF, EPS files at 300 dpi.

NEEDS Buys a few hundred freelance photos/year and lots of stock images. Photos for gift books; photos of wine, food, lifestyle, hobbies, and sports. Model/property release preferred. Photo captions preferred; include exact locations, names of pertinent items or buildings, names and dates for antiques or special items of interest.

TERMS Send URL and provide contact information. Do not send original art or anything that needs to be returned. Responds only if interested. Simultaneous submissions and previously published work OK. Pays $500–1,000 for color cover; $100–250 for inside. Pays 45 days after receipt of invoice. Credits listed on separate copyright or credit pages. Buys one-time rights.

RECENT TITLE(S) Examples of recently published titles: *Skinny Bitch, Eat What You Love, The Ultimate Book of Gangster Movies, Fenway Park, The Speedy Sneaky Chef, Les Petits Macarons, New York Fashion Week, I Love Lucy: A Celebration of All Things Lucy, Upcycling.*

TIPS Submission guidelines available online.

RYLAND PETERS AND SMALL

341 E. 116th St. New York NY 10029. (646)613-8682 or (646)613-8684 or (646)613-8685. Fax: (646)613-8683. E-mail: enquiries@rps.co.uk. Website: www.rylandpeters.com.

HOW TO CONTACT See website for details.

SEARCH PRESS USA

1338 Ross St. Petaluma California 94954-1117. (800)289-9276 or (707)762-3362. Fax: (707)762-0335. E-mail: northamerica@searchpress.com. Website: www.searchpressusa.com. Types of books published: art, craft. "We have 30+ years experience in publishing art and craft instruction books exclusively."

SIMON AND SCHUSTER

1230 Ave. of the Americas, New York NY 10020. (212)698-7000. Website: www.simonandschuster.com. *Accepts agented submissions only.*

HOW TO CONTACT Send query letter with tearsheets. Accepts disk submissions. Samples are filed and are not returned. Responds only if interested. Portfolios may be dropped off every Monday and Wednesday and should include tearsheets.

NEEDS Works with 50 freelance illustrators and 5 designers/year. Prefers freelancers with experience working with models and taking direction well. Uses freelancers for hand lettering, jacket/cover illustration and design and book design. 100% of design and 75% of illustration demand knowledge of Illustrator and Photoshop. Works on assignment only.

TERMS Buys all rights. Originals are returned at job's completion.

SKYHORSE PUBLISHING

307 W. 36th St., 11th Floor, New York NY 10018. (212)643-6816. Fax: (212)643-6819. E-mail: klim@skyhorsepublishing.com. Website: www.skyhorsepublishing.com. **Contact:** Kim Lim, assistant to publisher. Estab. 2006. Types of books published: general craft, sewing, crochet, knitting, paper craft, woodworking, interior decorating, household crafts, holiday crafts. Publishes hardcover originals, trade paperback originals, trade paperback reprints. Specialty: nonfiction. Titles can be found at Barnes and Noble, Amazon, Michaels. Publishes **10+** titles/year. Available online

HOW TO CONTACT Accepts unsolicited proposals and manuscripts; guidelines available on website. Does not keep information on file. If not filed, returned by SASE when specifically requested. Responds only if interested. Considers simultaneous submissions and previously published work.

NEEDS Negotiates rights. Finds authors through submissions, word-of-mouth, Internet. Works with never-before-published authors frequently. Looks for original concept, popluar concept, on-trend concept, large following on social media, existing fan base. Average book has 96–200 pages. Average craft/DIY book contains 45–100 projects/patterns. Author provides print-ready illustrations if book will be illustrated. Author provides photography.

TERMS Typical time frame from contract to manuscript due date is 6 months, but can vary. Payment based on royalty/advance. First-time authors typically paid $1,000–10,000.

RECENT TITLE(S) *Loom Magic*; *To Knit or Not to Knit*; *Rustic Garden Projects*; *Vintage Crafts*; *Warm Mittens and Socks*; *Fun with Yarn and Fabric*; *Swedish Christmas Crafts.*

TIPS "Please be sure to read submission guidelines and be courteous. Should you not receive a response from us, we often appreciate receiving one follow-up e-mail. We wish every craft author will submit full proposal: a summary, author biography, projected TOC, comp titles, sample projects, and sample photography."

STC CRAFT

Imprint of Abrams, 115 W. 18th St., New York NY 10011. E-mail: stccraft@abramsbooks. com; abrams@abramsbooks.com. Website: www.abramsbooks.com. **Contact:** STC craft editorial. Publishes a vibrant collection of exciting and visually stunning craft books specializing in knitting, sewing, quilting, felting, and other popular craft genres.

STC CRAFT/MELANIE FALICK BOOKS

115 W. 18th St., New York NY 10011. (212)206-7715. Fax: (212)519-1210. E-mail: abrams@ abramsbooks.com. Website: www.abramsbooks. com. Estab. 1949. Types of books published: art, photography, cooking, interior design, craft, fashion, sports, pop culture, as well as children's books and general interest. Publishes high-quality art and illustrated books. Titles can be found at Amazon.com, Barnes and Noble, Books-A-Million, IndieBound, !Indigo.

HOW TO CONTACT Accepts unsolicited proposals and manuscripts for STC Craft. No submission will be returned without SASE. Please submit via e-mail to stccraft@abramsbooks.com or mail your submission along with SASE.

RECENT TITLE(S) *Me and My Sewing Adventure*; *All-in-One Quilter's Reference Tool*, 2nd Ed.; *The Modern Applique Workbook*; *Foolproof Crazy Quilting*.

STOREY PUBLISHING

210 MASS MoCA Wy, North Adams MA 01247. (800)793-9396. Fax: (413)346-2196. E-mail: feedback@storey.com. Website: www.storey. com. Estab. 1983. Publishes hardcover and trade paperback originals and reprints. "The mission of Storey Publishing is to serve our customers by publishing practical information that encourages personal independence in harmony with the environment. We seek to do this in a positive atmosphere that promotes editorial quality, team spirit, and profitability. The books we select to carry out this mission include titles on gardening, small-scale farming, building, cooking, home brewing, crafts, part-time business, home improvement, woodworking, animals, nature, natural living, personal care, and country living. We are always pleased to review new proposals, that we try to process expeditiously. We offer both work-for-hire and standard royalty contracts." Publishes **40** titles/year. Book catalog available free.

TATE PUBLISHING

127 E. Trade Center Terrace, Mustang OK 73064. (888)361-9473 or (405)376-4900. Fax: (405)376-4401. Website: www.tatepublishing. com. "Tate Publishing and Enterprises, LLC, is a Christian-based, family-owned, mainline publishing organization with a mission to discover unknown authors. We combine unknown authors' undiscovered potential with Tate Publishing's unique approach to publishing and provide them with the highest-quality books and the most inclusive benefits package available."

HOW TO CONTACT "If you have a manuscript you would like us to consider for publication and marketed on nationwide television, please fill out the form on our website. If you choose to submit by postal mail or electronically, those manuscripts will not be returned and will be deleted or destroyed if not accepted for publication. Please retain at least one copy of your manuscript when submitting a hard copy or electronic version for our consideration and review."

THAMES AND HUDSON

500 Fifth Ave., New York NY 10110. (212)354-3763. Fax: (212)398-1252. E-mail: bookinfo@ thames.wwnorton.com. Website: www. thamesandhudsonusa.com. Estab. 1949.

HOW TO CONTACT "To submit a proposal by e-mail, please paste the text of your query letter and/or proposal into the body of the e-mail message. Please keep your proposal under 6 pages and do not send attachments. Please note that we cannot accept complete manuscripts via e-mail. We cannot open packages that are unsolicited or do not have a return address."

TRAFALGAR SQUARE BOOKS

388 Howe Hill Rd., P.O. Box 257, North Pomfret VT 05053. (802)457-1911. E-mail: submissions@trafalgarbooks.com. Website: www.horseandriderbooks.com. Estab. 1985. Publishes hardcover and trade paperback originals. "We publish high-quality instructional books for horsemen and horsewomen, always with the horse's welfare in mind." Publishes **12** titles/year. Catalog free on request and by e-mail.

RECENT TITLE(S) *The Art of Liberty Training for Horses*, by Jonathan Field; *When 2 Spines Align: Dressage Dynamics*, by Beth Baumert.

TIPS "Our audience is comprised of horse lovers and riders interested in pursuing their passion and/or sport while doing what is best for horses."

TUTTLE PUBLISHING

364 Innovation Dr., North Clarendon VT 05759. (802)773-8930. Fax: (802)773-6993. E-mail: submissions@tuttlepublishing.com. Website: www.tuttlepublishing.com. Estab. 1832. Publishes hardcover and trade paperback originals and reprints. Tuttle is America's leading publisher of books on Japan and Asia. "Familiarize yourself with our catalog and/or similar books we publish. Send complete book proposal with cover letter, table of contents, 1–2 sample chapters, target-audience description, SASE. No e-mail submissions." Publishes **125** titles/year.

HOW TO CONTACT Query with SASE.

NEEDS Terms Pays 5–10% royalty on net or retail price, depending on format and kind of book.

ULYSSES PRESS

Ulysses Press Main Office, P.O. Box 3440, Berkeley California 94703. (510)601-8301. Fax: (510)601-8307. E-mail: ulysses@ulyssespress.com. Website: www.ulyssespress.com. Available online

HOW TO CONTACT "We review unsolicited manuscripts on an ongoing basis." See website for submission guidelines. Please do not send e-mail submissions, attachments, or disks. Do not send original artwork, photographs, or manuscripts of that you do not retain a copy.

NEEDS "When it comes to finding new books, we are especially interested in titles that fill demonstrated niches in the trade book market. We seek books that take a specific and unique focus, a focus that can differentiate a book and make it stand out in a crowd."

USBORNE PUBLISHING

83-85 Saffron Hill, London En EC1N 8RT, UK. (44)207430-2800. Fax: (44)207430-1562. E-mail: mail@usborne.co.uk. Website: www.usborne. com. "Usborne Publishing is a multiple-award-winning, worldwide children's publishing company publishing almost every type of children's book for every age, from baby to young adult."

HOW TO CONTACT Works with 100 illustrators per year. Illustrations only: Query with samples. Samples not returned; samples filed.

TERMS Pays authors royalty.

TIPS "Do not send any original work and, sorry, but we cannot guarantee a reply."

WORKMAN PUBLISHING CO.

225 Varick St., New York NY 10014. E-mail: submissions@workman.com. Website: www.workman.com. Estab. 1967. Publishes hardcover and trade paperback originals, as well as calendars. "We are a trade paperback house specializing in a wide range of popular nonfiction. We publish no adult fiction and very little children's fiction. We also publish a full range of full-color wall and Page-A-Day calendars." Publishes **40** titles/year.

HOW TO CONTACT Query with SASE first for guidelines.

TIPS "We prefer electronic submissions."

[MAGAZINES]

A big part of building your craft business and boosting sales is name recognition. In an ever-growing sea of crafty celebrities, getting your name out there is critical to establishing yourself in the market as a resource, an expert, and a professional. Building name recognition requires constant work, especially in the beginning. Consistent social media, blogging, and representation at popular shows are important to making sure you are recognized in the industry, and magazines are a great way to reach your target demographic all at once. The listings in this section are geared toward craft magazines across the sub-genres.

Do your research. Peruse the listings in this book, visit your local bookstore, and search online to find the magazines that will be the best fit for your work, and that reach your target demographic. For example, not all quilt magazines are geared toward the same audience; some specifically target art quilters, while others cater to traditional or modern quilters. Be sure that you spend your precious time submitting only to those magazines that are a likely fit for your work and that will help grow your audience.

When you're ready to submit content to magazines, be sure to follow the publication's guidelines. Editors are busy people with tight deadlines and failure to follow their instructions might immediately disqualify your awesome project. Also, be patient after submitting. While it may feel like a lifetime to you, there are a million reasons why you may not hear back immediately from the editor. Don't get disheartened and don't give up!

Also, think creatively when it comes to magazine submissions. Is there a certain magazine that serves a demographic you'd like to reach but currently don't? Is there a way to tailor a project for them that still represents you while meeting the needs of their audience? Or maybe you are an expert at crochet joining techniques; instead of submitting a project idea, pitch an idea for an article—or, better yet, a series of articles—on different crochet joining methods.

As with book publishing, make sure that your goals and needs are in line with those of the magazine. If your primary goal is to build your audience, driving more people to your website or blog, or increasing your social media following, make sure that the magazine is willing to include your name, website, and social media informationrmation before signing an agreement.

Remember that magazines need a lot of quality content to fill the pages. If you have great ideas to share with the craft world, persistence pays off. Stick with it, keep generating quality content, and you're certain to find success in magazine publishing.

KEY TO SYMBOLS AND ABBREVIATIONS

☮	Canadian market
⬤	market located outside of the U.S. and Canada
⌂	market prefers to work with local artists/ designers
bandw	black and white (photo or illustration)
SASE	self-addressed, stamped envelope
SAE	self-addressed envelope
IRC	International Reply Coupon, for use when mailing to countries other than your own

- A great source for new magazine leads is in the business section of your local library. Ask the librarian to point out the business and consumer editions of the *Standard Rate and Data Service* (*SRDS*) and *Bacon's Media Directory*. These huge directories list thousands of magazines and will give you an idea of the magnitude of magazines published today. Another good source is a yearly directory called *Samir Husni's Guide to New Magazines*, also available in the business section of the public library and online at www.mrmagazine.com. *Folio* magazine provides informationrmation about new magazine launches and redesigns.

- Each year the Society of Publication Designers sponsors a juried competition, the winners of which are featured in a prestigious exhibition. For informationrmation about the annual competition, contact the Society of Publication Designers at (212)223-3332 or visit their website at www.spd.org.

- Networking with fellow artists and art directors will help you find additional success strategies. The Graphic Artists Guild (www.gag.org), The American Institute of Graphic Artists (www.aiga.org), your city's Art Directors Club (www.adcglobal.org) or branch of the Society of Illustrators (www.societyillustrators.org) hold lectures and networking functions. Attend 1 event sponsored by each organization in your city to find a group you are comfortable with, then join and become an active member.

ALTERED COUTURE

22992 Mill Creek Dr., Laguna Hills California 92653. E-mail: alteredcouture@stampington. com. Website: www.stampington.com/altered-couture. *Altered Couture* is a 160-page publication dedicated to altered and embellished clothing and accessories. It is filled with gorgeous photographs of altered jackets, T-shirts, sweaters, jeans, skirts, and more, accompanied by easy-to-understand techniques and endless inspiration. **HOW TO CONTACT** "We prefer submissions of original art. If original art is not available, our next preference is high-resolution digital images (300 dpi at 8¹/₂ x 10"). If hi-res digital images are not available, we will very rarely consider professional-quality transparencies or color slides. Color-copy submissions are not accepted. All artwork must be identified with the artist's name, address, e-mail, and phone number clearly printed on a label attached to each sample. Inscribe your name and address somewhere on each piece of art. If you desire acknowledgment of artwork receipt, please include a self-addressed stamped postcard. If the artwork is three-dimensional, please attach your identification with a removable string or pack the sample in a plastic bag with your identification. If you have a unique artistic technique you'd like to share with others, please send samples of your artwork accompanied by a query letter outlining your article idea to the respective managing editor at: Altered Couture, 22992 Mill Creek Dr., Laguna Hills CA 92653. Managing editors also welcome brief e-mail inquiries." **NEEDS** "Managing editors seek first-rate projects and encourage artists who have not published articles before to submit ideas, as editorial assistance will be provided." **TERMS** Competitive editorial compensation is provided for all published articles. "We may hold your sample for an extended period of time—9–12 months is common. Due to the large volume of artwork we receive, altered couture will return only those submissions accompanied by sufficient postage in the form of cash, check, or money order made out to Stampington and Company. We cannot offer delivery confirmation; however, we are happy to put insurance on the submission. If you wish to have your artwork insured for the return journey, please include sufficient funds and indicate your preference in a postcard or letter enclosed with your submission. Please do not attach postage to packaging and do not send loose postage stamps. Contributors from outside the US, please send cash, check, or money order in US funds to Stampington and Company. For questions regarding your artwork, please send inquiries to artmanagement@stampington.com."

AMERICAN CRAFT

American Craft Council, 1224 Marshall St. NE, Suite 200, Minneapolis MN 55413. (612)206-3115. E-mail: mmoses@craftcouncil.org; query@craftcouncil.org. Website: www.americancraftmag.org. **Contact:** Monica Moses, editor in chief. Estab. 1941. "American Craft Council is a national nonprofit aimed at supporting artists and craft enthusiasts. We want to inspire people to live a creative life. *American Craft* magazine celebrates the age-old human impulse to make things by hand." Circulation, 40,000. **HOW TO CONTACT** See writer's guidelines online. **TIPS** "Keep pitches short and sweet, a paragraph or two at most. Please include visuals with any pitches."

AMERICAN PATCHWORK AND QUILTING

E-mail: apq@meredith.com. Website: www.allpeoplequilt.com/magazines-more/american-patchwork-and-quilting. *American Patchwork and Quilting* magazine, part of the Better Homes and Gardens family, is the leading quilting magazine in the country.

AMERICAN QUILTER MAGAZINE

American Quilter's Society, PO Box 3290, Paducah KY 42001-3290. (270)898-7903. Fax: (270)898-1173. E-mail: angela.henry@americanquilter.com; ginny.borgia@americanquilter.com. E-mail: ginny.borgia@americanquilter.com. Website: www.americanquilter.com. **Contact:** Angela Henry, managing editor; Ginny Harris, editorial assistant. *American Quilter* Magazine is published 6 times per year and is the official publication of the American Quilter's Society. **HOW TO CONTACT** Quilting-related article ideas or queries may be submitted via e-mail to editor-in-chief Michele Duffy at micheleduffy@aqsquilt.com. Manuscripts may be submitted on a CD in .doc or .docx format with a hard copy printout accompanying the disk or via e-mail with "submission" in the subject field to Editorial Assistant Ginny Harris at ginnyharris@aqsquilt.com. Articles may range from 500 to 1,000 words and have accompanying images. "Furthermore, the inclusion of high-quality photos increases the chance of article acceptance; several images of each quilt or project allow the committee to see your submission at its best."

APRONOLOGY

22992 Mill Creek Dr., Laguna Hills California 92653. E-mail: customerservice@stampington.com. Website: www.stampington.com/apronology. This new publication flirts with the many uses and looks of the apron.

HOW TO CONTACT "We prefer submissions of original art. If original art is not available, our next preference is high-resolution digital images (300 dpi at $8^1/_2$ x 10"). If hi-res digital images are not available, we will very rarely consider professional-quality transparencies or color slides. Color-copy submissions are not accepted. All artwork must be identified with the artist's name, address, e-mail, and phone number clearly printed on a label attached to each sample. Inscribe your name and address somewhere on each piece of art. If you desire acknowledgment of artwork receipt, please include a self-addressed stamped postcard. If the artwork is three-dimensional, please attach your identification with a removable string or pack the sample in a plastic bag with your identification. If you have a unique artistic technique you'd like to share with others, please send samples of your artwork accompanied by a query letter outlining your article idea to the respective managing editor at: Apronology, 22992 Mill Creek Dr., Laguna Hills California 92653. Managing editors also welcome brief e-mail inquiries."

NEEDS "Managing editors seek first-rate projects and encourage artists who have not published articles before to submit ideas, as editorial assistance will be provided."

TERMS Competitive editorial compensation is provided for all published articles. "We may hold your sample for an extended period of time — 9–12 months is common. Due to the large volume of artwork we receive, *Apronology* will return only those submissions accompanied by sufficient postage in the form of cash, check, or money order made out to Stampington and Company. We cannot offer delivery confirmation; however, we are happy to put insurance on the submission. If you wish to have your artwork insured for the return journey, please include sufficient funds and indicate your preference in a postcard or letter enclosed with your submission. Please do not attach postage to packaging and do not send loose postage stamps. Contributors from outside the US, please send cash, check, or money order in US funds to Stampington and Company. For questions regarding your artwork, please send inquiries to artmanagement@stampington.com."

ART DOLL QUARTERLY

22992 Mill Creek Dr., Laguna Hills California 92653. E-mail: artdollquarterly@stampington.com. Website: www.stampington.com/art-doll-quarterly. "This full-color, 128-page publication is dedicated to art dolls and sculptural figures made from cloth, polymer clay, Creative Paperclay®, wire armatures, mixed media, and much more. In each issue, you will find original doll patterns, creative challenges, doll-artist profiles, convention listings and reviews, book and video reviews, and a 35-page gallery of art dolls made by our readers."

HOW TO CONTACT "We prefer submissions of original art. If original art is not available, our next preference is high-resolution digital images (300 dpi at 8½x10"). If hi-res digital images are not available, we will very rarely consider professional-quality transparencies or color slides. Color-copy submissions are not accepted. All artwork must be identified with the artist's name, address, e-mail, and phone number clearly printed on a label attached to each sample. Inscribe your name and address somewhere on each piece of art. If you desire acknowledgment of artwork receipt, please include a self-addressed stamped postcard. If the artwork is three-dimensional, please attach your identification with a removable string or pack the sample in a plastic bag with your identification. If you have a unique artistic technique you'd like to share with others, please send samples of your artwork accompanied by a query letter outlining your article idea to the respective managing editor at: Art Doll Quarterly, 22992 Mill Creek Dr., Laguna Hills California 92653. Managing editors also welcome brief e-mail inquiries."

NEEDS "Managing editors seek first-rate projects and encourage artists who have not published articles before to submit ideas, as editorial assistance will be provided."

TERMS Competitive editorial compensation is provided for all published articles. "We may hold your sample for an extended period of time—9–12 months is common. Due to the large volume of artwork we receive, *Art Doll Quarterly* will return only those submissions accompanied by sufficient postage in the form of cash, check, or money order made out to Stampington and Company. We cannot offer delivery confirmation; however, we are happy to put insurance on the submission. If you wish to have your artwork insured for the return journey, please include sufficient funds and indicate your preference in a postcard or letter enclosed with your submission. Please do not attach postage to packaging and do not send loose postage stamps. Contributors from outside the US, please send cash, check, or money order in US funds to Stampington and Company. For questions regarding your artwork, please send inquiries to artmanagement@stampington.com."

ARTFUL BLOGGING

Artful Blogging, 22992 Mill Creek Dr., Laguna Hills California 92653. E-mail: artfulblogging@stampington.com. Website: www.stampington.com/artful-blogging. "Allow yourself to be inspired as you flip through the pages of *Artful Blogging*. Join along with the growing community of artful bloggers as they continue to share their mesmerizing stories and captivating photographs."

HOW TO CONTACT "We prefer submissions of original art. If original art is not available, our next preference is high-resolution digital images (300 dpi at 8$1/2$ x 10"). If hi-res digital images are not available, we will very rarely consider professional-quality transparencies or color slides. Color-copy submissions are not accepted. All artwork must be identified with the artist's name, address, e-mail, and phone number clearly printed on a label attached to each sample. Inscribe your name and address somewhere on each piece of art. If you desire acknowledgment of artwork receipt, please include a self-addressed stamped postcard. If the artwork is three-dimensional, please attach your identification with a removable string or pack the sample in a plastic bag with your identification. If you have a unique artistic technique you'd like to share with others, please send samples of your artwork accompanied by a query letter outlining your article idea to the respective managing editor at: Artful Blogging, 22992 Mill Creek Dr., Laguna Hills California 92653. Managing editors also welcome brief e-mail inquiries."

NEEDS "Managing editors seek first-rate projects and encourage artists who have not published articles before to submit ideas, as editorial assistance will be provided."

TERMS Competitive editorial compensation is provided for all published articles. "We may hold your sample for an extended period of time—9–12 months is common. Due to the large volume of artwork we receive, *Artful Blogging* will return only those submissions accompanied by sufficient postage in the form of cash, check, or money order made out to Stampington and Company. We cannot offer delivery confirmation; however, we are happy to put insurance on the submission. If you wish to have your artwork insured for the return journey, please include sufficient funds and indicate your preference in a postcard or letter enclosed with your submission. Please do not attach postage to packaging and do not send loose postage stamps. Contributors from outside the US, please send cash, check, or money order in US funds to Stampington and Company. For questions regarding your artwork, please send inquiries to artmanagement@stampington.com."

ARTISTS' CAFÉ MAGAZINE

(949)380-9355. E-mail: submissions@stampington.com. Website: www.stampington.com/artists-cafe. The publishers of *Somerset Studio* invite you to explore the finest moments from over a decade in print with *Artists' Café*. This decadent, 144-page magazine is jam-packed with the best paper-crafting and mixed-media projects, as collected from past issues of *Somerset Studio, Somerset Apprentice, Sew Somerset, Art Journaling,* and *Somerset Workshop*. Relive favorite articles, discover techniques you may have missed, or get reacquainted with an admired artist.

ART JOURNALING

22992 Mill Creek Dr., Laguna Hills California 92653. E-mail: artjournaling@stampington.com. Website: www.stampington.com/art-journaling. "In every quarterly issue of *Art Journaling*, artists open their journals and share creative techniques for capturing their emotions. From stamping and collage art to painting and sketching, each journal is filled with innovative techniques that you'll want to try in your own art journal. Detailed photos and commentary will help you discover your journaling style, with hints and tricks for creating a stand-out page."

HOW TO CONTACT "We prefer submissions of original art. If original art is not available, our next preference is high-resolution digital images (300 dpi at $8^1/_2$ x 10"). If hi-res digital images are not available, we will very rarely consider professional-quality transparencies or color slides. Color-copy submissions are not accepted. All artwork must be identified with the artist's name, address, e-mail, and phone number clearly printed on a label attached to each sample. Inscribe your name and address somewhere on each piece of art. If you desire acknowledgment of artwork receipt, please include a self-addressed stamped postcard. If the artwork is three-dimensional, please attach your identification with a removable string or pack the sample in a plastic bag with your identification. If you have a unique artistic technique you'd like to share with others, please send samples of your artwork accompanied by a query letter outlining your article idea to the respective managing editor at: Art Journaling, 22992 Mill Creek Dr., Laguna Hills California 92653. Managing editors also welcome brief e-mail inquiries."

NEEDS "Managing editors seek first-rate projects and encourage artists who have not published articles before to submit ideas, as editorial assistance will be provided."

TERMS Competitive editorial compensation is provided for all published articles. "We may hold your sample for an extended period of time—9–12 months is common. Due to the large volume of artwork we receive, *Art Journaling* will return only those submissions accompanied by sufficient postage in the form of cash, check, or money order made out to Stampington and Company. We cannot offer delivery confirmation; however, we are happy to put insurance on the submission. If you wish to have your artwork insured for the return journey, please include sufficient funds and indicate your preference in a postcard or letter enclosed with your submission. Please do not attach postage to packaging and do not send loose postage stamps. Contributors from outside the US, please send cash, check, or money order in US funds to Stampington and Company. For questions regarding your artwork, please send inquiries to artmanagement@ stampington.com."

ART QUILTING STUDIO

22992 Mill Creek Dr., Laguna Hills California 92653. E-mail: artquiltingstudio@stampington. com. Website: www.stampington.com/art-quilting-studio. "*Art Quilting Studio* magazine provides a playful and informationrmative forum where quilt enthusiasts from all walks of life can cross-pollinate to share techniques, ideas, and inspiration."

HOW TO CONTACT "We prefer submissions of original art. If original art is not available, our next preference is high-resolution digital images (300 dpi at $8^1/_2$ x 10"). If hi-res digital images are not available, we will very rarely consider professional-quality transparencies or color slides. Color-copy submissions are not accepted. All artwork must be identified with the artist's name, address, e-mail, and phone number clearly printed on a label attached to each sample. Inscribe your name and address somewhere on each piece of art. If you desire acknowledgment of artwork receipt, please include a self-addressed stamped postcard. If the artwork is three-dimensional, please attach your identification with a removable string or pack the sample in a plastic bag with your identification. If you have a unique artistic technique you'd like to share with others, please send samples of your artwork accompanied by a query letter outlining your article idea to the respective managing editor at: Art Quilting Studio, 22992 Mill Creek Dr., Laguna Hills CA 92653. Managing editors also welcome brief e-mail inquiries."

NEEDS "Managing editors seek first-rate projects and encourage artists who have not published articles before to submit ideas, as editorial assistance will be provided."

TERMS Competitive editorial compensation is provided for all published articles. "We may hold your sample for an extended period of time —9–12 months is common. Due to the large volume of artwork we receive, *Art Quilting Studio* will return only those submissions accompanied by sufficient postage in the form of cash, check, or money order made out to Stampington and Company. We cannot offer delivery confirmation; however, we are happy to put insurance on the submission. If you wish to have your artwork insured for the return journey, please include sufficient funds and indicate your preference in a postcard or letter enclosed with your submission. Please do not attach postage to packaging and do not send loose postage stamps. Contributors from outside the US, please send cash, check, or money order in US funds to Stampington and Company. For questions regarding your artwork, please send inquiries to artmanagement@ stampington.com."

BEAD

E-mail: usoffice@ashdown.co.uk. Website: www. beadmagazine.co.uk. " Created by bead lovers, for bead lovers, each issue of *Bead* is packed full of beautiful beadwork, wirework, and stringing projects. Plus stylish and quality lampwork, metal clay, and polymer clay designs, and much more!"

BEAD & BUTTON

E-mail: editor@beadandbutton.com. Website: www.bnb.jewelrymakingmagazines.com. *Bead & Button* is a bimonthly magazine devoted to techniques, projects, and designs of beaded jewelry and accessories.

BEADS AND BEYOND

Traplet Publications Ltd., Traplet House, Pendragon Close Malvern WR14 1GA, UK. Website: www.beadsandbeyondmagazine.com. A monthly design-led craft magazine featuring jewelery-making projects, new techniques, stunning photography and inspiration, interviews, reviews, best buys, competitions, and prizes.

BEAD STYLE

21027 CrossRd.s Circle, P.O. Box 1612, Waukesha WI 53187-1612. E-mail: photostudio@ kalmbach.com. Website: http://bds. jewelrymakingmagazines.com/about-us/contact. *Bead Style*, the world's leading magazine for beaders. In every issue, *Bead Style* will deliver dozens of projects that show you how to make fast, fashionable, and fun jewelry that is uniquely you."

BEADWORK

Interweave, 201 E. Fourth St., Loveland CO 80537. E-mail: beadworksubmissions@ interweave.com. Website: www.beadingdaily. com. "*Beadwork* is a bimonthly magazine devoted to everything about beads and beadwork. Our pages are filled with projects for all levels of beaders, with a focus on the learning needs of those who seek to master beadweaving stitches. We pride ourselves on our easy-to-follow instructions and technical illustrations as well as our informationrmative and entertaining features."

HOW TO CONTACT Guidelines available on website. Query by e-mail or mail. If submitting a project idea, include high-resolution photo of project and contact information. If querying for a feature, submit proposal and contact information.

TERMS Acquires first rights and subsequent nonexclusive rights for use in print, electronic, or other Interweave publications and promotions.

BELLE ARMOIRE

22992 Mill Creek Dr., Laguna Hills California 92653. E-mail: bellearmoire@stampington.com. Website: www.stampington.com/belle-armoire. "*Belle Armoire* marries fabric arts with rubber stamping and embellishments—showcasing one-of-a-kind, handmade fashions and wearable-art projects. Whether you're an art stamper, embroidery artist, custom jewelry designer, fabric painter, or knitting and crocheting enthusiast, *Belle Armoire* provides the opportunity and inspiration to create fashions that are uniquely you."

HOW TO CONTACT "We prefer submissions of original art. If original art is not available, our next preference is high-resolution digital images (300 dpi at 8½ x 10"). If hi-res digital images are not available, we will very rarely consider professional-quality transparencies or color slides. Color-copy submissions are not accepted. All artwork must be identified with the artist's name, address, e-mail, and phone number clearly printed on a label attached to each sample. Inscribe your name and address somewhere on each piece of art. If you desire acknowledgment of artwork receipt, please include a self-addressed stamped postcard. If the artwork is three-dimensional, please attach your identification with a removable string or pack the sample in a plastic bag with your identification. If you have a unique artistic technique you'd like to share with others, please send samples of your artwork accompanied by a query letter outlining your article idea to the respective managing editor at: Belle Armoire, 22992 Mill Creek Dr., Laguna Hills California 92653. Managing editors also welcome brief e-mail inquiries."

NEEDS "Managing editors seek first-rate projects and encourage artists who have not published articles before to submit ideas, as editorial assistance will be provided."

TERMS Competitive editorial compensation is provided for all published articles. "We may hold your sample for an extended period of time—9–12 months is common. Due to the large volume of artwork we receive, *Belle Armoire* will return only those submissions accompanied by sufficient postage in the form of cash, check, or money order made out to Stampington and Company. We cannot offer delivery confirmation; however, we are happy to put insurance on the submission. If you wish to have your artwork insured for the return journey, please include sufficient funds and indicate your preference in a postcard or letter enclosed with your submission. Please do not attach postage to packaging and do not send loose postage stamps. Contributors from outside the US, please send cash, check, or money order in US funds to Stampington and Company. For questions regarding your artwork, please send inquiries to artmanagement@stampington.com."

BELLE ARMOIRE JEWELRY

22992 Mill Creek Dr., Laguna Hills California 92653. E-mail: bellearmoirejewelry@stampington.com. Website: www.stampington.com/belle-armoire-jewelry. "*Belle Armoire Jewelry* magazine is overflowing with exciting projects, such as necklaces, bracelets, earrings, and brooches. You'll be inspired by all of the projects, tips, and techniques you will find. Whether your passion is stringing, making polymer clay beads, or incorporating found or natural objects, you'll enjoy the artisan-made creations inside *Belle Armoire Jewelry*."

HOW TO CONTACT "We prefer submissions of original art. If original art is not available, our next preference is high-resolution digital images (300 dpi at 8¹/₂ x 10"). If hi-res digital images are not available, we will very rarely consider professional-quality transparencies or color slides. Color-copy submissions are not accepted. All artwork must be identified with the artist's name, address, e-mail, and phone number clearly printed on a label attached to each sample. Inscribe your name and address somewhere on each piece of art. If you desire acknowledgment of artwork receipt, please include a self-addressed stamped postcard. If the artwork is three-dimensional, please attach your identification with a removable string or pack the sample in a plastic bag with your identification. If you have a unique artistic technique you'd like to share with others, please send samples of your artwork accompanied by a query letter outlining your article idea to the respective managing editor. Managing editors also welcome brief e-mail inquiries."

NEEDS "Managing editors seek first-rate projects and encourage artists who have not published articles before to submit ideas, as editorial assistance will be provided."

TERMS Competitive editorial compensation is provided for all published articles. "We may hold your sample for an extended period of time—9–12 months is common. Due to the large volume of artwork we receive, *Belle Armoire Jewelry* will return only those submissions accompanied by sufficient postage in the form of cash, check, or money order made out to Stampington and Company. We cannot offer delivery confirmation; however, we are happy to put insurance on the submission. If you wish to have your artwork insured for the return journey, please include sufficient funds and indicate your preference in a postcard or letter enclosed with your submission. Please do not attach postage to packaging and do not send loose postage stamps. Contributors from outside the US, please send cash, check, or money order in US funds to Stampington and Company. For questions regarding your artwork, please send inquiries to artmanagement@ stampington.com."

BETTER HOMES AND GARDENS

Website: www.bhg.com. *Better Homes and Gardens* is the vibrant, down-to-earth guide for the woman who is passionate about her home and garden and the life she creates there.

BRITISH PATCHWORK AND QUILTING

Traplet Publications Ltd., Traplet House, Willow End Park, Blackmore Park Rd. Malvern WR13 6NN, UK. E-mail: joanna.kent@traplet.com. Website: www.pandqmagazine.com. **Contact:** Joanna Kent, editor. *British Patchwork and Quilting Magazine* is a monthly publication written by quilters, for quilters, with projects and features specifically to do with patchwork, quilting, appliqué, and textiles.

CARDMAKER

E-mail: submissions@cardmakermagazine. com. Website: www.cardmakermagazine. com. *CardMaker* is the leading print and digital publication for card-making enthusiasts on the market. Published quarterly.

HOW TO CONTACT "We prefer to receive submissions via e-mail. Please send a completed submittal form, including an image of your project, along with your complete contact informationrmation, to Submissions@ CardMakerMagazine.com. Your e-mail subject line should include the publication title and issue and project name—for example: CardMaker

Winter 2014, Warm Holiday Wishes. Please keep the attached file size under 2MG. Please send 1 project submission per e-mail."

NEEDS Original, attractive designs and patterns for card projects that will appeal to readers of all skill levels. Technique-based projects and articles that include, but are not limited to: rubber stamping, paper folding, interactive card construction, quilling, die cutting, paper piecing, dry and heat embossing, paper cutting, handmade paper, etc. Your ideas for issue themes, new techniques, and project types to feature.

TERMS "When your project and instructions are approved, we will send an agreement with our payment offer and a business reply envelope. You should complete it with your signature and date and return the original to us in the postage-paid envelope—the photocopy we send is for your records. If this is the first time we've worked with you or if it has been a while since we've accepted a project, you will also receive a W-9 (or a W-8 if you live outside the US) which must be completed and returned before payments can be issued. You will be issued a check for payment within 45 days of the date we received your signed contract. We will keep your project until the magazine issue is published. Your project will be returned to you after publication. All manuscripts, diagrams, etc., remain our property. Since we purchase all rights to designs, you should not sell that design—or 1 very similar to it—to another publication. If you have questions as to what constitutes an original design, please contact us."

CARD MAKING AND PAPER CRAFT

Website: www.cardmakingandpaper craft.com. *Cardmaking and Paper craft* is published 13 times a year by Immediate Media.

CLOTH PAPER SCISSORS

E-mail: submissions@clothpaperscissors. com. Website: www.clothpaperscissors.com. Published 6 times a year, *Cloth Paper Scissors* covers all types of fiber arts and collage work, including mixed media, assemblage, art dolls, visual art journals, rubber stamping, stamp carving, printmaking, creative embroidery, and book arts. Geared for the beginning artist/crafter as well as the advanced, *Cloth Paper Scissors* has a playful, positive tone, encouraging both the beginning and seasoned artist to try new techniques and share their work and expertise with a greater audience.

HOW TO CONTACT Please send the following to submissions@clothpaperscissors.com: 2–3 photos and/or sketches of the project(s) you'd like to write about; a short outline of the project, including a materials list; a 100-word biography; and your full address and contact informationrmation, including blog, website, and social media informationrmation. Please put I HEART PAPER in the subject line.

NEEDS Beautiful, decorative, and/or practical projects that showcase paper.

COMPLETE CARDMAKING

Website: www.paper craftmagazines.com/the-magazines/complete-cardmaking. *Complete Cardmaking* is the UK's first and only magazine dedicated to digital crafts, helping you make beautiful cards with your PC. This bimonthly magazine is the ideal accompaniment for the avid digital crafter, providing a free CD-ROM with every issue.

COUNTRY SAMPLER

707 Kautz Rd., St. Charles IL 60174. (630)377-8000. Fax: (630)377-8194. E-mail: editors@countrysampler.com. Website: www.countrysampler.com. "*Country Sampler* is a must-have, all-in-one resource for any country decorator. Our unbeatable combination of country-lifestyle articles and a complete catalog of decorating products provides all the tips and tools you need to make your house a country home."

CRAFTS

E-mail: crafts@craftscouncil.org.uk. Website: www.craftsmagazine.org.uk. Published 6 times a year and covering all disciplines, this is the perfect magazine for makers, collectors, and lovers of craft.

CRAFTS BEAUTIFUL

Aceville Publications, 1 Phoenix Court , Hawkins Rd. Colchester Essex CO8 8JY. 01206 505974. E-mail: sarah.crosland@aceville.co.uk. Website: www. crafts-beautiful.com. **Contact:** Sarah Crosland, editor. "Britain's best-selling craft magazine. Card making, paper craft, stitching, baking, and knits—we love it all!" Circulation 65,000.

CRAFTSELLER

E-mail: yourletters@craft-seller.com. Website: www.craft-seller.com. "An exciting magazine packed with projects, inspiration, and advice for anyone who loves crafting and wants to make and sell their handmade crafts."

CRAFT STAMPER

Traplet Publications Ltd., Traplet House, Pendragon Close Malvern WR14 1GA UK. E-mail: alix.merriman@traplet.com. Website: www.craftstamper.com. **Contact:** Alix Merriman, editor. The UK's best magazine for rubber-stamping enthusiasts.

CREATE WITH ME

22992 Mill Creek Dr., Laguna Hills California 92653. E-mail: createwithme@stampington.com. Website: www.stampington.com/create-with-me. "The articles cover a complete spectrum from fabric and wearable art to paint, papiér-mâche, card making, and bedroom dècor—and there is something for every age group."

HOW TO CONTACT "We prefer submissions of original art. If original art is not available, our next preference is high-resolution digital images (300 dpi at $8^{1}/_{2}$ x 10"). If hi-res digital images are not available, we will very rarely consider professional-quality transparencies or color slides. Color-copy submissions are not accepted. All artwork must be identified with the artist's name, address, e-mail, and phone number clearly printed on a label attached to each sample. Inscribe your name and address somewhere on each piece of art. If you desire acknowledgment of artwork receipt, please include a self-addressed stamped postcard. If the artwork is three-dimensional, please attach your identification with a removable string or pack the sample in a plastic bag with your identification. If you have a unique artistic technique you'd like to share with others, please send samples of your artwork accompanied by a query letter outlining your article idea to the respective managing editor at: Create With Me, 22992 Mill Creek Dr., Laguna Hills California 92653. Managing editors also welcome brief e-mail inquiries."

NEEDS "Managing editors seek first-rate projects and encourage artists who have not published articles before to submit ideas, as editorial assistance will be provided."

TERMS Competitive editorial compensation is provided for all published articles. "We may hold your sample for an extended period of time—9–12 months is common. Due to the large volume of artwork we receive, *Create With Me* will return only those submissions accompanied by sufficient postage in the form of cash, check, or money order made out to Stampington and Company. We can not offer delivery confirmation; however, we are happy to put insurance on the submission. If you wish to have your artwork insured for the return journey, please include sufficient funds and indicate your preference in a postcard or letter enclosed with your submission. Please do not attach postage to packaging and do not send loose postage stamps. Contributors from outside the US, please send cash, check, or money order in US funds to Stampington and Company. For questions regarding your artwork, please send inquiries to artmanagement@stampington.com."

CREATING KEEPSAKES

E-mail: editorial@creatingkeepsakes.com. Website: www.creatingkeepsakes.com. Estab. 1996. " *Creating Keepsakes* magazine is the leading magazine for inspiration and techniques for scrapbookers."

CREATIVE CARDMAKING

Website: www.creativemagazines.com. Each issue of *Creative Cardmaking* includes a FREE card-making kit and is packed full of fantastic ideas for using your craft stash as well as all of the latest products from your favorite craft companies.

CREATIVE KNITTING

E-mail: editor@creativeknittingmagazine.com. Website: www.creativeknittingmagazine.com. " *Creative Knitting* features clear instructions for classic and current trends in knitting design."

CREATIVE MACHINE EMBROIDERY

E-mail: information@cmemag.com. Website: www.cmemag.com. *Creative Machine Embroidery* is a bimonthly magazine devoted to all things embroidery.

CREATIVE STAMPING

Website: www.creativemagazines.com. " *Creative Stamping* is an amazing magazine devoted to the wonderful world of stamping."

CROCHET!

E-mail: editor@crochetmagazine.com. Website: www.crochetmagazine.com. **Contact:** Ellen Gormley, editor. *Crochet!* is a full-color 100-page full-size magazine published quarterly.

CROCHET WORLD

E-mail: editor@crochet-world.com. Website: www.crochet-world.com. **Contact:** Carol Alexander, editor. *Crochet World* magazine is published bimonthly. This 68-page magazine offers techniques and patterns with complete directions for all types of crochet.

HOW TO CONTACT Begin each submission with a sentence or 2 about why you designed it. Include all contact informationrmation with your query, including name, address, phone number, and e-mail address. If you want your projects returned, they must be accompanied by correct return postage, either check or money order ONLY. Project review: Reviews are held about every 8 weeks. Check the Editorial Calendar for dates. Many of these projects are seasonal.

TERMS "If we accept your design(s), we will contact you within 2 weeks after the review date. We may choose to hold on to a project that might fit in another issue. All others will be returned as soon as possible."

CROSS-STITCH&NEEDLEWORK

E-mail: jfranchuk@c-sn.com. Website: www.c-sn.com. "From beginner to advanced, there's something for every stitcher in *Cross-Stitch & Needlework* magazine. Each issue is packed with captivating designs, engaging feature articles and designer profiles, large full-color charts, fantastic finishing ideas, and easy-to-follow instructions for cross-stitch, needlepoint, embroidery, Hardanger, and more." Published bimonthly.

HOW TO CONTACT "We are always open to design submissions. Please send photos of stitched models or copies of the charted designs via e-mail or mail to Design Submissions, Bayview Publishing, P.O. Box 157, Plover WI 54467."

TERMS "All designs must be your original creations and may not have been previously published or sold. Please, do not send actual stitched models before contacting us first."

CROSS STITCH CARD SHOP

Website: www.cross-stitching.com/magazines/cross-stitch-card-shop.

CROSS STITCH COLLECTION

E-mail: csc@dennis.co.uk. Website: www.crossstitchcollection.com. " *Cross Stitch Collection* offers the most beautiful cross-stitch projects from the best designers, with high-value, top-quality charts."

CROSS STITCH CRAZY

Website: www.cross-stitching.com/magazines/cross-stitch-crazy.

CROSS STITCH FAVOURITES

Website: www.cross-stitching.com/magazines/cross-stitch-favourites.

CROSS STITCH GOLD

Website: www.cross-stitching.com/magazines/cross-stitch-gold.

DESIGNER KNITTING

E-mail: helen.chrystie@thegmcgroup.com. Website: www.thegmcgroup.com. "*Designer Knitting* (previously *Vogue Knitting*) offers undeniable style. For fascinating features, seasonable fashion, yarn news, and book reviews, this magazine is all you need and more."

EMBELLISH MAGAZINE

Website: www.artwearpublications.com.au/subscriptions/embellish-magazine.html. "*Embellish* magazine aims to fuse fashion, fantasy, and art into everyday items, gifts, and homewares. You will find in each issue a mix of techniques and articles as well as ideas and inspirational stories. Expect to see a range of projects including dye processes; fabric manipulation; knit and/or crochet embellished finishes; couture techniques; hand embellishing; machine embellishing; prints; custom designs; repurposed textiles and projects related to textile applications that incorporate fabric, yarn, felt, and/or fiber."

ENJOY CROSS STITCH

Website: www.cross-stitching.com/magazines/enjoy-cross-stitch.

FELT MAGAZINE

Website: www.artwearpublications.com.au/subscriptions/felt-magazine.html. *Felt Magazine* aims to inspire a new generation of fiber enthusiasts with comprehensive projects, articles, and an inspirational gallery. It includes a mix of easy, intermediate, and technical projects to suit a wide range of skill levels.

GENERATION Q MAGAZINE

6102 Ash St., Simi Valley California 93063. E-mail: melissa@generationqmagazine.com. Website: www.generationqmagazine.com. **Contact:** Melissa Thompson Maher. Estab. 2011. Bimonthly consumer magazine. *Generation Q magazine* is a lifestyle publication reflecting the interests and obsessions of the modern and contemporary quilter and sewist.Circulation 10,000. Available for $5.

HOW TO CONTACT Available for SAE and on website. Accepts unsolicited submissions. Approached by 30 project/pattern designers/year. Works with almost all freelancers. Has featured projects/patterns by Sara Lawson, Victoria Findlay Wolfe, Brigitte Heitland, Julie Herman, Heather Jones. Preferred subjects: sewing, quilting. Submission format: DOC files. Include sketch, photo, or other rendition with size information. Submit print-ready step-by-step/assembly diagrams. Model and property release preferred. Once agree to publish project, submit via e-mail as JPEG at 300 dpi. Only accepts DOC files for instructions and JPEGs or PDFs for illustrations.

TERMS Send e-mail with project concepts. Does not keep samples on file; samples are not returned. Responds in 2 months. Pays $200 minimum for project/pattern design and industry-related articles. Credit line given. Pays on publication. Buys rights for 6 months. Finds freelancers by submissions, word-of-mouth, online. Undergoes technical edit before publication.

TIPS "Our audience is a niche within the quilting/sewing world. We want projects that reflect modern and contemporary styles. We don't like working with single-fabric collection projects and we love newcomers!"

GOOD OLD DAYS

E-mail: editor@goodolddaysmagazine.com. Website: www.goodolddaysmagazine.com. *Good Old Days* magazine tells the real stories of the people who lived and grew up in "the good old days" (about 1935–1960). Available for $2.

HOW TO CONTACT "Manuscripts should be typed (preferably double-spaced) with the author's name, address, and phone number in the upper left-hand corner. Our preferred word length is 600–1,000 words. Please submit 1 manuscript at a time and enclose SASE (self-addressed stamped envelope) if you want your material acknowledged and/or returned. If your story is not accepted and you have enclosed SASE, you will receive it back after the review process has taken place—generally about 6 months. Send your submissions to: Good Old Days Submissions, 306 E. Parr Rd., Berne IN 46711. If you do not enclose an SASE, you will hear from us only if we offer you a contract for your story. We do accept submissions via e-mail (Editor@GoodOldDaysMagazine.com) or fax, but treat them the same as mailed unsolicited manuscripts without a SASE."

GREEN CRAFT

Green Craft Magazine, 22992 Mill Creek Dr., Laguna Hills California 92653. E-mail: greencraft@stampington.com. Website: www.stampington.com/greencraft-magazine. "*GreenCraft Magazine* provides ideas for upcycling trash to treasures by showcasing projects where waste is repurposed into ecologically chic creations. To support sustainable production, the entire publication is printed on 100% recycled paper."

HOW TO CONTACT "We prefer submissions of original art. If original art is not available, our next preference is high-resolution digital images (300 dpi at $8^{1}/_{2}$ x 10"). If hi-res digital images are not available, we will very rarely consider professional-quality transparencies or color slides. Color-copy submissions are not accepted. All artwork must be identified with the artist's name, address, e-mail, and phone number clearly printed on a label attached to each sample. Inscribe your name and address somewhere on each piece of art. If you desire acknowledgment of artwork receipt, please include a self-addressed stamped postcard. If the artwork is three-dimensional, please attach your identification with a removable string or pack the sample in a plastic bag with your identification. If you have a unique artistic technique you'd like to share with others, please send samples of your artwork accompanied by a query letter outlining your article idea to the respective managing editor at: Green Craft Magazine, 22992 Mill Creek Dr., Laguna Hills California 92653. Managing editors also welcome brief e-mail inquiries."

NEEDS "Managing editors seek first-rate projects and encourage artists who have not published articles before to submit ideas, as editorial assistance will be provided."

TERMS Competitive editorial compensation is provided for all published articles. "We may hold your sample for an extended period of time—

9–12 months is common. Due to the large volume of artwork we receive, *Green Craft Magazine* will return only those submissions accompanied by sufficient postage in the form of cash, check, or money order made out to Stampington and Company. We cannot offer delivery confirmation; however, we are happy to put insurance on the submission. If you wish to have your artwork insured for the return journey, please include sufficient funds and indicate your preference in a postcard or letter enclosed with your submission. Please do not attach postage to packaging and do not send loose postage stamps. Contributors from outside the US, please send cash, check, or money order in US funds to Stampington and Company. For questions regarding your artwork, please send inquiries to artmanagement@stampington.com."

HANDMADE BUSINESS

P.O. Box 5000, N7528 Aanstad Rd., Iola WI 54945. (715)445-5000. Fax: (715)445-4053. E-mail: stephanieh@jonespublishing.com. Website: www.handmade-business.com. **Contact:** Published monthly. Online publication. The mission of handmade business is to informationrm, instruct, and inspire both the beginning and the established crafts persona and crafts retailer. Circulation: 20,000. Sample copies available for $6.95 each. No submission guidelines available. Accepts unsolicited submissions from freelance writers/contributors/artists. Designers are responsible for submitting print-ready photography of the completed project. Freelancers should submit their work as 2400×1800 or larger color photos. Accepts images in digital format. Send via Zip and e-mail as TIFF, JPEG, or PNG. Prefer 2400×1800 or larger image size. Writers/artists should send query letter, e-mail, resume, project photographs, social media statistics, URL, and artist's biography. Keeps samples of resume, business card, and self-promotion piece on file. Samples are not returned. Responds to queries and submissions only if interested. Pays $25–$300 maximum for industry-related articles. Runs credit line with each designer's image. Freelance writers get paid within 60 days of publication. Rights purchased vary according to project. Willing to negotiate with designers unwilling to sell all rights. Finds freelancers via agents/reps, submissions, word-of-mouth, magazines, and Internet. Projects that are accepted for publication undergo a technical edit prior to printing. Read our magazine. Follow us on social media. Provide quality, usable images. Be creative. Be punctual with deadlines. Provide quality, usable images with proper photography credits/rights to reprint/publish. Estab. 1974.

HANDWOVEN

F+W, a Content and eCommerce Company, 4868 Innovation Dr., Fort Collins CO 80525. E-mail: osterhaug@att.net; cgarton@interweave.com; handwoven@interweave.com. Website: www.weavingtoday.com. Tamara Schmiege, editorial assistant; Kathy Mallo, managing editor. **Contact:** Anita Osterhaug, editor; Christina Garton, assistant editor. Estab. 1979. "The main goal of *Handwoven* articles is to inspire our readers to weave. Articles and projects should be accessible to weavers of all skill levels, even when the material is technical. The best way to prepare an article for *Handwoven* is to study the format and style of articles in recent issues."

HOW TO CONTACT Guidelines available on website.

HAUTE HANDBAGS

22992 Mill Creek Dr., Laguna Hills California 92653. E-mail: hautehandbags@stampington.com. Website: www.stampington.com/haute-handbags. "How do you carry it? That's the question Somerset Studio and *Belle Armoire* would like to help answer through our exciting special publication titled *Haute Handbags*. Whether we use purses, clutches, totes, portfolios, sacks, bags, or attachés, there are many styles made with an astounding array of materials emerging from all corners of the creative world— all vying to be made and enjoyed!"

HOW TO CONTACT "We prefer submissions of original art. If original art is not available, our next preference is high-resolution digital images (300 dpi at 8½ x 10"). If hi-res digital images are not available, we will very rarely consider professional-quality transparencies or color slides. Color-copy submissions are not accepted. All artwork must be identified with the artist's name, address, e-mail, and phone number clearly printed on a label attached to each sample. Inscribe your name and address somewhere on each piece of art. If you desire acknowledgment of artwork receipt, please include a self-addressed stamped postcard. If the artwork is three-dimensional, please attach your identification with a removable string or pack the sample in a plastic bag with your identification. If you have a unique artistic technique you'd like to share with others, please send samples of your artwork accompanied by a query letter outlining your article idea to the respective managing editor at: Haute Handbags, 22992 Mill Creek Dr., Laguna Hills California 92653. Managing editors also welcome brief e-mail inquiries."

NEEDS "Managing editors seek first-rate projects and encourage artists who have not published articles before to submit ideas, as editorial assistance will be provided."

TERMS Competitive editorial compensation is provided for all published articles. "We may hold your sample for an extended period of time—9–12 months is common. Due to the large volume of artwork we receive, *Haute Handbags* will return only those submissions accompanied by sufficient postage in the form of cash, check, or money order made out to Stampington and Company. We cannot offer delivery confirmation; however, we are happy to put insurance on the submission. If you wish to have your artwork insured for the return journey, please include sufficient funds and indicate your preference in a postcard or letter enclosed with your submission. Please do not attach postage to packaging and do not send loose postage stamps. Contributors from outside the US, please send cash, check, or money order in US funds to Stampington and Company. For questions regarding your artwork, please send inquiries to artmanagement@ stampington.com."

HOLIDAYS AND CELEBRATIONS

22992 Mill Creek Dr., Laguna Hills California 92653. E-mail: holidaysandcelebrations@ stampington.com. Website: www.stampington. com/somerset-holidays-and-celebrations.

Learn how to create a lasting impression on special occasions such as birthdays, Halloween, Christmas, Mother's Day, Valentine's Day, and more in each annual issue of *Somerset Holidays and Celebrations*—an endless source of handcrafted inspiration.

HOW TO CONTACT "We prefer submissions of original art. If original art is not available, our next preference is high-resolution digital images (300 dpi at 8 1/2 x 10"). If hi-res digital images are not available, we will very rarely consider professional-quality transparencies or color slides. Color-copy submissions are not accepted. All artwork must be identified with the artist's name, address, e-mail, and phone number clearly printed on a label attached to each sample. Inscribe your name and address somewhere on each piece of art. If you desire acknowledgment of artwork receipt, please include a self-addressed stamped postcard. If the artwork is three-dimensional, please attach your identification with a removable string or pack the sample in a plastic bag with your identification. If you have a unique artistic technique you'd like to share with others, please send samples of your artwork accompanied by a query letter outlining your article idea to the respective managing editor at: Holidays and Celebrations, 22992 Mill Creek Dr., Laguna Hills California 92653. Managing editors also welcome brief e-mail inquiries."

NEEDS "Managing editors seek first-rate projects and encourage artists who have not published articles before to submit ideas, as editorial assistance will be provided."

TERMS Competitive editorial compensation is provided for all published articles. "We may hold your sample for an extended period of time—9–12 months is common. Due to the large volume of artwork we receive, *Holidays and Celebrations* will return only those submissions accompanied by sufficient postage in the form of cash, check, or money order made out to Stampington and Company. We cannot offer delivery confirmation; however, we are happy to put insurance on the submission. If you wish to have your artwork insured for the return journey, please include sufficient funds and indicate your preference in a postcard or letter enclosed with your submission. Please do not attach postage to packaging and do not send loose postage stamps. Contributors from outside the US, please send cash, check, or money order in US funds to Stampington and Company. For questions regarding your artwork, please send inquiries to artmanagement@stampington.com."

INTERWEAVE CROCHET

F+W, a Content and eCommerce Company, 4868 Innovation Dr., Fort Collins CO 80525. E-mail: crochet@interweave.com. Website: www.crochetme.com. "*Interweave Crochet* is a quarterly publication for all those who love to crochet. In each issue, we present beautifully finished projects, accompanied by clear step-by-step instructions, as well as stories and articles of interest to crocheters. The projects range from quick but intriguing projects that can be accomplished in a weekend to complex patterns that may take months to complete. Engaging and informationrmative feature articles come from around the country and around the world. Fashion sensibility and striking examples of craft technique are important to us."

HOW TO CONTACT Guidelines available on website.

INTERWEAVE KNITS

F&W, 4868 Innvation Dr., Fort Collins CO 80525. E-mail: custserv@fwmedia.com. Website: www. knittingdaily.com. *Interweave Knits* is a quarterly publication of Interweave for all those who love to knit. In each issue, we present beautifully finished projects, accompanied by clear step-by-step instruction, and stories and articles of interest to knitters. The projects range from quick but intriguing items that can be accomplished in a weekend to complex patterns that may take months to complete. Feature articles (personally arresting but informationrmation rich) come from around the country and around the world. Fashion sensibility and striking examples of craft technique are important to us.

HOW TO CONTACT Guidelines available on website.

TIPS "Remember that your submission is a representation of who you are and how you work—if you send us a thoughtful, neat, and well-organized submission, we are likely to be intrigued."

JEWELRY AFFAIRE

22992 Mill Creek Dr., Laguna Hills California 92653. E-mail: jewelryaffaire@stampington.com. Website: www.stampington.com/jewelry-affaire. "*Jewelry Affaire* celebrates the beauty that can be found in easy-to-make jewelry. These pieces are not only feasts for the eyes, but they can easily dress up and adorn any outfit and its wearer. This jewelry is precious in its own right."

HOW TO CONTACT "We prefer submissions of original art. If original art is not available, our next preference is high-resolution digital images (300 dpi at $8^1/_2$ x 10"). If hi-res digital images are not available, we will very rarely consider professional-quality transparencies or color slides. Color-copy submissions are not accepted. All artwork must be identified with the artist's name, address, e-mail, and phone number clearly printed on a label attached to each sample. Inscribe your name and address somewhere on each piece of art. If you desire acknowledgment of artwork receipt, please include a self-addressed stamped postcard. If the artwork is three-dimensional, please attach your identification with a removable string or pack the sample in a plastic bag with your identification. If you have a unique artistic technique you'd like to share with others, please send samples of your artwork accompanied by a query letter outlining your article idea to the respective managing editor at: Jewelry Affaire, 22992 Mill Creek Dr., Laguna Hills California 92653. Managing editors also welcome brief e-mail inquiries."

NEEDS "Managing editors seek first-rate projects and encourage artists who have not published articles before to submit ideas, as editorial assistance will be provided."

TERMS Competitive editorial compensation is provided for all published articles. "We may hold your sample for an extended period of time—9–12 months is common. Due to the large volume of artwork we receive, *Jewelry Affaire* will return only those submissions accompanied by sufficient postage in the form of cash, check, or money order made out to Stampington and Company. We cannot offer delivery confirmation; however, we are happy to put insurance on the submission. If you wish to have your artwork insured for the return journey, please include sufficient funds and indicate your preference in a postcard or letter enclosed with your submission. Please do not attach postage to packaging and do not send loose postage stamps. Contributors from outside the US, please send cash, check, or money order in US funds to Stampington and Company. For questions regarding your artwork, please send inquiries to artmanagement@ stampington.com."

JEWELRY STRINGING

F+W Media, 4868 Innovation Dr, Fort Collins CO 80525. E-mail: stringingsubmissions@ interweave.com. Website: www. stringingmagazine.com. **Contact:** Debbie Blair. *Jewelry Stringing* magazine is published quarterly. Each issue of *Jewelry Stringing* includes more than 70 fabulous necklaces, bracelets, and earrings, accompanied by clear step-by-step instructions and beautiful photography. The projects range from quick and easy to more complex, but all are made using basic stringing, wireworking, and knotting techniques.

HOW TO CONTACT www.beadingdaily.com/ stringingcontributorguidelines. Please send the following to submissions@clothpaperscissors. com: 2–3 photos and/or sketches of the project(s) you'd like to write about; a short outline of the project, including a materials list; a 100-word biography; and your full address and contact informationrmation, including blog, website, and social media informationrmation.

JUST CROSSSTITCH

E-mail: editor@just-crossstitch.com. Website: www.just-crossstitch.com. Estab. 1983. *Just CrossStitch* is the first magazine devoted exclusively to counted cross-stitch and the only cross-stitch title written for the intermediate, to advanced-level hobbyist.

KNIT NOW MAGAZINE

Practical Publishing, Suite G2, St. Christopher House, 217 Wellington Rd. S., Stockport SK2 6NG, UK. Website: www.knitnowmag.co.uk. Estab. 2012. Four weekly (13 issues/year) consumer magazine. *"Knit Now Magazine* is the UK's best knitting magazine, focused on quick, simple, stylish knits. We are particularly committed to British wool, supporting independent designers, and publishing new and interesting knits every issue." Circulation 25,000 (per issue). Available by request.

HOW TO CONTACT Request via e-mail. Accepts unsolicited submissions. Approached by 300 project/pattern designers/year. Buys 130 project/pattern designs/year from freelancers. Preferred subjects: knitting, crochet. Submission format: PDF. Include swatch, sketch, and brief description.

TERMS Send PDF submission in response to a focused call for submission. Responds in 2 weeks. Pays $100 minimum, $320 maximum for project/pattern design. Credit line given. Pays on publication. Buys first rights. Finds freelancers through submissions, word-of-mouth. Undergoes technical edit before publication.

TIPS "See our blog post that offers advice for designers who want to work for us at www. knitnowmag.co.uk/item/193-submission-tips-for-designers. Be sure to include a clear swatch and sketch with submission."

KNITSCENE

E-mail: amy.palmer@fwcommunity.com. Website: www.knitscene.com. "In each issue, we feature up-and-coming designers, popular yarns, fun and concise tutorials, and fresh photography that invites the reader into a yarn-filled daydream. The projects are simple but intriguing, stylish but wearable, and designed for knitters of all ages and sizes."

KNIT SIMPLE

E-mail: helen.chrystie@thegmcgroup.com. Website: www.thegmcgroup.com. "*Knit Simple* with easy-to-use and well-organized instructions, this magazine offers exactly what it says in the title. Whatever your skill level, here is a great resource for casual creations and simple, easy-to-wear knits that accommodate all shapes and sizes."

THE KNITTER

E-mail: theknitter@futurenet.com. Website: www.theknitter.co.uk. *The Knitter* is the magazine for knitters seeking a creative challenge. Published 13 times a year.

KNITTER'S MAGAZINE

Knitter's Magazine Submissions, 1320 S. Minnesota Ave., Floor 2, Sioux Falls SD 57105. E-mail: managingeditor@xrx-inc.com. Website: www.knittinguniverse.com/K113. A quarterly publication featuring popular designers and the latest knitwear fashions, techniques, and supplies. **HOW TO CONTACT** All submissions should include a swatch, sketch, or picture of the project, and description of the design and techniques it will use. A short biography is helpful.

KNITTING

E-mail: helen.chrystie@thegmcgroup.com. Website: www.thegmcgroup.com. "K*nitting* is the UK's original and best magazine devoted to this popular craft. Bridging the divide between fashion and handknitting, each issue offers at least 25 new and contemporary patterns including knits for women, men, children, and the home."

KNIT TODAY

Website: www.knit-today.co.uk. "*Knit Today* magazine is for everyone who enjoys knitting. Whether you've just started knitting or an experienced knitter, you'll find lots to read and at least 20 great patterns in every single issue. All our patterns are brand-new so you won't have seen them anywhere else before. We pride ourselves on having the most accurate, easy-to-follow pattern instructions so you can enjoy knitting to the very last stitch!" Published 13 times a year.

LAPIDARY JOURNAL JEWELRY ARTIST

E-mail: ljeditorial@interweave.com. Website: www.jewelrymakingdaily.com/blogs/jewelryartistmagazine/default.aspx.

LET'S GET CRAFTING

Website: www.letsgetcrafting.com. "*LGC Knitting and Crochet* contains everything you need to get started right away! Perfect for both beginners and experienced crafters, each issue comes with a high-value yarn pack, plus knitting needles and a crochet hook. We'll guide you step-by-step through gorgeous projects from some of the UK's leading designers, plus we have all the latest news and gossip from the UK crafting community as well as shopping guides and informationrmative features."

LET'S KNIT

21-23 Phoenix Court, Hawkind Rd., Colchester Essex CO2 8JY, UK. E-mail: sarah.neal@aceville.co.uk. Website: www.letsknit.co.uk. **Contact:** Sarah Neal, editor. Estab. 2007. "*Let's Knit* is the UK's best knitting magazine! Every issue is packed with patterns for knitters of all ages and skill levels, with a fun and fashionable flavor that's perfect for today's knitter. It has all the practical help, informationrmative features, and shopping information you could possibly want, along with a fantastic high-value free gift with every issue."

LOVE CRAFTING

Website: www.cross-stitching.com/magazines/love-crafting. "*Love Crafting* is a brand-new magazine full of inspiration for crafters of all abilities. Inside our sewing special you will find over 50 amazing makes with easy-to-follow instructions and templates, plus our top budget buys!"

LOVE CROCHET

Website: www.immediate.co.uk/brands/love-crochet/. "*Love Crochet* is a quarterly magazine filled with over 30 beautiful crochet projects for clothes, accessories, and the home. As well as an inspiring mix of on-trend makes, you'll find all the latest crochet news plus designer interviews, blogs, courses, and kits. This is the perfect magazine for those who enjoy crochet or want to learn this exciting craft."

LOVE KNITTING

Website: www.immediate.co.uk/brands/love-knitting-for-baby. "*Love Knitting for Baby* is a bimonthly must-knit collection of beautiful clothes and accessories for babies and toddlers. Each issue includes over 25 knitting patterns, plus best buys, expert advice, baby yarn reviews, and interviews with top designers."

LOVE OF QUILTING

P.O. Box 171, Winterset NJ 50273. (515)462-1020. Fax: (515)462-5856. Website: www.fonsandporter.com. **Contact:** Diane Tomlinson, associate editor. Estab. 1996. Bimonthly consumer magazine. Also publishes special-interest issues (*Easy Quilts*, *Quilting Quickly*, *Scrap and Patriotic Quilts*) quarterly and biannually. Focus is quilting projects.Circulation 350,000. Available by request.

HOW TO CONTACT Available online. Accepts unsolicited submissions. Approached by 200 project/pattern designers/year. Buys 400 projects/pattern designs/year from freelancers. Has featured projects/patterns by Liz Porter, Marianne Fons, Nancy Mahoney. Preferred subjects: quilting. Submission format: PDF, JPEG, and Illustrator files. Include detailed descriptions including measurements and fabric.

TERMS Send e-mail. Does not keep samples on file; samples not returned. Responds in 1 month. Pay varies by project. Pays on acceptance. Buys all rights (for contracted period of time). Finds freelancers through submissions, word-of-mouth, magazines, online. Edits as required.

TIPS "We are looking for traditional, easy, and precut quilt ideas in all skill levels. Have good artwork and descriptions."

LOVE PATCHWORK AND QUILTING

Website: www.lovepatchworkandquilting.com. "*Love Patchwork and Quilting* is a dedicated modern quilting magazine from the makers of *Mollie Makes* and *Simply Crochet*. We publish 13 times a year, featuring projects, techniques, interviews, news, and reviews from the world of modern quilting. Every issue also comes with a FREE gift!"

MACHINE KNITTING MONTHLY

Website: www.machineknittingmonthly.net. *Machine Knitting Monthly* magazine is packed with great new pattern ideas, features on different stitches, letters, club news, reviews on related books and products, and much more.

MACHINE QUILTING UNLIMITED

P.O. Box 918, Fort Lupton CO 80621. E-mail: submissions@mqumag.com. Website: www.machinequilting.mqumag.com. "*Machine Quilting Unlimited Magazine* is for the machine-quilting enthusiast. We cover techniques and fundamentals, whether using a domestic sewing machine, a small- frame system, a midarm machine, or a longarm machine. There will also be design inspiration, profiles of your favorite quilting stars, reviews of products, books, and DVDs, ideas for setting up your studio or workroom, help for beginners, and a calendar of quilt shows and events."

MAKE

E-mail: editor@makezine.com. Website: www.makezine.com. Bimonthly magazine for DIY enthusiasts.

MAKING

E-mail: helen.chrystie@thegmcgroup.com. Website: www.thegmcgroup.com. "*Making* is the UK's first contemporary craft magazine, bringing its readers 25 bespoke projects every month. Filled with inspiration, beautiful projects, and stunning photography, *Making* is essential reading for the discerning crafter. Covering a wide range of techniques and disciplines, clear how-to's, and style advice along with regular features and shopping pages, *Making* is the perfect combination of craft and lifestyle for a creative audience."

MAKING JEWELLERY

E-mail: helen.chrystie@thegmcgroup.com. Website: www.thegmcgroup.com. "*Making Jewellery* is the UK's first and best-selling jewelery magazine. Each month, we feature more than 45 projects to make stylish, fashionable, and professional-looking jewelery. There are step-by step projects for every skill level using a variety of, techniques from simple stringing to metal clays, polymer, shrink plastic, wirework, silversmithing, resin, lampworking, and more. *Making Jewellery* offers an innovative approach to jewelery making with instruction on basic techniques and insight into the creative minds of leading makers."

MARTHA STEWART LIVING

E-mail: living@marthastewart.com. Website: www.marthastewart.com. Monthly magazine for gardening, entertaining, renovating, cooking, collecting, and creating.

MCCALL'S QUICK QUILTS

E-mail: mcq@creativecraftsgroup.com. Website: www.mccallsquilting.com. Bimonthly consumer publication, nationally distributed, and written for quilters of all skill levels.

MCCALL'S QUILTING

E-mail: mcq@creativecraftsgroup.com. Website: www.mccallsquilting.com. Bimonthly consumer publication, nationally distributed, and written for quilters of all skill levels.

MINGLE

22992 Mill Creek Dr., Laguna Hills California 92653. E-mail: mingle@stampington.com. Website: www.stampington.com/mingle. "*Mingle*, along with the uplifting stories behind uniquely creative get-togethers—from small and intimate "girls' nights in" to larger-scale art retreats. Discover creative ways for bringing friends and loved ones together—is complete with entertaining tips, one-of-a-kind invitations and party favor ideas, recipes, artful décor, creative inspiration, and an all-around good time! Make your next get-together "the talk of the town" with ideas from the pages of this photography-rich and engrossing magazine."

HOW TO CONTACT "We prefer submissions of original art. If original art is not available, our next preference is high-resolution digital images (300 dpi at 8$\frac{1}{2}$ x 10"). If hi-res digital images are not available, we will very rarely consider professional-quality transparencies or color slides. Color-copy submissions are not accepted. All artwork must be identified with the artist's name, address, e-mail, and phone number clearly printed on a label attached to each sample. Inscribe your name and address somewhere on each piece of art. If you desire acknowledgment of artwork receipt, please include a self-addressed stamped postcard. If the artwork is three-dimensional, please attach your identification with a removable string or pack the sample in a plastic bag with your identification. If you have a unique artistic technique you'd like to share with others, please send samples of your artwork accompanied by a query letter outlining your article idea to the respective managing editor at: Mingle, 22992 Mill Creek Dr., Laguna Hills California 92653. Managing editors also welcome brief e-mail inquiries."

NEEDS "Managing editors seek first-rate projects and encourage artists who have not published articles before to submit ideas, as editorial assistance will be provided."

TERMS Competitive editorial compensation is provided for all published articles. "We may hold your sample for an extended period of time—9–12 months is common. Due to the large volume of artwork we receive, *Mingle* will return only those submissions accompanied by sufficient postage in the form of cash, check, or money order made out to Stampington and Company. We cannot offer delivery confirmation; however, we are happy to put insurance on the submission. If you wish to have your artwork insured for the return journey, please include sufficient funds and indicate your preference in a postcard or letter enclosed with your submission. Please do not attach postage to packaging and do not send loose postage stamps. Contributors from outside the US, please send cash, check, or money order in US funds to Stampington and Company. For questions regarding your artwork, please send inquiries to artmanagement@stampington.com."

MODERN QUILTS UNLIMITED

Meander Publishing, Inc., P.O. Box 918, Fort Lupton CO 80621. E-mail: editor@mqumag. com. Website: www.modernquilts.mqumag.com. "*Modern Quilts Unlimited* is published quarterly and offers quilt, accessory, and home decoration patterns by exciting new designers, interviews with the innovators in this field, machine-quilting tips, and quilts and projects made by those who find that this new genre of quilting fits their needs and lifestyles."

◑ MOLLIE MAKES

Website: www.molliemakes.com. *Mollie Makes* brings you the best of craft online, a look inside the homes of the world's most creative crafters, tutorials on inspiring makes, roundups of the most covetable stash, and tours of the crafty capitals of the world.

◑ NEW STITCHES

E-mail: janice@ccpuk.co.uk. Website: www. newstitches.co.uk. Published monthly, *New Stitches* features designs for your favorite embroidery techniques such as cross-stitch, Hardanger, blackwork, and much more.

◑ ONLINE QUILT MAGAZINE

P.O. Box 57, Buxton NSW 2571, Australia. (61)2-4683-2912. E-mail: jody@onlinequiltmagazine. com. Website: www.onlinequiltmagazine.com. **Contact:** Jody Anderson, editor. Estab. 2010. Monthly online publication. "We publish a monthly online quilting magazine that has a large readership around the world. Our readers range from beginners to more experienced quilters, and as such we like to offer a variety of articles, 'how to's', and patterns so there is something to appeal to everyone. There is a smaller free version each month and a super-cheap twice-as-big paid issue as well." Circulation 20,000+. Available by request.

HOW TO CONTACT Request via e-mail. Accepts unsolicited submissions. Exchanges free publicity and ad space for project/pattern designs. Has featured projects/patterns by Pat Durbin, Jenny Bowker, Kathy McNeil, Frieda Anderson, Toby Lischko, Elaine Quehl. Preferred subjects: quilting. Submission format: DOC and JPEG files. E-mail with general idea before submitting materials/content. Responsible for submitting print-ready photos and step-by-step/assembly diagrams for completed project. Photo captions only required if needed to make photo clear. Accepts images in digital format only via e-mail as JPEG file.

TERMS Send e-mail with project concepts. Responds in 7 days. Offers free publicity and ad space in exchange for designs/articles. Credit line given. Finds freelancers through word-of-mouth, online. Edits as required.

TIPS "We welcome everyone! We're always looking for new projects and quilting articles, and whilst we can't pay money for your submissions, we do offer great advertising promotion to our large reader base in exchange. It's a great way of attracting traffic to your site! Please just get in touch with me!"

◑ PAPER CRAFTER MAGAZINE

E-mail: ella.johnston@aceville.co.uk. Website: www.paper craftermagazine.co.uk. **Contact:** Ella Johnston, editor. "*Paper crafter* is a must-buy magazine for makers who adore all things paper, offering everything you need to create cards and paper craft projects in 1 package. It comes with beautiful kits and paper books that are designed by a different illustrator every issue, giving projects a fresh new look and providing inspiration with every purchase."

◑ PAPER CRAFT ESSENTIALS

Website: www.paper craftmagazines.com/the-magazines/paper craft-essentials. "*Paper craft Essentials* is packed with fun cards you can make in an evening! With the emphasis on cute and traditional styles, the magazine combines quick makes for beginners with more in-depth projects for intermediate and advanced crafters."

◑ PAPER CRAFT INSPIRATIONS

E-mail: paper craft@futurenet.com. Website: www. paper craftinspirationsmagazine.co.uk. "Britain's best-selling card-making magazine—filled with help, advice, oodles of ideas, and techniques for card makers of all levels of experience!"

PAPER CRAFTS AND SCRAPBOOKING MAGAZINE

E-mail: editor@paper craftsmag.com. Website: www.paper craftsmag.com. *Paper Crafts and Scrapbooking* is an enthusiast-based magazine with worldwide circulation.

PIECEWORK MAGAZINE

F+W Media, 4868 Innovation Dr., Fort Collins CO 80537. (800) 272-2193. Fax: (970)669-6117. E-mail: piecework@interweave.com. Website: www.interweave.com. Estab. 1993. *PieceWork* celebrates the rich tradition of needlework and the history of the people behind it. Stories and projects on embroidery, cross-stitch, knitting, crocheting, and quilting, along with other textile arts, are featured in each issue. Circulation 30,000. Writer's guidelines available at pieceworkmagazine.com.

TIPS Submit a well-researched article on a historical aspect of needlework complete with informationrmation on visuals and suggestion for accompanying project.

◉ POPULAR PATCHWORK

E-mail: bridget.kenningham@myhobbystore. com. Website: www.popularpatchwork.com. **Contact:** Bridget Kenningham. "Bringing traditional and contemporary patchwork and quilting to the fabricaholics of the UK."

⊕ POPULAR WOODWORKING MAGAZINE

F+W, A Content + Ecommerce Company, 8469 Blue Ash Rd., Suite 100, Cincinnati OH 45236. (513)531-2690, ext. 11348. E-mail: megan. fitzpatrick@fwcommunity.com. Website: www. popularwoodworking.com. **Contact:** Megan Fitzpatrick. Estab. 1981. "*Popular Woodworking Magazine* invites woodworkers of all skill levels into a community of professionals who share their hard-won shop experience through in-depth projects and technique articles, which help readers hone their existing skills and develop new ones for both hand and power tools. Related stories increase the readers' understanding and enjoyment of their craft. Any project submitted must be aesthetically pleasing, of sound construction, and offer a challenge to readers. On the average, we use 5 freelance features per issue. Our primary needs are 'how-to' articles on woodworking. Our secondary need is for articles that will inspire discussion concerning woodworking. Tone of articles should be conversational and informationrmal but knowledgeable, as if the writer is speaking directly to the reader. Our readers are the woodworking hobbyist and small woodshop owner. Writers should have an extensive knowledge of woodworking and excellent woodworking techniques and skills." Circulation 150,000. Sample copy: $6.99 plus 9×12 SAE with 6 first-class stamps, or online.

HOW TO CONTACT Guidelines available online. Word length ranges from 1,200–2,500. Payment for features starts at $250 per contracted page (plus $75 per for images), depending on the total package submitted (including its quality) and the writer's level of woodworking and writing experience. "All submissions, except 'Out of the Woodwork' columns and 'Tricks of the Trade,' should be preceded by a query. We accept unsolicited manuscripts and artwork, although, if sent via post, they must be accompanied by a self-addressed stamped envelope to be returned. Digital queries are preferred. We try to respond to all queries within 60 days."

NEEDS "Our primary needs are how-to articles on woodworking projects, and instructional features dealing with woodworking and techniques. We rarely publish freelance articles about woodworkers and their particular work. The tone of articles should be conversational and informationrmal, as if the writer is speaking directly to the reader."

TIPS "Write an 'End Grain' column for us and then follow up with photos of your projects. Submissions should include materials list, SketchUp model or hand illustration (SU preferred), and discussion of the step-by-step process. We select attractive, practical projects with quality construction for which the authors can supply quality digital photography."

POTTERY MAKING ILLUSTRATED

600 N. Cleveland Ave., Suite 210, Westerville OH 43082. (614)895-4213. Fax: (614)891-8960. E-mail: editorial@potterymaking.org. Website: www.ceramicartsdaily.org/pottery-making-illustrated. *Pottery Making Illustrated* provides well-illustrated, practical, how-to instruction for all skill levels on all aspects of ceramic art.

HOW TO CONTACT "We require professional digital images for publication. Digital images should be delivered as uncompressed 4-color

(CMYK), 300 dpi image files with a minimum print size of 5" (preferably TIFF or EPS format). Image files should be burned to a CD and mailed to our editorial offices with your complete submission. Images can also be uploaded to our FTP site. Uploaded files must be stuffed or zipped. Include all captions on a separate sheet of paper. Each image or graphic element must have a caption. Make sure image file names clearly match up with caption numbers. Captions for processes and techniques should describe the activity shown. Captions for finished ware should include: the title, dimensions, specific ceramic medium (earthenware, porcelain, etc.), forming/glazing techniques, cone number and firing process (pit fired, high fire, raku, etc.). Provide a brief 1 or 2 sentence biography about yourself and include an e-mail address, Web address, fax number, or postal address if you want direct reader feedback. Our authors have indicated that this has been a valuable tool. If images or illustrations were provided by a third party, include her/his name so proper credit may be published. It is your responsibility to obtain the rights for any photographs, illustrations, or other third-party materials submitted."

TERMS "We ask for exclusive worldwide rights for the text (both print and electronic versions, including but not limited to publishing on demand, database online services, reprints, or books) and nonexclusive rights for use of the photographic materials in print or electronic media. This nonexclusive agreement allows for the continued use of the photographic material in any way the artist chooses after the article has appeared in *Pottery Making Illustrated*. When your article is published, you'll be paid at the current rate of $0.10 per word for text and $25 per image or graphic illustration."

PRIMITIVE QUILTS AND PROJECTS

E-mail: homespunmedia@aol.com. Website: www.primitivequiltsandprojects.com. "A premium quilting magazine dedicated to the primitive quilter, rug hooker, stitcher, and more! Each issue features at least 15 projects from some of the most admired designers in the primitive fiber arts world."

PRIMS

Prims, 22992 Mill Creek Dr., Laguna Hills California 92653. E-mail: prims@stampington. com. Website: www.stampington.com/prims. "*Prims* exclusively features art inspired by a bygone era. You will find artwork of primitive-, folk-, historic-, and early Americana-style artists that will captivate the imagination and enchant with their simple beauty. The traditional beauty of handcrafted art making includes dolls, paintings, and mixed-media artwork, along with teddy bears in Stampington and Company's unique publication."

HOW TO CONTACT "We prefer submissions of original art. If original art is not available, our next preference is high-resolution digital images (300 dpi at $8^1/2$ x 10"). If hi-res digital images are not available, we will very rarely consider professional-quality transparencies or color slides. Color-copy submissions are not accepted. All artwork must be identified with the artist's name, address, e-mail, and phone number clearly printed on a label attached to each sample. Inscribe your name and address somewhere on each piece of art. If you desire acknowledgment of artwork receipt, please include a self-addressed stamped postcard. If the artwork is three-dimensional, please attach your identification with a removable string or pack the sample in a plastic bag with your identification. If you have a unique artistic technique you'd like to share with others, please send samples of your artwork accompanied by a query letter outlining your article idea to the respective managing editor at: Prims, 22992 Mill Creek Dr., Laguna Hills California 92653. Managing editors also welcome brief e-mail inquiries."

NEEDS "Managing editors seek first-rate projects and encourage artists who have not published articles before to submit ideas, as editorial assistance will be provided."

TERMS Competitive editorial compensation is provided for all published articles. "We may hold your sample for an extended period of time—9–12 months is common. Due to the large volume of artwork we receive, *Prims* will return only those submissions accompanied by sufficient postage in the form of cash, check, or money order made out to Stampington and Company. We cannot offer delivery confirmation; however, we are happy to put insurance on the submission. If you wish to have your artwork insured for the return journey, please include sufficient funds and indicate your preference in a postcard or letter enclosed with your submission. Please do not attach postage to packaging and do not send loose postage stamps. Contributors from outside the US, please send cash, check, or money order in US funds to Stampington and Company. For questions regarding your artwork, please send inquiries to artmanagement@stampington.com."

QUICK AND EASY CROCHET

E-mail: shgrassroots@yahoo.com. Website: www.quickandeasycrochetmagazine.com. "America's No. 1 crochet magazine. Filled with easy-to-follow instructions for crocheted fashions, pillows, potholders, afghans, coverlets, bridal gowns, dollies, and more."

QUICK CARDS MADE EASY

Website: www.cardmakingandpaper craft.com/magazine/quickcards. *Quick Cards Made Easy* is packed with stylish card projects, for every occasion, each issue. Published 13 times a year.

QUILT

E-mail: quiltmag@epix.net. Website: www.quiltmag.com. "Published 6 times per year, *Quilt* will fulfill your every quilting need. Each issue is bursting with patterns in a variety of styles for all skill levels. Quilts are showcased in beautifully styled room settings, and clear directions and illustrations accompany each project. Our talented designers use current fabric collections, so you can create the exact quilt shown, and many projects include kit informationrmation for easy ordering."

QUILT ALMANAC

E-mail: quiltmag@epix.net. Website: www.quiltmag.com. "Published each January, *Quilt Almanac* features quilts for all seasons, from traditional to modern, and showcases a variety of techniques. This newsstand-only issue will provide you with inspiring projects to keep you busy all year long. Our designers create both quilts and small projects ideal for newer quilters or for experienced quilters looking for a quick and relaxing project."

QUILTER'S NEWSLETTER MAGAZINE

E-mail: questions@qnm.com. Website: www.quiltersnewsletter.com. *Quilters Newsletter* is a specialized publication for quilt lovers and quilt makers. Its domestic and international readership of about 200,000 includes professional and nonprofessional quilt makers, quilt collectors, historians, and teachers.

TERMS "Our rates depend on what rights we buy, how much editing or rewriting is required, if you can provide usable sewn samples, and whether we use your photos or do the photography in our studio. We reserve the right to use accepted material in any appropriate issue and for any editorial purpose. For general articles, as well as for each pattern that we develop from a submitted quilt, payment will be negotiated upon acceptance. We make no payment for material used in our News columns or for feature material sent by industry professionals or their representatives that promotes a person,event, or product. Payment for Top Tips used in Short Takes is $25. Payment for showcasing a quilt on our cover and presenting a pattern for a portion of or all of the quilt is $350 plus 10 copies of that issue. Payment for Photo Finish and About Space is $50 and 10 copies of that issue."

QUILTER'S WORLD

E-mail: editor@quiltersworld.com. Website: www.quiltersworld.com. Estab. 1979. *Quilter's World* features classic and current trends in quilt design.

QUILTING ARTS MAGAZINE

E-mail: submissions@quiltingarts.com. Website: www.quiltingdaily.com. "At *Quilting Arts*, we celebrate contemporary art quilting, surface design, mixed media, fiber art trends, and more. We are always looking for new techniques, innovative processes, and unique approaches to the art of quilting."

HOW TO CONTACT Guidelines available on website.

QUILTMAKER

E-mail: editor@quiltmaker.com. Website: www.quiltmaker.com. Quiltmaker publishes 6 regular issues per year, available by subscription (print and digital), at quilt shops and on newsstands.

QUILTMANIA

Website: www.quiltmania.com. *Quiltmania*, is published every 2 months in 3 versions: French, Dutch, and English.

QUILTS AND MORE

E-mail: apq@meredith.com. Website: www. allpeoplequilt.com/magazines-more/quilts-and-more.

QUILT SAMPLER

Website: www.allpeoplequilt.com/magazines-more/quilt-sampler.

QUILTY

E-mail: contributors@qnntv.com. Website: www. heyquilty.com. Quilting magazine.

RELOVED

E-mail: sally.fitzgerald@anthem-publishing.com. Website: www.relovedmag.co.uk. **Contact:** Sally Fitzgerald, editor. *Reloved* is the exciting new magazine at the heart of thrifting, shabby chic, and upcycling. With an emphasis on breathing new life into old, forgotten objects, it brings a hands-on approach to this thriving pastime.

SAMPLER AND ANTIQUE NEEDLEWORK QUARTERLY

E-mail: editor@sanqmagazine.com. Website: www.sanqmagazine.com. *Sampler and Antique Needlework Quarterly* is the premier magazine for those who look at the handwork from centuries past with a sense of awe, wonder, and inquisitiveness.

SCRAP 365

Traplet Publications Ltd., Traplet House, Pendragon Close Malvern WR14 1GA, UK. E-mail: scrap365@traplet.com. Website: www. inspiredtomake.com/zone/scrap-365/home. **Contact:** Alison Parris, editor. "Published 6 times a year, every issue is 90 pages stuffed with scrappy inspiration. As our strap line suggests, our magazine is aimed at keen scrapbookers who love and live their hobby."

SCRAPBOOK MAGAZINE

Website: www.paper craftmagazines.com/the-magazines/scrapbook-magazine. *Scrapbook Magazine* is Britain's biggest-selling scrapbook magazine. Published every 6 weeks, each issue shows you the ins and outs for bringing your photos and memories to life through the wonderful world of scrapbooking, allowing you to create stunning and personalized mini works of art using your photos, papers, found objects, and recycled elements.

SEW BEAUTIFUL

E-mail: editorial@sewbeautifulmag.com. Website: www.sewbeautifulmag.com. *Sew Beautiful* is 1 of the largest, most recognized heirloom sewing titles in the US

SEWING WORLD

Traplet Publications Ltd., Traplet House, Pendragon Close Malvern WR14 1GA, UK. Website: www.inspiredtomake.com/zone/sewing-world/home. *Sewing World* is a monthly magazine packed full of delicious, contemporary sewing projects as well as fabrics, techniques, products, features, and interviews.

SEW IT ALL

Website: www.sewitallmag.com. *Sew It All* is published once a year in December by Creative Crafts Group. It is a special newsstand issue brought to you by the editors of *Sew News*.

SEW MAGAZINE

E-mail: lorraine.luximon@aceville.co.uk. Website: www.sewmag.co.uk. **Contact:** Lorraine Luximon, editor. "Inspiration for you, your home, and the little ones—the UK's only sewing magazine that gives you a FREE full-sized dressmaker's pattern every month!"

SEW NEWS

Sew News Editor, 741 Corporate Circle, Suite A., Golden CO 80401. E-mail: sewnews@sewnews. com. Website: www.sewnews.com. *Sew News* is the go-to guide for the most current and relevant informationrmation that the sewing world has to offer.

HOW TO CONTACT Query by letter or e-mail; do not send finished manuscripts. Query should consist of a brief outline of the article, a sketch or photo of the intended project, a list of the illustrations or photographs you envision with it, an explanation of why your proposed article would be of interest to the *Sew News* reader, and why you are qualified to write it.

NEEDS Articles should teach a specific technique, inspire the reader to try a project, introduce the reader to a new product or company related to sewing, or informationrm the reader about current fashion and sewing trends.

TERMS When an article is accepted, you'll be sent an assignment sheet detailing what is expected of you for the assignment and the intended payment (from $50–500, new writers generally $50–150, depending on the length and complexity of the subject and the garment(s), samples, photography, illustrations, or sources to be supplied). After you receive the assignment, please sign and return it within 10 days. If you're unable to meet a deadline for any reason, please informationrm *Sew News* immediately. Failure to do so will void assignment. All articles, including those specifically assigned, are written "on speculation." All payments will be made upon publication. To receive the full payment suggested in the assignment sheet, the article must be submitted by the specified deadline, include all elements detailed in the assignment sheet, and be of acceptable quality (to be determined by the *Sew News* editorial staff). Payment may be decreased for late arrival, missing elements, or poor quality. *Sew News* reserves the right to return articles for rewriting or clarification of informationrmation, return samples for redo/corrections and, in extreme cases, to return them without payment.

SEW SIMPLE

Website: www.sewsimple.com. *Sew Simple* is right in tune with today's younger stitchers.

SEW SOMERSET

Sew Somerset, 22992 Mill Creek Dr., Laguna Hills California 92653. E-mail: sewsomerset@stampington.com. Website: www.stampington. com/sew-somerset. "*Sew Somerset* represents a new way of looking at sewn art. More than ever before, artists are discovering the joy of combining sewing with mixed-media projects, showing the world that stitches are not just for fabric anymore! In this 144-page publication, readers will find gorgeous photographs, easy-to-understand techniques, and endless inspiration. *Sew Somerset* will help crafters and artists alike learn how to add stitches of varied lengths, sizes, colors, and dimensions into their next project to create a look that is 'So Somerset!'"

HOW TO CONTACT "We prefer submissions of original art. If original art is not available, our next preference is high-resolution digital images (300 dpi at $8^1/2$ x 10"). If hi-res digital images are not available, we will very rarely consider professional-quality transparencies or color slides. Color-copy submissions are not accepted. All artwork must be identified with the artist's name, address, e-mail, and phone number clearly printed on a label attached to each sample. Inscribe your name and address somewhere on each piece of art. If you desire acknowledgment of artwork receipt, please include a self-addressed stamped postcard. If the artwork is three-dimensional, please attach your identification with a removable string or pack the sample in a plastic bag with your identification. If you have a unique artistic technique you'd like to share with others, please send samples of your artwork accompanied by a query letter outlining your article idea to the respective managing editor at: Sew Somerset, 22992 Mill Creek Dr., Laguna Hills California 92653. Managing editors also welcome brief e-mail inquiries."

NEEDS "Managing editors seek first-rate projects and encourage artists who have not published articles before to submit ideas, as editorial assistance will be provided."

TERMS Competitive editorial compensation is provided for all published articles. "We may hold your sample for an extended period of time—9–12 months is common. Due to the large volume of artwork we receive, *Sew Somerset* will return only those submissions accompanied by sufficient postage in the form of cash, check, or money order made out to Stampington and Company. We cannot offer delivery confirmation;

however, we are happy to put insurance on the submission. If you wish to have your artwork insured for the return journey, please include sufficient funds and indicate your preference in a postcard or letter enclosed with your submission. Please do not attach postage to packaging and do not send loose postage stamps. Contributors from outside the US, please send cash, check, or money order in US funds to Stampington and Company. For questions regarding your artwork, please send inquiries to artmanagement@stampington.com."

SIMPLE QUILTS AND SEWING

E-mail: quiltmag@epix.net. Website: www.quiltmag.com. Magazine about quilting and sewing.

THE SIMPLE THINGS

E-mail: thesimplethings@futurenet.com. Website: www.thesimplethings.com. *The Simple Things* is published 13 times a year and celebrates the things that matter most.

SIMPLY CARDS AND PAPER CRAFTS

Website: www.paper craftmagazines.com/the-magazines/simply-cards-paper craft. "*Simply Cards and Paper craft* is the UK's most inspirational paper craft magazine full of inspiration for quality cards for every occasion. It's full of the newest techniques, products, and up-to-the-minute ideas."

SIMPLY CROCHET

E-mail: simplycrochet@futurenet.com. Website: www.simplycrochetmag.co.uk. *Simply Crochet* is a dedicated crochet magazine from the makers of *Simply Knitting*, *The Knitter*, *Crochet Today!* and *Mollie Makes*. Featuring over 20 crochet patterns every month and technical advice, clear instructions, and crochet inspiration, *Simply Crochet* will get you hooked on handmade!

SIMPLY HOMEMADE

Website: www.simplyhomemademag.com. "*Simply Homemade* is a magazine designed specifically for those of us who love crafting and can't get enough of making things."

SIMPLY KNITTING

E-mail: simplyknitting@futurenet.com. Website: www.simplyknitting.co.uk. On sale 13 times a year, *Simply Knitting* is packed with patterns, yarn reviews, knitting tips, and knitting news.

SOMERSET APPRENTICE

22992 Mill Creek Dr., Laguna Hills California 92653. E-mail: somersetapprentice@stampington.com. Website: www.stampington.com/somerset-apprentice. "*Somerset Apprentice* takes its readers by the hand to teach them the fundamentals of creating *Somerset*-style art—one basic step at a time. Successful artists share their favorite tips and techniques, including layered collage, mixed media, and assemblage art, which are presented through detailed, close-up photographs and clear, concise instructions. Join the pros on a step-by-step journey as they complete an entire work of art! This top-selling magazine has everything you'll need to learn a new craft, fine-tune your technique, and gather inspiration for your creative adventure."

HOW TO CONTACT "We prefer submissions of original art. If original art is not available, our next preference is high-resolution digital images (300 dpi at $8^{1}/_{2}$ x 10"). If hi-res digital images are not available, we will very rarely consider professional-quality transparencies or color slides. Color-copy submissions are not accepted. All artwork must be identified with the artist's name, address, e-mail, and phone number clearly printed on a label attached to each sample. Inscribe your name and address somewhere on each piece of art. If you desire acknowledgment of artwork receipt, please include a self-addressed stamped postcard. If the artwork is three-dimensional, please attach your identification with a removable string or pack the sample in a plastic bag with your identification. If you have a unique artistic technique you'd like to share with others, please send samples of your artwork accompanied by a query letter outlining your article idea to the respective managing editor at: Somerset Apprentice, 22992 Mill Creek Dr., Laguna Hills California 92653. Managing editors also welcome brief e-mail inquiries."

NEEDS "Managing editors seek first-rate projects and encourage artists who have not published articles before to submit ideas, as editorial assistance will be provided."

TERMS Competitive editorial compensation is provided for all published articles. "We may hold your sample for an extended period of time—9–12 months is common. Due to the large volume of artwork we receive, *Somerset Apprentice* will return only those submissions accompanied by sufficient postage in the form of cash, check, or money order made out to Stampington and Company. We cannot offer delivery confirmation; however, we are happy to put insurance on the submission. If you wish to have your artwork insured for the return journey, please include sufficient funds and indicate your preference in a postcard or letter enclosed with your submission. Please do not attach postage to packaging and do not send loose postage stamps. Contributors from outside the US, please send cash, check, or money order in US funds to Stampington and Company. For questions regarding your artwork, please send inquiries to artmanagement@stampington.com."

SOMERSET DIGITAL STUDIO

Somerset Digital Studio, 22992 Mill Creek Dr., Laguna Hills California 92653. E-mail: somersetdigitalstudio@stampington.com. Website: www.stampington.com/somerset-digital-studio. "*Somerset Digital Studio* showcases some of the best digitally created artwork around, and these breathtaking samples of scrapbook pages, ATCs, and collages will have readers joining in this growing trend of creating digitally altered artwork in no time. Each of the 144 lush, full-color pages found in every issue contain captivating feature articles, a full gallery of digital eye candy, a digital dictionary, software comparison chart, digital tutorial, and more."

HOW TO CONTACT "We prefer submissions of original art. If original art is not available, our next preference is high-resolution digital images (300 dpi at 8$\frac{1}{2}$ x 10"). If hi-res digital images are not available, we will very rarely consider professional-quality transparencies or color slides. Color-copy submissions are not accepted. All artwork must be identified with the artist's name, address, e-mail, and phone number clearly printed on a label attached to each sample. Inscribe your name and address somewhere on each piece of art. If you desire acknowledgment of artwork receipt, please include a self-addressed stamped postcard. If the artwork is three-dimensional, please attach your identification with a removable string or pack the sample in a plastic bag with your identification. If you have a unique artistic technique you'd like to share with others, please send samples of your artwork accompanied by a query letter outlining your article idea to the respective managing editor at: Somerset Digital Studio, 22992 Mill Creek Dr., Laguna Hills California 92653. Managing editors also welcome brief e-mail inquiries."

NEEDS "Managing editors seek first-rate projects and encourage artists who have not published articles before to submit ideas, as editorial assistance will be provided."

TERMS Competitive editorial compensation is provided for all published articles. "We may hold your sample for an extended period of time—9–12 months is common. Due to the large volume of artwork we receive, *Somerset Digital Studio* will return only those submissions accompanied by sufficient postage in the form of cash, check, or money order made out to Stampington and Company. We cannot offer delivery confirmation; however, we are happy to put insurance on the submission. If you wish to have your artwork insured for the return journey, please include sufficient funds and indicate your preference in a postcard or letter enclosed with your submission. Please do not attach postage to packaging and do not send loose postage stamps. Contributors from outside the US, please send cash, check, or money order in US funds to Stampington and Company. For questions regarding your artwork, please send inquiries to artmanagement@stampington.com."

SOMERSET HOME

22992 Mill Creek Dr., Laguna Hills California 92653. E-mail: somersethome@stampington.com. Website: www.stampington.com/somerset-home. "*Somerset Home* magazine beautifully blends 'Somerset-esque' art together with functional everyday items to add an artful touch of décor. The result is a truly distinctive annual magazine that exemplifies creative living and showcases hundreds of tips, techniques, and charming accents designed to enlighten, organize, and beautify any dwelling place. When you wander through the inspiring pages of *Somerset Home*, you'll be enthralled by room after room of beautiful projects, and inside this inviting 160-page publication, you'll find unique and artistic creative ideas for every corner of your home."

HOW TO CONTACT "We prefer submissions of original art. If original art is not available, our next preference is high-resolution digital images (300 dpi at $8^{1}/_{2}$ x 10"). If hi-res digital images are not available, we will very rarely consider professional-quality transparencies or color slides. Color-copy submissions are not accepted. All artwork must be identified with the artist's name, address, e-mail, and phone number clearly printed on a label attached to each sample. Inscribe your name and address somewhere on each piece of art. If you desire acknowledgment of artwork receipt, please include a self-addressed stamped postcard. If the artwork is three-dimensional, please attach your identification with a removable string or pack the sample in a plastic bag with your identification. If you have a unique artistic technique you'd like to share with others, please send samples of your artwork accompanied by a query letter outlining your article idea to the respective managing editor at: Somerset Home, 22992 Mill Creek Dr., Laguna Hills California 92653. Managing editors also welcome brief e-mail inquiries."

NEEDS "Managing editors seek first-rate projects and encourage artists who have not published articles before to submit ideas, as editorial assistance will be provided."

TERMS Competitive editorial compensation is provided for all published articles. "We may hold your sample for an extended period of time—9–12 months is common. Due to the large volume of artwork we receive, *Somerset Home* will return only those submissions accompanied by sufficient postage in the form of cash, check, or money order made out to Stampington and Company. We cannot offer delivery confirmation; however, we are happy to put insurance on the submission. If you wish to have your artwork insured for the return journey, please include sufficient funds and indicate your preference in a postcard or letter enclosed with your submission. Please do not attach postage to packaging and do not send loose postage stamps. Contributors from outside the US, please send cash, check, or money order in US funds to Stampington and Company. For questions regarding your artwork, please send inquiries to artmanagement@stampington.com."

SOMERSET LIFE

22992 Mill Creek Dr., Laguna Hills California 92653. E-mail: somersetlife@stampington.com. Website: www.stampington.com/somerset-life. "Each issue of *Somerset Life* provides an abundance of inspiring ideas to infuse our daily lives with simple pleasures, art, romance, creativity, and beauty. Stunning photography and insightful and entertaining articles illustrate touching moments captured in poetry and artwork, unique ways to present gifts and treasured items, simple but beautiful remembrances, fresh ideas to elevate the art of letter writing, and many other imaginative ideas to enhance our lives with artful elements. *Somerset Life* will inspire you to make every day extraordinary!"

HOW TO CONTACT "We prefer submissions of original art. If original art is not available, our next preference is high-resolution digital images (300 dpi at $8^{1}/_{2}$ x 10"). If hi-res digital images are not available, we will very rarely consider professional-quality transparencies or color slides. Color-copy submissions are not accepted. All artwork must be identified with the artist's name, address, e-mail, and phone number clearly printed on a label attached to each sample. Inscribe your name and address somewhere on each piece of art. If you desire acknowledgment of artwork receipt, please include a self-addressed stamped postcard. If the artwork is three-dimensional, please attach your identification with a removable string or pack the sample in a plastic bag with your identification. If you have a unique artistic technique you'd like to share with others, please send samples of your artwork accompanied by a query letter outlining your article idea to the respective managing editor at: Somerset Life, 22992 Mill Creek Dr., Laguna Hills California 92653. Managing editors also welcome brief e-mail inquiries."

NEEDS "Managing editors seek first-rate projects and encourage artists who have not published articles before to submit ideas, as editorial assistance will be provided."

TERMS Competitive editorial compensation is provided for all published articles. "We may hold your sample for an extended period of time—9–12 months is common. Due to the large volume of artwork we receive, *Somerset Life* will return only those submissions accompanied by sufficient postage in the form of cash, check, or money order made out to Stampington and Company. We can not offer delivery confirmation; however, we are happy to put insurance on the submission. If you wish to have your artwork insured for the return journey, please include sufficient funds and indicate your preference in a postcard or letter enclosed with your submission. Please do not attach postage to packaging and do not send loose postage stamps. Contributors from outside the US, please send cash, check, or money order in US funds to Stampington and Company. For questions regarding your artwork, please send inquiries to artmanagement@stampington.com."

SOMERSET MEMORIES

Somerset Memories, 22992 Mill Creek Dr., Laguna Hills California 92653. E-mail: somersetmemories@stampington.com. Website: www.stampington.com/somerset-memories. "*Somerset Memories* provides a showcase for arts and crafts that feature family photographs and memorabilia. This unique semiannual magazine presents sophisticated scrapbook and journal pages, plus a gorgeous array of paper crafts, fabric arts, memorabilia, and mixed-media art made by our talented readers and contributors."

HOW TO CONTACT "We prefer submissions of original art. If original art is not available, our next preference is high-resolution digital images (300 dpi at 8 1/2 x 10"). If hi-res digital images are not available, we will very rarely consider professional-quality transparencies or color slides. Color-copy submissions are not accepted. All artwork must be identified with the artist's name, address, e-mail, and phone number clearly printed on a label attached to each sample. Inscribe your name and address somewhere on each piece of art. If you desire acknowledgment of artwork receipt, please include a self-addressed stamped postcard. If the artwork is three-dimensional, please attach your identification with a removable string or pack the sample in a plastic bag with your identification. If you have a unique artistic technique you'd like to share with others, please send samples of your artwork accompanied by a query letter outlining your article idea to the respective managing editor at: Somerset Memories, 22992 Mill Creek Dr., Laguna Hills California 92653. Managing editors also welcome brief e-mail inquiries."

NEEDS "Managing editors seek first-rate projects and encourage artists who have not published articles before to submit ideas, as editorial assistance will be provided."

TERMS Competitive editorial compensation is provided for all published articles. "We may hold your sample for an extended period of time—9–12 months is common. Due to the large volume of artwork we receive, *Somerset Memories* will return only those submissions accompanied by sufficient postage in the form of cash, check, or money order made out to Stampington and Company. We can not offer delivery confirmation; however, we are happy to put insurance on the submission. If you wish to have your artwork insured for the return journey, please include sufficient funds and indicate your preference in a postcard or letter enclosed with your submission. Please do not attach postage to packaging and do not send loose postage stamps. Contributors from outside the US, please send cash, check, or money order in US funds to Stampington and Company. For questions regarding your artwork, please send inquiries to artmanagement@stampington.com."

SOMERSET STUDIO

22992 Mill Creek Dr., Laguna Hills California 92653. E-mail: somersetstudio@stampington.com. Website: www.stampington.com/somerset-studio. "Paper crafting, art stamping, and the lettering arts are elevated to an artistic level in *Somerset Studio*! Come join in the celebration of these popular handcrafting styles by exploring the industry's most trusted and innovative mixed-media magazine, as you learn from fellow artists working with exotic papers, intriguing art stamps, fine calligraphy, and a variety of mediums."

HOW TO CONTACT "We prefer submissions of original art. If original art is not available, our next preference is high-resolution digital images (300 dpi at 8$\frac{1}{2}$ x 10"). If hi-res digital images are not available, we will very rarely consider professional-quality transparencies or color slides. Color-copy submissions are not accepted. All artwork must be identified with the artist's name, address, e-mail, and phone number clearly printed on a label attached to each sample. Inscribe your name and address somewhere on each piece of art. If you desire acknowledgment of artwork receipt, please include a self-addressed stamped postcard. If the artwork is three-dimensional, please attach your identification with a removable string or pack the sample in a plastic bag with your identification. If you have a unique artistic technique you'd like to share with others, please send samples of your artwork accompanied by a query letter outlining your article idea to the respective managing editor at: Somerset Studio, 22992 Mill Creek Dr., Laguna Hills California 92653. Managing editors also welcome brief e-mail inquiries."

NEEDS "Managing editors seek first-rate projects and encourage artists who have not published articles before to submit ideas, as editorial assistance will be provided."

TERMS Competitive editorial compensation is provided for all published articles. "We may hold your sample for an extended period of time—9–12 months is common. Due to the large volume of artwork we receive, *Somerset Studio* will return only those submissions accompanied by sufficient postage in the form of cash, check, or money order made out to Stampington and Company. We can not offer delivery confirmation; however, we are happy to put insurance on the submission. If you wish to have your artwork insured for the return journey, please include sufficient funds and indicate your preference in a postcard or letter enclosed with your submission. Please do not attach postage to packaging and do not send loose postage stamps. Contributors from outside the US, please send cash, check, or money order in US funds to Stampington and Company. For questions regarding your artwork, please send inquiries to artmanagement@ stampington.com."

SOMERSET STUDIO GALLERY

22992 Mill Creek Dr., Laguna Hills California 92653. E-mail: somersetstudiogallery@ stampington.com. Website: www.stampington. com/somerset-gallery. "*Somerset Studio Gallery* is filled with hundreds of samples of extraordinary artwork presented up close and in detail. Whether your passion is rubber stamping, calligraphy, or paper crafting, the newest *Gallery* features everything you love about *Somerset Studio* in 200 lush pages, including enlightening how-to articles, beautifully photographed projects, and hundreds of handmade creations by your favorite artists, as well as by you, our talented readers."

HOW TO CONTACT "We prefer submissions of original art. If original art is not available, our next preference is high-resolution digital images (300 dpi at 8$\frac{1}{2}$ x 10"). If hi-res digital images are not available, we will very rarely consider professional-quality transparencies or color slides. Color-copy submissions are not accepted. All artwork must be identified with the artist's name, address, e-mail, and phone number clearly printed on a label attached to each sample. Inscribe your name and address somewhere on each piece of art. If you desire acknowledgment of artwork receipt, please include a self-addressed stamped postcard. If the artwork is three-dimensional, please attach your identification with a removable string or pack the sample in a plastic bag with your identification. If you have a unique artistic technique you'd like to share with others, please send samples of your artwork accompanied by a query letter outlining your article idea to the respective managing editor at: Somerset Studio Gallery, 22992 Mill Creek Dr., Laguna Hills California 92653. Managing editors also welcome brief e-mail inquiries."

NEEDS "Managing editors seek first-rate projects and encourage artists who have not published articles before to submit ideas, as editorial assistance will be provided."

TERMS Competitive editorial compensation is provided for all published articles. "We may hold your sample for an extended period of time—9–12 months is common. Due to the large volume of artwork we receive, *Somerset Studio Gallery* will return only those submissions accompanied by sufficient postage in the form of cash, check, or money order made out to Stampington and Company. We cannot offer delivery confirmation; however, we are happy to put insurance on the submission. If you wish to have your artwork insured for the return journey, please include sufficient funds and indicate your preference in a postcard or letter enclosed with your submission. Please do not attach postage to packaging and do not send loose postage stamps. Contributors from outside the US, please send cash, check, or money order in US funds to Stampington and Company. For questions regarding your artwork, please send inquiries to artmanagement@stampington.com."

SOMERSET WORKSHOP

22992 Mill Creek Dr., Laguna Hills California 92653. E-mail: submissions@stampington.com. Website: www.stampington.com/somerset-workshop. "Learn fabulous techniques to help you make breathtaking projects that are illustrated from start to finish. All chapters in this 144-page book include simple stepped-out photographs with clear instructions to help you create exciting projects from some of the finest art and crafting instructors in our industry."

HOW TO CONTACT "We prefer submissions of original art. If original art is not available, our next preference is high resolution digital images (300 dpi at 8½ x 10"). If hi-res digital images are not available, we will very rarely consider professional-quality transparencies or color slides. Color-copy submissions are not accepted. All artwork must be identified with the artist's name, address, e-mail, and phone number clearly printed on a label attached to each sample. Inscribe your name and address somewhere on each piece of art. If you desire acknowledgment of artwork receipt, please include a self-addressed stamped postcard. If the artwork is three-dimensional, please attach your identification with a removable string or pack the sample in a plastic bag with your identification. If you have a unique artistic technique you'd like to share with others, please send samples of your artwork accompanied by a query letter outlining your article idea to the respective managing editor at: Somerset Workshop, 22992 Mill Creek Dr., Laguna Hills California 92653. Managing editors also welcome brief e-mail inquiries."

NEEDS "Managing editors seek first-rate projects and encourage artists who have not published articles before to submit ideas, as editorial assistance will be provided."

TERMS Competitive editorial compensation is provided for all published articles. "We may hold your sample for an extended period of time—9–12 months is common. Due to the large volume of artwork we receive, *Somerset Workshop* will return only those submissions accompanied by sufficient postage in the form of cash, check, or money order made out to Stampington and Company. We cannot offer delivery confirmation; however, we are happy to put insurance on the submission. If you wish to have your artwork insured for the return journey, please include sufficient funds and indicate your preference in a postcard or letter enclosed with your submission. Please do not attach postage to packaging and do not send loose postage stamps. Contributors from outside the US, please send cash, check, or money order in US funds to Stampington and Company. For questions regarding your artwork, please send inquiries to artmanagement@stampington.com."

SPIN-OFF

F&W, 4868 Innovation Dr., Fort Collins, CO 80525. E-mail: spinoff@interweave.com. Website: www.spinningdaily.com. "*Spin-Off* is a quarterly magazine devoted to the interests of handspinners at all skill levels. Informationrmative articles in each issue aim to encourage the novice, challenge the expert, and increase every spinner's working knowledge of this ancient and complex craft."

HOW TO CONTACT Guidelines available on website.

STEP BY STEP WIRE JEWELRY

E-mail: denise.peck@fwcommunity.com.
Website: www.jewelrymakingdaily.com.
Contact: Denise Peck. *Step by Step Wire Jewelry* is published 6 times/year by Interweave/ F+W Media. The magazine is project oriented, with step-by-step instructions for creating wire jewelry, as well as tips, tools, and techniques. Articles range from beginner to expert level. Writers must be able to substantiate that material submitted is an original design, accurate, and must make sure that all steps involved in the creation of the piece are feasible using the tools listed.

HOW TO CONTACT Guidelines available on website.

STUFFED

22992 Mill Creek Dr., Laguna Hills California 92653. E-mail: stuffed@stampington.com. Website: www.stampington.com/stuffed. *Stuffed* celebrates the loveable and huggable creatures known as "softies."

HOW TO CONTACT "We prefer submissions of original art. If original art is not available, our next preference is high-resolution digital images (300 dpi at 8$\frac{1}{2}$ x 10"). If hi-res digital images are not available, we will very rarely consider professional-quality transparencies or color slides. Color-copy submissions are not accepted. All artwork must be identified with the artist's name, address, e-mail, and phone number clearly printed on a label attached to each sample. Inscribe your name and address somewhere on each piece of art. If you desire acknowledgment of artwork receipt, please include a self-addressed stamped postcard. If the artwork is three-dimensional, please attach your identification with a removable string or pack the sample in a plastic bag with your identification. If you have a unique artistic technique you'd like to share with others, please send samples of your artwork accompanied by a query letter outlining your article idea to the respective managing editor at: Stuffed, 22992 Mill Creek Dr., Laguna Hills California 92653. Managing editors also welcome brief e-mail inquiries."

NEEDS "Managing editors seek first-rate projects and encourage artists who have not published articles before to submit ideas, as editorial assistance will be provided."

TERMS Competitive editorial compensation is provided for all published articles. "We may hold your sample for an extended period of time—9–12 months is common. Due to the large volume of artwork we receive, Stuffed will return only those submissions accompanied by sufficient postage in the form of cash, check, or money order made out to Stampington and Company. We cannot offer delivery confirmation; however, we are happy to put insurance on the submission. If you wish to have your artwork insured for the return journey, please include sufficient funds and indicate your preference in a postcard or letter enclosed with your submission. Please do not attach postage to packaging and do not send loose postage stamps. Contributors from outside the US, please send cash, check, or money order in US funds to Stampington and Company. For questions regarding your artwork, please send inquiries to artmanagement@ stampington.com."

⊕ SUNSHINE ARTIST

P.O. Box 5000 N7528 Aandstad Rd., Iola WI 54945, U.S. (800)597-2573. Fax: (715)445-4053. E-mail: stephanieh@jonespublishing. com. Website: www.sunshineartist.com. Estab. 1972. Published monthly. *Sunshine Artist* is the leading publication for art and craft show exhibitors, promoters, and patrons. Circulation 17,000. Sample copies are $5 each. Accepts unsolicited submissions from freelance writers/ contributors/artists. Designers are responsible for submitting print-ready photography of the completed project. Photo captions are preferred. Accepts images in digital format. Send via Zip or e-mail as TIFF, JPEG, PNG files at 300 dpi. Prefers 2400×1800 and larger. Writers/artists should send query letter, e-mail, résumé, project photographs, social media statistics, URL, and artist biography. Keeps samples of résumé, business cards and self-promotion pieces on file. Samples are not returned. Responds to queries only if interested. Pays designers $25–300 maximum for industry-related articles.

Credit line run with each designer's image. Pays within 60 days of publication. Rights purchased vary according to project. Finds freelancers via agents/reps, submissions, word-of-mouth, magazines, and Internet. Projects that are accepted for publication undergo a technical edit prior to printing. Read our magazine. Follow us on social media. Be creative. Be punctual with deadlines. Be active on the show-circuit scene. Provide quality, usable images with proper photography credits/rights to reprint/publish.

TAKE TEN

22992 Mill Creek Dr., Laguna Hills California 92653. E-mail: taketen@stampington.com. Website: www.stampington.com/take-ten. From the publisher that brings you *The Stampers' Sampler®* and *Somerset Studio®* comes a 144-page special issue brimming with card ideas. *Take Ten* offers rubber stamp enthusiasts of all levels great ideas for creating quick and easy cards in 10 minutes or less. You'll find hundreds of full-color samples inside each volume of this unique publication.

HOW TO CONTACT "We prefer submissions of original art. If original art is not available, our next preference is high-resolution digital images (300 dpi at 8$^{1}/_{2}$ x 10"). If hi-res digital images are not available, we will very rarely consider professional-quality transparencies or color slides. Color-copy submissions are not accepted. All artwork must be identified with the artist's name, address, e-mail, and phone number clearly printed on a label attached to each sample. Inscribe your name and address somewhere on each piece of art. If you desire acknowledgment of artwork receipt, please include a self-addressed stamped postcard. If the artwork is three-dimensional, please attach your identification with a removable string or pack the sample in a plastic bag with your identification. If you have a unique artistic technique you'd like to share with others, please send samples of your artwork accompanied by a query letter outlining your article idea to the respective managing editor at: Take Ten, 22992 Mill Creek Dr., Laguna Hills California 92653. Managing editors also welcome brief e-mail inquiries."

NEEDS "Managing editors seek first-rate projects and encourage artists who have not published articles before to submit ideas, as editorial assistance will be provided."

TERMS Competitive editorial compensation is provided for all published articles. "We may hold your sample for an extended period of time—9–12 months is common. Due to the large volume of artwork we receive, *Take Ten* will return only those submissions accompanied by sufficient postage in the form of cash, check, or money order made out to Stampington and Company. We can not offer delivery confirmation; however, we are happy to put insurance on the submission. If you wish to have your artwork insured for the return journey, please include sufficient funds and indicate your preference in a postcard or letter enclosed with your submission. Please do not attach postage to packaging and do not send loose postage stamps. Contributors from outside the US, please send cash, check, or money order in US funds to Stampington and Company. For questions regarding your artwork, please send inquiries to artmanagement@stampington.com."

🍥 TEXTILE FIBRE FORUM MAGAZINE

Website: www.artwearpublications.com.au/subscriptions/textile-fibre-forum-magazine.html. "*Textile Fibre Forum* has been in print since the 1980s. It has been under the ArtWear Publications banner since late 2011, with Janet De Boer and Marie-Therese Wisniowski as co-editors."

THE STAMPERS' SAMPLER

22992 Mill Creek Dr., Laguna Hills California 92653. E-mail: thestamperssampler@stampington.com. Website: www.stampington.com/the-stampers-sampler. "This delightful magazine provides over 200 cards and stamped project ideas—complete with detailed shots and step-by-step instructions to provide an added dose of paper-crafting inspiration. The artwork contributed by our talented readers is published in full color on gorgeous, glossy paper stock. Newly revamped, this quarterly publication comes complete with a free bonus artist paper and almost 40 more pages of featured hand-stamped projects tucked inside. In every issue, readers will also find a free Tempting Template and unique challenge results to help spark their creativity."

HOW TO CONTACT "We prefer submissions of original art. If original art is not available, our next preference is high-resolution digital images (300 dpi at 8$\frac{1}{2}$ x 10"). If hi-res digital images are not available, we will very rarely consider professional-quality transparencies or color slides. Color-copy submissions are not accepted. All artwork must be identified with the artist's name, address, e-mail, and phone number clearly printed on a label attached to each sample. Inscribe your name and address somewhere on each piece of art. If you desire acknowledgment of artwork receipt, please include a self-addressed stamped postcard. If the artwork is three-dimensional, please attach your identification with a removable string or pack the sample in a plastic bag with your identification. If you have a unique artistic technique you'd like to share with others, please send samples of your artwork accompanied by a query letter outlining your article idea to the respective managing editor at: The Stamper's Sampler, 22992 Mill Creek Dr., Laguna Hills California 92653. Managing editors also welcome brief e-mail inquiries."

NEEDS "Managing editors seek first-rate projects and encourage artists who have not published articles before to submit ideas, as editorial assistance will be provided."

TERMS Competitive editorial compensation is provided for all published articles. "We may hold your sample for an extended period of time—9–12 months is common. Due to the large volume of artwork we receive, *The Stampers' Sampler* will return only those submissions accompanied by sufficient postage in the form of cash, check, or money order made out to Stampington and Company. We cannot offer delivery confirmation; however, we are happy to put insurance on the submission. If you wish to have your artwork insured for the return journey, please include sufficient funds and indicate your preference in a postcard or letter enclosed with your submission. Please do not attach postage to packaging and do not send loose postage stamps. Contributors from outside the US, please send cash, check, or money order in US funds to Stampington and Company. For questions regarding your artwork, please send inquiries to artmanagement@stampington.com."

THREADS

The Taunton Press, Inc., 63 S. Main St., PO Box 5506, Newton CT 06470-5506. (800)309-9262. E-mail: th@taunton.com. Website: www.threadsmagazine.com. *Threads* is the trusted resource for both longtime sewers continuing to perfect their sewing skills and new sewers learning the fundamentals.

VINTAGE MADE MAGAZINE

Website: www.artwearpublications.com.au/subscriptions/vintage-made-magazine.html. "This great title is all about the love of vintage. It contains feature articles on dresses, hats, handbags and shoes, designer profiles, and items or places of historic interest. This is mixed with some handy tutorials, such as how to achieve that perfect vintage hairstyle or make that essential accessory. The feature of each issue is the full-size dress pattern! The dress range is from a 32-inch to 40-inch bust, with instructions and tips on where to make alterations. This has been multi-sized from a genuine vintage dress pattern."

VOGUE KNITTING INTERNATIONAL

Website: www.vogueknitting.com. "*Vogue Knitting* is the handknitting world's style leader and the magazine knitters turn to on a regular basis for inspirational patterns, chic styling, and compelling techniques."

WHERE WOMEN COOK

22992 Mill Creek Dr., Laguna Hills California 92653. E-mail: wherewomencook@stampington.com. Website: www.stampington.com/where-women-cook. "*Where Women Cook*, is an exciting publication packed to the brim with stunning photographs and heartwarming stories. Creative storage ideas, eye-catching décor, delicious food and drink recipes, and inspirational narratives will keep you intrigued from cover to cover."

HOW TO CONTACT "We prefer submissions of original art. If original art is not available, our next preference is high-resolution digital images (300 dpi at 8^1/$_2$ x 10"). If hi-res digital images are not available, we will very rarely consider professional-quality transparencies or color slides. Color-copy submissions are not accepted. All artwork must be identified with the artist's name, address, e-mail, and phone number clearly printed on a label attached to each sample. Inscribe your name and address somewhere on each piece of art. If you desire acknowledgment of artwork receipt, please include a self-addressed stamped postcard. If the artwork is three-dimensional, please attach your identification with a removable string or pack the sample in a plastic bag with your identification. If you have a unique artistic technique you'd like to share with others, please send samples of your artwork accompanied by a query letter outlining your article idea to the respective managing editor at: Where Women Cook, 22992 Mill Creek Dr., Laguna Hills California 92653. Managing editors also welcome brief e-mail inquiries."

NEEDS "Managing editors seek first-rate projects and encourage artists who have not published articles before to submit ideas, as editorial assistance will be provided."

TERMS Competitive editorial compensation is provided for all published articles. "We may hold your sample for an extended period of time—9–12 months is common. Due to the large volume of artwork we receive, *Where Women Cook* will return only those submissions accompanied by sufficient postage in the form of cash, check, or money order made out to Stampington and Company. We can not offer delivery confirmation; however, we are happy to put insurance on the submission. If you wish to have your artwork insured for the return journey, please include sufficient funds and indicate your preference in a postcard or letter enclosed with your submission. Please do not attach postage to packaging and do not send loose postage stamps. Contributors from outside the US, please send cash, check, or money order in US funds to Stampington and Company. For questions regarding your artwork, please send inquiries to artmanagement@ stampington.com."

WHERE WOMEN CREATE

22992 Mill Creek Dr., Laguna Hills California 92653. E-mail: wherewomencreate@ stampington.com. Website: www.stampington. com/where-women-create. "*Where Women Create* invites you into the creative spaces of the most extraordinary women of our time. Through stunning photography and inspirational stories, each issue of this quarterly magazine will nourish souls and motivate creative processes."

HOW TO CONTACT "We prefer submissions of original art. If original art is not available, our next preference is high-resolution digital images (300 dpi at 8^1/$_2$ x 10"). If hi-res digital images are not available, we will very rarely consider professional-quality transparencies or color slides. Color-copy submissions are not accepted. All artwork must be identified with the artist's name, address, e-mail, and phone number clearly printed on a label attached to each sample. Inscribe your name and address somewhere on each piece of art. If you desire acknowledgment of artwork receipt, please include a self-addressed stamped postcard. If the artwork is three-dimensional, please attach your identification with a removable string or pack the sample in a plastic bag with your identification. If you have a unique artistic technique you'd like to share with others, please send samples of your artwork accompanied by a query letter outlining your article idea to the respective managing editor at: Where Women Create, 22992 Mill Creek Dr., Laguna Hills California 92653. Managing editors also welcome brief e-mail inquiries."

NEEDS "Managing editors seek first-rate projects and encourage artists who have not published articles before to submit ideas, as editorial assistance will be provided."

TERMS Competitive editorial compensation is provided for all published articles. "We may hold your sample for an extended period of time—9–12 months is common. Due to the large volume of artwork we receive, *Where Women Create* will return only those submissions accompanied by sufficient postage in the form of cash, check, or money order made out to Stampington and Company. We cannot offer delivery confirmation; however, we are happy to put insurance on the submission. If you wish to have your artwork insured for the return journey, please include sufficient funds and indicate your preference in a postcard or letter enclosed with your submission. Please do not attach postage to packaging and do not send loose postage stamps. Contributors from outside the US, please send cash, check, or money order in US funds to Stampington and Company. For questions regarding your artwork, please send inquiries to artmanagement@stampington.com."

WILLOW AND SAGE

22992 Mill Creek Dr., Laguna Hills California 92653. E-mail: willowandsage@stampington.com. Website: www.stampington.com/willow-and-sage. "This brand-new publication features stunning photography, alongside recipes for creating handmade items that soothe and replenish both body and soul. In addition to showcasing natural bath salts and soaks, soaps, face masks, sugar scrubs, how-to-use essential oils, and more, *Willow and Sage* magazine highlights the art of presentation—giving special attention to beautiful packaging—and reveals how to create fragrant spa kits and must-have gift bundles for any occasion."

HOW TO CONTACT "We prefer submissions of original art. If original art is not available, our next preference is high-resolution digital images (300 dpi at 8$\frac{1}{2}$ x 10"). If hi-res digital images are not available, we will very rarely consider professional-quality transparencies or color slides. Color-copy submissions are not accepted. All artwork must be identified with the artist's name, address, e-mail, and phone number clearly printed on a label attached to each sample. Inscribe your name and address somewhere on each piece of art. If you desire acknowledgment of artwork receipt, please include a self-addressed stamped postcard. If the artwork is three-dimensional, please attach your identification with a removable string or pack the sample in a plastic bag with your identification. If you have a unique artistic technique you'd like to share with others, please send samples of your artwork accompanied by a query letter outlining your article idea to the respective managing editor at: Willow and Sage, 22992 Mill Creek Dr., Laguna Hills California 92653. Managing editors also welcome brief e-mail inquiries."

NEEDS "Managing editors seek first-rate projects and encourage artists who have not published

articles before to submit ideas, as editorial assistance will be provided."

TERMS Competitive editorial compensation is provided for all published articles. "We may hold your sample for an extended period of time—9–12 months is common. Due to the large volume of artwork we receive, *Willow and Sage* will return only those submissions accompanied by sufficient postage in the form of cash, check, or money order made out to Stampington and Company. We can not offer delivery confirmation; however, we are happy to put insurance on the submission. If you wish to have your artwork insured for the return journey, please include sufficient funds and indicate your preference in a postcard or letter enclosed with your submission. Please do not attach postage to packaging and do not send loose postage stamps. Contributors from outside the US, please send cash, check, or money order in US funds to Stampington and Company. For questions regarding your artwork, please send inquiries to artmanagement@stampington.com."

WOMAN'S DAY

300 W. 57th St., 28th Floor, New York NY 10019. (212)649-2000. E-mail: womansday@hearst.com. Website: www.womansday.com. "*Woman's Day* is an indispensable resource to 20 million women. The brand speaks to our reader's values and focuses on what's important. We empower her with smart solutions for her core concerns—health, home, food, style, and money, and celebrate the connection she cherishes with family, friends, and community. Whether in-book, online, mobile, or through social outlets, we provide inspiring insight and fresh ideas on how to get the most of everything."

HOW TO CONTACT "Our editors work almost exclusively with experienced writers who have clips from major national magazines. As a result, we accept unsolicited manuscripts only from writers with such credentials. There are no exceptions. If you do have significant national writing experience, and you have an idea or manuscript that you think might interest us, e-mail us at womansday@hearst.com and please include some of your most recent clips."

🌱 WOODCARVING

E-mail: helen.chrystie@thegmcgroup.com. Website: www.thegmcgroup.com. "*Woodcarving*'s inspiring features, projects, technical articles and reviews have wide appeal—it is read in 57 countries worldwide. Featuring the work of top professionals and the most talented amateur carvers from around the world, it has a new, picture-led design which offers insight into the process of creating both great and humble carvings."

WOODCARVING ILLUSTRATED MAGAZINE

Fox Chapel Publishing, 1970 BRd. St., East Petersburg PA 17520. E-mail: editors@woodcarvingillustrated.com. Website: www.woodcarvingillustrated.com. **Contact:** Mindy Kinsey. Estab. 1997. Fox Chapel Publishing publishes woodworking magazines and books, craft magazine and books, and lifestyle, travel, home improvement, and DIY books.Circulation 45,000; split between subscriptions and newsstand; international but mostly USA. By request.

HOW TO CONTACT on website; via e-mail by request

WOODCRAFT MAGAZINE

P.O. Box 7020, Parkersburg WV 26102-7020. (304)865-5268. Fax: (304)420-9840. E-mail: kiah_harpool@woodcraftmagazine.com. Website: www.woodcraftmagazine.com. **Contact:** Jim Harrold, editor in chief. Estab. 2005. Bimonthly trade magazine.Circulation 115,662. Available on request.

HOW TO CONTACT Request via e-mail. Accepts unsolicited submissions. Approached by 15 project/pattern designers/year. Has featured projects/patters by Andy Rae, Marlen Kemmet, Craig Bentzley. Preferred subjects: woodworking. Submission format: PDF or DOC files. Include brief description and photos. Submit print-ready photography and step-by-step/assembly diagrams for proposal. Model and property release required. Photo captions required. Submit color photos and illustrations via CD, zip, e-mail as TIFF or JPEG files.

TERMS Send e-mail with project text, concepts, samples, photographs, and website. Keeps samples on file; send business card. Responds only if interested. Will negotiate rights with designers unwilling to sell. Finds freelancers by word-of-mouth.

TIPS "Read and understand the magazine."

🌱 THE WORLD OF CROSS STITCHING

Immediate Media Co. Bristol, 9th Floor Tower House, Fairfax St., Bristol UK BS4 3DH. **Contact:** Ruth Southorn, editor. Estab. 1997. Four weekly (13 issues/year) consumer magazine. "*The World of Cross Stitching* is a special-interest magazine focusing on cross-stitch projects with related cross-stitch/needlework-based feature articles for an audience who are primarily women ranging in age from late twenties-early fifties." Circulation 39,457.

HOW TO CONTACT Request via e-mail. Accepts unsolicited submissions. Approached by 4 project/pattern designers/year. Buys 90 project/pattern designs per issue from freelancers. Has featured projects/patterns by Joan Elliott, Maria Diaz, Jenny Barton, Susan Bates, Rhona Norrie, Margaret Sherry. Preferred subjects: cross stitch. Submission format: JPEG, computer-generated cross-stitch charts. Include concept, sketch, or computer-designed chart. Model and property release preferred.

TERMS Send query letter or e-mail with résumé, project concepts, project samples, and website. Keeps samples on file; provide self-promotion piece to be kept for possible future assignment. Responds in 1 week. Pays $320 maximum for project/pattern design; $100 maximum for industry-related articles; pay also varies based on experience, design complexity, size of design. Credit line given. Pays on publication. Buys publication (digital and print) and syndication rights only. Finds freelancers through agent/reps, submissions, word-of-mouth, magazines, online. Undergoes technical edit before publication.

TIPS "Definitely read our magazine for indication of current style/fresh feel required. I am interested in a wide variety of design subject themes and techniques (e.g., whole stitch only vs. factional stitch, blackwork/assisi, techniques using specialty threads/metallic thread accents/

bead detailing for more complex designs). When contacting me, let me know some details of your typical design style/interests, details of any particular subject areas that you are specifically interested in, with my requirements in mind. It is imperative that I can rely on freelance designers to adhere to our strict deadlines. The majority of our projects are worked on 14-count white aida to suit our audience, however, evenweave/linen fabrics are regularly used, too, along with hand-dyed fabrics. Although it is not common for me to accept designs as a result of direct submission, it has occasionally happened. It is more common that I discover a new freelance designer as a result of them getting in touch. When submitting ideas please indicate: 1) a suggestion of the finished design size (stitch count) and suggestion(s) for fabric usage; 2) ideas of color palette to be used, if a pencil sketch only and color submission is not supplied; 3) indication of techniques involved, so that I might get an idea of what experience level of stitcher will enjoy this design; 4) any ideas for possible finishing."

☺ YARN MAGAZINE

Website: www.artwearpublications.com.au/subscriptions/yarn-magazine.html. "Features patterns covering a wide range of skill sets and techniques, from beginner to advanced.

[ONLINE COMMUNITIES]

The actual act of crafting—working with our hands to create a unique item—can be, by its very nature, solitary. Most of the time, crafting is a one-person job, and working from a home studio can be isolating. That's why it's so important to become part of the craft community. Connecting with other people who understand what you do and the personal toll it can take is valuable for myriad reasons. Not only do communities of like-minded people help encourage and inspire one another, they can be a valuable resource when questions arise. It's likely that you are not the first person to have a certain question or run up against a certain problem, and a member of your community will almost always be willing to lend a helping hand or offer an opinion. Remember to give back as much as you take! If you can help out another member of your community, lending a helping hand makes for a stronger group.

In the same way, keep in mind that the very community you look to for advice and support may also be your primary sales demographic! Joining a community as a member first and a seller second (or last!) makes real relationships built on trust—not commerce—possible. Look through the following listings for national organizations and online groups that are applicable to you and your craft, but also look into your local community for small craft groups that can provide in-person interaction. Searching through Meetup.com is a good way to find local groups with similar interests, as well as asking at your favorite craft store. If no groups exist, consider starting your own. Join a guild or take a class at a local shop, and begin building relationships. Soon, you'll know enough people to form a mini group with the exact focus you had in mind.

Break out of your studio every so often and check in with your fellow crafters. They may turn into your biggest supporters and your most reliable market research.

KEY TO SYMBOLS AND ABBREVIATIONS

❂	Canadian market
❧	market located outside of the U.S. and Canada
⌂	market prefers to work with local artists/ designers
bandw	black and white (photo or illustration)
SASE	self-addressed, stamped envelope
SAE	self-addressed envelope
IRC	International Reply Coupon, for use when mailing to countries other than your own

COMPLAINT PROCEDURE

If you feel you have not been treated fairly by a company listed in Crafter's Market, we advise you to take the following steps:

- First, try to contact the company. Sometimes one e-mail or letter can quickly clear up the matter.
- Document all your correspondence with the company. If you write to us with a complaint, provide the details of your submission, the date of your first contact with the company, and the nature of your subsequent correspondence.
- We will enter your complaint into our files.
- The number and severity of complaints will be considered in our decision whether to delete the listing from the next edition.
- We reserve the right to not list any company for any reason.

ALLIANCE FOR SUSTAINABLE ARTS PROFESSIONAL PRACTICES

Website: www.artflock.org. Estab. 2008. The Alliance for Sustainable Arts Professional Practices is a coalition of not-for-profit arts institutions in the New York area that share resources, methods, and best practices with artists as they build and manage their professional lives. Membership cost: Annual dues are based upon the organization's current operating budge (see website for details). Membership restrictions: nonprofit organizations offering professional practices programs. Goal/mission: "to identify overlaps and gaps in offerings, assist in inter-organizational collaborations, and to strengthen each individual organization's visibility and outreach to the arts community." Who should join: not-for-profit arts organizations and arts-related businesses dedicated to sharing professional development opportunities and best practice resources with artists in the New York City area.

AMERICAN CRAFT COUNCIL

1224 Marshall St. NE, Suite 200, Minneapolis MN 55413. (612)206-3100. E-mail: council@craftcouncil.org. Website: www.craftcouncil.org. Estab. 1943. National/international guild, professional resource. Membership cost: standard, $40/yr ($55/yr outside US); professional, $55/yr. Membership restrictions: standard, none; professional, craft artists. Goal/mission: "We champion craft." Who should join: students, collectors, scholars, enthusiasts, craft artists. Sells advertisement space on website, in magazine; contact Joanne Smith (jsmith@craftcouncil.org) for advertising rates.

AMERICAN NEEDLEPOINT GUILD

2424 American Lane, Madison WI 53704-3102. (608)443-2476. Fax: (608)443-2474 or (608)443-2478. E-mail: membership@needlepoint.org. Website: www.needlepoint.org. Estab. 1972. National/international guild, online community, online forum, professional resource. Membership cost: $40/yr; Canada/Mexico $52/yr; all other international $60/yr; lifetime $2,000; international lifetime $2,200. Membership restrictions: none. Goal/mission: "educational and cultural development through participation in and encouragement of interest in the art of needlepoint." Who should join: all stitchers.

AMERICAN QUILTER'S SOCIETY

PO Box 3290, Paducah KY 42002-3290. (270)898-7903 or (800)626-5420. Fax: (270)898-1173. Website: www.americanquilter.com. Estab. 1984. National/international guild, online community, online forum, professional resource. Membership cost: $25/yr. Membership restrictions: standard, none; professional, craft artists. Goal/mission: to provide a forum for quilters of all skill levels to expand their horizons in quilt-making, design, self-expression, and quilt collecting. Who should join: quilters. Sells advertisement space on website, in magazine; see website for media kit and advertising specifics.

AMERICAN SEWING GUILD

9660 Hillcroft, Suite 510, Houston TX 77096. (713)729-3000. Fax: (713)721-9230. Website: www.asg.org. Estab. 1984. National/international guild, online community, online forum, professional resource, professional networking tool. Membership cost: varies, see website. Membership restrictions: none. Goal/mission: to help members learn new sewing skills, network with others who share an interest in sewing, and participate in community service sewing projects. Who should join: sewing enthusiasts. Sells advertisement space through magazine; e-mail (advertising@asg.org) for rates.

THE ART QUILT ASSOCIATION

Grand Junction CO. E-mail: info@theartquiltassociation.com. Website: www.theartquiltassociation.com. Estab. 1996. National/international guild, professional resource. Membership cost: $25/yr. Membership restrictions: none. Mission/goal: "to explore textile manipulation and diversity of mixed media as an art form." Who should join: those interested in art quilt.

ASSOCIATION OF SEWING AND DESIGN PROFESSIONALS

2885 Sanford Ave SW #19588, Grandville MI 49418. (877)755-0303. E-mail: admin@sewingprofessionals.org. Website: www.paccprofessionals.org. Estab. 1984. National/international guild, online community, online forum, professional resource, professional networking tool. Membership cost: varies, see website. Membership restrictions: none. Goal/mission: to support individuals engaged in sewing and design related businesses, in both commercial and home-based settings. Educating the general public about the unique and valuable services offered by sewing and design professionals. Who should join: sewing professionals. Sells advertisement space in newsletter; e-mail (advertising@sewingprofessionals.org.) for rates or see website.

BURDA STYLE

Website: www.burdastyle.com. Estab. 2007. Online community, online forum. Membership cost: none. Membership restrictions: none. Goal/mission: to bring the traditional craft of sewing to a new generation of fashion designers, sewing hobbyists, DIYers, and anyone looking to sew something. Who should join: people passionate about sewing. Sells advertisement space; e-mail (maryeveholder@comcast.net) for rates or see website.

CERAMIC ARTS DAILY

600 N. Cleveland Ave., Suite 210, Westerville OH 43082. (614)794-5843. Fax: (614)794-5842. Website: www.ceramicartsdaily.org. Online community, online forum. Membership cost: none. Membership restrictions: none. Goal/mission: "CeramicArtsDaily.org provides a wide array of tools for learning about and improving skills, and is a place for artists to display their work and to share ideas and perspectives about how their art and life interact to shape each other." Who should join: active potters and ceramic artists; those interested in learning about ceramics. Sells advertisement space; e-mail (mbracht@ceramics.org) for rates or see website.

CLAYSTATION

Website: www.claystation.com. Online community, online forum. Membership cost: none. Membership restrictions: none. Goal/mission: "to be a social research network for the ceramic arts." Who should join: people with an interest in ceramic arts. Sells advertisement space; see website for rates.

CRAFT AND HOBBY ASSOCIATION

319 E. 54th St., Elmwood Park NJ 07407. (201)835-1200. E-mail: info@craftandhobby.org. Website: www.craftandhobby.org. Estab. 2004. National/international guild, online community, online forum, professional resource, virtual classroom, professional networking tool. Membership cost: varies. Membership restrictions: none. Goal/mission: "to create a vibrant industry with an exciting image, an expanding customer base, and successful members." Who should join: suppliers, buyers, industry professionals in craft. Sells advertisement space; see website for rates.

CRAFT BANTER

Website: www.craftbanter.com. Online forum. Membership cost: none. Membership restrictions: none. Goal/mission: "to be a craft forum acting as a gateway to the finest craft-related newsgroups." Who should join: people interested in crafts.

CRAFTSTER

Website: www.craftster.org. Online community. Membership cost: none. Membership restrictions: none. Goal/mission: provide a community for indie crafts. Who should join: people interested in crafts. Sells advertisement; see website for details.

CRAFT YARN COUNCIL OF AMERICA

(704)824-7838. Fax: (704)671-2366. Website: www.craftyarncouncil.com. Online community, online forum, professional resource. Membership cost: none. Membership restrictions: none. Goal/mission: "to provide educational resources." Who should join: yarn companies, accessory manufacturers, magazine, book publishers, and consultants in the yarn industry.

THE CROCHET CROWD

10 Mullen Dr., P.O. Box 473, Walkerton, Ontario N0G 2V0, Canada. E-mail: MikeysHelpDesk@hotmail.com. Website: www.thecrochetcrowd.com. Estab. 2008. Online community, online forum. Membership cost: none. Membership restrictions: none. Mission/goal: "to educate the consumer, which leads to confident feel-good buying power from the consumer that benefits distributors and manufacturers." Who should join: those interested in crochet. Sells advertisement; see website for details.

CROCHET GUILD OF AMERICA

1100-H Brandywine Blvd., Zanesville OH 43701. (740)452-4541. Fax: (740)452-2552. Website: www.crochet.org. National/international guild, online forum. Membership cost: varies. Membership restrictions: none. Goal/mission: to educate the public about crochet, provide education and networking opportunities, and set a national standard for the quality, art, and skill of crochet through creative endeavors. Who should join: all those who desire to perpetuate the art and skill of crochet.

CROCHET ME

Website: www.crochetme.com. Online community. Membership cost: free. Membership restrictions: none. Who should join: those interested in crochet. Sells advertisement; see website for information.

CROCHETVILLE

Website: www.crochetville.com. Estab. 2004. Online community. Membership cost: none. Membership restrictions: none. Who should join: those interested in crochet.

DEVIANTART

Website: www.deviantart.com. Online community. Preferred subjets: art. Membership cost: none. Membership restrictions: none. Goal/mission: "to entertain, inspire, and empower the artist in all of us." Who should join: artists and art enthusiasts. Sells advertisement on website.

EMBROIDERER'S GUILD OF AMERICA

1355 Bardstown Rd., Suite 157, Louisville KY 40204. (502)589-6956. Fax: (502)584-7900. Website: www.egausa.org. Estab. 1970. National/international guild. Membership cost: varies. Membership restrictions: none. Goal/mission: "to promote cooperation and the exchange of ideas among those who are engaged in needlework throughout the world." Who should join: anyone interested in embroidery.

GANOKSIN

E-mail: service@ganoksin.com. Website: www.ganoksin.com. Estab. 1970. Online community, online forum, professional resource. Preferred subjects: gem and jewelry. Membership cost: none. Membership restrictions: none. Goal/mission: "to educate, improve working conditions, and facilitate sharing between goldsmiths globally." Who should join: jewelers, professionals, hobbyists. Sells advertisement on website, e-mail blasts, and online video network; see website for rates.

☺ THE GUILD OF JEWELLERY DESIGNERS

Hockley, Birmingham West Midlands, UK. E-mail: alan@guildofjewellerydesigners.co.uk. Website: www.guildofjewellerydesigners.co.uk. International guild, online community, online forum. Membership cost: free; various paid options. Membership restrictions: none. Mission/goal: "to help promote UK jewelry designers." Who should join: Jewelry designers based in the UK. Sells advertisement; see website for details.

HANDMADE ARTISTS

P.O. Box 530, Point Pleasant NJ 08742. E-mail: admin@handmadeartistsshop.com. Website: www.handmadeartists.com. Online community, online forum. Membership cost: none. Membership restrictions: none. Goal/mission: "community of people banded together in an effort to support each other and handmade." Who should join: creative people who work with their hands.

HOME SEWING ASSOCIATION

P.O. Box 369, Monroeville PA 15146. Website: www.sewing.org. Online community, online forum. Membership cost: none. Membership restrictions: none. Sells advertisement; see website for rates.

INDIE BUSINESS NETWORK

206-B N. Hayne St., Monroe NC 28112. (908)444-6343. Website: www.indiebusinessnetwork. com. Online community, online forum, professional resource, professional networking tool. Membership cost: varies. Membership restrictions: none. Goal/mission: to empower and to encourage the success of creative entrepreneurs. Who should join: manufacturers of handmade soaps, cosmetics, candles, artisan perfumes, aromatherapy products, jewelry, baked goods, confections, and other artisanal consumer products.

INSTRUCTABLES

E-mail: info@instructables.com. Website: www. instructables.com. Online community, online forum, virtual classroom. Membership cost: free; paid options also available. Membership restrictions: none. Goal/mission: to share projects, connect with others, and make an impact on the world. Who should join: creative people who make things. Sells advertisement; See website for details.

INTERNATIONAL POLYMER CLAY ASSOCIATION

162 Lake St., Haverhill MA 01832. Website: www.theipca.org. National/international guild, professional resource. Membership cost: varies. Membership restrictions: none. Goal/mission: to educate the public about polymer clay, and to study and promote an interest in the use of polymer clay as an artistic medium. Who should join: those interested in the art of polymer clay.

INTERNATIONAL QUILT ASSOCIATION

7660 Woodway, Suite 550, Houston TX 77063. (713)781-6882. Fax: (713)781-8182. E-mail: iqa@ quilts.com. Website: www.quilts.org. Estab. 1979.

Nonprofit organization. Membership cost: varies. Membership restrictions: only open to individuals. Goal/mission: "dedicated to the preservation of the art of quilting, the attainment of public recognition for quilting as an art form, and the advancement of the state of the art throughout the world." Who should join: individuals interested in the art of quilting.

JEWELRY MAKING DAILY

Website: www.jewelrymakingdaily.com. Estab. 1979. Online community, online forum. Membership cost: free. Membership restrictions: none. Who should join: those interested in jewelry making. Sells advertisement; see website for details.

KNITPICKS

13118 NE Fourth St., Vancouver WA 98684. (800)574-1323. Website: www.knitpicks.com. "From beginners knitting tutorials to advanced techniques, our huge index of free videos and step-by-step tutorials on knitting, crocheting, and other fiber crafts will solve all of your 'how-to' questions."

KNITTER'S REVIEW

Website: www.knittersreview.com. Online community, online forum. Membership cost: free. Membership restrictions: none. Goal/mission: "to provide quality product information to help knitters make informed purchasing decisions and, ultimately, have a more fulfilling lifelong knitting experience." Who should join: serious fiber enthusiasts of all skill levels.

KNITTING AND CROCHET GUILD

Unit 4, Lee Mills Industrial Estate, St. Georges Rd. Scholes Holmfirth HD9 1RT, UK. E-mail: secretary@kcguild.org.uk. Website: www. kcguild.org.uk. Estab. 1978. International guild. Membership cost: about US$50. Membership restrictions: none. Goal/mission: "to share and develop skills, knowledge, and enthusiasm about hand-knitting, machine knitting, and crochet." Who should join: all levels of knitters, crocheters, from beginners to professionals.

KNITTING DAILY

Website: www.knittingdaily.com. Online community, online forum. Membership cost: free. Membership restrictions: none. Who should join: those interested in knitting. Sells advertisement; see website for details.

THE KNITTING GUILD ASSOCIATION

1100-H Brandywine Blvd., Zanesville OH 43701-7303. (740)452-4541. E-mail: TKGA@TKGA.com. Website: www.tkga.com. National/international guild, local guild, online community, online forum. Membership cost: varies. Membership restrictions: none. Mission/goal: "representing you and your stitching art to the world." Who should join: knitters. Sells advertisement in magazine; see website for details.

KNITTING HELP

P.O. Box 3306, Amherst MA 01004. Website: www.knittinghelp.com. Estab. 2004. Online community, online forum, virtual classroom. Membership cost: free. Membership restrictions: none. Who should join: those interested in knitting. Sells advertisement; contact sheldon@knittinghelp.com for details.

KNITTING PARADISE

382 NE 191st St., #74906, Miami FL 33179. E-mail: info@knittingparadise.com. Website: www.knittingparadise.com. Online community, online forum. Membership cost: free. Membership restrictions: none. Who should join: those interested in knitting.

KNITTING UNIVERSE

P. O. Box 965, Sioux Falls SD 57101-0965. (800)232-5648. Fax: (605)338-2994. Website: www.knittinguniverse.com. Online community. Membership cost: none. Membership restrictions: none. Who should join: all levels of knitters.

THE MODERN QUILT GUILD

4470 W. Sunset Blvd., #226, Los Angeles California 90027. (740)452-4541. E-mail: info@themodernquiltguild.com. Website: www.themodernquiltguild.com. Estab. 2009. National/international guild, local guild, online community, online forum. Membership cost: varies. Membership restrictions: none. Mission/goal: "to support and encourage the growth and development of modern quilting through art, education, and community." Who should join: modern quilters.

NATIONAL ACADEMY OF NEEDLE ARTS

E-mail: membership@needleart.org. Website: www.needleart.org. Estab. 1985. National/international guild, professional resource. Membership cost: varies. Membership restrictions: none. Mission/goal: "to educate and elevate needlework to NeedleART in the works of creative expression known as art." Who should join: those interested in needlework.

THE NATIONAL NEEDLE ARTS ASSOCIATION

1100-H Brandywine Blvd., Zanesville OH 43701-7303. (800)889-8662; (740)455-6773. E-mail: info@tnna.org. Website: www.tnna.org. Membership organization, professional resource, professional networking tool. Membership cost: varies. Membership restrictions: open only to verifiable businesses providing services and/or products for the needle-arts industry. Mission/goal: "The National Needle arts Association advances its community of professional businesses by encouraging the passion for needle arts through education, industry knowledge exchange, and a strong marketplace." Who should join: businesses providing services and/or products for the needle arts industry.

THE NATIONAL QUILTING ASSOCIATION

P.O. Box 12190, Columbus OH 43212-0190. (614)488-8520. Fax: (614)488-8521. Website: www.nqaquilts.org. Estab. 1970. Nonprofit organization. Membership cost: varies. Membership restrictions: none. Mission/goal: "The National Quilting Association, Inc., promotes the art, craft, and legacy of quiltmaking, encouraging high standards through education, preservation, and philanthropic endeavors." Who should join: quilters.

OH MY! HANDMADE GOODNESS
Website: www.ohmyhandmade.com. Estab. 2010. Online community, professional resource. Membership cost: see website. Membership restrictions: none. Mission/goal: "gather makers and entrepreneurs to cooperatively share their knowledge, resources, peer support, and mentorship." Who should join: creative makers and entrepreneurs. Sells advertisement; see website for details.

PALMER/PLETSCH
1801 NW, Upshur St., Suite 100, Portland OR 97209. Website: www.palmerpletsch.com. Professional resource, virtual classroom. Membership cost: see website for details. Membership restrictions: none. Who should join: those interested in sewing.

PINTEREST
Website: www.pinterest.com. Online community. Membership cost: free. Membership restrictions: none. Who should join: anyone.

PRECIOUS METAL CLAY GUILD
Website: www.pmcguild.com. National/international guild, local guild, online community, professional resource. Membership cost: free. Membership restrictions: none. Mission/goal: "to serve as the ambassador of Precious Metal Clay™." Who should join: those interested in working with Precious Metal Clay™.

QNNTV
54 Court, Winterset IA 50273. E-mail: customerservice@qnntv.com. Website: www.qnntv.com. Estab. 2007. Online community, virtual classroom. Preferred subjects: quilting. Membership cost: $69.99/yr. Membership restrictions: none. Goal/mission: "A division of F+W, A Content + eCommerce Company, QNNtv launched in 2007 and is your top online resource for quilting videos. QNNtv videos are streamed and available to members worldwide, 24/7, from any computer or handheld device with a high-speed Internet connection. The mobility of QNNtv makes it easy to watch the online quilting videos from the comfort of your home or on the go from your mobile device! Whether you want to perfect quilt-finishing techniques, learn how to resize quilt blocks, make a fast and easy quilt, or learn new quilting techniques, QNNtv has all the quilting videos you want and need to improve your skills. You will find quilting videos compatible with your current skill level, from instructors you can trust. Learn from experts like Patrick Lose in *Quilting Celebrations*, Eleanor Burns in *Quilt in a Day*, Mark Lipinski and Jodie Davis in *Quilt Out Loud*, Mary Fons in *Quilty*, and many, many more. If you're ready to propel yourself to advance your quilting skills, sign up for QNNtv with a membership option that's right for you." Who should join: open to all. Hires speakers/lecturers, class teachers, workshop/retreat leaders, pattern creators. Sells advertisement space on website, in newsletter and e-mail blast; **Contact** Cristy Adamski (Cristy.Adamski@fwcommunity.com) for advertising rates.

QUILTERS CLUB OF AMERICA
(888)253-0203. E-mail: admin@quiltersclubofamerica.com. Website: www.quiltersclubofamerica.com. Affinity quilting club, online community. Membership cost: $29.95/yr. Membership restrictions: none. Mission/goal: "to help members enhance their knowledge, skill, and enjoyment of quilting." Who should join: enthusiastic quilters.

QUILTING BOARD
E-mail: info@quiltingboard.com. Website: www.quiltingboard.com. Online forum. Membership cost: free. Membership restrictions: none. Who should join: quilters.

QUILTING DAILY
Website: www.quiltingdaily.com. Online community, online forum. Membership cost: free. Membership restrictions: none. Who should join: those interested in quilting. Sells advertisement; see website for details.

RAVELRY
203 Washington St., #244, Salem MA 01970. Website: www.ravelry.com. Online community. Membership cost: free. Membership restrictions: none. Who should join: knitters and crocheters. Sells advertisement; see website for details.

SCRAPBOOKING SOCIETY

Website: www.scrapbookingsociety.com. Online community. Membership cost: free. Membership restrictions: none. Who should join: those interested in scrapbooking. Sells advertisement; see website for details.

SEAMS

4921-C Broad River Rd., Columbia SC 29212. (803)772-5861. Fax: (803)731-7709. E-mail: info@seams.org. Website: www.seams.org. Non profit organization, professional resource. Membership cost: varies. Membership restrictions: none. Mission/goal: "to support the resurging US-sewn products industry by using membership networking and collaboration, offering members benefit packages that help control overhead expenses, giving members access to educational programs to help improve the quality and productivity of their companies and the industry as a whole, and keeping members informed about legislation in Washington, DC, that may impact the industry." Who should join: sewn products manufacturing and contract manufacturing companies and their suppliers.

STUDIO ART QUILT ASSOCIATES

P.O. Box 572, Storrs CT 06268-0572. (860)487-4199. E-mail: info@SAQA.com. Website: www.saqa.com. Estab. 1989. Nonprofit organization, professional resource. Membership cost: varies. Membership restrictions: none. Mission/goal: "to promote the art quilt through education, exhibitions, professional development, documentation, and publications." Who should join: artists, teachers, collectors, gallery owners, museum curators, and corporate sponsors.

THE SWITCHBOARDS

Website: www.theswitchboards.com. Online community, online forum, professional resource, professional networking tool. Membership cost: $12/month; $97/yr. Membership restrictions: none. Mission/goal: "TSB is an online hub that plays hostess to crafty and crafty service-related businesses." Who should join: crafters, bloggers, Web designers, photographers, artists, coaches.

TEXTILE SOCIETY OF AMERICA

P.O. Box 5617, Berkeley California 94705. (510)363-4541. E-mail: tsa@textilesociety.org. Website: www.textilesocietyofamerica.org. Estab. 1987. Non profit organization, professional resource. Membership cost: varies. Membership restrictions: none. Mission/goal: "dedicated to promoting and exchanging knowledge about textiles." Who should join: those interested in textiles.

WEAVOLUTION

7 St. Paul St., Suite 1660, Baltimore MD 21202. Website: www.weavolution.com. Online community, online forum. Membership cost: none. Membership restrictions: none. Mission/goal: "to have a website exclusively for handweavers where members could post drafts, pictures, details about their projects, and to share ideas and struggles with each other." Who should join: handweavers.

WOODWORKERS GUILD OF AMERICA

1903 Wayzata Blvd. E., Wayzata MN 55391. E-mail: wwgoasubscription@program-director.net. Website: www.wwgoa.com. **Contact:** George Vondriska, managing editor. National/international guild, online community, professional resource. Preferred subjects: woodworking. Membership cost: free or paid; premium membership $29.98/year. Membership restrictions: none. Goal/mission: "to provide our members with the best instructional woodworking videos, articles, and plans on the Internet, as well as foster a community where woodworkers can join together to share ideas and experiences." Who should join: woodworkers of all levels. Hires crafters/artisans as speakers/lecturers, blog/online article writers, online video talent. Sells advertisement space on website, newsletter, e-mail blasts; contact Jim Kopp (jimk@wwgoa.com) for advertising rates and options. Site traffic: 10,000 visits per day; 5,500 unique visits per day; 41,495 Facebook fans.

TIPS "Know the best practices when woodworking. From safety to tool use, to finishes and types of wood. It's important to have a wide range of woodworking knowledge and be able to express it on camera or in writing. Our videos and articles are a great resource for all level of woodworkers. We have over 400 articles and 400 videos that have in-depth woodworking instructions. We encourage woodworkers to get back in the shop."

[RETREATS]

Many crafters realize that the way to make their business a success is through diversification. Focusing on one specific area of sales can limit your potential income. So, when you run an online shop, sell at trade shows, have commissioned work in galleries and regularly work with a publisher, what's left? Teaching!

While you can certainly find ways to teach locally, many find teaching at art and craft retreats to be a wonderful way to reach new audiences, open up new revenue streams and, in some cases, relax at the same time. This section lists national and international retreats geared toward creative souls. If you haven't considered teaching at a retreat, you really should. These types of events are an investment on the student's part, and you'll find they are very eager learners. Quite often, students attend the same retreat year after year because of the wonderful sense of community and knowledge they take away. For more on teaching techniques and strategies, read Becka Rahn's article "The Art and Craft of the Class."

But what if you aren't ready to teach your own craft? If you're still growing your skills and expanding your knowledge on a particular subject, then this section is for you, too. Investing in attending a craft retreat centered around your specific medium can be an incredibly rewarding experience. Nicole Stevenson's article "The Value of In-Person Events" gives excellent perspective on how immersing yourself in your craft can feed your inspiration, develop your talents, and foster relationships with fellow attendees that last a lifetime. Take time to research the retreat you're considering taking, talk with other students and ask about their experiences. And when you get there, be open to the possibilities!

KEY TO SYMBOLS
AND ABBREVIATIONS

◉ Canadian market

◐ market located outside of
the U.S. and Canada

⌂ market prefers to
work with local artists/
designers

bandw black and white (photo or
illustration)

SASE self-addressed, stamped
envelope

SAE self-addressed envelope

IRC International Reply
Coupon, for use when
mailing to countries other
than your own

⊕ ADORN ME

Phoenix Rising Productions, P.O. Box 37338, Phoenix AZ 85069-7338. E-mail: info@artunraveled.com. Website: www.artunraveled.com. "Won't you join us for artful days filled with creativity, joy, and laughter? Join in the camaraderie and forge life-long friendships while learning and creating in workshops taught by internationally known artists. With over 50 workshops to choose from, there's something for everyone—this year we've added a few mixed-media workshops, so please check out the workshops page for the daily schedule. Come for one workshop or for many—we hope that you'll decide to join us to have the time of your life. Art experiences like no other!"

ALABAMA CHANIN

The Factory, 462 Lane Dr., Florence AL 35630. E-mail: office@alabamachanin.com. Website: www.alabamachanin.com. "We provide materials, know-how, local cuisine, and so much more at each of our workshops. Work with our instructors and immerse yourself in slow design and manufacturing."

AN ARTISTS' RETREAT WITH ANNA RHODES

(206)328-1788. E-mail: annarhodes@anartistsretreat.com. Website: www.anartistsretreat.com. "An Artists' Retreat™ with Anna Rhodes, for the inquisitive beginner, the seasoned artist, and anyone wishing to expand creative potential. This is an in-depth concentrated art course designed to encourage instinctive, confident creativity through developing skill and imagination within a creative community. Students experience the unfolding of their unique style and palette and will have the opportunity to explore the wonders of a wide array of the finest pigments, pencils, papers, and brushes. Through drawing and composing, painting and layering mixtures of mediums, personalized instruction and group discussion, we will use both experimental and traditional techniques to guide our travels through realism, impressionism, and into the realm of magic."

ARKANSAS FIBER FEST

E-mail: arfiberfest@gmail.com. Website: www.arfiberfest.com. Estab. 2007. "This is an annual gathering for knitters, crocheters, spinners, weavers, and all fiber arts lovers."

ARROW ROCK QUILT CAMP

(660)837-3268. E-mail: lblevins@iland.net. Website: www.arrowrockquiltcamp.com. "Arrow Rock Quilt Camp is all about giving quilters a relaxed atmosphere in which they can learn new techniques, eat well, make new friends, and have a good time."

ART AND SOUL MIXED MEDIA RETREATS

30231 SE Wheeler Rd. Boring OR 97009. E-mail: info@artandsoulretreat.com. Website: www.artandsoulretreat.com. Estab. 1999. "Art and Soul is the premier mixed-media art retreat in the United States. We offer an exciting week of classes taught by a select group of professional and inspiring instructors. Our diverse lineup of classes includes: mixed media, painting, fiber, encaustic, assemblage, metal, jewelry, fabric, and paper art. This event is more than a retreat and learning process, it's an unforgettable time spent with your artistic tribe that will create many happy memories. Art is created, friends are made, joy is everywhere. Join us for an amazing experience that feeds your heart and soul."

ARTISTIC ALCHEMY: A TAHOE RETREAT FOR CREATIVE SEWISTS AND QUILTERS

Website: www.artisticalchemyblog.wordpress.com. "We come together for this retreat, in a magical spot on Lake Tahoe, to offer you the chance to discover your own alchemy as you explore the concepts and techniques of quilting and clothing arts."

⊕ ART IS YOU

E-mail: visuallyspeakingllc@gmail.com. Website: www.eatcakecreate.com. Estab. 2005. "Our philosophy is to create a moment in time where artists, whether they be faculty or students, can come together to share in their passion for creativity. To create, self-nourish, replenish personal creative resources, and to nurture not only individual souls but the souls of those around them. Whether creating something is part of your daily routine or indeed the closest to creating has been using a glue stick, there is something for everybody."

ART QUILT SANTA FE
E-mail: aqsf@att.net. Website: www.artquiltsantafe. com. "Art Quilt Santa Fe is a quilt workshop, a fiber art workshop, and a quilt retreat dedicated to supplying a unique Santa Fe experience. We provide workshops that include quilting techniques, fiber art techniques, understanding color and design, working on and creating quilts under the mentoring and direction of experienced nationally known teachers and quilters."

ART RETREAT AT THE DESERT
E-mail: barb@vivimagoo.com. Website: www. vivimagoo.com/prairie. "Just one of a series of art retreats across our beautiful country! This retreat provides little bits of heaven where creative souls can meet, be inspired by each other, create unique art taught by renowned instructors, and return home energized and touched in some way by the experience."

ART RETREAT AT THE PRAIRIE
ViviMagoo.com, Round Top Texas. (602)509-6030. E-mail: barb@vivimagoo.com; erin@vivimagoo. com. Website: www.vivimagoo.com. Contact: Barb Solem. Estab. 2012. "Our outstanding lineup of instructors inspires our students to create beautiful pieces, and our amazing students create the most warm and welcoming atmosphere to create friendships. We hope you'll join us at the upcoming art retreat at the prairie."

☺ ART RETREAT CAMP
E-mail: susan@artstreamstudios.com. Website: www.artstreamstudios.com/arc/index.htm#. VZK95_IVhBc. "A private rustic island brimming with natural wonder surrounded by crystal-clear waters is nothing short of a breathtaking place to begin.This is the place to restart. To rediscover what is important within you from a place of wonder. The creative you will come out to PLAY. At artstream we take play seriously. We created this intimate summer retreat as a quiet experience for you to breathe in all that nature has to offer. While opening up to the creative play we have in store for you. With kindred spirits. And with expert guides that will help spark discovery through playful processes. It's a deeply refreshing experience unlike any other, and we want you to join us on the island this year."

BEAD CRUISE
(269)637-0682. E-mail: humblearts@gmail.com. Website: www.beadcruise.com. Contact: Heather Powers, event promoter. Estab. 2005. "The Bead Cruise is an annual event hosted by beadmaker, designer, and author Heather Powers. Each year, we travel to different locations and on a different ship, which makes it fun and exciting for those joining us again. Our incredible classes have something for everyone: off-loom beading, wirework, bead embroidery, metalwork, and unique bead-stringing projects. Our instructors teach all over the world, including at the biggest beading events in the country. Our cruise focuses on quality classes with innovative designers!"

BEADING BY THE BAY
(269)637-0682. E-mail: info@beadingbythebay. com. Website: www.beadingbythebay.com. Estab. 2008. "Beading by the Bay in beautiful San Francisco. Learn new off-loom seed bead techniques, create beautiful jewelry, and relax the weekend away with accomplished instructors."

BEADS ON THE VINE
2555 Biddle Ranch Rd., San Luis Obispo California 93401. (805)440-2613. Fax: (866)562-0452. E-mail: info@schoolofbeadwork.com. Website: www.beadsonthevine.com. Estab. 2002. "Experience 3 days of seed bead weaving in California's central coast wine country." **ADDITIONAL INFORMATION** Retreat held in July. Attendance: 48. Class size: 16. Geared toward handmade items. Focus: seed beads. Accepts Visa, MasterCard, American Express, PayPal, check.

BEADVENTURES

Beadventures, Inc., 2415 La Honda Dr., Anchorage AK 99517. (907)258-2331. Fax: (907)258-2332. E-mail: cfrasca@beadventures.com. Website: www.beadventures.com. Contact: Cheryl Frasca, owner. Estab. 1994. "We offer international travel to over 14 countries with many talented teachers and experts in the field of beadwork, beadmaking, fiber arts, and more. Creativity, sparked by culture and nurtured by talented teachers is what Beadventures is all about."

BENEATH THE SURFACE

E-mail: alisaburke@gmail.com. Website: www.shopalisaburke.com/collections/retreats-and-classes/products/beneath-the-surface-2-day-class. "Beneath the Surface is a 2-day class dedicated to designing and creating your very own unique and one-of-a-kind fabric. We will start with the design process and move into all kinds of techniques—screen printing, using dye, resists, painting, printmaking, stamp carving, and LOTS more! After 2 days of creativity you will walk away with all kinds of new techniques, inspiration, and a STACK of fabric to use in your own creative projects!"

BE PRESENT RETREATS

Website: www.bepresentretreats.com. "The Be Present Retreats are an invitation to pause in your life and gather in an intimate, creative community to explore, create, discover, and soak up the world around you. Each retreat includes creative play + adventures combined with stories and 'being present' exercises to encourage awareness of this moment. At each retreat, you will also be invited to practice self-care to rest and nurture yourself as needed."

BIG BEAR CRAFT COTTAGE

P.O. Box 6436, Big Bear Lake California 92315. (301)704-1796 or (909)281-4006. E-mail: bigbearcraftcottage@gmail.com. Website: www.bigbearcraftcottage.com. "Unwind from your busy schedule and escape to the beautiful mountains of Big Bear Lake for a relaxing weekend with your friends and family. If you are into hobbies such as crafting, quilting, reading, board games, paper crafts, puzzles, and more, we have an all-purpose Craft Room, with ample space for personal group gatherings. This is a great place for a girls' getaway weekend!"

BLUE BIRD LANE RETREATS

20531 S. Yale Ave., Mounds OK 74047. (918)633-6628. E-mail: reservations@bluebirdretreat.com. Website: www.bluebirdretreat.com. "Enjoy the songbirds from the front deck in the spring or keep cool behind our floor-to-ceiling window views during the summer heat. Find a rocking chair on the back balcony for the perfect fall evening, and when the winter turns frosty, cozy up with a warm cup of coffee in a comfy chair. Choose a relaxing 3-day weekend retreat with friends. Rent the entire facility for a family reunion, or stop by during the week to spend the day cropping. Every visit to The Lane is the perfect escape from the hustle and bustle of daily life."

BROWN BAG RETREATS

The Creation Station!, 252 E. Hwy. 246, Unit A, Buellton California 93427. (805)693-0174. Fax: (805)693-0164. E-mail: info@thecreationstation.com. Website: www.thecreationstation.com/brown-bag-retreats.htm. "It's a very friendly and fun gathering of quilters/sewers sharing a weekend together. We call it 'Brown Bag' because each retreater brings her/his own project to work on, and everyone brings something to share at the Friday night potluck. There are no classes, no schedules to adhere to, no workshop to follow—just you, your sewing machine, your project, and everyone else! Your weekend will be filled with good food, good fun, and good friends—we like to tell people you'll have nothing to do except 'graze and sew' (meaning enjoy the yummy snacks and food and then get back to sewing!)."

CAMP ARTSEEN

E-mail: fun@campartseen.com. Website: www.campartseen.com/summer-art-retreat/art-workshops-at-camp-artseen. "Camp ArtSeen is an annual weekend art retreat combining the playfulness of summer camp, the inspiration of art school, and the opportunity to just let go. Camp ArtSeen brings together working artists, aspiring makers, and curious creative types to make art and make friends in a beautiful, peaceful setting, far from the hustle and bustle of everyday life. Typical activities include art workshops, yoga, live music, movie night, glow-in-the-dark bocce ball, sunbathing and swimming, hiking, sharing organic meals, and plenty of free time to hike alone or share stories with fellow campers over a glass of wine."

CAROLINA FIBER FROLIC

411 Pine St., Ft. Mill SC 29715. (803)547-4299. E-mail: jan@carolinafiberfrolic.com. Website: www.carolinafiberfrolic.com. Contact: Jan Smiley, retreat organizer. Estab. 2010. "The Carolina Fiber Frolic is a friendly, welcoming retreat held all day Friday and Saturday, and until noon on Sunday in the North Carolina mountains. We embrace knitters, spinners, felters, crocheters, dyers, and weavers. The fall retreat is "all retreat," and people bring their own projects to work on. The spring retreat also hosts optional classes in a variety of fiber crafts that people sign up for ahead of time and take throughout the weekend. We have a fantastic caterer that supplies our lunches and dinner, and the conference center has 2 large double-sided fireplaces as well as wide covered porches with rocking chairs. Evening happy hour and activities, informal but informative after-lunch talks, door prizes, and Fashion Show and Tell round out a full and fun weekend at the Carolina Fiber Frolic."

ADDITIONAL INFORMATION Retreat held in March and November. Attendance: 40–50. Class size: 6–12. Geared toward handmade items. Focus: knitting, spinning, weaving, fiber arts. Accepts instructor applications online. Accepts PayPal, check.

CEDAR CHEST QUILT GUILD RETREAT

E-mail: Contact form on website. Website: www.cedarchestquiltersguild.org/retreat. "Experience 4 fun-filled days and nights of classes, trunk shows, meet-and-greet events, and an All-Night Sew with door prizes and drawings all night long. Learn new techniques and tricks from some great local and national teachers to hone your quilting skills and build some great friendships with fellow quilters."

CHICAGO ART RETREATS

(773)235-1408. E-mail: info@chicagoartretreats.org. Website: www.chicagoartretreats.org. "The Artist's Retreats are an invitation for artists of all disciplines to rediscover and be inspired by Chicago. Unfortunately, we cannot provide studio space, but you will be able to visit many of Chicago's museums, galleries, and urban treasures; we encourage research; time to be inspired by the cityscape; opportunity to share space and ideas with other artists in residence and artists from Chicago to forge lasting relationships. Salons are held on Saturday evening where residency participants and local artists will meet and talk."

CHICAGO URBAN ART RETREAT CENTER

1957 S. Spaulding Ave., Chicago IL 60623. (773)542-9126. E-mail: info@urbanartretreat.com. Website: www.urbanartretreat.com. Estab. 1984. "We are an oasis of peace and safety in an urban environment on public transportation with a direct route to downtown, plenty of outdoor space to enjoy, an art gallery, art studio, and friendly people. We specialize in working with talented artists and artisans, students who are testing out their artistic/creative abilities, and folks who enjoy a peaceful and satisfying experience. We are located in a real Chicago neighborhood that can be very inspiring. Our nonprofit organization often provides free creative experience for adults to enjoy and learn from where they can relax and be free from judgment. We are known for our artistic bohemian facility and small group workshops with plenty of one-on-one attention."

ADDITIONAL INFORMATION Retreat held weekly on Saturday mornings. Class size: 3–10. Geared toward handmade items. Focus: crochet, weaving, fiber arts, mixed media, paper craft, sewing, jewelry making, painting, collages, assemblage. Accepts instructor applications online. Accepts PayPal, check, or cash.

CHICKEN CREEK HEN HOUSE RETREAT

(918)457-3307. E-mail: darmstrong@lrec.org. Website: www.cchenhouseretreat.com. "The Hen House is a 2,100 sq. ft. constructed (2011) home for 'gatherings, getaways, and special events,' with a focus on quilting and scrapbooking retreats."

CONFERENCE OF NORTHERN CALIFORNIA HANDWEAVERS

E-mail: advisory@cnch.org. Website: www.cnch.org/conferences. "CNCH sponsors an annual conference for handweaving-related fiber arts. In even-numbered years, a full conference is hosted, featuring seminars, workshops, exhibits, shows, and a marketplace. In odd-numbered years, an alternative retreat-style conference is hosted, where the offerings vary."

CRAFT CRUISES

Website: www.craftcruises.com. "Cruising with a purpose is about collecting experiences and making new friends. If you have found yourself resisting cruising, then you may want to think again. Craft Cruises® is known for having the highest-quality educational programs on board award-winning cruise lines. Craft Cruises® carefully selects the cruise lines, ships, and itineraries used to ensure each passenger's safety, comfort, and enjoyment."

CRAFTING AT CAMP RETREAT

Website: www.cvillenaz.com/craft. "Our retreat is for women of all ages and experiences who enjoy crafts of all kinds. We get together at the Virginia Nazarene Camp in Buckingham several times a year to spend a weekend laughing, sharing, eating, crafting, and occasionally sleeping. We offer a 6 ft. table all your own, unlimited time to work on your projects (you don't have to sleep if you don't want to), a relaxed schedule with minimal distractions and interruptions. We may play a few games, give away a few prizes, and break for meals and devotions, but our main focus is uninterrupted time to work on your crafting projects. Cost for the retreat is $86, which includes 2 nights' lodging and 4 meals, and don't forget that exclusive 6 ft. table."

CRAFTY CHICKS RETREATS

(509)999-6187. E-mail: krystaws@comcast.net. Website: www.facebook.com/craftychicksretreats. "CCR appeals to all kinds of different crafters, such as painters, quilters, scrapbookers, crocheters, sewers, beaders, etc. Come relax, laugh, and make memories!"

CRAFTY RETREATS

44 (0)1566 776932. E-mail: info@craftyretreats.com. Website: www.craftyretreats.com. "Crafty Retreats offers exciting residential craft courses on a range of subjects in rural France. Although we are based in Cornwall, UK, all our holidays take place in our purpose-built center in the Limousin. We hope you will enjoy visiting and learning new skills with us."

CREATE, EXPLORE, DISCOVER

E-mail: sarah@red-line-design.com. Website: www.createexplorediscover.com. "Create.explore.discover is focused on guided hands-on projects and personal interaction with experienced artist-instructors. During the day retreats, in April and September, participants begin the day with a special welcome and 'art-awakening' session. You will then delve into a single-medium series of classes exploring the ins and outs with an expert. Beginners and advanced students alike will discover new techniques and unearth their own personal style. Following your day of creativity, participants and instructors will relax and unwind with an artists' reception and discussion-in-the-round to help participants reflect and appreciate the time spent on THEMSELVES. During the weekend retreat each participant experiences 3 unique guided art and creativity workshops, exploring the various art forms and media. The retreat kicks off on Friday evening with a welcome dinner with fellow participants and instructors. Saturday and Sunday mornings begin with a special 'art-awakening' session before your day of classes. On Saturday, an artists reception and discussion-in-the-round completes the first day of activities, with time to enjoy an evening meal in the historic Lake Tahoe town of Truckee, California. Sunday begins anew with a final workshop to complete your creative journey."

CREATIVE PASSIONS CROP AND QUILT RETREAT

203 Pearl St., Chesaning MI 48616. (989)845-2159. E-mail: lgreenfelder@hotmail.com. Website: www.creativepassionsllc.com. Contact: Laura Greenfelder. Estab. 2005. "Creative

Passions is an adult women's retreat, located in the cozy, historical village of Chesaning, Michigan, just off M-57 in southwest Saginaw County. The newly renovated church was built in 1868. It has some original stained-glass windows, as well as natural lighting. It is within walking distance from restaurants and small-town shops. With a ramp into the building and all work areas on the main floor, you can easily wheel in all your supplies."

ADDITIONAL INFORMATION Pedicures and massages are available on site.

CREATIVE SOUL RETREAT, THE

(928)282-3809. E-mail: sac@sedonaartscenter. org. Website: www.sedonaartscenter.org/ SedonaArtRetreats. "The Creative Soul Retreat offers a unique tour of self-discovery as you explore a world of creative possibilities. Sedona is known for three things: its beautiful and unique landscape, its art colony atmosphere and as a place for spiritual retreat. The Sedona Arts Center has wrapped these elements into a unique package where art and self-discovery fuse—creating the opportunity for artists and those who would consider themselves non-artists to engage fully in the experience of art. The retreat program is made of 6 hands-on experiences that become for each participant a personal creative path."

DOVER QUILT RETREAT

200 Titer Dr. Dover DE 19904. (302)734-0920. E-mail: info@doverquiltretreat.com. Website: www.doverquiltretreat.com. Contact: Nancy Quade. Estab. 2014. "Leave the solitude of your sewing room and have a great weekend or week-long retreat quilting with your friends at Dover Quilt Retreat. Nestled among Mennonite and Amish neighbors, enjoy the peaceful country setting of Kent County, Delaware."

EVERJEAN QUILT AND CRAFT RETREAT

(828)926-1381. E-mail: lapnc@aol.com. Website: www.everjeanquiltretreat.com. "Everjean Quilt and Craft Retreat is a home in the Smoky Mountains set up for quilt retreats and/or whatever hobby you may enjoy. Quilting, scrapbooking, knitting, we have the perfect place for you to plan your private retreat with your friends to meet, create, and complete your projects!"

FIBER RETREAT

E-mail: carroll-bartlettl@missouri.edu. Website: www.sites.google.com/site/fiberretreat2011/ schedule-at-a-glance-1/home. "We invite you with enthusiasm and excitement to join us in Jefferson City, Missouri, to participate in a learning experience with other fiber artists from around Missouri. We invite you to have a good time, make new friends, renew old acquaintances, and learn a new thing about spinning, weaving and natural dyeing, knitting, and crochet."

FIBERS OF FAITH KNITTING RETREAT

(888)863-2267. E-mail: retreats@singinghills. net. Website: www.singinghills.net. "Fibers of Faith Retreats combine Christian women, their faith, knitting, crocheting, and other fiber arts, at Singing Hills Christian Conference Center. Located in central New Hampshire, Singing Hills is easy to get to from all over New England."

FOCUS ON FIBER

Website: www.focusonfiberfloridastyle.com. "Enjoy a true retreat from the frantic fiber world at beautiful Atlantic Center for the Arts in New Smyrna Beach, Florida. Nothing is required of attendees other than they enjoy themselves and renew their spirits. Along with spacious studios specifically set up for computers, painting, dyeing, and sewing, there is room for sculpture, dance, yoga, and quiet spots for reading, writing, and communing with nature."

FRIENDS AND FIBERWORKS

E-mail: lisa@friendsandfiberworks.com. Website: www.friendsandfiberworks.com. "Three spectacular days of classes/workshops and FREE demonstrations! Artist and vendors from all over will feature workshops in felting, spinning, weaving, dyeing, knitting, crocheting, and much more!"

GATHERING, THE

85 E. Gay St., Suite 707, Columbus OH 43215. (614)222-2243. Fax: (614)222-2427. E-mail: admin@isgb.org. Website: www.isgb.org/ gathering.html. "The Gathering is an occasion to become involved in the glass world and make valuable contacts. There are a wide variety

of events at the conference to satisfy many interests. It is an opportunity for attendees to network with each other, gallery owners, collectors, technical vendors, and suppliers. It also gives technical vendors an opportunity to showcase new equipment, tools, supplies, and glass. Through demonstrations, lectures, panel discussions, and more, attendees can learn new techniques and business skills to further their glass-bead knowledge."

GRAND OAK RETREAT

10481 Scottsboro Hwy. Scottsboro AL 35769. (256)656-8917. Website: www.grandoakretreat. com. "Grand Oak Retreat is the perfect location for your next small group retreat, 24 people or less. Our focus is on crafting groups such as scrapbooking and quilting."

GREAT BEAD ESCAPE, THE

(772)359-0442. E-mail: jenny@ thegreatbeadescaperetreats.com. Website: www.thegreatbeadescaperetreats.com. "Our retreat is about learning something new, trying something different, making some wonderful new friends, all while making beautiful jewelry. Most of our classes are perfect for the beginner or someone that wants more practice in a certain area. There will be some advanced classes taught. Our retreat is all-inclusive. One price will cover 5 half-day classes of your choice, all materials, room, and meals. Each class is limited to 6 students."

GRIFFIN DYEWORKS FIBER RETREAT

Griffin Dyeworks and Fiber Arts, 13300 Victory Blvd. #311, Van Nuys California 91401. E-mail: info@griffindyeworks.com. Website: www. griffindyeworks.com/fiber-retreat. "Griffin Dyeworks sponsors a 3-day fiber retreat in the Los Angeles area. An exciting fiber adventure that will keep you busy all weekend, you'll do the crafts you love, meet local and faraway artists, and learn entirely new skills!"

HEAVENLY STITCHES QUILT RETREAT

(888)863-2267. E-mail: retreats@singinghills. net. Website: www.singinghills.net. "Heavenly Stitches Quilt Retreats combine Christian women, their faith, quilting, and sewing at Singing Hills Christian Conference Center. Located in central New Hampshire, Singing Hills is easy to get to from all over New England."

HISTORY UNWOUND RETREAT

P.O. Box 2381, Yorktown VA 23692. (757)726-7259. E-mail: kimberly@somebunnyslove. com; info@historyunwound.org. Website: www. historyunwound.org. "A 3-day retreat consisting of the education and learning of handcrafting textiles throughout history. A variety of lectures, classes, and demonstrations are held during this weekend."

HOPE HILL RETREAT

(903)583-2814. Website: www.hopehillretreat. com. "Hope Hill Retreat is a shabby chic rural getaway for scrapbooking, crafting, and quilting—nestled amongst several acres of beautiful countryside, 10 miles south of Bonham, Texas. The quiet country setting provides just the inspiration you need to complete your projects while enjoying the company of your friends."

☻ ISLAND CRAFT ADVENTURES

E-mail: truemana@telus.net. Website: www. islandcraftadventures.com. "Week-long knitting retreats on beautiful Salt Spring Island in British Columbia, Canada. Stay in a luxuriously rustic farmhouse overlooking the Pacific Ocean; eat fresh, delicious, professionally prepared meals; meet other eager knitters; and knit to your heart's content. What could be better?"

JEWELRY ARTISTS NETWORK RETREAT

(757)726-7259. Website: www. jewelryartistsnetwork.com. "The Jewelry Artists Network Retreat is an annual weeklong retreat held in October each year. For a week a group of artists gather together, sharing a house and creating from morning until late in the evening (or the wee hours of the morning, depending on who you are). We share tools and techniques. We share ideas and inspiration. We share meals and a lot of chatter and laughter."

JUST CROP! RETREATS

(714)309-9274. E-mail: justcropretreats@gmail. com. Website: www.justcropretreats.com. "Are you looking for a place where you can work on your scrapbooks/crafty projects without interruptions from your daily schedules and responsibilities at home? Just Crop! Retreats has just the place for you! We offer you a place where you can work on your projects that you have been longing to do. There are no interruptions from your daily routines or responsibilities that seem to stop you from working on your projects at home."

KANUGA KNITTING AND QUILTING RETREAT

Kanuga Conferences, Inc., P.O. Box 250, Hendersonville NC 28793-0250. (828)692-9136. E-mail: info@kanuga.org. Website: www.kanuga. org/conference-calendar/conference-calendar-details/kanuga-knitting-quilting-retreat. "Learn new techniques from patient experts as you enjoy the perfect weekend escape for knitters and quilters. Experience the casual, friendly atmosphere in the Blue Ridge Mountains that only Kanuga can offer. Knitters and quilters can choose a project to work on during this 3-day retreat. Projects will be offered for beginning to advanced knitters and beginning to intermediate quilters. You are also welcome to bring your own project to work on. In addition to daily classes, there will be get-togethers by the fire, time for hiking to scenic mountain overlooks, and visiting area yarn and quilting shops."

KATHY'S KAPTURED MOMENTS

8050 E. State Rd. 16, Twelve Mile IN 46988. (574)721-6876. E-mail: kbutch622@yahoo. com. Website: www.kathyskapturedmoments. com. "Kathy's Kaptured Moments was designed specifically for scrapbookers. It's the perfect place to kapture the important moments in our lives by recording them in scrapbooks. This retreat's upscale accommodations are also well designed for quilters, crafters of all kinds, and even those who just want to get away with friends."

KEEPING IT CRAFTY RETREATS AND MORE

(509)460-2264. E-mail: craftychicks@ clearwire.net. Website: www. craftychicksweekendgetaways.com. "Keeping It Crafty Retreats and More (previously known as Crafty Chicks Weekend Getaways) specializes in all-inclusive scrapbooking and craft retreats for women and is based in the southeast Washington community of the Tri-Cities (Richland-Pasco-Kennewick), Washington. With the inspiration of the mighty Columbia River and surrounded by the lush and beautiful vineyards of the Horse Heaven Hills and Red Mountain AVAs, Keeping It Crafty Retreats offers a unique and memorable experience at every retreat, party, and event. We coordinate the details while you enjoy your weekend, doing what you truly love to do: create!"

KENT NEEDLE ARTS RETREAT

(860)927-3808. Website: www. blacksheepyarnsct.com. "This is a getaway weekend where you can concentrate on developing your skills and taking your needlework to new heights; classes are available at all skill levels. Care has been taken to ensure there is a variety of activities including shopping the local stores, boutiques, restaurants, a special Retreat Marketplace with yarn tastings, and a gala dinner/fashion show."

KNITAWAY

(303)433-9205. E-mail: cheryl@cheryloberle.com. Website: www.cheryloberle.com/Knitaway.html. "Arrive at the Studio on Wednesday afternoon for the introductory get-together and then spend the next 3 1/2 days immersed in the session workshop in my knitting/teaching studio in the historic Highlands district of Denver, Colorado. I like to think of the studio as a playhouse for knitters. There's the yarn room, the knitting library, our 'snack time central' kitchen, and the meeting room where we will be sharing and exploring techniques all in one cozy place. With a knitting nest around your chair, a front porch and flower garden to enjoy, and anhistoric neighborhood to explore, you'll feel right at home."

KNITTER'S REVIEW RETREAT

Website: www.knittersreview.com. "The Knitter's Review Retreat is a special kind of gathering that mixes inspiration, learning, play, and a healthy dose of low-stress downtime with your peers. I take great care in pulling together just the right blend of people, vendors, and activities to create a weekend that leaves you feeling relaxed, inspired, and welcomed as part of a community."

KNITTING AND YOGA ADVENTURES

E-mail: knittingyogi@maine.rr.com. Website: www.knittingandyogaadventures.com. "Organized trips to wonderful locations featuring knitting workshops with nationally recognized knitting designers, yoga classes, massage therapy, and hikes."

KNITTING IN THE HILLS GETAWAY

(512)707-3396. Website: www.hillcountryweavers.com/pages/events. "Our retreat will be a time to relax, rejuvenate, and refresh in the beauty of the Hill Country. It will be a time to catch up with old friends and a chance to meet some new ones, too."

🌑 KNITTING RETREAT IN IRELAND

E-mail: victoria@ballycastleknits.com. Website: www.ballycastleknits.com/tours.htm. "Relax at the Dunloe, a 5-star luxury resort hotel located in Killarney, County Kerry. Renew your appreciation for crafting in beautiful places, refresh your knitting skills, and learn some new ones. This is a very ambitious knitting retreat and tour. Everything below is included in your tour package, but you may want to stay back at the hotel for a relaxing day in our private knitting lounge. Victoria will be your knitting instructor and is a member of several craft guilds. She will be there to help you work on your latest project or to start a new one. We will have a group project to start together as well. If you are bringing a non-knitter with you, consider some of the other activities for him or her—horseback riding, falcony, tennis, golf, hiking, fishing, and exploring."

KNITTREAT

5577 State Rte. 7, New Waterford OH 44445. (330)457-0351. E-mail: knittreat@gmail.com. Website: www.knittreat.com. Contact: Elaine Smith, organizer. Estab. 2013. "Knitting classes, fashion show, and 3 days and nights of fun."

ADDITIONAL INFORMATION Retreat held in November. Attendance: 65+. Class size: 20. Geared toward handmade items. Focus: knitting, crochet, jewelry making. Accepts instructor applications online. Accepts Visa, Mastercard, check.

LAKE ARROWHEAD RETREATS

(760)208-5514. E-mail: info@lakearrowheadretreats.com. Website: www.lakearrowheadretreats.com. "Imagine an uninterrupted 48 hours dedicated to the project of your choice. Immerse yourself in your favorite hobby together with friends or come on your own and make new friends! Whether quilting, scrapbooking, beading, or just getting away from it all, our goal is to provide a memorable weekend getaway with great food, good friends, and warm hospitality."

LA-LA LAND CRAFT RETREATS

E-mail: info@lalalandcrafts.com. Website: www.lalalandcrafts.com. Estab. 2012. "Enjoy 3 days full of classes, projects, games, and other events hosted by our talented International La-La Land Crafts Design Team while overlooking the gorgeous California coastline!"

LANTERN MOON RETREAT

7911 NE 33rd Dr., Suite 140, Portland OR 97211. (800)530-4170 or (503)460-0003. Fax: (503)284-6230. Website: www.lanternmoon.com. Estab. 2012. "Connect with your knitting sisters and share your love of the handcrafted arts at the Lantern Moon Retreat. We are heading to a place where the sun shines most of the year… central Oregon… and a quaint town full of arts and culture, including the international acclaimed Sisters Outdoor Quilt Show."

LAVENDERSAGE ART RETREAT

Website: www.janelafazio.com/lavender-sage-art-retreat. "On this retreat: You'll create your own unique sketchbook and fill it with drawings and watercolors and nature prints.You will learn to draw and watercolor and easy printmaking (or strengthen your existing skills) with Jane's gentle, honest, and insightful teaching.You'll experience the charming artsy town of Taos and stay at the restful, historic, and slightly magical Mabel Dodge Luhan Inn. You'll have a week just for yourself, shared with like-minded people."

LOFT ART RETREAT

E-mail: jenn@shurkus.com. Website: www.shurkus.com/artretreat. Contact: Jenn Shurkus. "Envision walking into a spacious, bright, inspiring loft—this is where you will start your creative journey. During these retreats you will create a unique project. It may be a stack of cards or a mixed-media creation. No matter if you are a card maker, a paper crafter, a scrapbooker, or all of the above, this retreat is for you!"

MAGNOLIA RIDGE HIDEAWAY RETREATS

(608)576-3623. E-mail: mail@bloomingescapes. com. Website: www.bloomingescapes.com/retreat.shtml. "Retreats for scrapbooking, quilting, and stamping in Wisconsin. Scrapbook, quilt, stamp, and craft in comfort for a girls' getaway."

MAINE KNITTING CRUISES

E-mail: sail@MaineWindjammer.com. Website: www.mainewindjammer.com/maine-knitting-cruises. "Various events with a variety of instructors throughout the year. Interested in putting together your own knitting or crochet cruise? Have a knitting group you'd like to travel with? The Riggin is available for sailing and knitting charters."

MAKE IT! MARK IT! MASK IT! MIXED-MEDIA MIDWEST—CHICAGO RETREAT

E-mail: registrar@scrap-a-thon.com. Website: www.makeit-markit-maskit-mixed-media.blogspot. com. This is a mixed-media art retreat hosted by artist LuLu Haynes, near Chicago. Ladies of all crafts and levels are welcome to attend.

MEADOWS CRAFT RETREAT , THE

(952)220-5910. E-mail: garden323@aol. com. Website: www.meadowsmn.com. "We have space for 12 crafting guests in a totally renovated 3,000-square-foot home set on a 13-acre farmstead. Relax and enjoy rural Midwest America rocking on the front porch, discovering one of the many garden destinations, strolling our meandering meadow paths, or chatting with friends on the patio."

MEMORY LANE CRAFTING RETREAT

10006 N. Rote Rd., Orangeville IL 61060. (815)868-2363. E-mail: memorylanecr@gmail. com. Website: www.memorylanecraftingretreat. com. "Memory Lane Crafting Retreat is the ideal place to spend time together, enjoying friendship and fun! Whether your passion is scrapbooking, quilting, knitting, spinning, beading, writing, or a girls' getaway, Memory Lane has it all! This is the perfect location to relax, laugh, and make memories. The retreat can accommodate up to 9 comfortably between 3 bedrooms and sitting area. The main floor crafting room is a beautiful south-facing room with plenty of natural light overlooking a pond and the picturesque countryside. Our fully stocked kitchen makes meal preparation easy. If you prefer not to cook, we can provide restaurant recommendations."

MENDOCINO ART CENTER RETREATS

(707)937-5818 or (800)653-3328. E-mail: register@mendocinoartcenter.org. Website: www.mendocinoartcenter.org/workshops.html. "The Mendocino Art Center is a highly regarded artistic and educational institution known for retreat-style classes led by superlative artist-instructors. About 200 2-to-5-day classes are offered each year in ceramics, fiber arts, fine art, jewelry/metalsmithing, and sculpture/blacksmithing."

MEN'S KNITTING RETREAT

Website: www.mensknittingretreat.com. "Letting men gather in beautiful settings and explore their passion for knitting, crocheting, spinning, and yarn. It's not often that men have the opportunity to get together in a supportive and educational environment to learn and ask about all aspects of crafting with yarn, including knitting, crocheting, weaving, spinning, tatting, embroidery, etc. With retreats specifically dedicated to providing workshops and support, the environment created often allows men to experience creativity outside the normal bounds of what they're used to."

MINNESOTA KNITTERS' GUILD YARNOVER

E-mail: sue_traczyk@yahoo.com; tabarrett0261@yahoo.com. Website: www. knitters.org/whats-yarnover. Contact: Sue Traczyk or Tracy Barrett. Estab. 1986. "Each year the Minnesota Knitters' Guild has a day-long event called Yarnover held in the Twin Cities metro area. Prestigious local and national instructors teach a variety of courses, and fiber vendors fill the Yarnover Market, which is free and open to the public."

MISSOURI BEAD RETREAT

E-mail: mobeadretreat@gmail.com. Website: www. mobeadretreat.wordpress.com. "BR is geared toward attracting new or seasoned artists who enjoy flameworking to make unique handcrafted items. Flameworking (also called lampworking) differs from traditional glassblowing since a torch is used to melt the glass instead of a furnace. Items made through flameworking also tends to be smaller in scale and more intricate in design."

MOONTIDE LACE KNITTING RETREAT

E-mail: mobeadretreat@gmail.com. Website: www.moonriselaceknitting.com/Moontide.htm. "Join us for a fabulous week spent with fellow knitters in beautiful, serene Wellfleet, Cape Cod. Focus on your knitting and enjoy a lovely beach vacation at the same time. Classroom time is mixed with free time for vacation activities and show/share/knit in the evenings. We stay right by the ocean, in a group of cottages that back up to the National Seashore, the same ones we've been enjoying for years. The pattern for the retreat project will be exclusively available only to the retreat attendees and is a strictly kept secret until the first day of the retreat! You'll advance both your technical skills and your ability to translate your creativity into a knittable piece. There will be about 24 hours of instruction at our main cabin, which has a large, comfortable classroom."

NEEDLEPOINTER RETREATS, THE

(425)252-2277 or (888)252-9733. E-mail: shop@theneedlepointer.com. Website: www. theneedlepointer.com/stitching-retreats. "We host 3 stitching retreats each year. They are a wonderful getaway weekend! Enjoy a relaxing time of stitching in the company of other stitchers. The retreat is held at The Inn at Port Gardner, a charming, cozy inn at the Everett waterfront marina. Complimentary continental breakfasts are provided by the inn (for those staying there). The retreat provides lunch on Saturday, a snack bar of goodies in the stitching room, surprise gifts throughout the weekend, and lots of time to stitch and relax. We have optional classes for you to take at the shop; check our classes page for details."

NEW ENGLAND FIBER ARTS RETREAT

(484)350-3022. E-mail: moonriselaceknitting@ gmail.com. Website: www.moonriselaceknitting. com/Moontide.htm. "Come join us for a week of fiber-filled fun in beautiful Mid-coast Maine. Whether you knit, crochet, spin, felt, dye, or weave, or if you've always wanted to learn how, this is the place for you! Enjoy the company of fellow fiber enthusiasts while you spin by the fireplace or knit in rocking chairs on the porch of our lodge. Work on a community weaving project throughout the week. Collect natural dyestuffs around camp and dye your own yarn and fiber. Most of all, relax!"

NORTH CAROLINA SCRAPBOOK RETREATS

Virginia Scrapbooking Weekend Retreats, 4140 Valencia Rd, Chesapeake VA 23321. (757)287-4774. E-mail: mertful@yahoo.com. Website: www.northcarolinascrapbookretreats.com. Contact: Mary Full. Estab. 2006. "Our retreats were created with you in mind where you can scrap with all your scrapbooking friends or family and work on your albums. We have some great scrapbook weekends planned. Our North Carolina Scrapbooking Retreats were created to meet the needs of overworked, stressed-out, seriously addicted scrappers. At our Scrappin' Retreats we give every scrapper a full 54 HOURS of uninterrupted cropping time by offering you these wonderful weekend scrapbooking events in Virginia and North Carolina. We have an atmosphere where you can relax in your jammies, stay up all night giggling with girlfriends, and create fabulous scrapbook pages. Won't you come join us?"

NORTHEAST ART WORKSHOPS AND RETREATS

19 Kettle Cove Ln., Bldg. C7, Gloucester MA 01930. (978)729-4970. Website: www.northeastartworkshops.com. Come bring your spirit and creativity to new levels along with the generous teachings from our internationally acclaimed artist-instructors. A uniquely unforgettable art experience of growth, inspiration, laughter, and lifelong friendships. Our spacious studio is a supportive atmosphere welcoming all ages and levels to America's oldest working Art Colony."

NORTHEAST KINGDOM RETREATS

(802)731-1049. E-mail: donna@sheeptoshawl.com. Website: www.nekretreats.com. "Nestled between the Green Mountains and the Connecticut River in northern Vermont, Vermont's Northeast Kingdom offers breathtaking scenery, outstanding lodging and dining, ecotourism and agritourism, Vermont-made products, a rich diversity of art, and recreational opportunities, which have gained the Northeast Kingdom national and international recognition. Vermont's Northeast Kingdom is revered by residents and visitors alike for its lovely countryside, abundant natural resources, and the preservation of traditional landscapes and lifestyles that have made the Vermont experience one to be cherished. Make plans to visit the Kingdom this summer for your Vermont vacation—take a hike, go for a paddle, hit the links, do some mountain biking, or just relax and get away from it all."

NORTHERN CALIFORNIA KNITTING RETREAT

E-mail: marlybuff@aol.com. Website: www.ravelry.com/groups/northern-california-knitting-retreat. "The Northern California Knitting Retreat takes place at the St. Francis Retreat Center in San Juan Bautista, California. The retreat is organized by a committee of friends brought together by their love of fiber craft and knitting from Northern California and by The 2 Knit Lit Chicks and The Yarniacs podcasts."

NORTHERN FIBERS RETREAT

E-mail: info@northhouse.org. Website: www.northhouse.org/programs/events/northernfibersretreat.htm. "What could be better than focusing on fibers in the heart of winter? This event celebrates all manner of fiber arts, featuring seminars and class offerings from longtime North House instructors."

PINE LILY RETREAT HOUSE

P.O. Box 864, Lacombe LA 70445. (985)768-6069. E-mail: pinelilyretreat@yahoo.com. Website: www.pinelilyretreat.com. "Pine Lily Retreat house is a cozy 2,000-square-foot newly renovated cottage with 3 bedrooms including an *extra-large* Craft Room. A fully complimented kitchen ready for you if you feel the need to cook, with a full dining room for group meals."

PINS AND NEEDLES RETREAT

(859)986-3832. E-mail: info@fiberfrenzy.net. Website: www.fiberfrenzy.net. "Pins and Needles Retreat is held at Boone Tavern in Berea, Kentucky, and includes knitting, quilting, and spinning."

POSIE PATCH RETREAT

(920)857-4025. E-mail: posiepatchretreat@yahoo.com. Website: www.posiepatchretreat.com. "The Posie Patch Retreat is a fabulous location for your next scrapbooking, quilting, stamping, or craft retreat. You will have 2,500 square feet of space to create to your heart's content in our studio."

POWELL RIVER FIBRE RETREAT

Website: www.prfiberfest.com. "Powell River, on the upper Sunshine Coast, is hosting the annual Vancouver Island Spinners and Weavers Retreat. Weavers and spinners from the islands and the Sunshine Coast will socialize and share their skills and stories."

QUILTERS' PARADISE RETREAT: QUILTING BY THE BEACH

E-mail: customerservice@quiltingbythebay.com. Website: www.quiltingbythebay.com. "Join the fun at Quilting by the Bay's Annual Quilters' Retreat!"

QUILT PLACE, THE

575 Barton Blvd., Rockledge FL 32955. (321)223-9969. E-mail: shop@thequiltplace. com. Website: www.thequiltplace.com. "This beautiful and relaxing spot is on the Indian River in Cocoa, Florida, and is only 31/2 miles from the shop in Rockledge. Imagine a relaxing weekend watching dolphins breaching, swimming in the pool, and of course lots of quilting. There will be no cooking, no cleaning, and no interruptions!"

QUILT RETREAT AT SEA

(210)858-6399. Website: www.quiltretreatatsea. com. "We organize fabulous quilt retreat events, both on land and at sea. Our quilt designer-teachers are chosen for their enthusiasm and experience. They design a new project for our events, and you should be able to complete this during our event."

QUILT ST. GEORGE RETREAT

Website: www.quiltstgeorge.com. "We have 23 teachers teaching everything from appliqué to basic patchwork, wool embroidery, traditional embroidery, quilting techniques, quilt design software, domestic machine quilting, antique-quilt lectures, and thread seminars. Come see what all the excitement is about! And did I mention delicious food, fantastic lecturers, prizes, Button Bingo with Chocolate, and Superior Threads Tours."

RED BARN RETREATS

(866)430-1717. Website: www.redbarnretreats. com. "Tools and supplies are available along with a large, well-lit, private workspace to comfortably work on your photographs, quilts, and sewing projects. Having our massage therapist come during your time has been very popular. An entire weekend for less than $100 per person!"

RED CEDAR HOUSE

(580)464-3495. E-mail: relax@redcedarhouse. net. Website: www.redcedarhouse.net. "Relax and enjoy a weekend designed just for you to work on your craft or hobby. At the Red Cedar House, you'll find the perfect getaway for scrapbookers, stampers, card makers, quilters, or any craft or hobby group. We're the perfect place for girlfriend getaways. Make memories by creating scrapbooks or quilts for your families to enjoy for years to come. Stay up all night, lounge by the pool, rock on the porch, watch a movie, take a relaxing walk around our property, or have a blissful massage from our massage therapist."

RED DOOR RETREAT

E-mail: reddoorretreat@gmail.com. Website: www.reddoorretreat.com. "An unhosted getaway for quilters, crafters, and other adults wanting relaxing time away."

RED ROOSTER RETREATS

(256)747-4295. E-mail: info@redroosterretreat. com. Website: www.redroosterretreat. com. "Specializes in crafting getaways for scrapbooking, quilting, and small church groups. Located on beautiful Smith Lake in north Alabama. Maximum group size is 23, minimum is 12. Meals, snacks, workspace, and a relaxing atmosphere provided."

REME RETREATS

706 E. Main St. Aberdeen NC 28315. E-mail: reme@remeretreats.com. Website: www. remeretreats.com. Jean Skipper. Contact: Jodi Ohl. Estab. 2013. "Borrowing the words of one of our students, ReMe has put the 'Retreat' back in retreats! We specialize in small intimate groups who share a love of creativity, peacefulness, good food, laughter, and desire much more than just art classes (although you will get plenty of those, too!). ReMe is more than just an art retreat, it is a Remarkable, Extraordinary, Memorable, Experience = ReMe."

RIPPLE WOMEN'S RETREATS

(970)349-7487. E-mail: melissa@crestedbuttearts.org. Website: www.crestedbuttearts.org/page.cfm?pageid=34582. "The Crested Butte Wildflower Festival in partnership with the Art Studio of the Center for the Arts brings you 'Ripple: Three-Day Women's Art Retreats.' Retreats in varying mediums are offered each year in March, June, July, and September. Participants are invited to immerse themselves in art surrounded by our majestic mountain scenery in a nonthreatening, relaxing, and pampered environment."

ROCKIN' REALITY CRAFT, FIBER AND ART RETREATS

E-mail: rena@rockinreality.com. Website: www.rockinreality.com. "Rockin' Reality Retreat Services hosts the ultimate scrapbook, quilting, and craft retreats in central Texas. Our retreats are held at Rockin' Reality Retreat Center, owned and operated by Rena and Don Cotti."

ROSE VILLA RETREAT

115 E. Grand River, P.O. Box 115, Laingsburg MI 48848. (517)258-1426. E-mail: rosevillaretreat@gmail.com. Website: www.rosevillaretreat.com. "A warm and inviting quilting, scrapbooking, stamping, and general hobby retreat located in the heart of Laingsburg, Michigan."

SANTA BARBARA QUILTING RETREATS

(805)705-5523. E-mail: info@santabarbaraquilting.com. Website: www.santabarbaraquilting.com. "We are a boutique retreat company operating in Santa Barbara County, California."

SCRAPAWAY

168 Point Plaza, Butler PA 16001. (724)287-4311. E-mail: contact@scrapbookstation.com. Website: www.scrapbookstation.com. "This retreat is for ladies who wish to avoid the circus-like atmosphere of large scrapbook vacations or conventions and concentrate on making friends and scrapping the weekend away. At our retreat you'll get plenty of workspace! You won't feel like a sardine when scrapping with us."

SCRAPPER'S RX SCRAPBOOKING WEEKEND RETREATS

(321)626-2767. E-mail: tammyandstacy@scrappersrx.com. Website: www.scrappersrx.com. "We provide scrapbookers a getaway that provides them the environment to preserve their family memories and a place to unwind from everyday responsibilities and truly enjoy themselves."

SCRAPPIN' HOME RETREATS

7433 Spout Springs Rd., Suite 7433 PMB 48, Flowery Branch GA 30542. (470)238-9730. E-mail: amy@victorycove.com. Website: www.scrappinretreats.com/homeretreats.htm. "Scrappin' HOME Retreats are Friday through Sunday weekends, located at our home in Flowery Branch, Georgia. Designed to accommodate up to 12 scrappers, Scrappin' HOME Retreats combines the high standards you've come to expect from Scrappin' Retreats with the affordability of small, intimate weekend retreats."

SEAMS LIKE HOME QUILTING RETREAT

(724)984-1399. Website: www.seamslikehomeretreat.com. "Seams Like Home is a quilting retreat and bed and breakfast located between Uniontown and Connellsville, Pennsylvania, in a beautiful rural setting that is peaceful and relaxing."

SEW DELIGHTFUL

(208)731-1391. E-mail: greenetj@msn.com. Website: www.sew-delightful.com. "We offer delightful quilters' retreats!"

SEW MANY MEMORIES

P.O. Box 338, Guttenburg IA 52052. (563)252-2389. E-mail: sewmanymemories@live.com. Website: www.sewmanymemoriesgetaway.com. "Sew Many Memories is an all-inclusive, pampered weekend retreat getaway for quilting or scrapbooking, located in the restored 1885 historic St. Clair hotel in Guttenberg. We are just one block from the picturesque Mississippi River in Iowa's 2006 Most Historic Town! Our weekends are designed to rejuvenate you in a stress-free environment, as we pamper you from Friday night to Sunday noon! Enjoy a favorite pastime of quilting or scrapbooking, or maybe even just time away with friends!"

SEW SOUTH

E-mail: jennifer@sewsouthretreat.com. Website: www.sewsouthretreat.com. "What's Sew South? It's a modern sewing retreat in Charlotte, North Carolina. It's a super fun weekend with friends old and new. It's sewing for the fun of it and making something for yourself. It's dusting off that WIP and having the time to make some headway! It's laughing, chatting, giggling, making connections, being creative, being yourself. It's staying up late or going to bed early, no cooking, no cleaning, no chores—just fun! It's creative, it's inspiring, it's relaxing. It's just the place for you!"

SEWTOPIA RETREAT

E-mail: info@gosewtopia.com. Website: www.gosewtopia.com. "Sewtopia is a weekend where attendees can leave all the stresses of daily life behind to indulge themselves, focus on sewing projects, and get together with friends, old and new. We will strive to do 2 amazing events each year. The Spring event will focus on education, and the fall event will be a retreat-style event."

SHEEP IN THE CITY GET WAY

E-mail: hello@just4ewe.com. Website: www.just4ewe.com/Sheep_in_the_City/Sheep_in_the_City/Welcome.html. "Come on and join in the fun. Three days of fiber overload, vendors, classes, door prizes, and party fun! Bring your wheel and or a project to work on and sit in the fiber circle with other addicts. Spend the day or the weekend! New vendors and new ideas."

SHEEPISH IN SEATTLE

E-mail: thetravelingewe@gmail.com. Website: www.thetravelingewe.com. "Join The Traveling Ewe for a weekend of yarn tourism in and around Seattle. Stops include local yarn shops, fiber galleries, and more."

SIMPLY STITCHING

(417)336-5016. Website: www.ceciliassamplers.com/classes.asp. "Simply Stitchin' is a 'no frills' weekend that you can spend stitching, visiting, shopping, and eating! It will be from Thursday afternoon until Sunday morning. We will include a welcome dinner catered to the conference room on Thursday evening. You will also receive a tote bag and T-shirt to commemorate the weekend. We will offer a 10% discount to all attendees for purchases in Cecilia's Samplers. The cost of the Simply Stitching retreat will be $50, which is payable at the time you make your reservation for the retreat. We'll still have a charity, with a $100 Cecilia's Samplers gift card as a prize. The trading table, the 50% off sale, and Buck-A-Bag fabric will still be included at the retreat. And, as usual, there's always one of us at the conference room with the group to answer questions, give directions, help with needlework questions, and to contact the shop for deliveries to the conference room. You are still welcome to bring snacks for the snack table, too!"

SPRING KNITTING RETREAT IN ICELANDIC NATURE

E-mail: helene@helenemagnusson.com. Website: www.icelandicknitter.com/en/travels/Spring-knitting-retreat-in-icelandic-nature/. "This 6-day retreat will take us to the beautiful west of Iceland where the enchanting landscape, the first flowers of Spring, the green moss, the utterly cute lambs and kids, the busy bird life, will inspire us as much as the knitting artifacts in the Textile Museum in Blönduós that we will have the chance to visit. Hélène will tell us about the Icelandic knitting traditions with a focus on the famous Icelandic lopi yoke sweater. We will meet with many local crafters, spinners, dyers, and tanners for an unforgettable insight into the Icelandic culture and knitting heritage. This trip does not include hiking, but participants will be provided with the opportunity of exploring and taking walks where we will be staying, enjoy some bird watching, or go horse riding."

SQUAM

Squam Art Workshops, 143 Ivy St., Providence RI 02906. E-mail: elizabeth@squamartworkshops.com. Website: www.squamartworkshops.com. "We teach, inspire, and heal. Our community receives encouragement, training, inspiration, and experience that expands their creative spirit. We help dissolve restrictions and limitations on the definition of what it means to be an artist."

STITCHING AT THE BEACH

E-mail: palsconvention@hotmail.com. Website: www.downsunshinelane.com/beach.htm. "We will be doing lots of stitching, chatting, laughing, shopping, eating, and more! We will be spending 4 days in an oceanfront conference center with our stitching and exchanges!"

STITCHIN' POST'S QUILT TIL YOU WILT BEACH RETREAT, THE

P.O. Box 280, Sisters OR 97759. (541)549-6061. E-mail: stitchin@stitchinpost.com. Website: www.stitchinpost.com/quilt-class-workshop-retreat/quilting-retreats-workshops.html. "Join us for a relaxing weekend getaway at the beach! Bring your sewing, knitting, or reading to the Overleaf Lodge in scenic Yachats, Oregon. Savor the many nearby coastal attractions and enjoy walks along the gorgeous rocky coastline. All of the Overleaf rooms have spectacular ocean views. Take advantage of the Overleaf in-house spa and be spoiled by the 'good fairies' available to help you with your projects. Register early, as this retreat fills quickly! Don't forget to bring an item to share at 'Show and Tell.'"

STITCHTOPIA KNITTING HOLIDAYS

01473 660800. E-mail: enquiries@arenatravel.com. Website: www.arenatravel.com/our-holidays/stitchtopia-knitting-crochet-holidays/view#. "Our knitting holidays, in association with Rowan, combine your passion for knitting with some amazing locations across the world. Each holiday is different, but the focus will always be on perfecting your craft with top experts, lovely hotels, inspiring destinations, and enjoying like-minded company."

STUDIO CRESCENDOH

E-mail: studio@crescendoh.com. Website: www.crescendoh.com/studio_crescendoh. "WORKSHOPS + LECTURES + SPECIAL EVENTS. Half-day, full-day, multi-day workshops, lectures, and special events are scheduled throughout the year. Once you purchase a workshop through PayPal or Google Checkout, you will be enrolled."

SUMMIT SEW AND QUILT RETREAT CENTER

Ponderosa Quilt retreat, Maggie Valley North Carolina 28751. (704)682-9567. E-mail: kim@summitquiltretreat.com. Website: www.summitquiltretreat.com. Contact: Kim Polson. Estab. 2009. "We offer sew and quilt retreats."

SUPER SUMMER KNITOGETHER

TheKnitGirllls, LLC, P.O. Box 876, Pomona NJ 08240. (662)626-7751. Website: www.supersummerknitogether.com. SSK is a 5-day knitting retreat.

SWANSEN'S KNITTING CAMPS, MEG

Schoolhouse Press, 800-you-knit. Fax: (715)884-2829. E-mail: info@schoolhousepress.com. Website: www.schoolhousepress.com/camp.htm. Estab. 1958. "Knitting Camp came into being when Elizabeth Zimmermann began teaching a weekend knitting course at an extension of the University of Wisconsin. Elizabeth Zimmermann passed the torch to her daughter, knitting designer Meg Swansen, and Schoolhouse Press now offers 4 sessions Thursday through Monday during 4 weekends in July. (Knitting Camp dates are posted by the end of August each year)."

TETON PATCHWORKS QUILTERS' RETREAT

(208)456-2130. E-mail: tetonpatchworks@aol.com. Website: www.tetonpatchworks.com. "Our retreat center is specially designed for up to eight quilters who want the ideal quilting retreat. The sewing room has 8 quilting stations distinctively designed with the quilter in mind. Each station has its own swivel chair and OTT light to provide true-color illumination. There is enough design wall space for everyone. The 2 spacious cutting tables are complete with large cutting mats and rulers. The 2 ironing stations have their irons ready to go. All you bring is your sewing machine and plenty of fabric!"

THREADS AND BEDS CREATIVE SEWING AND RETREAT CENTER

(217)431-9202. E-mail: reservations@ threadsoftimefab.com. Website: www. threadsandbedsretreat.com. "Our retreat center offers 10,000 square feet of spacious sewing area, comfortable accommodations, and kitchens. Whether you are a single sewer or a group, we have everything you need to plan your next sewing getaway!"

TIMBERHAZE RETREAT

Center City MN 55012. (651)257-1947. E-mail: stay@timberhazeretreat.com. Website: www.timberhazeretreat.com. Estab. 2015. "Timberhaze Retreat is designed for groups of up to 8 people to stay, relax, create, regenerate, or to simply enjoy spending time together. Our home features a large, well-lit craft room that is set up and equipped with sturdy tables, comfortable chairs, and a design wall (made especially with quilters in mind). The craft room is also an ideal workspace to inspire whatever your creative pursuit may be. Alternatively, use the craft room as a meeting space or for a place to just relax and hang out."

TWO RIVERS YARNS SPRING KNITTING RETREAT

E-mail: mary@tworiversyarns.com. Website: www.tworiversyarns.com. "After a long winter of gray days and cold temperatures, why not treat yourself to a weekend away: meet other knitters, learn something new, and experience the beauty of rural western Maryland. You will enjoy plenty of knitting time, instruction, catered organic meals, plus a soothing massage if you choose. We hope that this will be an experience to rejuvenate your body, mind, and spirit and leave behind the winter blues."

TYLER BEAD RETREAT

(870)615-2072. E-mail: belindajoann@yahoo. com. Website: www.tylerbeadretreat.com. 2-day retreat held in June and November.

UNWIND: A FIBER ARTS GETAWAY IN THE MOUNTAINS

E-mail: sue@unwindgetaway.com. Website: www.unwindgetaway.com. "Come unwind in Blowing Rock, North Carolina! This getaway is not just about education, but about community and relaxing, too. Take classes from fabulous instructors. Learn and share with old friends and new. Explore your surrounds, like nearby Grandfather Mountain and downtown Blowing Rock and the local yarn store, Unwound Yarn. And of course, unwind for awhile in the fantastic Meadowbrook Inn."

VASHON ISLAND SEWING RETREAT

P.O. Box 2143, Vashon WA 98070-2143. (206)567-5039. E-mail: penny@stitchinggirlssociety.org. Website: www.vashonislandsewingretreat.com. Estab. 1984. "Our Retreats are all about sewing, sharing, and having fun: sewing classes, sewing for fun; sharing ideas, sharing projects, sharing inspiration, sharing friendship and good times from sunup to sundown with no interruptions, wonderful food, beautiful scenery, and all the time in the world to sew. Retreaters sleep in cozy cabins nestled in the fir forest or the newer Retreat Center; hike the pebbled paths to the lodges, or around the peninsula loop trail, or down to the salt water beach; dine on the fabulous meals prepared especially for the Vashon Island Sewing Retreat by Camp Burton's Chef."

VERMONT SUMMER RETREATS, THE

Beth Brown-Reinsel's Vermont Retreats, Knitting Traditions, LLC, PO Box 124, Putney VT 05346. E-mail: beth@knittingtraditions.com. Website: www.knittingtraditions.com/workshops/ beths-vermont-retreats. Contact: Marilyn King: marilyn@abbeyyarns.com. Estab. 2003 was the first retreat. Knitting Traditions LLC, was created by Beth Brown-Reinsel in 1995 to promote traditional knitting through workshops, patterns that educate, books, and DVDs.

VIRGINIA SCRAPBOOK RETREATS

North Carolina Scrapbook Retreats, 4140 Valencia Rd. Chesapeake VA 23321. E-mail: mertful@yahoo.com. Website: www. virginiascrapbookretreats.com. Contact: Mary. Estab. 2006. Virginia Scrapbook retreats were created with you in mind, where you can scrap with all your scrapbooking friends or family and work on your albums. We have some great scrapbook weekends planned. We offer weekend getaways to meet the needs of overworked, stressed-out, seriously addicted scrappers. At our Scrappin' Retreats we give every scrapper a full 72 HOURS plus of uninterrupted cropping time by offering you these wonderful 4-day weekend scrapbooking events in Virginia, Maryland,Tennessee, Pennsylvania, South Carolina, and North Carolina. We have an atmosphere where you can relax in your jammies, stay up all night giggling with girlfriends, and create fabulous scrapbook pages. Won't you come join us?"

WHISTLESTOP QUILT RETREAT

134 Head of Creek Rd., Sweetwater TN 37874. (865)684-6858. E-mail: jodi@ whistlestopquiltretreat.com. Website: www. whistlestopquiltretreat.com. "The Whistlestop Quilt Retreat, located in Sweetwater, Tennessee, is a 150-year-old farmhouse on 7 acres of picturesque farmland where you can step back in time and gather with friends. Experience Whistlestop with your private group of up to 18 friends, or join us for a Whistlestop Open Retreat workshop, or class."

WINDY STITCHES RETREAT

(406)539-6144. E-mail: lori@windystitches. com. Website: www.windystitches.com. "Windy Stitches Retreat is a wonderful place where quilters, knitters, scrapbookers, and other crafters can get away and relax in the company of friends. Our 3-bedroom, 2-bath retreat has comfortable accommodations for up to 8 people."

WOODLAND RIDGE RETREAT

P.O. Box 27, Downsville WI 54735. (715)664-8220. E-mail: dyecandy@gmail.com. Website: www.woodlandridgeretreat.com. Contact: Chris Daly. Estab. 2013. "Woodland Ridge Retreat is a creative getaway for quilters, knitters, fiber artists, scrapbookers, and artists. Located in the rural village of Downsville, Wisconsin, this idyllic property overlooks the scenic Red Cedar River Valley in the west-central part of the state.

Our retreat offers deluxe accommodations and brightly lit gathering rooms. The facility is on one level with ADA-accessible guest accommodations. Join us for a workshop or getaway with your favorite girlfriends."

WOOLEN WILLOW RETREATS

E-mail: woolenwillowretreats@yahoo.com. Website: www.woolenwillowretreats.weebly.com. "Woolen Willow Retreats hosts retreats each year dedicated to all styles of quilters and rug hookers. Simply click on one of the tabs at the top of the website page and begin your retreat planning!"

YARN CUPBOARD RETREAT

(315)399-5148. E-mail: info@yarncupboard. com. Website: www.yarncupboard.com/festival. "The Yarn Cupboard has many opportunities for instruction with a full roster of classes. We believe at the Yarn Cupboard we go beyond just supplying beautiful fibers or providing help. We are a fiber arts community."

YARNOVER SLEEPOVER RETREAT

E-mail: yarnoversleepover@gmail.com. Website: www.yarnoversleepover.com. "Wake up in stitches… This is a yarn retreat for knitters and crocheters looking for fun classes with fabulous teachers and delicious food."

YOUR TIME ARTS AND CRAFTS RETREATS

808 Montrose Blvd., Buffalo MN 55313. (763)682-2061. E-mail: yourtimecrafts@gmail. com. Website: www.yourtimecrafts.com. James McCarty. Contact: Cynthia McCarty. Estab. 2015. "Your Time Arts and Crafts Retreat is a crafters' paradise. Located in historic Buffalo, Minnesota, just 40 miles from the Twin Cities, our retreat offers the perfect place to visit with old and new friends, share your creativity, have fun, and enjoy personal time away from home. We offer full-service accommodations in our fully restored home nestled in a quiet and serene small-town village atmosphere."

ZOMBIE KNITPOCALYPSE RETREAT

Website: www.zombieknitpocalypse.com. "ZK is an urban knitting retreat hosted in downtown Rochester, Minnesota. The retreat runs Wednesday afternoon through Sunday midday, with a relaxed atmosphere that encourages knitting, meeting new friends, shopping, and eating great food at the wonderful restaurants centrally located in downtown Rochester. In fact, once you get to the hotel, there is very little need for a car, as everything is within walking distance. While the retreat atmosphere is laid-back, there are also many optional opportunities to get involved. You can pack your weekend with as many fun activities as you care to join."

[INDUSTRY SHOWS]

Attending an industry trade show can be an eye-opening experience. For the craft industry, there are niche trade shows that take place multiple times a year in various parts of the country, each with potentially hundreds of top-name exhibitors. Attend one of these shows and you'll see just how popular sewing, quilting, scrapbooking, jewelry making, needlearts, and craft in general continue to be. This section includes listings of major industry shows in different niches of the craft industry, as well as some that are not craft specific but still may be good places to exhibit your handmade goods.

Simply attending one of these shows and walking the floor as a new business owner can be helpful. You'll be able to see the wide variety of items produced in your industry, and identify major competitors or those that you might want to work with down the line. You will certainly have the chance to network with your peers and those who inspire you. Nicole Stevenson's article "The Value of Attending In-Person Events" gives great perspective on the professional and personal benefits of attending shows like this.

All trade shows have different restrictions on who can attend the show. Most are open only to buyers or industry professionals, not the general public, so be sure to find out if you are eligible to attend a show before showing up. You may be required to submit your business identification number, wholesale receipts, tax information, or other paperwork showing that you are indeed a professional in the industry.

A major step for any professional crafter is to exhibit at an industry show. Doing so can be expensive and time-consuming, but the benefits are great. Exhibiting as a vendor at one of these shows puts you in contact with retailers from around the world who are at the show specifically to place wholesale orders and stock their store. Depending on the items you sell, exhibiting at one of the major trade shows could provide you with a major increase in sales. If you are interested in exhibiting at a trade show in your industry niche, be sure to do your research. There will most likely be a lengthy application process to complete. You will also want to know how large your booth is so you can dress it well. Many booths are decorated to the gills at these events to draw in potential buyers. Make sure you are able to put your best foot forward if you choose to exhibit. Also, think through your sales process for these types of events. You'll need order sheets, sales slips, receipts, the ability to take payment information, etc. Finally, reach out to someone who's "been there, done that" before you exhibit for the first time. They will be able to provide you with invaluable insight as you gear up for your first show.

KEY TO SYMBOLS & ABBREVIATIONS

☘	Canadian market
⬛	market located outside of the U.S. and Canada
⌂	market prefers to work with local artists/ designers
b&w	black & white (photo or illustration)
SASE	self-addressed, stamped envelope
SAE	self-addressed envelope
IRC	International Reply Coupon, for use when mailing to countries other than your own

ALASKA WHOLESALE GIFT & FOOD SHOW

Alaska Genesis Productions, P.O. Box 200846, Anchorage AK 99520. (907)929-2822. E-mail: info@alaskagiftshow.com. Website: www.alaskagiftshow.com. Annual wholesale/cash and carry show held in January. Indoors. Open to trade only. Accepts handmade craft merchants, pattern, magazine, book publishers, and other mediums. Number of exhibitors: see website. Number of attendees: see website. Admission: see website. Apply online. Deadline for entry: see website. Application fee: none. Space fee: varies. Exhibition space: 10×10. For more information, exhibitors should e-mail, visit website, or call.

☾ ALBERTA GIFT FAIR

42 Voyager Court S., Toronto, Ontario M9W5M7 Canada. (416)679-0170. Fax: (800)611-6100. E-mail: alberta@cangift.org. Website: www.albertagiftfair.org. Annual wholesale show held in spring/fall. Indoors. Open to trade only. Accepts handmade craft merchants, gifts, collectibles, and other mediums. Number of exhibitors: 800. Number of attendees: 16,000. Admission: see website. Apply online. Deadline for entry: see website. Application fee: none. Space fee: varies. Exhibition space: 10×10. For more information, e-mail, visit website, or call.

AMERICAN BEAD & JEWELRY SHOWS

P.O. Box 490803, Atlanta GA 30349. (770)739-0057. Fax: (866)311-7774. E-mail: info@americangemexpo.com. Website: www.americanbeadshows.com. Annual wholesale show held multiple times per year. Indoors. Open to public. Accepts handmade craft merchants, beads, jewelry, gems, gifts, body products, and more. Number of exhibitors: see website. Number of attendees: varies. Admission: see website. Apply online. Deadline for entry: varies by date. Application fee: none. Space fee: varies. Exhibition space: varies. For more information, e-mail, visit website, call.

AMERICAN CRAFT RETAILER EXPO— LAS VEGAS

P.O. Box 4597, Mooresville NC 28117-4597. (888)427-2381. E-mail: service@wholesalecrafts.com. Website: www.acrelasvegas.com. Currently boasting 1,200 artists and 16,000 retailer members, Wholesalecrafts.com is the only successful online trade show of its kind. See website for details.

AMERICAN CRAFT RETAILER EXPO— ORLANDO

P.O. Box 4597, Mooresville NC 28117-4597. Website: www.wholesalecrafts.com. Currently boasting 1,200 artists and 16,000 retailer members, Wholesalecrafts.com is the only successful online trade show of its kind. See website for details.

AMERICAN MADE SHOW

3000 Chestnut Ave., Suite 300, Baltimore MD 21211. (410)889-2933, ext. 227. E-mail: jenm@rosengrp.com. Website: www.americanmadeshow.com. **Contact:** Jen Menkhaus, exhibits manager. Estab. 1983. Annual wholesale show held in winter. Indoors. Open to trade only. Accepts handcrafted artist-made goods. Awards/prizes: Merit Awards. Number of exhibitors: 800. Number of attendees: 4,500. Admission: see website. Apply online. Deadline for entry: see website. Application fee: none. Space fee: varies. Exhibition space: 6×10; 10×10. For more information, e-mail, visit website, or call.

ATLANTA INTERNATIONAL GIFT & HOME FURNISHINGS

Website: www.americasmart.com. "We know your time is money, so we strive to make your experience at AmericasMart productive and profitable. As the leading international source for consumer goods, AmericasMart remains unmatched in convenience, amenities, and professionalism. Experience AmericasMart for yourself and make it your business advantage. We've got an edge over our national competitors: nation's largest single product collection. By design, the airport connects to rapid rail that takes you directly to the heart of downtown, where AmericasMart is located." See website for more information.

ATLANTIC CRAFT TRADE SHOW (ACTS), THE

1574 Argyle St., Suite 15, Box 3, Halifax, Nova Scotia B3J 2B3 Canada (902)492-2773. Fax: (902)429-9059. E-mail: acts@craftalliance.ca. Website: www.actshow.ca/EN/. Estab. 1977. Annual wholesale show held in February. Indoors. Open to trade only. Accepts handmade craft merchants, giftware. Juried. Number of exhibitors: see website. Number of attendees: see website. Admission: see website. Apply online. Deadline for entry: see website. Application fee: none. Space fee: see website. Exhibition space: see website. For more information, e-mail, visit website, or call.

BEAD & BUTTON SHOW

E-mail: lkollatz@kalmbach.com. Website: www. beadandbuttonshow.com. Over 300 vendors will be selling one-of-a-kind finished jewelry plus precious gems, pearls, art beads, gold and silver, beading supplies, and books. The show will also feature a juried exhibit of inspiring bead art and over 700 bead and jewelry classes. See website for more information.

BEAD FEST

(513)531-2690. Fax: (610)232-5754. E-mail: beadfest@fwmedia.com. Website: www.bead-fest.com. Estab. 2001. Bead Fest is an annual beading and jewelry-making event held several times throughout the year in various locations. Bead Fest started in our Philadelphia location back in 2001. The program includes 100+ workshops and classes for jewelry makers of all skill levels, presented by some of the top instructors in the country. Bead Fest also features a large Shopping Expo, where exhibitors display beads, gems, stones, and other jewelry-making supplies and tools in one convenient location. It's the ideal venue for jewelry makers who don't have easy access to abundant supplies and a welcome opportunity for vendors to increase sales and meet their customers face-to-face. Bead Fest is presented by Interweave, publisher of *Beadwork, Step by Step Wire Jewelry, Lapidary Journal Jewelry Artist, Jewelry Stringing* and *Handcrafted Jewelry*. Interweave's parent company, F+W, a community-focused content creator and marketer of products and services for enthusiasts.

BILOXI WHOLESALE GIFT SHOW

E-mail: biloximarket@gmail.com. Website: www. wmigiftshows.com. "Buyers attending the Biloxi Wholesale Gift Show will experience over 300 booths with manufacturers from 22 states and a huge selection of new and trendy merchandise including holiday, home décor, tabletop, garden accessories, souvenirs, gourmet, jewelry, apparel, floral, gift wrap, and much more." See website for more information.

BOSTON GIFT SHOW

415 Summer St., Boston MA 02210. (800)318-2238. Fax: (678)285-7469. E-mail: info@urban-expositions.com. Website: www.bostongiftshow. com. **Contact:** Erica Davidson, show director. Cash and carry/wholesale show held annually in March. Indoors. Open to trade only; must show business ID to enter. Accepts handmade craft merchants, pattern, magazine, book publishers, functional and decorative accessories, fashion. Juried. Number of exhibitors: 500. Number of attendees: 4,000. Admission: no fee, open to trade only. Apply online. Deadline for entry: August. Application fee: none. Space fee: $1,690. Exhibition space: 10×10. For more information, e-mail, visit website, or call.

BRITISH CRAFT TRADE FAIR

E-mail: info@bctf.co.uk. Website: www.bctf.co.uk. "The British Craft Trade Fair (BCTF) is a three-day event that takes place in April each year at the scenic Great Yorkshire Showground in beautiful Harrogate, Yorkshire. The fair is strictly trade-only and showcases work from exclusively British and Irish makers. BCTF differs from other trade fairs in that no mass-manufactured products or products made overseas are allowed. Visitors can be confident that they will be presented with a selection of the best handmade British giftware available from more than 500 talented makers." See website for more information.

BUYER'S CASH & CARRY—MADISON

(717)796-2377. E-mail: mktsqr@epix.net. Website: www.marketsquareshows.com. Select from a large variety of unusual gift items, handcrafted furniture, gourmet food products, jewelry, as well as handcrafted quality reproductions. All for immediate inventory needs. See website for more information.

BUYER'S CASH & CARRY—MARLBOROUGH
(717)796-2377. E-mail: mktsqr@epix.net. Website: www.marketsquareshows.com. Select from a large variety of unusual gift items, handcrafted furniture, gourmet food products, jewelry, as well as handcrafted quality reproductions. All for immediate inventory needs. See website for details.

BUYER'S CASH & CARRY—VALLEY FORGE
(717)796-2377. E-mail: mktsqr@epix.net. Website: www.marketsquareshows.com. Hand pick holiday collectibles, folk art, handcrafted furniture, and speciality foods. All available for immediate inventory needs. See website for more information.

⟳ BY HAND
113 Murray St., Ottawa, Ontario K1N 5M5, Canada. (888)773-4444. Fax: (613)241-5678. E-mail: info@byhand.ca. Website: www.byhand.ca. "Canada's premier wholesale marketplace allows buyers the opportunity to discover the very best in Canadian handmade products. Buyers who visit By Hand will see the finest in handmade glass, ceramics, mixed media, fashion, jewelry, leather, art, wood, metal, raku, home décor, stone, pottery, photography, sculpture, toys, and more. At By Hand you will find new and exciting product designs that will delight your customers and separate you from your competition. By Hand is a juried show where you will meet the designers and makers of the products and come to understand the joy and passion artisans have for their work." See website for more information.

CALIFORNIA GIFT SHOW
(800)318-2238. E-mail: eshoda@urban-expo.com. Website: www.californiagiftshow.com. See website for more information and to apply.

CHICAGO GIFT MARKET
E-mail: kzwirkoski@mmart.com. Annual wholesale show that takes place 4 times a year. See website for more information and to apply.

COLUMBUS MARKETPLACE
E-mail: info@thecolumbusmarketplace.com. Website: www.thecolumbusmarketplace.com. "The Columbus MarketPlace is a permanent wholesale market center offering the newest and finest lines of gifts, collectibles, home furnishings, accessories, housewares, stationery, and floral items. This array of trend-setting merchandise is displayed in permanent showrooms in an easy-to-shop, single-floor layout." See website for more information.

⟲ CRAFT
E-mail: craft@clarionevents.com. Website: www.craft-london.com. "Covering basketry, blacksmithing, book art, ceramics, enameling, fashion accessories, furniture, glass, interiors, non-precious and precious jewelry, knitwear, leather, lettering, metalwork, wood, millinery, mosaic, paper, printmaking, product design, sculptural, recycled, stone carving, textiles, traditional, and more, CRAFT fills a gap in the UK market for a high-quality, juried trade event that enables over 150 leading makers and artisans to meet a substantial audience of international retailers, galleries, museums, professional buyers, and collectors within a dedicated trade event in London."

⟲ CRAFT AND HOBBY ASSOCIATION 2016 MEGA CONFERENCE & TRADE SHOW
(201)835-1200. E-mail: info@craftandhobby.org. Website: www.craftandhobby.org. Celebrating Creativity and 75 Years of Connecting the Creative Arts and Craft Industry! The CHA MEGA Show is the only place you can conduct a year's worth of business in 6 days! There is no better place to discover new products and trends, participate in hands-on product education and business classes, and attend special networking events designed to grow your professional connections and improve your business. The CHA MEGA Show connects the entire industry, making it essential to all facets of your business. Visit www.chamegashow.org for more information.

⟲ CRAFT HOBBY & STITCH INTERNATIONAL
E-mail: info@chsi.co.uk. Website: www.chsi.co.uk. "Europe's No. 1 trade show for the creative craft sector provides suppliers of creative

art, craft, needlecraft, and hobby products with a fantastic platform to showcase their products to a worldwide audience."

DALLAS TEMP SHOW
E-mail: jlugannani@mcmcmail.com. Website: www.dallasmarketcenter.com. See website for more information.

DALLAS TOTAL HOME & GIFT SHOW
E-mail: jlugannani@mcmcmail.com. Website: www.dallasmarketcenter.com. "The premier product destination offering more than 20,000 gift and home décor lines within a convenient, easy-to-shop marketplace."

GALVESTON GIFT & RESORT MERCHANDISE SHOW
5600 Seawall Blvd., Galveston TX 77554. (800)318-2238. Fax: (678)285-7469. E-mail: info@urbanexpositions.com. Website: www. galvestongiftshow.com. **Contact:** Christina Bell, show director. Wholesale show held annually in October. Indoors. Open to trade only. Accepts handmade craft merchants, pattern, magazine, and book publishers. Number of exhibitors: see website. Number of attendees: see website. Admission: none. Apply online. Deadline for entry: see website. Application fee: none. Space fee: $645. Exhibition space: 10×10. For more information, e-mail cbell@urban-expo.com.

GEM AND LAPIDARY WHOLESALERS SHOW
E-mail: info@glwshows.com. Website: www.glwshows.com. G&LW trade shows are produced in many major trade centers across the United States for the convenience of retail dealers.

HAWAII MARKET MERCHANDISE EXPO
Website: www.douglastradeshows.com. Featured products are: jewelry, gift, apparel, fashion accessories, leather goods, art, and collectibles in addition to products manufactured in Hawaii. The expos are designed specifically to serve Hawaii's business buyers and sellers. The expos are not open to the public. The cash and carry format of immediate release of merchandise encourages

thousands of business owners, managers, and professional trade buyers to purchase hundreds of products for use or resale in their businesses.

INTERNATIONAL QUILT MARKET
E-mail: shows@quilts.com. Website: www.quilts.com. See website for more information.

LAS VEGAS MARKET
(702)599-9621. E-mail: info@imcenters.com. Website: www.lasvegasmarket.com. "Las Vegas Market is the most comprehensive furniture, home décor, and gift market in the US, presenting a unique cross-section of 2,000+ resources in an unrivaled market destination. With two markets each year, retailers and designers can shop a broad assortment of product from thousands of manufacturers of furniture, mattress, lighting, decorative accessories, floor coverings, home textiles, tabletop, general gift, and more delivering the most complete, cross-category wholesale trade show for the furniture, home décor, and gift industries in the US."

LAS VEGAS SOUVENIR & RESORT GIFT SHOW
3150 Paradise Rd., Las Vegas NV 89109. (800)318-2238. Fax: (678)285-7469. E-mail: info@urbanexpositions.com. Website: www. lvsouvenirshow.com. **Contact:** Lisa Glosson, show director. Wholesale show held annually in September. Indoors. Open to trade only. Accepts handmade craft merchants, pattern, magazine, book publishers. Number of exhibitors: see website. Number of attendees: see website. Admission: none. Apply online. Deadline for entry: see website. Application fee: none. Space fee: $1,950. Exhibition space: 10×10. For more information, e-mail lglosson@urban-expo.com.

LOUISVILLE GIFT SHOW
P.O. Box 17112, Cincinnati OH 45217. (513)861-1139. Fax: (513)861-1557. E-mail: lpharris42@hotmail.com. Website: www.stlouisgiftshow.com. **Contact:** Larry Harris, president. Estab. 1960s. Wholesale show (some cash and carry and order writing) held semiannually in February and August. Indoors. Not open to public. Accepts handmade craft merchants, pattern, magazine, book pub

lishers, USA made, imports. Number of exhibitors: 70. Number of attendees: 800. Admission: none. Apply online. Deadline for entry: open until filled. Application fee: none. Space fee: $525 (10×8); $625 (10×10). Exhibition space: 10×8; 10×10. For more information, e-mail or visit website. **TIPS** "Product presentation."

⏱ MAKE IT!—EDMONTON
E-mail: april@aprilcommunications.co.uk. Website: www.make-it.org.uk. "Make it! continues to be one of the biggest and most popular papercrafting events in the South of England, attracting the most celebrated companies in the craft world and thousands of enthusiastic visitors each year. Make it! brings you the best in paper and card craft from over a hundred exhibiting companies."

⏱ MAKE IT!—VANCOUVER
E-mail: april@aprilcommunications.co.uk. Website: www.make-it.org.uk. "Make it! continues to be one of the biggest and most popular papercrafting events in the South of England, attracting the most celebrated companies in the craft world and thousands of enthusiastic visitors each year. Make it! brings you the best in paper and card craft from over a hundred exhibiting companies."

MINNEAPOLIS MART GIFT HOME & ACCESSORY SHOW
10301 Bren Rd. W., Minnetonka MN 55343. (952)932-7200 or (800)626-1298. Fax: (952)932-0847. E-mail: mart@mplsmart.com. Website: www.mplsmart.com. Annual wholesale show held 4 times a year (see website for dates). Indoors. Open to trade only. Accepts home décor, accessories and apparel merchandise. Number of exhibitors: see website. Number of attendees: see website. Admission: see website. Apply online. Deadline for entry: see website. Application fee: see website. Space fee: varies. Exhibition space: varies. For more information, e-mail, visit website, or call.

MJSA EXPO
57 John L. Dietsch Square, Attleboro Falls MA 02763. (774)225-6014. E-mail: lucy.ferreira@mjsa.org. Website: www.mjsa.org. **Contact:** Lucy Ferreira. Annual wholesale show held in spring (check website for dates). Indoors. Open to trade only. Accepts jewelry machinery, supplies, components, services, and finished product. Number of exhibitors: see website. Number of attendees: see website. Admission: see website. Apply online. Deadline for entry: see website. Application fee: none. Space fee: varies. Exhibition space: varies. For more information, e-mail, visit website, or call.

NAMTA ART MATERIALS WORLD
20200 Zion Ave., Cornelius NC 28031. (704)892-6244. Fax: (704)892-6247. E-mail: rmunisteri@namta.org. Website: www.namta.org. **Contact:** Rick Munisteri, director of meetings. Annual conference and wholesale show held in spring. Indoors. Open to trade only. Accepts art and craft materials. Number of exhibitors: see website. Number of attendees: see website. Admission: see website. Apply online. Deadline for entry: see website. Application fee: see website. Space fee: varies. Exhibition space: 10×10. For more information, e-mail, visit website, or call.

NATIONAL NEEDLEARTS ASSOCIATION TRADE SHOW, THE
1100-H Brandywine Blvd. Zanesville OH 43701-7303. (800)889-8662 or (740)455-6773. E-mail: info@tnna.org. Website: www.tnna.org. Annual wholesale show held winter, spring, fall. Indoors. Open to trade only. Accepts needle arts. Number of exhibitors: see website. Number of attendees: see website. Admission: see website. Apply online. Deadline for entry: see website. Application fee: none. Space fee: varies. Exhibition space: see website. For more information, e-mail, visit website, or call.

NEW YORK INTERNATIONAL GIFT FAIR, THE
(914)421-3395. E-mail: paula_bertolotti@glmshows.com. Website: www.nynow.com. **Contact:** Paula Bertolotti. Estab. 2001. Annual wholesale market held semiannually. Indoors. Open to trade only. Accepts home, lifestyle, and gift vendors. Number exhibitors: 2,800. Number attendees: 35,000. Admission: see website. Apply online. Deadline for entry: see website. Application fee: none. Space fee: varies. Exhibition space: varies. For more information, e-mail, visit website, or call.

NORTHEAST MARKET CENTER
2 Cabot Rd., Hudson MA 01749. (800)435-2775. E-mail: info@northeastmarketcenter.com. Website: www.northeastmarketcenter.com. **Contact:** Cathryn Fridell, director. Wholesale marketplace open several times a year. Indoors. Open to trade only. Accepts gifts, decorative accessories. Number of exhibitors: see website. Number of attendees: see website. Admission: see website. Apply online. Deadline for entry: see website. Application fee: see website. Space fee: varies. Exhibition space: see website. For more information, e-mail, visit website, or call.

OASIS GIFT SHOWS
15591 W. Yucatan Dr., Surprise AZ 85379. (602)952-2050 or (800)424-9519. Fax: (602)445-6936. E-mail: information@oasis.org. Website: www.oasis.org. Estab. 1976. Wholesale show, not open to public, held in January and September. Indoors. NOT open to public. Accepts giftware. Number of exhibitors: see website. Number of attendees: 1,000–2,000 per show. Admission: see website. Apply online. Deadline for entry: see website. Application fee: see website. Space fee: varies. Exhibition space: 10×10. For more information, e-mail, visit website, or call.

OCEAN CITY RESORT & GIFT EXPO
4001 Coastal Hwy., Ocean City MD 21842. (800)318-2238. Fax: (678)285-7469. E-mail: info@urbanexpositions.com. Website: www.oceancitygiftshow.com. **Contact:** Russ Turner, show director. Wholesale show held annually in October/November. Indoors. Open to trade only. Accepts handmade craft merchants, pattern, magazine, and book publishers. Number of exhibitors: 200. Number of attendees: see website. Admission: none. Apply online. Deadline for entry: see website. Application fee: none. Space fee: $890. Exhibition space: 10×10. For more information, e-mail rturner@urban-expo.com.

OFFINGER'S MARKETPLACES
1100-H Brandywine Blvd., Zanesville OH 43701-7303. (740)452-4541. Fax: (740)452-2552. E-mail: contact@offingersmarketplaces.com. Website: www.offingersmarketplaces.com. Estab. 1930. Annual wholesale show held 4 times a year (see website for dates). Indoors. Open to trade only. Accepts handmade craft merchants, giftware, home décor, and other mediums. Number of exhibitors: see website. Number of attendees: see website. Admission: see website. Apply online. Deadline for entry: see website. Application fee: see website. Space fee: varies. Exhibition space: 12×10. 24× 20. For more information, e-mail, visit website, or call.

PHILADELPHIA GIFT SHOW, THE
100 Station Ave., Oaks PA 19456. (800)318-2238. Fax: (678)285-7469. E-mail: manderson@urban-expo.com. Website: www.philadelphiagiftshow.com. **Contact:** Marilyn Anderson, show director. Estab. 1996. Wholesale show held semiannually in January and July. Indoors. Open to trade only. Accepts pattern, magazine, and book publishers. Number of exhibitors: see website. Number of attendees: see website. Admission: none. Apply online. Deadline for entry: see website. Application fee: none. Space fee: $1,785 plus a $100 show promotional fee for the first booth. Exhibition space: 10×10. For more information, e-mail manderson@urban-expo.com.

⊕ PIEDMONT CRAFTSMEN'S FAIR
601 N. Trade St., Winston-Salem NC 27101. (336)725-1516. E-mail: craftsfair@piedmontcraftsmen.org. Website: www.piedmontcraftsmen.org/programs/crafts-fair. **Contact:** Deborah Britton, fair coordinator. Estab. 1963. Annual showcase held 3rd weekend in November. Indoors. Open to public. Accepts clay, wood, glass, fibers, leather, metal, photography, printmaking, and mixed media. Number of exhibitors: see website. Number of attendees: see website. Admission: $7 adults; $6 students/seniors; children 12 and under free; weekend pass $11. Apply online. Deadline for entry: mid-April. Application fee: $35. Space fee: starts at $625. Exhibition space: see website. For more information, e-mail, visit website, or call.

⟳ QUEBEC GIFT FAIR
42 Voyager Court S., Toronto, Ontario M9W 5M7, Canada. (416)679-0170; (800)611-6100. Fax: (416)385-1851; (877)373-7555. E-mail: quebec@cangift.org. Website: quebecgiftfair.org. Wholesale show held semiannually in spring/fall. Indoors. Open to trade only. Accepts giftware

merchants. Awards/prizes: Best Booth Awards. Number of exhibitors: see website. Number of attendees: see website. Admission: see website. Apply online. Deadline for entry: see website. Application fee: none. Space fee: varies. Exhibition space: varies. For more information, e-mail, visit website, or call.

SEATTLE GIFT SHOW, THE
800 Convention Place, Seattle WA 98101-2350. (800)318-2238. Fax: (678)285-7469. E-mail: info@urbanexpositions.com. Website: www.seattlegiftshow.com. **Contact:** Lisa Glosson, show director. Cash and carry/wholesale show held semiannually in January and August. Indoors. Open to trade only. Accepts handmade craft merchants, pattern, magazine, and book publishers. Number of exhibitors: see website. Number of attendees: see website. Admission: no fee for retail buyers; $30 guest fee. Apply online. Deadline for entry: see website. Application fee: none. Space fee: see website. Exhibition space: 10×10. For more information, e-mail lglosson@urban-expo.com.

ST. LOUIS GIFT SHOW
P.O. Box 17112, Cincinnati OH 45217. (513)861-1139. Fax: (513)861-1557. E-mail: lpharris42@hotmail.com. Website: www.stlouisgiftshow.com. **Contact:** Larry Harris, president. Estab. 1970s. Wholesale show (some cash and carry and order writing) held semiannually in January and August. Indoors. Not open to public. Accepts handmade craft merchants, pattern, magazine, book publishers, USA made, imports. Number of exhibitors: 80. Number of attendees: 800. Admission: none. Apply online. Deadline for entry: open until filled. Application fee: none. Space fee: $525 (10×8); $625 (10×10). Exhibition space: 10×8; 10×10. For more information, visit website. **TIPS** "Presentation of product."

STITCHES EXPOS
P.O. Box 965, Sioux Falls SD 57101-0965. (800)237-7099. Fax: (605)338-2994. E-mail: stitchesregistration@xrx-inc.com. Website: www.knittinguniverse.com/STITCHES/. Annual conference and market held 4 times a year. Indoors. Open to public. Accepts fiber. Number of exhibitors: see website. Number of attendees: see website. Admission: $10/1-day pass; $15/2-day pass;

$20/3-day pass. Apply online. Deadline for entry: see website. Application fee: none. Space fee: see website. Exhibition space: see website. For more information, e-mail, visit website, or call.

☁ TORONTO GIFT FAIR
42 Voyager Court S., Toronto, Ontario M9W 5M7, Canada. (416)679-0170 or (800)611-6100. Fax: (416)679-0175 or (800)496-2966. E-mail: toronto@cangift.org. Website: torontogiftfair.org. Wholesale show held semiannually in spring/fall. Indoors. Open to trade only. Accepts innovative tabletop, housewares, gourmet food, garden accessories, collectibles, handmade, stationery, home décor, bath, bed, and linen products. Number of exhibitors: 900. Number of attendees: 26,000. Admission: see website. Apply online. Deadline for entry: see website. Application fee: none. Space fee: see website. Exhibition space: see website. For more information, e-mail, visit website, or call.

WHOLESALECRAFTS.COM
P.O. Box 4597, Mooresville NC 28117-4597. (888)427-2381. E-mail: ACREinfo@wholesalecrafts.com. Website: www.wholesalecrafts.com. Estab. 1998. Annual wholesale show held 3 times a year. Indoors. Open to trade only. Accepts handmade craft merchants. Number of exhibitors: see website. Number of attendees: see website. Admission: see website. Apply online. Deadline for entry: see website. Application fee: none. Space fee: see website. Exhibition space: see website. For more information, e-mail, visit website, or call.

WINTER SEATTLE MARKET WEEK: GIFT & HOME ACCESSORIES SHOW
6100 4th Ave. S., Seattle WA 98108. (206)767-6800 or (800)433-1014. Fax: (206)767-5449. E-mail: info@pacmarket.com. Website: www.pacificmarketcenter.com. Wholesale show held semiannually. Indoors. Number exhibitors: see website. Number attendees: see website. Admission: see website. Apply online. Deadline for entry: see website. Application fee: none. Space fee: see website. Exhibition space: see website. For more information, e-mail, visit website, or call.

REGIONAL CRAFT SHOW INDEX

[SUBJECT INDEX]

Floral Craft

Folk and Native American Art

Gourmet/Artisan Foods

Performance Art

Photography

GENERAL INDEX

[OTHER BOOKS IN THE MARKET SERIES]

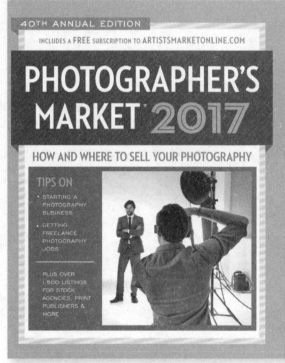

These and other F+W titles are available online, or from your favorite craft retailer or bookstore.